Lecture Notes in Artificial Intelligence   997

Subseries of Lecture Notes in Computer Science
Edited by J. G. Carbonell and J. Siekmann

Lecture Notes in Computer Science
Edited by G. Goos, J. Hartmanis and J. van Leeuwen

Springer
Berlin
Heidelberg
New York
Barcelona
Budapest
Hong Kong
London
Milan
Paris
Santa Clara
Singapore
Tokyo

Klaus P. Jantke Takeshi Shinohara
Thomas Zeugmann (Eds.)

Algorithmic Learning Theory

6th International Workshop, ALT '95
Fukuoka, Japan, October 18-20, 1995
Proceedings

 Springer

Series Editors

Jaime G. Carbonell, Carnegie Mellon University, USA

Jörg Siekmann, University of Saarland, DFKI, Germany

Volume Editors

Klaus P. Jantke
Fachbereich für Informatik, Mathematik und Naturwissenschaften, FH Leipzig
Postfach 66, D-04251 Leipzig, Germany

Takeshi Shinohara
Department of Artificial Intelligence, Kyushu Institute of Technology
Iizuka 820, Japan

Thomas Zeugmann
Research Institute of Fundamental Information Science, Kyushu University 33
Fukuoka 812, Japan

Cataloging-in-Publication Data applied for

Die Deutsche Bibliothek - CIP-Einheitsaufnahme

Algorithmic learning theory : 6th international workshop ;
proceedings / ALT '95, Tokyo, Japan, October 18 - 20, 1995.
Klaus P. Jantke ... (ed.). - Berlin ; Heidelberg ; New York ;
Barcelona ; Budapest ; Hong Kong ; London ; Milan ; Paris ;
Tokyo : Springer, 1995
　　(Lecture notes in computer science ; 997 : Lecture notes in artificial
　　intelligence)
　　ISBN 3-540-60454-5
NE: Jantke, Klaus P. [Hrsg.]; ALT <6, 1995, Tōkyō>; GT

CR Subject Classification (1991): I.2.6, I.2.3, F.4.1, I.2.7

ISBN 3-540-60454-5 Springer-Verlag Berlin Heidelberg New York

© Springer-Verlag Berlin Heidelberg 1995
Printed in Germany

Typesetting: Camera ready by author
SPIN 10485854　　06/3142 – 5 4 3 2 1 0　　Printed on acid-free paper

Preface

This volume contains all the papers presented at the Sixth International Workshop on Algorithmic Learning Theory (ALT '95), held at the Recent Hotel, Fukuoka, Japan, October 18–20, 1995. The ALT'95 technical program included 21 papers selected for presentation by the program committee from 46 submissions. Additionally, three invited talks presented by Yves Kodratoff of Université Paris, Ming Li of University of Waterloo, and Yasubumi Sakakibara of Fujitsu Labs., Numazu, respectively, were featured at the conference.

This workshop is the sixth in a series of annual conferences established in 1990. The ALT series is focusing on all areas related to algorithmic learning theory including (but not limited to): the theory of machine learning, the design and analysis of learning algorithms, computational logic of/for machine discovery, inductive inference of recursive functions and recursively enumerable languages, learning via queries, learning by artificial and biological neural networks, pattern recognition, learning by analogy, statistical learning, Bayesian/MDL estimation, inductive logic programming, robotics, application of learning to databases, gene analyses, etc.

The diversity of approaches presented in this and the other ALT proceedings reflects the broad spectrum of relevant disciplines. The many possible aspects of learning that can be formally investigated and the variety of viewpoints expressed in the technical contributions clearly indicate that developing models of learning is still particularly important to broaden our understanding of what learning really is. This ALT conference as well as its predecessors aimed to extend and to intensify the communication in the continuously growing scientific community interested in the phenomenon of learning. Continuation of the ALT series is supervised by its steering committee consisting of Setsuo Arikawa (chair, Kyushu Univ.), Takashi Yokomori (University of Electro-Communications, Tokyo), Hiroshi Imai (Univ. of Tokyo), Teruyasu Nishizawa (Niigata Univ.), Akito Sakurai (Hitachi, Tokyo), Taiske Sato (Tokyo Inst. Technology), Takeshi Shinohara (Kyushu Inst. Technology), Masayuki Numao (Tokyo Inst. Technology), and Yuji Takada (Fujitsu, Numazu).

The 6th International Workshop on Algorithmic Learning Theory (ALT'95) has been sponsored by the Japanese Society for Artificial Intelligence (JSAI), by the Kyushu Institute of Technology, and by the Human Genome Center, University of Tokyo.

The ALT'95 Conference Chair was

> Takeshi Shinohara (Kyushu Inst. Techn., Iizuka, Japan),

and the Local Arrangement Chair was

> Masateru Harao (Kyushu Inst. Techn., Iizuka, Japan).

We would like to express our immense gratitude to all the members of the Program Committee, which consisted of:

N. Abe (NEC, Kawazaki, Japan)
N. Cesa-Bianchi (Univ. Milano, Italy)
R.P. Daley (Univ. Pittsburgh, USA)
P.A. Flach (Tilburg Univ., Netherlands)
M. Hagiya (Univ. Tokyo, Japan)
M. Haraguchi (Hokkaido Univ., Sapporo, Japan)
H. Ishizaka (Kyushu Inst. Techn., Iizuka, Japan)
K.P. Jantke (HTWK Leipzig, Germany)
P.M. Long (Research Triangle Inst.)
Y. Mansour (Tel Aviv Univ., Israel)
A. Maruoka (Tohoku Univ., Sendai, Japan)
T. Sato (Tokyo Inst. Techn., Japan)
A. Sharma (Univ. New South Wales, Sydney, Australia)
H.-U. Simon (Univ. Dortmund, Germany)
T. Takagi (Univ. Tokyo, Japan)
T. Yokomori (Univ. Electro-Comm., Tokyo, Japan)
T. Zeugmann (Kyushu Univ., Fukuoka, Japan, chair).

They and the subreferees they enlisted put a huge amount of work into reviewing the submissions and judging their importance and significance.

We would like to thank everybody who made this meeting possible: the authors for submitting papers, the invited speakers for accepting our invitation and providing us their insight into the recent development of their research area, the conference and local arrangement chair, the Steering Committee, the sponsors, Fukuoka Science and Technology Foundation and Telecommunications Advancement Foundation for providing generous financial support, and Springer-Verlag. Finally, the Program Committee heartily thanks the following person who served as subreferees for ALT'95:

Sumitaka Akiba	Satoshi Kobayashi	Yasubumi Sakakibara
Jun Arima	Takeshi Koshiba	Seiichiro Sakurai
Hiroki Arimura	Steffen Lange	Takeshi Shinohara
Hideki Asoh	Eiji Maeda	Noriko Sugimoto
Mike Bain	Tetsuhiro Miyahara	Yuji Takada
Peter Bartlett	Chowdhury R. Mofizur	Jun'ichi Takeuchi
Claudio Ferretti	Anna Morpurgo	Ichiro Tajika
Koichi Hirata	Atsuyoshi Nakamura	Eiji Takimoto
Eiju Hirowatari	Tetsuro Nishino	Mitsuo Wakatsuki
Hitoshi Iba	Masayuki Numao	Osamu Watanabe
Sanjay Jain	Francesco Ravasio	Akihiro Yamamoto
Shuji Jimbo	Takashi Saitoh	
Shyam Kapur	Yoshifumi Sakai	

Fukuoka, July 1995

Klaus P. Jantke
Takeshi Shinohara
Thomas Zeugmann

Table of Contents

SESSION 6

SESSION 7

SESSION 8

SESSION 9

SESSION 10

Editors' Introduction

Learning is a fascinating phenomenon of natural intelligence. In particular, humans have developed the ability to acquire knowledge, and to generalize or specify it in dependence on their actual needs. Also, humans are very good in learning their maternal languages as well as other languages. These abilities have always been considered the hallmark of intelligence. Therefore, learning is a central issue of research undertaken in the field of artificial intelligence, too. The challenge to design an "intelligent" computer has led to growing interest in learning within the computer science community. Nowadays, machine learning is sought after in a wider range of industrial and scientific applications, e.g., in molecular biology, in knowledge engineering, in financial prediction, in robotics, in pattern recognition, in natural language processing, and in machine discovery.

Various machine learning techniques have been developed during the last decade to satisfy this demand. Given this, it is important to elaborate a thorough theory to be able to provide, for example, performance guarantees. Additionally, it is necessary to develop a unified theory of learning as well as techniques to translate the resulting theory into applications. However, this is easier said than done. Algorithmic learning theory aims to develop mathematically based models of learning and to derive results within the models. Clearly, both parts are important. However, our understanding of learning is still too limited to allow the ultimate definition of learning. Therefore, the first part is of particular importance. Unlike in other areas of computer science, there are many interesting and contending models for learning giving vastly different result concerning the learnability and non-learnability, respectively, of target concepts. Nevertheless, all these models considerably help to broaden our understanding of what learning really is. As it turns out, there is at least one common feature shared by all learning models, i.e., recognizing regularities in the data provided and expressing the regularities found by compressing the data received. Usually, the data provided are incomplete. Moreover, in many applications one has to handle sometimes noisy or erroneous information.

The general theory studying learning from incomplete information is usually referred to as *inductive inference* which goes back at least to the seminal work of Solomonoff and of Gold. Inductive inference mainly emphasizes to answer what can be learned computationally at all. In particular, it studies the impact of several postulates on the behavior of learners to their learning power. The insight obtained is often valuable in enlarging our general understanding of learning. However, it is often much less satisfactory from the standpoint of computational efficiency. This led to the development of a variety of learning models emphasizing on the feasibility of learning. The present proceedings reflect a broad variety of the currently intensively studied areas in algorithmic learning theory.

Formal Language Learning

Inductive inference of formal languages is the study of algorithms that map evidence on a language into hypotheses about it. The investigation of scenarios in which the sequence of computed hypotheses stabilizes to an accurate and finite description (e.g., a grammar) of the target language has attracted considerable attention during the last decades. The source of information may vary from augmenting initial segments of the sequence of all positive and negative examples (all strings over the underlying alphabet are classified with respect to their containment in the target language), positive data only (any infinite sequence of strings exhausting just the target in the limit) to queries, i.e., the learner is allowed to ask particular types of questions to gain information concerning the target. Commonly used types of questions are membership queries (asking whether or not a particular string belongs to the target language) and equivalence queries (asking whether or not a particular finite description generates the target language and nothing else). If the proposed description does not generate the target, a counterexample drawn from the symmetric difference of the target and the proposed description is returned, too. Learning from examples usually results in identification in the limit, i.e., after having seen only finitely many examples the learner stabilizes its output to a correct description of the target. However, usually it is not decidable whether or not the learner has already converged. In contrast, learning via queries requires the learner to clearly indicate that it has learned by stopping asking questions and outputting a correct description of the target.

The invited paper by Yasubumi Sakakibara surveys grammatical inference with an emphasis on constructive approaches rather than enumerative ones (cf. Section 1). Starting with the learnability of regular languages and subsets thereof the paper introduces various models of grammatical inference including but not restricted to the classical model of learning in the limit and Angluin's minimally adequate teacher. Next, the learnability of context free languages from structural information and membership as well as equivalence queries is considered and the author gives a detailed account of his and his co-workers contributions to this interesting area. Subsequently, we are guided to the emerging and important field of inferring stochastic grammars which allows nice applications in molecular biology. Finally, the author deals with non-grammatical inference and outlines recently obtained results in the setting of cased-based learning of formal languages.

Section 2 starts with Fahmy and Ross' paper on efficient learning of real time one counter automata from equivalence and membership queries. Note that these languages are in general not regular. The resulting algorithm is more efficient than the known one for deterministic one counter automata. Applying Fahmy's decomposition theorem the learning can be divided into two steps. First, an initial segment of the Nerode-automaton is inferred by using Angluin's algorithm. Then, this segment is decomposed into the control and data structure of the target real time one counter automaton.

Koshiba, Makinen and Takada prove strongly deterministic even linear languages to be learnable from positive data. The target class of languages is a proper subset of the set of all context free languages. First, the target class is characterized in terms of a universal grammar and reversible control sets. The resulting learning algorithm is a generalization of Angluin's work on reversible automata and Takada's approach to learn even linear grammars.

Sakamoto introduces the notion of characteristic examples for parenthesis grammars, i.e., examples which exercise every production in the target grammar for their derivation. The main result is a learning algorithm that, given characteristic examples as input, learns by additionally asking membership queries. The construction resembles Sakakibara's approach to learn context free languages from structured examples by asking membership and equivalence queries. This also shows that characteristic examples are quite helpful, since they allow to avoid asking equivalence queries.

The polynomial time learnability of unions of at most k tree patterns via membership and equivalence queries is established by Arimura, Ishizaka, and Shinohara. Note that neither membership nor equivalence queries alone are sufficient to achieve learning of the same target class in polynomial time. Furthermore, the authors introduced a technique called *conservative refinement* that allows updating of the actual hypotheses in a way such that the size of the conjectured number of tree patterns in the target is never exceeded.

Further papers dealing with language learning are presented in Sections 6 and 10. Meyer studies probabilistic language learning of recursively enumerable families of uniformly recursive languages (abbr. indexed families) from positive examples. In this setting, the learner is allowed to flip a coin each time it reads a new example, and to branch its computation in dependence of the outcome of the coin flip. This model has been initiated by Freivalds in 1979. Subsequently, various authors studied the learning capabilities of probabilistic learners in dependence on the success probability required. Interestingly enough, all approaches undertaken so far led to discrete hierarchies. Looking at probabilistic learners that are required to fulfill the subset principle to avoid overgeneralization (guesses describing proper supersets of the target) Meyer discovers a *new* phenomena, i.e., the learning capabilities have a *dense* structure and are strictly decreasing as the success probability converges to 1.

Stephan deals with noisy inference from both positive and negative and only positive examples. The model of noise is as follows. Correct data are required to be presented infinitely often while incorrect data (the noise) is restricted to be presented only finitely often. The main result shows that learning in the limit with noise from positive and negative examples is equivalent to finite learning from noise-free data provided the finite learner has access to an oracle for the halting problem. Variants thereof are proved for learning from noisy positive examples.

Finally, Kobayashi and Yokomori investigate the approximate identification of languages in the limit from positive data. The starting point of their research is to take into account that prior knowledge concerning a suitable hypothesis space is often not available. Hence, one might be forced to perform learning with respect to an *a priori* chosen hypothesis space possibly not containing the target. Clearly, under such circumstances it seems highly desirable to learn the best possible approximation available. Therefore, the authors investigate the learnability of arbitrary target languages with respect to some given indexed family as hypothesis space. Different formalizations of "best possible approximation" are introduced. The resulting learning models are completely characterized with respect to the topological properties the relevant hypothesis spaces must possess in order to achieve approximate learning.

Interestingly, results obtained in language learning can be sometimes applied to solve learning problems arising in different areas. Gavalda and Guijarro (cf. Section 7) study the learnability of Boolean functions. The description chosen are ordered binary decision diagrams, a representation of Boolean functions that has nice computational properties. Assuming a fixed ordering over the set of variables, their algorithm learns a minimal ordered binary decision diagram with respect to that ordering for the target

Boolean function by asking polynomially many equivalence and membership queries. This result is obtained by a reduction to learning regular languages represented by deterministic finite automata. Moreover, since the range of the reduction does not exhaust the whole class of deterministic finite automata the number of queries needed can be reduced.

Learning logic programs

Logic programming and learning logic programs has attracted serious attention at least during the last decade, and constitutes another core area of this conference series. The basic scenario can be described as follows. The learner is generally provided background knowledge B as well as (sequences of) positive (E^+) and negative examples (E^-) (all of which can be regarded as logic programs, too). However, E^+ and E^- usually contain only ground clauses with empty body. The learning goal consists in inferring a hypothesis H (again a logic program) such that E^+ can be derived from $B \wedge H$ while $B \wedge H \wedge E^-$ is contradiction free. Again, if growing initial segments of E^+ and E^- are provided, we arrive at learning in the limit. Variations of this model include the use of membership queries to obtain E^+ and E^- and of equivalence queries (or disjointness queries) to terminate the learning process. Alternatively, E^+ and E^- may be drawn randomly with respect to some unknown probability distribution, and the learner is required to produce with high confidence a hypothesis that has small error (both measured with respect to the underlying probability distribution).

In Section 3, De Raedt and Van Lear propose a new approach to learning first order logic programs from positive and negative examples. The key idea is to view examples as interpretations which are true or false in the target theory instead of taking them as true and false ground facts, i.e., they are taken as a Herbrand model of the target theory. As a result, the role of positive and negative examples has to be changed. This approach has been successfully implemented, and the authors provide experimental data showing that their system can learn classification rules previous systems failed to handle.

Rao studies incremental learning of logic programs. In his setting, incremental means learning predicates in terms of previously learned predicates. This is a nonstandard idea. Combining this idea with the known approach to treat background knowledge as function symbols evaluated in process of resolution by E-unification he arrives at a learning systems that is more powerful than previously designed ones. (cf., e.g., Yamamoto, ALT'93).

Sadohara and Haraguchi present an algorithm for analogical logic program synthesis from positive and negative examples for linear logic programs with a certain restriction. The novelty is to search the hypothesis space for a program that is similar to the target by refuting inappropriate similarities. Interestingly enough, the idea to refute hypothesis spaces born in the field of language learning (cf. Mukouchi and Arikawa, ALT'93) proved to be useful in this rather different setting.

Learning logic formulae

The polynomial time learnability of CNF and DNF formulae is a long standing open problem in algorithmic learning theory. These classes are of special interest, since they provide a natural and universal description of all Boolean concepts. In Section 3, Miyashiro et al. contribute to the analysis of the DNF learning problem.

They consider the learnability of orthogonal F-Horn formulae defined as follows. An F-Horn clause is a disjunction of negative literals and at most one function from the function class F. A k-F-Horn formula is the disjunction of at most k F-Horn clauses with distinct sets of literals (called body). Orthogonal F-Horn formulae have pairwise incomparable bodies with respect to set inclusion. This concept class is a natural generalization of k-quasi Horn formulae. If k-quasi Horn formulae could be proved to be exactly learnable using membership and equivalence queries than DNF formulae are PAC-learnable (cf. Angluin, Frazier and Pitt, *Machine Learning* 9, 147 - 164, 1992). In particular, Miyashiro *et al.* extend the latter result by showing the following. If F is the set of monotone ℓ-CNF formulae then the exact learnability of k-F-Horn formulae via membership and equivalence queries implies the PAC learnability of CNF and DNF with membership queries.

There is another paper closely related to the learnability of monotone DNF, i.e., learning minor closed graph classes by Domingo and Shawe-Taylor (cf. Section 7).

Inferring a DNA sequence

In his invited lecture, Ming Li addresses the problem of how to infer an original DNA sequence with high probability from erroneous copies. A satisfactory solution to this problem is of central importance to the Human Genome Project. The approach developed by Li and his co-authors Kececioglu and Tromp focuses on reconstruction of an original DNA sequence from a small number of erroneous copies, thereby dealing with insertion, deletion, and substitution errors. The main progress made is reducing the number of copies needed from exponentially many to polylogarithmically many. Furthermore, the convergence rate is proved to be polynomial in the length of the copies, and independent of the number of erroneous copies, thus considerably improving known techniques. The analysis of the algorithm developed makes heavy use of Kolmogorov complexity.

Learning recursive functions

Starting with Gold's and Putnam's pioneering work, inductive inference of recursive functions has been widely studied. The source of information provided are arbitrary sequences of input/output pairs of the target function drawn from an infinite set of recursive functions. Admissible hypothesis spaces are recursive enumerations of partial recursive functions the range of which comprises the target set, e.g., an acceptable programming system. The learning goal consists in identifying in the limit a number (program) in the relevant enumeration such that the enumerated function correctly computes the target with respect to the correctness criterion introduced. Many variations of this basic setting have been intensively studied, and the present volume provides further specifications designed to answer questions studied elsewhere. Case *et al.* look at machine induction without revolutionary paradigm shifts. In their model, a paradigm shift is associated with a significant change in the hypothesis guessed by the learner. As a first approach to model "significant" the *length* of a hypothesis is considered. Informally, a revolutionary paradigm shift is one performing an extreme variation in the size from the previously guessed hypothesis to the actual one. The influence of forbidding revolutionary paradigm shifts to the learning power is considered in two variations. First, all hypotheses generated must be not too far (measured by a recursive factor) from the minimal possible size. Second, all guessed hypotheses must be close to each other (again measured by a recursive factor). Finally, the authors combine this approach with the number of paradigm shifts expressed by the number of performed mind changes. Fixing the number of mind changes *a priory* it is shown that one more mind change can be much more liberating than removing the non-revolutionary constraint (in the second formalization).

Kalyanasundaram and Velauthapillai study an old problem that has resisted several attacks. The scenario considered deals with pluralistic learners modeled as a team. A team is said to learn successfully if one of its members infers the target function. The problem addressed is, given two teams with a bounded number of learners each of which is restricted to an *a priory* bounded number of mind changes (one bound for each team) and demanded to infer programs that are correct for all but an *a priory* bounded number of inputs (again one bound for each team), which of them, if any, can learn more than the other. This problem is usually referred to as the six parameter problem, and its complete solution is sought after for roughly 15 years. In particular, the authors provide a complete solution to the four parameter problem (both teams are requested to converge to an error free program).

The question whether or not learning devices are capable to "reflect" about their own competence is addressed by Jantke. Two formalizations are proposed, i.e., immediately reflecting and reflecting, respectively. In both cases, the learner is required to either learn the target function or to detect its incompetence in doing so. Immediately reflecting learners are demanded to detect there inability as soon as there is enough evidence that the initial segment of the target seen so far differs from all functions it can learn. Reflecting machines are allowed to use more time, and possibly more input data before detecting their failure to learn. Though seemingly contradicting our intuition, both formalizations are proved to be equivalent. Morever, the author provides evidence that reflecting about its own competence is possible if and only if there is no need to do so.

Finally, there is a paper dealing with the complexity of learning recursive functions. The model investigated goes back to Freivalds, Kinber and Smith. In their setting, a learner has access to a long term and a short term memory, respectively. Before reading the next input bit, the short term memory is cleared. All information the learner wants to maintain has to be stored in the long term memory. After having read the next input bit the learner can exploit its short term memory to perform all necessary computations to produce its guess as well as to decide which of the data it wants to store in its long term memory. While it was known that every function identifiable at all can be learned with linear long term memory and no short term memory, it remained open how much short term memory must be provided in the worst-case if the long term memory is required to be sublinear. Ambainis presents a complete solution to this problem by showing that every sublinear long term memory may force the learner to exceed any recursively bounded short term memory. As far as we are concerned this result provides evidence that a distinction between long and short term memory might be not appropriate for practical purposes.

Knowledge discovery in databases

In his invited lecture, Yves Kodratoff addresses the emerging topic of knowledge discovery in databases. Nowadays huge databases are available in various fields and there is a growing need for knowledge discovery in such huge databases. Knowledge discovery aims at transforming the information contained in the database into knowledge about it. Starting point is data mining, i.e., the discovery of patterns in the data. Once such patterns have been recognized they should be further processed with the overall goal to interpret them. Clearly, what kind of interpretation is desired may considerably vary in dependence on the envisaged users and goals. Kodratoff provides a thorough overview of the issues addressed and the techniques applied in this important field.

Miscellaneous

Auer (cf. Section 4) investigates the learnability of nested differences of intersection closed concept classes in the presence of malicious noise. The learning models dealt with are the on-line learning model (mistake bound), and the PAC model with malicious noise. The author proves matching upper and lower bounds. It is worth noticing that the tolerable noise rate exclusively depends on the complexity of the target concept *class*, and not on the target itself.

Nakamura and Miura (cf. Section 4) address the problem to learn a $GF(2)$-valued or real-valued function over a finite domain by querying the function values of the target at points the learner can choose. The complexity of learning is measured by the number of queries needed. Since the learning domain is finite, say N, every such function class can be represented by a linear space whose basis B consists of N pairwise independent functions. Then, every function from the concept class possesses a representation as a linear combination of basis functions. The size s of the function is the number of non-zero coefficients in the representation. The query complexity is analyzed in dependence on the domain size N and the target size s. Clearly, the target size depends on the basis, and so may the learnability. Lower and upper bounds are derived that are fairly close to each other.

In Section 7, Castro and Balcazar study simple PAC learning of decision lists. Simple PAC learning is the same as PAC learning except that the class of probability distributions is restricted to simple distributions, assuming that the examples are drawn with respect to the universal distribution. These distributions have been introduced by Li and Vitanyi (*Siam J. Comp.* 20, 911 - 935, 1991) who also showed that simple distributions form a wide and interesting class. In particular, the paper resolves the learnability of simple decisions list that remained open in Li and Vitanyi.

Last but not least, Pinter (cf. Section 7) resolves an open problem from Blum and Rivest (*Machine Learning: From Theory to Applications* 9 - 28, Springer 1993). The problem addressed concerns training very simple neural nets. Consider a fully connected layered neural net whose units compute linear threshold functions that consists of *one* layer and k units. Pinter shows that training such networks is already NP-complete.

Fukuoka, July 1995

Klaus P. Jantke
Takeshi Shinohara
Thomas Zeugmann

Grammatical Inference:
An old and new paradigm

Yasubumi Sakakibara

Institute for Social Information Science, Fujitsu Laboratories Ltd.,
140, Miyamoto, Numazu, Shizuoka 410-03, Japan
(email: yasu@iias.flab.fujitsu.co.jp)

Abstract. In this paper, we provide a survey of recent advances in the
field "grammatical inference" with a particular emphasis on the results
concerning the learnability of target classes represented by deterministic
finite automata, context-free grammars, hidden Markov models, stochastic context-free grammars, simple recurrent neural networks, and case-
based representations.

1 Introduction

Loosely speaking, Grammatical Inference is an inductive inference problem where
the target domain is a formal language and the representation class is a family of grammars. The learning task is to identify a "correct" grammar for the
(unknown) target language, given a finite number of examples of the language.
Grammatical Inference is a well-established research field in Artificial Intelligence as it dates back to the 60s. Gold [25] originated this study and introduced
the notion of *identification in the limit*. His motivation for studying the problem
is to construct a formal model of human language acquisition. Since his seminal
work, there has been a remarkable amount of work to establish a theory of grammatical inference, to find effective and efficient methods for inferring grammars,
and to apply those methods to practical problems.

Grammatical inference has been investigated, more or less independently,
within many research fields, including machine learning, computational learning
theory, pattern recognition, computational linguistics, neural networks, formal
language theory, information theory, and many others. Recently, the international conference on Grammatical Inference has been established with an aim to
bring together researchers from diverse fields and to bring about a stimulating
interdisciplinary interaction between them. The first colloquium on grammatical inference was held in U.K. in April 1993, and the second one in Spain in
September 1994 [19].

There are several excellent survey articles on the field of grammatical inference. An early survey on inductive inference is Angluin and Smith's article [14].
An early good introduction to grammatical inference is Miclet's article [38]. A
recent extensive survey of the inference of deterministic finite automata is Pitt's
paper [42].

Much of the recent research activities on grammatical inference have been stimulated by the new learning models proposed recently within computational learning theory framework: the query learning model of Angluin [10] and the PAC (probably approximately correct) learning model of Valiant [59]. These new models put much more emphasis on the computational efficiency of the inference algorithm. A good introduction to computational learning theory is Laird's paper [34], and a very recent survey of computational learning theory is Angluin's paper [12]. Thus grammatical inference is an old and new paradigm in artificial intelligence.

This paper, rather than being a thorough survey on the topic, is intended mainly as a review of the research carried out by the Machine Learning group at Fujitsu Laboratories Ltd. and related work done at other institutions. The interested reader can consult the above cited survey papers. Also, an important subject which we won't deal with here is inductive inference of *indexable classes* of formal languages (e.g., see [14] and [63] for references). This is because, while we acknowledge that enumeration is a powerful and useful technique in inductive inference, we are more interested in "constructive" methods in the sense that the grammars are constructed directly from training examples rather than by enumeration.

We will begin with the problem of identifying deterministic finite automata (DFAs) from examples. DFAs are the bottom class of formal grammars in the Chomsky hierarchy, and the problem of identifying DFAs from examples has been studied quite extensively [14, 42]. We will pick up several interesting results on identifying DFAs: polynomial-time identification of DFAs from queries, identification of subclasses of DFAs from positive data, computationally hardness results, and identification from erroneous examples. In Section 4, we will consider the problem of identifying context-free grammars (CFGs) because the questions of whether there are analogous results held for context-free grammars would be more interesting and important. The results contain identification of CFGs from examples in the form of structured strings, polynomial-time reduction to identification of finite automata, and efficient identifications of several subclasses of CFGs. In Section 5, since stochastic modeling is very important for practical applications, we will consider the problem of identifying stochastic grammars. A stochastic grammar is obtained by specifying a probability for each production in a grammar. We will review some fundamental methods for training probabilistic parameters in the grammar based on expectation maximization (EM), and their applications to biological sequence analyses. In Section 6, we will see two special topics which use non-grammatical representations for grammatical inference or language learning. One is simple recurrent neural networks and the other is case-based representations.

2 The Learning Models

Within computational learning theory, there are three major established formal models for learning from examples or inductive inference: the *identification in the limit* by Gold [25], the *query learning model* by Angluin [10], and the *PAC learning model* by Valiant [59]. Each model provides a learning protocol and a criterion for the success of learning. Identification in the limit views learning as an infinite process and provides a learning model where an infinite sequence of examples of the unknown grammar G is presented to the inference algorithm M and the eventual or limiting behavior of the algorithm is used as the criterion of its success. A *complete presentation* of the unknown grammar G is an infinite sequence of ordered pairs $\langle w, l \rangle$ from $\Sigma^* \times \{0, 1\}$ such that $l = 1$ if and only if w is generated by G, and such that every string w of Σ^* appears at least once as the first component of some pair in the sequence, where Σ is the terminal alphabet. If after some finite number of steps in a complete presentation of G, M guesses a correct grammar which is equivalent to the unknown grammar G and never changes its guess after this, then M is said to *identify G in the limit from complete presentations.*

Angluin [10] has considered a learning situation in which a teacher is available to answer specific kind of queries on the unknown grammar G and devised an elegant formulation of such a teacher and learner paradigm. In this setup, we can expect the inference algorithm be the *exact identification*, which means the algorithm outputs a correct grammar in a certain finite time. This is no longer a limiting criterion of learning. In the query learning model, a teacher is a fixed set of *oracles* that can answer specific kinds of queries made by the inference algorithm on the unknown grammar G. For example, the following two types of queries are typical:

1. *Membership.* The input is a string $w \in \Sigma^*$ and the output is "yes" if w is generated by G and "no" otherwise.
2. *Equivalence.* The input is a grammar G' and the output is "yes" if G' is equivalent to G (i.e., G' generates the same language as G) and "no" otherwise. If the answer is "no", a string w in the symmetric difference of the language generated by G and the language generated by G' is returned.

For the equivalence query, the returned string w is called a *counter-example*. A membership query returns one bit of information. Nevertheless it often plays an important role in efficient exact identification.

Valiant [59] has introduced the distribution-independent probabilistic model of learning from random examples, which is called *probably approximately correct learning* (PAC learning, for short). In the PAC learning model, we assume that random samples are drawn independently from the domain Σ^* whose probability distribution D may be arbitrary and unknown. The inference algorithm takes a sample as input and produces a grammar as output. The success of identification is measured by two parameters: the accuracy parameter ϵ and the confidence parameter δ, which are given as inputs to the inference algorithm. A successful inference algorithm is one that *with high probability* (at least $1 - \delta$) finds a grammar *whose error is small* (less than ϵ).

We measure the efficiency of the inference algorithm with respect to relevant parameters: the size of examples and the size of the unknown grammar. The *Size* of an example in the form of string is the length of the string. The *Size* of the unknown grammar is usually the number of states, in the case of finite automata, and the number of production rules, in the case of context-free grammars.

3   Learning Finite Automata

The study of the identifiability of deterministic finite automata is an excellent mean for studying a number of general aspects of inductive inference and grammatical inference [42]. In this section, we will review several important results and useful techniques related to computationally efficient identifications of deterministic finite automata.

A *deterministic finite (state) automaton* (DFA) is defined by a 5-tuple $A = (Q, \Sigma, \delta, q_0, F)$, where Q is a finite set of *states*, Σ is an alphabet of input symbols, δ is the *state-transition function* $\delta : Q \times \Sigma \rightarrow Q$, $q_0 \in Q$ is the *initial state*, and $F \subseteq Q$ is a set of *final states*. The *language accepted* by a DFA A is denoted by $L(A)$.

3.1   Learning from representative samples

When trying to identify an unknown DFA $A = (Q, \Sigma, \delta, q_0, F)$ from examples, a useful information about A is the *representative sample S* of A, that is, a finite subset of $L(A)$ that exercises every live transition in A. Taking the set $R(S)$ of all prefixes of strings in S, for every live state q of A, there must exist a string u in $R(S)$ such that $\delta(q_0, u) = q$. Further, for every state q and every transition $\delta(q, a)$ from q where $a \in \Sigma$, there exists a string va in $R(S)$ such that $\delta(q_0, v) = q$ and $\delta(q, a) = \delta(q_0, va) = q'$. Thus every state and transition are represented by strings in $R(S)$. It remains to distinguish two states q_u and q_v represented by two strings u and v in $R(S)$, i.e., $q_u = \delta(q_0, u)$ and $q_v = \delta(q_0, v)$, if q_u and q_v are different states in A. Angluin [7] has given an efficient procedure to solve this problem using membership queries. A *membership query* made by an inference algorithm proposes a string w and asks whether $w \in L(A)$, where A is the unknown DFA. The answer is either "yes" or "no".

Theorem 1 [7]. *The class of deterministic finite automata can be identified in polynomial time from a representative sample and using membership queries.*

3.2   Learning with teachers

Angluin [9] has considered a learning protocol which is based on what is called "minimally adequate teacher". This teacher can answer two types of queries about the unknown DFA A made by an inference algorithm: *membership query* and *equivalence query*. An *equivalence query* proposes a conjecture A' of DFA and asks whether $L(A) = L(A')$. The answer is either "yes" or "no". If it is "no", then it provides a *counterexample*, an arbitrary string w in the symmetric difference of $L(A)$ and $L(A')$. Angluin [9] has shown that the equivalence query compensates for the lack of representative samples, and presented an efficient inference algorithm for identifying DFAs using equivalence and membership queries.

Theorem 2 [9]. *The class of deterministic finite automata can be identified in polynomial time using equivalence queries and membership queries.*

Yokomori [61] has studied efficient identification of *non-deterministic* finite automata from equivalence and membership queries.

3.3 Learning from positive data

One interesting and important topic on the Gold's framework of identification in the limit for language learning is identification from positive data. A *positive presentation* of the unknown DFA A is any infinite sequence of examples such that the sequence contains all and only the strings in the language $L(A)$. Gold [25] has shown that there is a fundamental, important difference in what could be learned from *positive* versus *complete* presentations, and shown a negative result that no "superfinite" class of languages can be identified in the limit from positive presentation. Since the class of regular languages is superfinite, we need to restrict DFAs somehow to subclasses to establish identifiability results from positive presentation.

The problem is to avoid "overgeneralization", which means guessing a language that is a strict superset of the unknown language. Angluin [8] has introduced a series of subclasses of DFAs, called k-reversible automata for $k = 0, 1, 2, \ldots$, and shown that the existence of characteristic samples is sufficient for identification from positive presentation (to avoid overgeneralization) for k-reversible automata and there exist such characteristic samples for the class of k-reversible automata. A *characteristic sample* of a k-reversible automaton A is a finite sample $S \subset L(A)$ such that $L(A)$ is the smallest k-reversible language that contains S. It turns out that any characteristic sample is a representative sample for k-reversible automata.

As we have seen in Section 3.1, a representative sample provides enough information for reconstructions of states and state transitions. By utilizing the structural properties specific to k-reversible automata, we could accomplish the main task of state distinctions in identifying k-reversible automata without the use of membership queries. For example, a *zero-reversible automaton* is a DFA such that it has at most one final state and no two edges entering any state are labeled with the same symbol. Given a representative sample S for the unknown zero-reversible automaton, we construct the prefix tree automaton A' that precisely accepts the set S, and then merge states in A' to satisfy the conditions for zero-reversible automata.

Theorem 3 [8]. *The class of k-reversible automata, for $k = 0, 1, 2, \ldots,$ can be identified in the limit from positive presentation.*

Furthermore, the inference algorithm updates a conjecture in time polynomial in the size of the inputs.

Another interesting class of DFAs which can be identified in the limit from positive presentation is the class of strictly deterministic automata investigated by Yokomori [62]. A *strictly deterministic automaton* is a DFA such that the set of labels W for state-transition edges is extended to be a finite subset of strings over Σ, each edge has the unique label (no same label is attached to different edges), and for each symbol $a \in \Sigma$ there is at most one label in W starting with a.

Theorem 4 [62]. *The class of strictly deterministic automata can be identified in the limit from positive presentation.*

An inference algorithm can be constructed so that it not only runs in time polynomial in m, the maximum length of all positive examples provided, but also makes at most a polynomial number of *implicit errors of prediction* in m and n, the size of the unknown strictly deterministic automaton.

Other interesting topics and results on identification from positive presentation which may not directly be related to DFAs are Angluin's characterization of identifiability from positive presentation [6], Angluin's *pattern languages* [5], Koshiba's extension to *typed pattern languages* [32], Shinohara's general result for identifiability from positive presentation [55], and Oncina et al.'s *subsequential transducers* [40].

3.4 Hardness results

There are many computationally hardness results related to identifying DFAs. Gold [26] has shown that the problem of finding a DFA with a minimum number of states consistent with a given finite sample of positive and negative examples is NP-hard. This result is generally interpreted as indicating that even a very simple case of grammatical inference, identifying DFA from positive and negative examples, is computationally intractable. Further, Pitt and Warmuth [43] have proven a stronger result, namely that it is NP-hard to find a DFA of at most $n^{(1-\epsilon)\log\log n}$ states consistent with a given finite sample of positive and negative examples for any constant $\epsilon > 0$, where n is the number of states of a minimum DFA consistent with the given sample.

Angluin [11] has shown negative results for efficient identifications of various classes of grammars from equivalence queries only. She has developed the useful technique of "approximate fingerprints" to obtain negative results for identification from equivalence queries only.

3.5 Learning from erroneous examples

In practice, it is natural to assume that the examples may contain some noise. There are fewer works to study the effect of noise on learning from queries in the Valiant's probabilistic framework of PAC-learnability.

Sakakibara [48] has defined a benign model for errors in the responses to membership queries where answers to queries are subject to random independent noise (i.e., for each query there is some independent probability to receive an incorrect answer and these errors are not persistent), and shown that these errors can be effectively removed by repeating the query until the confidence in the correct answer is high enough.

Ron and Rubinfeld [46] have considered a model of *persistent* noise in membership queries in which a fixed but randomly chosen fraction of membership queries are answered incorrectly but any additional query on the same string is answered consistently when queried again. They have shown by modifying Angluin's algorithm (Theorem 2) for identifying DFAs using equivalence and membership queries that DFAs can be learned in polynomial time from membership queries with persistent noise under the uniform distribution on inputs.

Sakakibara and Siromoney [53] have studied a noise model which is specific to language learning where the examples are corrupted by purely random errors affecting only the strings (and not the labels). They have considered three types of errors on strings, called *EDIT operation errors*. EDIT operations consist of "insertion", "deletion", and "change" of a symbol in a string. They have shown efficient identification from random examples with EDIT noise for a small subclass of regular languages defined by containment decision lists, a variant of *decision list* [45] to represent languages.

4 Learning Context-Free Grammars

As we have seen in the previous sections, there has been extensive research into the problem of identifying DFAs from examples. The question of whether there are analogous results for context-free grammars is important because context-free grammars are a more interesting class of grammars from the practical point of view.

A *context-free grammar* (CFG) is defined by a quadruple $G = (N, \Sigma, P, S)$, where N is an alphabet of *nonterminal symbols*, Σ is an alphabet of *terminal symbols* such that $N \cap \Sigma = \emptyset$, P is a finite set of production rules of the form $A \rightarrow \alpha$ for $A \in N$ and $\alpha \in (N \cup \Sigma)^*$, and S is a special nonterminal called the *start symbol*. The *language generated* by a CFG G is denoted $L(G)$.

Angluin [11] has shown that the whole class of CFGs cannot be identified in polynomial time using equivalence queries only. Furthermore, Angluin and Kharitonov [13] have shown that the problem of identifying the class of CFGs from membership and equivalence queries is computationally as hard as the cryptographic problems for which there is currently no known polynomial-time algorithm. Despite these negative results, we will present in the following sections several positive results for identifying the whole class of CFGs with additional information or identifying subclasses of CFGs efficiently.

4.1 Learning from structural information

We consider an identification problem for CFGs where, besides given examples, some additional information is available for the inference algorithm. A useful (and maybe reasonable) information would be information on the grammatical structure of the unknown CFG. We assume example presentations in the form

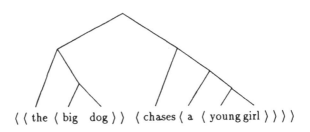

⟨ ⟨ the ⟨ big   dog ⟩ ⟩   ⟨ chases ⟨ a ⟨ young girl ⟩ ⟩ ⟩ ⟩

Fig. 1. An example of structured string for "the big dog chases a young girl".

of strings with grammatical structure. Levy and Joshi [36] have already suggested the possibility of efficient grammatical inferences in terms of strings with grammatical structure.

A string with grammatical structure, called *a structured string* or *a structural description* (of string), is a string with some parentheses inserted to indicate the shape of the derivation tree of a CFG, or equivalently an unlabeled derivation tree of the CFG, that is, a derivation tree whose internal nodes have no labels. (See Figure 1.) It is known that the set of derivation trees of a CFG constitutes a rational set of trees, where a *rational set* of trees is a set of trees which can be recognized by some tree automaton. Further, the set of unlabeled derivation trees of a CFG also constitutes a rational set of trees. Based on these observations, the problem of identifying CFGs from structured strings is reduced to the problem of identifying tree automata.

Sakakibara [47] has shown by extending Angluin's inference algorithm (Theorem 2) for DFAs to tree automata that the class of CFGs can be identified in polynomial time using structural membership queries and structural equivalence queries.

Theorem 5 [47]. *The class of context-free grammars can be identified in polynomial time using structural equivalence queries and structural membership queries.*

A *structural membership query* is a membership query for a structured string, and a *structural equivalence query* returns "yes" if a queried CFG is *structurally equivalent* to the unknown CFG and returns "no" with a counterexample otherwise.

Since the class of CFGs is superfinite, Gold's negative result [25] on identifiability from positive presentation implies that the class of CFGs cannot be identified in the limit from positive presentation. Sakakibara [49] has demonstrated that, here also, information on the grammatical structure of the unknown CFG could help the inference. He has shown that there exists a class of CFGs, called *reversible context-free grammars*, which can be identified in the limit from positive presentations of structured strings, that is, all and only unlabeled derivation trees of the unknown CFG, and shown that the reversible context-free grammar is a normal form for CFGs, that is, reversible context-free grammars can generate all the context-free languages.

A *reversible context-free grammars* is a CFG $G = (N, \Sigma, P, S)$ such that $A \to \alpha$ and $B \to \alpha$ in P implies that $A = B$ and $A \to \alpha B \beta$ and $A \to \alpha C \beta$ in P implies that $B = C$, where A, B, and C are nonterminals, and $\alpha, \beta \in (N \cup \Sigma)^*$.

Theorem 6 [49]. *The class of reversible context-free grammars can be identified in the limit from positive presentation of structured strings.*

Since the inference algorithm for reversible context-free grammars is an extension of Angluin's inference algorithm which identifies zero-reversible automata (Theorem 3), the algorithm updates a conjecture in time polynomial in the size of the inputs. Note that the above result does not imply that the whole class of CFGs can be identified from positive presentation of structured strings.

A related early work to identifying CFGs from positive presentation of structured strings is Crespi-Reghizzi's [20]. He has described a constructive method for identifying a subclass of CFGs, which is a different class from reversible CFGs, from positive samples of structured strings. His class of CFGs defines only a subclass of context-free languages, called *noncounting context-free languages*. Mäkinen [37] has refined Sakakibara's inference algorithm for reversible CFGs to gain more efficiency, and also investigated a subclass of reversible CFGs, called *type invertible grammars*, that can be identified from positive presentation of structured strings in time linear in the size of the inputs.

4.2 Reductions to finite-automata learning problems

A well-known technique often used to establish identifiability results is a *reduction* technique that reduces an inference problem to an other inference problem whose result is known. Takada [57] has shown that the inference problem for even linear grammars can be solved by reducing it to the one for DFAs, and presented a polynomial-time algorithm for the reduction. For example, we can identify the class of even linear grammars using equivalence and membership queries in polynomial time by employing Angluin's efficient algorithm for DFAs (Theorem 2) via reduction.

An *even linear grammar* is a CFG that has productions only of the form $A \to uBv$ or $A \to w$ such that u and v have the same length, where A and B are nonterminals and u, v and w are strings over Σ. Let $G = (N, \Sigma, P, S)$ be an even linear grammar. We write $x \overset{\pi}{\Longrightarrow} y$ to mean that y is derived from x applying the production π in P, where $x, y \in (N \cup \Sigma)^*$. We denote a derivation from x_0 to x_k obtained by applying a sequence $\gamma = \pi_1 \pi_2 \cdots \pi_k$ of productions by $x_0 \overset{\gamma}{\Longrightarrow} x_n$. γ is called an *associate word* and a set of associate words is called a *control set* on G. The language generated by G with a control set C is defined by $L(G, C) = \{w \in \Sigma^* \mid S \overset{\gamma}{\Longrightarrow} w \text{ and } \gamma \in C\}$. It can be shown that there is a universal even linear grammar G_U such that for any even linear grammar G, $L(G) = L(G_U, C)$ for some regular control set C.

Theorem 7 [57]. *The problem of identifying the class of even linear grammars is reduced to the problem of identifying the class of finite automata.*

Note that the class of even linear languages properly contains the class of regular languages and is a proper subclass of context-free languages. By iteratively applying the above reduction technique, Takada [58] has further developed an infinite hierarchy of families of languages whose identification problems are reduced to the identification problem of DFAs.

4.3 Learning subclasses of context-free grammars

Because the whole class of CFGs seems to be hard to be identified efficiently without any additional information, there have been some attempts to design polynomial-time algorithms for identifying *subclasses* of CFGs from examples.

Ishizaka [30] has investigated a subclass of CFGs, called *simple deterministic grammars*, and gave a polynomial-time algorithm for exactly identifying it using equivalence and membership queries in terms of general CFGs. This inference algorithm may sometimes ask an equivalence query for a CFG which is not simple deterministic.

A CFG $G = (N, \Sigma, P, S)$ in 2-standard form is called *simple deterministic* if $A \rightarrow a\alpha$ and $A \rightarrow a\beta$ in P implies that $\alpha = \beta$, where A and B are nonterminals, a is a terminal, and $\alpha, \beta \in (N \cup \Sigma)^*$.

Theorem 8 [30]. *The class of simple deterministic grammars can be identified in polynomial time using equivalence queries and membership queries in terms of general context-free grammars.*

Note that given any regular language L, the language $L\#$ is simple deterministic, where $\#$ is a special symbol not in Σ. In this sense, the class of simple deterministic languages properly contains the class of regular languages.

Yokomori [60] has considered a smaller class of simple deterministic grammars with the goal of finding a polynomial-time algorithm to identify it in the limit from positive presentation. A CFG $G = (N, \Sigma, P, S)$ in Greibach normal form is called *very simple* if for each terminal symbol a in Σ, there exists exactly one production rule starting with a (i.e., exactly one production rule of the form $A \rightarrow a\alpha$, where $\alpha \in (N \cup \Sigma)^*$). He has shown that the class of very simple grammars can efficiently be identified in the limit from positive presentation, and this result has provided the first instance of language class containing non-regular languages that can be identified in the limit in polynomial time in the sense of Pitt [42], that is, the time for updating a conjecture is bounded by a polynomial in the size n of the unknown grammar and the sum of lengths of examples provided, and the number of times the inference algorithm makes a wrong conjecture is bounded by a polynomial in n.

Theorem 9 [60]. *The class of very simple grammars can be identified in the limit from positive presentation in polynomial time.*

From this result, it immediately follows that the class of very simple grammars can be identified in polynomial time using only equivalence queries.

Related to identification of very simple grammars, Burago [18] has investigated the structurally reversible context-free grammars, and shown that the class of structurally reversible CFGs can be identified in polynomial time using equivalence queries and membership queries. A CFG is called *structurally reversible* if among all nonterminal strings that might derive a given terminal string, no one is an extension of the other. The class of structurally reversible CFGs is a subclass of CFGs and the class of structurally reversible context-free languages properly contains the class of very simple languages.

Other representation forms for languages which are not in the form of grammars sometimes help understanding the mathematical structures and designing efficient inference algorithms. Fahmy and Biermann [23] have investigated identification of *real time acceptors*. The class of languages accepted by real time acceptors is a subclass of context-sensitive languages and incomparable with the class of context-free languages.

5 Learning Stochastic Grammars

Another major research topic in grammatical inference is stochastic modeling and training of stochastic grammars. Stochastic modeling has become increasingly important for applications such as speech recognition, natural language processing, and biological sequence analysis. A *stochastic grammar* is obtained by specifying a probability for each production in a grammar. A stochastic grammar assigns a probability to each string which it derives and hence defines a probability distribution on the set of strings. Stochastic (probabilistic) automata are the probabilistic counterpart of finite automata that are known as *hidden Markov models* (HMMs) and very extensively used in speech recognition. *Stochastic context-free grammars* (SCFGs) is a superclass of and goes one step beyond hidden Markov models in the Chomsky hierarchy.

The problem of identifying stochastic grammars has two aspects: determining the discrete structure (topology) of the grammar and estimating probabilistic parameters in the grammar. Based on the maximum likelihood criterion, efficient estimation algorithms for probabilistic parameters have been proposed: *forward-backward algorithm* for HMMs [44] and *inside-outside algorithm* for SCFGs [16, 35]. The relative success of stochastic grammars in real tasks is due to the existence of these techniques for automatic estimation of probabilities and distributions. Both algorithms are iterative algorithms which are based on the expectation-maximization (EM) technique that increases the likelihood of the training sample in each step until a local maximum is reached. Therefore, the initialization in the iterative process is a crucial point since it affects the speed of convergence and the goodness of the results. On the other hand, finding an appropriate discrete structure of the grammar is a harder problem. In certain cases, it might be possible to consider the inference of the discrete structure as a result of the probability estimation process. For example, in the case of HMM, we start with a fully connected HMM, get a locally maximum estimation of probabilities, and obtain a structure of HMM by pruning out zero or low probability transitions. However, this method does not seem to be effective or efficient. In fact, Abe and Warmuth [2] have shown a computationally hardness result for the inference of probabilistic automata.

In the remaining of this section, we will focus on probability estimation procedures for HMM and SCFG.

5.1 Hidden Markov models

A *Hidden Markov Model* (HMM) is defined by a 5-tuple $\lambda = (Q, \Sigma, T, O, \pi)$, where Q is a finite set of states, Σ is an alphabet of output symbols, T is a state transition probability distribution, O is an output symbol probability distribution, and π is an initial state distribution. Let $Q = \{q_1, \ldots, q_n\}$. T is the set $\{t_{ij} \mid 1 \leq i, j \leq n\}$ of state transition probabilities where t_{ij} is a state transition probability from state q_i to state q_j, O is the set $\{o_j(a) \mid 1 \leq j \leq n, a \in \Sigma\}$ of output symbol probabilities where $o_j(a)$ is a probability to output a at state q_j, and π is the set $\{\pi_i \mid 1 \leq i \leq n\}$ of initial state probabilities where π_i is the probability to start at state q_i.

Given a HMM λ, there are three basic problems for dealing with λ: given a string $w = a_1 \cdots a_m$,

1. calculate $\Pr(w|\lambda)$, the probability of the string w,
2. find the most probable path $s = q_{i_1} \cdots q_{i_l}$ of states to maximize $\Pr(s|w, \lambda)$,
3. estimate the parameters in λ to maximize $\Pr(w|\lambda)$.

These problems can be solved efficiently using dynamic programming techniques [44]. A polynomial-time algorithm for solving the second algorithm is known as *Viterbi* algorithm, and a polynomial-time algorithm for the third problem is known as *Forward-Backward (Baum-Welch)* algorithm. To solve the first problem, we consider the forward variable $\alpha_k(q_i)$ defined as $\alpha_k(q_i) = \Pr(a_1 \cdots a_k, q_i|\lambda)$, i.e., the probability of the initial segment $a_1 \cdots a_k$ of the string w and state q_i at time k. The probability $\alpha_k(q_i)$ can be calculated inductively as follows:

1. Initialization:
$$\alpha_1(q_i) = \pi_i o_i(a_1)$$

2. Induction:
$$\alpha_{k+1}(q_j) = \left(\sum_{i=1}^{N} \alpha_k(q_i) t_{ij} \right) o_j(a_{k+1})$$

3. Termination:
$$\Pr(w|\lambda) = \sum_{i=1}^{N} \alpha_m(q_i).$$

The forward-backward algorithm is an EM (expectation maximization) algorithm which finds parameters in the HMM λ to maximize $\Pr(w|\lambda)$. It proceeds as follows:

1. Let λ_{old} be an initial guess for the parameters.
2. Based on λ_{old} and the given string w,
   (a) For each pair q_i, q_j of states, estimate the fraction of times a transition is made from q_i to q_j among all transitions out of q_i. In λ_{new}, set t_{ij} to this value.
   (b) For each state q_j and output symbol a, estimate the fraction of times that a is output in state q_j. In λ_{new}, set $o_j(a)$ to this value.
3. Set $\lambda_{old} = \lambda_{new}$ and iterate starting at step 2 until there are no significant changes in λ_{old}.

The forward-backward algorithm for HMMs is very efficient because of the use of dynamic programming techniques, including the forward procedure and the symmetric "backward" procedure. Each iteration in the algorithm increases $\Pr(w|\lambda)$, but the algorithm can still get caught in local maxima. The algorithm is easily extended to handle a set of strings, but the algorithm suffers from the usual problems with maximum likelihood estimates: when it observe something 0 times, it sets the probability to 0.

5.2 Stochastic context-free grammars

A *stochastic context-free grammar* (SCFG) G consists of a set of nonterminal symbols N, a terminal alphabet Σ, a set P of production rules with associated probabilities, and the start symbol S. The associated probability for every production $A \rightarrow \alpha$ in P is denoted $\Pr(A \rightarrow \alpha)$, and a probability distribution exists over the set of productions which have the same nonterminal on the left-hand sides.

The three basic problems to deal with SCFGs which are same as in HMMs can be solved efficiently. The first two problems, calculating the probability $\Pr(w|G)$ of a given string w assigned by a SCFG G and finding the most likely derivation tree of w by G, can be solved using dynamic programming methods analogous to the Cocke-Kasami-Young or Early parsing methods [4]. There is a standard method for estimating the parameters of an SCFG (i.e. the probabilities of the productions) from a set of training strings. This procedure is known as the *inside-outside* algorithm [35]. Just like the forward-backward algorithm for HMMs, this procedure is an expectation-maximization (EM) method for obtaining maximum likelihood of the grammar's parameters. However, it requires the grammar to be in Chomsky normal form, which is inconvenient to handle in many practical problems (and requires more nonterminals). Further, it takes time at least proportional to n^3, whereas the forward-backward procedure for HMMs takes time proportional to n^2, where n is the length of the typical string. There are also many local maxima in which the method can get caught.

To avoid such problems, Sakakibara et al. [50] have developed a new method for training SCFGs that is a generalization of the forward-backward algorithm to tree grammars and which is more efficient than the inside-outside algorithm. The new algorithm, called Tree-Grammar EM, requires structured strings as training examples. This algorithm uses a similar idea to identification of CFGs from structured strings shown in Section 4.1. Since information on the grammatical structure is given explicitly in training strings, Tree-Grammar EM does not have to (implicitly) consider *all* possible derivations of the training strings when reestimating the grammar's parameters, as the inside-outside algorithm must do. This reduces the time complexity to a time proportional to n per training string of length n, and hence may be practical on longer strings. Tree-Grammar EM also tends to converge faster because each training structured string is much more informative.

Sakakibara et al. [50] have also modified the algorithm to train SCFGs even from (unstructured) strings. If only unstructured training strings are available, we iteratively estimate the structure of the training strings as follows:

1. Start with a initial grammar and parse the training strings to obtain a set of partially structured strings.
2. Estimate a new SCFG using the partially structured strings and the estimation algorithm Tree-Grammar EM.
3. Use the trained grammar to obtain more accurately structured training strings.
4. Repeat steps 2 and 3 until finding the structures stabilizes.

In natural language processing, Pereira and Schabes [41] have developed a similar method to Tree-Grammar EM for training SCFGs from bracketed sentences to incorporate linguistic information. Their method utilizes phrase bracketing information during the estimation process of the inside-outside algorithm to get a linguistically-motivated maximum.

Stolcke and Omohundro [56] have considered identification of a discrete structure of the stochastic grammar. They have proposed efficient heuristic methods for finding the topology of HMM and for finding an appropriate set of production rules of SCFG based on Bayesian criterion, and shown some experimental results.

5.3 Applications to molecular sequence analyses

Attempts to understand the folding, structure, function and evolution of molecules have resulted in the confluence of many diverse disciplines ranging from structural biology and chemistry, to computer science and computational linguistics. Rapid generation of sequence data in recent years thus provides abundant opportunities for developing new approaches, to problems in computational biology [29]. Determining common or consensus patterns among a family of sequences, producing a multiple sequence alignment, discriminating members of the family from non-members and discovering new members of the family will continue to be some of the most important and fundamental tasks in mathematical analysis and comparison of macromolecular sequences.

Recently, Searls [54, 29] has argued the benefits of viewing the biological strings representing DNA, RNA and protein as sentences derived from a formal grammar. In this new direction of computational biology research, stochastic context-free grammars have been applied to the problems of folding, aligning and modeling families of tRNA sequences [50]. SCFGs capture the sequences' common primary and secondary structure (See Figure 2) and generalize the HMMs used in related work on protein and DNA. Results show that after having been trained on as few as 20 tRNA sequences from only two tRNA sub-families (mitochondrial and cytoplasmic), the model can discern general tRNA from similar-length RNA sequences of other kinds, can find secondary structure of new tRNA sequences, and can produce multiple alignments of large sets of tRNA sequences. Figure 3 shows an example of multiple sequence alignment (which is a central problem in computational biology) produced by the learned grammar: the learned grammar has successfully produced a very accurate multiple alignments for some family (gene) of molecular sequences, called tRNA.

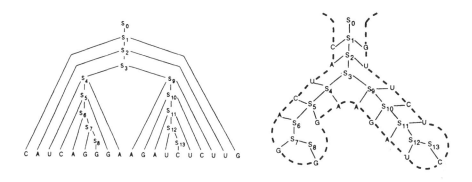

Fig. 2. A derivation tree (left) generated by a simple CFG for RNA molecules and the physical secondary structure (right) of the RNA sequence which is a reflection of the derivation tree.

Related to the above work, Krogh et al. [33] have applied HMMs to the problems of statistical modeling, database searching and multiple sequence alignment of protein families and protein domains. These methods are demonstrated on the globin family, the protein kinase catalytic domain, and the EF-hand calcium binding motif. In each case, the parameters of an HMM are estimated from a training set of unaligned sequences. The HMM produces multiple alignments of good quality that agree closely with the alignments produced by programs that incorporate three-dimensional structural information. When employed in discrimination tests, the HMM is able to distinguish members of these families from non-members with a high degree of accuracy.

Recently, Abe and Mamitsuka [1] have studied a more powerful class of grammars, called *stochastic ranked node rewriting grammars*, than SCFGs and applied it to the problem of secondary structure prediction of proteins.

```
     <     D-domain    > <   Anticodon   >< Extra ><    T-domain    >
 ((((  ((((              )))) ((((( === )))))            (((((      )))))))
AAGGUGGCAGAGUUCGGCCUAACGCGGCGGCCUGCAGAGCCGCUC----AUCGCCGGUUCAAAUCCGGCCCU
CGUGUGGCGUAGUC-GGU--AGCGCGCUCCCUUAGCAUGGGAGAG----GUCUCCGGUUCGAUUCCGGACUC
CCCAUCGUCUAGA--GGCCUAGGACACCUCCCUUUCACGGAGGCG----A-CGGGGAUUCGAAUUCCCUGG
GGCAUAGCCAAGC--GGU--AAGGCCGUGGAUUGCAAAUCCUCUA----UUCCCCAGUUCAAAUCUGGGUGC
UUUGUAGUUUAUGUG-----AAAAUGCUUGUUUGUGAUAUGAGUGAAAU-----------------UGG

 ((((  ((((              )))) ((((( === )))))            (((((      )))))))
AAGGUGGCAG.AGUUcGGccUAACGCGGCGGCCUGCAGAGCCGCUC---AUCGCCGGUUCAAAUCCGGCCCU
CGUGUGGCGU.AGUC.GG..UAGCGCGCUCCCUUAGCAUGGGAGAGG---UCUCCGGUUCGAUUCCGGACUC
CC-AUCGUCU.AGAG.GCc.UAGGACACCUCCCUUUCACGGAGGCG----ACGGGGAUUCGAAUUCCCCU-G
GGCAUAGCCA.AGC-.GG..UAAGGCCGUGGAUUGCAAAUCCUCUA---UUCCCCAGUUCAAAUCUGGGUGC
UUUGUAGUUU.A--U.GU..GAAAAUGCUUGUUUGUGAUAUGAGUGA--AAU----------------UGG
```

Fig. 3. Comparison of the alignment of several representative tRNAs produced by trained (learned) grammar (bottom) with that from the biologically trusted database (top). Parentheses indicate base-paired positions; === the anticodon.

6 Learning with non-grammatical representations

In grammatical inference, formal grammars or finite automata are usually used to represent the unknown languages. There are many other forms of representations which define languages. A typical example of representations which are not in the form of grammars is *regular expressions* for regular languages. Brāzma and Čerāns [17] have studied efficient identification of regular expressions from good examples. Arikawa et al. [15] have considered *elementary formal systems*, a variant of logic programs, for identification of context sensitive languages.

In this section, we study two non-grammatical representation classes which are very hot and interesting topics in machine learning: one is simple recurrent neural networks and the other is case-based representations.

6.1 Connectionist approach

In neural network studies, recurrent neural networks have been shown to have the potential to encode *temporal* properties of a sequence of inputs. There have been proposed many recurrent neural network models [28] for dealing with temporal sequences, and here we consider variations of the *simple recurrent neural network* introduced by Elman [22]. In addition to the input and hidden units, the architecture of simple recurrent networks has an extra hidden layer of *context units* which acts as the memory or the internal state of the network (Figure 4). Thus the simple recurrent network is a two-layer feedforward network augmented by the context units and the feedback connections to context units. There has been a great deal of interest in training simple recurrent networks to recognize grammars and simulate finite automata [24].

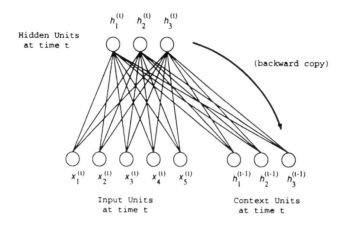

Fig. 4. Simple recurrent neural network.

Sakakibara and Golea [51] have proposed the simple recurrent network of Figure 4. The random variables represented by the input units take real values in $\mathcal{R}$, and the hidden variables represented by the hidden units take values in $\{0,1\}$. The hidden variables represented by context units also take values in $\{0,1\}$. The context units simply hold a *copy* of the activations (state) of the hidden units from the previous time step. Thus the next state of the hidden units is determined by the inputs and the state of the context units, the latter is equal to the previous state of the hidden units. From the finite-automata point of view, this dynamic structure is a finite-state machine and the simple recurrent network represents a state-transition function. Hence simple recurrent networks should be able to perform the same type of computations as finite automata and solve grammatical inference problems.

Sakakibara and Golea [51] have proposed these simple recurrent neural networks as probabilistic models for representing and predicting time-sequences, and shown that the model can be viewed as a generalized hidden Markov model with distributed representations. First, the state transition and the output probability functions are nonlinear. Second, the model can deal with high-dimensional, real valued vectors as output symbols. Third, it has an efficient learning algorithm using dynamic programming based on gradient descent (the algorithm can be seen as an extension of back-propagation). Moreover, compared to the previous attempts to link neural nets and HMM, the present model is more appealing because it does not require a specifically tailored architecture, e.g. *second order connections* where the multiplication operation is used between connection weights [24].

The model of Sakakibara and Golea [51] provides a new probabilistic formulation of learning in simple recurrent networks. They have presented some very preliminary simulation results to demonstrate the potential capabilities of the model. The very simple test uses a simple recurrent network with one input, two hidden units, and two context units to learn the periodic sequence "$-2, 0, 2, -2, 0, 2, -2, 0, 2, ...$". The learned recurrent network is shown in Figures 5 and 6. It is easy to see that the network represents a probabilistic finite automaton (HMM) and that each binary vector in the hidden layer corresponds to a state in the automaton. The output probability distribution is a time-varying (state-dependent) mixture of four basic Gaussians with variance $\sigma = 1$ and means 0, w_1, w_2, and $w_1 + w_2$. It is interesting to see how the learned recurrent network encodes the state transition function and the output function of the finite automaton in a distributed manner. For example, the learned network starts with two initial states, represented by the vectors "$(0, 0)$" and "$(0, 1)$", which have significant initial probabilities, and then repeats a sequence of state transitions: "$(0, 1) \rightarrow (1, 0) \rightarrow (1, 1) \rightarrow (0, 1)$".

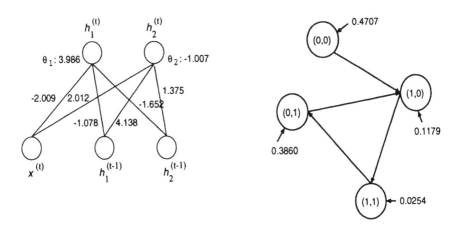

Fig. 5. The learned RNN and its equivalent probabilistic FA.

Golea et al. [27] have also presented another experimental results that use simple recurrent networks for time series prediction, and shown that the learned network is robust for outliers in noisy time sequences.

Giles et al. [24] has enhanced simple recurrent networks by connecting to an external analog stack memory. It is called a *neural net pushdown automaton*, and manipulates the operations "push" and "pop" of the external stack and reads the top of the stack. They have tested its ability to learn some simple context-free grammars.

6.2 Case-based representation and learning

Case-based reasoning is deemed an important technology to alleviate the bottle-neck of knowledge acquisition in Artificial Intelligence. In case-based reasoning,

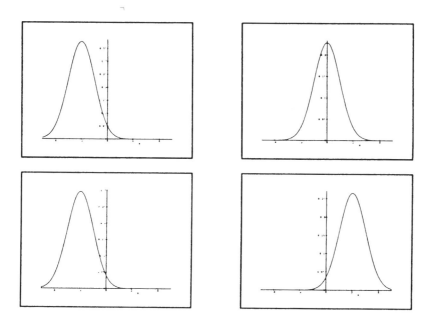

Fig. 6. Output probability distributions for state transitions: left-upper for $(0,0) \rightarrow (1,0)$, left-lower for $(0,1) \rightarrow (1,0)$, right-upper for $(1,0) \rightarrow (1,1)$, and right-lower for $(1,1) \rightarrow (0,1)$

knowledge is represented in the form of particular cases with an appropriate similarity measure rather than any form of rules. The main task of case-based learning is to collect good cases which will be stored in the case base for describing knowledge and classifying unknown examples [3]. Thus, case-based learning algorithms do not construct explicit generalizations from examples which most other supervised learning algorithms derive.

A *similarity measure* σ on Σ^* which defines a similarity between two strings is a computable function from $\Sigma^* \times \Sigma^*$ to real interval $[0,1]$. A *case base CB* is a finite subset of $\Sigma^* \times \{0,1\}$. We call a case $(w,1)$ in CB a *positive case* and $(w,0)$ a *negative case*. The language $L(CB,\sigma)$ represented by a similarity measure σ and a finite case base CB is defined as follows.

$$L(CB,\sigma) = \{w \in \Sigma^* \mid \exists (u,1) \in CB \ [\ \sigma(u,w) > 0 \ \wedge$$
$$\forall (v,0) \in CB \ [\ \sigma(u,w) > \sigma(v,w)]\}$$

We restrict all positive cases to be taken from the unknown language and all negative cases to be taken from the complement of the language.

A formal framework for case-based learning has recently been developed by Jantke and Lange [31] in an inductive inference manner. Sakakibara et al. [52] have investigated the power and the limitations of such case-based learning algorithms for formal languages in this framework. They have first shown that any indexable class of recursive languages is case-based representable, but many

Grammar   Case-based representation

$$G = \left\{ \begin{array}{l} S \rightarrow AB, \ B \rightarrow cBd, \\ A \rightarrow aAb, \ B \rightarrow cd, \\ A \rightarrow ab \end{array} \right\} \qquad \left\{ \begin{array}{l} (abcd, 1) \\ (aabbccdd, 1) \\ (abcccddd, 1) \\ (aac, 0) \\ (bbb, 0) \end{array} \right\} + \sigma(x, y)$$

$\qquad\qquad\qquad\qquad\qquad\qquad\qquad\quad$ *case base* $\qquad$ *similarity measure*

Fig. 7. An example of grammatical representation and case-based representation for the language $\{a^m b^m c^n d^n \mid m, n > 0\}$.

classes of languages including the class of all regular languages are not case-based learnable with a fixed universal similarity measure, even if both positive and negative examples are presented.

Theorem 10 [52]. *Let $\mathcal{L}$ be any indexed class of recursive languages. There is a universal similarity measure σ such that every language L in $\mathcal{L}$ can be represented by σ and a finite case base CB of positive and negative cases, i.e., $L = L(CB, \sigma)$.*

For a complete presentation s and a natural number n, let $s_{\leq n}$ denote the initial segment of s of length n. A class of languages $\mathcal{L}$ is *case-based learnable (in the limit) from complete presentation* if and only if there are an algorithm M and a similarity measure σ such that for all $L \in \mathcal{L}$ and for all complete presentation s of L, there exists some case base CB:

1. $\forall n \in \mathbb{N} : M(s_{\leq n}) = CB_n$ is defined,
2. $\forall n \in \mathbb{N} : \emptyset \subseteq CB_1 \subseteq \{(w_1, l_1)\}$ and $CB_n \subseteq CB_{n+1} \subseteq CB_n \cup \{(w_{n+1}, l_{n+1})\}$,
3. $\lim_{n \rightarrow \infty} M(s_{\leq n}) = CB$,
4. $L = L(CB, \sigma)$.

Theorem 11 [52]. *Let $\mathcal{L}$ be the class of all finite and all co-finite languages. Then $\mathcal{L}$ is not case-based learnable from complete presentation.*

Next Sakakibara et al. [52] have considered a framework of case-based learning where the learning algorithm is allowed to learn similarity measures, too. An interesting and important method for learning similarity measures is given by adopting weighting scheme for cases like the weighted nearest neighbor algorithm. This scheme is based on the idea that some cases stored within the case base are more reliable than others. This can be accomplished with the weights in similarity measures: reliable strings are given larger weights making them more similar to strings in the target domain. Then by allowing only to learn parameters of the weights in the similarity measures, they have shown that any indexable class of recursive languages is case-based learnable. This implies, in particular, that all context-free languages are case-based learnable by collecting cases and learning parameters of the similarity measure.

7 Conclusions

We have reviewed many recent advances in the grammatical inference research. Grammatical inference is considered a main subject of inductive inference, and grammars are important representations to be investigated in machine learning from both theoretical and practical points of view. In particular, recent research activities appeal more to the practical aspects such as computational linguistics and molecular sequence processing.

Since stochastic modeling would strongly be required for practical applications, an important future problem is to find efficient algorithms which solve both problems of determining the structure of the grammar and estimating the probabilistic parameters on identifying stochastic grammars. Those algorithms should be guaranteed theoretically for their correctnesses of identifiabilities and efficiencies. Other interesting topic which we have not dealt with in this article is Genetic Search for identification of the grammars, i.e., a search using genetic algorithm techniques for finding (approximating) the target grammar. Some works (e.g., [21]) have been done to see the effectiveness of genetic search for grammatical inference problems. Finally, the formal language domain (in particular, DFAs) has been studied quite well in the PAC learning model (e.g., [39]) while we have reviewed only a few works for PAC learnabilities of formal languages.

Acknowledgements

We would like to thank Mostefa Golea, Takashi Yokomori, Takeshi Koshiba and Mitsuhiko Toda for their reading the draft and providing many valuable comments. Especially, Mostefa has helped very much for improving the paper. We also greatly thank our colleagues at the Machine Learning group at Fujitsu Labs., Hiroki Ishizaka (currently, at Kyushu Institute of Technology), Takeshi Koshiba, Masahiro Matsuoka, Yuji Takada, and Takashi Yokomori (currently, at University of Electro-Communications) for their excellent contributions to grammatical inference and enjoyable discussions.

References

1. N. Abe and H. Mamitsuka. A new method for predicting protein secondary structures based on stochastic tree grammars. In *Proceedings of 11th International Conference on Machine Learning*, 1994.
2. N. Abe and M. K. Warmuth. On the computational complexity of approximating distributions by probabilistic automata. *Machine Learning*, 9:205–260, 1992.
3. D. W. Aha, D. Kibler, and M. K. Albert. Instance-based learning algorithms. *Machine Learning*, 6:37–66, 1991.
4. A. V. Aho and J. D. Ullman. *The Theory of Parsing, Translation and Compiling, Vol. I: Parsing.* Prentice Hall, Englewood Cliffs, N.J., 1972.
5. D. Angluin. Finding patterns common to a set of strings. *Journal of Computer and System Sciences*, 21:46–62, 1980.

6. D. Angluin. Inductive inference of formal languages from positive data. *Information and Control*, 45:117–135, 1980.

7. D. Angluin. A note on the number of queries needed to identify regular languages. *Information and Control*, 51:76–87, 1981.

8. D. Angluin. Inference of reversible languages. *Journal of the ACM*, 29:741–765, 1982.

9. D. Angluin. Learning regular sets from queries and counter-examples. *Information and Computation*, 75:87–106, 1987.

10. D. Angluin. Queries and concept learning. *Machine Learning*, 2:319–342, 1988.

11. D. Angluin. Negative results for equivalence queries. *Machine Learning*, 5:121–150, 1990.

12. D. Angluin. Computational learning theory: survey and selected bibliography. In *Proceedings of 24th Annual ACM Symposium on Theory of Computing*, pages 351–369. ACM Press, 1992.

13. D. Angluin and M. Kharitonov. When won't membership queries help? In *Proceedings of 23rd Annual ACM Symposium on Theory of Computing*, pages 444–454. ACM Press, 1991.

14. D. Angluin and C. H. Smith. Inductive inference : Theory and methods. *ACM Computing Surveys*, 15(3):237–269, 1983.

15. S. Arikawa, T. Shinohara, and A. Yamamoto. Elementary formal systems as a unifying framework for language learning. In *Proceedings of 2nd Workshop on Computational Learning Theory*, pages 312–327. Morgan Kaufmann, 1989.

16. J. K. Baker. Trainable grammars for speech recognition. *Speech Communication Papers for the 97th Meeting of the Acoustical Society of America*, pages 547–550, 1979.

17. A. Brāzma and K. Čerāns. Efficient learning of regular expressions from good examples. In *Proceedings of 4th International Workshop on Analogical and Inductive Inference (AII'94)*, Lecture Notes in Artificial Intelligence 872, pages 76–90. Springer-Verlag, 1994.

18. A. Burago. Learning structurally reversible context-free grammars from queries and counterexamples in polynomial time. In *Proceedings of 7th Workshop on Computational Learning Theory (COLT'93)*, pages 140–146. ACM Press, 1994.

19. R. C. Carrasco and J. Oncina, editors. *Proceedings of Second International Colloquium on Grammatical Inference (ICGI-94)*, Lecture Notes in Artificial Intelligence 862. Springer-Verlag, 1994.

20. S. Crespi-Reghizzi. An effective model for grammar inference. In B. Gilchrist, editor, *Information Processing 71*, pages 524–529. Elsevier North-Holland, 1972.

21. P. Dupon. Regular grammatical inference from positive and negative samples by genetic search: the GIG method. In *Proceedings of Second International Colloquium on Grammatical Inference (ICGI-94)*, Lecture Notes in Artificial Intelligence 862, pages 236–245. Springer-Verlag, 1994.

22. J. L. Elman. Distributed representations, simple recurrent networks, and grammatical structure. *Machine Learning*, 7:195–225, 1991.

23. A. F. Fahmy and A. W. Biermann. Synthesis of real time acceptors. *Journal of Symbolic Computation*, 15:807–842, 1993.

24. C. L. Giles, G. Z. Sun, H. H. Chen, Y. C. Lee, and D. Chen. Higher order recurrent networks & grammatical inference. In *Advances in Neural Information Processing Systems 2*, pages 380–387. Morgan Kaufmann, 1990.

25. E. M. Gold. Language identification in the limit. *Information and Control*, 10:447–474, 1967.

26. E. M. Gold. Complexity of automaton identification from given data. *Information and Control*, 37:302–320, 1978.
27. M. Golea, M. Matsuoka, and Y. Sakakibara. Unsupervised learning of time-varying probability distributions using two-layer recurrent networks. Unpublished manuscript, 1995.
28. J. Hertz, A. Krogh, and R. G. Palmer. *Introduction to the Theory of Neural Computation*. Addison-Wesley, 1991.
29. L. Hunter. *Artificial Intelligence and Molecular Biology*. AAAI Press/MIT Press, 1993.
30. H. Ishizaka. Polynomial time learnability of simple deterministic languages. *Machine Learning*, 5:151–164, 1990.
31. K. P. Jantke and S. Lange. Case-based representation and learning of pattern languages. In *Proceedings of 4th Workshop on Algorithmic Learning Theory (ALT'93)*, Lecture Notes in Artificial Intelligence 744, pages 87–100. Springer-Verlag, 1993.
32. T. Koshiba. Typed pattern languages and their learnability. In *Proceedings of 2nd European Conference on Computational Learning Theory (EuroCOLT'95)*, Lecture Notes in Artificial Intelligence 904, pages 367–379. Springer-Verlag, 1995.
33. A. Krogh, M. Brown, I. S. Mian, K. Sjölander, and D. Haussler. Hidden Markov models in computational biology: Applications to protein modeling. *Journal of Molecular Biology*, 235:1501–1531, Feb. 1994.
34. P. D. Laird. A survey of computational learning theory. In R. B. Banerji, editor, *Formal Techniques in Artificial Intelligence - A Sourcebook*, pages 173–215. Elsevier Science Publishers, 1990.
35. K. Lari and S. J. Young. The estimation of stochastic context-free grammars using the inside-outside algorithm. *Computer Speech and Language*, 4:35–56, 1990.
36. L. S. Levy and A. K. Joshi. Skeletal structural descriptions. *Information and Control*, 39:192–211, 1978.
37. E. Mäkinen. On the structural grammatical inference problem for some classes of context-free grammars. *Information Processing Letters*, 42:193–199, 1992.
38. L. Miclet. Grammatical inference. In H. Bunke and A. Sanfeliu, editors, *Syntactic and Structural Pattern Recognition - Theory and Applications*, pages 237–290. World Scientific, 1986.
39. S. Miyano, A. Shinohara, and T. Shinohara. Which classes of elementary formal systems are polynomial-time learnable? In *Proceedings of 2nd Workshop on Algorithmic Learning Theory (ALT'91)*, pages 139–150. Japanese Society for Artificial Intelligence, Ohmsha, Ltd, 1991.
40. J. Oncina, P. Garcia, and E. Vidal. Learning subsequential transducers for pattern recognition interpretation tasks. *IEEE Transactions on Pattern Analysis and Machine Intelligence*, 15:448–458, 1993.
41. F. Pereira and Y. Schabes. Inside-outside reestimation for partially bracketed corpora. In *Proceedings of 30th Annual Meeting of the Association for Computational Linguistics*, pages 128–135, 1992.
42. L. Pitt. Inductive inference, DFAs, and computational complexity. In *Proceedings of AII-89 Workshop on Analogical and Inductive Inference (Lecture Notes in Computer Science, 397)*, pages 18–44. Springer-Verlag, 1989.
43. L. Pitt and M. K. Warmuth. The minimum consistent DFA problem cannot be approximated within any polynomial. In *Proceedings of 21st Annual ACM Symposium on Theory of Computing*. ACM Press, 1989.
44. L. R. Rabiner. A tutorial on hidden Markov models and selected applications in speech recognition. *Proc IEEE*, 77(2):257–286, 1989.

45. R. L. Rivest. Learning decision lists. *Machine Learning*, 2:229–246, 1987.
46. D. Ron and R. Rubinfeld. Learning fallible deterministic finite automata. *Machine Learning*, 18:149–185, 1995.
47. Y. Sakakibara. Learning context-free grammars from structural data in polynomial time. *Theoretical Computer Science*, 76:223–242, 1990.
48. Y. Sakakibara. On learning from queries and counterexamples in the presence of noise. *Information Processing Letters*, 37:279–284, 1991.
49. Y. Sakakibara. Efficient learning of context-free grammars from positive structural examples. *Information and Computation*, 97:23–60, 1992.
50. Y. Sakakibara, M. Brown, R. Hughey, I. S. Mian, K. Sjolander, R. C. Underwood, and D. Haussler. Stochastic context-free grammars for tRNA modeling. *Nucleic Acids Research*, 22:5112–5120, 1994.
51. Y. Sakakibara and M. Golea. Simple recurrent networks as generalized hidden markov models with distributed representations. Unpublished manuscript, 1995.
52. Y. Sakakibara, K. P. Jantke, and S. Lange. Learning languages by collecting cases and tuning parameters. In *Proceedings of 5th International Workshop on Algorithmic Learning Theory (ALT'94)*, Lecture Notes in Artificial Intelligence 872, pages 532–546. Springer-Verlag, 1994.
53. Y. Sakakibara and R. Siromoney. A noise model on learning sets of strings. In *Proceedings of 5th Workshop on Computational Learning Theory (COLT'92)*, pages 295–302. ACM Press, 1992.
54. D. B. Searls. The linguistics of DNA. *American Scientist*, 80:579–591, Nov.–Dec. 1992.
55. T. Shinohara. Inductive inference from positive data is powerful. In *Proceedings of 3rd Workshop on Computational Learning Theory*, pages 97–110. Morgan Kaufmann, 1990.
56. A. Stolcke and S. Omohundro. Inducing probabilistic grammars by bayesian model merging. In *Proceedings of Second International Colloquium on Grammatical Inference (ICGI-94)*, Lecture Notes in Artificial Intelligence 862, pages 106–118. Springer-Verlag, 1994.
57. Y. Takada. Grammatical inference for even linear languages based on control sets. *Information Processing Letters*, 28:193–199, 1988.
58. Y. Takada. A hierarchy of language families learnable by regular language learners. In *Proceedings of Second International Colloquium on Grammatical Inference (ICGI-94)*, Lecture Notes in Artificial Intelligence 862, pages 16–24. Springer-Verlag, 1994.
59. L. G. Valiant. A theory of the learnable. *Communications of the ACM*, 27:1134–1142, 1984.
60. T. Yokomori. Polynomial-time learning of very simple grammars from positive data. In *Proceedings of 4th Workshop on Computational Learning Theory (COLT'91)*, pages 213–227. Morgan Kaufmann, 1991.
61. T. Yokomori. Learning nondeterministic finite automata from queries and counterexamples. In Furukawa, Michie, and Muggleton, editors, *Machine Intelligence 13*, pages 169–189. Oxford Univ. Press, 1994.
62. T. Yokomori. On polynomial-time learnability in the limit of strictly deterministic automata. To appear in *Machine Learning*, 1995.
63. T. Zeugmann and S. Lange. A guided tour across the boundaries of learning recursive languages. GOSLER-Report 26, TH Leipzig, FB Mathematik und Informatik, 1994.

Efficient Learning of Real Time One-Counter Automata

Amr F. Fahmy[1] and Robert S. Roos[2]

[1] (**Contact author.**) Aiken Computation Lab, Harvard University,
Cambridge MA 02138, USA (`amr@das.harvard.edu`).
Research supported in part by ARPA contract no. F19628-92-C-0113
and by NSF grant CDA-9308833.
[2] Department of Computer Science, Smith College,
Northampton MA 01063, USA (`roos@cs.smith.edu`).

Abstract. We present an efficient learning algorithm for languages accepted by deterministic real time one-counter automata (ROCA). The learning algorithm works by first learning an initial segment, B_n, of the infinite state machine that accepts the unknown language and then decomposing it into a complete control structure and a partial counter. A new, efficient ROCA decomposition algorithm, which will be presented in detail, allows this result. The decomposition algorithm works in time $O(n^2 log(n))$ where nc is the number of states of B_n for some language-dependent constant c. If Angluin's algorithm for learning regular languages is used to learn B_n and the complexity of this step is $h(n, m)$, where m is the length of the longest counterexample necessary for Angluin's algorithm, the complexity of our algorithm is $O(h(n, m) + n^2 log(n))$.

1 Introduction

We present an efficient learning algorithm for languages accepted by deterministic real time one-counter automata (ROCA). The learning algorithm works by first learning an initial segment, B_n, of the infinite state machine that accepts the unknown language L and then decomposing it into a complete control structure and a partial counter. A new, efficient ROCA decomposition algorithm, which will be presented in detail, allows this result. The decomposition algorithm works in $O(n^2 log(n))$ where nc is the number of states of B_n, c being an upper bound on the number of states in a control structure that accepts L. The minimum value of n needed to achieve decomposition could be exponentially larger than c for some ROCA languages, but we claim that this n is a more natural measure of the complexity of the language L.

If Angluin's algorithm for learning regular languages (appropriately modified) is used to construct B_n, and the complexity of this step is $h(n, m)$, where m is the length of the longest counterexample necessary for Angluin's algorithm, the complexity of our algorithm is $O(h(n, m) + n^2 log(n))$.

Roos and Berman [2] and Roos [8] were the first to find a polynomial time algorithm for the exact learning of deterministic one-counter automata (DOCA) as defined by Valiant and Paterson in [9]. The polynomial is of large degree, thus motivating this work to find a practical algorithm. (The differences between ROCA and

DOCA are described in Section 3.) Fahmy and Biermann [4] and Fahmy [5] introduced the idea of learning by automata decomposition. The method is applicable to a very wide class of real time languages using a variety of data structures such as counters, stacks, queues, and double counters; however, the algorithms they present are of exponential time in the worst case. The definitions of control structures, data structures, and behavior graphs that we use here and the relations between them were first given in [3] and subsequently in [4].

A discussion and an example of the learning process will be presented in Section 2. Following this, definitions of the control structure, the counter, the behavior graph, and the relations between them are given in Section 3. In Section 4 the decomposition theorem and decomposition algorithm will be presented.

2 The Learning Algorithm

We will present the learning process for a ROCA language using an example.

Consider the language $L = \{a^n ccb^n d \mid n > 0\} \cup \{a^n d \mid n > 0\}$. This language is not regular and is accepted by an infinite state machine that we call the *behavior graph* (b.g.), denoted by B. An "initial segment" of B—the submachine of B induced by all the states that are distance n or less from the initial state of B—will be denoted by B_n. The b.g. for our example appears in Figure 1.

A ROCA $A = (C, D)$ for L is a pair of state machines that also accepts L. C is a finite state machine called the *control structure* (c.s.), and D, called the *data structure* (d.s.), is an infinite state machine that simulates a counter. State diagrams for a counter and c.s. that accept L also appear in Figure 1. L is accepted by A in the following manner. Input symbols are read by C which, using the symbol, its current state, and the state of the counter, changes its state. While it is changing its state it sends a single instruction to the counter which it uses to change its state, too. The triples $(sym, val, instr)$ appear on the transitions of the c.s. in Figure 1 where sym is the input symbol, val is 0 if the counter state is 0 and $\neg 0$ otherwise, and $instr$ is the instruction sent to the counter. If the final symbol of an input string causes C to end up in a final state then we say that the ROCA has accepted the input string.

The learning process for a ROCA language L with behavior graph B starts by constructing a machine that contains B_n, for some natural number n. This is done using a slight modification of Angluin's learning algorithm for regular languages. One of our modifications to Angluin's "minimally adequate teacher" permits the ability to test the equivalence of a given submachine (the learner's guess for the initial segment B_n) with the behavior graph of a ROCA language L. We note that Angluin's algorithm will not terminate if the state machine that accepts L has an infinite number of states (as in the case of ROCAs). Thus, we will assume that the teacher will choose a suitable depth n and request that the learner decompose B_n after constructing it using Angluin's algorithm. (See remarks below on removing this requirement.) In addition, we assume that our teacher is "helpful" in the sense of fully exercising the counter; in other words, the teacher's counterexamples will enable the full graph B_n to be constructed. These assumptions simplify our presentation; our algorithm makes no further use of the teacher once B_n has been constructed. If

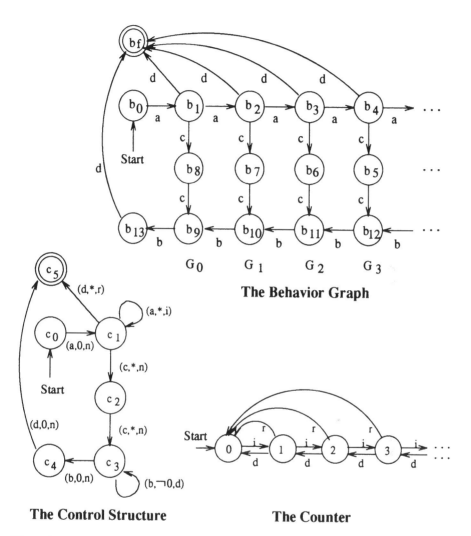

The Behavior Graph

The Control Structure　　　　**The Counter**

Fig. 1. The b.g. for the language $L = \{a^n ccb^n d \mid n > 0\} \cup \{a^n d \mid n > 0\}$, the state diagram for a c.s. for this language and the state diagram of the counter. Transitions to dead states in the b.g. and the c.s. are not shown. A "*" indicates a "don't care" value. Also the error state of the counter and transitions from states to themselves are not shown for clarity.

we slightly strengthen the teacher to permit full ROCA equivalence testing and we perform our algorithm in several "rounds" of ROCA equivalence queries, we need make no assumptions about the kinds of counterexamples returned. In addition, the use of multiple rounds eliminates any need for the teacher to choose the value of n for us.

(For the rest of the discussion of the example, assume that we are working with an initial segment containing the states $b_0, \ldots, b_13, b_f$ in Figure 1.) After constructing B_n (if n is large enough), the learning algorithm will be able to decompose B_n

into a complete c.s. and a finite d.s. consisting of a single counter. The finite counter is then replaced with an infinite one and the learning algorithm will have constructed a complete ROCA for the unknown language. The decomposition is done by performing what we call a *parallel breadth first traversal* (PBFT) from a certain set of starting states. The PBFT marks certain states of B_n; in our example, the PBFT starts at states b_1, b_2, b_3, and b_4.

The marks made during the parallel traversals must trace out isomorphic submachines of B_n. In our example these isomorphic graphs are labeled G_0, G_1, G_2 and G_3 in Figure 1. These marks are then used to construct partitions over the set of states of B_n that are necessary for the decomposition. Using the partitions it is then easy to construct the c.s. and the finite counter.

To identify the states where the PBFT must start, a string w identifying a path from the initial state of B_n to an "exit point" must be identified. (In B, if $\delta_B(p, a) = q$ is any transition such that p belongs to B_n and q belongs to $B - B_n$, we say that $\delta_B(p, a)$ is an exit point of B_n.) Some prefix of w is then broken into a string of the form xw' where w' is of the form y^k for some $k \geq 2$. The PBFT starts from the states reachable using the strings xy^i for $1 \leq i \leq k$. In our example there will be only one exit point for any sufficiently large value of n; e.g., if we assume $n = 5$, this exit point is reachable using the string $w = a^5$. Letting $x = a$ and $y = a$, the PBFT starts at states b_1, b_2, b_3, and b_4. The BFTs are performed in a manner that guarantees that the resulting graphs are all isomorphic. In our example, the transitions $\delta(b_1, c)$, $\delta(b_2, c)$, $\delta(b_3, c)$ and $\delta(b_4, c)$ are all examined in parallel. If, for any one of the traversals, a transition is missing, then the PBFT is declared a failure. If the traversals collide then we require that they all collide in a single state, as in state b_f for this example, or that they collide in a well defined manner—the traversal numbered i can encounter states marked by traversals numbered $i + 1$ or $i - 1$, and it is required that all traversals collide in the same way. In general, it is possible to have more than one exit point and the process would be repeated for each one.

In the rest of this paper we formalize the notions presented in this section and prove them correct.

3 Definitions and Properties

3.1 The Counter

Considered as a subclass of general real-time deterministic automata, ROCA are characterized by a common data structure, a counter.

Definition 1. A *counter* is defined by

$$D = \{S_D, \Sigma_D, O_D, \delta_D, d_0, \lambda_D\}$$

where

- $S_D = N \cup \{E\}$ is the set of states, where N is the set of natural numbers and E is an error state.
- $\Sigma_D = \{i, d, n, r\}$ is the input alphabet.
- $O_D = \{0, \neg 0, error\}$ is the output alphabet.

– δ_D, the transition function, is defined by: $\forall x \in N$,

$$\delta_D(x, i) = x + 1$$
$$\delta_D(x, n) = x$$
$$\delta_D(0, d) = E$$
$$\delta_D(x, d) = x - 1, \quad x \neq 0$$
$$\delta_D(x, r) = 0$$
$$\delta_D(E, I) = E \ \ \forall I \in \{i, d, n, r\}$$

– $d_0 = 0$ is the start state.
– λ_D is the output function that assigns an output value from O_D to each state d and is defined as follows $\forall d \in N, d \neq 0$:

$$\lambda_D(d) = \neg 0$$
$$\lambda_D(0) = 0$$
$$\lambda_D(E) = error$$

Figure 1 contains a diagram of a counter (state E has been omitted).

A counter can be thought of as the memory of a computing device; it cannot, on its own, accept or reject input strings since it has no final states. It is a means by which a ROCA can count the number of occurrences of some event, such as the appearance of a certain string in the input.

3.2 The Control Structure

The second component of a ROCA is the *control structure*. Its next state depends on its own current state, the output value of the current state of the counter, and the input symbol. The control structure issues instructions to the counter while it is changing states, i.e., instructions to the counter appear in the control structure's transitions.

Definition 2. A *control structure* is a state machine $C = \{S_C, \Sigma_C, O_C, \delta_C, c_0, \lambda_C, F_C\}$ where:

– S_C is a finite nonempty set of states.
– Σ_C is a finite set of symbols called the *input alphabet* to C. Σ_C is the cross product of two alphabets: the finite nonempty *input alphabet* from the outside world, Σ, and the output alphabet of the counter, O_D. Thus, $\Sigma_C = \Sigma \times O_D$.
– O_C is the set of instructions that can be issued to the counter, i.e., $O_C = \Sigma_D = \{i, d, n, r\}$.
– $\delta_C : S_C \times \Sigma_C \longrightarrow S_C$ is a mapping by which C changes states, called the *transition function* of C.
– c_0 is the *initial state* of C.
– $\lambda_C : S_C \times \Sigma_C \longrightarrow \Sigma_D$ is a mapping that assigns to each transition of C an instruction to the counter called the *instruction assignment function*.
– $F_C \subset S_C$ is a set of *final states* of C.

3.3 Real Time One Counter Automata

A *Real Time One Counter Automaton* (ROCA) A is a pair of state machines (C, D) where C is a control structure and D, the data structure, is an infinite state machine that is isomorphic to a counter.

The following definitions explain, in a more formal manner, how a ROCA works and how it accepts strings. An *instantaneous description* (ID) of a ROCA is given by the pair $< c, d >$ where c and d are the current states of its c.s. and d.s., respectively. The *initial ID* of the ROCA is the ID $< c_0, d_0 >$. If the current ID of ROCA A is $< c, d >$, the following events take place when A reads an input symbol α:

$$\delta_C(c, (\alpha, \lambda_D(d))) = c' \quad \text{(Compute next state of C)}$$
$$\lambda_C(c, (\alpha, \lambda_D(d))) = I \quad \text{(Send instruction to D)}$$
$$\delta_D(d, I) = d' \quad \text{(Compute next state of D)}$$

A ROCA A *accepts* a string $\sigma \in \Sigma^*$ iff the sequence of transitions induced by the letters of σ leads from $< c_0, d_0 >$ to $< c', d' >$ where $c' \in F_C$ and the counter never enters its error state. Let $\mathcal{L}(A)$ denote the language accepted by A, that is $\mathcal{L}(A) = \{\sigma \in \Sigma^* \mid A \text{ accepts } \sigma. \}$ Such a language will be called a ROCA language.

The Real Time Constraint From the previous definitions we can see that the c.s. of a ROCA, when given an input string of length n, can issue exactly n instructions (one instruction per input symbol), some of which could be the null or do nothing instruction, to the counter. So, for example, if the current state of the counter is d and if the current input string is of length n, then after the c.s. reads the input string, it can leave the counter in a state d' such that

$$d - n \leq d' \leq d + n$$

In this respect the ROCA is more restricted than the DOCA since DOCAs can change the value of the counter by more than one per input symbol and also because ROCAs are not allowed to make epsilon transitions. Consequently, ROCA are less concise than DOCA: a language accepted by a c-state DOCA might require a ROCA whose control structure has a number of states exponential in c.

3.4 The Behavior Graph of a ROCA

A ROCA works in much the same way as finite state machines that accept the regular languages work. It consumes one input symbol at a time and after each such symbol we can determine if it has accepted the input. We shall now define a single infinite state machine that can do the work that a ROCA does.

Definition 3. The *behavior graph* (b.g.) of a ROCA A is the reduced Moore-type state machine

$$B = \{S_B, \Sigma, \delta_B, b_0, F_B\}$$

that accepts $L = \mathcal{L}(A)$.

The b.g. is reduced in the sense that among its states, no two are equivalent. The b.g. of a ROCA is unique, up to isomorphism.

If π_L is the right invariant equivalence relation defined by L over Σ^*, $\beta_{\pi_L}(\sigma)$ is the block of π_L that contains σ, and $T_L(\sigma)$ is the set of suffixes of σ with respect to L, then B is defined as follows:

- $S_B = \pi_L$: the set of states of the b.g. is the set of blocks of the partition π_L where $\sigma_1 \equiv \sigma_2 \, (\pi_L)$ iff $T_L(\sigma_1) = T_L(\sigma_2)$.
- Σ is the same input alphabet as that of A.
- $\delta_B : S_B \times \Sigma \longrightarrow S_B$ is defined as follows: $\delta_B(\beta_{\pi_L}(\sigma), \alpha) = \beta_{\pi_L}(\sigma\alpha)$.
- $b_0 = \beta_{\pi_L}(e)$, where e is the null string. The initial state of B is the unique block of π_L that contains the null string.
- $F_B = \{\beta_{\pi_L}(\sigma) \mid e \in T_L(\sigma)\}$: the set of final states of B is the set of blocks of π_L such that the null string is a suffix for strings in the block.

δ_B is well defined since π_L is a right invariant equivalence relation, i.e., if $\sigma_1 \equiv \sigma_2 \, (\pi_L)$ then $\forall \alpha \in \Sigma, \sigma_1\alpha \equiv \sigma_2\alpha \, (\pi_L)$. A string σ is accepted by a b.g. if it drives B from its initial state b_0 to a state $b \in F_B$, i.e., if the null string is in $T_L(\sigma)$.

So far we have two different views of the language accepted by a ROCA: the c.s. and the counter of the ROCA working together to accept strings in the language, and the b.g. that accepts the language. In the next section we will relate the two views. Our goal is to show that the c.s. and d.s. are a *decomposition* of the b.g.

3.5   The Product of a Control Structure by the Counter

Let $A = \{C, D\}$ be a ROCA, The product of the c.s. by the counter is going to be a machine $M_{C\times D}$. The set of states of the product machine is a subset of $S_C \times S_D$. The alphabet of the product machine is going to be the input alphabet, Σ of the ROCA. To connect state (c, d) to state (c', d'), there must be a transition from c to c' in C and a transition from d to d' in D. The instruction labeling the transition from c to c' must be the same as that leading from d to d'. Also the transition from c to c' must be labeled with a test value from O_D which is the same as that of d. The initial state of the product machine is (c_0, d_0). State (c, d) will be labeled as a final state of the product machine if c is a final state of C. Notice that the product machine will contain many useless states, i.e. states that are unreachable and states that have no tails. If all the useless states are deleted from the set of states of the product machine, it will not affect the language it accepts. Formally,

Definition 4. For a ROCA, $A = \{C, D\}$ where

$$C = \{S_C, \Sigma_C, O_C, \delta_C, c_0, \lambda_C, F_C\} \text{ and } D = \{S_D, \Sigma_D, O_D, \delta_D, d_0, \lambda_D\}$$

the *product* $C \times D$ is the Moore-type machine $M_{C\times D} = \{S_{C\times D}, \Sigma, \delta_{C\times D}, p_0, F_{C\times D}\}$ where

- $S_{C\times D} \subseteq S_C \times S_D$.
- $\forall \alpha \in \Sigma, \delta_{C\times D}((c, d), \alpha) = (\delta_C(c, (\alpha, \lambda_D(d))), \delta_D(d, I))$, where $I = \lambda_C(c, (\alpha, \lambda_D(d)))$.
- $p_0 = (c_0, d_0)$.
- $(c, d) \in F_{C\times D}$ if $c \in F_C$.

The following theorem characterizes the language accepted by $M_{C \times D}$ and relates it to B.

Theorem 5. *Let* $A = \{C, D\}$ *be a RTA with b.g.* B, *we have*

$$\mathcal{L}(B) = \mathcal{L}(M_{C \times D}).$$

Proof. A proof is immediate by induction on the length of strings accepted by A and $M_{C \times D}$.

3.6 The Repetitive Structure of the Behavior Graph

Define the mapping g from the set of configurations to the set of states in the b.g. so that each state of $M_{C \times D}$ is mapped to the state corresponding to it. Then $g(p, i) = g(q, j)$ iff (p, i) is equivalent to (q, j). In other words, g maps configurations, (c, d)-pairs into their equivalence classes, which, in turn, are the states of the b.g. Extend g to submachines in the obvious way, i.e., map transitions using $g(\delta_{C \times D}((p, i), a)) = \delta_B(g(p, i), a)$. (Observe that g is not, in general, a one-to-one mapping.) Then a subgraph of $M_{C \times D}$ is mapped into a subgraph of the b.g.

Let X be a set of configurations, let $G(X)$ be the graph induced by X, i.e., the portion of the configuration graph containing X and all transitions among elements of X. Let $X_{m,n}$ be the set of reachable configurations $X_{m,n} = \{(p, i) : p \in S_C, m \leq i < n\}$ We call this a "slice" of the configuration graph; it consists of all configurations with counter values bounded above and below by fixed constants.

The overall goal is to prove that:

There exist two constants, H and K, such that the graphs

$$G(X_{H,H+K}), G(X_{H+K,H+2K}), G(X_{H+2K,H+3K}), \ldots.$$

all have isomorphic images under the mapping g. Moreover, either all these images coincide, or they are all distinct subgraphs of the b.g.

Because a ROCA can distinguish only between zero and nonzero counter values, the infinite transition diagram of the automaton $M_{C \times D}$ has a special kind of translational invariance with respect to the counter value. More precisely, if $\delta_{C \times D}((p, i), a) = (q, j)$, for $i, j > 0$, then $\delta_{C \times D}((p, i + k), a) = (q, j + k)$ for any $k > 0$, and if $\delta_{C \times D}((p, i), a) = (q, 0)$ for some $i > 1$, then $\delta_{C \times D}((p, i + k), a) = (q, 0)$ for all $k > 0$.

We now show that we can assign artificial counter values to the states of the behavior graph B to give it a similar repetitive structure; one way to do this is by examining the equivalence classes of the reachable states in $M_{C \times D}$. We will drop the subscript "$C \times D$" on our transition function δ in the following discussion.

We need the following fact, whose proof should be self-evident:

Lemma 6. *If* $\delta((p, i), w)$ *is final and* $\delta((p, j), w)$ *is nonfinal, for some* $i, j > 0$, *then at least one of the two computations on* w *must visit a state* $(q, 0)$ *without performing a reset.*

The next fact is an immediate consequence of the preceding one:

Lemma 7. *For each $w \in \Sigma^*$, for each $p \in S_C$, there is a threshold value t (no larger than $1 + |w|$) such that the states $\delta((p, t + i), w)$ are all final or are all nonfinal for every $i \geq 0$.*

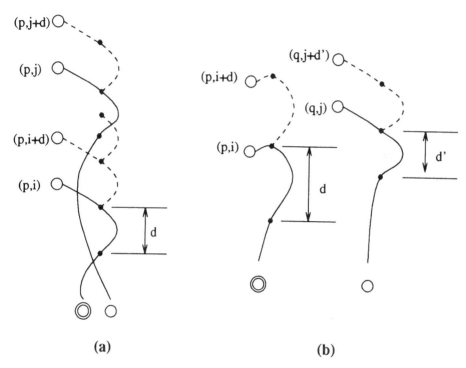

Fig. 2. (a) Lemma 8; (b) Lemma 10

Lemma 8. *For each $p \in S_C$, there are constants t and k such that for each j, $0 \leq j < k$, either:*

- *all states $(p, t + j + rk), r \geq 0$, are pairwise nonequivalent, or*
- *all states $(p, t + j + rk), r \geq 0$, are equivalent*

Proof. Suppose there exist $i_1, j_1 > |S_c|$ such that (p, i_1) and (p, j_1) are nonequivalent. Let w_1 be a (smallest) witness to their nonequivalence. By the pigeonhole principle applied to a sequence of states with decreasing counter values, the computation paths traced by $\delta((p, i_1), w_1)$ and $\delta((p, j_1), w_1)$ must contain a *descending loop* (a path that loops in the control structure while decreasing the counter). Write $w_1 = \alpha_1 \beta_1 \gamma_1$, where $\beta_1 \neq \epsilon$ is the loop. The "drop" d_1 of β_1 can be bounded by $|S_C|$ (consider only the states in the computation path that have counter components between $i_1 - |S_C|$ and i_1). Consider the infinite family of witnesses $\{\alpha_1 \beta_1^i \gamma_1 : i \geq 0\}$. These can be used to prove that $(p, i_1 + t_1 + rd_1)$ is not equivalent to $(p, j_1 + t_1 + sd_1)$ for any $r, s \geq 0$, for some threshold t_1 bounded by $|w_1| + 1$. In addition, for at least one of the two values i_1 and j_1, say i_1, we have the pairwise nonequivalence of all states in the set $\{(p, i_1 + t_1 + rd_1) : r \geq 0\}$. (The latter follows from the fact that, because w_1 was chosen smallest, $\alpha_1 \gamma_1$ is not a witness between (p, i_1) and (p, j_1); hence, it *is* a witness between either (p, i_1) and $(p, i_1 - d_1)$ or (p, j_1) and $(p, j_1 - d_1)$; now we can "pump" β_1.) See Figure 2(a).

If an infinite number of nonequivalences among p-states remain unaccounted for, repeat this construction on other pairs of p-states (p, i_r), (p, j_r), $r = 2, 3, \ldots$, obtaining witnesses w_r. This process cannot continue forever; at any stage, the set of p-states containing nonequivalent pairs that have not been accounted for will be a union of periodic (with respect to the counter) sets, with period at most the least common multiple of all of the loop drops used so far. The above construction shows that some infinite periodic subset of this, with period bounded by $|S_C|$, will be covered in the next step. Therefore, we will achieve the lemma with a threshold t that is no more than the maximum of all $|w_r| + 1$ and a value of k that is no worse than the least common multiple of the d_r.

Corollary 9. *There is some threshold t and constant k such that, for any $p \in S_C$, the results of the previous lemma hold.*

Proof. Repeat the lemma for each state; take the largest threshold and the least common multiple of all the ks.

Lemma 10. *Let p and q be any two states. There is a threshold t and a constant k such that, for each $i, j, 0 \leq i, j < k$, either:*

- *all states $(p, t + i + mk)$ and $(q, t + j + mk)$ are nonequivalent for each $m \geq 0$;*

or
- *all states $(p, t + i + mk)$ and $(q, t + j + mk)$ are equivalent for all $m \geq 0$.*

Proof. Choose constants t_0 and k_0 using the construction of corollary 9. Suppose neither condition of the lemma holds. Then we have a witness w_1 to the nonequivalence of some state pair (p_1, i_1) and (q_1, j_1), where $i_1, j_1 > t_0$. Consider the sequence of state pairs visited during the computations of $\delta((p_1, i_1), w_1)$ and $\delta((q_1, j_1), w_1)$. If neither contains a state with zero counter value, or if both reach zero states using the reset operation, we can extend the nonequivalence to infinitely many state pairs $(p_1, i_1 + r)$, $(q_1, j_1 + s)$ using the same witness. Therefore, assume at least one computation descends to zero by counting down. If t_0 is at least $|S_C|^2$, some pair of states repeats in the two computations, forming loops in both computations over the same substring β_1. This repetition can be chosen so that the loop is descending in at least one of the computations (specifically, the one that "counts down").

Let $w_1 = \alpha_1 \beta_1 \gamma_1$. For each state $r \geq 0$, let m_r denote the smallest value of m such that $\{\delta((p_1, i_1 + d_1 r), \alpha_1 \beta_1^m \gamma_1), \delta((p_1, i_1 + d_1 r), \alpha_1 \beta_1^{m-1} \gamma_1)\}$ contains both a final and a nonfinal state. Let n_r be the smallest n such that $\{\delta((q_1, j_1 + d_1' r), \alpha_1 \beta_1^n \gamma_1), \delta((q, j_1 + d_1 r), \alpha_1 \beta_1^{n-1} \gamma_1)\}$ contains a final and a nonfinal state. When both $d_1 r$ and $d_1' r$ are greater than $|w_1|$, each of these sequences will be either constant or will consist of consecutive integers. If both are constant, w is a witness between any pair of states

$(p_1, i_1 + d_1 r)$, $(q_1, j_1 + d_1' s)$ (since it was a witness between (p_1, i_1) and (q_1, j_1). If either or both sequences consist of consecutive integers, a witness between $(p_1, i_1 + d_1 r)$ and $(q_1, j_1 + d_1' s)$ is $\alpha_1 \beta_1^k \gamma_1$, where $k = \min(m_r, n_s)$. See Figure 2(b).

Let $t_1 = \min(t_0, |w_1| + 1)$, let k_1 be the least common multiple of k_0 and the drops d_1, d_1'.

If there are still unaccounted-for nonequivalences among states, repeat the process on state pairs $(p_2, i_2), (q_2, j_2), \ldots$. The process must halt after only a finite number of steps.□

We can now observe the desired regularity condition in B by assigning the labels to its states. Let t and k be the constants guaranteed by the lemma. For each state s of B, consider the set $E(s)$ of states of $M_{C \times D}$ that are equivalent to s. Uniformly choose some representative state (p, i) from $E(s)$ (e.g., the lowest-numbered state in the equivalence class, and the lowest counter value appearing with that state). If $E(s)$ is an infinite set, or if it contains only states whose counter values are less than the threshold t determined by the last lemma, assign a unique state name and a counter value of zero to s. Otherwise, i is of the form $t + kr + j$, so assign s the name $[p, j]$ and the counter value r. The translational invariance now holds.

Now that we know that a labeling exists which establishes the regular structure of B, we know that any search for such a labeling will take place in a nonempty search space (although we will obtain our labels in a different way).

4 Decomposing the Behavior Graph

4.1 Partitions and Partition Pairs

Hartmanis and Stearns [6] developed a theory for the decomposition of finite state machines in the early sixties. By decomposing a state machine into a number of state machines that emulate the behavior of the composite machine they were able to use fewer electronic components to realize the machine. In this section, we use their theory to find the conditions under which a behavior graph B is decomposable into a control structure and a counter.

Definition 11. A *partition*, π, on a set S is a collection of pairwise disjoint subsets of S whose union is S. Each subset is called a *block* of the partition. If two elements, s and t of S, are in the same block of π, we shall write $s \equiv t \ (\pi)$. The block of π containing an element s will be denoted by $\beta_\pi(s)$. If π_1 and π_2 are two partitions on a set S then the *product* of π_1 and π_2 denoted by $\pi_1.\pi_2$ is also a partition on the set S such that $s \equiv t \ (\pi_1.\pi_2)$ iff $s \equiv t \ (\pi_1)$ and $s \equiv t \ (\pi_2)$. The partition that puts every element in a block by itself is called the *zero partition* and will be denoted by **0**. If π_1 and π_2 are two partitions on a set S, then π_2 is said to be *larger than or equal to* π_1, denoted by $\pi_1 \leq \pi_2$, if every block of π_1 is a subset of a block of π_2. It is clear that $\pi_1 \leq \pi_2$ iff $\pi_1.\pi_2 = \pi_1$.

Let π be a partition over the set of states of some machine M. π will be called *output consistent* iff $b \equiv b'(\pi)$ implies that either both states are final or both are non final. The largest output consistent partition will be denoted π_F and is the unique partition that groups all the final states in one block and all non-final states in another block.

Definition 12. Let π and π' be two partitions on the set of states, S, of some machine M. The ordered pair (π, π') is called a *partition pair* (pp) iff

$$\forall s, t \in S, \forall \alpha \in \Sigma, s \equiv t \ (\pi) \Rightarrow \delta(s, \alpha) \equiv \delta(t, \alpha) \ (\pi')$$

If (π, π') is a pp then from the block of π that contains the current state of the machine we can find the block of π' that contains the next state on every letter of the alphabet. We can see that $\delta(\beta_\pi, \alpha) \subseteq \beta_{\pi'}$.

A partial ordering, $\leq$, is defined on pps by comparing the respective components of pps. If (π, π') and (τ, τ') are two pps then $(\pi, \pi') \leq (\tau, \tau')$ iff $\pi \leq \tau$ and $\pi' \leq \tau'$. See [6] for more properties of partition pairs.

The basic idea behind decomposition is to merge states, and thus the use of partitions, while preserving the transitions. Merged states in one machine must not be merged in at least one other component machine. In this section we discuss the decomposition theorem that will tell us exactly when a decomposition is possible.

4.2 The Associated Partitions of a ROCA

Given a ROCA and its b.g., Theorem 5 states that every state of the b.g. is equivalent to a state of $M_{C \times D}$ and vice versa. We shall define two partitions over the states of the b.g. that group states with the same components in the same block. One partition groups states of the b.g. that have the same c.s. component in the same block and the second groups states of the b.g. that have the same counter component in the same block. Using these two partitions we can decompose the b.g. into a c.s. and a counter.

Definition 13. Given a ROCA $A = \{C, D\}$ with b.g. B, let b_1 and b_2 be two states of the b.g., c_1, c_2 be states of the c.s. and d_1, d_2 be two states of the counter such that

$$b_1 = (c_1, d_1) \quad \text{and} \quad b_2 = (c_2, d_2)$$

We define the four partitions π_C, π_D, ρ_{CD} and ρ_{DC} over the set of states of B as follows

- $b_1 \equiv b_2 \ (\pi_C)$ iff $c_1 = c_2$.
- $b_1 \equiv b_2 \ (\pi_D)$ iff $d_1 = d_2$.
- $b_1 \equiv b_2 \ (\rho_{CD})$ iff $\forall \alpha \in \Sigma, \forall v \in O_D, \lambda_C(c_1, (\alpha, v)) = \lambda_C(c_2, (\alpha, v))$. Two states of B share the same block of ρ_{CD} iff, for every letter of the alphabet and every test value of the d.s., the c.s.-components of the behavior states send the same instructions to the d.s.
- $b_1 \equiv b_2 \ (\rho_{DC})$ iff $\lambda_D(d_1) = \lambda_D(d_2)$. Two states of B share the same block of ρ_{DC} iff the d.s.-components of the two behavior states have the same test value.

The four partitions are called the *associated partitions* of ROCA A over the set of states of B. They tell us which states of the b.g. will have the same properties when B is decomposed into C and D.

4.3 The Decomposition Theorem

The following theorem gives us sufficient conditions for when a b.g. can be decomposed into a c.s. and a counter given a set of partitions over the set of states of the b.g. This theorem is a special case of a theorem that appeared in [4], [5] and [6] and thus will be stated here without proof.

Theorem 14. *Let* π_C, π_D, ρ_{CD} *and* ρ_{DC} *be four partitions over the set of states of a behavior graph* B. *These four partitions define a ROCA* A *and are the associated partitions of* A *over the behavior graph* B *if*

1. $(\pi_C.\rho_{DC}, \pi_C)$ *is a partition pair.*
2. $(\pi_D.\rho_{CD}, \pi_D)$ *is a partition pair.*
3. $\pi_C \leq \rho_{CD}$
4. $\pi_D \leq \rho_{DC}$
5. $\pi_C.\pi_D = \mathbf{0}$
6. *The number of blocks of* π_C *is finite.*
7. $\pi_C \leq \pi_F$, *i.e.* π_C *is output consistent.*
8. *The machine* $D = \{S_D, \Sigma_D, O_D, \delta_D, d_0, \lambda_D\}$ *is isomorphic to a counter where* D *is defined by*
   - $S_D = \pi_D$.
   - $\Sigma_D \subseteq \rho_{CD} \times \rho_{DC} \times \Sigma$.
   - $O_D = \rho_{DC}$.
   - $d_0 = \beta_{\pi_D}(b_0)$.
   - $\lambda_D(\beta_{\pi_D}) = \beta_{\rho_{DC}}(\beta_{\pi_D})$.
   - $\delta_D(\beta_{\pi_D}(b), (\beta_{\rho_{CD}}(b), \beta_{\rho_{DC}}(b), \alpha)) = \beta_{\pi_D}(\delta_B(b, \alpha))$

4.4 A Decomposition Algorithm

Given B_n, our aim now is to describe an algorithm that will mark states of B_n with (c, d)-pairs such that the necessary partitions for the decomposition can be created.

Since B_n is a submachine of B there are transitions in B_n that lead to states that are not in B_n, such transitions will be called *exit points*. Note that there exist only a constant number of exit points in B_n; this constant is independent of n.

Let w be a shortest string that leads from the initial state of B_n to an exit point e in B_n. Such strings can be found in an efficient manner. The algorithm in Figure 3 uses w to identify a periodic structure in B_n (and, hence, B).

The outer loop searches for a prefix of w sufficiently long to reach states above some (unknown) threshold t. The inner loop searches for a pair of states, p_0 and p_1, that are isomorphic under some periodic description of B, then uses the substring y to try to determine additional isomorphic copies of these states. Procedure **PARBFT** is described below; it performs breadth-first traversals "in parallel" from each of the states $p_1, p_2, \ldots$ and succeeds if it detects a periodic structure. (The precise mechanism for simulating this parallelism is unimportant.) Traversals are synchronized so that, for any string m that labels a path from the root of a BFT tree, the traversals simultaneously visit the nodes $\delta_{B_n}(p_i, m)$, for $i = 0, 1, \ldots$.

A single breadth-first traversal from state p_i marks nodes with a "traversal number" i and a word m (which describes the path used to reach that node). A BFT

```
for each prefix x of w do
    let w = xw'
    let p₀ = δ_Bₙ(q₀, x)
    for each prefix y of w' do
        let pᵢ = δ_Bₙ(p₀, yⁱ) for i = 1, 2, ..., until
        pᵢ = e for some i or until a state is repeated.
        if e reached in previous step then
            if PARBFT(p₀, p₁, ...) returns "success" then
                exit;
            end if
        end if
    end for
end for
```

Fig. 3. Finding a periodic structure in B_n

halts when it can't extend the traversal without using nodes that are already labelled (possibly by one of the traversals operating in parallel with it). Each individual BFT is a standard queue-based breadth first traversal; the queue contains (state,string) pairs, and initially contains (p_i, ϵ). When we remove (q, m) from the queue, we label it (i, m) and then, for each $a \in \Sigma$ and each neighbor r of q, we add (r, ma) to the queue if r has not already been labelled.

Two graphs G_i and G_j visited by $\text{BFT}(p_i, i)$ and $\text{BFT}(p_j, j)$ are called isomorphic if there is a one-to-one correspondence f between their nodes that preserves membership in F_n, the set of final states, and such that $p = f(q)$ if and only if, for some constant c and for each $a \in \Sigma$, $\delta_{B_n}(p, a) = f(\delta_{B_n}(f(q), a))$, the label of p is (i, m) and the label of q is $(i + c, m)$ (for some string m). A finite sequence of graphs $G_0, G_1, \ldots$ satisfies the property **isom** if there is a nonempty subsequence $G_i, G_{i+1}, G_{i+2}, \ldots$ such that G_i is isomorphic to G_{i+1} with constant $c = 1$.

Finally, algorithm **PARBFT** is given in Figure 4; k is a small constant which may be used to ignore "bad" traversals caused by being too near the zero counter states or too near the exit points:

4.5 Complexity of The Learning Algorithm

We measure the complexity of the learning algorithm in terms of the number of states of B_n, nc for some constant c. Assume that Angluin's algorithm is used to construct B_n and assume that the complexity of this step is in $O(h(n, m))$ steps where m is the length of the longest counter example necessary for this algorithm. The decomposition step first searches for a string w to an exit point which can be found in $O(n)$ steps. The string w is then partitioned into the form xw' which can be done in $O(n)$ steps. For each such x, w' is partitioned into a string of the form y^i in another $O(n)$ steps for a total of $O(n^2)$ steps to rewrite w in the form xy^i. See [7] for an $O(n \log(n))$ to perform this last step. For each such form of w, a PBFT

PARBFT$(p_0, p_1, \ldots)$:
for $i = 0, 1, \ldots$ **paralleldo**
    $G_i = \mathbf{BFT}(p_i, i)$;
    if $k < i < n - k$ and G_i and G_{i+1} violate the **isom** property **then**
        return failure
    end if
end for
return success;

Fig. 4. Parallel bread-first traversal

must be performed. If there are k such BFTs then each must be of depth n/k and the complexity is $O(n)$. The complexity of the decomposition step is thus $O(n^3)$ or $O(n^2 log(n))$ if the algorithm in [7] is used. The complexity of the learning algorithm is thus $O(h(n, m) + n^2 log(n))$.

5 Conclusions and Further Work

We have shown that the family of languages accepted by real time one-counter automata can be learned efficiently using a thirty-year-old automata decomposition method due to Hartmanis and Stearns, combined with Angluin's algorithm and a parallel breadth-first traversal algorithm. This is an exponential improvement over the learning algorithms described in [4] and [5]. Although ROCA are, in general, less concise than the DOCA examined in [2] and [8], the method promises to compare favorably with the algorithm described in those papers for a large class of DOCA languages.

The technique of automata decomposition is applicable to many more data structures than simple counters; therefore, the methods described in this paper should be extendable to other classes of real-time acceptors (and, thus, to other language classes)—multiple-counter real time machines, queue-based machines, and so on.

References

1. Angluin, D.: Learning regular sets from queries and counter examples. Information and Computation **75** (1987) 87–106
2. Berman, P., Roos, R.: Learning one-counter languages in polynomial time. *Proceedings of the 28th IEEE Symposium on Foundations of Computer Science* (1987) 61–67
3. Biermann, A.W.: A fundamental theorem for real time programs. Duke Univerity Department of Computer Science technical report (1977)
4. Fahmy, A. F., Biermann, A. W.: Synthesis of real time acceptors. Journal of Symbolic Computation **15** (1993) 807–842
5. Fahmy, A. F.: *Synthesis of Real Time Programs*. PhD thesis, Duke University, 1989

6. Hartmanis, J., Stearns, R.E.: *Algebraic Structure Theory of Sequential Machines*. (1966: Prentice-Hall)

7. Main, M., Lorentz, R.: An $O(n \log(n))$ algorithm for finding all repetitions in a string. *Journal of Algorithms* **5** (1984) 422–432

8. Roos, R.: *Deciding Equivalence of Deterministic One-Counter Automata in Polynomial Time with Applications to Learning*. PhD thesis, The Pennsylvania State University, 1988

9. Valiant, L. G., Paterson, M. S.: Deterministic one-counter automata. *Journal of Computer and System Sciences* **10** (1975) 340–350

Learning Strongly Deterministic Even Linear Languages from Positive Examples

Takeshi Koshiba[1], Erkki Mäkinen[2] and Yuji Takada[3]

[1] *First Research Lab., Institute for Social Information Science,*
Fujitsu Laboratories Ltd.,
140 Miyamoto, Numazu-shi, Shizuoka 410-03, Japan.
Email: koshiba@iias.flab.fujitsu.co.jp
[2] *Department of Computer Science, University of Tampere,*
P.O.Box 607, SF-33101, Tampere, Finland.
Email: em@cs.uta.fi
[3] *Second Research Lab., Institute for Social Information Science,*
Fujitsu Laboratories Ltd.,
1-9-3 Nakase, Mihama-ku, Chiba-shi, Chiba 261, Japan.
Email: yuji@iias.flab.fujitsu.co.jp

Abstract. We consider the problem of learning deterministic even linear languages from positive examples. By a "deterministic" even linear language we mean a language generated by an $LR(k)$ even linear grammar. We introduce a natural subclass of $LR(k)$ even linear languages, called $LR(k)$ *in the strong sense*, and show that this subclass is learnable in the limit from positive examples. Furthermore, we propose a learning algorithm that identifies this subclass in the limit with almost linear time in updating conjectures. As a corollary, in terms of even linear grammars, we have a learning algorithm for k-reversible languages that is more efficient than the one proposed by Angluin[Ang82].

1 Introduction

An even linear language is a language generated by an even linear grammar that has productions only of the form $A \rightarrow uBv$ or $A \rightarrow w$ such that u and v have the same length, where A and B are nonterminals and u, v and w are strings over terminal symbols. Amar and Putzolu [AP64] have proposed even linear grammars and have shown that the class of even linear languages properly contains the class of regular languages.

Interesting even linear languages are sets of palindromic strings; a string w is called *palindromic* if and only if $w = a_1 a_2 \cdots a_n b a_n \cdots a_2 a_1$, where each a_i $(1 \leq i \leq n)$ is a terminal symbol and b is a terminal symbol or the null string. Characterizing palindromic strings by grammars is interesting from biological point of view. Many palindromic strings are observed in DNA and RNA sequences [Lew94]. They have a possibility of forming special kinds of secondary structures like cruciforms in double-stranded DNA and hairpins in single-stranded RNA. Characterizing palindromic strings by grammars offers a

systematic way to analyze these structures of DNA and RNA sequences. Therefore, an inductive learning method for the grammars offers a way to guess regularity behind those sequences.

In this paper, we consider the problem of learning deterministic even linear
languages from positive examples. By a "deterministic" even linear language we
mean a language generated by an $LR(k)$ even linear grammar. We introduce
a natural subclass of $LR(k)$ even linear languages, called $LR(k)$ *in the strong
sense*. Intuitively speaking, an even linear grammar is $LR(k)$ in the strong sense,
abbreviated $LRS(k)$, if in any sentential form, an applied production can be determined by looking at strings of length k before and after the substring of the
sentential form that corresponds to the right hand side of the production. Following [Tak88], it is shown that $LRS(k)$ even linear languages are generated by
a fixed even linear grammar *with k-reversible control sets*. Then, with Angluin's
result [Ang82], we have the desired result on the problem of learning $LRS(k)$
even linear languages from positive examples. Moreover, since we need only a
proper subclass of k-reversible languages, we have a learning algorithm for the
subclass that updates conjectures in almost linear time. Using this algorithm,
we also have a learning algorithm for $LRS(k)$ even linear languages that updates
conjectures in almost linear time.

One of the interesting corollaries of our results is that, in terms of $LRS(k)$
even linear grammars, we have a learning algorithm for k-reversible languages
that is more efficient than Angluin's algorithm [Ang82]. This follows from our
present results together with results given in [Tak94]. Namely, Takada has created a hierarchy of language classes in which the learning problem for each class
is reduced to the one for k-reversible languages. The hierarchy has language
classes incomparable with the class of context-free languages but not beyond
the class of context-sensitive languages. Our results also mean that all classes
in the hierarchy are learnable from positive examples with almost linear time in
updating conjectures.

2   Preliminaries

Let Σ denote an alphabet and let Σ^* denote the set of all strings over Σ including
the null string λ. We denote by $|u|$ the length of a string u.

We denote a finite automaton by a quintuple $M = (Q, \Sigma, \delta, I, F)$, where Q
is a finite nonempty set of states, Σ is a finite nonempty set of input symbols, δ
is a transition function from $Q \times \Sigma$ to the power set of Q, I and F are subsets of
Q. The elements of I and F are called initial states and final states, respectively.
A language accepted by a finite automaton is called *regular*. A finite automaton
M is *deterministic* if and only if there is at most one initial state and for any
state $q \in Q$ and for any symbol $a \in \Sigma$ there is at most one element in $\delta(q, a)$.
Let k be a fixed nonnegative integer. The string u is said to be a *k-follower*
of the state q if and only if $|u| = k$ and $\delta(q, u) \neq \emptyset$. M is *deterministic with
lookahead k* if and only if for any pair of distinct states q_1 and q_2, if $q_1, q_2 \in I$
or $q_1, q_2 \in \delta(q_3, a)$ for some $q_3 \in Q$ and for some symbol $a \in \Sigma$, then there is

no string that is a k-follower of both q_1 and q_2. The *reverse* of δ, denoted δ^r, is defined by $\delta^r(q, a) = \{q' \mid q \in \delta(q', a)\}$ for all $a \in \Sigma$ and $q \in Q$. The *reverse* of M is $M^r = (Q, \Sigma, \delta^r, F, I)$. A finite automaton M is said to be k-*reversible* if and only if M is deterministic and M^r is deterministic with lookahead k. A k-*reversible language* is the language accepted by a k-reversible finite automaton.

For any language L and for any string $w \in \Sigma^*$, the *left-quotient* of L and w is a set $T_L(w) = \{v \mid wv \in L\}$.

Proposition 1 [Ang82]. *Let L be a regular language. Then L is k-reversible if and only if whenever $u_1 vw$ and $u_2 vw$ are in L and $|v| = k$, $T_L(u_1 v) = T_L(u_2 v)$.*

An *even linear grammar*, abbreviated ELG, is a quadruple $G = (N, \Sigma, P, S)$. N is a finite nonempty set of *nonterminals*. P is a finite nonempty set of *productions*; each production in P is of the form

$$\pi_n : A \rightarrow uBv \quad \text{or} \quad \pi_t : A \rightarrow w,$$

where $A, B \in N$, $u, v, w \in \Sigma^*$, and $|u| = |v|$. π_n and π_t are labels of productions; we assume that each production is labeled by a unique label symbol and therefore uniquely referable with its label. S is a special nonterminal called the *start symbol*. We assume $N \cap \Sigma = \varnothing$ and denote $N \cup \Sigma$ by V.

Let $G = (N, \Sigma, P, S)$ be an ELG. We write $x \xrightarrow[G]{\pi} y$ to mean that y is derived from x using the production π. Let $x_0, x_1, \ldots, x_n$ be strings over V. If

$$x_0 \xrightarrow[G]{\pi_1} x_1, \; x_1 \xrightarrow[G]{\pi_2} x_2, \; \ldots, \; x_{n-1} \xrightarrow[G]{\pi_n} x_n,$$

then we denote $x_0 \xrightarrow[G]{\alpha} x_n$, where $\alpha = \pi_1 \pi_2 \cdots \pi_n$, which is called a *derivation* from x_0 to x_n with the associate word α in G. The *language generated by G* is the set

$$L(G) = \{w \mid S \xrightarrow[G]{\alpha} w \text{ and } w \in \Sigma^*\}$$

and the *Szilard language of G* is the set

$$Sz(G) = \{\alpha \mid S \xrightarrow[G]{\alpha} w \text{ and } w \in \Sigma^*\}.$$

An *even linear language* is the language generated by an ELG.

Any even linear language can be generated by an ELG $G = (N, \Sigma, P, S)$ that has productions only of the form

$$\pi_n : A \rightarrow bBc \quad \text{or} \quad \pi_t : A \rightarrow a,$$

where $A, B \in N$, $a \in \Sigma \cup \{\lambda\}$ and $b, c \in \Sigma$ [AP64]. We can also assume that any even linear language is generated by a *reduced ELG*, that is, an ELG that has no useless nonterminals and no useless productions. Throughout this paper, we assume that ELGs are reduced and in this normal form if not otherwise stated.

Definition 2. Let $G = (N, \Sigma, P, S)$ be an ELG. A subset C of P^* is said to be a *control set on G* and

$$L(G, C) = \{w \in \Sigma^* \mid S \underset{G}{\overset{\alpha}{\Longrightarrow}} w \text{ and } \alpha \in C\}$$

is called the *language generated by G with the control set C.*

Definition 3. A *universal ELG over an alphabet Σ* is an ELG $U = (\{S\}, \Sigma, \Psi, S)$ such that Ψ consists of the following productions:

$$\Psi = \{\psi_n : S \to aSb \mid a, b \in \Sigma\} \cup \{\psi_t : S \to a \mid a \in \Sigma\} \cup \{\psi_\lambda : S \to \lambda\}.$$

Lemma 4. *For any alphabet Σ, a universal ELG U has the following properties:*

1. $L(U) = \Sigma^*$,
2. U is unique up to renaming of the start symbol,
3. if the cardinality of Σ is n then the number of productions of U is $n^2 + n + 1$,
4. U is unambiguous, that is, for any $w \in \Sigma^*$, $S \underset{U}{\overset{\alpha}{\Longrightarrow}} w$ and $S \underset{U}{\overset{\beta}{\Longrightarrow}} w$ imply $\alpha = \beta$.

Let $G = (N, \Sigma, P, S)$ be an ELG and $G^0 = (\{S\}, \Sigma, \Psi, S)$ be a universal ELG. We define a *universal homomorphism h* from P^* to Ψ^* as

$$h(\pi) = \begin{cases} \psi_t, & \text{where } \psi_t : S \to a \text{ is in } \Psi, & \text{if } \pi : A \to a, \\ \psi_n, & \text{where } \psi_n : S \to bSc \text{ is in } \Psi, & \text{if } \pi : A \to bBc, \end{cases}$$

where $A, B \in N$, $a \in \Sigma \cup \{\lambda\}$ and $b, c \in \Sigma$.

Proposition 5 [Tak88]. *For any language L, L is an even linear language if and only if L is generated by a universal ELG U with a unique regular control set $C \subseteq Sz(U)$.*

We note that a finite automaton that accepts C has only one final state.

The following example may help to understand Proposition 5. Let $L = \{a^n d(b + c)^{n-1} c \mid n \geq 1\}$. Since L is generated by the ELG $G_0 = (N, \Sigma, P, S)$, where $N = \{S, A\}$, $\Sigma = \{a, b, c, d\}$ and

$$P = \{\pi_1 : S \to aAc, \ \pi_2 : A \to aAb, \ \pi_3 : A \to aAc, \ \pi_4 : A \to d\},$$

L is an even linear language. Consider a corresponding universal ELG $U = (\{S\}, \Sigma, \Psi, S)$ and the following universal homomorphism h:

$$h(\pi_1) = h(\pi_3) = \psi_c : S \to aSc,$$
$$h(\pi_2) = \psi_b : S \to aSb,$$
$$h(\pi_4) = \psi_d : S \to d.$$

Define the finite automaton $M_C = (N \cup \{q_f\}, \Sigma, \delta, \{S\}, \{q_f\})$ in the following way:

- $E \in \delta(D, \psi_n)$ if $\psi_n = h(\pi_n)$ and $\pi_n : D \to eEf$,
- $q_f \in \delta(D, \psi_t)$ if $\psi_t = h(\pi_t)$ and $\pi_t : D \to e$,

where $q_f \notin N$ and $e, f \in \Sigma \cup \{\lambda\}$. It is easy to show that L is generated by U with the regular control set accepted by M_C.

3 A Grammatical Characterization of Deterministic Even Linear Languages

In this section, we shall reveal a relation between deterministic even linear languages and k-reversible control sets. Deterministic even linear languages are defined by $LR(k)$ ELGs.

For any string w and for any nonnegative integer i, we define

$$pref(w, i) = \begin{cases} w & \text{if } |w| < i, \\ \text{the prefix of } w \text{ of length } i & \text{if } |w| \geq i. \end{cases}$$

Definition 6. Let $G = (N, \Sigma, P, S)$ be an ELG. G is said to be $LR(k)$ if and only if, for each $u, v, v' \in \Sigma^*$, $x \in V^*$, $A, A' \in N$ and $\pi, \pi' \in P$, if

1. $S \overset{\alpha}{\underset{G}{\Rightarrow}} uAv \overset{\pi}{\underset{G}{\Rightarrow}} uxv$,
2. $S \overset{\alpha'}{\underset{G}{\Rightarrow}} uA'v' \overset{\pi'}{\underset{G}{\Rightarrow}} uxv'$, and
3. $pref(v, k) = pref(v', k)$,

then $\pi = \pi'$.

This definition for ELGs is induced from the general definition for context-free grammars. We note that every universal ELG is $LR(0)$.

An even linear language L is $LR(k)$ if and only if there exists an $LR(k)$ ELG generating L.

We first show that the $LR(k)$ property introduces a proper subclass of even linear languages.

Proposition 7. *There exists an even linear language that is not $LR(k)$ for any nonnegative integer k.*

Proof. Consider the language

$$L = \{ ad^n fe^n b \mid n \geq 0 \} \cup \{ a(dd)^m f(ee)^m c \mid m \geq 0 \},$$

where $(dd)^i$ denotes the string $d \cdots d$ of the length $2i$. This language is an even linear language. In fact, L is generated by an ELG $G_1 = (N, \Sigma, P, S)$, where

$$N = \{S, A, B, C\},$$
$$\Sigma = \{a, b, c, d, e, f\},$$
$$P = \{\pi_1 : S \to aAb, \ \pi_2 : S \to aBc, \ \pi_3 : A \to dAe, \ \pi_4 : B \to dCe,$$
$$\pi_5 : C \to dBe, \ \pi_6 : A \to f, \ \pi_7 : B \to f\}.$$

Let k be a nonnegative integer and let G' be an $LR(k)$ ELG generating L. Since L has strings $ad^n fe^n b$ for any nonnegative integer n, by the "pumping lemma" for context-free languages G' must have a nonterminal A such that

$A \underset{G'}{\overset{\alpha}{\Longrightarrow}} dAe$ and $A \underset{G'}{\overset{\beta}{\Longrightarrow}} f$. Since G' is an ELG, this implies that G' has productions $\pi_n : A \to dAe$ and $\pi_t : A \to f$. For any integer i, G' must have derivations

$$S \underset{G'}{\overset{\gamma}{\Longrightarrow}} ad^{2i} Ae^{2i} b \underset{G'}{\overset{\pi_t}{\Longrightarrow}} ad^{2i} fe^{2i} b$$
$$S \underset{G'}{\overset{\gamma'}{\Longrightarrow}} ad^{2i} Be^{2i} c \underset{G'}{\overset{\pi'_t}{\Longrightarrow}} ad^{2i} fe^{2i} c.$$

If we choose $2i \geq k$, the $LR(k)$ property of G' implies that $A = B$. Hence, G' generates the string $ad^{2i+1} fe^{2i+1} c$, which is not in L. □

Proposition 8. *Let L be an even linear language. If L is generated by a universal ELG with a k-reversible control set, then L is an $LR(k)$ even linear language.*

Proof. We assume that L is generated by a universal ELG U with a k-reversible control set $C \subseteq Sz(U)$. Let M be a k-reversible automaton accepting C. Using the technique of [Tak88], we can obtain from M and U an ELG G such that $L = L(G)$. Let h be a universal homomorphism from the productions of G to the productions of U. Let

$$S \underset{G}{\overset{\tau\alpha}{\Longrightarrow}} uAv \underset{G}{\overset{\pi}{\Longrightarrow}} uxv \quad \text{and}$$
$$S \underset{G}{\overset{\tau'\alpha'}{\Longrightarrow}} uA'v' \underset{G}{\overset{\pi'}{\Longrightarrow}} uxv'$$

be derivations in G, where $u, v, v' \in \Sigma^*$, $x \in V^*$ and π, π' are labels of productions of G. We note that $h(\pi) = h(\pi')$. We also have $|u| = |v| = |v'|$ which implies $|\tau\alpha| = |\tau'\alpha'| = |v|$.

We show $\pi = \pi'$ in each case of (1) $|v| \geq k$ and (2) $|v| < k$. In the case (1), since C is k-reversible, if $h(\alpha) = h(\alpha')$ and $|h(\alpha)| = |h(\alpha')| = k$ then we have $\delta(q_0, h(\tau\alpha)) = \delta(q_0, h(\tau'\alpha'))$, where q_0 is the initial state of M. By the construction of G, this implies $A = A'$ and therefore $\pi = \pi'$. In the case (2), we have only to consider the case $v = v'$. Since M is deterministic and $h(\tau\alpha\pi) = h(\tau'\alpha'\pi')$, we obtain $A = A'$ and therefore $\pi = \pi'$. Hence, G is an $LR(k)$ grammar. □

The converse of Proposition 8 does not hold. Let $G_2 = (N, \Sigma, P, S)$ be an ELG, where

$N = \{S, A, B, C\}$,

$\Sigma = \{a, b, c, d, e, f, g\}$, and

$P = \{\pi_1 : S \to aAb, \ \pi_2 : S \to cBd, \ \pi_3 : A \to eAf, \ \pi_4 : B \to eCf,$
$\qquad \pi_5 : C \to eBf, \ \pi_6 : A \to g, \ \pi_7 : B \to g\}$.

It is easy to see that G_2 is $LR(k)$, for all $k \geq 0$, because symbols a and c are unique to productions π_1 and π_2, respectively. However, $h(Sz(G_2))$ is not reversible. Let $U = (\{S\}, \Sigma, \Psi, S)$ be a universal ELG, where

$$\Psi \supseteq \{\psi_1 : S \to aSb, \ \psi_2 : S \to cSd, \ \psi_3 : S \to eSf, \ \psi_4 : S \to g\}.$$

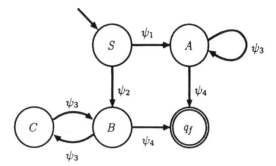

Fig. 1. A nonreversible automaton for an $LR(k)$ ELG

The finite automaton illustrated in Fig.1 accepts $h(Sz(G_2))$, but $h(Sz(G_2))$ is not k-reversible for any k [Ang82].

We can have the converse of Proposition 8 with the following additional condition on the $LR(k)$ property. For a string w and a nonnegative integer i, we define

$$suff(w, i) = \begin{cases} w & \text{if } |w| < i, \\ \text{the suffix of } w \text{ of length } i & \text{if } |w| \ge i. \end{cases}$$

Definition 9. Let $G = (N, \Sigma, P, S)$ be an ELG. G is said to be $LR(k)$ in the *strong sense*, abbreviated $LRS(k)$, if and only if G is *in the normal form* and, for each $u, u', v, v' \in \Sigma^*$, $x \in V^*$, $A, A' \in N$ and $\pi, \pi' \in P$, if

1. $S \overset{\alpha}{\underset{G}{\Longrightarrow}} uAv \overset{\pi}{\underset{G}{\Longrightarrow}} uxv$,
2. $S \overset{\alpha'}{\underset{G}{\Longrightarrow}} u'A'v' \overset{\pi'}{\underset{G}{\Longrightarrow}} u'xv'$,
3. $pref(v, k) = pref(v', k)$, and
4. $suff(u, k) = suff(u', k)$,

then $\pi = \pi'$.

An even linear language L is $LRS(k)$ if and only if there exists an $LRS(k)$ ELG generating L. We note that if G is $LRS(k)$ then G is $LR(k)$ but the converse is not true in general.

Lemma 10. *If an ELG G is $LRS(k)$ then $h(Sz(G))$ is k-reversible.*

Proof. Using the technique of [Tak88], we construct a deterministic finite automaton M that accepts $h(Sz(G))$ and further, we obtain an ELG G' from M. Then by the result of [Tak88], we have $L(G) = L(G')$. Moreover, since each non-terminal in G' is a subset of nonterminals of G, it is easy to verify that G' is also $LRS(k)$. We also note that $h(Sz(G)) = h(Sz(G'))$. The construction of G' ensures that $\alpha = \alpha'$ for any two derivations $S \overset{\alpha}{\underset{G'}{\Longrightarrow}} uAv$ and $S \overset{\alpha'}{\underset{G'}{\Longrightarrow}} uA'v$ in G'.

Let
$$S \xRightarrow[G']{\tau\alpha} uxAyv \xRightarrow[G']{\pi} uxzyv \text{ and}$$
$$S \xRightarrow[G']{\tau'\alpha'} u'xA'yv' \xRightarrow[G']{\pi'} u'xzyv'$$

be derivations in G', where $u, u', v, v', x, y \in \Sigma^*$, $z \in V^*$ and π, π' are labels of productions of G'. Since G' is in the required normal form, we have $h(\alpha) = h(\alpha')$ and $h(\pi) = h(\pi')$. Assume now that $|\alpha| = k$. Since G' is $LRS(k)$, the above fact concerning derivations in G' implies that the derivations given above are unique for $uxzyv$ and $u'xzyv'$, respectively. We have $\pi = \pi'$ and therefore $T_{h(Sz(G'))}(h(\tau\alpha)) = T_{h(Sz(G'))}(h(\tau'\alpha'))$. It then follows from Proposition 1 that $h(Sz(G'))$ is k-reversible. Since $h(Sz(G)) = h(Sz(G'))$, $h(Sz(G))$ is k-reversible. □

Lemma 11. *Let G be an ELG. If $h(Sz(G))$ is k-reversible then there exists an $LRS(k)$ ELG G' such that $L(G) = L(G')$.*

Proof. (sketch) Let M be a k-reversible automaton accepting $h(Sz(G))$. As in the proof of Lemma 10, we can obtain an *ELG* G' such that $L(G) = L(G')$. We note that $h(Sz(G)) = h(Sz(G'))$ and therefore $h(Sz(G'))$ is k-reversible.

The proof can be completed as in the case of Proposition 8. □

Lemmas 10 and 11 mean that for any $LRS(k)$ ELG G, $L(G) = L(U, h(Sz(G)))$, where U is a universal *ELG*. Hence, together with Proposition 5, we have the following theorem.

Theorem 12. *Let L be an even linear language. L is generated by a universal ELG with a unique k-reversible control set if and only if L is an $LRS(k)$ even linear language.*

It is well known that for any $k \geq 1$ an $LR(k)$ context-free language is generated by an $LR(1)$ context-free grammar. However, as the following proposition says, there is a hierarchy in the class of $LRS(k)$ even linear languages.

Proposition 13. *For any nonnegative integer k, let $\mathcal{L}_k$ denote the class of all languages generated by $LRS(k)$ ELGs. Then $\mathcal{L}_k$ is properly contained in $\mathcal{L}_{k+1}$.*

Proof. Let k be a nonnegative integer. By [Ang82] and Theorem 12, $\mathcal{L}_k \subseteq \mathcal{L}_{k+1}$. Consider the language $L = \{a^n ba^n \mid n \geq k+1\}$. L is generated by a universal *ELG* U that has productions $\psi_1 : S \to aSa$ and $\psi_2 : S \to b$ with a control set $C = \{\psi_1^n \psi_2 \mid n \geq k+1\}$. Anglin [Ang82] has shown that C is $(k+1)$-reversible but not k-reversible. It follows from Theorem 12 that L is generated by an $LRS(k+1)$ ELG but not an $LRS(k)$ ELG. □

Next we consider the relationship between $LRS(1)$ ELGs and so called almost terminal-fixed *ELGs* introduced in [Mäk94]. An *ELG* G is said to be *almost terminal-fixed* if $A \to aBb$ and $C \to aDb$ in G always imply $B = D$.

Proposition 14. *Almost terminal-fixed ELGs are $LRS(1)$ ELGs and therefore $LR(1)$ ELGs.*

4 Learning Deterministic Even Linear Languages from Positive Examples

Consider now the class of languages obtained as universal homomorphic images from the Szilard languages of $LRS(k)$ ELGs. We have seen that this class, hereafter called the class of LRS k-reversible languages, is a proper subclass of all k-reversible languages. Each k-reversible automaton accepting an LRS k-reversible language can be reduced to a k-reversible automaton having just one final state without changing the language accepted. We call such an automaton a *canonical LRS k-reversible automaton*.

Let E be a nonempty finite set of strings over Σ. We define the *prefix tree automaton* for E, $PT(E) = (Q, \Sigma, \delta, I, F)$, as follows:

$$Q = \{u \mid u \text{ is a prefix of } w \in E\},$$
$$I = \{\lambda\},$$
$$F = E,$$
$$\delta(u, a) = ua \quad \text{if } u, ua \in Q.$$

If E is a set of positive examples for an LRS k-reversible language, the out degree of each final state of the prefix tree automaton for E is zero because LRS k-reversible languages are prefix-free.

Now, in Fig.2, we describe the algorithm k-LRSRI to infer LRS k-reversible automata from positive examples. k-LRSRI is almost the same as ZR in [Ang82] except for looking ahead with strings of length at most k. In the sequel, we generally use the same terminology as [Ang82]. For any input E, let $M_0 = PT(E) = (Q_0, \Sigma, \delta_0, \{\lambda\}, F_0)$ be the prefix tree automaton for E. Let $\Sigma^{\leq k}$ denote the set of all strings of length less than or equal to k. *table* is a function from $Q_0 \times \Sigma^{\leq k}$ to $\{0, 1\}$, where 0 and 1 are logical truth values. This function can be represented as a table whose columns are named by the states of Q_0 and whose rows are named by the strings of $\Sigma^{\leq k}$. $\vee$ and $\wedge$ denote the logical disjunction and conjunction, respectively. Subprocedures FIND and UNION are from [Tar75]; they operate on subsets of Q_0. The final output $M_f = (Q_f, \Sigma, \delta_f, \{\lambda\}, F_f)$ is defined in the following way: Q_f is the set of all blocks left after all merging by UNION operations and F_f is the block which has a final state of M_0. For each blocks B_1 and B_2 and each symbol $a \in \Sigma$, $B_2 \in \delta_f(B_1, a)$ if and only if $q_2 \in \delta_0(q_1, a)$ for $q_1 \in B_1$ and $q_2 \in B_2$.

Lemma 15. *The output M_f of the algorithm k-LRSRI is always a canonical LRS k-reversible automaton.*

Proof. (sketch) For FIND and UNION operations, every subset of Q_0 is represented as a tree structure. We have only to check the table information of two states associated with the roots. Therefore, for each UNION operation, the only *table* function values to be updated are those related to the new root. This guarantees that the table information is always supplied correctly.

The proof can be completed as in [Ang82]. □

Algorithm k-LRSRI

Input: A set E of positive examples;
Output: A canonical *LRS* k-reversible automaton;

begin
  $M_0 = PT(E) = (Q_0, \Sigma, \delta_0, \{\lambda\}, F_0)$.
  foreach (q, w) in $(Q_0, \Sigma^{\leq k})$
    if $(|w| < k$ and $q = \delta_0(\lambda, w))$ or
                       $(|w| = k$ and $q = \delta_0(\lambda, vw)$ for some $v \in \Sigma^*)$ **then**
    $table(q, w) = 1$ else $table(q, w) = 0$;
  foreach (q, a) in (Q_0, Σ)
    $succ(\{q\}, a) = \delta_0(q, a); \;\; pred(\{q\}, a) = \delta_0^r(q, a)$;
  choose some $q' \in F_0$;
  $\mathsf{LIST} = \Big[(q', q)\Big]_{q \in F_0 \setminus \{q'\}}$;
  while $\mathsf{LIST} \neq \varnothing$ **do**
    begin
      remove some element (q_1, q_2) from LIST;
      $B_1 = FIND(q_1); \;\; B_2 = FIND(q_2)$;
      if $B_1 \neq B_2$ **then**
        begin
          $B_3 = UNION(B_1, B_2)$;
          foreach w in $\Sigma^{\leq k}$
            $table(B_3, w) = table(B_1, w) \vee table(B_2, w)$; /* updating *table* function */
          foreach a in Σ
            begin
              if $succ(B_1, a) \neq \varnothing$ and $succ(B_2, a) \neq \varnothing$ **then**
                place $(succ(B_1, a), succ(B_2, a))$ on LIST;
              if $succ(B_1, a) \neq \varnothing$ **then** $succ(B_3, a) = succ(B_1, a)$
                          else $succ(B_3, a) = succ(B_2, a)$;
              if $pred(B_1, a) \neq \varnothing$ and $pred(B_2, a) \neq \varnothing$
                and $\displaystyle\bigvee_{w \in \Sigma^{\leq k}} (table(B_1, w) \wedge table(B_2, w)) = 1$ **then**
                place $(pred(B_1, a), pred(B_2, a))$ on LIST;
              if $pred(B_1, a) \neq \varnothing$ **then** $pred(B_3, a) = pred(B_1, a)$
                          else $pred(B_3, a) = pred(B_2, a)$;
            end
        end
    end
  output M_f
end.

Fig. 2. The algorithm k-LRSRI to infer *LRS* k-reversible automata

With the above lemma, the following can be proved in a way analogous to [Ang82].

Lemma 16. *Let M_f be the output by k-LRSRI with an input E. Then $L(M_f)$ is the smallest LRS k-reversible language containing E.*

Our criterion for successful learning is "identification in the limit" [Gol67]. The following lemma means that the class of all *LRS* k-reversible languages is learnable in the limit from positive examples.

Lemma 17. *Let L be an LRS k-reversible language and let $w_1, w_2, w_3, \ldots$ be a positive presentation of L. On this input, the sequence of outputs converges to a canonical LRS k-reversible automaton accepting L.*

The time complexity of k-LRSRI is similar to that of ZR in [Ang82]. Let α denote a functional inverse of Ackermann's function. We note that this function is very slowly growing.

Lemma 18. *Let E be the set of input strings and let n be one more than the sum of the lengths of the strings in E. The algorithm k-LRSRI runs in time $O(n\alpha(n))$.*

Proof. The prefix tree automaton M_0 is constructed in time $O(n)$ and contains at most n states. The initial *table* function is constructed in time $O(n)$ since $|Q_0 \times \Sigma^{\leq k}|$ is $O(n)$. The partition of Q_0 is queried and updated using FIND and UNION operations described and analyzed by Tarjan [Tar75]. Processing each pair of states from LIST entails two FIND operations to determine the subsets containing two states. If the subsets are distinct, which can occur at most $n - 1$ times, they are merged with a UNION operation in time $O(1)$. Each merging process causes at most $2|\Sigma|$ new pairs to be placed on LIST. At most $(4|\Sigma| + 2)(n - 1)$ FIND operations and $n - 1$ UNION operations are required, which run in total time $O(n\alpha(n))$. Each logical operation runs in $O(1)$. Therefore, we conclude that the running time is $O(n\alpha(n))$. □

To construct a learning algorithm for the class of $LRS(k)$ even linear languages, we have only to prepare a front-end processing algorithm and add it to k-LRSRI. The front-end processing algorithm has the following two tasks:

- converting a string to an associate word by parsing in a universal *ELG*, and
- constructing an $LRS(k)$ *ELG* from a universal *ELG* and an *LRS* k-reversible automaton.

The configuration of a learning algorithm is illustrated in Fig.3. The front-end processing algorithm reduces the problem of identifying an $LRS(k)$ even linear language to the problem of identifying an *LRS* k-reversible automaton. We note that, since any universal *ELG* U is $LR(0)$, the time complexity of parsing a string in U is $O(m)$, where m is the length of the string. The time complexity of constructing an $LRS(k)$ *ELG* from a universal *ELG* and an *LRS* k-reversible

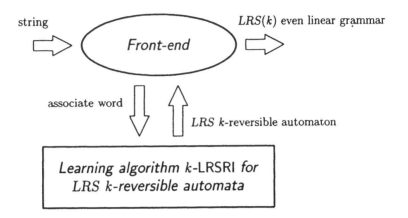

Fig. 3. The configuration of a learning algorithm for $LRS(k)$ even linear languages

automaton is bounded by the size of the automaton, which is bounded by the size of the input strings. Therefore, it is possible to construct an $LRS(k)$ ELG in time $O(n)$, where n is the size of the input strings. These observations immediately give us the time complexity of a learning algorithm for $LRS(k)$ even linear languages. Hence, by Theorem 12 and Lemmas 17 and 18, we have the following theorem.

Theorem 19. *The class of all $LRS(k)$ even linear languages is learnable in the limit from positive examples. Updating conjectures takes time $O(n\alpha(n))$.*

Takada [Tak94] has shown the existence of a hierarchy of language classes, in which the learning problem for each class is reduced to the problem for k-reversible languages. Let k be a fixed nonnegative integer. We denote the class of k-reversible languages by $\mathcal{R}^k$ and the class of context-sensitive languages by $\mathcal{CS}$.

Definition 20. Let $\mathbf{U}$ be the collection of all universal ELGs. Define $\mathcal{L}_i^k$ for any integer $i \geq 0$ inductively as follows:

$$\mathcal{L}_0^k = \mathcal{R}^k,$$
$$\mathcal{L}_i^k = \{L(U, C) \mid U \in \mathbf{U} \text{ and } C \in \mathcal{L}_{i-1}^k\} \quad \text{for any integer } i \geq 1.$$

Proposition 21 [Tak94]. $\mathcal{R}^k = \mathcal{L}_0^k \subsetneq \mathcal{L}_1^k \subsetneq \mathcal{L}_2^k \subsetneq \cdots \subsetneq \mathcal{CS}$.

Now, we apply our results to this hierarchy. The configuration of a learning algorithm for each class $\mathcal{L}_i^k$ is analogous to Fig.3. In this case, the front-end processing algorithm parses input strings iteratively in universal ELGs and outputs LRS k-reversible automata with universal ELGs.

Proposition 22. *For any fixed integers $i \geq 1$ and $k \geq 0$, the class $\mathcal{L}_i^k$ is learnable in the limit from positive examples. Updating conjectures takes time $O(n\alpha(n))$.*

As a corollary of this proposition, we obtain a learning algorithm for k-reversible languages which is more efficient than Angluin's algorithm in terms of $LRS(k)$ ELGs.

Corollary 23. *In terms of $LRS(k)$ ELGs, the class of k-reversible languages is learnable in the limit from positive examples with $O(n\alpha(n))$ updating time.*

5 Concluding Remarks

In this paper, we have shown that the class of $LRS(k)$ even linear languages is learnable in the limit from positive examples. The proposed learning algorithm updates conjectures in almost linear time of the size of input strings. We have also extended these to a hierarchy of language classes proposed by Takada [Tak94]. As a corollary of this, in terms of $LRS(k)$ even linear grammars, we have a learning algorithm for k-reversible languages that is more efficient than the one proposed by Angluin [Ang82].

The time complexity of the algorithm k-LRSRI is dominated by the set union problem. There exist some special cases where the set union problem can be solved in linear time [GI91]. Using these results, there would be a possibility to obtain an algorithm that runs in linear time.

The hierarchy of language classes and the learning algorithms of these languages are interesting from biological point of view. Each class $\mathcal{L}_i^k$ contains the language $\{a_1^n a_2^n \cdots a_{2i}^n \mid n \geq 0\}$, where i is a nonnegative integer and each a_j is a terminal symbol. These languages describe more context dependencies than context-free languages. Therefore, with our method, we can analyze more complicated context dependencies of palindromic sequences of DNA and RNA. One of our future work is analyzing these sequences by our algorithm.

Acknowledgments

We are grateful to thank Yasubumi Sakakibara, You Matsuo, and Steffen Lange for their valuable comments and suggestions.

References

[Ang82] D. Angluin. Inference of reversible languages. *Journal of the Association for Computing Machinery*, Vol. 29, No. 3, pp. 741–765, 1982.

[AP64] V. Amar and G. Putzolu. On a family of linear grammars. *Information and Control*, Vol. 7, No. 3, pp. 283–291, 1964.

[GI91] Z. Galil and G. F. Italiano. Data structures and algorithms for disjoint set union problems. *ACM Computing Surveys*, Vol. 23, No. 3, pp. 319–344, 1991.

[Gol67] E. M. Gold. Language identification in the limit. *Information and Control*, Vol. 10, No. 5, pp. 447–474, 1967.

[Har78] M. A. Harrison. *Introduction to Formal Language Theory*. Addison-Wesley, 1978.

[Lew94] B. Lewin. *Genes V.* Oxford University Press, 1994.

[Mäk94] E. Mäkinen. A note on the grammatical inference problem for even linear languages. Report A-1994-9, University of Tampere, 1994. To appear in *Fundamenta Informaticae.*

[Tak88] Y. Takada. Grammatical inference for even linear languages based on control sets. *Information Processing Letters*, Vol. 28, No. 4, pp. 193–199, 1988.

[Tak94] Y. Takada. A hierarchy of languages families learnable by regular language learning. Research Report ISIS-RR-94-15E, ISIS, Fujitsu Laboratories Ltd., 1994. To appear in *Information and Computation.*

[Tar75] R. E. Tarjan. Efficiency of a good but not linear set union algorithm. *Journal of the Association for Computing Machinery*, Vol. 22, No. 2, pp. 215–225, 1975.

Language Learning from Membership Queries and Characteristic Examples

Hiroshi Sakamoto

Research Institute of Fundamental Information Science
Kyushu University 33, Fukuoka 812-81, Japan
email hiroshi@rifis.kyushu-u.ac.jp

Abstract. This paper introduces the notion of characteristic examples and shows that the notion contributes to language learning in polynomial time. A characteristic example of a language L is an element of L which includes, in a sense, sufficient information to represent L. Every context-free language can be divided into a finite number of languages each of which has a characteristic example and it is decidable whether or not a context-free language has a characteristic example. We present an algorithm that learns parenthesis languages using membership queries and characteristic examples. Our algorithm runs in time polynomial in the number of production rules of a minimal parenthesis grammar and in the length of the longest characteristic example.

1 Introduction

An algorithm which learns a language with queries receives yes/no answers according to the criteria of the queries. Angluin [Ang87b] introduced a learning model with two types of queries (i.e., membership queries and equivalence queries). For a membership query of a string, an oracle returns 'yes' if the string is an element of a target language; otherwise it returns 'no'. For an equivalence query of a language, an oracle returns 'yes' if the language is equivalent to a target language; otherwise it returns a counterexample.

After her work, many researchers have studied language learning with queries (cf., e.g., [Sak90, Ang87a, BR87, Tak88]). Most of the methods applied in those papers are based on the notion of observation tables introduced by Angluin [Ang87b]. Ishizaka [Ish90] proposed another method based on the theory of model inference (cf. [Sha83]) and presented an algorithm that learns a simple deterministic language using membership queries and extended equivalence queries. He showed that his algorithm runs in time polynomial in the length of the longest counterexample and in the number of nonterminals in a minimal grammar for a target language. Sakakibara [Sak90] studied the problem of learning the whole class of context-free grammars from structured strings using queries. He defined a nondeterministic tree automaton that accepts a set of trees over an alphabet and presented an algorithm using two types of queries (i.e., structural membership queries and structural equivalence queries). He also showed that the algorithm runs in time polynomial in the number of states of a minimal tree automaton and in the length of the longest counterexample.

The learning ability of an algorithm depends on the information oracles provide. As an example, we consider the case that a target language can be divided into some disjoint sub-languages. If oracles give the algorithm no information about such a sub-language (i.e., no example is given from such a sub-language), then the algorithm can never identify the whole language. Consequently, it is reasonable to assume that an oracle carefully selects examples from a target language. Informally, the task of the oracle is described as follows. The oracle divides a target language into a finite number of sub-languages each of which has a kind of representative elements. A representative element of a language is a terminal string derived using all production rules of a grammar that generates the language. Such sub-languages and representative elements are called *complete* languages and *characteristic examples*, respectively.

In this paper, we consider the problem of learning parenthesis languages using characteristic examples and membership queries. A parenthesis language is a context-free language in which ambiguity is avoided by the systematic and tedious use of parentheses such that a sentence (or terminal string) wears its syntactic structure on its sleeve (cf. [McN67]). Thus, for parenthesis languages, every example is a structural example in the sense of Sakakibara [Sak90]. We present an algorithm that learns parenthesis languages using membership queries and characteristic examples. Our algorithm runs in time polynomial in the number of production rules of a minimal parenthesis grammar and in the length of the longest characteristic example.

2 Preliminaries

An alphabet is a finite non-empty set of distinct symbols. Let Σ be an alphabet, then Σ^* denotes the set of all finite strings of symbols from Σ. For a finite set S, let $|S|$ denote the cardinality of S. Every subset $L \subseteq \Sigma^*$ is called a language.

A *context-free grammar* is a 4-tuple $G = (N, \Sigma, P, S)$, where N is an alphabet of *nonterminals*, Σ is an alphabet of *terminals* such that $N \cap \Sigma = \phi$, $S \in N$ is the *start symbol* and P is a finite set of *production rules* of the form $A \to w$ ($A \in N, w \in (N \cup \Sigma)^*$). For strings $\alpha, \beta \in (N \cup \Sigma)^*$, the binary relation $\Rightarrow$ is defined as follows: $\alpha \Rightarrow \beta$ if and only if there exist strings $\gamma_1, \gamma_2 \in (N \cup \Sigma)^*$ and a production rule $A \to w \in P$ such that $\alpha = \gamma_1 A \gamma_2$ and $\beta = \gamma_1 w \gamma_2$. A *derivation* from α to β is a finite sequence of strings $\alpha = \alpha_0, \alpha_1, \cdots, \alpha_n = \beta$ such that for each i, $\alpha_i \Rightarrow \alpha_{i+1}$. If there is a derivation from α to β, then we denote it by $\alpha \Rightarrow^* \beta$, that is, the relation $\Rightarrow^*$ is the reflexive and transitive closure of $\Rightarrow$. The language of a nonterminal A, denoted $L(A)$, is the set of all $w \in \Sigma$ such that $A \Rightarrow^* w$. The language of a grammar G, denoted $L(G)$, is just $L(S)$, where S is the start symbol of G. A language L is said to be *context-free* if there exists a context-free grammar G such that $L = L(G)$.

A derivation tree T of a grammar $G = (N, \Sigma, P, S)$ is a tree such that each internal node of T is labeled by an element of N, each leaf of T is labeled by an element of Σ and for each internal node labeled by $A \in N$, there exists a production rule $A \to w$ in P, where w is the concatenation of labels of its children in left-to-right order.

A production rule of the form $A \to \varepsilon$ is said to be an ε-*production*, where ε is the empty string. A grammar is said to be ε-*free* if it has no ε-production except $S \to \varepsilon$. Note that for any context-free grammar G, there exists a grammar G' such that G' is ε-free and $L(G) = L(G')$. In this paper, we assume that context-free grammars are ε-free.

A grammar G is said to be *unambiguous* if for every terminal string $w \in L(G)$, there exists exactly one derivation tree of G. A *context* β is a string with one blank and we write $\beta[w]$ for the context β with its blank replaced by the string w. Two nonterminals A_1 and A_2 of G are said to be *equivalent* if either both $\beta[A_1]$ and $\beta[A_2]$ are derived from G or none of them. A nonterminal A of G is said to be *useless* if no $\beta[A]$ is derived from G or no terminal string is derived from A. A grammar G is said to be *reduced* if no two distinct nonterminals of G are equivalent and G has no useless nonterminal.

A *parenthesis grammar* is a context-free grammar all of whose production rules are of the from $A \to (w)$, where w contains no occurrence of '(' or of ')'. A *backwards deterministic* parenthesis grammar is one in which no two production rules have the same right side. Note that a backwards deterministic parenthesis grammar is unambiguous.

Theorem 1 (McNaughton). Every parenthesis grammar has an equivalent backwards deterministic parenthesis grammar effectively obtainable from it.

Theorem 2 (McNaughton). There is an algorithm that computes for every backwards deterministic parenthesis grammar G a reduced backwards deterministic parenthesis grammar G' such that $L(G) = L(G')$.

3 Characteristic Examples

In this section, we provide the theoretical background for our learning algorithm. In particular, we introduce the notion of a characteristic example. Next, we establish the decomposability of context-free languages into sublanguages possessing characteristic examples (cf. Proposition 4). Finally, we ask whether or not it is decidable if a context-free grammar has a characteristic example. The answer is provided by Theorem 10.

3.1 Definition and basic properties

Definition 3. A terminal string w is said to be a *characteristic example* of a grammar G if w is derived using all production rules of G. A grammar G is said to be *complete* if G has a characteristic example.

Clearly, there exists a grammar that is not complete.

Proposition 4. Let $G = (N, \Sigma, P, S)$ be a context-free grammar. There exists a set $S_G = \{G_1, G_2, \cdots, G_k\}$ of complete grammars such that $\cup_{i \leq k} G_i = G$ and $k \leq |P|$, where $\cup_{i \leq k} G_i = (\cup_{i \leq k} N_i, \cup_{i \leq k} \Sigma_i, \cup_{i \leq k} P_i, S)$.

Proof. Since G is ε-free, if $\varepsilon \in L(G)$, then there exists a grammar G' such that $L(G) = L(G') \cup L(G_\varepsilon)$ and $L(G') \cap L(G_\varepsilon) = \phi$, where $G_\varepsilon = (\{S\}, \{\varepsilon\}, \{S \to \varepsilon\}, S)$. Thus, without loss of generality, we assume that $\varepsilon \notin L(G)$.

For grammars $G_i = (N_i, \Sigma_i, P_i, S)$ $(1 \le i \le 2)$, let $G_1 \sqsubseteq G_2$ iff $N_1 \subseteq N_2$, $\Sigma_1 \subseteq \Sigma_2$, and $P_1 \subseteq P_2$. For a set $S_G = \{G_1, \cdots, G_k\}$ of grammars, let $\sqcup S_G$ denote $\cup_{i \le k} G_i$.

For any $w \in L(G)$, there exists a grammar $G' \sqsubseteq G$ such that w is a characteristic example of G'. Since the number of non-empty subset of P is $2^{|P|} - 1$, there exists a set $S_G = \{G_1, \cdots, G_k\}$ of complete grammars such that $\sqcup S_G = G$ and $|S_G| \le 2^{|P|} - 1$. If $|S_G| > |P|$, then

1. there exists a set $S'_G \subset S_G$ of grammars such that $\sqcup S'_G \sqsubseteq G'$ for a grammar $G' \in S_G - S'_G$, or
2. there exists a grammar $G' \in S_G$ such that $G' \sqsubseteq S'_G$ for a set $S'_G \subset S_G - \{G'\}$ of grammars.

In Condition 1, $\sqcup S_G = \sqcup \{S_G - S'_G\} = G$. In Condition 2, $\sqcup S_G = \sqcup \{S_G - \{G'\}\} = G$. Thus, there exists a set S_G of complete grammars such that $\sqcup S_G = G$ and $|S_G| \le |P|$.
□

For a grammar G, a set S_G of grammars that satisfies the condition in Proposition 4 is said to be a set of complete grammars *with respect to G*.

Proposition 5. Let G be a backwards deterministic parenthesis grammar and let $S_G = \{G_1, G_2, \cdots, G_m\}$ be a set of complete grammars with respect to G. Let W_i and W_j be sets of characteristic examples from G_i and G_j $(1 \le i, j \le m)$, respectively. Then W_i and W_j are disjoint if and only if $i \ne j$.

Proof. If $i = j$, then $W_i = W_j$. Let $i \ne j$. By Proposition 4, $G_i \nsqsubseteq G_j$ and $G_j \nsqsubseteq G_i$. Let $G_i = (N_i, \Sigma_i, P_i, S)$ and $G_j = (N_j, \Sigma_j, P_j, S)$. If $P_i \nsqsubseteq P_j$, then $N_i \sqsubseteq N_j$ and $\Sigma_i \nsqsubseteq \Sigma_j$. Thus, $P_i \nsqsubseteq P_j$, that is, there exists a production rule $r \in P_i - P_j$. Every $w_i \in W_i$ is derived using all production rules in P_i and every $w_j \in W_j$ is not derived using the production rule $r \in P_i$. Since G is unambiguous, G_i and G_j both are unambiguous. Hence, $W_i \cap W_j = \phi$.
□

3.2 Decision problem

Let $G = (N, \Sigma, P, S)$ be a grammar. For a nonterminal $A \in N$, we write $\alpha \Rightarrow^*_A \beta$ if there exists a derivation from α to β such that $\alpha \Rightarrow^* \gamma_1 A \gamma_2 \Rightarrow^* \beta$. For a production rule $A \to w \in P$, we write $\alpha \Rightarrow^*_{A \to w} \beta$ if there exists a derivation from α to β such that $\alpha \Rightarrow^* \gamma_1 A \gamma_2 \Rightarrow \gamma_1 w \gamma_2 \Rightarrow^* \beta$.

For a derivation tree T of G, let $d(T)$ denote the depth of T. For a nonterminal $A \in N$, let $n(T)_A$ denote the number of internal nodes of T labeled by A. For a production rule $A \to w \in P$, let $n(T)_{A \to w}$ denote the number of internal nodes of T labeled by A such that w is concatenation of labels of its children. For a set $P' \subseteq P$ of production rules, let $T_{P'}$ denote a derivation tree such that for every $r \in P'$, $n(T_{P'})_r \ge 1$.

Definition 6. Let A be a nonterminal of a grammar G. A is said to be *bounded* if there exists a constant k such that for every derivation tree T of G, $n(T)_A \leq k$.

Definition 7. Let r be a production rule of a grammar G. r is said to be *bounded* if there exists a constant k such that for every derivation tree T of G, $n(T)_r \leq k$.

Lemma 8. It is decidable whether or not a nonterminal of a context-free grammar is bounded.

Proof. Let $G = (N, \Sigma, P, S)$ be a context-free grammar. First we prove that the following conditions are equivalent.

1. A nonterminal $A \in N$ is not bounded.
2. For a nonterminal $A \in N$, there exists a nonterminal $B \in N$ such that $B \Rightarrow_A^* \beta[B]$.

It is clear that 2 implies 1. Now, we assume that there exists no $B \in N$ that satisfies Condition 2. Let T be a derivation tree of G. For any subtree of T whose root a_1 is labeled by A, it has no internal node labeled by A except a_1. If the length of the path of T from the root to a_1 is greater than $|N|$, then there exist two or more internal nodes of T labeled by $B \in N$ in the path. Let b_1 and b_2 be such internal nodes in root-to-leaf order. Let T_1 and T_2 be subtrees of T whose root are b_1 and b_2, respectively. Since both T_1 and T_2 have exactly one internal node labeled by A and T_2 is a subtree of T_1, the tree that is obtained by replacing T_1 of T by T_2 is a derivation tree of G. Thus, for any derivation tree T of G, there exists a derivation tree T' of G such that $n(T)_A = n(T')_A$ and $d(T') \leq |N|$, thus, A is bounded. □

We note that for every context-free grammar $G = (N, \Sigma, P, S)$ and every strings $\alpha, \beta \in (N \cup \Sigma)^*$, it is decidable whether or not $\alpha \Rightarrow^* \beta$. Let m be the maximum length of right sides of production rules in P. For every $B \in N$ and $\beta[B]$, we can decide whether or not $B \Rightarrow^* \beta[B]$, where the length of $\beta[B]$ is at most $m^{|P|}$. If $B \Rightarrow_A^* \beta[B]$, then A is not bounded; otherwise A is bounded.

Lemma 9. It is decidable whether or not a production rule of a context-free grammar is bounded.

Proof. Let $G = (N, \Sigma, P, S)$ be a context-free grammar. Clearly, every production rule of the form $S \rightarrow w_S$ ($w_S \in (N \cup \Sigma)^*$) is bounded. Without loss of generality, let a production rule $r \in P$ be of the form $A \rightarrow w_A$ ($A \in N - \{S\}, w_A \in (N \cup \Sigma)^*$). We prove that the following conditions are equivalent.

1. $r \in P$ is not bounded.
2. There exists $B \in N$ such that
   (a) $B \Rightarrow^* \beta[B]$ and $\beta[B]$ contains A, or
   (b) $B \Rightarrow^* \beta_1[A]$ and $A' \Rightarrow^* \beta_2[B]$, where $A' \in N$ is contained in w_A.

It is clear that 2 implies 1. Now, we assume Condition 1. Since A is not bounded, there exists $B \in N$ such that $B \Rightarrow_A^* \beta[B]$, that is, $B \Rightarrow^* \alpha_1 A \alpha_2 \Rightarrow^* \beta[B]$ for some strings $\alpha_1, \alpha_2 \in (N \cup \Sigma)^*$. If B is derived from a nonterminal contained in α_1 or α_2, then (a) holds. If B is derived from a nonterminal contained in w_A, then (b) holds.

Otherwise for any derivation tree T of G, $n(T)_r$ is less than the number of internal nodes of a derivation tree of G having depth less than or equal to $|N|$, thus, r is bounded. This contradicts that r is not bounded. Hence, Condition 2 holds.

Similarly as above, for any production rule in P, we can decide whether or not (a) or (b) holds. $\square$

Theorem 10. It is decidable whether or not a context-free grammar has a characteristic example.

Proof. Let $P' \subseteq P$ be a set of bounded production rules of a context-free grammar $G = (N, \Sigma, P, S)$. By Lemma 9, membership in P' is decidable. First we prove that the following conditions are equivalent.

1. G has a characteristic example.
2. There exists a derivation tree $T_{P'}$ of G.

It is clear that 1 implies 2. For the converse direction, assume Condition 2. Let $r \in P - P'$. There exists $A_1 \in N$ such that $A_1 \Rightarrow_r^* \beta_1[A_1]$. If $T_{P'}$ has an internal node labeled by A_1, then there exists a derivation tree T of G such that $n(T_{P'})_{r' \in P'} \leq n(T)_{r' \in P'}$ and $n(T)_r \geq 1$. Otherwise any production rule $r_1 \in P$ which contains A_1 is not bounded. If there exists no $A_2 \in N$ such that $A_2 \Rightarrow_{r_1}^* \beta_2[A_2]$ and $A_2 \neq A_1$, then A_1 must be contained in the right side of a production rule of the form $S \to w_S \in P'$. This contradicts that $T_{P'}$ has no internal node labeled by A_1. Thus, $A_2 \neq A_1$. Since there are only finitely many nonterminals, we can find $A_k \in N$ such that $A_k \Rightarrow_{r_{k-1}}^* \beta_k[A_k], \cdots, A_2 \Rightarrow_{r_1}^* \beta_2[A_2], A_1 \Rightarrow_r^* \beta_1[A_1]$ and $T_{P'}$ has an internal node labeled by A_k, namely, there exists a derivation tree T of G such that $n(T_{P'})_{r' \in P'} \leq n(T)_{r' \in P'}$ and $n(T)_r \geq 1$. Thus, 2 implies 1.

Finally, we prove that it is decidable whether or not there exists $T_{P'}$. Let T be a derivation tree of G. If $d(T) > |N|$, then for a production rule $A \to w \in P$, there exists an internal node a_1 of T labeled by A such that w is the concatenation of labels of its children and $n(T_1)_{A \to w} \geq 2$, where T_1 is the subtree of T whose root is a_1. Since $n(T_1)_{A \to w} \geq 2$, there exists an internal node a_2 ($\neq a_1$) of T_1 labeled by A such that w is the concatenation of labels of its children. Let T_2 be a subtree of T_1 whose root is a_2. A tree obtained by replacing T_1 of T by T_2 is a derivation tree of G. Thus, there exists a derivation tree T' of G such that $n(T)_{r' \in P'} = n(T')_{r' \in P'}$ and $d(T') \leq |N|$. Hence, we can decide whether or not there exists $T_{P'}$ by enumerating all derivation trees of depth less than or equal to $|N|$. $\square$

4   Learning Algorithm

Our algorithm takes as input a set of characteristic examples of a target language. For a characteristic example, our algorithm determines a derivation tree. For a derivation tree, our algorithm computes a grammar and outputs the union of the grammars computed as a parenthesis grammar for the target language. In order to determine a derivation tree, our algorithm uses membership queries. In this section, we describe the procedure $\mathcal{M}$ to determine derivation trees for characteristic examples. The procedure $\mathcal{M}$ is the main part of our algorithm.

4.1 Membership query for frontier

Definition 11. A *frontier* of a tree is the concatenation of labels of its leaves in left-to-right order.

Definition 12 (Sakakibara). A *skeletal alphabet* Sk is a ranked alphabet consisting of only the special symbol σ with the rank relation $r_{Sk} \subseteq \{\sigma\} \times \{1, 2, \cdots, m\}$ for some m. A tree defined over $Sk \cup V_0$ is called a *skeleton*, where V_0 is an alphabet.

Let T be a derivation tree of a grammar $G = (N, \Sigma, P, S)$. A *skeletal description* of T is a skeleton over $Sk \cup \Sigma$ obtained by replacing all labels of internal nodes of T by σ. In this paper, a skeleton means a skeletal description of a derivation tree of a grammar.

Let a be an internal node of a tree s, and let s' be a tree. $s(a)$ denotes a subtree of s whose root is a and $s(a, s')$ denotes a tree obtained by replacing $s(a)$ of s by s'.

Definition 13. Let s and s' be skeletons for derivation trees of a grammar G. Let a and a' be internal nodes of s and s', respectively. The relation $\equiv_{G(s, s')}$ is defined as follows: $a \equiv_{G(s_i, s_j)} a'$ if and only if two frontiers of $s(a, s'(a'))$ and $s'(a', s(a))$ are in $L(G)$.

Definition 14. Let G be a grammar, and let s be a tree. A *membership query* for the frontier of s is defined as follows: if the frontier is in $L(G)$, then the answer *yes* is returned; otherwise *no* is returned.

Example 1. For a terminal string $((((a)(b)))(((a)(b))(b)))$ of a parenthesis grammar, Figure 1 depicts the skeleton s and its replacement. σ_i $(1 \leq i \leq 9)$ of s denotes a label of node i. The tree $s(5, s(6))$ is obtained by replacing $s(5)$ of s by $s(6)$. The frontier of $s(5, s(6))$ is the string $(((a)((a)(b)))(((a)(b))(b)))$.

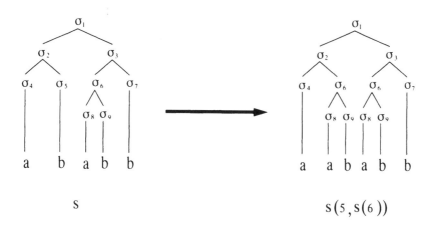

Fig. 1. A skeleton and its replacement

4.2 Procedure $\mathcal{M}$ for skeletons

In Table 1, we give the procedure $\mathcal{M}$ that determines derivation trees of character-istic examples with membership queries. As input, $\mathcal{M}$ takes a set of characteristic examples of complete grammars with respect to a parenthesis grammar that gener-ates a target parenthesis language L_T. $\mathcal{M}$ outputs a set of derivation trees for the characteristic examples given as input.

Procedure $\mathcal{M}$
Input: a set $\hat{s} = \{s_1, s_2, \cdots, s_m\}$ of skeletons
Output: derivation trees

begin
    for each $s_i \in \hat{s}$ $(1 \leq i \leq m)$ /* First loop */
        for each nodes j, k of s_i
            if $j \equiv_{G_U(s_i, s_i)} k$, then   (make membership queries)
                rename σ_k by σ_j $(j < k)$ or σ_j by σ_k $(k < j)$;
            else;

    for each $s_i, s_j \in \hat{s}$ $(1 \leq i \leq m - 1, i < j)$ /* Second loop */
        for each nodes i' of s_i and j' of s_j
            if $i' \equiv_{G_U(s_i, s_j)} j'$, then   (make membership queries)
                rename $\sigma_{j'}$ by $\sigma_{i'}$ $(i' < j')$ or rename $\sigma_{i'}$ by $\sigma_{j'}$ $(j' < i')$;
            if $i' \not\equiv_{G_U(s_i, s_j)} j'$ and $i' = j'$, then
                rename $\sigma_{j'}$ by a new label $\sigma_{k'}$
            else;

    output $\hat{s}$;
end

Table 1. The procedure $\mathcal{M}$ to decide derivation trees

Let $\hat{s} = \{s_1, s_2, \cdots, s_m\}$ be the set of skeletons for m characteristic examples of L_T. First, for any two nodes i and j of a skeleton s_k $(1 \leq k \leq m)$, $\mathcal{M}$ uses a membership query. The membership query proposes two frontiers of $s_k(i, s_k(j))$ and $s_k(j, s_k(i))$. If these two frontiers are both in L_T, then the answer yes is returned; otherwise no is returned. If yes is returned, then $\mathcal{M}$ renames σ_j by σ_i if $i < j$ or renames σ_i by σ_j if $j < i$.

Then, for any node i' of a skeleton s_i and any node j' of another skeleton s_j $(1 \leq i \leq m-1, i < j)$, $\mathcal{M}$ uses a membership query. The membership query proposes two frontiers of $s_i(i', s_j(j'))$ and $s_j(j', s_i(i'))$. If these two frontiers are both in L_T, then the answer yes is returned; otherwise no is returned. If yes is returned, then $\mathcal{M}$ renames $\sigma_{j'}$ of s_j by $\sigma_{i'}$ of s_i if $i' < j'$ or renames $\sigma_{i'}$ of s_i by $\sigma_{j'}$ of s_j if $j' < i'$. If no is returned and $i' = j'$, then $\mathcal{M}$ renames $\sigma_{j'}$ of s_j by $\sigma_{k'}$, where no skeleton $s_k \in \hat{s}$ has a label $\sigma_{k'}$.

Finally, $\mathcal{M}$ outputs a refined $\hat{s}$ as a set of derivation trees of a grammar for the target parenthesis language L_T. Our algorithm computes a parenthesis grammar $G = (N, \Sigma, P, S)$ using such a refined $\hat{s} = \{s_1, s_2, \cdots, s_m\}$. Since each s_i $(1 \leq i \leq m)$ is a derivation tree for a characteristic example, N, Σ and P are computable. For example, if $s \in \hat{s}$ has an internal node labeled by σ such that $\sigma_{i_1} \cdots \sigma_{i_k}$ is the concatenation of labels of its children, then our algorithm makes a rule $\sigma \rightarrow \sigma_{i_1} \cdots \sigma_{i_k}$.

5 Correctness and Complexity

Lemma 15. Let a and b be internal nodes of a derivation tree T of a reduced backwards deterministic parenthesis grammar G. Let s be a skeleton of T. Two labels of a and b of T are equal if and only if $a \equiv_{G(s,s)} b$.

Proof. Clearly, if two labels of a and b are equal, then $a \equiv_{G(s,s)} b$. We assume $a \equiv_{G(s,s)} b$. Let σ_a and σ_b denote the labels of a and b of T, respectively. Since G is backwards deterministic, if two frontiers of $s(a)$ and $s(b)$ are equal, then σ_a and σ_b are equal.

Let two frontiers of $s(a)$ and $s(b)$ be not equal. G has two production rules of the form $\sigma \rightarrow (w_1 \sigma_a w_2)$ and $\sigma' \rightarrow (w_1' \sigma_b w_2')$ for nonterminals σ and σ', strings w_1, w_2, w_1' and w_2', respectively. G also has two production rules of the form $\sigma \rightarrow (w_1 \sigma_b w_2)$ and $\sigma' \rightarrow (w_1' \sigma_a w_2')$. Then, any $\beta[\sigma_a]$ and $\beta[\sigma_b]$ derived from G are of the form $W_1(w_1 \sigma'' w_2)W_2$ or $W_1'(w_1' \sigma'' w_2')W_2'$ for a nonterminal $\sigma'' \in \{\sigma_a, \sigma_b\}$, strings W_1, W_2, W_1' and W_2'. Thus, $\beta[\sigma_a]$ is derived from G if and only if $\beta[\sigma_b]$ is derived from G. Since G is reduced, no two distinct nonterminals of G are equivalent. Hence, σ_a and σ_b are equal. □

Lemma 16. Let a and a' be internal nodes of derivation trees T and T' of a reduced backwards deterministic parenthesis grammar G, respectively. Let s and s' be skeletons for T and T', respectively. Two labels of a of T and a' of T' are equal if and only if $a \equiv_{G(s,s')} a'$.

Proof. The proof of this lemma is analogous to that of Lemma 15. □

From Lemma 15 and 16, we conclude that for a target parenthesis language, our algorithm eventually terminates and outputs a parenthesis grammar which generates the target parenthesis language. We now analyze the time complexity of our algorithm.

Lemma 17. The time used by $\mathcal{M}$ is bounded by a polynomial in the number of characteristic examples and in the length of the longest characteristic example.

Proof. It is sufficient to show that the total number of membership queries is bounded by a polynomial in the number of characteristic examples and in the length of the longest characteristic example. Let m be the number of characteristic examples, and let n be the length of the longest characteristic example.

For a characteristic example w, its skeleton has at most $c|w|^2$ internal nodes for a constant c. In order to decide whether or not any two labels of internal nodes of the skeleton are equal, $\mathcal{M}$ uses membership queries at most $(c|w|^2 - 1) + (c|w|^2 - 2) + \cdots + (c|w|^2 - (c|w|^2 - 1)) = \frac{1}{2}(c|w|^2 + 2)(c|w|^2 - 1)$. For two characteristic examples w_1 and w_2 ($|w_1| \leq |w_2|$), their skeletons have at most $c|w_2|^2$ internal nodes for a constant c. In order to decide whether or not any two labels of internal nodes of the skeletons are equal, $\mathcal{M}$ uses membership queries at most $c^2|w_2|^4$.

Thus, the total number of membership queries $\mathcal{M}$ uses is at most $\frac{1}{2}m(cn^2 + 2)(cn^2 - 1) + \frac{1}{2}c^2(m-1)(m-2)n^4 = \mathcal{O}(m^2n^4)$. □

Lemma 18. The total number of characteristic examples to decide a parenthesis grammar for a target language is bounded by the number of production rules of a minimal reduced backwards deterministic parenthesis grammar.

Proof. By Proposition 4, for any reduced backwards deterministic parenthesis grammar $G = (N, \Sigma, P, S)$, there exists a set $S_G = \{G_1, \cdots, G_k\}$ of complete grammars such that $\sqcup S_G = \cup_{i \leq k} G_i = G$ and $k \leq |P|$. Let w_i be a characteristic example of $G_i \in S_G$. By Proposition 5, w_i is not a characteristic example of $G_j \in S_G - \{G_i\}$. By Lemma 15 and 16, a grammar G_i' is decidable such that $L(G_i) = L(G_i')$ and $L(G_i') \neq L(G_j)$ for any $G_j \in S_G - \{G_i\}$. Thus, for a set $\{w_1, \cdots, w_k\}$ of characteristic examples of grammars in S_G, a set S_G' of grammars is decidable such that $L(\sqcup S_G') = L(\sqcup S_G) = L(G)$ and $|S_G'| = |S_G| \leq |P|$. □

Theorem 19. There is an algorithm that learns parenthesis languages using membership queries and characteristic examples of complete grammars with respect to a parenthesis grammar for a target language. Moreover, the time used by the algorithm is bounded by a polynomial in the number of production rules of a minimal reduced backwards deterministic parenthesis grammar for a target language and in the length of the longest characteristic example.

6 Concluding Remarks

We have introduced the notion of characteristic examples and discussed their properties. In particular, it is decidable whether or not a context-free grammar has a characteristic example. Consequently, in this paper, we assumed characteristic examples as input for our algorithm instead of using equivalence queries.

The method used in our algorithm to decide derivation trees of characteristic examples heavily depends on the structural properties of parenthesis grammars (for example, the uniqueness of a left-most derivation). Then, it seems that the method is not applicable to the class containing an ambiguous grammar. In future, we would like to find more practical solutions to this problem.

We have not analyzed the size of characteristic examples. In our setting, the size of characteristic examples of a grammar depends on the size of terminal strings derived from nonterminals of the grammar. Then, the size of a minimal characteristic example of a grammar may not be bounded by a polynomial in the size of the grammar. It is an open problem whether the size of a minimal characteristic example of a grammar can be reduced by, for example, dividing the grammar into a polynomial number of subgrammars.

Acknowledgment. The author would like to thank Setsuo Arikawa, Thomas Zeugmann, Hiroki Ishizaka, and Hiroki Arimura for helpful advice and encouragements.

References

[Ang88]   Dana Angluin. *Queries and concept learning.* Machine Learning, 2:319-342, 1988.

[Ang87a] Dana Angluin. *Learning k-bounded context-free grammars.* Technical Report YALEU/DCS/RR-557, Department of Computer Science, Yale University, 1987.

[Ang87b] Dana Angluin. *Learning regular sets from queries and counterexamples.* Information and Computation, 75:87-106, 1987.

[Ang81]   Dana Angluin. *A note on the number of queries needed to identify regular languages.* Information and Control, 51:76-87, 1981.

[BR87]   Piotr Berman and Pobert Roos. *Learning one-counter languages in polynomial time.* Proceedings of 28th IEEE Symposium on Foundations of Computer Science, pages 61-67. IEEE Computer Society Press, 1987.

[Har78]   Michael A. Harrison. *Introduction to Formal Language Theory.* Reading, MA:Addison-Wesley, 1978.

[Ish90]   Hiroki Ishizaka. *Polynomial time learnability of simple deterministic languages.* Machine Learning, 5:151-164, 1990.

[Knu67]   Donald E. Knuth. *Characterization of Parenthesis Languages.* Information and Control, 11:269-289, 1967.

[McN67]   Robert McNaughton. *Parenthesis Grammars.* Journal of the ACM, 14:490-500, 1967.

[Sak90]   Yasubumi Sakakibara. *Learning context-free grammars from structural data in polynomial time.* Theoretical Computer Science, 76:223-242, 1990.

[Sha83]   Ehud Y. Shapiro. *Algorithmic program debugging.* Cambridge, MA: MIT Press, 1983.

[Tak88]   Yuji Takada. *Grammatical inference for even linear languages based on control sets.* Information Processing Letters, 28:193-199, 1988.

Learning Unions of Tree Patterns Using Queries

Hiroki Arimura, Hiroki Ishizaka, Takeshi Shinohara

Department of Artificial Intelligence
Kyushu Institute of Technology
Kawazu 680-4, Iizuka 820, Japan
{arim,ishizaka,shino}@ai.kyutech.ac.jp

Abstract. This paper characterizes the polynomial time learnability of TP^k, the class of collections of at most k first-order terms. A collection in TP^k defines the union of the languages defined by each first-order terms in the set. Unfortunately, the class TP^k is not polynomial time learnable in most of learning frameworks under standard assumptions in computational complexity theory. To overcome this computational hardness, we relax the learning problem by allowing a learning algorithm to make membership queries. We present a polynomial time algorithm that exactly learns every concept in TP^k using $O(kn)$ equivalence and $O(k^2 n \cdot \max\{k, n\})$ membership queries, where n is the size of longest counterexample given so far. In the proof, we use a technique of replacing each restricted subset query by several membership queries under some condition on a set of function symbols. As corollaries, we obtain the polynomial time PAC-learnability and the polynomial time predictability of TP^k when membership queries are available. We also show a lower bound $\Omega(kn)$ of the number of queries necessary to learn TP^k using both types of queries. Further, we show that neither types of queries can be eliminated to achieve efficient learning of TP^k. Finally, we apply our results in learning of a class of restricted logic programs, called unit clause programs.

1   Introduction

Inductive learning is a process of finding general concepts from their concrete examples. In this paper, we consider the learnability of the class C^k of unions, which is the collection of unions $c_1 \cup \ldots \cup c_n$ of at most k concepts $c_1, \cdots, c_n$ ($n \leq k$) in a concept class C. In particular, this paper focuses on the polynomial time learnability of TP^k, the class of unions of at most k tree pattern languages.

A *tree pattern* is a first-order term in formal logic, and the *language defined by a tree pattern* p is the set of all the tree patterns obtained by replacing each variable in p with a tree pattern containing no variable. A set of tree patterns represents the union of the languages of each tree pattern in the set. For a non-negative integer k, TP^k is the class of sets of at most k tree patterns. Although concepts in TP^k are simple, they have characteristics common to a variety of representation frameworks for structured objects such as knowledge representation languages [7, 10], logic programming languages [6, 13], and combinatorial objects like string patterns [1, 3, 5, 9]. Furthermore, computational problems related to tree patterns are more efficiently solvable than the other representation frameworks; for example, the membership and the containment problems are polynomial time solvable for tree patterns, while the membership problem is NP-complete [1] and the containment problem is undecidable for string patterns [9]. For these reasons, it is a basic but useful practice in machine learning to capture the efficient learnability of TP^k.

Plotkin [16] and Reynolds [17] introduced a *subsumption relation* $\preceq$ over TP^1, and developed a polynomial time algorithm for computing the least upper bound of a given set of tree patterns, called the *lgg*. By computing the lgg of positive examples, TP^1 is polynomial time PAC-learnable, or polynomial time exact learnable using equivalence queries [1].

This subsumption relation $\preceq$ can be extended for a powerset relation $\sqsubseteq$ over TP^k by defining as $P \sqsubseteq Q$ iff $(\forall p \in P)(\exists q \in Q)\ p \preceq q$ for any unions P, Q. Arimura et al. [4] developed a polynomial time algorithm that finds one of the minimal upper bounds (called *mmg*) of a given set of tree patterns with respect to $\sqsubseteq$. Using this algorithm, they showed that the class TP^k is *identifiable in the limit from positive data with consistent and conservative polynomial time update*.

Unfortunately, the convergence time of the algorithm has not been proved to be bounded by any polynomial. The reason is that there may exist several mmg's of the set, while the lgg is unique. In fact, we can prove that for every $k \geq 2$ the class TP^k of unions is not polynomial time learnable in PAC-learning model or exact learning model mentioned above under some assumption in complexity theory, while TP^1 is polynomial time learnable in both models.

One approach to overcome this computational hardness is to relax the problem by allowing a learning algorithm to make *membership queries*. A membership query is any word w, and its answer is "yes" or "no" according to whether w is contained in the target concept. By using membership queries, a learning algorithm can actively collect information on a target concept. Ishizaka *et al.* [8] considered a decision problem closely related to the learnability of TP^k, called the *consistency problem*, and showed that the problem is polynomial time solvable using membership queries for $k = 2$.

In this paper, we present a polynomial time algorithm for learning TP^k using equivalence and membership queries. Under some condition on a set of function symbols, our algorithm LEARN exactly identifies every target concept in TP^k, and outputs "failed" for every target concept not in TP^k. Further, LEARN runs in polynomial time in k and n making $O(kn)$ equivalence queries and $O(k^2 n \cdot \max\{k, n\})$ membership queries, where n is the size of the longest counterexample. Then, the result of Ishizaka *et al.* is generalized by this algorithm for arbitrary positive integer k. Since the algorithm is presented in the paradigm of exact learning by Angluin [2], we can transform in a standard way our learning algorithm into either a *polynomial time PAC-learning algorithm using membership queries* [2], or a *polynomial time prediction algorithm with a polynomial mistake bound using membership queries* [11].

---

[1] In exact learning of TP^1, we have to assume that there exists the bottom element $\perp$ of TP^1, or that one positive example is initially given to a learning algorithm.

The paper is organized as follows. Section 3 gives a polynomial time learning algorithm using equivalence and restricted subset queries, and shows the correctness and the complexity. Next, Section 4 shows that a subset query can be replaced with several membership queries under some condition on a set of function symbols. Then, we show a polynomial time algorithm for learning TP^k using $O(kn)$ equivalence queries and $O(k^2 n \cdot \max\{k, n\})$ membership queries. We also show that any algorithm using equivalence and membership queries requires $\Omega(kn)$ queries. Section 5 shows that neither types of queries can be eliminated to learn TP^k in polynomial time. Section 6 describes an application of the results in Section 3.2 in learning restricted logic programs whose computational mechanisms are only disjunctive definition and unification. Finally, Section 7 concludes the results.

2 Preliminaries

2.1 Unions of tree patterns

Let Σ be a finite alphabet. Each element of Σ is called a *function symbol* and associated with a non-negative integer called an *arity*. A function symbol with arity 0 is also called a *constant*. We assume that Σ contains at least one constant. Let V be a countable set of symbols disjoint from Σ. Each element of V is called a *variable*.

A *first-order term* over Σ is an expression defined recursively as follows: (1) a function with arity 0 or a variable is a first-order term; (2) For a function f with arity n $(n \geq 1)$ and first-order terms $t_1, \ldots, t_n$, $f(t_1, \ldots, t_n)$ is a first-order term. Throughout this paper, we will refer to the first-order terms as *tree patterns* by analogy with string patterns [1]. A tree pattern is said to be *ground* if it contains no variable. Tree patterns will normally be denoted by letters p, q, r, and h, and sets of tree patterns will normally be denoted by capital letters P, Q, R, and H, possibly subscripted.

The set of all the tree patterns is denoted by TP and the set of all the ground tree patterns is denoted by $TP(\Sigma)$. For a non-negative integer k, the class of all the sets consisting of at most k tree patterns is denoted by TP^k. Each element in TP^k is called a *union of at most k tree patterns*. Note that TP^0 includes only one element $\emptyset$.

For a set S, $|S|$ denotes the number of elements in S, and 2^S denotes the powerset of S. The *size* of a tree pattern p, denoted by $size(p)$, is the number of symbol occurrences in p minus the number of distinct variables occurring in p. For example, $size(f(g(X, Y), h(X, Z), Y)) = 8 - 3 = 5$. For a set P of tree patterns, $size(P)$ is defined as $\sum_{p \in P} size(p)$. Note that if a tree pattern p contains no variable then $size(p)$ is the total number of symbol occurrences in p.

A *substitution* is a finite set of the form $\{X_1/t_1, \ldots, X_n/t_n\}$, where X_i is a variable, each t_i is a tree pattern different from X_i, and $X_1, \ldots, X_n$ are mutually distinct. An *instance* of a tree pattern p by a substitution $\theta = \{X_1/t_1, \ldots, X_n/t_n\}$, denoted by $p\theta$, is the tree pattern obtained by simultaneously replacing each occurrences of the variable X_i with the term t_i $(1 \leq i \leq n)$.

For tree patterns p and q, if there exists a substitution θ such that $p = \theta(q)$, then q is said to be a *generalization* of p, and denoted by $p \preceq q$. If $p \preceq q$ but $q \not\preceq p$, then we define $p \prec q$. If both $p \preceq q$ and $q \preceq p$ hold, then we define $p \equiv q$. In what follows, we do not distinguish any tree patterns which are the same modulo $\equiv$. Now, we extend the relation $\preceq$ for unions. Let $P, Q \in TP^k$. If $(\forall p \in P)(\exists q \in Q)\ p \preceq q$ then P is said to be a *refinement* of Q, or Q is a *generalization* of P, and denoted by $P \sqsubseteq Q$. A refinement P of a union Q is said to be *conservative* if for any $q \in Q$ there is at most one $p \in P$ such that $p \preceq q$. For a tree pattern h and a set H of tree patterns, we write $h \preceq H$ if $\{h\} \sqsubseteq H$ holds.

For a tree pattern p, the *language of p*, denoted by $L(p)$, is the set of all the ground instances of p. More precisely, $L(p) = \{\, w \in TP(\Sigma) \mid w \preceq p \,\}$. For a set P of tree patterns, the *language* of P is also denoted by $L(P)$ and defined as $L(P) = \bigcup_{p \in P} L(p)$. If no confusion arises, we denote also by TP^k the class of languages defined by sets of at most k tree patterns. For example, if Σ is an alphabet $\{tom, bob, mom(\cdot), likes(\cdot, \cdot), \ldots\}$ and P is a union $\{likes(X, X), likes(Y, mom(Y))\}$, the language of P is the following set:

$$L(P) = \left\{ \begin{array}{l} likes(tom, tom),\ likes(bob, bob),\ likes(mom(tom), mom(tom)),\ \ldots \\ likes(tom, mom(tom)),\ likes(mom(tom), mom(mom(tom))),\ \ldots \end{array} \right\}.$$

For sets P, Q of tree patterns, if $L(P) = L(Q)$ then P is said to be *equivalent* to Q. A set P of tree patterns is said to be *reduced* if there is no $p, q \in P\ (p \not\equiv q)$ such that $p \preceq q$. For any set $P \in TP^k$ of tree patterns, there exists the unique reduced set $\widetilde{P} \in TP^k$ that is equivalent to P. The following property is called the *compactness* of tree pattern languages [4].

Proposition 1. *Suppose that $|\Sigma| \geq k+1$. Then, for any tree patterns $p, p_1, \ldots, p_k$, $L(p) \subseteq L(p_1) \cup \cdots \cup L(p_k)$ if and only if $p \preceq p_i$ for some $1 \leq i \leq k$.*

For a nonempty set S of tree patterns, a tree pattern p is said to be a *common generalization* of S if $p \succeq q$ for any q in S. A *least general generalization (lgg)* of S is a common generalization p of S such that $p \preceq q$ for every common generalization q of S. For any set S of tree patterns, a lgg of S always exists, is unique modulo $\equiv$, and is polynomial time computable [16, 17]. For tree patterns p, q, we denote by $p \sqcup q$ the lgg of the pair $\{p, q\}$. Furthermore, the following properties hold (see e.g. [16, 17]).

Proposition 2. *Let p, q be tree patterns, w be a ground tree patterns, and $H, H' \in TP^k$ be finite sets of tree patterns. Suppose that $|\Sigma| > 1$. Then the following propositions hold.*

1. *If $p \preceq q$ then $size(p) \geq size(q)$, and if $p \prec q$ then $size(p) > size(q)$.*
2. *$p \succeq q$ if and only if $L(p) \supseteq L(q)$.*
3. *$H \sqsubseteq H'$ if and only if $L(H) \subseteq L(H')$ when $|\Sigma| > k$.*
4. *$w \preceq H$ if and only if $w \in L(H)$.*
5. *If $H \sqsubseteq H'$ and $h \preceq H'$ then $H \cup \{h\} \sqsubseteq H'$*

2.2 The learning problem

We employ the standard protocol of exact learning from equivalence and membership queries [2]. Let $H_* \in TP^k$ be the *target* union to be identified. A *learning algorithm* $\mathcal{A}$ may collect information about H_* using equivalence and membership queries. An *equivalence query* is to propose any hypothesis H in TP^k. If $L(H) = L(H_*)$ then the answer to the query is "yes," and $\mathcal{A}$ has succeeded in the inference task. Otherwise, the answer is "no," and $\mathcal{A}$ receives any ground tree pattern w in the symmetric difference $L(H) \oplus L(H_*)$ as a *counterexample*. A counter example w is said to be *positive* if $w \in L(H_*)$ and *negative* if $w \in L(H)$. A *membership query* is to propose a ground tree pattern w. The answer to the membership query is "yes" if $w \in L(H_*)$, and "no" otherwise. An equivalence and a membership queries are denoted by $EQUIV(H)$ and $MEMB(w)$, respectively. The goal of a learning algorithm $\mathcal{A}$ is *exact identification* in polynomial time, that is, $\mathcal{A}$ must halt and output a union $H \in TP^k$ that is equivalent to H_*. Furthermore at any stage in learning, the running time of $\mathcal{A}$ must be bounded by a polynomial in the size of H_* and the size of the longest counterexample returned by equivalence queries so far.

Because the problem of determining whether two unions in TP^k are equivalent is solvable in polynomial time [10], both types of queries are efficiently computable by a teacher.

3 Learning Unions of Tree Patterns Using Queries

In this section, we first prove that there exists a polynomial time algorithm that correctly identifies any union in TP^k using equivalence and restricted subset queries. Then in the next section, we prove that every restricted subset query made in LEARN can be replaced with several membership queries. This yields a modified version of the algorithm that exactly learns every union in TP^k in polynomial time using equivalence and membership queries.

3.1 The learning algorithm

Figure 1 gives our learning algorithm LEARN, which uses equivalence and restricted subset queries to learn TP^k. A *restricted subset query*, denoted by $SUBSET(H)$, is to propose any hypothesis H in TP^k, and the answer is either "yes" or "no" according to whether $L(H) \subseteq L(H_*)$. The algorithm starts with the most specific hypothesis $\emptyset$, and searches hypotheses space TP^k from more specific to more general. The algorithm carefully generalizes each element of a hypothesis by making restricted subset queries so that only positive counterexamples are provided.

We give an example to illustrate the operation of the algorithm. Suppose that the alphabet is $\Sigma = \{ \text{cat, dog, beef, pork, orange, banana, } h(\cdot), f(\cdot), eat(\cdot, \cdot) \}$ and the target concept is $H_* = \{ eat(X, m(Y)), eat(h(X), Y) \}$, where h and m are abbreviations of *hungry* and *meat*, respectively. The following table shows the computation of LEARN. In each row, the tree pattern underlined in the fourth column denotes the updated element in H_n. At each stage $n \geq 1$ LEARN asks an equivalence query with a hypothesis H_{n-1}, receives a counterexample w_n if H_{n-1} is not equivalent to the target, and updates the hypothesis H_n by either replacing some element $h \in H_{n-1}$ with the lgg $h \sqcup w_n$ (Gen), or simply adding w_n into H_{n-1} (Add). At stage 6, LEARN receives "yes" as the answer to the equivalence query, and then succeeds in learning H_*.

n	counterexample w_i	update	hypothesis H_n
0	—	—	$\{\,\}$
1	$eat(cat, m(beef))$	Add	$\{\underline{eat(cat, m(beef))}\}$
2	$eat(dog, m(beef))$	Gen	$\{\underline{eat(X, m(beef))}\}$
3	$eat(h(cat), orange)$	Add	$\{eat(X, m(beef)), \underline{eat(h(cat), orange)}\}$
4	$eat(h(dog), m(pork))$	Gen	$\{\underline{eat(X, m(Y))}, eat(h(cat), orange)\}$
5	$eat(h(dog), banana))$	Gen	$\{eat(X, m(Y)), \underline{eat(h(X), Y)}\}$
6	"yes"	—	—

3.2 The correctness and the complexity of the learning algorithm

Let Σ be the alphabet such that $|\Sigma| > k$, and $H_* \in TP^k$ be the target union. In what follows, let $H_0, H_1, \ldots, H_i, \ldots$ and $w_1, w_2, \ldots, w_i, \ldots$ $(i \geq 0)$, respectively, be the sequence of hypotheses asked in the equivalence queries by LEARN and the sequence of counterexamples returned by the queries. H_0 is the initial hypothesis $\emptyset$, and at each stage $i \geq 1$, LEARN makes an equivalence query $EQUIV(H_{i-1})$, receives a counterexample w_i to the query, and produce a new hypothesis H_i from w_i and H_{i-1}.

Lemma 3. *For each $i \geq 0$, w_i is a positive counterexample and H_i is a refinement of H_*.*

Proof. The proof is by induction on the number of iterations $i \geq 0$ of the main loop. If $i = 0$ then the result immediately follows since the hypothesis $H_0 = \emptyset$ defines the smallest language $\emptyset$.

Assume inductively that the result holds for any number of iteration of the main loop less than i, and H_i is defined. Since $H_{i-1} \sqsubseteq H_*$ by induction hypothesis, and since w_i is a counterexample witnessing $L(H_{i-1}) \neq L(H_*)$, we know $L(H_{i-1}) \subset L(H_*)$ by Proposition 2. Thus, w_i must be positive.

On the other hand, H_i is obtained from both of H_{i-1} and w_i at Line 5 of Figure 1. There are two cases for the construction of H_i. (i) If the answer to the query $SUBSET(h \sqcup w_i)$ is "yes" for some $h \in H_i$, then $h \sqcup w_i \preceq H_*$ by (3) of Proposition 2. By induction hypothesis, we know $H_{i-1} \sqsubseteq H_*$. Thus, we have $H_i = (H_{i-1} - \{h\}) \cup \{h \sqcup w_i\} \sqsubseteq H_*$ by (5) of Proposition 2. (ii) Otherwise,

Procedure: *LEARN*

Given: the equivalence and the subset oracles for the target set $H_* \in TP^k$.

Output: a set H of at most k tree patterns equivalent to H_*.

begin

1    $H := \emptyset$;

2   **until** $EQUIV(H)$ returns "yes" **do**

3   **begin**

4   let w be a counterexample returned by the equivalence query;

5   **if** there is some $h \in H$ such that $SUBSET(h \sqcup w)$ returns "yes" **then**

6   generalize H by replacing h with $h \sqcup w$

7   **else if** $|H| < k$ **then**

8   generalize H by adding w into H

9   **else**

10   return "failed"

11   **endif**

12   **end** /* main loop */

13   return H;

end

Fig. 1. A learning algorithm for TP^k using equivalence and restricted subset queries.

$H_{i-1} \sqsubseteq H_*$ by induction hypothesis. Since $w_i \in L(H_*)$ holds from the induction hypothesis, we have $w_i \preceq H_*$ by (4) of Proposition 2. Thus, (5) of Proposition 2 shows that $H_i = H_{i-1} \cup \{w_i\} \sqsubseteq H_*$. $\square$

The next lemma states that the number of tree patterns in a produced hypothesis H_i does not diverge in the learning process. This makes it possible for LEARN to reject every target concept that does not belong to TP^k.

Lemma 4. *For each $i \geq 0$, H_i is a conservative refinement of H_*.*

Proof. If $i = 0$ then $H_0 = \emptyset$ is obviously a conservative refinement of H_*. Assume inductively that H_{i-1} is a conservative refinement of H_*, and H_i is defined. By Lemma 3, we know that H_i is a refinement of H_*. There are two cases for the construction of H_i. (i) If the answer to the query $SUBSET(h \sqcup w_i)$ at Line 5 of Figure 1 is "yes" for some $h \in H_{i-1}$, then $h \sqcup w_i \preceq h_*$ for some $h_* \in H_*$ by (3) of Proposition 2. Since h is the unique tree pattern in H_{i-1} satisfying $h \preceq h_*$ from the conservativeness of H_{i-1}, $h \sqcup w_i$ is also the unique tree pattern in H_i satisfying $h \sqcup w_i \preceq h_*$. (ii) Otherwise, there is no tree pattern h in H_{i-1} satisfying $h \sqcup w_i \preceq h_*$ for some $h_* \in H_*$. Therefore, w_i is the only tree pattern h in H_i satisfying $h \preceq h_*$ because w_i is a positive counterexample and $H_i = H_{i-1} \cup \{w_i\}$. Combining (i) and (ii) above, we prove the result. $\square$

Corollary 5. *For each $i \geq 0$, $H_i \in TP^k$.*

To prove the termination of the algorithm, we need the following technical lemma. Let $\mathbf{N}_\infty = \mathbf{N} \cup \{\infty\}$. For k-tuples of elements in $\mathbf{N}_\infty$, we define a strict partial order on k-tuples as $\langle x_1, \ldots, x_k \rangle > \langle y_1, \ldots, y_k \rangle$ iff $x_i \geq y_i$ for all i and $x_i > y_i$ for some i.

Lemma 6. *Let* $Z_0 > Z_1 > \cdots > Z_i > \cdots (Z_i \in (N_\infty)^k, i \geq 0)$ *be the properly decreasing sequence of k-tuples of elements in* $\mathbf{N}_\infty$. *If n is the maximum finite integer appearing in the sequence then the length of the sequence is at most $k(n+2)$.*

Theorem 7. *Let k be any positive integer and $|\Sigma| > k$. Then, the algorithm LEARN exactly identifies every set H_* of at most k tree patterns in time polynomial in k and n making $O(kn)$ equivalence queries and $O(k^2n)$ restricted subset queries, where n is the size of the longest counterexample seen so far.*

Proof. By the construction of the algorithm, if the algorithm terminates then the last hypothesis H_i is equivalent to the target H_*. Further from Corollary 5, we know that all the hypotheses produced so far are members in TP^k. Therefore, it is sufficient to show the termination in polynomial time.

Let $\perp$ be a special tree pattern such that $\perp \prec p$ for any tree pattern p and $size(\perp) = \infty$. Suppose H_* is reduced and has k elements. For each $n \geq 0$, we associate with H_n a k-vector $\tilde{H}_n$ over $TP \cup \{\perp\}$ as follows. First, for $H_* = \{h_1^*, \ldots, h_k^*\}$, let $\tilde{H}_*$ be any k-vector $\langle h_1^*, \ldots, h_k^* \rangle$. For each H_n $(n \geq 0)$, let $\tilde{H}_n$ be a vector $\langle h_1, \ldots, h_k \rangle$ such that $h_i \in H_n$ and $h_i \preceq h_i^*$ for each $1 \leq i \leq k$. We put $h_i = \perp$ if there is no $h \in H_n$ satisfying $h \not\preceq h_i^*$. Since each H_n is a conservative refinement of H_*, $\tilde{H}_n$ is uniquely determined.

Let H_n be defined, and let $H_{n-1} = \langle p_1, \ldots, p_k \rangle$ and $H_n = \langle q_1, \ldots, q_k \rangle$. By construction, there is exactly one $1 \leq i \leq k$ such that $p_i \neq q_i$ and $p_j = q_j$ for all $j \neq i$. Then, we show $p_i \prec q_i$ as follows. (i) The case where H_n is obtained from H_{n-1} by replacing p_i with $p_i \sqcup w_n$ at Line 6 of Figure 1. From the proof of Lemma 4, we observe that $p_i \sqcup w_n$ is the unique member h of H_n such that $h \preceq h_i^*$. Thus, q_i must be $p_i \sqcup w_n$, and $p_i \preceq (p_i \sqcup w_n)$. Since w_n is a positive counterexample, we have $w_n \not\preceq p_i$. Hence, $p_i \prec (p_i \sqcup w_n) = q_i$.

(ii) The case where H_n is obtained from H_{n-1} by adding w_n into H_{n-1} at Line 8 of Figure 1. Since queries $SUBSET(h \sqcup w_n)$ returns "no" for all $h \in H_{n-1}$, we can see that p_i must be $\perp$. Thus $p_i = \perp \prec w_n = q_i$.

Consider the sequence $Z_0, Z_1, \ldots, Z_n, \ldots$ of k-vectors over $\mathbf{N}_\infty$, where $\tilde{H}_n = \langle h_1^n, \ldots, h_k^n \rangle$ and $Z_n = \langle size(h_1^n), \ldots, size(h_k^n) \rangle$ for all $n \geq 0$. Combining (i) and (ii) above, for each $n \geq 0$ we have $h_i^{n-1} \preceq h_i^n$ for all i and $h_i^{n-1} \prec h_i^n$ for some i. From (1) of Proposition 2, we know the sequence $Z_0, Z_1, \ldots, Z_n, \ldots$ satisfies the condition of Lemma 6. Thus, the length of the sequence is at most $k(n+2)$, where n is the size of the longest counterexample given so far. Since the lgg is polynomial time computable, the computation time of the algorithm is clearly bounded by a polynomial in k and n. The numbers of equivalence and restricted subset queries are bounded by $k(n+2)$ and $k^2(n+2)$, respectively. This completes the proof. $\square$

4 Replacing a Subset Query with Membership Queries

In this section, we show that a modified version of our learning algorithm which uses several membership queries instead of a restricted subset query also works well under some condition for Σ.

Lemma 8. *Let k be a positive integer. Suppose that $|\Sigma| > k$ and that Σ contains at least $k - 1$ function symbols of nonzero arity. Then, for any tree pattern r with n variables there exists a finite set $G(r)$ of $k + n - 1$ ground instances of r satisfying the following: for any tree patterns $p_1, \ldots, p_l$ ($l \leq k$), $G(r) \subseteq L(p_1) \cup \cdots \cup L(p_l)$ if and only if $r \preceq p_i$ for some $1 \leq i \leq l$.*

Proof. The if part of the statement is trivial. Thus, we show the only-if part. Without loss of generality, we may assume that Σ contains $k - 1$ unary function symbols $f_1, \ldots, f_{k-1}$ and two constants a, b. For function symbols of arity more than one, we can fill the extra places by some dummy symbol, say a. If r is ground then the proof is done. Thus, we assume that r contains n variables $x_1, \ldots, x_n$. Let $\sigma_1, \ldots, \sigma_{k-1}$ and $\theta_1, \ldots, \theta_n$ be the substitutions that replace each variable by some ground tree pattern as defined in the followings. For each $i = 1, \ldots, k - 1$ and for each $j = 1, \ldots, n$, let

$$\sigma_i(x_j) = \overbrace{f_i(f_i(\cdots f_i(a) \cdots))}^{j}.$$

For each $i = 1, \ldots, n$ and for each $j = 1, \ldots, n$, let

$$\theta_i(x_j) = \begin{cases} a & \text{, if } i = j, \\ b & \text{, otherwise.} \end{cases}$$

Let $G(r) = \{\sigma_1(r), \ldots, \sigma_{k-1}(r), \theta_1(r), \ldots, \theta_n(r)\}$. Suppose to the contrary that $r \not\preceq p_i$ for any $1 \leq i \leq l$.

Consider the case where $l = k$. For any $1 \leq i \leq k$, if $L(p_i)$ contains $\sigma_{j_1}(r)$ and $\sigma_{j_2}(r)$ for distinct j_1, j_2, then $r \preceq p_i$ holds. This is the contradiction. Thus, we needs at least $k - 1$ distinct tree patterns to contain all of ground tree patterns $\sigma_1(r), \ldots, \sigma_{k-1}(r)$. Without loss of generality, assume that $\sigma_1(r) \in L(p_1), \ldots, \sigma_{k-1}(r) \in L(p_{k-1})$. If $L(p_i)$ contains at least one $\theta_j(r)$ for some $1 \leq j \leq n$, then $r \preceq p_i$ immediately holds, and the contradiction also follows. Thus, $\theta_j(r)$ is contained by none of $L(p_1), \ldots, L(p_{k-1})$ for any $1 \leq j \leq n$. This implies that $L(p_k)$ must contain all of ground tree patterns $\theta_1(r), \ldots, \theta_n(r)$. Since the least common generalization of $\theta_1(r), \ldots, \theta_n(r)$ is r, we have $r \preceq p_k$. This derives the contradiction. Hence, $r \preceq p_i$ for some $1 \leq i \leq k$. A similar discussion can prove the result for the cases where $l < k$. □

By the lemma shown above, it is easily seen that $L(r) \subseteq L(H_*)$ if and only if $w \in L(H_*)$ for all $w \in G(r)$. Therefore, we can replace each restricted subset query made in the learning algorithm LEARN by at most $k + n - 1$ membership queries, where n is the size of the maximum pattern in the current hypothesis H (Figure 2). Since n is bounded by the size of the longest counterexample seen so far, we have the following theorem from Theorem 7 in the previous section.

Procedure: $SUBSET(p)$
Input: a tree pattern p.
Given: the membership oracle for the target set H_*.
Output:"yes" if $L(p)$ is a subset of $L(H_*)$, and "no" otherwise.
begin
    for each $r \in G(p)$ **do** query $MEMB(r)$;
    if all the answers returned by the membership queries are "yes" **then**
        return "yes"
    else
        return "no"
    endif
end

Fig. 2. A procedure for replacing a subset query with several membership queries

Theorem 9. *Suppose that $|\Sigma| > k$ and that Σ contains at least $k - 1$ function symbols of nonzero arity. For each positive integer k, the algorithm LEARN exactly identifies every set H_* of at most k tree patterns in time polynomial in k and n making $O(kn)$ equivalence queries and $O(k^2 n \cdot \max\{k, n\})$ membership queries, where n is the size of the longest counterexample seen so far.*

Corollary 10. *Let k be any positive integer. Suppose that $|\Sigma| > k$ and that Σ contains at least $k - 1$ function symbols of nonzero arity. Then, the following statements hold.*

- *There exists a polynomial time PAC-learning algorithm for TP^k using membership queries. (See Angluin [2] for definitions.)*

- *There exists a polynomial time prediction algorithm for TP^k with a polynomial mistake bound using membership queries (excluding the element to be predicted). (See Littlestone [11] for definitions.)*

- *There exists a polynomial time algorithm that solves the consistency problem for TP^k using membership queries, given a minimally consistent membership oracle. (See Ishizaka et al. [8] for definitions.)*

Proof. For proofs of (a) and (b), see Angluin [2] and Littlestone [11]. The transformations describes in these literatures also works when membership queries are allowed. To prove (c), we describe an algorithm $\mathcal{C}$ that solves the consistency problem for TP^k working as an environment of the learning algorithm LEARN. $\mathcal{C}$ receives sets Pos and Neg of positive and negative examples, and answers queries asked by LEARN as follows. Let $H_* \in TP^l(l \geq 0)$ be a hypothesis of the smallest cardinality that is consistent with Pos and Neg. For an equivalence query with H, the answer to LEARN is "yes" if H is consistent with Pos and Neg. Otherwise, the answer to LEARN is "no," and $\mathcal{C}$ returns any elements w in

$Pos - L(H)$ or $Neg \cap L(H)$ as a counterexample. For a membership query with w, C asks the *minimally consistent membership oracle* [8] whether $w \in L(H_*)$, and returns this answer to LEARN. Since C correctly answers any queries made by LEARN as though H_* is the target hypothesis, if H_* belongs to TP^k then LEARN eventually finds a hypothesis consistent with Pos and Neg, and at worst LEARN may find H_*. Otherwise, LEARN returns "failed." It is easy to observe that the time complexity of C is bounded by the total size of examples in Pos and Neg. □

We also have the following lower bound from a general lower bound result of Maass and Turán [12].

Theorem 11. *Any algorithm that exactly identifies all the unions of at most k tree patterns using equivalence and membership queries must make $\Omega(kn)$ queries in the worst case, where n is the size of the longest counterexample seen so far.*

Proof. We say a concept class C *shatters* a set $U \subseteq \Sigma^*$ if $\{U \cap c \mid c \in C\} = 2^U$ holds. The *VC-dimension* of C is the cardinality of the largest set $U \subseteq \Sigma^*$ that is shattered by C. Let TP_n^k be the subclass of TP^k for which all tree patterns are of size at most n. We first show that the the VC-dimension of TP_n^k is $\Omega(kn)$. Suppose that Σ contains at least two constants $0, 1$, and k binary function symbols $f^{(1)}, \ldots, f^{(k)}$. Let f be any binary symbol, and let $S = \{w_1, \ldots, w_n\}$ be the set of tree patterns over $\{0, 1, f\}$, where w_i is a tree pattern in TP_{2n-1}

$$w_i = \overbrace{f(b_1, f(\cdots f(b_{n-1}, b_n) \cdots))}^{n},$$

such that b_j is 0 if $j = i$ and 1 otherwise. Elements of S correspond with bit-vector representations of the elements of the set $\{1, \ldots, n\}$. Consider tree patterns in TP_{2n-1} of the form

$$\overbrace{f(t_1, f(\cdots f(t_{n-1}, t_n) \cdots))}^{n}, \qquad (t_1 \cdots t_{n-1} t_n \in \{x, 0\}^n),$$

which correspond with the bit-vector representations of all the subsets of $\{1, \ldots, n\}$. Then, we can observe that for any subset $T \subseteq S$, there is a tree pattern p of this form such that $T = L(p) \cap S$. Thus, we know TP_{2n-1} shatters a set S of cardinality n.

We generalize this construction for TP_{2n-1}^k. Let $S_1, \ldots, S_k$ be mutually disjoint sets of tree patterns such that S_l is the set obtained from S by replacing each occurrence of f with $f^{(l)}$ $(1 \leq l \leq k)$, and let U be the direct sum $S_1 \cup \cdots \cup S_k$ of cardinality kn. Then, a similar argument shows that TP_{2n-1}^k shatters the set U, and thus the VC-dimension of TP_n^k is $\Omega(kn)$.

Maass and Turán [12] show that any algorithm that exactly learns a concept class C using equivalence and membership queries must make $\Omega(d)$ queries even when arbitrary hypotheses are allowed, where d is the VC-dimension of C. Further, the adversary described in [12] can be modified to choose counterexamples only from U. Since U contains only tree patterns of size at most $2n - 1$, the total number of queries are bounded below by $\Omega(kn)$, where n is the size of the longest counterexample given so far. □

5 Insufficiency of Learning with Membership Queries Alone

In this section, we show that membership queries alone are insufficient for learning of TP^k. Since Ishizaka et $al.$ [8] has shown that the problem of finding a union in TP^k consistent with given examples is NP-complete, we know from [14] that equivalence queries alone are insufficient in exact learning model assuming $P \neq NP$, and that random examples alone are insufficient in PAC-learning model assuming $RP \neq NP$. Combining these results and the following theorem, neither equivalence nor membership queries can be eliminated to learn TP^k.

Theorem 12. *Any algorithm that exactly identifies all the unions of at most k tree patterns using membership queries alone must make $\Omega(2^n)$ queries in the worst case, where n is the longest counterexample, even when Σ contains one binary symbol and two constants.*

Proof. Suppose that Σ contains at least two constants $0, 1$, and one binary symbol f. Consider tree patterns over Σ that have the form

$$\overbrace{f(b_1, f(\cdots f(b_{n-1}, b_n)\cdots))}^{n}, \qquad (b_1 \cdots b_{n-1}b_n \in \{0,1\}^n)$$

which correspond with all binary sequences of length $n \geq 1$. There are 2^n such tree patterns, and the intersection of the languages of two tree patterns is empty if they are distinct. Thus by [2], we show that any algorithm using membership queries alone requires at least $2^n - 1$ queries in the worst case. $\qquad\square$

6 Application to Learning from Entailment

In this section, we describe an application of the results in Section 3 to learning from entailment. *Learning from entailment* is exact learning suitable for learning logic programs. In learning from entailment [7, 13], a hypothesis is any logic program H and an example is any clause F in the same class. An equivalence test "$L(G) = L(H)$?" and a membership test "$F \in L(H)$?" are replaced by a logical equivalence "$G \Leftrightarrow H$?" and an entailment "$H \models F$?", respectively. Exact learning and PAC-learning based on entailment are defined similarly as usual one.

We consider a class of a restricted logic programs that consists of only unit clauses. We call the class *unit clause programs* and denote by UCP. The predictability and the learnability of general DNF has been a long-standing open problem in computational learning theory. It is easy to see that a log-space transformation from the consistency problem for k-term DNF to that for TP^k given in [8] is actually a prediction preserving reduction of Pitt and Warmuth [15] from DNF to $\bigcup_{k \geq 0} TP^k$. Thus, we have the following theorem.

Theorem 13. *If UCP are polynomial time predictable with polynomial mistake bound with respect to entailment then so are general DNF, even when Σ contains only two binary symbols and one constant.*

Since each clause is unit, we can characterize the entailment $\models$ by the subsumption $\sqsupseteq$ as follows; $\forall(A_1)\&\cdots\&\forall(A_n) \models \forall(B_1)\&\cdots\&\forall(B_n)$ if and only if $\{A_1,\ldots,A_n\} \sqsupseteq \{B_1,\ldots,B_n\}$. Since the running time of the algorithm LEARN is a polynomial in k and n, the next theorem immediately follows from Theorem 7.

Theorem 14. *Let Π be any set of predicate symbols and Σ any set of function symbols. Then, there exists an algorithm that exactly identifies every program H_* in UCP in time polynomial in the size of H_* as a string and the size of the maximum counterexample seen so far, using equivalence and membership queries with respect to entailment.*

These results indicate that membership queries are necessary for learning even very restricted logic programs whose computational mechanisms are only disjunctive definition and unification.

7 Concluding Remarks

In this paper, we investigated efficient learning of TP^k, and presented a polynomial time learning algorithm using equivalence and membership queries. We also showed several hardness results, which suggests that membership queries are necessary for efficiently learning TP^k, in addition to equivalence queries or random examples.

In Section 5, we proved that TP^k is neither polynomial time exact-learnable nor polynomial time PAC-learnable in terms of TP^k when membership queries are not available. Note, however, that this negative result does not eliminate the possibility of a polynomial time learning algorithm in terms of a larger hypothesis space than TP^k, or a polynomial time prediction algorithm with polynomial mistake bound. Hence, it is a future problem to investigate the polynomial time predictability of TP^k in mistake bound model without membership queries.

For some subclasses PAT of string pattern languages, a minimal upper bounds of a finite set is efficiently computable in terms of PAT^k [5]. However, the convergence of the algorithm is not shown to be polynomial. Thus, it is another future problem to generalize the result of the paper for unions of string patterns.

Constrained atoms are nonrecursive definite Horn clauses with a subterm property, and the class of sets of constrained atoms includes the class UCP. Page Jr. independently showed in his PhD. thesis an extension of our Theorem 14 in Section 6 (personal communication, June 1995). He showed that the class of finite sets of constrained atoms is efficiently learnable using equivalence and membership queries in the framework of learning from entailment. However, it is still open whether we can use the techniques developed in Section 3 to achieve efficient learning of sets of constrained atoms without entailment queries.

Acknowledgements

The first author would like to thank Steffen Lange, David Page Jr., Sin-ichi Shimozono, and Kouichi Hirata for discussions and suggestions on this issue. He also thanks the anonymous referees for their valuable comments to improve this paper.

References

1. D. Angluin. Finding patterns common to a set of strings. *Journal of Computer and System Sciences*, 21:46–62, 1980.
2. D. Angluin. Queries and concept learning. *Machine Learning*, 2:319–342, 1988.
3. S. Arikawa, S. Kuhara, S. Miyano, A. Shinohara, and T. Shinohara. A learning algorithm for elementary formal systems and its experiments on identification of transmembrane domains. In *Proc. the 25th HICSS*, 675–684, 1992.
4. H. Arimura, T. Shinohara, and S. Otsuki. A polynomial time algorithm for finding finite unions of tree pattern languages. In *Proc. the 2nd NIL*, LNAI 659, Springer-Verlag, 118–131, 1991.
5. H. Arimura, T. Shinohara, and S. Otsuki. Finding minimal generalizations for unions of pattern languages and its application to inductive inference from positive data. In *Proc. the 11th STACS*, LNCS 775, Springer-Verlag, 649–660, 1994.
6. H. Arimura, H. Ishizaka, T. Shinohara, and S. Otsuki. A generalization of the least general generalization. *Machine Intelligence*, 13, 59–85, Oxford Univ. Press, 1994.
7. M. Frazier and L. Pitt. CLASSIC Learning. In *Proc. COLT'94*, 23–34, 1994.
8. H. Ishizaka, H. Arimura, and T. Shinohara. Finding tree patterns consistent with positive and negative examples using queries In *Proc. ALT'94*, LNAI872, 317–332, 1994.
9. T. Jiang, A. Salomaa, K. Salomaa, and S. Yu. Inclusion is undecidable for pattern languages. In *Proc. 20th ICALP*, pp. 301–312, LNCS 700, Springer, 1993.
10. G. Kuper, K. McAloon, K. Palem, K. Perry. Efficient Parallel Algorithm for Anti-Unification and Relative Complement. In *Proc. the 3rd LICS*, 111–120, 1988.
11. N. Littlestone. Learning quickly when irrelevant attributes abound: A new linear-threshold algorithm. *Machine Learning*, 2, 285–318, 1988.
12. W. Maass and G. Turán. Lower bound methods and separation results for on-line learning models. Machine Learning, 9, 107–145, 1992.
13. C. D. Page Jr. and A. M. Frisch. Generalization and Learnability: A Study of Constrained Atoms. S. Muggleton, editor, *Inductive Logic Programming*, 29–61, 1992.
14. L. Pitt and L. G. Valiant. Computational limitations on learning from examples. *JACM*, 35:965–984, 1988.
15. L. Pitt and M. K. Warmuth. Prediction preserving reduction. JCSS, 41:430–467, 1990.
16. G. D. Plotkin. A note on inductive generalization. In *Machine Intelligence 5*, 153–163. Edinburgh University Press, 1970.
17. J. C. Reynolds. Transformational systems and the algebraic structure of atomic formulas. In *Machine Intelligence 5*, 135–152. Edinburgh University Press, 1970.

Inductive Constraint Logic

Luc De Raedt and Wim Van Laer

Department of Computer Science, Katholieke Universiteit Leuven
Celestijnenlaan 200A, B-3001 Heverlee, Belgium
Email:{Luc.DeRaedt,Wim.VanLaer}@cs.kuleuven.ac.be

Abstract. A novel approach to learning first order logic formulae from positive and negative examples is presented. Whereas present inductive logic programming systems employ examples as true and false ground facts (or clauses), we view examples as interpretations which are true or false for the target theory. This viewpoint allows to reconcile the inductive logic programming paradigm with classical attribute value learning in the sense that the latter is a special case of the former. Because of this property, we are able to adapt AQ and CN2 type algorithms in order to enable learning of full first order formulae. However, whereas classical learning techniques have concentrated on concept representations in disjunctive normal form, we will use a clausal representation, which corresponds to a conjuctive normal form where each conjunct forms a constraint on positive examples. This representation duality reverses also the role of positive and negative examples, both in the heuristics and in the algorithm. The resulting theory is incorporated in a system named ICL (Inductive Constraint Logic).

1 Introduction

Present work on inductive concept-learning is usually classified as belonging to either the attribute value learning paradigm (see [Quinlan, 1986; Michalski, 1983; Clark and Niblett, 1989], etc.) or the inductive logic programming paradigm [Muggleton and De Raedt, 1994; Muggleton, 1992]. The differences between the two paradigms are due to the representation formalism employed. Although the inductive logic programming paradigm is generally believed to be more expressive, there is no straightforward and generally accepted way to represent an attribute value learning problem as an inductive logic programming task. A possible explanation for this comes from the fact that in attribute value learning examples are true and false interpretations (models and non-models, or positive and negative examples) of a target theory, whereas in inductive logic programming, examples are true and false facts (or clauses). Recently, [De Raedt and Džeroski, 1994] have suggested this is as a possible explanation why PAC-learning results for inductive logic programming are so hard to obtain and mostly negative. They have also sketched a PAC-learning algorithm to learning (a certain class of) clausal theories from models (i.e. positive examples) of that theory. In this paper, we will further the ideas of De Raedt and Džeroski from a practical perspective. To this aim, we will define a notion of concept-learning in first order logic, in which examples are true and false interpretations of a target theory, and the target theory is a set of clauses. It will be convenient to view each clause in the target theory as a constraint, hence the term *inductive constraint logic.* Indeed, the aim of learning will be to induce a set of clauses (or constraints) such that every positive example p is true for *all* of the clauses (i.e. p is covered by all the clauses) and every negative example n is false for *at least one* of the clauses . This corresponds to learning a conjunctive normal form instead of a disjunctive normal form. Therefore the role of positive and negative examples is swapped, as compared to the usual covering approach of AQ and CN2 type systems. Nevertheless, this will enable us to develop the ICL algorithm, which is essentially a covering approach with the role of positive and negative examples reversed. Furthermore, as examples are interpretations, most of the other attribute value learning techniques, such as noise handling heuristics, will nicely upgrade towards our framework. Some of these ideas (like the swapping of positives and negatives) can also be found in [Mooney, 1995]. However, our approach is more general, as we work with a first order logic representation and with examples as interpretations.

The paper is organized as follows: in Section 2, we introduce the inductive constraint logic framework; in Section 3, we sketch the ICL algorithm for inducing clausal theories, in Section 4, we report on some preliminary experiments, and in Section 5 we discuss related and further work and finally conclude in Section 6.

2 Inductive constraint logic: definitions and framework

We assume familiarity with first order logic and model theory (see [Lloyd, 1987; Genesereth and Nilsson, 1987] for an introduction).

A first order alphabet is a set of predicate symbols, constant symbols and functor symbols. A clause is a formula of the form $A_1; ...; A_m \leftarrow B_1, ..., B_n$ where the A_i and B_i are logical atoms. An atom $p(t_1, ..., t_n)$ is a predicate symbol p followed by a bracketed n-tuple of terms t_i. A term t is a variable V or a function symbol $f(t_1, ..., t_k)$ immediately followed by a bracketed n-tuple of terms t_i. Constants are function symbols of arity 0. *Functor-free* clauses are clauses that contain only variables as terms.

The above clause can be read as A_1 or ... or A_m if B_1 and ... and B_n. All variables in clauses are universally quantified, although this is not explicitly written. Extending the usual convention for *definite clauses* (where $m = 1$), we call $A_1, ..., A_m$ the *head* of the clause and $B_1, ..., B_n$ the *body* of the clause. A *fact* is a definite clause with an empty body, $(m = 1, n = 0)$. Throughout the paper, we shall assume that all clauses are *range restricted*, which means that all variables occurring in the head of a clause also occur in its body.

A *Herbrand interpretation* over a first order alphabet is a set of ground facts constructed with the predicate, constant and functor symbols in the alphabet. A Herbrand interpretation I is a model for a clause c if and only if for all grounding substitutions θ of c : $body(c)\theta \subset I \rightarrow head(c)\theta \cap I \neq \emptyset$. We also say c is true in I or c makes the interpretation I true, or even I is a true interpretation for c. If a herbrand interpretation I is not a model for a clause c, we say that c is false in interpretation I. A Herbrand interpretation I is a model for a clausal theory T if and only if it is a model for all clauses in T. Roughly speaking, the truth of a clause c in an interpretation I can be determined by running the query $? - body(c), not\ head(c)$ on a database containing I using a theorem prover (such as Prolog). If the query succeeds, the clause is false in I. If it finitely fails, the clause is true.

By now we can intuitively describe our inductive constraint logic setting. One starts from a set of positive and negative examples (true and false interpretations or models and non-models of a target theory) and aims at finding a clausal theory for which all positive examples are models and none of the negative examples is a model. A definite clause background theory can be used as follows. Rather than starting from complete interpretations of the target theory, examples are a kind of partial interpretations I (set of facts) and are completed by taking the minimal Herbrand model $M(B \cup I)$ of background theory B plus the partial interpretation I. Note that the completion need not be computed explicitly, but can be left to the theorem-prover[1]. The minimal Herbrand model of a definite clause theory contains the set of all ground facts that are logically entailed by that theory[2]. Formally, this setting thus becomes:

- **Given**
  - P is a set of interpretations such that for all $p \in P$, $M(B \cup p)$ is a true interpretation of the unknown target theory;
  - N is a set of interpretations such that for all $n \in N$, $M(B \cup n)$ is a false interpretation of the unknown target theory;
  - a definite clause background theory B;
- **Find**: a clausal theory H such that
  - for all $p \in P$, $M(B \cup p)$ is a true interpretation of H (Completeness)
  - for all $n \in N$, $M(B \cup n)$ is a false interpretation of H (Consistency).

In the following, each example will be completed implicitly with the background knowledge. So whenever we say an example e is true (false) for a clause (or theory), we mean that $M(B \cup e)$ is true (false) for that clause (theory).

This setting is illustrated in Examples 1, 2 and 3.

Example 1. The well-known autolander problem (from the Irvine database) is described by a table (see figure 1) in attribute value representation (only a part is shown).

This attribute value learning problem can directly be specified in terms of our framework. E.g. the interpretation $I_1 = \{$stability(stab), error(mm), sign(pp), wind(tail), magnitude(strong), visibility(yes)$\}$ (last line) corresponds to a positive example, and $I_2 = \{$stability(stab), error(mm), sign(pp), wind(head), magnitude(strong), visibility(yes)$\}$ is a negative example. Given this problem (with no background knowledge), the ICL technique derives the following clausal theory for the positive class.

visibility(no) ← *stability(xstab)*
visibility(no) ← *magnitude(out-of-range)*
visibility(no) ← *error(xl)*
visibility(no) ← *error(lx)*

---

[1] Using Prolog, one could assert background theory and interpretation into the knowledge base, and run the query $? - body(c)$, *not head(c)*, in order to test whether a clause c makes an interpretation true or not.

[2] The setting can easily be extended to handle program clauses including negation, provided that the model of background theory and interpretation is unique. Such a semantics is provided for instance by the preferred model semantics.

stability	error	sign	wind	magnitude	visibility	CLASS
xstab	XL	nn	head	Low	no	⊕
...	...	...	...	...	no	⊕
xstab	XL	nn	head	Low	yes	⊖
xstab	...	...	...	...	...	⊖
stab	LX	nn	head	Low	yes	⊖
stab	LX	...	...	...	yes	⊖
stab	XL	nn	head	Low	yes	⊖
stab	XL	...	...	...	yes	⊖
stab	MM	nn	tail	Low	yes	⊖
stab	MM	nn	tail	...	yes	⊖
xstab	XL	nn	head	OutOfRange	yes	⊖
...	...	...	...	OutOfRange	yes	⊖
stab	SS	nn	head	Low	yes	⊕
stab	SS	...	...	Low	yes	⊕
stab	SS	nn	head	Medium	yes	⊕
stab	SS	...	...	Medium	yes	⊕
stab	SS	nn	head	Strong	yes	⊕
stab	SS	...	...	Strong	yes	⊕
stab	MM	pp	head	Low	yes	⊕
stab	MM	pp	head	Medium	yes	⊕
stab	MM	pp	tail	Low	yes	⊕
stab	MM	pp	tail	Medium	yes	⊕
stab	MM	pp	head	Strong	yes	⊖
stab	MM	pp	tail	Strong	yes	⊕

Fig. 1. The Autolander input

$visibility(no);error(ss) \leftarrow sign(nn)$
$visibility(no);error(ss);wind(tail) \leftarrow magnitude(strong)$

Notice that I_1 is true for all clauses, whereas I_2 is false for the last clause and thus for the clausal theory.

Example 2. The *Bongard Problems* are general problems developed by the Russian scientist M. Bongard in his book *Pattern recognition* (a nice overview can be found in Gödel, Escher and Bach, Douglas R. Hofstadter). Each problem exists of 12 figures, six of class ⊕ and six of class ⊖. One example problem can be found in figure 2, based on the *Bongard Problem 47*. The goal is to discriminate between the two classes.

Each figure consists of lines, points, squares, triangles, circles,... which can be white, black, small, large, horizontal,... So each of these figures can be described by a set of facts. Take for instance the upper left figure in our example problem. It consists of a small triangle, pointing up, which is in a large circle. This figure can thus be described as : $I = \{triangle(f1), small(f1), up(f1), circle(f2), large(f2), in(f1,f2)\}$.

In our setting, each interpretation (example) is a set of facts, describing one figure. The following theory is consistent and complete (found by ICL in a few seconds) :

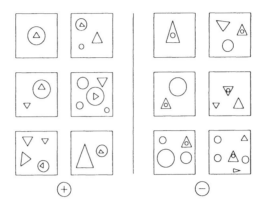

Fig. 2. A Bongard Problem

$$false \leftarrow circle(Y), in(Y,X)$$

This constraint says that for each figure of class $\oplus$, there is no circle that is inside another object. This can also be read as : if a figure has a circle inside another object, it is of class $\ominus$.

Example 3. A well known problem in the context of inductive logic programming is the card game of Eleusis. The problem was first decribed by Dietterich and Michalski [Dietterich and Michalski, 1985], and later employed by Quinlan [Quinlan, 1990], and Lavrac and Dzeroski [Lavrač and Džeroski, 1994]. There are two players. One of them has to guess the secret rule the other player has in mind.

main line	J♣	4♣	Q♡	3♠	Q♢	9♡	Q♣	7♡	Q♢	9♢	Q♣	3♡	K♡
side lines	K♣	5♠				4♠		10♢					
		7♠											
main (ctd)	4♣	K♢	6♣	J♢	8♢	J♡	7♣	J♢	7♡	J♡	6♡	K♢	
mainline	4♡	5♢	8♣	J♠	2♣	5♠	A♣	5♠	10♡				
side line	7♣	6♠	K♣	A♡		6♣		A♠					
	J♡	7♡	3♡	K♢									
	4♣	2♣		Q♠									
	10♠	7♠											
	8♡	6♢											
	A♢	6♡											
	2♢	4♣											

Fig. 3. Two Eleusis layouts

Two example sequences can be found in figure 3 (from [Lavrač and Džeroski, 1994]). Two consecutive cards on the main line satifies the secret rule. These can be used as positive examples. Each card on a side line is an illegal successor of the corresponding card on the main line. So these two cards can be seen as a negative example. Each example (a set of two cards) is translated (as in [Van Laer *et al.*, 1994]) into one fact of the form: $canfollow(R_2, S_2, R_1, S_1)$, which states that a card of rank R_2 and suit S_2 can follow a sequence ending with a card of rank R_1 and suit S_1. In this way, each interpretation contains one fact. For example in the first sequence, one positive model might be $canfollow(Q, \heartsuit, 4, \clubsuit)$, while a negative model might be $canfollow(5, \spadesuit, 4, \clubsuit)$.

Note that these interpretations are (implicitly) completed with the background knowledge, which contains the definitions of *red, black, samecolor, number, face, precedesrank, lowerrank, precedessuit.*

In the first sequence, the intended rule was "Play alternate face and non-face cards". Following our setting, ICL found the following constraints on the positive examples (in about 10 sec):

$face(R_2) \leftarrow canfollow(R_2,S_2,R_1,S_1),number(R_1)$
$number(R_2) \leftarrow canfollow(R_2,S_2,R_1,S_1),face(R_1)$

which states the intended rule. Contrast this with the kind of rules LINUS or FOIL learns:

$canfollow(R_2,S_2,R_1,S_1) \leftarrow face(R_2), number(R_1)$
$canfollow(R_2,S_2,R_1,S_1) \leftarrow face(R_1), number(R_2)$

The intended rule for the second layout is "Play a higher card in the suit preceding that of the last card; or, play a lower card in the suit following that of the last card". ICL learns three constraints on the positive models:

$precedes\_suit(S1,S2) \leftarrow can\_follow(R2,S2,R1,S1),lower\_rank(R1,R2)$
$lower\_rank(R1,R2) \leftarrow can\_follow(R2,S2,R1,S1),red(S1)$
$precedes\_suit(S2,S1) \leftarrow can\_follow(R2,S2,R1,S1),lower\_rank(R2,R1)$

A nicer result is obtained when the positive and negative models are switched, which gives us constraints on the negative models :

$lower\_rank(R2,R1) \leftarrow can\_follow(R2,S2,R1,S1),precedes\_suit(S1,S2)$
$lower\_rank(R1,R2) \leftarrow can\_follow(R2,S2,R1,S1),precedes\_suit(S2,S1)$

This is very simular to the result obtained by LINUS.

The view that examples are interpretations and that the aim is to discriminate between two classes of examples is similar to classical learning from positive and negative examples. This is illustrated by the fact that an attribute value learning task (the Autolander problem) can be represented in a straightforward way in our framework. Furthermore, for many complex and structural induction problems the view that examples are interpretations is a very natural one, cf. for instance the drug activity problem [King *et al.*, 1992] the mutagenicity [Srinivasan *et al.*, 1994] and Michalski's classical eastbound - westbound train problem [Michalski and Stepp, 1983] that was recently used as the basis for a machine learning competition.

3 Inductive Constraint Logic: a first algorithm

The key observation to arrive at the ICL algorithm is the following. Each clause belonging to the target theory will have to make *all* positive examples true, and will have to exclude *some* of the negatives. This contrasts with the classical attribute value learning setting where each conjunctive rule has to cover some of the positives and none of the negatives. This contrast is actually a duality because clauses are to be considered as disjunctions of literals, rather than as conjunctions. So, clausal theories correspond to a conjunctive normal form (a conjunction of disjunctions) whereas classical attribute value learning has concentrated on learning a disjunctive normal form (a disjunction of conjunctions). A conjunctive normal form formula is of roughly the following structure:

$$(l_{1,1} \lor ... \lor l_{1,n_1}) \land ... \land (l_{m,1} \lor ... \lor l_{m,n_m})$$

and for a disjunctive normal form formula:

$$(l_{1,1} \land ... \land l_{1,n_1}) \lor ... \lor (l_{m,1} \land ... \land l_{m,n_m}).$$

This duality is further illustrated in Example 4 for the autolander problem.

Example 4. The results generated by CN2 for the Autolander problem (negative class) is:

$(stability(xstab) \land visibility(yes)) \lor$
$(error(xl) \land visibility(yes)) \lor$
$(error(lx) \land visibility(yes)) \lor$
$(magnitude(outofrange) \land visibility(yes)) \lor$
$(error(mm) \land sign(nn) \land visibility(yes)) \lor$
$(error(mm) \land wind(head) \land magnitude(strong) \land visibility(yes))$

It is easily verified that the negation of this description corresponds to the clausal form formula in Example 1. The negation of the negative class in DNF will for boolean learning problems always correspond to the positive class in CNF. However, when variables appear in clauses, complications arise because of quantifiers. As a result, the negation of the negative class may no longer be expressible in clausal form, cf. also Section 5.

The duality between CNF and DNF can easily be exploited by inversing well-known algorithms (such as AQ and CN2) that learn disjunctive normal forms to learn CNF formula (cf. also [Haussler, 1988]). It is because of this property that we will pursue a covering approach on the negatives instead of the positives, and also generally invert the role of positives and negatives. Also, in the heuristics the role of positives and negatives will be swapped. Furthermore, as examples are interpretations, the heuristics will count interpretations. This contrasts ICL from other ILP algorithms (such as FOIL [Quinlan, 1990]) where one counts facts and/or substitutions. The ICL algorithm derived from CN2 [Clark and Niblett, 1989] by exploiting this duality is shown in Figures 4 and 5

Figure 4 contains the covering algorithm. Given a background theory B and a set of positive examples P and negative examples N, the algorithm produces a theory H. Initially the hypothesis is empty, and the algorithm repeatedly tries to find interesting clauses c to add to the hypothesis. Each clause added will make all positive examples true and will make some negatives false. After a clause is found, the negatives that are false interpretations for the clause (i.e. not covered by the clause) are discarded. This process continues until no significant clause can be found, or a complete and consistent hypothesis is discovered.

Inductive-Constraint-Logic(P,N,B);

1. Initialize $H := \emptyset$
2. **repeat until** *best clause* c not found **or** N is empty
   (a) find *best clause* c
   (b) **if** *best clause* c found **then**
       i. add c to H
       ii. remove from N all interpretations that are false for c
3. **return** H

Fig. 4. ICL covering algorithm

Find-Best-Clause(P,N,B);

1. Initialize $Beam := \{false \leftarrow true\}$
2. Initialize $BestClause := \emptyset$
3. **while** $Beam$ is not empty **do**
   (a) Initialize $NewBeam := \emptyset$
   (b) **for each** clause c in $Beam$ **do**
       i. **for each** refinement Ref of c **do**
          A. **if** Ref is better than $BestClause$
             and Ref is statistically significant
             then $BestClause := Ref$
          B. **if** Ref is not to be pruned
             then
             $-$ add Ref to $NewBeam$
             $-$ **if** size of $NewBeam > MaxBeamSize$
                then remove worst clause from $NewBeam$
   (c) $Beam := NewBeam$
4. **return** $BestClause$

Fig. 5. ICL beam search algorithm

The search algorithm for the best clause is shown in figure 5. As in CN2, we use beam search as search strategy. A classical refinement operator under θ-subsumption (Plokin 70, Shapiro 83) is used together with CLAUDIEN's mechanism to specify the declarative bias (i.e. the syntax of well-formed clauses in hypotheses), cf. [Van Laer et al., 1994; Adé et al., 1995] and below. (Notice that whenever a clause c is true in an interpretation I, all refinements of c are also true in I.)

The search starts with the most general clause of the refinement graph (namely $false \leftarrow true$, for wich each example model is false). During the search, ICL keeps a $Beam$ of candidate clauses and the best clause found sofar ($BestClause$ in 2.). At each step in the beam search, all the possible refinements Ref of the clauses in $Beam$ are considered and evaluated (see A and B in figure 5). Depending on the evaluation, Ref becomes the $CurrentBest$ and/or Ref is added to $NewBeam$ (such that only the $MaxBeamSize$ best candidate clauses remain in the beam).

ICL makes use of two heuristic evaluation functions. The first one estimates the $quality\ of\ a\ clause$. This measure is used to direct the search (as only the best $MaxBeamSize$ clauses are placed in the beam) and to determine the best clause found during the beam search. The quality of a clause c is determined by the probability that an example interpretation is negative, given that clause c is false in the interpretation, i.e. $p(\ominus|\bar{c})$. Notice the difference with classical attribute value learning, where $p(\oplus|c)$ is used (see [Lavrač and Džeroski, 1994]). We use the Laplace estimate (as default) to measure this probability :

$$HV(c) = p(\ominus|\bar{c}) = \frac{n^{\ominus}(\bar{c}) + 1}{n(\bar{c}) + 2}$$

where $n(\bar{c})$ is the number of examples that are false for clause c and $n^{\ominus}(\bar{c})$ is the number of negative examples that are false for c.

The second evaluation function tests whether a clause is statistically significant, to ensure that the clause represents a genuine regularity in the examples and not a regularity which is due to chance (see [Lavrač and Džeroski, 1994; Clark and Niblett, 1989]). The statistical significance test is based on the likelihood ratio statistic, which is also employed in CN2. This gives

$$LR(c) = 2n(c) \times (p(\oplus|c)log(\frac{p(\oplus|c)}{p_a(\oplus)}) + p(\ominus|c)log(\frac{p(\ominus|c)}{p_a(\ominus)}))$$

where $n(c)$ is the number of interpretations covered by c (true for c), $p_a(\oplus)$ and $p_a(\ominus)$ are the prior probabilities of classes $\oplus$ and $\ominus$ (= relative frequency of positive and negative examples in the training set), $p(\oplus|c)$ is the probability (estimated by relative frequency) that an example is positive given that c is true for that example, and $n(c)$ is the total number of examples satisfying clause c. This statistic is distributed approximately as χ^2 with one degree of freedom. We say that a clause c is significant, if $LR(c) > T$, with T a certain significance treshold (for example 6.64 for 99 per cent significance).

Based on these two heuristics, we can do some additional pruning. First of all, a clause c can be pruned if no refinements of c can become better than the best clause at that moment (the best value we can achieve with further refinements of a clause, is a clause that is false for the same negative models and true for all positive models) (cfr. gain pruning in FOIL). Secondly, we can stop refining a clause when it's not possibly statistically significant (cfr. mFoil [Lavrač and Džeroski, 1994]).

Notice that the refinement operator in ICL is a classical one based on Plotkin's θ-subsumption [Plotkin, 1970]. Though a complete refinement operator for clausal logic could be employed by ICL (as is given in for instance in [Shapiro, 1983; van der Laag and Nienhuys-Cheng, 1993], we choose to enhance ICL with a declarative bias mechanism for restricting the search space. The declarative bias is the same as that in the CLAUDIEN system [Van Laer et al., 1994] and in NINA [Adé et al., 1995]. Basically, clause models are used to define the syntax of clauses that can appear in hypotheses. From the models, one can automatically derive a refinement operator that only generates clauses that are allowed by the syntax. A full discussion of this declarative bias mechanism is outside the scope of this paper, but see [Adé et al., 1995; Van Laer et al., 1994] for more details.

4 Experiments

In this section, we report on an experiment in the King-Rook-King domain of [Muggleton et al., 1989]. The experiment mainly serves to demonstrate the performance of ICL on a larger domain involving noise. The same experimental setting and the same data as [Lavrač and Džeroski, 1994] was employed. The significance level of ICL was set to 99 per cent. There were for all different noise levels, 5 runs of 100 examples (60 positive examples and 40 negatives), whereas the testset contained 5000 examples. The results are averaged over the 5 runs and compared to the results for mFOIL using the Laplace heuristic (see Figure 6 and 7)[3]. A noise level of x per cent in the arguments means that in x per cent of the examples the values of one of the arguments was replaced by a random value. Similarly, a noise level of x per cent in the class means that in x per cent of the examples the classification was assigned randomly.

In order to make the comparison easier, we learned the negative concept. As outlined in the example for the Autolander problem, the negation of the negative concept in the form of clausal constraints (CNF) corresponds roughly to the definition of the positive concept in DNF format. An example output (for the noise free runs) is:

$false \leftarrow wk(WKf,WKr),wr(WRf,WRr),bk(BKf,BKr),WRf=BKf$
$false \leftarrow wk(WKf,WKr),wr(WRf,WRr),bk(BKf,BKr),WRr=BKr$
$false \leftarrow wk(WKf,WKr),wr(WRf,WRr),bk(BKf,BKr),adj\_file(WKf,BKf),adj\_rank(WKr,BKr)$
$false \leftarrow wk(WKf,WKr),wr(WRf,WRr),bk(BKf,BKr),WKf=BKf,adj\_rank(WKr,BKr)$
$false \leftarrow wk(WKf,WKr),wr(WRf,WRr),bk(BKf,BKr),adj\_file(WKf,BKf),WKr=BKr$
$false \leftarrow wk(WKf,WKr),wr(WRf,WRr),bk(BKf,BKr),WKf=BKf,WKr=BKr$
$false \leftarrow wk(WKf,WKr),wr(WRf,WRr),bk(BKf,BKr),adj\_rank(WRr,BKr),WKf=WRf$

As one can see ICL performs roughly the same as mFOIL on these data.

---

[3] For ease of comparison we choose to compare with the Laplace estimate in mFOIL and not with the best m-value, because ICL also uses the Laplace heuristic though ICL could also employ the m-estimate.

System	Noise in Arguments							
	0	5	10	15	20	30	50	80
mFOIL - Laplace	95.14	90.11	80.41	78.32	73.66	72.57	67.91	59.20
ICL	95.26	90.78	79.04	78.46	72.22	72.36	66.44	62.14
System	Noise in Class							
	0	5	10	15	20	30	50	80
mFOIL - Laplace	95.14	92.71	88.90	86.40	84.58	83.75	73.74	60.25
ICL	95.26	92.78	88.84	86.12	82.28	83.04	76.84	63.96
System	Noise in Class and Arguments							
	0	5	10	15	20	30	50	80
mFOIL - Laplace	95.14	85.36	75.76	75.08	71.69	64.22	61.38	57.58
ICL	95.26	90.66	78.58	74.86	74.10	65.90	64.64	59.14

Fig. 6. Results of the King-Rook-King experiment

5 Discussion

In this section we discuss the strenghts and the weaknesses of ICL as compared to other approaches.

First, notice that ICL is meant to learn binary concepts from examples. As such it addresses the same task as propositional learners (but in a more expressive framework) and it does not learn logic programs from examples as many ILP systems do cf. [Muggleton and De Raedt, 1994]. In ILP, examples are usually true and false ground facts of a target predicate, and the result is a logic program. For instance when applying ILP to program synthesis, the examples show the input-output behaviour of the target predicate, and the resulting program can be used to produce the output for a given input. Inducing a logic program involves learning a more complex behaviour than inducing a classifier as the latter can only be used to produce a true/false answer.

A second difference with the majority of ILP systems, is that there is a clear view of how to use examples in heuristics. This is because in ICL one interpretation counts as one example. In many ILP systems (such as e.g. Quinlan's FOIL) it is unclear what counts as an example. At some points, FOIL counts facts, and at other points it counts substitutions. We believe this is one of the reasons that heuristics for attribute value learning are much better understood than for ILP. Our framework resolves this confusion and allows to carry over the results of a lot of research on using heuristics in attribute value learning to inductive constraint logic.

Third, let us mention that ICL assumes that the examples are finite sets of facts because it is decidable for all clauses and for all finite interpretations whether or not the interpretation is a model for the clause. Notice that this property also holds for recursive clauses. F.i. it is decidable whether or not $ancestor(X, Y) \leftarrow parent(X, Z) \wedge ancestor(Z, Y)$ makes any finite interpretation true. This means that ICL has no problems learning recursive clauses, which contrasts again with most of the other ILP approaches. However, when interpretations may be infinite (f.i. in the presence of functor symbols), testing for coverage is no longer decidable. A (rather technical) approach to circumventing this problem based on [Rouveirol, 1994], is given in [De Raedt and Džeroski, 1994]. Another point of difference is that in ICL

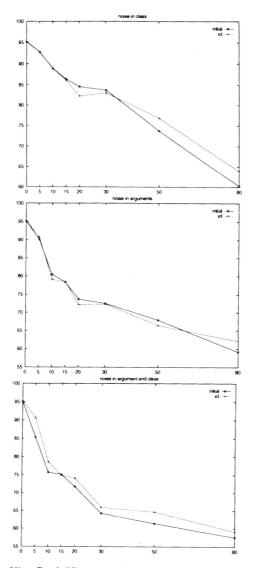

Fig. 7. Results of the King-Rook-King experiment

all clauses are considered independent constraints, whereas in ILP clauses may be mutually dependent, complicating coverage tests [De Raedt *et al.*, 1993].

Fourth, the clausal logic we employ allows to easily express some concepts which are hard (or impossible) to express using the normal inductive logic programming paradigm and definite clauses. For instance, a concept such as all wagons are black or white, can very naturally be represented by $black(X) \vee white(X) \leftarrow wagon(X)$.

Fifth, whereas some forms of existential quantification are easily handled in the normal inductive logic programmign setting using definite clauses, ICL cannot (yet) learn concepts involving existential quantifiers. A possible target concept could be the following expression in prenex conjunctive normal form

$$\exists W : wagon(W) \wedge black(W) \wedge small(W)$$

(In words: there is a wagon that is black and small. This concept could be expressed in normal ILP by a clause such as $positive(T) \leftarrow wagon(T, W) \wedge black(W) \wedge small(W)$.) The reason that this cannot directly be translated in clausal logic is that the translation from predicate calculus to clausal logic involves skolemization (see Genesereth and Nillson 87), which essentially introduces names for all existential quantifiers. Thus the corresponding clausal logic formula (after skolemization) would be:

$$wagon(sk) \wedge small(sk) \wedge wagon(sk)$$

Now it is easy to find interpretations that are models for the prenex conjunctive normal form but not for skolemized version of it. At present we are working on an extension of ICL that learns formula in prenex conjunctive normal form rather than clausal form. One complication in this context is that disjunctions (or clauses) can no longer be considered independently of each other. F.i. in the above target concept, the three constraints (wagon, black and small) have to be considered at the same time in order to test coverage.

6 Related Work and Conclusions

ICL forms the practical counterpart to the PAC-learning framework presented by De Raedt and Džeroski who also view examples as interpretations of a clausal theory. Secondly, some of the ideas on reversing the role of positives and negatives when going from CNF to DNF or vice versa, were presented in [Haussler, 1988] and in [Mooney, 1995]. Given Haussler's results it was relatively easy to turn ideas of Clark and Niblett's CN2 into ICL. Finally, we believe ICL is also similar in spirit as Michalski's work [Michalski, 1983] on learning structural concept definitions, in that it addresses the same learning task. However, the use of a formal logical framework as well as more advanced attribute value learning techniques distinguishes ICL from AQ.

We have outlined a novel approach to learn classification rules in the predicate calculus. Whereas the large majority of results of induction in first order logic views examples as ground facts or clauses, we view examples as interpretations. This corresponds to learning a conjunctive normal form instead of a disjunctive one. The presented technique seems promising for learning classification rules because it inherits many well-known techniques from attribute value learning as well as the much more expressive framework of inductive logic programming.

Just before submitting this article, it was brought to our attention that there are some unpublished results on learning propositional CNF formulas by Ray Mooney, which would be to appear in the MLJournal. In a final version of this paper, we hope to elaborate on this.

Acknowledgements

Luc De Raedt and Wim Van Laer are supported by the Belgian National Fund for Scientific Research and by the ESPRIT project no. 6020 on Inductive Logic Programming, co-financed by the Flemish Government under contract no. 93/14. They would like to thank Sašo Džeroski, Nada Lavrač and Maurice Bruynooghe for interesting discussions and earlier work that finally lead to this paper and Sašo Džeroski for supplying the data for the KRK experiment.

References

[Adé et al., 1995] H. Adé, L. De Raedt, and M. Bruynooghe. Declarative Bias for Specific-To-General ILP Systems. *Machine Learning*, 1995. To appear.

[Clark and Niblett, 1989] P. Clark and T. Niblett. The CN2 algorithm. *Machine Learning*, 3(4):261–284, 1989.

[De Raedt and Džeroski, 1994] L. De Raedt and S. Džeroski. First order jk-clausal theories are pac-learnable. *Artificial Intelligence*, 70:375–392, 1994.

[De Raedt et al., 1993] L. De Raedt, N. Lavrač, and S. Džeroski. Multiple predicate learning. In *Proceedings of the 13th International Joint Conference on Artificial Intelligence*, pages 1037–1042. Morgan Kaufmann, 1993.

[Dietterich and Michalski, 1985] T.G. Dietterich and R.S. Michalski. Discovering patterns in sequences of events. *Artificial Intelligence*, 25:257–294, 1985.

[Genesereth and Nilsson, 1987] M. Genesereth and N. Nilsson. *Logical foundations of artificial intelligence*. Morgan Kaufmann, 1987.

[Haussler, 1988] D. Haussler. Quantifying inductive bias : AI learning algorithms and Valiant's learning framework. *Artificial Intelligence*, 36:177 – 221, 1988.

[King et al., 1992] R.D. King, S. Muggleton, R.A. Lewis, and M.J.E. Sternberg. Drug design by machine learning: the use of inductive logic programming to model the structure-activity relationships of trimethoprim analogues binding to dihydrofolate reductase. *Proceedings of the National Academy of Sciences*, 89(23), 1992.

[Lavrač and Džeroski, 1994] N. Lavrač and S. Džeroski. *Inductive Logic Programming: Techniques and Applications*. Ellis Horwood, 1994.

[Lloyd, 1987] J.W. Lloyd. *Foundations of logic programming*. Springer-Verlag, 2nd edition, 1987.

[Michalski and Stepp, 1983] R.S. Michalski and R.E. Stepp. Learning from observation: conceptual clustering. In R.S Michalski, J.G. Carbonell, and T.M. Mitchell, editors, *Machine Learning: an artificial intelligence approach*, volume 1. Tioga Publishing Company, 1983.

[Michalski, 1983] R.S. Michalski. A theory and methodology of inductive learning. In R.S Michalski, J.G. Carbonell, and T.M. Mitchell, editors, *Machine Learning: an artificial intelligence approach*, volume 1. Morgan Kaufmann, 1983.

[Mooney, 1995] R.J. Mooney. Encouraging experimental results on learning cnf. *Machine Learning*, 19:79–92, 1995.

[Muggleton and De Raedt, 1994] S. Muggleton and L. De Raedt. Inductive logic programming : Theory and methods. *Journal of Logic Programming*, 19,20:629–679, 1994.

[Muggleton et al., 1989] S. Muggleton, M. Bain, J. Hayes-Michie, and D. Michie. An experimental comparison of human and machine learning formalisms. In *Proceedings of the 6th International Workshop on Machine Learning*, pages 113–118. Morgan Kaufmann, 1989.

[Muggleton, 1992] S. Muggleton, editor. *Inductive Logic Programming*. Academic Press, 1992.

[Plotkin, 1970] G. Plotkin. A note on inductive generalization. In *Machine Intelligence*, volume 5, pages 153–163. Edinburgh University Press, 1970.

[Quinlan, 1986] J.R. Quinlan. Induction of decision trees. *Machine Learning*, 1:81–106, 1986.

[Quinlan, 1990] J.R. Quinlan. Learning logical definitions from relations. *Machine Learning*, 5:239–266, 1990.

[Rouveirol, 1994] C. Rouveirol. Flattening and saturation: Two representation changes for generalization. *Machine Learning*, 14:219–232, 1994.

[Shapiro, 1983] E.Y. Shapiro. *Algorithmic Program Debugging*. The MIT Press, 1983.

[Srinivasan *et al.*, 1994] A. Srinivasan, S.H. Muggleton, R.D. King, and M.J.E. Sternberg. Mutagenesis: Ilp experiments in a non-determinate biological domain. In S. Wrobel, editor, *Proceedings of the 4th International Workshop on Inductive Logic Programming*, volume 237 of *GMD-Studien*, pages 217–232. Gesellschaft für Mathematik und Datenverarbeitung MBH, 1994.

[van der Laag and Nienhuys-Cheng, 1993] P.R.J. van der Laag and S.-H. Nienhuys-Cheng. Subsumption and refinement in model inference. In P. Brazdil, editor, *Proceedings of the 6th European Conference on Machine Learning*, volume 667 of *Lecture Notes in Artificial Intelligence*, pages 95–114. Springer-Verlag, 1993.

[Van Laer *et al.*, 1994] W. Van Laer, L. Dehaspe, and L. De Raedt. Applications of a logical discovery engine. In *Proceedings of the AAAI Workshop on Knowledge Discovery in Databases*, pages 263–274, 1994.

Incremental Learning of Logic Programs

M. R. K. Krishna Rao

Computer Science Group, Tata Institute of Fundamental Research,
Colaba, BOMBAY 400 005, INDIA, e-mail: **krishna@tifrvax.bitnet**
and
Max-Planck-Institut für Informatik, Im Stadtwald,
66123 Saarbrücken, GERMANY, e-mail: **krishna@mpi-sb.mpg.de**

Abstract. In this paper, we identify a class of polynomial-time learnable logic programs. These programs can be learned from examples in an incremental fashion using the already defined predicates as background knowledge. Our class properly contains the class of innermost simple programs of [20] and the class of hereditary programs of [12, 13]. Standard programs for `multiplication`, `quick-sort`, `reverse` and `merge` are a few examples of programs that can be handled by our results but not by the earlier results of [12, 13, 20].

1 Introduction

Starting with the seminal work of Shapiro [17, 18], the problem of learning logic programs from examples has attracted a lot of attention in the last ten years (see a.o., [16, 12, 13, 2, 5, 8, 20]). Many techniques and systems for learning logic programs are developed and used in many applications [14]. In this paper, we identify a class of polynomial-time learnable logic programs and present an algorithm for learning these programs.

Our work has been inspired by the works of Miyano et. al. [12, 13, 2] and Yamamoto [20]. Miyano et. al. [12, 13, 2] identified a class of elementary formal systems (EFSs) – which are a special kind of logic programs manipulating character strings – and presented a polynomial-time algorithm to learn these programs from examples without asking any queries. This class, called *hereditary programs*,[1] contains logic programs with the following property: all the terms appearing in the body of a clause are subterms in the head. The standard append program is an example of hereditary programs. The condition that all the terms appearing in the body of a clause are subterms in the head is a bit restrictive from the programming point of view. It is not easy to write hereditary programs even for simple tasks like `reverse`, `merge`, `quick-sort` and `multiplication`.

Yamamoto [20] generalized the results of [12, 13, 2] using generalized unification as the background knowledge in the learning process. The approach can

---

[1] Though Miyano et. al. only considered EFSs, but all their definitions and results can be generalized to the usual logic programs.

be paraphrased as follows. In learning a program for reverse, one can use the knowledge about the append program already known and use the knowledge about addition in learning a program for multiplication. Essentially, the program append (resp. addition) is used as a background knowledge in learning reverse (resp. multiplication). This way, one can learn (or synthesize) programs in an incremental fashion. With the following background knowledge

$$app([\,], Ys) = Ys$$
$$app([X|Xs], Ys) = [X|app(Xs, Ys)]$$

about append, one can come up with the following program for reverse which satisfies the requirement of hereditary programs that all the terms in the body are subterms in the head.

$$reverse([\,],[\,]) \leftarrow$$
$$reverse([X|Xs], app(Ys, [X])) \leftarrow reverse(Xs, Ys)$$

The background theory about app can be used in the execution of reverse employing generalized unification (also called E-unification) instead of the usual unification. Though the list constructors [ ] and [·|·] as well as app are used as function symbols in this program, they are used for two different purposes. The list constructors [ ] and [·|·] are used for data structor building and app is used to manipulate lists. We call app a defined symbol and [ ] and [·|·] constructor symbols (terminology borrowed from term rewriting literature). The above reverse program is essentially a functional logic program (see, [6]) and can be transformed into an equivalent logic program through the flattening operation of [4].

Yamamoto [20] identified a class (called innermost simple programs) of logic programs which can be learned in polynomial-time with certain restrictions on the background knowledge employed. The background knowledge about append and addition do not satisfy the restrictions of [20] and hence the standard programs for multiplication, quick-sort, reverse cannot be certified as polynomial-time learnable programs. Due to a syntactic condition of innermost simple programs, the standard merge program falls beyond the scope of the results of [20].

In this paper, we identify a class of polynomial-time learnable logic programs by relaxing certain syntactic conditions and the requirements on the background knowledge presented in [20]. Our class properly contains the class of innermost simple programs and multiplication, quick-sort, reverse and merge programs can be certified as polynomial-time learnable programs using our results.

The rest of the paper is organized as follows. The next section gives preliminary definitions and results needed. Section 3 explains 'E-unification as background knowledge'. We identify a class of programs, called generalized hereditary programs, and a class of background knowledges and prove some lemmata about SLD-derivations of these programs in section 4 and establish polynomial-time learnability of these programs in section 5. A comparison with related works is given in section 6 and section 7 concludes with a summary.

2 Preliminaries

We assume that the reader is familiar with the basic terminology of logic programming and machine learning and use the standard terminology from [11, 14, 15].

In the following, $T(\Sigma, \mathcal{X})$ denotes the set of terms constructed from set of function symbols Σ and set of variables X and $\mathcal{A}(\Pi, \Sigma, \mathcal{X})$ denotes the set of atoms constructed from these terms and predicate symbols in Π. Throughout the paper, we use Π and Σ to denote the sets of predicate and function symbols under consideration. The size of a term $t \in T(\Sigma, \mathcal{X})$, denoted by $|t|$, is the number of symbols occurring in it and $var(t)$ is the set of variables in t. Terms which do not contain any variable are called ground terms and $T(\Sigma)$ denotes the set of ground terms constructed from Σ. Atoms constructed from ground terms are ground atoms. A context over Σ is a term in $T(\Sigma \cup \{\Box\}, \mathcal{X})$, where $\Box$ is a special symbol called *hole*. If $C[\Box, \cdots, \Box]$ is a context with n holes, $C[t_1, \cdots, t_n]$ denotes the term obtained by substituting the terms $t_1, \cdots, t_n$ for the n holes in the context C from left to right. We denote arity of a predicate/function symbol f by $arity(f)$. As mentioned in the introduction, we partition Σ into two disjoint sets (i) Γ, the set of constructor symbols (corresponding to data structures) and (ii) Δ, the set of defined symbols (corresponding to predicates already known/defined). A constructor term is a term in $T(\Gamma, \mathcal{X})$ and a constructor context is a context over Γ. We denote by $B(p)$, the set of atoms $\mathcal{A}(\{p\}, \Gamma, \phi)$.

Definition 1 The size of an atom $p(t_1, \ldots, t_n)$ is defined as $|p(t_1, \ldots, t_n)| = max(|t_1|, \ldots, |t_n|)$. For a set S of atoms and an integer n, we define $S_n = \{A \in S; |A| \le n\}$.

Definition 2 A logic Program P is a finite set of definite clauses of the form $H \leftarrow B_1, \ldots, B_n$, where $H, B_1, \ldots, B_n$ are atoms. The atom H is the head of this clause and $B_1, \ldots, B_n$ is the body of this clause. The length of a program P, denoted by $length(P)$, is defined as follows:

- $length(t) = 0$ if t is a constructor term,
- $length(c) = 1$ if c is a defined/predicate symbol with $arity(c) = 0$,
- $length(f(t_1, \ldots, t_m)) = m + length(t_1) + \cdots + length(t_m)$ if $f \in \Delta \cup \Pi$ and $m > 0$,
- length of a clause $C = H \leftarrow B_1, \ldots, B_n$ is defined as
  $length(C) = length(H) + length(B_1) + \cdots + length(B_n)$ and
- $length(P)$ is maximum over the lengths of clauses in P.

Informally, length of a clause is the sum of the arities of predicate/defined symbols in it plus the number of predicate/defined symbols of arity 0 in it.

We recall the following notions from [15, 12, 20]. In the following, we use a special predicate symbol c to denote the target predicate to be learned.

Definition 3 A *concept* is a subset I of $B(c)$ and a *concept class* C is a subset of $2^{B(c)}$. For a concept class C, we define $C_n = \{I \cap B(c)_n; I \in C\}$ and $dim(C_n) = log_2|C_n|$.

Definition 4 A concept class C is of *polynomial dimension* if there is a polynomial $d(n)$ such that $dim(C_n) \leq d(n)$ for all $n \geq 0$.

Definition 5 An *example* is a tuple $\langle A, a \rangle$ where $A \in B(c)$ and $a = 1$ or 0. It is *positive* if $a = 1$ and *negative* otherwise. A concept I is *consistent* with a sequence of examples $\langle A_1, a_1 \rangle, \ldots, \langle A_m, a_m \rangle$ if $A_i \in I$ is equivalent to $a_i = 1$ for each $i \in [1, m]$.

Definition 6 A *polynomial-time fitting* for a concept class C is a polynomial-time algorithm that takes a sequence of examples and returns a concept in C consistent with the sequence.

The following result from [3, 15] is useful in identifying polynomial-time learnable classes of concepts.

Theorem 1 *A concept class C is polynomial-time learnable if and only if C is of polynomial dimension and there is a polynomial-time fitting for C.*

3 Background Knowledge: E-Unification

In this paper, we use logic programs defining the already known predicates as background knowledge in learning a new predicate. This background knowledge is presented in the form of an equality theory B over the defined and constructor symbols, Δ and Γ respectively. There are many techniques to derive a term rewrite system (i.e., a set of directed equations) from a given logic program (see e.g. [9, 19, 10, 1]). The derived rewrite systems have a nice property that *in the left-hand sides, defined symbols occur only at the outermost level and constructor symbols do not occur at the outermost level.* Such rewrite systems are called *constructor systems.* Any equality theory B presented by such a rewrite system has the property: for every pair of constructor terms s and t, $B \models s = t$ if and only if s and t are syntactically identical. For an equality theory B presented by a confluent and terminating constructor system, *narrowing* serves as a sound and complete E-unification method [7]. Throughout the paper, we consider equality theories presented by confluent and terminating constructor systems.

Example 1 The equality theory presented by the following rewrite system is a background knowledge B about append.

$$\text{app}([\,],\text{Ys}) \rightarrow \text{Ys}$$
$$\text{app}([X|Xs],\text{Ys}) \rightarrow [X|\text{app}(Xs,\text{Ys})]$$

One can see the similarity of this term rewrite system and a logic program defining append. □

Definition 7 A *unifier* of two terms s and t in $T(\Sigma,\mathcal{X})$ *w.r.t* B is a substitution θ such that $B \models s\theta = t\theta$. A *unifier* of two atoms $p(s_1,\cdots,s_n)$ and $p(t_1,\cdots,t_n)$ *w.r.t* B is a substitution θ such that $B \models s_1\theta = t_1\theta \wedge \cdots \wedge s_n\theta = t_n\theta$. Two terms (or atoms) are *unifiable* if there exist a unifier for them.

Definition 8 A unifier $\theta = \{X_1/s_1,\ldots,X_n/s_n\}$ of two terms (or atoms) s and t is *relevant* if $\{X_1,\ldots,X_n\} \subseteq var(s) \cup var(t)$.

Example 2 The following are some of the relevant unifiers of terms $s = \text{app}(X,Y)$ and $t = [1,2,3]$ with respect to the background knowledge B given in the above example.

$$\theta_1 = \{X/[\,],\ Y/[1,2,3]\};$$
$$\theta_2 = \{X/[1],\ Y/[2,3]\};$$
$$\theta_3 = \{X/[1,2],\ Y/[3]\};$$
$$\theta_4 = \{X/[1,2,3],\ Y/[\,]\}$$

4 Generalized Hereditary Programs and Regular Background Knowledge

In this section, we define a class of logic programs and a class of background knowledges and study certain properties of SLD-derivations (with E-unification) of these programs.

Definition 9 A definite clause $H \leftarrow B_1,\ldots,B_n$ is *generalized-hereditary* if

(a) all the arguments of defined symbols occurring in H are constructor terms and

(b) all the arguments of $B_1,\ldots,B_n$ are subterms of constructor terms in H.

A logic program is *generalized-hereditary* if each clause in it is generalized-hereditary.

Informally, the arguments of H are either constructor terms or terms containing both constructor and defined symbols but without any nesting of defined symbols. The arguments in the body are constructor terms occurring in H as subterms of its arguments.

Example 3 The following program for reverse is generalized-hereditary.

$$\text{reverse}([\,],[\,]) \leftarrow$$
$$\text{reverse}([X|Xs], \text{app}(Ys,[X])) \leftarrow \text{reverse}(Xs,Ys)$$

The background knowledge $\mathcal{B}$ given in Example 1 defines the symbol app. □

To establish polynomial-time learnability of generalized-hereditary programs, we need to put some restrictions on the background knowledge employed. We explain these restrictions in the following and by $\mathcal{B}$, we denote the background knowledge under consideration.

Definition 10 A defined symbol $f \in \Delta$ is *solvable* if there exists an algorithm which takes a term $t \in \mathcal{T}(\Gamma)$ as input and outputs all the tuples $\langle t_1, \cdots, t_n \rangle$ of ground constructor terms satisfying $\mathcal{B} \models f(t_1, \cdots, t_n) = t$ if exists and reports failure otherwise. A defined symbol f is *polynomial-time solvable* if the algorithm runs in polynomial-time of $|t|$.

The following two examples give polynomial-time solvable functions.

Example 4 Consider the background knowledge $\mathcal{B}$ presented in Example 1. The defined symbol app is polynomial-time solvable, as list of length $n \geq 1$ can be broken into two sublists in $n + 1$ different ways. □

Example 5 Consider the background knowledge $\mathcal{B}$ about add presented by the following rewrite system.

$$\text{add}(0, Y) \rightarrow Y$$
$$\text{add}(s(X), Y) \rightarrow s(\text{add}(X, Y))$$

The defined symbol add is polynomial-time solvable, as a positive integer n can be split into two non-negative integers in $n + 1$ different ways. □

Definition 11 A defined symbol $f \in \Delta$ is *increasing* if $|t| \geq |t_i|$ for each $i \in [1, n]$ whenever $\mathcal{B} \models f(t_1, \cdots, t_n) = t$ and $t_1, \cdots, t_n, t$ are constructor terms.

Example 6 It is very easy to see that the defined symbols app and add given above are increasing. □

Remark: Yamamoto [20] defines a defined symbol $f \in \Delta$ to be *increasing* if $|t| > |t_1| + \cdots + |t_n|$ whenever $\mathcal{B} \models f(t_1, \cdots, t_n) = t$. With respect to his definition, neither app nor add is increasing as $\mathcal{B} \models \text{app}([\,], L) = L$ but $|L| \not> 1 + |L| = |[\,]| + |L|$ for any list L and $\mathcal{B} \models \text{add}(0, n) = n$ but $|n| \not> 1 + |n| = |0| + |n|$ for any positive integer n.

To capture the set of all terms that occur in an SLD-derivation starting from a query, we introduce the following notion of *dependent set* of [20].

Notation: For two ground constructor terms s and t, the expression $p_f^i(t, s)$ denotes the fact that there are ground constructor terms $s_1, \ldots, s_{i-1}, s_{i+1}, \ldots, s_n$ such that $B \models f(s_1, \ldots, s_{i-1}, s, s_{i+1}, \ldots, s_n) = t$. Note that f can be either defined or constructor symbol.

Now, we define the notion of *dependent set*.

Definition 12 The *dependent set* $D(t)$ of a ground constructor term t is defined as

1. $t \in D(t)$ and
2. $s \in D(t)$ if $s' \in D(t)$ and $p_f^i(s', s)$ for some $f \in \Sigma$ and $i \le arity(f)$.

It is easy to see that $D(t)$ is closed under subterms, i.e., every subterm of s is in $D(t)$ if $s \in D(t)$. The following lemma shows that the size of the terms in $D(t)$ is bounded by the size of t, when each defined symbol is increasing.

Lemma 1 Let B be a background knowledge such that all the defined symbols are increasing. Then *for each term* $s \in D(t)$, $|s| \le |t|$.

Proof: We show that $|s'| \le |s|$ whenever $p_f^i(s, s')$ and the lemma follows from this by induction. If f is a constructor symbol, s' is a subterm of s and obviously $|s'| < |s|$. If f is a defined symbol then $B \models f(\ldots, s', \ldots) = s$. Since $f \in \Delta$ is increasing, it follows that $|s'| \le |s|$. □

Definition 13 A background knowledge B has *polynomial dependency property* if $|D(t)|$ is bounded by a polynomial in $|t|$.

Example 7 Consider the background knowledge B about app given in Example 1. For a list L, $D(L)$ is the set of sublists of L. The number of sublists of a list L of length n is $(n+1)_{C_2}$, which of the order $O(n^2)$. Therefore, B has polynomial dependency property.

Basically, a sublist of L can be identified by its two end-points. So to compute the number of sublists, we need to compute the number of possible ways of choosing two points on a line with $n+1$ points. That's, the number of sublists of a list L of length n is $(n+1)_{C_2}$.

Similarly, the background knowledge B about add given in Example 5 has polynomial dependency property as $D(n)$ is the set of non-negative integers less than or equal to n. □

Definition 14 A background knowledge B is *regular* if it has the polynomial dependency property and each defined symbol in it is increasing and polynomial-time solvable.

Example 8 The background knowledge B about app given in Example 1 is regular as we have proved all the three requirements in the above examples. Similarly, the background knowledge B about add given in Example 5 is regular. □

Now, we prove some lemmas about the SLD-derivations of generalized-hereditary programs with regular background knowledge. We say a goal is a ground constructor goal if every term in it is a ground constructor term.

Lemma 2 If P is a generalized-hereditary program with a regular background knowledge B and G is a ground constructor goal, then *every resolvent of G is a ground constructor goal.*

Proof: Let A be an atom in G and $H \leftarrow B_1, \ldots, B_n$ be a clause in P such that A and H are unifiable (w.r.t. B). Since A is a ground constructor atom and B is regular, the unifier θ instantiates variables in H by ground constructor terms. Since every argument of $B_1, \ldots, B_n$ is a subterm of a constructor term in H, all the arguments in $B_1\theta, \ldots, B_n\theta$ are ground constructor terms. □

By induction on length of the SLD-derivations, we get the following lemma.

Lemma 3 If P is a generalized-hereditary program with a regular background knowledge B and G is a ground constructor goal, then *all the goals in any SLD-derivation starting with G is a ground constructor goal.*

Lemma 4 If P is a generalized-hereditary program with a regular background knowledge B and $\leftarrow p(t_1, \cdots, t_n)$ is a ground constructor goal, then *all the terms occurring in any SLD-derivation starting with $\leftarrow p(t_1, \cdots, t_n)$ are in $S = D(t_1) \cup \cdots \cup D(t_n)$.*

Proof: Induction on the length l of the SLD-derivation.

Basis: $l = 0$. The lemma follows from the fact that $t \in D(t)$ for any term t.

Induction Hypothesis: Assume that the lemma holds for all SLD-derivations of length $l < k$.

Induction Step: Now, we establish that it holds for $l = k$. Let A be the selected atom and $H \leftarrow B_1, \ldots, B_n$ be the input clause used in the last resolution step. By the above lemma, all the arguments of A are ground constructor terms which are in S by the induction hypothesis. We have to show that all the arguments of $B_1\theta, \ldots, B_n\theta$ are ground constructor terms in S, where θ is a unifier of A and H.

Consider an argument $t\theta$ in $B_1\theta, \ldots, B_n\theta$. Since P is a generalized-hereditary program, t is a constructor subterm of an argument (say, s) in H. Let s' be the term in the corresponding argument-position of A. By the induction hypothesis, $s' \in S$. If s is a constructor term it is obvious that $t\theta$ is a subterm of $s\theta \equiv s'$.

Since $s' \in S$, all its subterms are in S as well and hence $t\theta \in S$. If s contains defined symbols, it can be written as $C[s_1, \ldots, s_m]$, where is C is a context of constructor symbols and variables and $root(s_i)$ is a defined symbol for each $i \in [1, m]$. It is clear that s' can be written as $C[s'_1, \ldots, s'_m]$ and each $s'_i \in S$. Now, t is either a subterm of C or one of s_i. If t is a subterm of C, it can be proved $t\theta \in S$ as above. Let us now consider the case that t is a subterm of s_i. Since, P is a generalized-hereditary program, s_i is of the form $f(t_1, \ldots, t_h)$, where $f \in \Delta$ and each t_i is constructor term. Since θ is a unifier of A and H, it follows that $\mathcal{B} \models f(t_1\theta, \ldots, t_h\theta) = s'_i$. Since $s'_i \in S$ it follows from Definition 12 that each $t_j\theta \in S$. Since t is a constructor subterm of s_i, it must be a subterm of some t_j and $t\theta$ a subterm of $t_j\theta$ and hence $t\theta \in S$. □

From this lemma and lemma 1, we get the following theorem.

Theorem 2 If P is a generalized-hereditary program with a regular background knowledge $\mathcal{B}$ and $\leftarrow p(t_1, \cdots, t_n)$ is a ground constructor goal, then *all the atoms occurring in any SLD-derivation starting with $\leftarrow p(t_1, \cdots, t_n)$ are of size less than or equal to $|p(t_1, \cdots, t_n)|$.*

5 Polynomial-time Learnability

In this section, we prove polynomial-time learnability of generalized-hereditary programs with regular background knowledge. We prove that the class $\mathcal{C}$ of the concepts definable by these programs is of *polynomial dimension* and there is a polynomial-time fitting for $\mathcal{C}$.

Definition 15 For a generalized-hereditary program P, we define the semantics[2] $M(P)$ as $\{A \in B(\Gamma);$ there is an SLD-refutation starting with atom $A\}$.

Definition 16 For $\mathbf{k}, \mathbf{1} \geq 0$, $\mathtt{GH}(\mathbf{k}, \mathbf{1})$ is the class of concepts definable by the generalized-hereditary programs P satisfying $|P| \leq \mathbf{k}$ and $length(P) \leq \mathbf{1}$.

We need the following lemma.

Lemma 5 Let H be the head of a generalized-hereditary clause and $\mathcal{B}$ be a regular background knowledge. If H unifies with a ground constructor atom of A of size n w.r.t. $\mathcal{B}$, the size of each constructor subterm in H and each constructor context in H is less than or equal to n.

Proof: Since $|A| = n$, each argument s of A has $|s| \leq n$. Now, consider an argument t of H and the corresponding argument s of A. If t is a constructor term, it is

---

[2] The semantics $M(P)$ can also be defined as the least fixpoint of a monotonic operator (similar to the T_P operator in [11]) in a straightforward way.

obvious that $|t| \leq n$ as it is unifying with a ground constructor term s with $|s| \leq n$. Otherwise, t can be written as $C[f_1(t_{11}, \ldots, t_{1n_1}), \ldots, f_m(t_{m1}, \ldots, t_{mn_m})]$ such that C is a context of constructor symbols and variables, $f_i \in \Delta$ for each $i \in [1, m]$ and each t_{ij} is a constructor term. It is obvious that $|C| \leq n$ as s should be of the form $C[\ldots]$. Each $f_i(t_{i1}, \ldots, t_{in_i})$ unifies with a subterm s_i of s and $|s_i| \leq n$. That's, $B \models f_i(t_{i1}\theta, \ldots, t_{in_i}\theta) = s_i$. Since B is regular, $|t_{ij}\theta| \leq |s_i| \leq n$ for each $j \in [1, n_i]$. Hence $|t_{ij}| \leq n$ for each $j \in [1, n_i]$. $\qquad\square$

Theorem 3 The class $\text{GH}(\mathbf{k}, 1)$ is of polynomial dimension if the background knowledge B is regular.

Proof: We evaluate $|\{I \cap B(c)_n; \ I \in \text{GH}(\mathbf{k}, 1)\}|$ for $n \geq 0$. Let P be a generalized-hereditary program with $|P| \leq \mathbf{k}$ and $length(P) \leq 1$ and $C = H \leftarrow B_1, \ldots, B_h$ be a clasue in P. By Theorem 2, all the atoms in an SLD-derivation starting with a goal $\leftarrow A$ such that $A \in I \cap B(c)_n$ are of size less than or equal to n. By the above lemma, $M(P) \cap B(c)_n = M(P - \{C\}) \cap B(c)_n$ if there is a constructor subterm/context of size more than n in H. If there is a predicate p which occurs in C but does not occur in the head of any clause in P, $M(P) = M(P - \{C\})$. So, we can assume that $\Pi = \{p_1, \ldots, p_{\mathbf{k}}\}$, the target predicate $c = p_1$ and the $arity(p_i) \leq 1$. By the definition of $length$, the number of constructor terms/contexts in H is at most 1 and hence the number of variables in H is at most $n.1$. We need to consider programs consisting of $\mathbf{k}$ clauses of length at most 1 such that the constructor terms in the clauses are of size at most n. The number of such programs are bounded by

$$N = (\mathbf{k}.|\Delta|^1.(n.1 + |\Gamma|)^{n.1}.(\mathbf{k}.(n.1 + |\Gamma|)^{n.1} + 1)^1)^{\mathbf{k}}.$$

Since $log_2(N) = O(n.log_2(n))$, the class $\text{GH}(\mathbf{k}, 1)$ is of polynomial dimension. $\quad\square$

Now, we give our main result.

Definition 17 For $\mathbf{k}, 1, \mathbf{m} \geq 0$, $\text{GH}(\mathbf{k}, 1, \mathbf{m})$ is the class of concepts definable by generalized-hereditary programs P having at most $\mathbf{m}$ variables in any clause and satisfying $|P| \leq \mathbf{k}$ and $length(P) \leq 1$.

Note that the number of defined symbols in a clause is bounded by 1.

Theorem 4 If the background knowledge B is regular, *there exists a polynomial-time fitting for the class* $\text{GH}(\mathbf{k}, 1, \mathbf{m})$ *for any* $\mathbf{k}, 1, \mathbf{m} \geq 0$.

Proof: Let P be a program in $\text{GH}(\mathbf{k}, 1, \mathbf{m})$. We can assume that the set of predicate symbols $\Pi = \{p_1, \ldots, p_{\mathbf{k}.(1+1)}\}$, $arity(p_i) = i \bmod (1 + 1)$ and the target predicate $c = p_j$ for some $j \in [1, \mathbf{k}.(1 + 1)]$. The idea behind the learning algorithm is essentially same as that in [12, 13, 20] and is based on generate-and-test method. Given a sequence S of examples, it produces a program P consistent with S. Let S^+ be the set of positive examples in S. If $S^+ = \phi$, the algorithm returns $P = \phi$. Otherwise, let $S = \{t \in \mathcal{T}(\Gamma); t = t_i$ for some $c(t_1, \ldots, t_n) \in S\}$. For each $p_i, i \in [1, \mathbf{k}.(1 + 1)]$, let H_i denote the set of atoms $\{p_i(t_1, \ldots, t_h); h = i \bmod (1+1)$ and $t_1, \ldots, t_h \in \bigcup_{t \in S} D(t)\}$. By the polynomial dependency property of $\mathcal{B}$, $|H_i|$ is polynomial in $\sum_{s \in S} |s|$ for every p_i.

The algorithm generates a set $\mathcal{P}$ of all programs P satisfying: (1) P is a generalized-hereditary program, $|P| \leq \mathbf{k}$ and $length(P) \leq 1$, (2) at most $\mathbf{m}$ variables in any clause C in P and (3) if there is a clause $H \leftarrow B_1, \ldots, B_n$ in P and the predicate symbol of H is p_i then there exists a $A \in H_i$ such that A and H are unifiable w.r.t $\mathcal{B}$.

Then the algorithm checks for each $P \in \mathcal{P}$ whether $s \in M(P)$ or not for each $s \in S$ as required for the consistency, by constructing a bottom-up proof for s. By lemma 4, all the atoms appearing in the proof are in the set $\bigcup_{i \in [1, \mathbf{k}.(1+1)]} H_i$. Hence the proof goes in polynomial in $\sum_{s \in S} |s|$. Since $\mathbf{k}, 1, \mathbf{m}$ are fixed, $|\mathcal{P}|$ is polynomial in $\sum_{s \in S} |s|$. The algorithm runs in polynomial-time. $\qquad \Box$

From the above two theorems, we get our main result.

Theorem 5 If the background knowledge $\mathcal{B}$ is regular, *the class* GH$(\mathbf{k}, 1, \mathbf{m})$ *of concepts is polynomial-time learnable for any* $\mathbf{k}, 1, \mathbf{m} \geq 0$.

Now, we give a series of examples illustrating our main result.

Example 9 The reverse program given in Example 3 with the regular background knowledge $\mathcal{B}$ about append is polynomial-time learnable as it is in GH$(2, 6, 3)$. $\qquad \Box$

Example 10 The following program for multiplication with the background knowledge $\mathcal{B}$ about add is a generalized-hereditary program.

```
mult(0,Y,0) ←
mult(s(X),Y,add(Y,Z)) ← mult(X,Y,Z)
```

This program is polynomial-time learnable as it is in GH$(2, 8, 3)$ and $\mathcal{B}$ is regular. $\qquad \Box$

Example 11 The following program for merge is a generalized-hereditary program.

```
merge([ ],[ ],[ ]) ←
merge([X|Xs],[Y|Ys],[X|Zs]) ← X < Y, merge(Xs,[Y|Ys],Zs)
merge([X|Xs],[Y|Ys],[Y|Zs]) ← X ≥ Y, merge([X|Xs],Ys,Zs)
```

This program is polynomial-time learnable as it is in GH$(3, 8, 5)$. $\qquad \Box$

Example 12 The following program for quick-sort over lists of distinct elements (need not be natural numbers but on any set with a total order) with the background knowledge $\mathcal{B}$ about append is a generalized-hereditary program.

This program is non-conventional and needs an explanation. The lack of local variables (which occur in body but not in head) in generalized-hereditary programs contributes to the non-simplicity of the program. The second clause of qs says that app($A,[H|B]$) is the result of (quick) sorting $[H|L]$ if A is the sorted list of all the elements in L smaller than H (implied by the atoms less(H,L,A) and qs(A,A) in the body) and B is the sorted list of all the elements in L bigger than H (implied by the atoms great(H,L,B) and qs(B,B) in the body). The atom ls1(H,L,A) stands for the fact that A contains all the elements in L smaller than H and the atom ls2(H,A) stands for the fact that all the elements in A are smaller than H. The meanings of predicates gr1 and gr2 are similar.

$$qs([\ ],[\ ]) \leftarrow$$
$$qs([H|L], app(A,[H|B])) \leftarrow less(H,L,A),\ great(H,L,B),\ qs(A,A),\ qs(B,B)$$

$$less(H,L,A) \leftarrow subset(A,L),\ ls1(H,L,A),\ ls2(H,A)$$
$$ls1(H,[\ ],A) \leftarrow$$
$$ls1(H,[Y|Ys],A) \leftarrow H > Y,\ member(Y,A),\ ls1(H,Ys,A)$$
$$ls1(H,[Y|Ys],A) \leftarrow H < Y,\ ls1(H,Ys,A)$$
$$ls2(H,[\ ]) \leftarrow$$
$$ls2(H,[Y|Ys]) \leftarrow H > Y,\ ls2(H,Ys)$$

$$great(H,L,A) \leftarrow subset(A,L),\ gr1(H,L,A),\ gr2(H,A)$$
$$gr1(H,[\ ],A) \leftarrow$$
$$gr1(H,[Y|Ys],A) \leftarrow H < Y,\ member(Y,A),\ gr1(H,Ys,A)$$
$$gr1(H,[Y|Ys],A) \leftarrow H > Y,\ gr1(H,Ys,A)$$
$$gr2(H,[\ ]) \leftarrow$$
$$gr2(H,[Y|Ys]) \leftarrow H < Y,\ gr2(H,Ys)$$

$$subset([\ ],L) \leftarrow$$
$$subset([X|Xs],L) \leftarrow member(X,L),\ subset(Xs,L)$$

$$member(H,[H|L]) \leftarrow$$
$$member(H,[Y|Ys]) \leftarrow member(H,Ys)$$

This program is polynomial-time learnable as it is in GH($18, 14, 4$) and B is regular. □

6 Comparison with Related Works

Our work is inspired by the works of Miyano et. al. [12, 13, 2] and Yamamoto [20]. The results in Yamamoto [20] are generalizations of the results in Miyano et. al. [12, 13, 2] (see statement 1 below for a small clarification). In the following, we compare our results with those of [20].

Our results are generalizations of the results in Yamamoto [20] in the following respects:

1. The class of innermost-simple programs [20] is a proper subclass of the class of generalized-hereditary programs, as innermost-simple programs allow only variables in the body and these variables should occur in the head of the clause. For this reason, the class of innermost-simple programs [20] does

not contain the hereditary programs of [12, 13, 2]. Generalized-hereditary programs allow non-variable constructor terms in the body if these terms are subterms of the terms in the head of the clause. The class of generalized-hereditary programs contain both the class of hereditary programs and the class of innermost-simple programs.

2. Yamamoto [20] needs that each defined symbol is *completely defined* (over $T(\Gamma)$). For the quick-sort program (with constructors: [ ], [·|·] and natural numbers), it is not clear how to make the defined function append a completely defined one as append is defined only on lists (but not on natural numbers). We do not need this requirement. Our requirement that the rewrite system presenting the background knowledge is confluent ensures that for any tuple $\langle t_1, \ldots, t_n \rangle$ of ground constructor terms there is at most one ground constructor term t such that $\mathcal{B} \models f(t_1, \ldots, t_n) = t$ for any defined symbol $f \in \Delta$.

3. Yamamoto [20] needs that each defined symbol is *injective* in the following sense that for any ground constructor term t there is at most one tuple $\langle t_1, \ldots, t_n \rangle$ of ground constructor terms such that $\mathcal{B} \models f(t_1, \ldots, t_n) = t$ for any defined symbol $f \in \Delta$. We do not need this requirement and find *injectivity* very restrictive. Defined symbols app and add are not injective. In the revised version of [20], the requirement of injectivity is omitted.

4. Our notion of *increasing* function is a generalization of the corresponding notion in [20]. Our notion only needs that $|t| \geq |t_i|$ for each $i \in [1, n]$ when $\mathcal{B} \models f(t_1, \ldots, t_n) = t$. While the notion in [20] needs that $|t| \geq |t_1| + \cdots + |t_n|$ when $\mathcal{B} \models f(t_1, \ldots, t_n) = t$. For this reason, defined symbols add and append given in the previous sections are not increasing in the sense of [20].

None of the above programs reverse, multiplication, quick-sort and merge can be certified as polynomial-time learnable by the results of [20]. Programs reverse, multiplication and quick-sort cannot be certified as the defined symbols append and add are not increasing in the sense of [20]. Program merge cannot be certified as there are nonvariable terms [X|Xs] and [Y|Ys] in the bodies of the two non-unit clauses. However, a slightly different program for reverse can be proved as polynomial-time learnable by the results of [20].

Example 13 The following program and background knowledge $\mathcal{B}$ about addlast are from [20].

$$\text{reverse}([\,],[\,]) \leftarrow$$
$$\text{reverse}([X|Xs],\text{addlast}(X,Ys)) \leftarrow \text{reverse}(Xs,Ys)$$

$\mathcal{B}$: $\text{addlast}(X,[\,]) \rightarrow [X]$
$\text{addlast}(X,[Y|Ys]) \rightarrow [Y|\text{addlast}(X,Ys)]$

This background knowledge is regular in the sense of [20] (as well as our sense) and the program is innermost-simple. Hence it is polynomial-time learnable. □

The function addlast is specialized version of app to append an element at the end of a given list. These two are equally efficient in this special case. Apparently, multiplication, quick-sort and merge cannot be certified as polynomial-time learnable by the results of [20] through modifications as in the case of reverse.

For the sake of completeness, we discuss an example which is beyond the scope of our results (as well as [12, 13, 20]). A program for merge-sort with a background knowledge about merge cannot be handled by our results, as the defined symbol merge does not have polynomial dependency property (unlike app). For any ground list L of length n there are 2^n pairs of ground lists satisfying $\mathcal{B} \models \text{merge}(L_1, L_2) = L$.

7 Conclusion

In this paper, we study incremental learning of logic programs. In this approach, logic programs defining the already known predicates are used as background knowledge in learning new predicates. We identify a class of polynomial-time learnable logic programs and present an algorithm for learning these programs. A comparison with the known results is provided and it is shown that our results generalize the existing results.

We first learn a functional logic program from a given sequence of examples using the already defined predicates as a background knowledge (a term rewrite system) and then transform it into a logic program using flattening [4]. The logic programs learned by the algorithm are some times very inefficient (the quick-sort program given above is an example) and some of the transformations known in the logic programming literature may be used in deriving efficient programs from them.

References

1. G. Aguzzi and U. Modigliani (1993), *Proving termination of logic programs by transforming them into equivalent term rewriting systems*, Proc. of FST&TCS'93, LNCS 761, pp. 114-124.

2. S. Arikawa, S. Miyano, A. Shinohara, T. Shinohara and A. Yamamoto (1992), *Algorithmic learning theory and elementary formal systems*, IEICE Trans. Inf. & Sys. E75-D, pp. 405-414.

3. A. Blumer, A. Ehrenfeucht, D. Haussler and M.K. Warmuth (1989), *Learnability and Vapnik-Chervonenkis dimension*, JACM 36, pp. 929-965.

4. P.G. Bosco, E. Giovannetti and C. Moiso (1988), *Narrowing vs. SLD-resolution*, Theoretical Computer Science 59, pp. 3-23.

5. S. Dzeroski, S. Muggleton and S. Russel (1992), *PAC-learnability of determinate logic programs*, Proc. of COLT'92, pp. 128-135.

6. M. Hanus (1994), *The integration of functions into logic programming: a survey*, J. Logic Prog. **19/20**, pp. 583-628.

7. J.-M. Hullot (1980), *Canonical forms and unification*, Proc. of CADE'80, LNCS **87**, pp. 318-334.

8. K. Ito and A. Yamamoto (1992), *Polynomial-time MAT learning of multilinear logic programs*, Proc. of ALT'92, LNAI **743**, pp. 63-74.

9. M.R.K. Krishna Rao, D. Kapur and R.K. Shyamasundar (1991), *A Transformational methodology for proving termination of logic programs*, Proc. of CSL'91, LNCS **626**, pp. 213-226.

10. M.R.K. Krishna Rao, D. Kapur and R.K. Shyamasundar (1993), *Proving termination of GHC programs*, Proc. of ICLP'93, pp. 720-736.

11. J. W. Lloyd (1987), *Foundations of Logic Programming*, Springer-Verlag.

12. S. Miyano, A. Shinohara and T. Shinohara (1991), *Which classes of elementary formal systems are polynomial-time learnable?*, Proc. of ALT'91, pp. 139-150.

13. S. Miyano, A. Shinohara and T. Shinohara (1993), *Learning elementary formal systems and an application to discovering motifs in proteins*, Tech. Rep. RIFIS-TR-CS-37, RIFIS, Kyushu University.

14. S. Muggleton and L. De Raedt (1994), *Inductive logic programming: theory and methods*, J. Logic Prog. **19/20**, pp. 629-679.

15. B.K. Natarajan (1991), *Machine Learning: A Theoretical Approach*, Morgan-Kaufmann.

16. Y. Sakakibara (1990), *Inductive inference of logic programs based on algebraic semantics*, New Gen. Comp. **7**, pp. 365-380.

17. E. Shapiro (1981), *Inductive inference of theories from facts*, Tech. Rep., Yale Univ.

18. E. Shapiro (1983), *Algorithmic Program Debugging*, MIT Press.

19. R.K. Shyamasundar, M.R.K. Krishna Rao and D. Kapur (1992), *Rewriting concepts in the study of termination of logic Programs*, Proc. of ALPUK'92 conf. (edited by K. Broda), Workshops in Computing series, pp. 3-20, Springer-Verlag.

20. A. Yamamoto (1993), *Generalized unification as background knowledge in learning logic programs*, Proc. of ALT'93, LNAI **744**, pp. 111-122. Revised version appears as *Learning logic programs using definite equality theories as background knowledge*, IEICE Trans. Inf. & Syst. **E78-D**, May 1995, pp. 539-544.

Learning Orthogonal F-Horn Formulas

Akira Miyashiro[1], Eiji Takimoto[2], Yoshifumi Sakai[3] and Akira Maruoka[2]

[1] Second Department of Energy Research, Hitachi Research Laboratory, Hitachi, Ltd.
7-1-1 Omika-Cho, Hitachi, Ibaraki, 319-12, Japan
miyasiro@hrl.hitachi.co.jp
[2] Graduate School of Information Sciences, Tohoku University
Sendai, 980-77, Japan
{t2, maruoka}@ecei.tohoku.ac.jp
[3] Department of Information and Computer Sciences, Faculty of Engineering, Toyo
University
2100, Kujirai, Kawagoe, 350, Japan
sakai@csgwy.cs.toyo.ac.jp

Abstract. In the PAC-learning, or the query learning model, it has been an important open problem to decide whether the class of DNF and CNF formulas is learnable. Recently, it was pointed out that the problem of PAC-learning for these classes with membership queries can be reduced to that of query learning for the class of k-quasi Horn formulas with membership and equivalence queries. A k-quasi Horn formula is a CNF formula with each clause containing at most k unnegated literals. In this paper, notions of F-Horn formulas and l-F-Horn formulas, which are extensions of k-quasi formulas, are introduced, and it is shown that the problem of PAC-learning for DNF and CNF formulas with membership queries can be reduced to that of query learning for l-F-Horn formulas with membership and equivalence queries for an appropriate choice of F. It is shown that under some condition, the class of orthogonal F-Horn formulas is learnable with membership, equivalence and subset queries. Moreover, it is shown that under some condition the class of orthogonal l-F-Horn formulas is learnable with membership and equivalence queries.

1 Introduction

One of the central issues of the computational learning theory is to determine, among various interesting classes of functions, which class is learnable and which is not. Especially, the DNF and CNF formulas are considered to be one of the most important classes to be investigated because they are natural and universal to describe Boolean concepts. Although much effort has been devoted to decide whether the DNF and CNF formulas are learnable, the problem for various cases is not yet solved. More precisely, the various learning problems, such as the problem of deciding whether DNF and CNF formulas are PAC learnable (i.e., learnable by randomly drawn examples), that of deciding whether they are PAC learnable using membership queries, and that of deciding whether they are exactly learnable using membership and equivalence queries, are all left open.

On the other hand, some restricted classes of DNF(CNF) formulas were shown to be learnable. For examples, k-DNF formulas (DNF formulas with each term containing at most k literals) are PAC learnable and also exactly learnable using equivalence queries[Val85]. Monotone k-DNF formulas are exactly learnable using membership queries. Monotone DNF formulas[Ang88][Val84], log-term-DNF formulas (DNF formulas with at most $O(\log n)$ terms where n is the number of variables)[BR92], Horn formulas (CNF formulas with each clause containing at most one unnegated literal)[AFP92], CDNF formulas(DNF formulas that can be represented by CNF formulas with sizes polynomially larger) [Bsh93] are all exactly learnable using membership and equivalence queries. (In the result on CDNF formulas, the hypotheses output by the learning algorithm are not necessarily DNF formulas). Moreover, a simple argument of reduction of learning shows that the dual classes of the classes mentioned above such as k-CNF formulas, monotone CNF formulas, etc. are also learnable. Furthermore, since an equivalence query can be simulated by some appropriate number of randomly drawn examples[Ang88], those classes that are exactly learnable using membership and equivalence queries are also PAC learnable using membership queries.

Kearns, Li, Pitt and Valiant introduced a methodology about the reduction of learning called the substitution argument, and showed that if monotone DNF formulas are PAC learnable, then DNF formulas are also PAC learnable [KLPV87]. The result was epoch-making because this implies that the learning problems for the (unrestricted) DNF formulas can be reduced to the learning problems for some restricted DNF formulas. Pitt and Warmuth developed the methodology and established the notion of prediction preserving reductions[PW90]. Using the methodology of prediction preserving reductions, Angluin, Frazier and Pitt showed that if k-quasi Horn formulas (CNF formulas with each clause containing at most k unnegated literals) are exactly learnable using membership and equivalence queries, then DNF formulas are PAC learnable using membership queries[AFP92]. Angluin and Kharitonov used the methodology to show that under some conditions, if DNF formulas are PAC learnable using membership queries, then DNF formulas are PAC learnable without membership queries[AK91]. These results suggest the significance of exploring the learnability of k-quasi Horn formulas.

In this paper, extending the notion of k-quasi Horn formulas, we introduce a notion of F-Horn formulas and investigate the learnability of this class. Let F be a class of formulas. Then, an F-Horn clause is a disjunction of some negated literals and at most one formula in F. For examples, if $f \in F$, then $(x_1 \vee x_3 \vee x_4 \vee f)$ is an F-Horn clause. Here, the set $\{x_1, x_3, x_4\}$ is referred to as the body of this F-Horn clause. An F-Horn formula is a conjunction of F-Horn clauses with distinct bodies. Note that if F is the class of (monotone) k-CNF formulas, then F-Horn formulas turns out to be identical to the class of k-quasi Horn formulas. We call an F-Horn formula with no body containing others an orthogonal F-Horn formula. We show that, under some condition on class F, orthogonal F-Horn formulas are exactly learnable using membership, equivalence and subset queries, and from this result we show that orthogonal k-quasi Horn formulas are exactly learnable using equivalence and subset queries. Moreover, we introduce a notion of l-F-Horn formulas. An l-F-Horn formula is an F-Horn formula with at most l clauses containing an element of F (and other clauses consisting of only negative literals). Although the class of l-F-Horn formulas seems too restricted to be investigated, the class is very important because the reduction by [AFP92] mentioned above can be restated in terms of l F-

Horn formulas as follows: If F is taken to be the class of monotone k-CNF formulas, then the PAC learning with membership queries problem for DNF formulas can be reduced to the exact learning with membership and equivalence queries problem for l-F-Horn formulas. In this paper, we show that, under some condition (which is satisfied when F is the class of monotone k-CNF formulas), orthogonal l-F-Horn formulas is exactly learnable using membership and equivalence queries.

In Section 2, we give the framework of exact learning with queries, and in Section 3, we give the definition of F-Horn formulas and show that if l-F-Horn formulas with F being the class of monotone k-CNF formulas are exactly learnable using membership and equivalence queries, then CNF formulas (and thus DNF formulas by duality) are PAC learnable using membership queries. In Section 4, we give a learning algorithm for orthogonal F-Horn formulas using membership, equivalence and subset queries, and give the correctness of the algorithm in Section 5. In Section 6, we give a learning algorithm for orthogonal l-F-Horn formulas using membership and equivalence queries. Finally in Section 7, we relate our results to the PAC learning problem for DNF and CNF formulas with membership queries.

2 Learning Model

Let F be a class of formulas and function $size_F$ from F to the natural numbers be associated with F. For $f \in F$, $size_F(f)$ is regarded as the complexity of f and we call it the size of f. Usually, the size of a formula f is defined to be the length (or something polynomially equivalent) of the description of f. In what follows, we sometimes omit the subscript F and simply denote $size(f)$ unless confusion arises. For natural numbers n and s, $F_{n,s}$ denotes the set of formulas in F with domain being $\{0,1\}^n$ and size at most s. That is,

$$F_{n,s} = \left\{ f \in F \mid f : \{0,1\}^n \to \{0,1\}, size(f) \leq s \right\}.$$

Clearly, $F = \bigcup_{n \geq 1} \bigcup_{s \geq 1} F_{n,s}$ holds.

In the query learning model, a teacher of the learning algorithm is assumed to exist and give partial information about a formula f to be learned when a query is arisen from the algorithm. Invoking the teacher many times, the learning algorithm outputs a formula h in F that would be equivalent to f. Here, the formula f to be learned and the formula h output by the algorithm are called the target formula and the hypothesis, respectively. More precisely, the set of queries available to the learning algorithm is specified in advance, and for each query a device called an oracle is attached to the algorithm that, when invoked, replies an answer of the query to the algorithm. Therefore, the learnability of F strongly depends on the set of queries available. Many kinds of queries have been proposed, and those considered to be reasonable and often used are membership queries(MQ), equivalence queries(EQ), subset queries(SubQ), superset queries(SupQ), and so on. In what follows, we identify a query with an oracle that accepts the query.

In the following, let the target formula be $f \in F_{n,s}$. A vector $\mathbf{v}$ such that $f(\mathbf{v}) = 1$ ($f(\mathbf{v}) = 0$) is called a positive (negative, resp.) example of f.

A membership query MQ, when invoked with a vector $\mathbf{v} \in \{0,1\}^n$ as its argument, returns the value $f(\mathbf{v})$. An equivalence query EQ, when invoked with a formula

$h \in F$ as its argument, returns "yes" if h is equivalent to f, and a counter example **v** (i.e., **v** such that $f(\mathbf{v}) \neq h(\mathbf{v})$) otherwise. A subset query SubQ, when invoked with a formula $h \in F$ as its argument, returns "yes" if h implies f (i.e., $h^{-1}(1) \subseteq f^{-1}(1)$), and a counter example **v** (i.e., **v** such that $f(\mathbf{v}) = 0$ and $h(\mathbf{v}) = 1$) otherwise. A superset query SupQ, when invoked with a formula $h \in F$ as its argument, returns "yes" if f implies h (i.e., $h^{-1}(1) \supseteq f^{-1}(1)$), and a counter example **v** (i.e., **v** such that $f(\mathbf{v}) = 1$ and $h(\mathbf{v}) = 0$) otherwise.

Now we give the definition of the learnability of a class of formulas. In the definition below, we take into account the time spent by the learning algorithm. An oracle, when invoked, is assumed to return a value in one unit time.

Definition 1. A class of formulas F is exactly learnable using queries $Q_1, \ldots, Q_k$ if there exists a learning algorithm A with oracles $Q_1, \ldots, Q_k$ for F such that for any $n, s \geq 1$ and any target formula $f \in F_{n,s}$, A halts in time polynomial in n and s, and outputs a formula $h \in F$ that is equivalent to f.

In the above definition, note that the hypothesis output by the learning algorithm must be in the target class F, and note that the queries EQ, SubQ and SupQ are so defined that the arguments of them are also restricted to formulas in F. Removing these restrictions from learning algorithms, we have the weaker notion of exact learning, which we call "non-proper" exact learning.

3 F-Horn formulas

In this section, we give the definitions of F-Horn formulas and l-F-Horn formulas.

A literal is a variable x_i or its negation $\bar{x}_i$. Especially, a variable x_i is called a positive literal and a negation $\bar{x}_i$ a negative literal. A Horn clause is a disjunction of negative literals and at most one positive literals. For example, $(x_1 \vee \bar{x}_3 \vee \bar{x}_5 \vee x_2)$ is a Horn clause. Note that the clause is equivalent to $(x_1 x_3 x_5 \Rightarrow x_2)$, where $\Rightarrow$ denotes the implicative operation, i.e., $(a \Rightarrow b) \equiv (\bar{a} \vee b)$. Therefore, Horn clauses correspond to those used in logic programs such as Prolog. A Horn formula is a conjunction of a finite number of Horn clauses. Clearly, the class of Horn formulas is a subclass of the class of CNF formulas.

Angluin, Frazier and Pitt showed that Horn formulas are exactly learnable using membership and equivalence queries[AFP92]. This result shows a new approach to learning of DNF formulas, as well as the fact that some class of logic programs is learnable. Taking duals of Horn formulas, we have the class of DNF formulas with each term containing at most one negative literal, which is the first subclass of DNF formulas shown to be learnable that properly contains monotone DNF formulas. Furthermore, as stated in the introduction, Horn formulas are important when considering PAC learning problem of (unrestricted) DNF formulas with membership queries. Using the methodology of prediction preserving reductions, [AFP92] showed that if k-quasi Horn formulas (with $k \geq 2$ being a constant) are exactly learnable using membership and equivalence queries, then DNF and CNF formulas are PAC learnable using membership queries. Here, a k-quasi Horn formula is a CNF formula with each clause containing at most k positive literals. Clearly, since by definition

1-quasi Horn formulas are Horn formulas, they are exactly learnable using membership and equivalence queries, and thus they are PAC learnable using membership
queries. Therefore, if unrestricted DNF formulas are not PAC learnable using membership queries, then there would be a large computational gap between the problem
of learning 1-quasi Horn formulas and that of learning k-quasi Horn formulas with
$k \geq 2$. Below we briefly review the reduction shown by [AFP92] from learning CNF
formulas to learning k-quasi Horn formulas. Let the target formula be a CNF formula f over n variables. Replacing each x_i occurring in f with $\bar{x}_{n+i}$, we have a CNF
formula consisting of only negative literals. Let $\tilde{f}$ be the conjunction of the CNF for-
mula obtained and the special clauses $(x_1 + x_{n+1})(\bar{x}_1 + \bar{x}_{n+1}) \cdots (x_n + x_{2n})(\bar{x}_n + \bar{x}_{2n})$.
Clearly $\tilde{f}$ is a 2-quasi Horn formula over $2n$ variables. For example, if

$$f = (x_1 + \bar{x}_2 + x_3)(\bar{x}_1 + x_2),$$

then

$$\tilde{f} = (x_4 + \bar{x}_2 + \bar{x}_6)(\bar{x}_1 + \bar{x}_5)(x_1 + x_4)(\bar{x}_1 + \dot{x}_4)(x_2 + x_5)(\bar{x}_2 + \bar{x}_5)(x_3 + x_6)(\bar{x}_3 + \bar{x}_6).$$

For a vector $\mathbf{w} \in \{0,1\}^{2n}$, let the vectors consisting of the first and the last n bits of
$\mathbf{w}$ be denoted by $\mathbf{w}_1$ and $\mathbf{w}_2$, respectively. It is easily seen that for any $\mathbf{w} \in \{0,1\}^{2n}$,
$\tilde{f}(\mathbf{w}) = f(\mathbf{w}_1)$ if $\mathbf{w}_2 = \bar{\mathbf{w}}_1$ and $\tilde{f}(\mathbf{w}) = 0$ otherwise. Here, $\bar{\mathbf{w}}_1$ denotes the vector
obtained by taking bitwise complement of $\mathbf{w}_1$. From this fact, we can construct the
membership query $\mathrm{MQ}_{\tilde{f}}$ and the equivalence query $\mathrm{EQ}_{\tilde{f}}$ for $\tilde{f}$ from the membership
query MQ_f and random examples for f as follows. $\mathrm{MQ}_{\tilde{f}}$, when invoked with $\mathbf{w} \in$
$\{0,1\}^{2n}$, returns 0 if $\mathbf{w}_2 \neq \bar{\mathbf{w}}_1$, and $f(\mathbf{w}_1)$ otherwise. $\mathrm{EQ}_{\tilde{f}}$, when invoked with h,
returns "yes" if $h(\mathbf{v}\bar{\mathbf{v}}) = a$ for sufficiently many random examples $(\mathbf{v}, a)$ of f, and
otherwise returns $\mathbf{v}\bar{\mathbf{v}}$ such that $h(\mathbf{v}\bar{\mathbf{v}}) \neq a$, where $\mathbf{v}\bar{\mathbf{v}}$ denotes the concatenation of $\mathbf{v}$
and $\bar{\mathbf{v}}$. Then, using the argument of prediction preserving reductions, we can show
that if 2-quasi Horn formulas is exactly learnable using membership and equivalence
queries, then CNF formulas (and hence, DNF formulas by duality) are PAC-learnable
using membership queries.

In this paper, extending the notion of Horn formulas, we introduce notions of
F-Horn formulas and l-F-Horn formulas.

Let F be a class of formulas. An F-Horn clause is a disjunction of some negative
literals and at most one formula in F. For example, for $f \in F$, $(\bar{x}_1 \vee \bar{x}_3 \vee \bar{x}_4 \vee f)$ is
an F-Horn clause.

Definition 2. Let C be an F-Horn clause. Let $neg(C)$ denote the set of indices i
of variables x_i occurring as a negative literal in C. Let $cons(C)$ denote a formula
in F occurring in C. Note that for any F-Horn clause C, C is represented by $C =$
$\bigvee_{j \in neg(C)} \bar{x}_j \vee cons(C)$.

Definition 3. An F-Horn formula is a conjunction of a finite number of F-Horn
clauses C with distinct index sets $neg(C)$. Let the size of an F-Horn formula f be
the sum of $size_F(f_i)$ for all $f_i \in F$ occurring in f plus the number of Horn clauses
m of f.

Although an F-Horn formula f is restricted so that the index sets $neg(C)$ are
different from each other, the class of F-Horn formulas can contain Horn formulas.

This is because using the fact $(A + B)(A + C) = A + BC$ we can rewrite a Horn formula as an F-Horn formula with F being the class of monotone monomials. Similarly, k-quasi Horn formulas can be rewritten as F-Horn formulas with F being the class of monotone k-CNF formulas.

Restricting the number of occurrences of formulas in F, we have the notion of l-F-Horn formulas.

Definition 4. An l-F-Horn formula is an F-Horn formula with at most l clauses containing a formula in F (and other clauses consisting of only negative literals).

Although the class of l-F-Horn formulas seems unnaturally restricted, it is an important class to be investigated because the formula reduced from a CNF formula shown above is just an 1-F-Horn formula with F being the class of monotone 2-CNF formulas. Thus, we have the following theorem.

Theorem 5. Let $l \geq 1$ and $k \geq 2$ be constants and F be the class of monotone k-CNF formulas. Then, if l-F-Horn formulas are exactly learnable using membership and equivalence queries, then DNF and CNF formulas are PAC learnable using membership queries.

We introduce a notion of orthogonality for F-Horn formulas so that orthogonal F-Horn formulas and orthogonal l-F-Horn formulas are learnable as seen in the subsequent sections.

Definition 6. An F-Horn formula $f = C_1 \wedge \cdots \wedge C_m$ is said to be orthogonal if for any i and j such that $1 \leq i \neq j \leq m$, $neg(C_i) \not\subseteq neg(C_j)$.

Note that the dual of a monotone DNF formula is an orthogonal F-Horn formula (with each clause containing no formula in F). So, the dual class of monotone DNF formulas is properly contained in the class of orthogonal F-Horn formulas for appropriate choice of F. Therefore, the fact that orthogonal F-Horn formulas are learnable implies that a class larger than monotone DNF formulas are learnable.

4 Learning orthogonal F-Horn formulas

A class of formulas F is learnable with one-sided error if F is still learnable under the condition where equivalence queries are restricted to accepting only formulas h with one-sided error, i.e., $h^{-1}(1) \subseteq f^{-1}(1)$ for any target formula f. Note that for any hypothesis h with one-sided error, the counter example returned by the equivalence query is always positive.

Now, we give one of the main theorems of this paper.

Theorem 7. Let a class of monotone formulas F be exactly learnable using equivalence queries with one-sided error. Then, orthogonal F-Horn formulas are exactly learnable using membership, equivalence and subset queries.

Let f be a target formula. Clearly, for any vector $\mathbf{v} = (v_1, \ldots, v_n) \in \{0, 1\}^n$, $f(\mathbf{v}) = 1$ if and only if the monomial $\bigwedge_{j : v_j = 0} \bar{x}_j \wedge \bigwedge_{j : v_j = 1} x_j$ is contained in f. This implies that the value of $f(\mathbf{v})$ can be obtained without membership queries by invoking a subset query with this monomial. However, if the monomial cannot be represented by an F-Horn formula, we cannot use a subset query with the monomial as its argument by definition. (Recall that if we permit the usage of that kind of queries, then we only say that the class are "non-properly" learnable using equivalence and subset queries.)

Of course, if monomials are contained in the target class, then we do not need membership queries. Furthermore, if monotone monomials are contained in F, then we can show that a membership query can be simulated by a subset query in a similar way. For vector $\mathbf{v}$, we define a formula $h_\mathbf{v}$ as follows:

$$h_\mathbf{v} = \bigwedge_{j : v_j = 1} (\bar{x}_j \vee m_\mathbf{v}) \wedge \bigwedge_{j : v_j = 0} \bar{x}_j,$$

where $m_\mathbf{v}$ is the monotone monomial $\bigwedge_{j : v_j = 1} x_j$. Clearly, the vectors satisfying $h_\mathbf{v}$ are $\mathbf{v}$ and $\mathbf{0}$. That is, $h_\mathbf{v}^{-1}(x) = \{\mathbf{v}, \mathbf{0}\}$. Since $m_\mathbf{v} \in F$ by assumption, $h_\mathbf{v}$ is an orthogonal F-Horn formula. So, we can use a subset query with $h_\mathbf{v}$ as its argument. Without loss of generality, we can assume that $f(\mathbf{0}) = 1$ because otherwise f consists of only one clause C such that $C = f$ (i.e., $neg(C) = \phi$ and $cons(C) = f$), and hence f is exactly learnable using only equivalence queries by assumption. Thus, we can assume that $f(\mathbf{0}) = 1$. Then, a subset query with $h_\mathbf{v}$ returns "yes" if and only if $f(\mathbf{v}) = 1$.

Since the class of monotone k-CNF formulas contains monotone monomials and is exactly learnable using equivalence queries with one-sided error[Val84], we have the following corollary.

Corollary 8. Orthogonal k-quasi Horn formulas are exactly learnable using subset and equivalence queries.

We prove Theorem 7 by giving a learning algorithm $A_{F\text{-Horn}}$ for orthogonal F-Horn formulas. We give the learning algorithm $A_{F\text{-Horn}}$ in this section and the correctness of the algorithm in the next section. First we give the outline of the algorithm.

Let the learning algorithm that exactly learns F using equivalence queries with one-sided error be denoted by A_F. Without loss of generality, we assume the first hypothesis with which A_F invokes the equivalence query to be FALSE (the formula taking value 0 identically). Let the target formula be $f = C_1 \wedge \cdots \wedge C_m$, where C_i is an F-Horn clause. In order to learn $cons(C_i)$'s, algorithm $A_{F\text{-Horn}}$ runs A_F's independently for each $1 \leq i \leq m$. For notational convenience, these executions of A_F's are referred to as $A_{F,1}, \ldots, A_{F,m}$.

For $\mathbf{v} = (v_1, \ldots, v_n) \in \{0, 1\}^n$ and $1 \leq j \leq n$, let $\mathbf{v}^{(j)}$ denote the vector obtained by replacing the j-th component of $\mathbf{v}$ by 0. Let $true(\mathbf{v})$ be the set of indices of the components of $\mathbf{v}$ taking value 1. That is, $\mathbf{v}^{(j)} = (v_1, \ldots, v_{j-1}, 0, v_{j+1}, \ldots, v_n)$ and $true(\mathbf{v}) = \{j | v_j = 1, 1 \leq j \leq n\}$.

Algorithm $A_{F\text{-Horn}}$ consists of two phases, each computing the ingredients of the clauses of the target formula: One computing the negative literal sets, denoted

begin
    $h :=$ TRUE;
    {Phase 1}
    until $\mathrm{SubQ}(h) =$ "yes" **do**
        begin
            $\mathbf{v} := \mathrm{SubQ}(h)$;
            {minimize $\mathbf{v}$}
            for n **times do**
                forall $j \in true(\mathbf{v})$ **do**
                    if $\mathrm{MQ}(\mathbf{v}^{(j)}) = 0$ **then**
                        $\mathbf{v} := \mathbf{v}^{(j)}$;
            $h := h \wedge (\bigvee_{j \in true(\mathbf{v})} \bar{x}_j)$;
        end
    {Let the hypothesis at this point be $h = N_1 \wedge \cdots \wedge N_m$.}
    {Phase 2}
    for $i := 1$ **to** m **do**
        $h_i := A_{F,i}()$;
    $h := (N_1 \vee h_1) \wedge \cdots \wedge (N_m \vee h_m)$;
    until $\mathrm{EQ}(h) =$ "yes" **do**
        begin
            $\mathbf{v} := \mathrm{EQ}(h)$;
            forall i **such that** $(N_i \vee h_i)(\mathbf{v}) = 0$ **do**
                $h_i := A_{F,i}(\mathbf{v})$;
            $h := (N_1 \vee h_1) \wedge \cdots \wedge (N_m \vee h_m)$;
        end
    output h;
end.

Fig. 1. Algorithm $A_{F\text{-Horn}}$

N_i's, using only negative counter examples (Phase 1), and the other computing the monotone formulas, denoted f_i's, using only positive counter examples (Phase 2).

In Phase 1, putting the initial hypothesis h to be TRUE (the formula taking value 1 identically), algorithm $A_{F\text{-Horn}}$ repeats the following procedure. Let the hypothesis obtained at the beginning of the k-th iteration of the procedure be denoted by $h = N_1 \wedge \cdots \wedge N_{k-1}$. (Note that $h =$ TRUE for $k = 1$.) First invoke the subset query SubQ with h as its argument. If $\mathrm{SubQ}(h)$ returns "yes", then terminate Phase 1 and proceed to Phase 2. Otherwise, receive the counter example $\mathbf{v}$ from $\mathrm{SubQ}(h)$ and obtain a negative vector $\mathbf{v}'$ using membership queries so that $true(\mathbf{v}')$ is a minimal subset of $true(\mathbf{v})$. Then, let the k-th clause be $N_k := \bigvee_{j \in true(\mathbf{v}')} \bar{x}_j$ and modify the hypothesis by $h := h \wedge N_k$.

Note that at the end of Phase 1, the algorithm has $h = N_1 \wedge \cdots \wedge N_m$ as the current hypothesis, where each clause N_i consists of only negative literals.

In Phase 2, run $A_{F,i}$ for $1 \leq i \leq m$ independently and suspend the executions when $A_{F,i}$'s invoke equivalence queries with some hypotheses h_i's. (Actually, the h_i's are all FALSE because the initial hypothesis of A_F is assumed to be FALSE.) Then, repeat the following procedure with $h = (N_1 \vee h_1) \wedge \cdots \wedge (N_m \vee h_m)$. First invoke the equivalence query with h as its argument. If EQ(h) returns "yes", then output h as the final hypothesis and halt. Otherwise, receive the counter example $\mathbf{v}$ from EQ(h) and for all $1 \leq i \leq m$ such that the i-th clause $(N_i \vee h_i)$ is not satisfied with $\mathbf{v}$, feed $\mathbf{v}$ to $A_{F,i}$ as a counter example of h_i and continue the execution of $A_{F,i}$ until it invokes the equivalence query with some hypothesis h_i, and suspend it again. Then, modify the i-th clause by $(N_i \vee h_i)$.

The detailed algorithm $A_{F\text{-Horn}}$ is shown in Figure 1. For notational convenience, let the hypothesis h_i with which $A_{F,i}$, when given $\mathbf{v}$, invokes the equivalence query be denoted by $A_{F,i}(\mathbf{v})$. Also, let the initial hypothesis of $A_{F,i}$ be denoted by $A_{F,i}()$.

5   The correctness of $A_{F\text{-Horn}}$

In this section, we prove that algorithm $A_{F\text{-Horn}}$ exactly learns orthogonal F-Horn formulas by showing two lemmas. In what follows, fix the target formula to be $f = C_1 \wedge \cdots \wedge C_m$, and let N_i denote $\bigvee_{j \in neg(C_i)} \bar{x}_j$ and let f_i denote $cons(C_i)$ for $1 \leq i \leq m$. Note that $C_i = N_i \vee f_i$.

Lemma 9. In Phase 1, invoking SubQ m times and MQ at most nm times, $A_{F\text{-Horn}}$ obtains $h = N_1 \wedge \cdots \wedge N_m$.

Proof. We show the lemma by an induction on the number of the iterations of **until** statement (i.e., the number of invoking SubQ). We may assume that the hypothesis obtained at the beginning of the k-th iteration is $h = N_1 \wedge \cdots \wedge N_{k-1}$. Now we show in the k-th iteration a new clause $N \in \{N_k, \ldots, N_m\}$ is obtained.

First we show that h is not contained in f. Note that the target formula is represented as $f = (N_1 \vee f_1) \wedge \cdots \wedge (N_m \vee f_m)$. Choose $N_j \in \{N_k, \ldots, N_m\}$ arbitrarily, and let $\mathbf{u}$ be the vector such that $true(\mathbf{u}) = neg(N_j)$. Clearly $\mathbf{u}$ is a minimal vector among $\mathbf{v}$'s such that $N_j(\mathbf{v}) = 0$. So, we may assume that $f_j(\mathbf{u}) = 0$, and hence $f(\mathbf{u}) = 0$ because otherwise $N_j \vee f_j$ would take value 1 identically by the monotonicity of f_j. On the other hand, we have $h(\mathbf{u}) = 1$ by the orthogonality of $\{N_1, \ldots, N_m\}$. This implies $h^{-1}(1) \not\subseteq f^{-1}(1)$. Therefore, SubQ($h$) returns a negative counter example $\mathbf{v}$. That is, $f(\mathbf{v}) = 0$ and $h(\mathbf{v}) = 1$. Let the $\mathbf{v}$ be denoted by $\mathbf{v}_0$.

In the procedure of minimizing $\mathbf{v}$, let $\mathbf{v}_i$ denote the vector $\mathbf{v}$ obtained at the end of the i-th iteration of **for** statement ($1 \leq i \leq n$). Now suppose inductively that $\mathbf{v}_{i-1}$ is a negative counter example, i.e., $f(\mathbf{v}_{i-1}) = 0$ and $h(\mathbf{v}_{i-1}) = 1$. (This holds for $i = 1$.) This implies that there exists a clause $C \in \{C_k, \ldots, C_m\}$ such that $C(\mathbf{v}_{i-1}) = 0$, i.e., $neg(C) \subseteq true(\mathbf{v}_{i-1})$) and $cons(C)(\mathbf{v}_{i-1}) = 0$. Assume that $neg(C) \neq true(\mathbf{v}_{i-1})$, that is, there exists a $j \in true(\mathbf{v}_{i-1}) - neg(C)$. Then, since $cons(C)$ is a monotone formula, $\mathbf{v}_{i-1}^{(j)}$ does not satisfy C, that is, $\mathbf{v}_{i-1}^{(j)}$ remains a negative example. This implies that at the i-th iteration of **for** statement, $\mathbf{v}$ is replaced by $\mathbf{v}^{(j)}$, i.e., $\mathbf{v}_i = \mathbf{v}_{i-1}^{(j)}$ for some j. Moreover, since $h(\mathbf{v}_{i-1}) = 1$ and h consists of only negative literals, $h(\mathbf{v}_i) = 1$ holds as well. From these facts, we can see that $\mathbf{v}_i$ remains a negative counter example and $true(\mathbf{v}_i) \subsetneq true(\mathbf{v}_{i-1})$ holds.

Thus, the sequence $\mathbf{v}_1, \mathbf{v}_2, \ldots$ converges to some $\mathbf{v}$ such that $neg(C) = true(\mathbf{v})$ for some $C \in \{C_k, \ldots, C_m\}$. Therefore, a new clause $N = \bigvee_{j \in true(\mathbf{v})} x_j = \bigvee_{j \in neg(C)} x_j$ is found in $\{N_k, \ldots, N_m\}$. It is easily seen that for each iteration, SupQ is invoked just once and MQ is invoked at most n times.

Since A_{F_i} exactly learns F using equivalence queries, there exists a polynomial p such that for any $f_i \in F_{n,s_i}$, A_{F_i} halts after at most $p(n, s_i)$ equivalence queries are invoked.

Lemma 10. In Phase 2, $A_{F\text{-Horn}}$ calls A_{F_i} at most $p(n, size_F(f_i))$ times for any $1 \le i \le m$.

Proof. It suffices to show that when an equivalence query is arisen from some A_{F_i}, $A_{F\text{-Horn}}$ correctly feeds a counter example for f_i to A_{F_i}. We show this by an induction on the number t of the iterations of **until** statement.

Before the iterations starts, since each h_i is the initial hypothesis of A_{F_i}, we can say that A_{F_i} is on the execution of learning of f_i as its target formula. Note that since $h_i = \text{FALSE}$ is contained in f_i, h is also contained in f.

Assume at the beginning of the t-th iteration that h is contained in f and for any $1 \le i \le m$, A_{F_i} is on the execution of learning of f_i as its target formula. Clearly, this holds for $t = 1$. The hypothesis h can be represented as $h = (N_1 \vee h_1) \wedge \cdots \wedge (N_m \vee h_m)$. Since h is contained in f, $EQ(h)$ always returns a positive counter example $\mathbf{v}$. So, there exists an i such that $(N_i \vee h_i)(\mathbf{v}) = 0$ and $(N_i \vee f_i)(\mathbf{v}) = 1$, which implies $h_i(\mathbf{v}) = 0$ and $f_i(\mathbf{v}) = 1$. This implies that $\mathbf{v}$ is a counter example of h_i for the target formula f_i. Thus, A_{F_i}, when given $\mathbf{v}$, continues the execution of learning of f_i and modifies the h_i, which is contained in f_i because A_{F_i} learns F with one-sided error.

By the above two lemmas, we can easily see that algorithm $A_{F\text{-Horn}}$ halts in time polynomial in n and the size of f $(m + \sum_{i=1}^{m} size_F(f_i))$ and outputs a formula that is equivalent to f, completing the proof of Theorem 7.

6 Learning orthogonal l-F-Horn formulas

Inspecting Algorithm $A_{F\text{-Horn}}$ closely, we find in $A_{F\text{-Horn}}$ that two types of counter examples are separately used to construct a hypothesis, negative ones to find $neg(C_i)$ for some clause C_i not yet found, and positive ones to learn $cons(C_i)$ for some clause C_i already found. This causes us to form an idea to combine two phases into one so that the algorithm may appropriately choose which phase to go depending on the types of counter examples. More precisely, invoking the equivalence query with the current hypothesis $h = (N_1 \vee h_1) \wedge \cdots \wedge (N_t \vee h_t)$ and receiving a counter example $\mathbf{v}$, the algorithm executes the procedure of minimizing $\mathbf{v}$ to find a new N_{t+1} if $\mathbf{v}$ is negative, or executes A_{F_i} to modify h_i if $\mathbf{v}$ is positive. In fact, if $\mathbf{v}$ is a positive counter example, then the same argument as Lemma 10 holds and A_{F_i} proceeds on the right way of learning of f_i. Moreover, if $\mathbf{v}$ is a negative counter example satisfying $N_1, \ldots, N_t$, then the same argument as Lemma 9 also holds and a new N_{t+1} is found. The only problem is that a negative counter example $\mathbf{v}$ is drawn

```
begin
    h := TRUE;
    until EQ(h) = "yes" do
        begin
            {Let the hypothesis of this point be h = (N₁ ∨ h₁) ∧ ··· ∧ (Nₜ ∨ hₜ). }
            v := EQ(h);
            if h(v) = 1 then        {a negative counter example }
                begin
                    I := {i|Nᵢ(v) = 0, 1 ≤ i ≤ t};
                    { Let I = {i₁,...,iₛ}. Note that s ≤ l. }
                    find j₁ ∈ neg(Nᵢ₁),...,jₛ ∈ neg(Nᵢₛ) such that
                        MQ(v^({j₁...jₛ})) = 0;
                    v := v^({j₁...jₛ});
                    for n times do
                        for j ∈ true(v) do
                            if MQ(v^(j)) = 0 then
                                v := v^(j);
                    N_{t+1} := ⋁_{j∈true(v)} x̄ⱼ;
                    h_{t+1} := A_{F,t+1}();
                    h := h ∧ (N_{t+1} ∨ h_{t+1});
                end
            else        {a positive counter example }
                begin
                    forall i such that (Nᵢ ∨ hᵢ)(v) = 0 do
                        hᵢ := A_{F,i}(v);
                    h := (N₁ ∨ h₁) ∧ ··· ∧ (Nₜ ∨ hₜ);
                end
            endif
        end
    output h;
end.
```

Fig. 2. A learning algorithm for orthogonal l-F-Horn formulas

such that $\mathbf{v}$ does not satisfy N_i for some $1 \leq i \leq t$. Note in this case that $\mathbf{v}$ satisfies h_i instead because $\mathbf{v}$ is positive for h. So, this can happen only for the clauses C with $cons(C)$ being not the identical formula FALSE, which are at most l if f is an l-F-Horn formula. Let I denote the set of indices i's such that $\mathbf{v}$ does not satisfy N_i, and let N denote a clause in $\{N_{t+1},\dots N_m\}$ such that $N(\mathbf{v}) = 0$. Note that $|I| \leq l$. Since h is an orthogonal F-Horn formula, there exists a $j_i \in neg(N_i) - neg(N)$, for any i in I. Therefore, letting J denote the set $\bigcup_{i \in I}\{j_i\}$, we have $\mathbf{v}^{(J)}$ that satisfies all $N_1, \dots, N_t$ and still does not satisfy f, where $\mathbf{v}^{(J)}$ denotes the vector obtained by replacing the j-th component of $\mathbf{v}$ by 0 for all $j \in J$. Then, the same argument of Lemma 9 follows. However, it may be hard to find the set J since $neg(N)$ is unknown. To overcome this difficulty, the algorithm simply enumerates all $J = \bigcup_{i \in I}\{j_i\}$ for all combinations of $j_i \in neg(N_i)$. Since the size of J is at most $|I| \leq l$, the enumeration completes in polynomial time when l is a constant. Thus, we have the following theorem.

Theorem 11. Let a class of monotone formulas F be exactly learnable using equivalence queries with one-sided error. Then, for any constant l, orthogonal l-F-Horn formulas are exactly learnable using membership and equivalence queries.

The detailed learning algorithm for orthogonal l-F-Horn formulas is given in Figure 2.

7 Concluding remarks

Although there has been a great deal of interest in developing PAC learning algorithms for the class of DNF and CNF formulas, nobody has succeeded to develop one for these classes even if the usage of membership queries are permitted. Recently, Jackson partially solved the problem by giving a PAC learning algorithm with membership queries for DNF formulas provided that the examples are drawn according to the uniform distribution[Jac94]. But, the hypotheses produced are not DNF formulas (.i.e., the algorithm non-properly learns DNF formulas) and it remains open whether DNF and CNF formulas are PAC learnable with membership queries in the distribution-free setting.

One of the hopeful strategies to attack the problem is to develop an exact learning algorithm for some subclass of DNF and CNF formulas instead, as pointed in [AFP92]. In this paper, we restated this reduction of learning in terms of l-F-Horn formulas as follows. Let F be the class of monotone k-CNF formulas for $k \geq 2$. Then, if l-F-Horn formulas are exactly learnable with membership and equivalence queries for some $l \geq 1$, then DNF and CNF formulas are PAC learnable with membership queries. Since the class of l-F-Horn formulas is very restricted subclass of CNF formulas, it seems easier to cope with this class, rather than to cope with CNF and DNF formulas themselves.

On the other hand, some researchers suspect that DNF and CNF formulas are not PAC learnable (even with membership queries). For example, Kharitonov used cryptographic assumptions to show that the class AC^0 is not PAC learnable with membership queries[Kha93]. While this result does not immediately apply to subclasses of AC^0 such as DNF formulas, it might provide a circumstantial evidence of the hardness of PAC learning of DNF formulas. If it is true, then our reduction result would imply that l-F-Horn formulas are also hard to learn with membership and equivalence queries.

In order to break the hardness, we introduced the notion of orthogonality and showed that orthogonal l-F-Horn formulas are exactly learnable with membership and equivalence queries (with F being monotone k-CNF formulas). Since the condition of orthogonality makes l-F-Horn formulas learnable, there would be a large computational gap between with and without the orthogonality for learning l-F-Horn formulas. Recall, however, that the l-F-Horn formula reduced from a CNF formula in Theorem 5 is *almost* orthogonal, i.e., all clauses except the clause $((x_1 + x_{n+1}) \cdots (x_n + x_{2n}))$ are orthogonal and have no formula in F. This special clause

C' is of the form $(0 + f)$ with f being a monotone 2-CNF formula. Note that $neg(C')$ is the empty set and contained in $neg(C_i)$ for any other clause C_i. (This is because the reduced l-F-Horn formula is not orthogonal.) Note also that the only formula f in F appeared in the reduced l-F-Horn formula is known and need not be inferred. Therefore, the only thing to do for learning DNF and CNF formulas is to infer the orthogonal clauses other than the special clause of the reduced l-F-Horn formula. This implies that the computational gap would lie between with and without the special clause, rather than with and without the orthogonality.

References

[AFP92] Dana Anguin, Michael Frazier, and Leonard Pitt. Learning conjunctions of Horn clauses. *Machine Learning*, 9:147–164, 1992.

[AK91] Dana Anguin and Michael Kharitonov. When won't membership queries help? In *Proceedings of the 23rd Annual ACM Symposium on Theory of Computing*, pages 444–454. Association for Computing Machinery, 1991.

[Ang88] Dana Anguin. Queries and concept learning. *Machine Learning*, 2:319–342, 1988.

[BR92] Avrim Blum and Steven Rudich. Fast learning of k-term DNF formulas with queries. In *Proceedings of the 24th Annual ACM Symposium on Theory of Computing*, pages 382–389. Association for Computing Machinery, 1992.

[Bsh93] Nader H. Bshouty. Exact learning via the monotone theory. In *Proceedings of the 34th Annual IEEE Symposium on Foundations of Computer Science*, pages 302–311. IEEE, 1993.

[Jac94] Jeffrey Jackson. An efficient membership-query algorithm for learning DNF with respect to the uniform distribution. In *Proceedings of the 35th Annual IEEE Symposium on Foundations of Computer Science*, pages 42–53, 1994.

[Kha93] Michael Kharitonov. Cryptographic hardness of distribution-specific learning. In *Proceedings of the 25th Annual ACM Symposium on Theory of Computing*, pages 372–381, 1993.

[KLPV87] Michael Kearns, Ming Li, Leonard Pitt, and Leslie G. Valiant. On the learnability of Boolean formulae. In *Proceedings of the 19th Annual ACM Symposium on Theory of Computing*, pages 185–294. Association for Computing Machinery, 1987.

[PW90] Leonard Pitt and Manfred K. Warmuth. Prediction-preserving reducibility. *Journal of Computer and System Sciences*, 41:430–467, 1990.

[Val84] Leslie G. Valiant. A theory of the learnable. *Communications of the ACM*, 27(11):1134–1142, 1984.

[Val85] Leslie G. Valiant. Learning disjunctions of conjunctions. In *Proceedings of the 9th International Joint Conference on Artificial Intelligence*, volume 1, pages 1134–1142, Los Angeles, Aug. 1985.

Learning Nested Differences in the Presence of Malicious Noise

Peter Auer [*]

University of California at Santa Cruz, Santa Cruz, CA 95064, USA

Abstract. We investigate the learnability of nested differences of intersection-closed classes in the presence of malicious noise. Examples of intersection-closed classes include axis-parallel rectangles, monomials, linear sub-spaces, and so forth. We present an on-line algorithm whose mistake bound is optimal in the sense that there are concept classes for which each learning algorithm (using nested differences as hypotheses) can be forced to make at least that many mistakes. We also present an algorithm for learning in the PAC model with malicious noise. Surprisingly enough, the noise rate tolerable by these algorithms does not depend on the complexity of the target class but depends only on the complexity of the underlying intersection-closed class.

1 Introduction and preliminaries

We are interested in the implications of noise when learning nested differences of intersection-closed classes. For the noise-free case the learnability of nested differences was analyzed in [HSW90]. The main focus of our work is the tolerable amount of noise such that learning is still possible. The learning models we will consider are the on-line learning model [Ang88, Lit88] and the PAC-learning model with malicious noise [Val84, KL93]. In both learning models the learner has to discover some fixed target concept $C \subseteq X$ over the domain X, where it is known that $C \in \mathcal{C}$ for some given concept class $\mathcal{C}$ of subsets of X. We will not distinguish between a concept C and the corresponding function $C(x) = \begin{cases} + & \text{if } x \in C \\ - & \text{if } x \notin C \end{cases}$.

We use the formalization of the on-line learning model in [Ang88], where in each trial $t \geq 1$ the learner has to produce a hypothesis H_t, and if H_t is considered to be different from the target concept C, then the learner receives a counterexample (x_t, l_t), $l_t \in \{+, -\}$, to hypothesis H_t, where $H_t(x_t) \neq l_t$. If $l_t = C(x_t)$ then (x_t, l_t) is a correct counterexample, if $l_t \neq C(x_t)$ then the counterexample is noisy. The preformance of the learner is measured by its number of mistakes, i.e. by the number of counterexamples it receives until it has learned the target concept. We denote by $\text{MB}(A, \mathcal{C}, N)$ the maximal number of mistakes algorithm A makes while learning a concept from $\mathcal{C}$ if at most N of the counterexamples are noisy. For $N = 0$ we abbreviate $\text{MB}(A, \mathcal{C}) := \text{MB}(A, \mathcal{C}, 0)$. Furthermore we denote by $\text{MB}(A, C)$ the number of mistakes algorithm A makes when learning a fixed concept C. It must be

---

[*] Also with Graz University of Technology, Austria. Supported by grant J01028-MAT from the Fonds zur Förderung der wissenschaftlichen Forschung, Austria.

observed that in the on-line model we do not explicitely introduce a noise rate as was done in [Aue93, AC94]. Nevertheless a lower bound of $\frac{1}{R}$ on the tolerable noise rate can be derived from a result like $MB(A, C, N) \leq RN + M_0$, see [AC94].

In the original PAC-learning model [Val84] the learner receives a sample $(x_1, C(x_1)), \ldots, (x_m, C(x_m))$ labeled by the target concept C where the x_i are independently drawn from a probability distribution $\mathcal{D}$ on X. The learner successfully learns C if for most (measured by the confidence parameter δ) of the random sample draws the learner produces a hypothesis H which is ϵ-close to C, i.e. $\mathcal{D}\{x : H(x) \neq C(x)\} < \epsilon$, where ϵ is the precision parameter. In the malicious PAC model [KL93] a certain fraction (measured by the noise rate η) of the examples is noisy. Formally, for each example $(x_i, C(x_i))$ of the sample an independent Bernulli experiment with success probability $1 - \eta$ determines if the example is affected by noise. On success the original example $(x_i, C(x_i))$ is passed to the learner, on failure an arbitrary (x_i', l_i') chosen by an adversary is passed to the learner. As in the original PAC model, with high probability the learner has to produce a hypothesis H which is ϵ-close to the target concept C.

Definition 1. Let C be a concept class over domain X. Algorithm A (ϵ, δ)-learns C with malicious noise rate η if there is an $m(\epsilon, \delta, \eta)$ such that the following condition is fulfilled: for any concept $C \in C$ and for any probability distribution $\mathcal{D}$ on X, the probability that a sample of size $m(\epsilon, \delta, \eta)$ is given to algorithm A such that the algorithm's hypothesis H is not ϵ-close to the target C is at most δ. The sample is drawn accordingly to $\mathcal{D}$ and C and it is affected by a noise rate of at most η .

After defining the learning models we turn to nested differences of intersection-closed classes. A class C is intersection-closed if $\bigcap_{C' \in C'} C \in C$ for any subclass $C' \subseteq C$, and if $\emptyset \in C$. Intersection-closed classes can be learned using the Closure Algorithm (ClosAlg) [HLW88, HSW90, Nat91, HSW92], which uses as hypothesis the closure of all positive (counter)examples seen so far. For any concept class C the closure operator $CL_C : 2^X \to 2^X$ is defined as $CL_C(S) = \bigcap_{C \in C, S \subseteq C} C$. If not stated otherwise we assume from now on that C is an intersection-closed concept class and for convenience we write CL instead of CL_C. If S is a set of labeled examples we write $CL(S, l) := CL(\{x : (x, l) \in S\}), l \in \{+, -\}$, for the closure of the positive or negative examples in S. Since the Closure Algorithm always produces the smallest hypothesis consistent with all positive examples, in the noise-free case this hypothesis is also consistent with the negative examples. For the noisy case the Closure Algorithm was extended in [AC94]. Intersection-closed classes have the following important property which we will use to construct our algorithms. For any finite set $S \subseteq X$ there is a minimal basis $\text{Base}(S) \subseteq S$, such that $CL(S) = CL(\text{Base}(S))$ and $B' \subset \text{Base}(S)$ implies $CL(B') \subset CL(S)$. The basis $\text{Base}(S)$ can be constructed by removing elements from S as long as the closure of the remaining elements equals the closure of the original set S, see Figure 1. Observe that the basis of a set S is not uniquely determined. For a labeled sample S we again define $\text{Base}(S, l) = \text{Base}(\{x : (x, l) \in S\})$. The size of any basis is bounded by the VC-dimension [VC71] of C.

Lemma 2 [HSW90]. *For any intersection-closed concept class C over X and any set $S \subseteq X$.*

$$|\text{Base}(S)| \leq \text{VC-dim}(C).$$

---
1. $B := S$.
2. WHILE $\exists r \in B : CL(B \setminus \{r\}) = CL(B)$ DO $B := B \setminus \{r\}$.
3. OUTPUT B.

Fig. 1. Construction of a basis B for set S.

The nested difference C of the concepts $C_1, \ldots, C_K \in C$ is defined as

$$C = C_1 \setminus (C_2 \setminus (C_3 \setminus \cdots)). \tag{1}$$

We call each C_i in (1) a shell of C. To simplify notation we define

$$\langle C_1, \ldots, C_K \rangle := C_1 \setminus (C_2 \setminus \ldots (C_{K-1} \setminus C_K)).$$

If $C = \langle C_1, \ldots, C_K \rangle$ then $C(r) = \ell_i$ where $i = \max\{j \geq 0 : r \in C_j\}$ (we assume $C_0 = X$) and

$$\ell_i = \begin{cases} + & \text{if } i \text{ odd} \\ - & \text{if } i \text{ even} \end{cases}.$$

Two examples of nested differences of rectangles are show in Figure 2. The concept

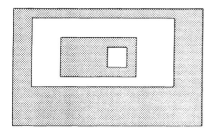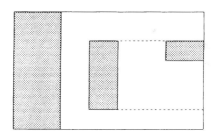

Fig. 2. Examples of nested differences of rectangles with 4 and 5 shells.

class of nested differences with K shells is defined as

$$C^{(K)} = \{\langle C_1, \ldots, C_K \rangle : C_i \in C\}$$

and the class of nested differences with an unbounded number of shells is $C^{(*)} = \bigcup_{K \geq 1} C^{(K)}$. For intersection-closed classes C we always can obtain a normal form of a nested difference $C \in C^{(K)}$.

Fact 3 *Let C be an intersection-closed concept class. Then for any $C \in C^{(K)}$ there are $C_1 \supset C_2 \supset \cdots \supset C_k \neq \emptyset$, $C_i \in C$, $k \leq K$, with $C = \langle C_1, \ldots, C_k \rangle$.*

Proof. Assume that $C = \langle C'_1, \ldots, C'_K \rangle$. Then also $C = \langle C''_1, \ldots, C''_K \rangle$ where $C''_i = \bigcap_{1 \le j \le i} C'_j$. Clearly $C''_1 \supseteq C''_2 \supseteq \cdots \supseteq C''_K$. If $C''_i = C''_{i+1}$ for some $i = 1, \ldots, K-1$ then $\langle C''_1, \ldots, C''_K \rangle = \langle C''_1, \ldots, C''_{i-1}, C''_{i+2}, \ldots, C''_K \rangle$. Thus we can remove all duplicates among the $C''_1, \ldots, C''_K$ and get $C = \langle C_1, \ldots, C_{k'} \rangle$ with $C_1 \supset \cdots \supset C_{k'}$. Finally, if $C_{k'} = \emptyset$ then $\langle C_1, \ldots, C_{k'} \rangle = \langle C_1, \ldots, C_{k'-1} \rangle$, which completes the proof. □

In [HSW90] the Inclusion-Exclusion-Algorithm, Figure 3, was used to learn

---

1. Set $S_0 := X$.
2. FOR $i := 1, \ldots, K$ DO $S_i := \{x \in \mathrm{CL}(S_{i-1}) : (x, \ell_i) \in S\}$.
3. OUTPUT $H = \langle \mathrm{CL}(S_1) \ldots, \mathrm{CL}(S_K) \rangle$.

Fig. 3. The Inclusion-Exclusion-Algorithm computes a hypothesis from $C^{(K)}$ consistent with the noise-free sample S.

nested differences of intersection-closed classes. It first computes the closure of all positive examples, obtaining the first shell of the hypothesis. In general, this shell contains some negative examples, so that the closure of these negative examples must be subtracted from the first shell. This closure of the negative examples (only the negative examples in the first shell are considered) forms the second shell. Of course in this shell there again might be positive examples, and a third, positive shell must be subtracted from the second, negative shell. This continues until a nested difference consistent with all examples is found. It can be proven that this algorithm works well in the noise-free case, but there is a problem in the noisy case. Consider Figure 4 where in the second shell there is a noisy positive example. Given by the

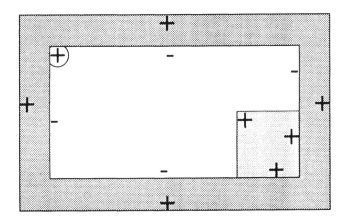

Fig. 4. The noisy example $\oplus$ causes the Inclusion-Exclusion-Algorithm to loop forever.

closure of all positive examples in the second shell the third shell equals the second shell. The fourth shell, given by the closure of all negative examples in the third shell, again equals the second shell. Thus for this set of examples the Inclusion-Exclusion-Algorithm will not make any progress and cannot compute a consistent hypothesis. This is not surprising at all since for this set of examples there is no consistent hypothesis from $C^{(*)}$.

Lemma 4. *Let C be any intersection-closed concept class. Then there is no hypothesis in $C^{(*)}$ consistent with examples $(x_1, +), \ldots, (x_n, +), (y_1, -), \ldots, (y_{n'}, -)$ if $CL(\{x_1, \ldots, x_n\}) = CL(\{y_1, \ldots, y_{n'}\})$.*

Proof. Assume that $H = \langle H_1, \ldots, H_k \rangle$ is consistent with the examples above and normalized such that $H_1 \supset \cdots \supset H_k \neq \emptyset$. Since $CL(\{x_1, \ldots, x_n\}) = CL(\{y_1, \ldots, y_{n'}\})$ we have for any $i = 1, \ldots, k$: $x_j \in H_i$ for all $j = 1, \ldots, n$ iff $y_j \in H_i$ for all $j = 1, \ldots, n'$. Since H is consistent with the examples, all $x_j \in H_1$. Thus also all $y_j \in H_1$. Again, since H is consistent, all $y_j \in H_2$. And this implies that all $x_j \in H_2$. Continuing with this argument we finally find that all $x_j \in H_k$ and all $y_j \in H_k$. Hence H classifies all x_j and y_j with ℓ_k which contradicts that H is consistent with the examples. □

To overcome the difficulty that there is no hypothesis in $C^{(*)}$ consistent with all examples, one can construct a hypothesis which is not consistent, without being explicit about which of the examples are labeled inconsistently. We use this approach in Section 2 to get an on-line learning algorithm which can tolerate a noise rate of $\frac{1}{2m}$, $m = \mathrm{MB}(\mathrm{ClosAlg}, C)$. We also show that this noise tolerance is optimal among all algorithms which use $C^{(*)}$ as their hypothesis class.

Alternatively, one can explicitly remove some of the examples and come up with a hypothesis consistent with the remaining sub-sample. This approach was taken in [AC94] to make the Closure Algorithm noise robust. In Section 3 we follow this line and obtain a PAC-learning algorithm which tolerates a malicious noise rate up to $\Omega(\frac{\epsilon}{\mathrm{VC\text{-}dim}(C)})$. For some concept classes this result gives the best known noise tolerance[2].

We conclude this section by proving that for any intersection-closed class C the number of shells in the normal form of any nested difference is bounded by $m = \mathrm{MB}(\mathrm{ClosAlg}, C)$.

Lemma 5. *If $C_1 \supset C_2$ then $\mathrm{MB}(\mathrm{ClosAlg}, C_1) \geq \mathrm{MB}(\mathrm{ClosAlg}, C_2) + 1$.*

Proof. Consider a sequence of counterexamples to ClosAlg when learning C_2. Since in the noisy-free case ClosAlg receives only positive counterexamples all these counterexamples are in C_2. Thus all these counterexamples are also counterexamples to ClosAlg when learning C_1. After this sequence of counterexamples the hypothesis of ClosAlg is a subset of C_2. Hence any $x \in C_1 \setminus C_2$ is an additional counterexample to ClosAlg when learning C_1. Therefore ClosAlg makes at least one more mistake when learning C_1 than when learning C_2. □

Thus $C = \langle C_1, \ldots, C_{m+1} \rangle$ with $C_i \supset C_{i+1}$ and $m = \mathrm{MB}(\mathrm{ClosAlg}, C)$ implies $\mathrm{MB}(\mathrm{ClosAlg}, C_{m+1}) = 0$ and hence $C_{m+1} = \emptyset$. Since each concept in $C^{(k)}$ has a normal form with at most k shells we have the following corollary.

---

[2] We consider only time-efficient algorithms.

Corollary 6. *Let C be any intersection-closed concept class. Then for any $k \geq m = $ $\mathrm{MB}(\mathrm{ClosAlg}, C)$ we have $C^{(k)} = C^{(m)}$.*

2 On-line learning of nested differences in the presence of noise

In this section we present the algorithm XInclusionExclusion, Figure 5, which is an

---

Algorithm XInclusionExclusion maintains a sequence of sets of counterexamples $S = \langle S_1, \ldots, S_n \rangle$, $n \geq 0$, such that $\mathrm{CL}(S_i) \supseteq \mathrm{CL}(S_{i+1})$ for all $i = 1, \ldots, n-1$.

Initialization:
Initialize S to the empty sequence. $S := \langle \rangle$, $n := 0$.

Construction of the hypothesis:
In each trial $t \geq 1$ set $H_t := \langle \mathrm{CL}(S_1), \ldots, \mathrm{CL}(S_n) \rangle$. ($H_1 = \langle \rangle = \emptyset$.)

Update:
Let (x_t, l_t) be the counterexample to H_t.
Set $i := \min\{j \geq 1 : x_t \notin \mathrm{CL}(S_j)\}$. If $x_t \in \mathrm{CL}(S_j)$ for all j then $i := n+1$.
Update S by setting $S_i := S_i \cup \{x_t\}$. If $i = n+1$ set $S_{n+1} := \{x_t\}$ and $n := n+1$.

Fig. 5. Algorithm XInclusionExclusion for the on-line learning of nested differences with noise.

extension of the Inclusion-Exclusion-Algorithm and has the advantage that in the presence of noise it still produces a hypothesis consistent with most of the counterexamples seen so far. We start with an informal description of the algorithm. Like the Inclusion-Exclusion-Algorithm its hypothesis H_t is the nested difference of the closures of some sets of counterexamples $S_1, S_2, \ldots$ For each trial the Inclusion-Exclusion-Algorithm calculates these sets from scratch, such that S_1 is the set of all positive counterexamples seen so far, S_2 is the set of all negative counterexamples in the closure of S_1, and so on. In contrast algorithm XInclusionExclusion updates the sets $S_1, S_2, \ldots$ incrementally: the counterexample x_t is added to the set S_i with the smallest index i such that $x_t \notin \mathrm{CL}(S_i)$. Since before the update $x_t \in \mathrm{CL}(S_{i-1}) \setminus \mathrm{CL}(S_i)$ and x_t was a counterexample to H_t, the label of x_t is l_i. While the hypothesis of the Inclusion-Exclusion-Algorithm is always consistent with all counterexamples seen so far (therefore the Inclusion-Exclusion-Algorithm cannot tolerate noisy counterexamples), the hypothesis of algorithm XInclusionExclusion is in general not consistent with all the counterexamples (which enables the algorithm to deal with noise), see Figure 6. We get the following mistake bound for algorithm XInclusionExclusion and show that this bound is optimal.

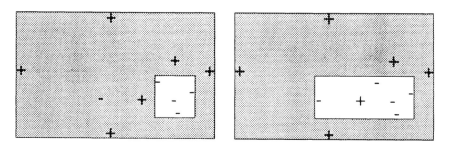

Fig. 6. The new negative counterexample, added to S_2, enlarges the second shell of the hypothesis. Since all positive counterexamples remain in S_1, one of them (not necessarily a noisy one if the target is from $C^{(3)}$) is misclassified by the hypothesis.

Theorem 7. *For any intersection-closed concept class C and for any $2 \leq K \leq$ $\mathrm{MB}(\mathrm{ClosAlg}, C)$ and any $N \geq 0$*

$$\mathrm{MB}(\mathrm{XInclusionExclusion}, C^{(K)}, N) \leq (2N + K)\mathrm{MB}(\mathrm{ClosAlg}, C) - \frac{K(K-1)}{2}$$

where algorithm XInclusionExclusion uses hypotheses from $C^{(K+2N)}$ and runs in time polynomial in K, N, and the maximal time taken by ClosAlg to learn a concept from C.

Theorem 8. *For any $m \geq 2$ there is an intersection-closed concept class C with $\mathrm{MB}(\mathrm{ClosAlg}, C) = m$ such that*

$$\mathrm{MB}(A, C, N) \geq (2N + K)m - \frac{K(K-1)}{2}$$

for any $N \geq 0$ and $2 \leq K \leq m$ and for any algorithm A which uses hypotheses from $C^{(*)}$.

To prove the mistake bound on algorithm XInclusionExclusion we show that each set S_i contains at most $\mathrm{MB}(\mathrm{ClosAlg}, C)$ examples and that the number of sets n is at most $K + 2N$, where K is the number of nested differences in the target concept and N is the number of noisy examples. The bound on the size of S_i is obtained easily: since an example is added to S_i only if it is not in the closure of S_i, the examples in S_i form a sequence of counterexamples to the Closure Algorithm and therefore their number is bounded by $\mathrm{MB}(\mathrm{ClosAlg}, C)$. To bound the number of sets n we argue that besides the K sets which correspond to the shells of the target each noisy counterexample generates at most 2 additional sets: roughly speaking, each noisy counterexample can be "covered" by adding 2 additional shells to the target, see Figure 7. The following lemma bounds the number of additional shells generated by noisy counterexamples.

Lemma 9. *Let C be any intersection-closed concept class and $C = \langle C_1, \ldots, C_K \rangle \in$ $C^{(K)}$ some target concept. Furthermore let $S_1, \ldots, S_n \subseteq X$ be a sequence of sets of*

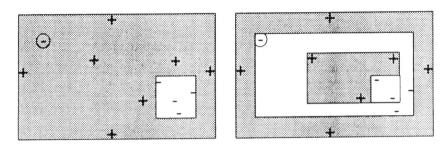

Fig. 7. The noisy example $\ominus$ is covered by an additional shell. Another shell is used to cover the positive examples which would be misclassified otherwise.

examples such that the label of an example $x \in S_i$ is ℓ_i. If $\mathrm{CL}(S_1) \supseteq \mathrm{CL}(S_2) \supseteq \cdots \supseteq$ $\mathrm{CL}(S_n) \neq \emptyset$ and at most N examples in $\bigcup_{1 \leq i \leq n} S_i$ are noisy (in respect to C) then $n \leq K + 2N$. Moreover there are $n - 2N \leq k \leq K$ indices $1 \leq i_1 < \cdots i_k \leq n$ with $S_{i_j} \subseteq C_j$ for $j = 1, \ldots, k$.

Proof. At first we construct the indices i_j. We set $i_0 = 0$, $C_0 = S_0 = X$, $C_{K+1} = \emptyset$, and $i_{j+1} = \min\{i_j + 1 + 2s : s \geq 0, S_{i_j+1+2s} \subseteq C_{j+1}\}$ for $j = 0, \ldots, K$ (we assume $S_i = \emptyset$ for $i > n$). Observe that $\ell_{i_j} = \ell_j$. Let k be the number of indices i_j with $1 \leq i_j \leq n$. Obviously this choice of indices satisfies $S_{i_j} \subseteq C_j$ for $j = 1, \ldots, k$. By the construction of the i_j and the prerequisite of the lemma we have $C_j \supseteq \mathrm{CL}(S_{i_j}) \supseteq S_{i_j+1+2s}$ for all $s \geq 0$ and all $j = 0, \ldots, k$. Since all examples in S_{i_j+1+2s} have label ℓ_{j+1} all correct examples in $S_{i_j+1+2s} \subseteq C_j$ are in C_{j+1}. Thus $S_{i_j+1+2s} \not\subseteq C_{j+1}$ only if S_{i_j+1+2s} contains at least one noisy example. Hence for $j = 0, \ldots, k$ each $S_{i_j+1}, S_{i_j+3}, \ldots, S_{i_{j+1}-2}$ contains at least one noisy example. Counting these sets for all j gives

$$N \geq \sum_{j=0}^{k} \frac{i_{j+1} - i_j - 1}{2} = \frac{i_{k+1} - i_0 - (k+1)}{2} \geq \frac{n-k}{2}$$

and the lemma. $\qquad\square$

Proof of Theorem 7. We use the notation of Figure 5. Let $C = \langle C_1, \ldots, C_{K'} \rangle$, $K' \leq K$, be the normalized target concept. Since the sets S_i fulfill the prerequisite of Lemma 9 we have $n \leq K + 2N$ and there are $n - 2N \leq k \leq K$ indices $1 \leq i_1 < \cdots < i_k \leq n$ with $S_{i_j} \subseteq C_j$. Furthermore observe that counterexample x_t is added to set S_i only if $x_t \notin \mathrm{CL}(S_i)$. Thus the sequence of counterexamples $x_{t_1}, x_{t_2}, \ldots$ added to set S_i is also a sequence of counterexamples to the Closure Algorithm when learning the concept class C. Moreover, the sequence $x_{t_1}, x_{t_2}, \ldots$ added to a set S_{i_j} is a sequence of counterexamples to the Closure Algorithm when learning C_j. Hence $|S_i| \leq \mathrm{MB}(\mathrm{ClosAlg}, C)$ for all $1 \leq i \leq n$. Using the fact that $C_1 \supseteq \cdots \supseteq C_{K'}$ and Lemma 5 we find $|S_{i_j}| \leq \mathrm{MB}(\mathrm{ClosAlg}, C_j) \leq \mathrm{MB}(\mathrm{ClosAlg}, C) - j + 1$. Since $n = 2N + k$ summing over all sets S_i gives the theorem. $\qquad\square$

2.1 Proof of Theorem 8

Let C be the concept class C of all linear sub-spaces of the vector space $\mathbf{Z}_p^m$ over the field $\mathbf{Z}_p$, where p is an arbitrary prime $p > m$. It is known that for this concept class $\mathrm{MB}(\mathrm{ClosAlg}, C) = m$ [AC94]. For this choice of C Theorem 8 lower bounds the number of mistakes for any learning algorithm which uses hypotheses from $C^{(*)}$. The main idea of the proof is to give to the algorithm m linearly independent positive and m linearly independent negative counterexamples. The order in which the counterexamples are given to the algorithm depends on the hypotheses of the algorithm. Since both the positive and the negative counterexamples span the whole vector space there is no hypothesis consistent with all counterexamples, hence one of the counterexamples is noisy. We will show that the learning algorithm cannot figure out which of the counterexamples is noisy, and thus essentially has to discard all the counterexamples. Doing this N times, once for each noisy counterexample, gives a total of $2Nm$ counterexamples. The remaining $Km - \frac{K(K-1)}{2}$ counterexamples are necessary to finally learn the target concept.

We start proving the theorem for the case $m = K = 2$ which gives an idea how the proof in the general case works. Observe that for vectors $\boldsymbol{x}_1, \ldots, \boldsymbol{x}_n \in \mathbf{Z}_p^m$ the closure $\mathrm{CL}(\{\boldsymbol{x}_1, \ldots, \boldsymbol{x}_n\})$ is the linear sub-space spanned by these vectors. We set $\boldsymbol{b}_1 = (1, 0)$, $\boldsymbol{b}_2 = (0, 1)$, $\boldsymbol{u}_1 = (1, 1)$, and $\boldsymbol{u}_2 = (1, -1)$. Since $\mathrm{CL}(\{\boldsymbol{b}_1, \boldsymbol{b}_2\}) = \mathrm{CL}(\{\boldsymbol{u}_1, \boldsymbol{u}_2\}) = \mathbf{Z}_p^2$ there is no concept in $C^{(*)}$ consistent with the labels $(\boldsymbol{b}_1, +), (\boldsymbol{b}_2, +), (\boldsymbol{u}_1, -), (\boldsymbol{u}_2, -)$ by Lemma 4. Thus among the $(\boldsymbol{b}_1, +), (\boldsymbol{b}_2, +), (\boldsymbol{u}_1, -), (\boldsymbol{u}_2, -)$ there is a counterexample to any hypothesis from $C^{(*)}$. After $4N + 3$ trials one of these counterexamples has been given at most N times so that we consider this counterexample to be noisy. If $(\boldsymbol{b}_1, +)$ is this noisy counterexample than the remaining counterexamples are consistent with $\mathrm{CL}(\{\boldsymbol{b}_2\})$ (analogously if $\boldsymbol{b}_2$ is the noisy counterexample). If $(\boldsymbol{u}_1, -)$ is the noisy counterexample than the remaining counterexamples are consistent with $\mathrm{CL}(\{\boldsymbol{b}_1, \boldsymbol{b}_2\}) \setminus \mathrm{CL}(\{\boldsymbol{u}_2\})$ (analogously for $\boldsymbol{u}_2$). Thus for each algorithm there is a hypothesis from $C^{(2)}$ which can force $4N + 3$ mistakes of the algorithm if N of the counterexamples might be noisy.

For the case $m \geq 3$ we use a somewhat more sophisticated argument and some tools from linear algebra. Let $\boldsymbol{x}\boldsymbol{y}$ denote the inner product of the vectors $\boldsymbol{x}, \boldsymbol{y} \in \mathbf{Z}_p^m$. Furthermore we call vectors $\boldsymbol{x}_1, \ldots, \boldsymbol{x}_n \in \mathbf{Z}_p^m$ orthonormal if $\boldsymbol{x}_i \boldsymbol{x}_i \equiv 1(p)$ for all $i = 1, \ldots, n$, and $\boldsymbol{x}_i \boldsymbol{x}_j \equiv 0(p)$ for $i \neq j$. We will make use of the following lemma.

Lemma 10. *If for $n \geq 3$ $\boldsymbol{b}_1, \ldots, \boldsymbol{b}_n$ are orthonormal vectors from $\mathbf{Z}_p^m$ then there are also orthonormal vectors $\boldsymbol{u}_1, \ldots, \boldsymbol{u}_n \in \mathbf{Z}_p^m$ such that*

1. $\mathrm{CL}(\{\boldsymbol{b}_1, \ldots, \boldsymbol{b}_n\}) = \mathrm{CL}(\{\boldsymbol{u}_1, \ldots, \boldsymbol{u}_n\})$.
2. $\boldsymbol{b}_i \notin \mathrm{CL}(U)$ for all $\boldsymbol{b}_i$ and any subset U of at most $n - 1$ vectors from $\boldsymbol{u}_1, \ldots, \boldsymbol{u}_n$.
3. $\boldsymbol{u}_i \notin \mathrm{CL}(B)$ for all $\boldsymbol{u}_i$ and any subset B of at most $n - 1$ vectors from $\boldsymbol{b}_1, \ldots, \boldsymbol{b}_n$.

Proof. Basicly we get the $\boldsymbol{u}_i$ by rotating the $\boldsymbol{b}_i$. We set

$$\boldsymbol{u}_i = \left(\sum_{j \neq i} \boldsymbol{b}_j + (1 - 2^{-1}n)\boldsymbol{b}_i \right) 2n^{-1}$$

where x^{-1} denotes the multiplicative inverse in the field $\mathbf{Z}_p$. Since the b_i are orthonormal we find

$$u_i u_i \equiv \left(n - 1 + (1 - 2^{-1} n)^2\right) 4 n^{-2} \equiv 1(p)$$

and

$$u_i u_j \equiv \left(n - 2 + 2(1 - 2^{-1} n)\right) 4 n^{-2} \equiv 0(p)$$

for $i \neq j$. Thus the vectors $u_1, \ldots, u_n$ are orthonormal and therefore linear independent. Since $\mathrm{CL}(\{u_1, \ldots, u_n\}) \subseteq \mathrm{CL}(\{b_1, \ldots, b_n\})$ and the linear sub-space spanned by $u_1, \ldots, u_n$ has dimension n as the linear sub-space spanned by $b_1, \ldots, b_n$, we have $\mathrm{CL}(\{u_1, \ldots, u_n\}) = \mathrm{CL}(\{b_1, \ldots, b_n\})$. Furthermore $b_i u_j \not\equiv 0(p)$ for all i and j implies that no b_i can be expressed as the linear combination of at most $n - 1$ of the vectors u_j and vice versa. □

We are ready now to prove Theorem 8 for $m \geq 3$. Let the b_i be the unit vectors of $\mathbf{Z}_p^m$ (which obviously are orthonormal) and let $u_1, \ldots, u_m$ be the alternate orthonormal vectors given by Lemma 10. We label all b_i with $+$ and all u_i with $-$. Since $\mathrm{CL}(\{b_1, \ldots, b_m\}) = \mathrm{CL}(\{u_1, \ldots, u_m\})$ there is no hypothesis in $\mathcal{C}^{(*)}$ consistent with all these labels and one of the labeled vectors can be given as counterexample to any hypothesis. After $2mN + 2m - 1$ trials one of the vectors was given as a counterexample at most N times and we consider this labeled vector to be the noisy counterexample. If b_i is the noise vector then the labels of all other vectors are consistent with $\mathrm{CL}(\{b_1, \ldots, b_{i-1}, b_{i+1}, \ldots, b_m\})$ since no u_j is in this closure by Lemma 10. If u_j is the noisy vector then $\mathbf{Z}_p^m \setminus \mathrm{CL}(\{u_1, \ldots, u_{j-1}, u_{j+1}, \ldots, u_m\})$ is consistent with the labels of the remaining vectors. So after $2mN + 2m - 1$ counterexamples (where N of them have been noisy) we have a consistent hypothesis $\langle C_1 \rangle$ or $\langle C_1, C_2 \rangle$ where C_1 resp. C_2 is spanned by $m - 1$ orthonormal vectors.

We proceed by proving by induction that for any $2 \leq K \leq m - 1$ we can force any learner to make at least $2mN + \sum_{k=0}^{K-1}(m - k)$ mistakes while there is still a concept in $\mathcal{C}^{(K)}$ consistent with all but the N noisy counterexamples. Obviously this gives the theorem for $2 \leq K \leq m - 1$. Above we have already proven this for $K = 2$. To get the remaining number of mistakes we basicly use the fact that in the noisy-free case any algorithm makes at least $m - k$ mistakes when learning a linear sub-space of dimension $m - k$. Since the shells $C_1, C_2, \ldots, C_K$ have dimensions $m, m - 1, \ldots, m - K + 1$ we get the result. But of course we have to take care that a counterexample given while learning C_i does not help the learner when learning C_j for some $j > i$.

For $K \geq 3$ let $\langle C_1, \ldots, C_k \rangle$, $k \leq K - 1$, be the concept consistent with previous correct counterexamples such that the following holds: C_k is spanned by orthonormal vectors $b_1, \ldots, b_{m-K+2}$, no previous counterexamples besides the $b_1, \ldots, b_{m-K+2}$ are elements of C_k, and the learner has already made $2mN + \sum_{k=0}^{K-2}(m - k)$ mistakes. By the constructions in the above paragraph these conditions are fulfilled for $K = 3$. Let $u_1, \ldots, u_{m-K+2}$ be the alternate orthonormal vectors given by Lemma 10. We label all u_i with ℓ_{k+1}. If the learner's hypothesis is consistent with the labels of all u_i then it is not consistent with the labels of all $b_1, \ldots, b_{m-K+2}$ (which are all ℓ_k) by Lemma 4. Thus in this case one of the b_i can be given as counterexample to the learner's hypothesis. If the learner's hypothesis is not consistent with the label of one of the u_i this vector is given as counterexample. This is done

$m - K + 1$ times, forcing $m - K + 1$ mistakes. After at most $m - K + 1$ of the u_i have been given as counterexamples (we denote them by $u_{i_1}, \ldots, u_{i_{m-K+1}}$) the concept $\langle C_1, \ldots, C_k, C_{k+1}\rangle \in C^{(K)}$, $C_{k+1} = \mathrm{CL}(\{u_{i_1}, \ldots, u_{i_{m-K+1}}\})$, is consistent with all correct counterexamples (note that none of the u_i was noisy). By Lemma 10 no b_i is contained in C_{k+1}, and since $C_{k+1} \subseteq C_k$ also no of the other previous counterexamples is contained in C_{k+1}. Thus all requirements for the next induction step are met.

At last we have to deal with the case $K = m \geq 3$. From the above considerations we know that there is a concept $\langle C_1, \ldots, C_k\rangle$, $k \leq m - 1$, consistent with all previous correct counterexamples such that C_k is spanned by orthonormal vectors b_1, b_2, no other counterexample is element of C_k, and the learner has already made $2mN + \sum_{k=0}^{m-2}(m-k)$ mistakes. Let $u_1 = b_1 + b_2$ and $u_2 = b_1 - b_2$. We assign the label ℓ_{k+1} to u_1 and u_2. If the learner's hypothesis is consistent with these labels then it is not consistent with the labels of b_1 or b_2 by Lemma 4. Thus in this case one of the b_i can be given as counterexample to the learner's hypothesis. If the learner's hypothesis is not consistent with the label of u_1 then u_1 is given as counterexample (analogously for u_2). Since this forces an additional mistake of the learner and $\langle C_1, \ldots, C_k, C_{k+1}\rangle$ with $C_{k+1} = \mathrm{CL}(\{u_1\})$ is consistent with this counterexample, this concludes the proof.

3 Learning of nested differences in the malicious PAC-model

In this section we present another extension of the Inclusion-Exclusion-Algorithm. Algorithm RobustInclusionExclusion (Figure 8) performs in two phases. At first it removes examples from the sample until there is a hypothesis in $C^{(*)}$ which is consistent with the remaining sub-sample. In general this hypothesis consists of many shells. The results of the previous section, especially Lemma 9, indicate that the number of shells might be as large as the number of noisy examples in the sample. Since the number of noisy examples is a certain fraction of the sample size, the complexity of the hypothesis increases with the sample size. On the other hand the sample size which is necessary to produce an ϵ-close hypothesis increases with the complexity of the hypothesis class. Thus increasing the sample size increases the number of noisy examples, which increases the complexity of the hypothesis, which implies that the sample size must be increased. To break this vicious circle, in the second phase algorithm RobustInclusionExclusion removes more examples from the sample until there is a simple hypothesis consistent with the remaining sub-sample. We will show that at most $4dN$ examples are removed from the sample if there are N noisy examples in the sample ($d = \mathrm{VC\text{-}dim}(C)$). To get an ϵ-close hypothesis it will suffice that $4dN < \epsilon m$ where m is the sample size. Solving for N yields $N < \frac{\epsilon}{4d}m$ which gives a tolerable noise rate of $\frac{\epsilon}{4d}$.

In the first phase algorithm RobustInclusionExclusion has to detect noisy examples which cause any hypothesis from $C^{(*)}$ to be inconsistent with the sample. Recall that the Inclusion-Exclusion-Algorithm does not make progress only if two consecutive shells of its "hypothesis" are equal. Hence in this case algorithm RobustInclusionExclusion removes the bases of these shells. Since the closures of both bases are equal and the examples in one base are labeled + and the the ex-

```
Input: Sample S.

Phase 1:

1. n := 1. S₁ := {r : (r, +) ∈ S}.
2. n := n + 1. Sₙ := {r ∈ CL(Sₙ₋₁) : (r, ℓₙ) ∈ S}.
3. IF Sₙ = ∅ THEN n := n − 1. GOTO Phase 2.
4. IF CL(Sₙ₋₁) = CL(Sₙ)
   THEN S := S \ ({(r, ℓₙ₋₁) : r ∈ Base(Sₙ₋₁)} ∪ {(r, ℓₙ) : r ∈ Base(Sₙ)}). GOTO 1
   ELSE GOTO 2.

Phase 2:

1. IF n ≤ 2K
   THEN OUTPUT ⟨CL(S₁), ..... CL(Sₙ)⟩ and STOP
   ELSE S := S \ ⋃₁≤ᵢ≤ₙ{(r, ℓᵢ) : r ∈ Base(Sᵢ)}.
2. n := 1. S₁ := {r : (r, +) ∈ S}.
3. n := n + 1. Sₙ := {r ∈ CL(Sₙ₋₁) : (r, ℓₙ) ∈ S}.
4. IF Sₙ = ∅
   THEN n := n − 1. GOTO 1
   ELSE GOTO 3.
```

Fig. 8. Algorithm RobustInclusionExclusion constructs a hypothesis from $C^{(2K)}$.

amples in the other base are labeled $-$, at least one of these examples is noisy by Lemma 4. Thus in one step the algorithm removes at least 1 noisy example and at most $2d - 1$ correct examples. Phase 1 stops as soon as there are only examples left which are consistent with some hypothesis in $C^{(*)}$. In Phase 2 examples are removed until there is a consistent hypothesis in $C^{(2K)}$. If the current hypothesis has $n > 2K$ shells and the target is in $C^{(K)}$ then by Lemma 9 $\frac{n-K}{2}$ of the sets S_i contain noisy examples. Thus removing the bases of all sets S_i removes at least $\frac{n-K}{2}$ noisy examples and less than dn correct examples. Since the number of noisy examples is reduced there is now a consistent hypothesis with fewer shells. Repeating this process yields a hypothesis in $C^{(2K)}$. To prove the theorem below we finally have to bound the total number of removed examples and apply known results on the sample size sufficient for PAC-learning.

Theorem 11. Let C be any intersection-closed concept class with VC-dim(C) $= d < \infty$ and let $K \geq 1$. Then for any $\epsilon, \delta > 0$ and any $\eta = \frac{\epsilon}{4d} - \alpha$, $\alpha > 0$, algorithm RobustInclusionExclusion (ϵ, δ)-learns $C^{(K)}$ in the malicious PAC model with noise rate η when provided with a sample S of size $m \geq \max\left\{\frac{16\epsilon}{\alpha^2}\left(2dK\ln\frac{48\epsilon}{\alpha^2} + \ln\frac{8}{\delta}\right), \frac{8}{\alpha^2}\log\frac{2}{\delta}\right\}$. Algorithm RobustInclusionExclusion outputs a hypothesis from $C^{(2K)}$ and runs in time polynomial in the sample size m and the time needed to compute the closure and a basis of a set of size m.

Remark. Algorithm RobustInclusionExclusion can be modified so that it tolerates a noise rate up to $\frac{\epsilon}{2d}$. This can be done by changing the termination condition in step 1 of Phase 2 of the algorithm. Instead of producing a hypothesis from $C^{(2K)}$

the modified algorithm produces a hypothesis whose number of shells depends on $\frac{1}{2d} - \eta$. Another modification of RobustInclusionExclusion gives an algorithm which outputs a hypothesis from $C^{(K)}$. The drawback of this algorithm is that it tolerates only a noise rate of $O(\frac{\epsilon}{Kd})$.

Remark. We made no attempt to optimize the bound on the sample size. There might be some room for future work.

3.1 Proof of Theorem 11

Assume that $S' \subseteq S$ is the sub-sample which was not effected by noise. We set $m' = |S'|$ so that $N = m - m'$ is the number of noisy examples. Since the examples which were effected by noise were chosen randomly, S' is a noise-free sample in the sense of the original PAC-model. Thus we will bound the number of examples in S' which are misclassified by the algorithm's hypothesis and then apply the following result from PAC-learning theory. Essentially the lemma states that with high probability a hypothesis which makes few mistakes on a noise-free sample, is close to the target concept.

Lemma 12 (Adapted from [AST93]). *Let C be any target concept and $\mathcal{H}$ any hypothesis class on a domain X, $d = $ VC-dim($\mathcal{H}$). Furthermore let $\mathcal{D}$ be any distribution on X, and choose $\epsilon, \delta, \alpha > 0$. Then with probability at most δ a sample of size $m' \geq \frac{8\epsilon}{\alpha^2}\left(d\ln\frac{48\epsilon}{\alpha^2} + \ln\frac{4}{\delta}\right)$ is drawn accordingly to $\mathcal{D}$ and labeled by C, such that there is an $H \in \mathcal{H}$ which is not ϵ-close to C and makes at most $(\epsilon - \alpha)m$ mistakes on the sample.*

To bound the number of misclassified examples in S' we bound the number of examples removed from S' by the algorithm. Since all remaining examples are classified correctly this gives the desired estimate. Let s_1 and s_2 be the number of examples removed from S' during Phase 1 and Phase 2, respectively, and let N_1 and N_2 be the number of noisy examples removed during Phase 1 and Phase 2, respectively.

In Phase 1 the examples in Base(S_{n-1}) and Base(S_n) are removed from the sample iff CL(Base(S_{n-1})) = CL(Base(S_n)). By Lemma 4 at least one of these examples is noisy. Since $|\text{Base}(S_{n-1}) \cup \text{Base}(S_n)| \leq 2d$, with each noisy example at most $2d - 1$ correct examples are removed from S'. Thus we find $s_1 \leq (2d - 1)N_1$.

In Phase 2 the bases of all sets S_i are removed from the sample. Since the bases Base(S_i), $i = 1, \ldots, n$, fulfill the prerequisite of Lemma 9 at least $\frac{n-K}{2}$ bases contain a noisy example. Thus by removing all bases at least $\frac{n-K}{2}$ noisy examples are removed. Since at most a total number of dn examples is removed at most $dn - \frac{n-K}{2}$ examples are removed from S'. Thus per noisy example at most

$$\frac{dn - \frac{n-K}{2}}{\frac{n-K}{2}} = \frac{2dn}{n - K} - 1 \leq \frac{4dK}{K} - 1 = 4d - 1$$

examples from S' are removed. Hence we get $s_2 \leq (4d - 1)N_2$.

Summing over Phase 1 and Phase 2 we find that $s_1 + s_2 \leq (4d - 1)N$. Now we have to bound the number of noisy examples N. The number of noisy examples is the sum of m independent Bernoulli trials whose probability of success is at most η.

Thus we get by standard Höffding bounds that $N \leq m(\eta + \frac{\alpha}{2})$ with probability at least $1 - \frac{\delta}{2}$ if $m \geq \frac{8}{\alpha^2} \log \frac{2}{\delta}$. Therefore with probability at least $1 - \frac{\delta}{2}$ the algorithm's hypothesis misclassifies at most a fraction of

$$\frac{(4d-1)N}{m'} = \frac{(4d-1)N}{m-N} \leq \frac{(4d-1)(\eta+\alpha/2)}{1-\eta-\alpha/2} = \frac{(4d-1)(\frac{\epsilon}{4d}-\alpha/2)}{1-\frac{\epsilon}{4d}+\alpha/2} \tag{2}$$

examples in S'. Some algebra shows that $(2) \leq \epsilon - \alpha$ for $0 < \epsilon, \alpha < 1$. By applying Lemma 12 with $\mathcal{H} = \mathcal{C}^{(2k)}$, ϵ, $\delta/2$, and α, we get that with probability $1 - \frac{\delta}{2}$ the algorithm's hypothesis is ϵ-close to the target if

$$m' \geq \frac{8\epsilon}{\alpha^2} \left(\text{VC-dim}(\mathcal{C}^{(2K)}) \ln \frac{48\epsilon}{\alpha^2} + \ln \frac{8}{\delta} \right), \tag{3}$$

provided that $N \leq m(\eta + \frac{\alpha}{2})$. The VC-dimension of $\mathcal{C}^{(2K)}$ is bounded by the following lemma.

Lemma 13 [HSW90]. *For any intersection-closed class $\mathcal{C}$*

$$\text{VC-dim}(\mathcal{C}^{(K)}) \leq K \cdot \text{VC-dim}(\mathcal{C}).$$

At last we have with probability $1 - \frac{\delta}{2}$ that $m' = m - N \geq m(1 - \eta - \frac{\alpha}{2}) \geq \frac{m}{2}$ (for $0 < \epsilon < 1$) which implies (3). Summing up we find that with probability $1 - \delta$ the algorithm's hypothesis is ϵ-close to the target, which gives the theorem.

3.2 Discussion and related results

In [KL93] Kearns and Li presented a general technique to make a PAC-learning algorithm noise robust. They show that any time-efficient learning algorithm for the noise-free PAC model which uses a sample of size m, can be turned into a time-efficient PAC learning algorithm tolerating a malicious noise rate up to $\Omega\left(\frac{\log m}{m}\right)$. In general, $\mathcal{C}^{(K)}$ can be (ϵ, δ)-learned in the noise-free case using a sample of size $m = O\left(\frac{1}{\epsilon} \log \frac{1}{\delta} + \frac{dK}{\epsilon} \log \frac{1}{\epsilon}\right)$ ([HSW90]), where $d = \text{VC-dim}(\mathcal{C})$. Applying the result of Kearns and Li gives for small ϵ a tolerable noise rate of $\Omega\left(\frac{\epsilon}{dK}\right)$. While this bound on the tolerable noise rate depends on the number of shells, our general result gives an error tolerance of $\Omega\left(\frac{\epsilon}{d}\right)$ which is independent of the number of shells. The error tolerance of our algorithm is the best known for example for the class of nested differences of axis-parallel rectangles. Talking about achievable noise tolerance one has to be aware of the fact that we are considering only time-efficient algorithms. Time-efficiency essentially means that the algorithms run in time polynomial in the sample complexity. If the run time of the learning algorithm is not constrained then the optimal noise tolerance of $\frac{\epsilon}{1+\epsilon}$ can be achieved. This is done by searching for a hypothesis which misclassifies a minimal number of examples in the sample. The optimality of $\frac{\epsilon}{1+\epsilon}$ was proven in [KL93].

4 Conclusion

We investigated the learnability of nested differences in the presence of noise, both in the on-line and in the malicious PAC-model. For both models we presented general algorithms which were based on the Closure Algorithm and the Inclusion-Exclusion-Algorithm. Our on-line learning algorithm was proven to obtain the best possible general mistake bound. The learning algorithm for the malicious PAC-model achieves a noise tolerance which is superior to previously known results.

Acknowledgments

We want to thank Nicolò Cesa-Bianchi, David Haussler, Christiane Michel, and Manfred Warmuth for very fruitful discussions.

References

[AC94]   Peter Auer and Nicolò Cesa-Bianchi. On-line learning with malicious noise and the closure algorithm. In Setsuo Arikawa and Klaus P. Jantke, editors, *Algorithmic Learning Theory. ALT'94. ALT'94*, pages 229–247. Lecture Notes in Artificial Intelligence 872. Springer, 1994.

[Ang88]   D. Angluin. Queries and concept learning. *Machine Learning*, 2(4):319–342, April 1988.

[AST93]   M. Anthony and J. Shawe-Taylor. A result of Vapnik with applications. *Discrete Applied Mathematics*, 47:207–217, 1993.

[Aue93]   Peter Auer. On-line learning of rectangles in noisy environments. In *Proceedings of the Sixth Annual ACM Conference on Computational Learning Theory*, pages 253–261. ACM Press, 1993.

[HLW88]   D. Haussler, N. Littlestone, and M. K. Warmuth. Predicting {0,1} functions on randomly drawn points. In *Proceedings of the 29th Annual IEEE Symposium on Foundations of Computer Science*, pages 100–109. IEEE Computer Society Press, 1988.

[HSW90]   David Helmbold, Robert Sloan, and Manfred K. Warmuth. Lerning nested differences of intersection-closed concept classes. *Machine Learning*, 5:165–196, 1990.

[HSW92]   D. Helmbold, R. Sloan, and M. K. Warmuth. Learning integer lattices. *SIAM J. Comput.*, 21(2):240–266, 1992.

[KL93]   M. Kearns and M. Li. Learning in the presence of malicious errors. *SIAM J. Comput.*, 22:807–837, 1993.

[Lit88]   N. Littlestone. Learning quickly when irrelevant attributes abound: A new linear-threshold algorithm. *Machine Learning*, 2:285–318, 1988.

[Nat91]   B. K. Natarajan. *Machine Learning: A Theoretical Approach*. Morgan Kaufmann, San Mateo, CA, 1991.

[Val84]   L. G. Valiant. A theory of the learnable. *Commun. ACM*, 27(11):1134–1142, November 1984.

[VC71]   V. N. Vapnik and A. Y. Chervonenkis. On the uniform convergence of relative frequencies of events to their probabilities. *Theory of Probab. and its Applications*, 16(2):264–280, 1971.

Learning Sparse Linear Combinations of Basis Functions over a Finite Domain

Atsuyoshi Nakamura and Shinji Miura

C&C Research Laboratories, NEC Corporation
4-1-1 Miyazaki Miyamae-ku, Kawasaki 216, Japan
E-mail: {atsu.miura}@sbl.cl.nec.co.jp.

Abstract. We study the problem of identifying a $GF(2)$-valued ($\{0,1\}$-valued) or real-valued function over a finite domain by querying the values of the target function at points of the learner's choice. We analyze the *(function value query) learning complexity* of subclasses of such functions, namely, the number of queries needed to identify an arbitrary function in a given subclass. Since the whole class of $GF(2)$-valued functions, and the class of real-valued functions, over a domain with cardinality N is each an N-dimensional vector space, an arbitrary function in each of these classes can be written as a linear combination of N functions from an arbitrary basis. *The size of function f with respect to basis B* is defined to be the number of non-zero coefficients in the unique representation of f as a linear combination of functions in B. We show upper and lower bounds on the learning complexity of the size-k subclasses for various basis, including the basis that enjoys the minimum learning complexity (among all bases). We also consider subclasses of real-valued functions representable by a linear combination of basis functions *with non-negative coefficients*. We analyze the learning complexity of such subclasses for two bases, and show that neither of them attains the lower bound we obtained for the basis with the minimum learning complexity.

1 Introduction

We consider the learning problem of $GF(2)$-valued ($\{0,1\}$-valued) or real-valued functions over a finite domain via function value queries, i.e., queries which ask for the values of the target function at points of the learner's choice. As an illustrative example, consider an answer sheet of a certain test in which 40 (yes or no) answers are filled. These 40 answers determine the testee's score on the test. If the scores are given by real numbers, we can regard the score of an answer sheet as a real-valued function on $\{\text{yes,no}\}^{40}$. Supposing that the scoring method for the sheets has not been announced, how can you determine that method by asking for the scores of a number of answer sheets that you are allowed to make up? For which sheets and in what order should you ask what the scores are, if you wish to use as small a number of queries as possible ? In this case, determining the scoring method corresponds to learning a function on $\{\text{yes,no}\}^{40}$, and asking for the score of a certain sheet corresponds to a function value query.

Since, for an arbitrary field F, we can view an F-valued function on a domain with cardinality N as an N-dimensional vector space F^N over F, the whole class of such functions can be represented by a linear space whose basis consists of N mutually independent functions. We define *the size of function f with respect to basis B* to be the number of non-zero coefficients in the representation of f as a linear combination of functions in B. We analyze the *(function value query) learning complexity* — the number of function value queries needed to identify a target function — of some subclasses of $GF(2)$-valued and real-valued functions, as a function of domain size N and target function size s (or its known upper bound k).

As a basis of Boolean functions on $\{0,1\}^n$, which can be viewed as $GF(2)$-valued functions on a domain with cardinality 2^n, the set of functions representable by the product of a subset of n Boolean variables is well-known, and linear combinations of these basis functions are known as multivariate polynomials over $GF(2)$ (or as $GF(2)$ polynomials). Roth and Benedek [RB91] and Hellerstein and Warmuth [HW] studied the learning complexity of the size-k (k-sparse) subclass of this function class. What motivate this research are the following questions: What basis achieves the least learning complexity for its size-k subclass, and how does the learning complexity of the size-k subclass vary depending on the choice of the basis ? This paper partially resolves these questions.

For the $GF(2)$-valued function class, we generalize the relation between Reed-Muller code [MS77] and the learning complexity of the size-k subclass of multivariate polynomials over $GF(2)$ discussed in [RB91]. We show that the existence of a binary linear code of length N, of dimension at least m and minimum distance at least $2k + 1$, insures the existence of a basis on a domain with cardinality N such that the learning complexity of its size-k subclass is at most $N - m$. We see that the *BCH Basis*, derived from the parity check matrix of a binary BCH code, achieves the optimal complexity $O(k \log N)$ among all bases.

For the real-valued function class, we only consider the bases composed of $\{0,1\}$-valued functions only. Any basis of the $GF(2)$-valued function class is also a basis of the real-valued function class [NA93], and so we can obtain the same upper bound of $O(k \log N)$ on the complexity of the size-k subclass for the BCH Basis, which is nearly optimal because we also show a lower bound of $\Omega(k(\log N)/\log k)$ for any basis..

Concerning the real-valued function class, we also considered the subclasses composed of functions representable by a linear combination of basis functions *with nonnegative coefficients*. We analyzed the learning complexity of such subclasses $\mathcal{F}^+_{LB}(\Re)$ for *Linear Basis* and $\mathcal{F}^+_{SB}(\Re)$ for *Set Lattice Basis*. We generalize algorithm 'Identify' [NA95], which learns $\mathcal{F}^+_{SB}(\Re)$, to 'G-Identify' which learns $\mathcal{F}^+_{LB}(\Re)$ as well as $\mathcal{F}^+_{SB}(\Re)$ with at most $(\lceil \log N \rceil - \lfloor \log s \rfloor + 1)s$ function value queries, where N is the domain size and s is the target size. (This algorithm can identify any target without knowing its size.) The existence of this algorithm proves that the learning complexity of $\mathcal{F}^+_{LB}(\Re)$ and $\mathcal{F}^+_{SB}(\Re)$ are both $O(s \log N)$. In fact, we show that the learning complexity of $\mathcal{F}^+_{LB}(\Re)$ is $\Theta(s \log N)$ by proving a lower bound $\Omega(s \log N)$. As for $\mathcal{F}^+_{SB}(\Re)$, we show that its complexity is *not* $O(s(\log N)/\log s)$, which means that Set Lattice Basis does not attain the lower bound $\Omega(s(\log N)/\log s)$ we obtained on the learning complexity of a subclass of this kind for any basis.

2 Preliminaries

Let $\mathcal{F}(F)$ denote the class of F-valued functions on finite domain D with cardinality N, where F is $GF(2)$ or $\Re$. We can view $\mathcal{F}(F)$ as an N-dimensional vector space F^N over F, which is a linear space spanned by a basis consisting of N mutually independent vectors. In this paper, we consider bases of $\mathcal{F}(F)$ which are composed of $\{0,1\}$-valued functions only, even when $F = \Re$. Since any set of vectors which are mutually independent in the vector space $GF(2)^N$ over $GF(2)$ are also mutually independent in the vector space $\Re^N$ over $\Re$ [NA93], every basis of $\mathcal{F}(GF(2))$ is also a basis of $\mathcal{F}(\Re)$.

We define a partial order ' $\preceq$ ' on functions as follows:

$$f \preceq g \overset{def}{\Leftrightarrow} \forall a \in D \, [f(a) \leq g(a)].$$

The next three examples are bases of $\mathcal{F}(GF(2))$ as well as $\mathcal{F}(\Re)$.

Example 1. **Disjoint Basis (DB):**
$\quad DB = \{f_a : f_a(x) = 1 \text{ iff } x = a, a \in D\}$
Every pair in DB are incomparable with respect to ' $\preceq$ '.

Example 2. **Linear Basis (LB):** $D = \{1, 2, ..., N\}$.
$\quad LB = \{f_i : f_i(x) = 1 \text{ iff } x \leq i, i \in D\}$
Every pair in LB are comparable with respect to ' $\preceq$ '.

Example 3. **Set Lattice Basis (SB):** $D = \{0,1\}^n$ $(2^n = N)$.
$\quad SB = \{\prod_{i \in S} x_i : S \subseteq \{1, ..., n\}\}$.
where x_i is a variable for the i'th component of D. $(SB, \preceq)$ has a lattice structure.

The next example is a basis of $\mathcal{F}(\Re)$ but not of $\mathcal{F}(GF(2))$.

Example 4. **Parity Basis (PB):** $D = \{0,1\}^n$ $(2^n = N)$,
$\quad PB = \{\bigoplus_{i \in S} x_i : S \subseteq \{1, ..., n\}\}$.
where $[\bigoplus_{i \in S} x_i](b_1, ..., b_n) = 1$ iff $|\{i \in S : b_i = 1\}| = 0 \; (mod \; 2)\}$.

For $f \in \mathcal{F}$, we define $size_B(f)$ to be the number of non-zero coefficients when f is represented by a linear combination of functions in B. For example, consider function $\mathbf{1}$ whose value is 1 at every assignment in D. For this function, $size_{LB}(\mathbf{1}) = size_{SB}(\mathbf{1}) = size_{PB}(\mathbf{1}) = 1$ but $size_{DB}(\mathbf{1}) = N$. Although in general one only has $size_B(f) \leq N$, here we assume for all bases B considered that

$$size_B(f) \leq N^{c_0}, \text{ where } c_0 \text{ is a constant with } 0 < c_0 < 1.$$

We call this condition the *sparsity condition*.

We let $\mathcal{F}_B^k(F)$ denote the subclass of $\mathcal{F}(F)$ composed of all functions with $size_B(f) \leq k$. $\mathcal{F}_B^+(\Re)$ denotes the subclass of $\mathcal{F}(\Re)$ representable by a linear combination of functions in B with non-negative coefficients. In this paper, all logarithms are to the base 2.

3 Function value query learning complexity

A *function value query* (*membership query* when f is $\{0.1\}$-valued) is a query which asks for the value $f(a)$ of an unknown function f at a certain point a. Let $\mathcal{A}$ denote the set of algorithms which identify an arbitrary function f in a function class $\mathcal{G}$ using function value queries only. For $A \in \mathcal{A}$ and $f \in \mathcal{G}$, $NFQ_A(f)$ denotes the number of function value queries needed for A to identify f. We then define $CFQ_A(\mathcal{G})$ and $CFQ(\mathcal{G})$ as follows[1] :

$CFQ_A(\mathcal{G}) = \max_{f \in \mathcal{G}} NFQ_A(f)$. and

$CFQ(\mathcal{G}) = \min_{A \in \mathcal{A}} CFQ_A(\mathcal{G})$.

We call $CFQ(\mathcal{G})$ the *function value query learning complexity* of $\mathcal{G}$. or simply the learning complexity of $\mathcal{G}$.

In this paper. we analyze $CFQ(\mathcal{F}_B^k(F))$ as a function of domain size N and known upper bound k on the target function size and $CFQ(\mathcal{F}_B^+(\Re))$ as a function of domain size N and target function size s.

We sometimes consider for any function class $\mathcal{G}$ the learning complexity $CFQ^{batch}(\mathcal{G})$ in a nonadaptive (batch) learning model. in which the sequence of queries made by a learning algorithm cannot depend on the answers to earlier queries.

Here. we use the notation[2] $CFQ(\mathcal{G}_B) = O(g(N.s))$. where N is the domain size of functions in $\mathcal{G}_B$ and $s = size_B(f)$ for a target function f. in the following sense:

$$\exists c(> 0). \exists N_0. \exists s_0 \text{ s.t. } \forall N \geq N_0. N^{c_0} \geq \forall s \geq s_0 [CFQ(\mathcal{G}_B) \leq cg(N.s)].$$

Notice that the sparsity condition is incorporated in this definition. The definition of $CFQ(\mathcal{G}_B) = \Omega(g(N.s))$ is similar to the above except that the last inequality is replaced by $CFQ(\mathcal{G}_B) \geq cg(N.s)$. We then define $CFQ(\mathcal{G}_B) = \Theta(g(N.s))$ by $CFQ(\mathcal{G}_B) = O(g(N.s)) = \Omega(g(N.s))$ and $CFQ(\mathcal{G}_B) = \omega(g(N.s))$ by $CFQ(\mathcal{G}_B) \neq O(g(N.s))$.

4 Learning $GF(2)$-valued functions

As is discussed on p.293 in [RB91]. there exists a certain relation between binary linear coding theory and learning from function value queries. First. we generalize the relation noted in [RB91].

Definition 1 [MS77]. $C \subseteq GF(2)^N$ is said to be a *binary linear code of length N and dimension m* if a matrix H having N columns and $N - m$ mutually independent rows composed of elements in $GF(2)$ exists such that $C = \{\mathbf{x} : H\mathbf{x} = \mathbf{0}\}$, where $\mathbf{0}$ is a vector composed of 0 only. A matrix H satisfying $C = \{\mathbf{x} : H\mathbf{x} = \mathbf{0}\}$ is called a *parity check matrix* of C.

The *minimum distance of C* is defined to be the minimum Hamming distance between two distinct vectors in C.

---

[1] In this paper. we only consider function classes over a finite domain. so max and min always exist.

[2] As for $\mathcal{F}_B^k(F)$. we use the same notation with k in place of s.

Theorem 2. *There exists a binary linear code of length N, of dimension at least m and minimum distance at least $2k + 1$, if and only if there exists a basis B of $\mathcal{F}(GF(2))$ on a domain of cardinality N such that[3] $CFQ^{batch}(\mathcal{F}_B^k(GF(2))) \leq N - m$.*

Proof. Assume that C is a binary linear code of length N, of dimension $m_0 \geq m$ and minimum distance at least $2k + 1$. Let H denote the parity check matrix of C composed of $N - m_0$ mutually independent rows. Then, the mapping ϕ_H from $GF(2)^N$ to $GF(2)^{N-m_0}$ defined by $\phi_H(x) = Hx$ is an injection on $X = \{\mathbf{x} \in GF(2)^N$: The Hamming distance between $\mathbf{x}$ and $\mathbf{0}$ is at most $k\}$, since otherwise, there would exist two distinct vectors $\mathbf{x}, \mathbf{y} \in X$ such that $H\mathbf{x} = H\mathbf{y}$, and the Hamming distance between $\mathbf{x} - \mathbf{y} \in C$ and $\mathbf{0} \in C$ would be at most $2k$, contradicting the assumption that the minimum distance of C is $2k + 1$. Now define an $N \times N$ matrix H' whose rows are mutually independent by adding m_0 rows to H as the $(N - m_0 + 1)$th row,....,the Nth row. Define a function $f_j \in \mathcal{F}(GF(2))$ on domain $D = \{1, ..., N\}$ as $f_j(i) = H'(i, j)$ for $j = 1, ..., N$. Let $B = \{f_1, ..., f_N\}$. We show that the function values at $1, ..., N - m_0$ are enough to identify any function in $\mathcal{F}_B^k(GF(2))$. For $f = \sum_{i=1}^N a_i f_i \in \mathcal{F}(GF(2))$, let $\mathbf{f}$ denote the vector whose ith component is a_i. Then, $\{\mathbf{f} : f \in \mathcal{F}_B^k(GF(2))\}$ coincides with X defined above. If $H'(i)$ denotes the ith row of H', then $H'(i) \cdot \mathbf{f} = f(i)$. Thus, $H\mathbf{f} = \begin{pmatrix} f(1) \\ \vdots \\ f(N - m_0) \end{pmatrix}$

by the definition of H'. Since ϕ_H is an injection on X, any f in $\mathcal{F}_B^k(GF(2))$ can be identified from $f(1), ..., f(N - m_0)$.

On the other hand, assume the existence of basis $B = \{f_1, ..., f_N\}$ satisfying $CFQ^{batch}(\mathcal{F}_B^k(GF(2))) \leq N - m$. Without loss of generality, we can assume that every $f \in \mathcal{F}_B^k(GF(2))$ can be identified from its values at $1, ..., N - m$. Define $(N - m) \times N$ matrix H as $H(i, j) = f_j(i)$. Consider the binary linear code C defined by the parity matrix H. Since the mapping defined by H is an injection on X defined above, the minimum distance of C is at least $2k + 1$. □

The proof of Theorem 2 implies the next corollary.

Corollary 3. *Let H be a $GF(2)$-valued $N \times N$ regular matrix and $B = \{f_1, ..., f_N\}$ be a basis of $\mathcal{F}(GF(2))$ on the domain $\{1, ..., N\}$. Assume that $f_j(i) = H(i, j)$ for all $i, j \in \{1, ..., N\}$. Let $C_N(k)$ be a code of length N, of dimension at least $m(k)$ and minimum distance at least $2k + 1$ for each $k \in \{0, 1, ..., \lfloor (N - 1)/2 \rfloor\}$. Then, the following two conditions are equivalent.*

1. *For each $k \in \{0, ..., \lfloor (N - 1)/2 \rfloor\}$, some submatrix H' composed of at most $N - m(k)$ rows of H is a parity check matrix of $C_N(k)$.*
2. *$CFQ^{batch}(\mathcal{F}_B^k(GF(2))) \leq N - m(k)$ for all $k \in \{0, ..., \lfloor (N - 1)/2 \rfloor\}$.*

Proof. This corollary can be proven similarly to Theorem 2. □

Example 5 (r 'th order Reed-Muller code [RB91]). This code has length $N = 2^n$, dimension $m = \sum_{i=0}^r \binom{n}{i}$, and minimum distance $d = 2^{n-r}$ (See [MS77]). By

---

[3] CFQ^{batch} is the learning complexity of nonadaptive learning defined in Section 3.

setting $k = 2^{n-r-1} - 1$, we get $N - m = \sum_{i=0}^{\log(k+1)} \binom{n}{i} \leq \sum_{i=0}^{\lfloor \log k \rfloor + 1} \binom{n}{i}$. By Theorem 2, there exists basis B of $\mathcal{F}(GF(2))$ such that $CFQ^{batch}(\mathcal{F}_B^k(GF(2))) \leq \sum_{i=0}^{\lfloor \log k \rfloor + 1} \binom{n}{i} = O(n^{\lfloor \log k \rfloor + 1})$. Moreover, it can be shown that for each $k \in \{0, \ldots, 2^{n-1} - 1\}$ there is a Reed-Muller code $C_N^{RM}(k)$ of length N, of dimension at least $N - \sum_{i=0}^{\lfloor \log k \rfloor + 1} \binom{n}{i}$ and minimum distance at least $2k + 1$ by chosing an appropriate r. For this $C_N^{RM}(k)$, there exists an $N \times N$ matrix H satisfying condition 1 in Corollary 3, and for such an H, SB on the domain $\{0, 1\}^n$ (defined in Example 3) corresponds to B in Corollary 3. Thus, $CFQ^{batch}(\mathcal{F}_{SB}^k(GF(2))) \leq \sum_{i=0}^{\lfloor \log k \rfloor + 1} \binom{n}{i}$ for all $k \in \{0, \ldots, 2^{n-1} - 1\}$. $\mathcal{F}_{SB}^k$ is the class of k-sparse multivariate polynomials over $GF(2)$. Roth and Benedek invented a polynomial (in n) time algorithm[4] using $\sum_{i=0}^{\lfloor \log k \rfloor + 1} \binom{n}{i}$ function value queries.

Example 6 (binary BCH code). It is well-known that for each $k \in \{0, \ldots, 2^{n-1} - 1\}$ there exists a binary BCH code $C_N^{BCH}(k)$ of length $N = 2^n - 1$, of dimension at least $N - nk$ and minimum distance at least $2k + 1$ such that the first l rows (such that $l \leq nk$) of some regular matrix H is a parity check matrix of $C_N^{BCH}(k)$ for all $k \in \{0, \ldots, 2^{n-1} - 1\}$. (See [MS77].) Thus by Corollary 3, the basis B corresponding to this H satisfies $CFQ^{batch}(\mathcal{F}_B^k(GF(2))) \leq nk$ for all $k \in \{0, \ldots, 2^{n-1} - 1\}$. If there is no integer n satisfying $N = 2^n - 1$, let $N' = 2^{\lceil \log(N+1) \rceil} - 1$ and consider an $N' \times N'$ matrix H' satisfying that the first l' rows (such that $l' \leq k\lceil \log(N + 1) \rceil$) of H' is a parity check matrix of $C_{N'}^{BCH}(k)$ for all $k \in \{0, \ldots, \lfloor (N' - 1)/2 \rfloor\}$. Let H be an $N \times N$ regular submatrix of H' composed of the first N rows of H'. It is easy to see that for each $k \in \{0, \ldots, \lfloor (N - 1)/2 \rfloor\}$ there is a code $C_N(k)$ of length N, of dimension at least $N - k\lceil \log(N + 1) \rceil$ and minimum distance $2k + 1$ such that the first l' rows of H give a parity check matrix of $C_N(k)$ for all $k \in \{0, \ldots, \lfloor (N - 1)/2 \rfloor\}$. Then, the basis B corresponding to this H satisfies $CFQ^{batch}(\mathcal{F}_B^k(GF(2))) \leq k\lceil \log(N + 1) \rceil$ for all $k \in \{0, \ldots, \lfloor (N - 1)/2 \rfloor\}$.

We call a basis constructed in this fashion a *BCH Basis (BB)*.

From this example, we can obtain the next theorem.

Theorem 4. *There exists a basis B of $\mathcal{F}(GF(2))$ on a domain of cardinality N such that $CFQ^{batch}(\mathcal{F}_B^k(GF(2))) \leq k\lceil \log(N + 1) \rceil = O(k \log N)$.*

Proof. BCH basis defined in Example 6 satisfies the condition. □

By the next theorem, we will see that the BCH Basis is optimal within a constant factor with respect to $CFQ(\mathcal{F}_B^k(GF(2)))$ among all bases B of $\mathcal{F}(GF(2))$.

Theorem 5. *For every basis B of $\mathcal{F}(GF(2))$ on a domain of cardinality N,*
$$CFQ(\mathcal{F}_B^k(GF(2))) \geq \log \sum_{i=0}^{k} \binom{N}{i} \geq k(\log N - \log k) = \Omega(k \log N).$$

---

[4] Note that the cardinality of SB is 2^n

Proof. It is trivial that at least $\log |\mathcal{F}_B^k|$ function value queries are necessary to identify an arbitrary function in $\mathcal{F}_B^k$. Since $|\mathcal{F}_B^k| = \sum_{i=0}^{k} \binom{N}{i}$, the first inequality holds. The last equality follows from the definition of Ω in Section 3. $\square$

5 Learning real-valued functions

In this section, we analyze $CFQ(\mathcal{F}_B^k(\Re))$ for bases B of $\mathcal{F}(\Re)$ composed of $\{0,1\}$-valued functions only[5].

Using the fact that vectors that are mutually independent in the vector space $GF(2)^N$ over $GF(2)$ are also mutually independent in the vector space $\Re^N$ over $\Re$, BCH basis also achieves the upper bound $O(k \log N)$ as a basis of $\mathcal{F}(\Re)$.

Corollary 6. *There exists a basis B of $\mathcal{F}(\Re)$ (composed of $\{0,1\}$-valued functions only) on a domain of cardinality N such that $CFQ^{batch}(\mathcal{F}_B^k(\Re)) \leq k\lceil\log(N+1)\rceil = O(k \log N)$.*

The lower bound corresponding to Theorem 5 is a little worse for real-valued functions.

Theorem 7. *For every basis B of $\mathcal{F}(\Re)$ (composed of $\{0,1\}$-valued functions only) on a domain of cardinality N, $CFQ(\mathcal{F}_B^k(\Re)) \geq (\log \sum_{i=0}^{k} \binom{N}{i})/\log(k+1) \geq k(\log N - \log k)/\log(k+1) = \Omega(k(\log N)/\log k)$.*

Proof. Let $\mathcal{G}$ be a subclass of $\mathcal{F}_B^k(\Re)$ composed of functions representable by a linear combination of B with coefficients 0's and 1's only. Then, the function value of $f \in \mathcal{G}$ at any point is $0, ..., k-1$ or k. Thus, l function value queries can distinguish at most $(k+1)^l$ functions from each other, and this number must be at least $|\mathcal{G}|$ to distinguish all functions in $\mathcal{G}$ from each other. Since $|\mathcal{G}| = \sum_{i=0}^{k} \binom{N}{i}$, the theorem follows. $\square$

Remark 1. From the way $\mathcal{G}$ is constructed in the proof of Theorem 7, it trivially follows that the above lower bound holds for the size-k subclass of $\mathcal{F}_B^+(\Re)$, for which a lower bound of the same order was proved for the case $B = SB$ by a similar method in [NA95].

6 Learning non-negative functions

In this section, we consider the learning complexity of $\mathcal{F}_B^+(\Re)$ as a function of domain size N and target function size s with respect to B, where B is a basis of $\mathcal{F}(\Re)$ composed of $\{0,1\}$-valued functions only. Upper and lower bounds on $\min_B CFQ(\mathcal{F}_B^+(\Re))$ are $O(s \log N)$ and $\Omega(s(\log N)/\log s)$ by Theorem 3.1 in [NA95] (See Corollary 12 in this paper) and Remark 1. Here, we analyze $CFQ(\mathcal{F}_B^+(\Re))$ for two specific bases B, Linear Basis and Set Lattice Basis.

---

[5] If any basis B of $\mathcal{F}(\Re)$ is allowed, then we can find B such that $CFQ^{batch}(\mathcal{F}_B^k(\Re)) = 2k$ for all N.

6.1 Classes of non-negative functions with Linear Bases

First, we describe a general algorithm that exactly learns both $\mathcal{F}_{LB}^{+}(\Re)$ and $\mathcal{F}_{SB}^{+}(\Re)$. For $f \in B$, we call the point $a \in D$ a *representative point* of f if the following condition holds : $\forall g \in B[f \preceq g \Leftrightarrow g(a) = 1]$. Let $\mathcal{G}_f = \{g \in \mathcal{G} : f \preceq g\}$ for any function class $\mathcal{G}$ and its element $f \in \mathcal{G}$. We call f the *midpoint* of $\mathcal{G}$ when $||\mathcal{G}_f| - |\mathcal{G} - \mathcal{G}_f|| \leq 1$. We say that $\mathcal{G}$ *can be halved recursively* if $\mathcal{G}$ has the following property (1) :

(1) $\mathcal{G}$ is composed of only one element or has a midpoint f such that both $\mathcal{G}_f$ and $\mathcal{G} - \mathcal{G}_f$ can be halved recursively.

```
procedure G-Identify return(H)
H ∈ F⁺_B(ℜ)
(T : target function in F⁺_B(ℜ)
a : a representative point of a minimum element in B)
begin
        p = T(a)
        if p = 0 then return(0) else return(Divide-two(B, p, 0))
end
procedure Divide-two(𝒢, p, H) return(H_out)
𝒢 : a subset of B that can be halved recursively and
            whose every element has its representative point in D
p : the value of ∑_{f∈𝒢} c_f      (T = ∑_{f∈B} c_f f)
H, H_out ∈ F⁺_B(ℜ)
begin
        while |𝒢| > 1
                f : a midpoint of 𝒢
                a : a representative point of f
                q := T(a) − H(a)
                if q = p then 𝒢 := 𝒢_f
                else if q = 0 then 𝒢 := 𝒢 − 𝒢_f
                else exit while
        end while
        if |𝒢| = 1 then
                f : the unique element in 𝒢
                return(H + pf)
        else begin
                H' := Divide-two(𝒢_f, q, H)
                return(Divide-two(𝒢 − 𝒢_f, p − q, H'))
            end
end
```

Fig. 1. Algorithm 'G-Identify'

The next theorem says that Algorithm 'G-Identify' (See Fig. 1) learns $\mathcal{F}_B^{+}(\Re)$ exactly with $CFQ_{G-Identify}(\mathcal{F}_B^{+}(\Re)) \leq (\lceil \log N \rceil - \lfloor \log s \rfloor + 1)s$ if the basis B satisfies certain conditions.

Theorem 8. $CFQ_{G-Identify}(\mathcal{F}_B^+(\Re)) \leq (\lceil \log N \rceil - \lfloor \log s \rfloor + 1)s$ *for every basis* B *satisfying the following conditions :*

1. *There exists a minimum element in* $(B, \preceq)$.
2. *Every element in* B *has a representative point in* D.
3. B *can be halved recursively.*

We omit the proof of Theorem 8 because it is a simple generalization of the proof of Theorem 3.1 in [NA95]. Here, we only give an overview of how algorithm 'G-Identify' works.

Let $T \in \mathcal{F}_B^+(\Re)$ be a target function represented by $\sum_{h \in B} c_h h$. One positive coefficient c_f can be found as follows. We can get the value of $\sum_{h \in B} c_h$ by asking for the function value at a representative point of a minimum element in B. The returned positive value indicates the existence of positive values in $\{c_h : h \in B\}$. Assume $\sum_{h \in B} c_h > 0$. Let $\mathcal{G} = B$ initially. Let f be the midpoint of $\mathcal{G}$ and a be a representative point of f. We can get the value of $\sum_{h \in \mathcal{G}_f} c_h$ by asking for the function value at a. If $\sum_{h \in \mathcal{G}_f} c_h > 0$, replace $\mathcal{G}$ with $\mathcal{G}_f$. Otherwise, replace $\mathcal{G}$ with $\mathcal{G} - \mathcal{G}_f$. After repeating this procedure at most $\lceil \log |B| \rceil$ times, $\mathcal{G}$ contains only one basis function whose coefficient is the function value at a representative point of the unique $f \in \mathcal{G}$.

In fact, we can find all positive coefficients c_f. Assume that the value of the positive coefficients of $f_1, f_2, ..., f_l$ are known and there are other positive coefficients. Then, we can find another positive coefficient by applying the same procedure to the function $T - \sum_{i=1}^l c_{f_i} f_i$. Thus, by repeating this process until all positive coefficients are found, we can identify the target function.

Algorithm 'G-Identify' is a generalization of algorithm 'Identify' in [NA95]. It searches for all positive coefficients efficiently by branching in the case that both $\mathcal{G}_f$ and $\mathcal{G} - \mathcal{G}_f$ contain basis functions having positive coefficients.

Corollary 9. $CFQ(\mathcal{F}_{LB}^+(\Re)) \leq (\lceil \log N \rceil - \lfloor \log s \rfloor + 1)s = O(s \log N)$

Proof. The minimum element of LB is f_1 and the representative point of f_i is i. The midpoints of LB are $f_{\lfloor N/2 \rfloor}$ and $f_{\lceil N/2 \rceil}$. Trivially, LB can be halved recursively. Thus, LB satisfies the condition of Theorem 8. □

Next, we show a lower bound on $CFQ(\mathcal{F}_{LB}^+(\Re))$.

Theorem 10. $CFQ(\mathcal{F}_{LB}^+(\Re)) \geq s \log \lfloor N/s \rfloor = \Omega(s \log N)$

Proof. We show that learning the size-k subclass of $\mathcal{F}_{LB}^+(\Re)$ needs at least $k \log \lfloor N/k \rfloor$ function value queries. Let $D = \{1, 2, ..., N\}$ and $LB = \{f_i : f_i(x) = 1 \text{ iff } x \leq i, i \in D\}$. We divide D into k almost-equal-sized subsets $S_1, ..., S_k$:

$$S_j = \{i \in D : \frac{(j-1)N}{k} < i \leq \frac{jN}{k}\}, \quad j = 1, 2, ..., k.$$

Consider a subclass $\mathcal{G}$ of $\mathcal{F}_{LB}^+(\Re)$ defined as $\mathcal{G} = \{\sum_{j=1}^k f_{i_j} : \forall j [i_j \in S_j]\}$.

Assume that the target function is $T = \sum_{j=1}^k f_{i_j}$, where $i_j \in S_j$. $T(i)$ for $i \in S_j$ is $k - (j-1)$ or $k - j$, and $k - (j-1)$ implies $i \leq i_j$ and $k - j$ implies $i > i_j$. Notice that we know nothing about the other i_h's ($h \neq j$) from $T(i)$ for $i \in S_j$. This means that the problem of identifying T can be reduced to k independent subproblems of finding i_j in S_j. Assume that $i_j \in S_j$ is known to satisfy $a_j < i_j \leq b_j$. When asked the function value at $i \in S_j$ with $a_j < i \leq b_j$, the adversary answers $k - (j - 1)$ if $i - a_j - 1 \leq b_j - i + 1$ and answers $k - j$ if $i - a_j - 1 > b_j - i + 1$. Then the number of elements in S_j which may be i_j does not become less than a half by every query for $i \in S_j$. Since $|S_j| \geq \lfloor N/k \rfloor$, the number of function value queries needed to find i_j is at least $\log |S_j| \geq \log \lfloor N/k \rfloor$. Thus, to identify $T \in \mathcal{G}$, we need at least $k \log \lfloor N/k \rfloor$ function value queries. Now the equality of the theorem follows from the definition of Ω in Section 3. $\qquad \square$

Corollary 11. $CFQ(\mathcal{F}_{LB}^+(\mathfrak{R})) = \Theta(s \log N)$

6.2 Classes of non-negative functions with Set Lattice Bases

In this subsection, we assume that $D = \{0,1\}^n$ and SB is the set of functions representable by a product of variables in $\{x_1, \ldots, x_n\}$, where x_i is a variable for the i'th component of D (See Sec. 2). Algorithm 'G-Identify' shown in the previous subsection also learns $\mathcal{F}_{SB}^+(\mathfrak{R})$ exactly using a number of queries bounded above by the same bound as that for $\mathcal{F}_{LB}^+(\mathfrak{R})$. The next corollary follows from Theorem 8.

Corollary 12 (Theorem 3.1 in [NA95]). $CFQ(\mathcal{F}_{SB}^+(\mathfrak{R})) \leq (n - \lfloor \log s \rfloor + 1)s = O(sn)$

Proof. The minimum element of SB is $x_1 x_2 \ldots x_n$ and the representative point of $\prod_{i \in S} x_i$ is the assignment $(a_1, \ldots, a_n)$, where $a_i = 1$ if and only if $i \in S$. The midpoints of SB are $\prod_{i \neq 1} x_i, \ldots, \prod_{i \neq n-1} x_i$ and $\prod_{i \neq n} x_i$. It is easy to see that SB can be halved recursively. Thus, SB satisfies the conditions of Theorem 8. $\qquad \square$

In the previous subsection, we showed $CFQ(\mathcal{F}_{LB}^+(\mathfrak{R})) = \Omega(s \log N)$, but does it hold that $CFQ(\mathcal{F}_{SB}^+(\mathfrak{R})) = \Omega(sn)$? We have not been able to answer this question, but we can show that $CFQ(\mathcal{F}_{SB}^+(\mathfrak{R})) = \omega(sn/\log s) \neq O(sn/\log s)$. Note that $CFQ(\mathcal{F}_{SB}^+(\mathfrak{R})) = \Omega(sn/\log s)$ by Remark 1.

First, we consider the following problem which we call *Pairing(n)*.

Pairing(n) Assume that each element of $P_n = \{1, \ldots, 2n\}$ is paired with another element of P_n, but no pair is known at the beginning. Find all pairs in P_n using queries $pair(i, j)$, $i, j \in \{1, \ldots, 2n\}$ for which 1 is returned when i and j are a pair and 0 otherwise.

Deciding all the pairings of P_n yields a partition of P_n of size n, and we call the resulting partition a *pair partition*. We use the following notation.

$\mathcal{D}_n = \{D : D \text{ is a pair partition of } P_n\}$

$q_n(A, D)$: the number of queries required for Algorithm A
to identify a pair partition $D \in \mathcal{D}_n$

$q_n(A) = \max_{D \in \mathcal{D}_n} q_n(A, D)$

$q_n = \min_{A \in \mathcal{A}} q_n(A)$, where $\mathcal{A}$ is the set of algorithms solving $Pairing(n)$.

Lemma 13. $q_n = n(n-1)$

Proof. $(q_n \geq n(n-1))$: Assume that the adversary returns 0 for each query $pair(i,j)$ as long as possible, that is, it returns 0 except when i and j are a pair in all partitions in $\mathcal{D}_n$ consistent with all answers of queries asked so far. Under this assumption, 1 is returned only when we already know the answer before making the query. Thus, we can assume that all answers are 0's. Consider a graph whose vertices are $1, \ldots, 2n$, and whose edges (i,j) are pairs of vertices for which a query $pair(i,j)$ has been asked before. Note that every edge (i,j) means that i and j are known not to be a pair. Now assume that there is only one pair partition $D = \{p_1, \ldots, p_n\}$ consistent with all answers to queries asked so far. Then, the following holds for every pair $\{p_i, p_j\}$ in D : there exist more than two edges between elements in p_i and elements in p_j. For $p_i = \{i_1, i_2\}$ and $p_j = \{j_1, j_2\}$, assume that there is only one edge (i_1, j_1) between them. Then another pair partition made by substituting $\{i_1, j_2\}$ and $\{j_1, i_2\}$ for p_i and p_j is also consistent, that contradicts the assumption that D is a unique consistent partition. We can similarly lead to contradiction in the other cases when there is at most one edge between p_i and p_j. Thus $q_n \geq 2 \binom{n}{2} = n(n-1)$.

$(q_n \leq n(n-1))$: Consider the following algorithm :

Initial value $S = \{1, \ldots, 2n\}, D = \emptyset$

Step 1 If $S = \emptyset$, then stop. Otherwise, remove $i \in S$ from S.

Step 2 Find an element j in S paired with i.

(The number of queries required is at most $|S| - 1$.)

Step 3 Add the pair $\{i, j\}$ to D. Remove $j \in S$ from S. Return to Step 1.

The number of queries needed for this algorithm in the worst case is $(2n-2)+(2n-4) + \ldots + 2 = n(n-1)$. $\qquad\square$

Theorem 14. *Let* $k \leq n/2$ *and* $\mathcal{G} = \{\sum_{p \in D} t_p : D \in \mathcal{D}_k\}$, *where* $t_{\{i,j\}} = \prod_{l \neq i,j} x_l$. *Then* $CFQ(\mathcal{G}) = k(k-1)$.

Proof. Without loss of generality, we can restrict the set of variables to $V = \{x_1, \ldots, x_{2k}\}$. For $U \subseteq V$, $\mathbf{0}_U$ denotes an assignment that assigns 0 to a variable $x \in V$ if and only if $x \in U$. For all $f \in \mathcal{G}$,

$f(\mathbf{0}_\emptyset) = k$,

$f(\mathbf{0}_U) = 1$ for $|U| = 1$, and

$f(\mathbf{0}_U) = 0$ for $|U| \geq 3$.

Therefore, we can get no information by asking for the value of $f(\mathbf{0}_U)$ for $|U| \neq 2$. Assume that the target function is $f = \sum_{p \in D} t_p$. For $|U| = 2$,

$$f(\mathbf{0}_U) = \begin{cases} 1 \text{ if } U \in D \\ 0 \text{ otherwise } . \end{cases}$$

This means that we must solve $Pairing(k)$ to identify f using function value queries. Thus, $CFQ(\mathcal{G}) = q_k = k(k-1)$. $\qquad\square$

Corollary 15. $CFQ(\mathcal{F}_{SB}^+(\Re)) = \omega(sn/\log s)$.

Proof. We show that the size-k subclass of $\mathcal{F}_{SB}^+(\Re)$ is not learnable from $O(kn/\log k)$ function value queries. Let $g(n,k)$ be the learning complexity of the size-k subclass of $\mathcal{F}_{SB}^+(\Re)$ and $h(n,k) = kn/\log k$. We show

$$\forall c > 0. \forall n_0. \forall k_0. \exists n \geq n_0. 2^{c_0 n} \geq \exists k \geq k_0 [g(n,k) > ch(n,k)].$$

Consider the case with $k = n/2$. Let $\mathcal{G}$ be the subset of the size-k subclass defined in Theorem 14. Since $g(n,k) \geq CFQ(\mathcal{G}) = n(k-1)/2$ by Theorem 14.

$$\frac{g(n,k)}{h(n,k)} \geq \frac{(k-1)\log k}{2k} \xrightarrow{k \to \infty} \infty.$$

Thus, for all $c > 0$, $g(n,k) > ch(n,k)$ holds for a large enough n and $k(= n/2)$. □

7 Concluding remarks and open problems

Basis B	$CFQ(\mathcal{F}_B^k(GF(2)))$	$CFQ(\mathcal{F}_B^k(\Re))$	$CFQ(\mathcal{F}_B^+(\Re))$	note
DB		N		
LB		N	$\Theta(s\log N)$ Cor.11	$k \geq 2$
SB	$O((\log N)^{\lfloor \log k \rfloor + 1})$, $\Omega((\log N/\lfloor \log k \rfloor)^{\lfloor \log k \rfloor})$ [RB91]Lem.2.1,[NA95]Th.4.1		$O(s\log N).\omega(s(\log N)/\log s)$ Cor.12,Cor.15	$N = 2^n$
BB		$O(k\log N)$ Th.4,Cor.6	$O(N)$	Ex.6
any	$\Omega(k\log N)$ Th.5	$\Omega(k(\log N)/\log k)$ Th.7	$\Omega(s(\log N)/\log s)$ Rem.1	

Table 1. CFQ's of $\mathcal{F}_B^k(GF(2))$, $\mathcal{F}_B^k(\Re)$ and $\mathcal{F}_B^+(\Re)$ for various bases B

In this paper, we analyzed the learning complexity of subclasses of the $GF(2)$-valued function class $\mathcal{F}(GF(2))$ and the real-valued function class $\mathcal{F}(\Re)$ on a finite domain with cardinality N. For an arbitrary basis B of $\mathcal{F}(GF(2))$, we considered subclass $\mathcal{F}_B^k(GF(2))$ composed of functions representable by a linear combination of at most k basis functions in B. For an arbitrary basis B of $\mathcal{F}(\Re)$ consisting of $\{0,1\}$-valued functions only, we considered subclass $\mathcal{F}_B^+(\Re)$ composed of functions representable by a linear combination of basis functions in B with non-negative coefficients, as well as $\mathcal{F}_B^k(\Re)$, which is defined similarly to $\mathcal{F}_B^k(GF(2))$.

Table 1 is the summary of our results. This table contains a few results that have not been shown in the body of this paper which we will briefly explain here. First, $CFQ(\mathcal{F}_{DB}^k(GF(2))) = CFQ(\mathcal{F}_{DB}^k(\Re)) = CFQ(\mathcal{F}_{DB}^+(\Re)) = N$ holds, because these subclasses contain $DB \cup \{0\}$, where 0 is the constantly 0-valued function, and 0 and one in DB remain consistent after any $N-1$ function value queries. Next, we explain why $CFQ(\mathcal{F}_{LB}^k(F)) = N$ holds for $F = GF(2)$ or $\Re$ when $k \geq 2$. Let $D = \{1, ..., N\}$. $DB = \{f_i : f_i(j) = 1 \text{ iff } j = i, i \in D\}$ and $LB = \{g_i : g_i(j) = 1 \text{ iff } j \leq i, i \in D\}$.

Then, an arbitrary element f_i of DB can be written as $f_i = g_i - g_{i-1}$ for $i \geq 2$ or $f_1 = g_1$, and this means $\mathcal{F}_B^2(F)$ contains $DB \cup \{0\}$. Thus, the complexity is N when $k \geq 2$ by the above argument. Finally, note that that $CFQ(\mathcal{F}_{BB}^+(\Re)) = O(N)$ is trivial. We are not aware of any non-trivial upper bound in the absence of information on the size of the target function.

Finally, we list some open problems.

We showed that BCH Basis is optimal within a constant factor among bases of $\mathcal{F}(GF(2))$ with respect to the learning complexity. However, the upper bound of $CFQ(\mathcal{F}_{BB}^k(\Re))$ shown in this paper differs by $\log k$ factor from the lower bound shown for any basis of $\mathcal{F}(\Re)$. Is there a basis B such that $CFQ(\mathcal{F}_B^k(\Re))$ is less than $O(k \log N)$ or can we get a lower bound for all bases of $\mathcal{F}(\Re)$ that is better than $\Omega(k(\log N)/\log k)$? A similar question arises with respect to $CFQ(\mathcal{F}_B^+(\Re))$. In this case, if the lower bound were tight, SB would not be optimal within a constant factor.

Concerning $\mathcal{F}_B^+(\Re)$, we showed that $CFQ(\mathcal{F}_{LB}^+(\Re)) = CFQ(\mathcal{F}_{SB}^+(\Re)) = O(s \log N)$ and $CFQ(\mathcal{F}_{LB}^+(\Re)) = \Omega(s \log N)$, but we could not prove that $CFQ(\mathcal{F}_{SB}^+(\Re)) = \Omega(s \log N)$. Is there any gap between $CFQ(\mathcal{F}_{LB}^+(\Re))$ and $CFQ(\mathcal{F}_{SB}^+(\Re))$, namely, can the upper bound of $CFQ(\mathcal{F}_{SB}^+(\Re))$ be improved ?

Acknowledgement

The authors thank Dr. Naoki Abe of C&C Research Laboratories and Dr. Kai Werther at Bonn University for valuable discussions and their helpful comments. The authors also acknowledge Mr. Katsuhiro Nakamura and Mr. Tomoyuki Fujita of C&C Research Laboratories for their encouragement.

References

[HW]   L. Hellerstein and M. Warmuth, "Interpolating GF[2] polynomials." Unpublished manuscript.

[MS77]   F. J. MacWilliams and N. J. A. Sloane, *The Theory of Error-Correcting Codes*, *Noth-Holland, Amsterdam*, 1977.

[NA93]   A. Nakamura and N. Abe, "Exact Learning of Linear Combination of Monotone Terms from Function Value Queries." Proceedings of 4th International Workshop, ALT'93 (*Lecture Notes in Artificial intelligence* 744), pp.300-313, 1993.

[NA95]   A. Nakamura and N. Abe, "Exact Learning of Linear Combination of Monotone Terms from Function Value Queries." *Theoretical Computer Science* 137, pp.159-176, 1995. (Journal version of [NA93])

[RB91]   R. M. Roth and G. M. Benedek, "Interpolation and approximation of sparse multivariate polynomials over GF[2]." *SIAM J. Comput.* 20(2), pp.291-314, 1991.

Inferring a DNA Sequence from Erroneous Copies (Abstract)

John Kececioglu[1] and Ming Li[2] and John Tromp[2]

[1] University of Georgia, Athens, GA 30602, USA
[2] University of Waterloo, Waterloo, Ont N2L 3G1, Canada

We are interested in the problem of how to infer an original DNA sequence from erroneous copies, with high probability.

DNA sequencing is a key step and a major bottleneck in the Human Genome Project. It is a relatively slow and expensive process (~$1 per base with current techniques). Since the human genome comprises no less than 3 billion bases, the development of faster and cheaper sequencing methods is crucial to this project.

Certain technologies promise the ability to obtain long DNA sequences fast but with lots of errors. In *single-molecule DNA sequencing*, the DNA strand is passed by a cutter, that cuts off a single base at a time, which then flows down a microscopic tube at high speed past an optical device. This excites the individual molecule and reads off which type of base it is. The order in time of the bases as they flow down the tube past the reader is hopefully the order of bases along the DNA strand. The process doesn't always flow smoothly, sometimes sputtering (especially at the beginning and the end), hence the presence of long deletions.

In this talk, we study the problem of how to reconstruct an original DNA sequence from a small number of erroneous copies. We deal with three types of commonly considered errors: insertion, deletion, and substitution.

There are several difficulties. First of all, given k sequences, doing multiple sequence alignment on those sequences by any known algorithm that guarantees optimality takes $\Omega(n^k)$ time. Second, even if we can do multiple alignment efficiently, is this guaranteed to yield the real sequence? And if it does, how many sequences do we need to stand a high chance of converging to the real sequence? Blackwell [1] has shown that if one takes the maximum likelihood point, then, in the limit, we can converge to the real sequence. With high probability, after sampling an exponential number of erroneous copies, we are bound to converge to the original sequence. But this approach is clearly not practical because n, the length of the sequence, is usually very large, in the hundreds or thousands. With our approach, we will need only a polylogarithmic number of copies. With k erroneous copies, and some reasonable assumptions, our algorithm converges in polynomial time independent of k, rather than in time n^k.

The analysis of our algorithm makes heavy use of Kolmogorov complexity [2]. Intuitively, the Kolmogorov complexity of a finite sequence is the length of the shortest program that prints the sequence. Kolmogorov complexity has found many applications in learning as well as in other areas of computer science such as proving lower bounds and the average case analysis of algorithms, see [2].

References

1. T. Blackwell, Ph.D. Thesis, Harvard University, 1994.
2. M. Li and P. Vitányi, *An introduction to Kolmogorov complexity and its applications.* Springer-Verlag, 1993.

Machine Induction Without Revolutionary Paradigm Shifts

John Case[1] and Sanjay Jain[2] and Arun Sharma[3]

[1] Department of Computer and Information Sciences, University of Delaware, Newark, DE 19716, USA, Email: case@cis.udel.edu

[2] Department of Information Systems and Computer Science, National University of Singapore, Singapore 0511, Republic of Singapore, Email: sanjay@iscs.nus.sg,

[3] School of Computer Science and Engineering, The University of New South Wales, Sydney, NSW 2052, Australia, Email: arun@cse.unsw.edu.au

Abstract. This paper provides a beginning study of the effects on inductive inference of paradigm shifts whose absence is approximately modeled by various formal approaches to forbidding large changes in the size of programs conjectured.

One approach, called *severe parsimony*, requires all the programs conjectured on the way to success to be nearly (i.e., within a recursive function of) minimal size. It is shown that this very conservative constraint allows learning infinite classes of functions, but *not* infinite r.e. classes of functions.

Another approach, called *non-revolutionary*, requires all conjectures to be nearly the same size as one another. This quite conservative constraint is, nonetheless, shown to permit learning some infinite r.e. classes of functions. Allowing, up to one extra *bounded size* mind change towards a final program learned certainly doesn't appear revolutionary. However, somewhat surprisingly for scientific (inductive) inference, it is shown that there are classes learnable *with* the non-revolutionary constraint (respectively, with severe parsimony), up to $(i+1)$ mind changes, and no anomalies, which classes can*not* be learned with no size constraint, an unbounded, finite number of anomalies in the final program, but with no more than i mind changes. Hence, in some cases, the possibility of one extra mind change is considerably more liberating than removal of very conservative size shift constraints. The proof of these results is also combinatorially interesting.

1 Introduction

The present paper is a beginning study of the phenomenon of paradigm shift (see Kuhn [19]) in the context of machine inductive learning/inference. The issues are difficult to formalize directly mathematically, so instead of tackling them directly, we take an indirect approach and investigate the effects on induction of disallowing *certain formalizable kinds of* paradigm shift. A number of mathematical formulations that capture some interesting notions of paradigm shift are proposed. The induction task we chose for this investigation is the identification of computer programs for computable functions from their graphs.[4]

---

[4] Several papers in computational learning theory, which investigate identification of computer programs for computable functions, have already provided explicit insights into inductive inference in science (see, for example, [22, 4, 11, 8, 2, 7, 14, 20]).

A paradigm shift is usually associated with a significant change in the hypothesis conjectured by the "learner." A plausible, though possibly overly simple expectation is that a significant change in hypotheses is also accompanied by a significant change in the size of the hypotheses. Thus, keeping learners from conjecturing hypotheses of extreme variation in size may be seen as disallowing a kind of paradigm shift. This assumption forms the basis of our beginning attempts herein to model induction without paradigm shifts.

Learning machines may be thought of as Turing machines computing a mapping from "finite sequences of data" into computer programs. A typical variable for learning machines is **M**. A *function learning machine* may be thought of as a learning machine that at any given time, takes an initial segment of the graph of a function as input and outputs the index of a computer program in some fixed acceptable programming system [25, 21, 27]. We now describe what it means for such a machine to learn a function.

Let N denote the set of natural numbers. Let f be a computable function, and let $n \in N$. Then, the initial segment of f of length n is denoted $f[n]$. The following definition is essentially Gold's [15] criterion for successful identification of functions by learning machines.

Definition 1. [15]

(a) **M Ex**-identifies f just in case **M**, fed the graph of f, converges to a program for f. In this case we say that $f \in \mathbf{Ex}(\mathbf{M})$.

(b) **Ex** denotes the set of all collections S of computable functions such that some machine **Ex**-identifies each function in S.

The class **Ex** is a set theoretic summary of the capability of single machines to **Ex**-identify collections of functions.

As noted, in the present study, we will view disallowing paradigm shift in terms of restrictions regarding the size of a machine's conjectures on the graph of a function. It is instructive, then, to review studies of size restriction on hypotheses in the inductive inference literature. Freivalds [13] was the first to consider a criterion of success in which a learning machine was required to conjecture the minimal size program for the function being identified. Unfortunately, this criterion of success turned out to be mathematically problematical since the collections of functions that could be identified according to this criterion were dependent on the acceptable programming system used to interpret a learner's conjectures. Freivalds relaxed this stringent requirement to introduce a criterion of success called *nearly minimal identification* according to which a learner need converge only to a program for the function whose size is within a computable "fudge factor" of the minimal size program for the function. This criterion, called herein **MEx** and which is acceptable programming system independent, turned out to be a useful notion and was extended by Chen [12]. However, it is easy to see that nearly minimal identification does not provide a suitable model for inference without paradigm shift because, although there is a size restriction placed on the final hypothesis, a learner is free to conjecture hypotheses of arbitrary size before the onset of convergence.[5] Addressing

---

[5] It does quite importantly model the possible goal in science of eventually finding *parsimonious* explanations.

this objection yields our first model of induction without paradigm shift. This formulation, referred to as *severely parsimonious identification*, requires that a learner not only conjecture a final program that is within a computable fudge factor of minimal size, but all its conjectures on the function being identified are required to be within that computable fudge factor of minimal size. We clarify this notion in the next definition.

Definition 2. (a) **M** is *severely parsimonious* on a collection of functions S just in case there exists a computable function h such that, for each $f \in S$, **M**, fed f, outputs only programs that are smaller in size than h(minimal size program for f).

(b) **SpEx** denotes the set of collections of functions, S, such that there exists a machine that is severely parsimonious on S and that **Ex**-identifies S.

A somewhat stronger requirement in which the learner behaves severely parsimoniously on every computable function is referred to as *globally severely parsimonious* identification. The class **gSpEx** is defined to be the collection of sets of functions, S, such that there exists a machine that is severely parsimonious on every computable function and that **Ex**-identifies S. This latter, global version of severe parsimony turns out to be too restrictive since we are able to show that only finite collections of functions can be identified by globally severely parsimonious learners. On the other hand there are infinite collections of functions that can be identified by severely parsimonious learners. However, no *infinite* r.e. class of (total) computable functions is identifiable by severely parsimonious machines! Surprisingly, then, standard classes easily and naturally identifiable without the constraint of severe parsimony (for example, by the enumeration technique [15, 4]) are no longer identifiable with this constraint.

The simplicity of severely parsimonious identification notwithstanding, it suffers from a crucial drawback as a model of induction without paradigm shift. The following argument illuminates this point.

There is nothing that prevents a learner from going from a small size conjecture to a large size conjecture: The restriction is due to the size of the programs conjectured in relation to the minimal size program for the function being learned, and not due to the sizes of the various conjectured programs. To see this point, suppose on successive initial segments a learner outputs a very small size program and a very large size program. It is not clear if a paradigm shift (of the kinds we are considering) has taken place. One cannot be sure that such a paradigm shift has taken place since later parts of the function may be complex enough so that the size of minimal program for the function is huge, hiding all the earlier differences in the conjectures. Although the global version of severe parsimony avoids this problem, as noted above, it turns out to be too restrictive.

To address these concerns, we introduce another approach to modeling induction without paradigm shifts. This new approach considers learners that, on any computable function, conjecture programs which differ only "slightly" in size from each other. We make this idea precise with the help of some technical machinery. Suppose **M** is a learning machine and f is a computable function. Then, ProgSet(**M**, f) is defined to be the collection of programs that are output by **M** on any initial segment of f.

Definition 3. A learning machine **M** is said to be *non-revolutionary* just in case there exists a computable function h such that for *each* computable f,

$$\max(\mathrm{ProgSet}(\mathbf{M}, f)) \leq h(\min(\mathrm{ProgSet}(\mathbf{M}, f))).$$

In other words, the range of a non-revolutionary machine's conjectures on any computable function is limited in terms of size, in fact there is a bound on how large the largest size conjecture can be in relation to the smallest size conjecture and this bound is uniform across every computable function.

Definition 4. **NrEx** denotes the set of collections of functions, S, such that some non-revolutionary machine **Ex**-identifies each function in S.[6]

Clearly, non-revolutionary learners capture an interesting notion of induction without paradigm shifts.

In the present paper we completely compare the power of all criteria considered (with and without anomalies allowed and/or mind change bounds [11]), and below are some interesting highlights.

Of course we would (correctly) expect the non-revolutionary restriction to limit learning power, i.e., we expect and have (from Theorem 31) that $(\mathbf{Ex} - \mathbf{NrEx}) \neq \emptyset$. Surprisingly, though, this theorem says, moreover, that *some* classes can be learned with severe parsimony, no anomalies and at most one mind change, which classes can*not* be learned by a non-revolutionary machine even with no restrictions on mind changes and allowing an unbounded, finite number of anomalies in the final programs learned! By contrast, however, we see below from the proof of Corollary 16(a) and from Proposition 30 that **NrEx**, unlike **SpEx**, *does* contain some infinite r.e. classes of (total) computable functions; hence, the quite conservative non-revolutionary restriction is, in *some other and important cases*, not as strongly deleterious to learning power as severe parsimony.

Of course the non-revolutionary constraint is quite conservative (as is severe parsimony). Allowing, say, up to one extra mind change toward a final program learned under the non-revolutionary constraint is seemingly trivially liberal—one little mind change *of bounded size* doesn't seem to make a revolution. *However*, by Theorem 34, somewhat surprisingly, there are classes learnable *with* the non-revolutionary constraint, up to $(i+1)$ mind changes, and no anomalies, which classes can*not* be learned with no size constraint, an unbounded, finite number of anomalies in the final program, but with no more than i mind changes. Hence, in some cases, the possibility of one extra mind change is considerably more liberating than removal of the quite conservative non-revolutionary constraint. The proof of this result is combinatorially interesting.

Also, we have, by Corollary 33(a), that possible anomalies, like possible mind changes, in some cases, liberate more learning power than permitting revolutionary shifts in program size. This result, however, follows easily from prior results in the literature.

---

[6] It is easily seen that, were we to require instead in the definition of **NrEx** that some machine **M** **Ex**-identifies each function in S, where **M**'s non-revolutionary behavior is exhibited on all $f \in S$ (and not necessarily on all computable f), the class **NrEx** would be the same. Likewise, it would be the same were we to require the non-revolutionary behavior on all f computable or not.

Theorems 25 and 23 provide results similar to those of the just above two para-
graphs, but for the very conservative constraint of severe parsimony.

Though this paper is mostly concerned with function identification, the above
notions have counterparts in language identification which will be discussed more
fully in a later version of the present paper. Most results carry over to the language
learning context; however, the picture, for language learning without paradigm shift,
is more complicated for vacillatory identification [6, 9, 18]. Later versions of the
paper will also report on slightly less conservative criteria in which the fudge factor
functions h are allowed to be limiting-recursive [28, 10].

We now proceed formally. Section 2 introduces the notation and preliminary
notions from inductive inference literature. Severely Parsimonious Identification is
considered in Section 3. Non-revolutionary identification is studied in Section 4. Section 5 deals with issues arising out of behaviorally correct and vacillatory function
learning, each without paradigm shift. Our proofs of many of the theorems in this
paper involve complicated combinatorial arguments.

2 Notation and Preliminaries

Recursion-theoretic concepts not explained below are treated in [26]. N denotes the
set of natural numbers. $*$ denotes a non-member of N and is assumed to satisfy
$(\forall n)[n < * < \infty]$. We let $e, i, j, k, l, m, n, p, r, s, t, x, y$, and z, with or without
decorations, range over N. We let a, b, c, and d, with or without decorations, range
over $N \cup \{*\}$. We let P, S, X, with or without decorations, range over subsets of
N and we let D range over finite subsets of N. $\in, \subseteq, \subset, \supseteq, \supset$, respectively denote
membership, subset, proper subset, superset and proper superset relations for sets.
$\emptyset$ denotes emptyset. $\operatorname{card}(P)$ denotes the cardinality of P. So then, '$\operatorname{card}(P) \leq *$'
means that $\operatorname{card}(P)$ is finite. $\min(P)$ and $\max(P)$ respectively denote the minimum
and maximum element in P. We take $\min(\emptyset)$ to be ∞ and $\max(\emptyset)$ to be 0.

$\langle \cdot, \cdot \rangle$ denotes a 1-1 mapping from pairs of natural numbers onto natural numbers.
π_1, π_2 are the corresponding projection functions. $\langle \cdot, \cdot \rangle$ is extended to n-tuples in a
natural way.

η, with or without decorations, ranges over partial functions. For $a \in N \cup \{*\}$,
$\eta_1 =^a \eta_2$ means that $\operatorname{card}(\{x \mid \eta_1(x) \neq \eta_2(x)\}) \leq a$. $\operatorname{domain}(\eta)$ and $\operatorname{range}(\eta)$
respectively denote the domain and range of partial function η.

$\mathcal{R}$ denotes the class of all *recursive* functions, i.e., total computable functions
with arguments and values from N. f, g, h, with or without decorations, range over
$\mathcal{R}$. $\mathcal{C}$ and $\mathcal{S}$, with or without decorations, range over subsets of $\mathcal{R}$. ψ ranges over
acceptable programming systems for the partial computable functions: $N \to N$. ψ_i
denotes the partial function computed by the i-th program in the ψ programming
system. φ denotes a fixed *acceptable* programming system. φ_i denotes the partial
computable function computed by program i in the φ-system. We let Φ be an arbitrary Blum complexity measure [5] associated with the acceptable programming system φ; such measures exist for any acceptable programming system [5]. For a given
total computable function f, we define $\operatorname{MinProg}(f)$ to denote $\min(\{i \mid \varphi_i = f\})$.

2.1 Function Identification in the Limit

We first describe function learning machines. We assume, without loss of generality, that the graph of a function is fed to a machine in canonical order. For $f \in \mathcal{R}$ and $n \in N$, we let $f[n]$ denote the finite initial segment $\{(x, f(x)) \mid x < n\}$. Clearly, $f[0]$ denotes the empty segment. SEG denotes the set of all finite initial segments, $\{f[n] \mid f \in \mathcal{R} \wedge n \in N\}$. We let σ, with or without decorations, range over SEG.

Definition 5. [15] A *function learning machine* is an algorithmic device that computes a mapping from SEG into $N \cup \{?\}$.

Intuitively, "?" above denotes the case when the machine may not wish to make a conjecture. Although it is not necessary to consider learners that issue "?" for identification in the limit, it becomes useful when the number of mind changes a learner can make is bounded. In this paper, we assume, without loss of generality, that once a function learning machine has issued a conjecture on some initial segment of a function, it outputs a conjecture on all extensions of that initial segment. This is without loss of generality, because a machine wishing to emit "?" after making a conjecture can instead be thought of as repeating its old conjecture. We let $\mathbf{M}$, with or without decorations, range over learning machines.

Since the set of all finite initial segments, SEG, can be coded onto N, we can view these machines as taking natural numbers as input and emitting natural numbers or ?'s as output. The next definition describes identification in the limit of functions. We also consider the case in which the final program is allowed to have anomalies. Some notation about anomalous programs is in order. For $a \in N \cup \{*\}$, a partial recursive function η, and a recursive function f, we say that $\eta =^a f$ (read: η is an a-variant of f) just in case card($\{n \mid \eta(n) \neq f(n)\}$) $\leq a$. It is helpful to think of a program i for η as an "anomalous explanation" for f, that is, an explanation with a finite number of anomalies (in fact, $\leq a$ anomalies) in its predictions. In this case i is referred to as an a-error program for f. Finally, we say that $\mathbf{M}(f)$ converges to i (written: $\mathbf{M}(f){\downarrow} = i$) iff $(\overset{\infty}{\forall} n)[\mathbf{M}(f[n]) = i]$; $\mathbf{M}(f)$ is undefined if no such i exists.

Definition 6. [15, 4, 11] Let $a, b \in N \cup \{*\}$.

(a) $\mathbf{M}$ $\mathbf{Ex}_b^a$-*identifies* f (read: $f \in \mathbf{Ex}_b^a(\mathbf{M})$) just in case there exists an a-error program i for f such that $\mathbf{M}(f){\downarrow} = i$ and card($\{n \mid ? \neq \mathbf{M}(f[n]) \neq \mathbf{M}(f[n + 1])\}$) $\leq b$ (i.e., $\mathbf{M}$ makes no more than b mind changes on f).
(b) $\mathbf{Ex}_b^a = \{\mathcal{S} \subseteq \mathcal{R} \mid (\exists \mathbf{M})[\mathcal{S} \subseteq \mathbf{Ex}_b^a(\mathbf{M})]\}$.

The relationship between the above criteria is summarized in the following theorem.

Theorem 7. [11, 4]

(a) Let $b \in N \cup \{*\}$. Then, $\mathbf{Ex}_b = \mathbf{Ex}_b^0 \subset \mathbf{Ex}_b^1 \subset \mathbf{Ex}_b^2 \subset \cdots \subset \mathbf{Ex}_b^*$.
(b) Let $a \in N \cup \{*\}$. Then, $\mathbf{Ex}_0^a \subset \mathbf{Ex}_1^a \subset \mathbf{Ex}_2^a \subset \cdots \subset \mathbf{Ex}_*^a$.
(c) $(\forall a, b, c, d \in N \cup \{*\})[\mathbf{Ex}_b^a \subseteq \mathbf{Ex}_d^c \iff (a \leq c) \wedge (b \leq d)]$.

2.2 Nearly Minimal Identification

Since our study of induction without paradigm shift is intimately related to identification of succinct programs, we next define the notion nearly minimal identification considered by Freivalds [13] and extended by Chen [12].

Definition 8. [13, 12] Let $a, b \in N \cup \{*\}$.

(a) **M MEx$_b^a$-identifies** f, with recursive fudge factor h, (written: $f \in$ **MEx$_b^a$(M, h)**) iff **M Ex$_b^a$-identifies** f and $\mathbf{M}(f) \leq h(\text{MinProg}(f))$.
(b) **M MEx$_b^a$-identifies** S, iff there exists a recursive fudge factor h such that, $S \subseteq$ **MEx$_b^a$(M, h)**.
(c) **MEx$_b^a$** $= \{S \subseteq \mathcal{R} \mid (\exists \mathbf{M})[\mathbf{M} \text{ MEx}_b^a\text{-identifies } S]\}$.

We write **MEx** for **MEx$_*^0$** and **MEx^a** for **MEx$_*^a$**.

The following is a theorem relating **MEx**-identification and **Ex**-identification.

Theorem 9. [12, 16] Let $a, b, c, d \in N \cup \{*\}$ and $n \in N$. Then

(a) $\mathbf{MEx}_b^a \subseteq \mathbf{Ex}_d^c \iff (a \leq c) \wedge (b \leq d)$.
(b) $\mathbf{Ex}_n^a \subseteq \mathbf{MEx}_*^a$.
(c) $\mathbf{Ex}_0^0 - \mathbf{MEx}_n^* \neq \emptyset$.
(d) $\mathbf{Ex}^0 - \mathbf{MEx}^n \neq \emptyset$.
(e) $\mathbf{Ex}^* = \mathbf{MEx}^*$.

3 Severely Parsimonious Identification

As noted in the introductory section, the constraint of severe parsimony requires a learning machine to emit programs of size within a computable "fudge" factor of the minimal size program. We formalize this notion in the next definition. In doing so we also consider the following two modifications on the constraint of severe parsimony as described in the introduction.

(a) Allowing the final programs to contain errors.
(b) Introducing a bound on the number of mind changes before the onset of convergence.

Definition 10. Let $a, b \in N \cup \{*\}$.

(a) **M** is *severely parsimonious on* $S \subseteq \mathcal{R}$ just in case there exists a recursive function h such that, for each $f \in S$, for each $n \in N$, $\mathbf{M}(f[n]) \leq h(\text{MinProg}(f))$.
(b) **M** is *globally severely parsimonious* just in case **M** is severely parsimonious on $\mathcal{R}$.
(c) **gSpEx$_b^a$** $= \{S \subseteq \mathcal{R} \mid (\exists \mathbf{M})[\mathbf{M} \text{ is globally severely parsimonious and } \mathbf{M} \text{ Ex}_b^a\text{-identifies } S]\}$.
(d) **SpEx$_b^a$** $= \{S \subseteq \mathcal{R} \mid (\exists \mathbf{M})[\mathbf{M} \text{ is severely parsimonious on } S \text{ and } \mathbf{M} \text{ Ex}_b^a\text{-identifies } S]\}$.

Intuitively, $\mathbf{SpEx}_b^a$ denotes the class of sets of functions, $\mathcal{S}$, such that some machine that is severely parsimonious on $\mathcal{S}$ $\mathbf{Ex}_b^a$-identifies $\mathcal{S}$. On the other hand $\mathbf{gSpEx}_b^a$ denotes the class of sets of functions that can be identified by a globally severely parsimonious machine. It is easy to see that for all $a, b \in N \cup \{*\}$,

$$\mathbf{gSpEx}_b^a \subseteq \mathbf{SpEx}_b^a.$$

Clearly, $\mathbf{SpEx}$ is $\mathbf{SpEx}_*^0$. Also, by $\mathbf{SpEx}^a$ we mean $\mathbf{SpEx}_*^a$. We first show the following result which shows that, if a machine $\mathbf{M}$ is severely parsimonious on an r.e. collection of functions $\mathcal{S}$, then $\mathbf{M}$ outputs only finitely many programs on initial sequences drawn from functions in $\mathcal{S}$. This result is used to show that $\mathbf{gSpEx}$ is a trivial class.

Theorem 11. *Suppose $\mathcal{S}$ is an r.e. class of recursive functions and $\mathbf{M}$ is severely parsimonious on $\mathcal{S}$. Then* $\mathrm{card}(\{\mathbf{M}(f[n]) \mid f \in \mathcal{S} \wedge n \in N\}) < \infty$.

Proof. Let $\mathcal{S}$ be an r.e. class of recursive functions. Suppose by way contradiction that $\mathbf{M}$ is severely parsimonious on $\mathcal{S}$ and $\mathrm{card}(\{\mathbf{M}(f[n]) \mid f \in \mathcal{S} \wedge n \in N\}) = \infty$. Then for all i, there exists an $f \in \mathcal{S}$ and $n \in N$ such that $\mathbf{M}(f[n]) > i$.

Let h be such that, for all $f \in \mathcal{S}$ and $n \in N$, $\mathbf{M}(f[n]) \leq h(\mathrm{MinProg}(f))$. Without loss of generality we can assume that h is an increasing function. Now, by the implicit use of Kleene's recursion theorem [26], there exists an e such that φ_e may be defined as follows.

begin {Definition of φ_e}
    Search for an $f \in \mathcal{S}$ and $n \in N$ such that $\mathbf{M}(f[n]) > h(e)$.
    {This search is possible because $\mathcal{S}$ is r.e. and because of the supposition.}
    If and when such an f, n are found, let $\varphi_e = f$.
end {Definition of φ_e}

It is easy to see that $\varphi_e \in \mathcal{S}$ and for some n, $\mathbf{M}(\varphi_e[n]) > h(e)$. A contradiction. Thus, if $\mathbf{M}$ is severely parsimonious on $\mathcal{S}$, then $\mathrm{card}(\{\mathbf{M}(f[n]) \mid f \in \mathcal{S} \wedge n \in N\}) < \infty$. $\quad\square$

As an immediate corollary of the above result, we have that, if $\mathbf{M}$ is severely parsimonious on $\mathcal{R}$, then range of $\mathbf{M}$ consists of only finitely many conjectures.

Corollary 12. $(\forall \mathcal{S} \subseteq \mathcal{R})[\mathcal{S} \in \mathbf{gSpEx} \iff \mathrm{card}(\mathcal{S}) < \infty]$.

Thus, globally parsimonious machines can $\mathbf{Ex}$-identify only finitely many functions.[7] The non-global version of severe parsimony, however, is not so restrictive since it can potentially identify classes that are not r.e. This is the subject of the next theorem.

Theorem 13. $(\exists \mathcal{S} \subseteq \mathcal{R})[\mathrm{card}(\mathcal{S}) = \infty \wedge \mathcal{S} \in \mathbf{SpEx}_0^0]$.

---

[7] Even for identification with anomalies globally parsimonious machines cannot identify much since all the functions identified by the machines must be within the specified error bound of functions computed by finitely many programs.

Proof. We will construct an acceptable programming system ψ such that an infinite class of functions is $\mathbf{SpEx}_0^0$ identifiable in the programming system ψ. Since the class $\mathbf{SpEx}_b^a$ is acceptable programming system independent, we have our result. Define ψ as follows.

Let $\psi_{3i} = \varphi_i$. Note that this makes ψ acceptable. For j not divisible by 3, let ψ_j be defined as follows: $\psi_j(x) = j$, for all x. Let $S = \{\varphi_j \mid j$ is not divisible by 3 and $\mathrm{MinProg}(\varphi_j) = j\}$. It is easy to see that S is an infinite class.

Define a machine $\mathbf{M}$ as follows: for $n > 0$, $\mathbf{M}(f[n]) = f(0)$. It is easy to see that $\mathbf{M}$ witnesses $S \in \mathbf{SpEx}_0^0$. □

An immediate corollary of the above two theorems follows:

Corollary 14. $\mathbf{gSpEx} \subset \mathbf{SpEx}$.

As a contrast to Theorem 13, we have the following result that says that no infinite r.e. class of recursive functions can be identified by a machine that is severely parsimonious on the class. This follows directly from Theorem 11.

Corollary 15. *Suppose S is an infinite r.e. class of recursive functions. Then, $S \notin \mathbf{SpEx}$.*

3.1 Severe Parsimony and Nearly Minimal Identification

Because of the results in the previous section, we only investigate the non-global version of severe parsimony. Our first aim is to compare the effects of altering the parameters a and b in $\mathbf{SpEx}_b^a$. This is facilitated by looking at $\mathbf{SpEx}_b^a$ in relation to nearly minimal identification, that is classes $\mathbf{MEx}_b^a$. It is easy to verify that for all $a, b \in N \cup \{*\}$,

$$\mathbf{SpEx}_b^a \subseteq \mathbf{MEx}_b^a.$$

First, we would like to find out how does $\mathbf{SpEx}^0$ compare with $\mathbf{Ex}_0^0$. To this end it is helpful to consider the class $S^0 = \{f \mid \varphi_{f(0)} = f\}$. It can be shown that S^0 contains an infinite r.e. class as a subset. It is also easy to see that $S^0 \in \mathbf{Ex}_0^0$. Thus, as an immediate consequence of Theorem 15 above we have Corollary 16(a) below which says that there are collections of functions that can be finitely identified, but which cannot be identified in the limit by severely parsimonious learners. Additionally, since Chen [12] showed that $S^0 \in \mathbf{MEx}^0$, we also get Corollary 16(b).

Corollary 16.

(a) $\mathbf{Ex}_0^0 - \mathbf{SpEx}^0 \neq \emptyset$.
(b) $\mathbf{MEx}^0 - \mathbf{SpEx}^0 \neq \emptyset$.

A natural question is, if the anomalous version of severe parsimony is considered, does Part (a) of the above corollary still hold (i.e., is $\mathbf{Ex}_0^0 - \mathbf{SpEx}^* \neq \emptyset$?). To answer this question, we introduce the following technical definition.

Definition 17. Let $a \in N \cup \{*\}$.

(a) A finite set D *a-supports* a class of recursive functions S just in case, for each $f \in S$, there exists an $i \in D$ such that $\varphi_i =^a f$.

(b) $S \subseteq \mathcal{R}$ is *a-supportable* just in case there exists a finite set that a-supports S.

Intuitively, D a-supports S iff, for each $f \in S$, D contains a program for an a-variant of f. The next corollary is a counterpart of Corollary 15 for $\mathbf{SpEx}^a$. It follows immediately from Theorem 11.

Corollary 18. *Let* $a \in N \cup \{*\}$. *Suppose* S *is r.e. and not* a-*supportable. Then* $S \notin \mathbf{SpEx}^a$.

It can be shown that S^0 contains r.e. classes of functions that are not a-supportable for any $a \in N \cup \{*\}$. Hence, an immediate consequence of Corollary 18 is that $S^0 \notin \mathbf{SpEx}^a$ for any $a \in N \cup \{*\}$. This yields the following corollary.

Corollary 19.

(a) $\mathbf{Ex}_0^0 - \mathbf{SpEx}^* \neq \emptyset$.
(b) $\mathbf{MEx}^0 - \mathbf{SpEx}^* \neq \emptyset$.

We now consider whether Part (b) of the above corollary can be further strengthened when mind changes are introduced in the class $\mathbf{MEx}^0$. Also, the following proposition is immediate.

Proposition 20. *Let* $a \in N \cup \{*\}$. $\mathbf{MEx}_0^a \subseteq \mathbf{SpEx}_0^a$.

A natural question is what happens to the above proposition if we allow up to one mind change in nearly minimal identification. That is, we would like to know, if by allowing extra mind changes in nearly minimal identification, can we get out of severely parsimonious identification. The answer to this question turns out to be affirmative as implied by the following theorem.

Theorem 21. $\mathbf{MEx}_1^0 - \mathbf{SpEx}^* \neq \emptyset$.

Proof. We will construct an acceptable programming system ψ and a class $\mathcal{C}_\psi$ such that, with respect to this programming system, $\mathcal{C}_\psi$ is in $\mathbf{MEx}_1^0 - \mathbf{SpEx}_*^*$. (Since the inference classes $\mathbf{MEx}_1^0$ and $\mathbf{SpEx}_*^*$ are acceptable programming system independent, we will have our result.)

Let $\mathcal{C}_\psi^0 = \{f \in \mathcal{R} \mid (\forall x)[f(x) = \mathrm{MinProg}_\psi(f)]\}$.

Let $\mathcal{C}_\psi^1 = \{f \in \mathcal{R} \mid (\exists y > 0)[f(y) = \mathrm{MinProg}_\psi(f) \ \wedge \ (\forall x < y)[f(x) = f(0) \neq f(y)] \ \wedge \ (\forall x > y)[f(x) = f(y)]]\}$.

Let $\mathcal{C}_\psi = \mathcal{C}_\psi^0 \cup \mathcal{C}_\psi^1$.

It is easy to see that, for each acceptable programming system ψ, $\mathcal{C}_\psi \in \mathbf{MEx}_1^0$.

We will now construct an acceptable programming system ψ such that $\mathcal{C}_\psi \notin \mathbf{SpEx}_*^*$.

Let, $\psi_{4i} = \varphi_i$. Note that this makes ψ acceptable.

For all i, for all j, such that $4^{2i+1} < j < 4^{2i+2}$, for all x, let $\psi_j(x) = j$.

Let $S_i = \{\varphi_j \mid 4^{2i+1} < j < 4^{2i+2}\}$. Note that for any i, at least $\mathrm{card}(S_i) - (4^{2i+1} + 1)$ of the functions in S_i are in $\mathcal{C}_\psi^0$. This ensures that any $\mathbf{M}$ that witnesses $\mathcal{C}_\psi \in \mathbf{SpEx}_*^*$ must output arbitrarily large programs on functions in $\mathbf{CONST} = \{f \mid (\forall x)[f(x) = f(0)]\}$. We will use this fact to define ψ_j, where $4^{2i} < j < 4^{2i+1}$.

Let g_i denote the constant function $\lambda x.[i]$, i.e., for all x, $g_i(x) = i$.

Let $X_{k,l} = \{i > 4^{2\langle k,l\rangle+1} \mid \varphi_l(4^{2\langle k,l\rangle+1})\downarrow \wedge (\exists n)[\mathbf{M}_k(g_i[n]) > \varphi_l(4^{2\langle k,l\rangle+1})]\}$.

Intuitively, $X_{k,l}$ is used to collect the functions g_i, such that $\mathbf{M}_k$ on g_i outputs a large program (a program larger than $\varphi_l(4^{2\langle k,l\rangle+1})$). Note that if $\mathbf{M}_k$ witnesses that $\mathcal{C}_\psi \in \mathbf{SpEx}_*^*$ then $X_{k,l}$ must be infinite.

We are now ready to define ψ_j, where $4^{2i} < j < 4^{2i+1}$, for some i.

For j, such that $4^{2\langle k,l\rangle} < j < 4^{2\langle k,l\rangle+1}$, ψ_j is defined as follow: Let i be $(j - 4^{2\langle k,l\rangle})$-th element in some fixed 1-1 r.e. enumeration of $X_{k,l}$. Let n be such that $\mathbf{M}_k(g_i[n]) > \varphi_l(4^{2\langle k,l\rangle+1})$. Let ψ_j be defined as follows: $\psi_j(x) = i$, if $x \leq n$; $\psi_j(x) = j$ otherwise.

We now show that $\mathcal{C}_\psi \notin \mathbf{SpEx}_*^*$. So suppose by way of contradiction that $\mathbf{M}_k$ witnesses $\mathcal{C}_\psi \in \mathbf{SpEx}_*^*$, where the recursive fudge factor is φ_l. Without loss of generality we assume that φ_l is increasing. Now let us consider the functions ψ_j, where $4^{2\langle k,l\rangle} < j < 4^{2\langle k,l\rangle+1}$. It is easy to see (by the construction of these ψ_j's) that each of these ψ_j's are total, distinct, and on each of them $\mathbf{M}_k$ outputs a program larger than $\varphi_l(4^{2\langle k,l\rangle+1})$. Also, at least one of these ψ_j's is in $\mathcal{C}_\psi^1$ (since at most $4^{2\langle k,l\rangle} + 1$ of these ψ_j's do not belong to $\mathcal{C}_\psi^1$). This contradicts the assumption that $\mathbf{M}_k$ witnesses $\mathcal{C}_\psi \in \mathbf{SpEx}_*^*$ where the recursive fudge factor is φ_l. Thus, no such $\mathbf{M}_k$ can exist and we have $\mathcal{C}_\psi \notin \mathbf{SpEx}_*^*$. $\qquad\square$

As a corollary to the above results, we have:

Corollary 22. *Suppose* $a, b, c, d \in N \cup \{*\}$. $\mathbf{MEx}_b^a \subseteq \mathbf{SpEx}_d^c \iff (b = 0) \wedge (a \leq c)$.

3.2 Anomaly Hierarchy for Severe Parsimony

Using Proposition 20 and Theorem 9 we get the next result which says that there are collections of functions that can be severely parsimoniously identified with up to $i + 1$ errors in the final program, but that cannot be identified by allowing only up to i errors in the final program.

Theorem 23. $(\forall i \in N)[\mathbf{SpEx}_0^{i+1} - \mathbf{Ex}^i \neq \emptyset]$.

This result yields the following anomaly hierarchy that underscores the fact that allowing extra errors in the final program makes larger collections of functions identifiable by severely parsimonious machines.

Corollary 24. $\mathbf{SpEx} \subset \mathbf{SpEx}^1 \subset \mathbf{SpEx}^2 \subset \cdots \subset \mathbf{SpEx}^*$.

3.3 Mind Changes and Severe Parsimony

We now consider bounding the number of mind changes in severely parsimonious identification. We are able to establish the following result which says that there are collections of functions for which 0-error programs can be identified by severely parsimonious learners by allowing up to $i + 1$ mind changes, but for which even a finite variant program cannot be $\mathbf{Ex}$-identified if up to only i mind changes are allowed. Due to space considerations, we omit the proof.

Theorem 25. $(\forall i \in N)[\mathbf{SpEx}_{i+1} - \mathbf{Ex}_i^* \neq \emptyset]$.

The above theorem yields the following hierarchy with the moral that allowing extra mind changes before the onset of convergence makes larger collections of functions identifiable with respect to severely parsimonious identification.

Corollary 26. *Let* $a \in N \cup \{*\}$. $\mathbf{SpEx}_0^a \subset \mathbf{SpEx}_1^a \subset \cdots \subset \mathbf{SpEx}_*^a$

As a corollary to Theorems 23 and 25, we have

Corollary 27. *Let* $a, b, c, d \in N \cup \{*\}$. *Suppose* $I \in \{\mathbf{Ex}, \mathbf{SpEx}, \mathbf{MEx}\}$. *Then,* $\mathbf{SpEx}_b^a \subseteq I_d^c \iff (a \leq c) \wedge (b \leq d)$.

4 Non-Revolutionary Identification

As noted in the introductory section, the notion of severe parsimony has some drawbacks as a model for induction without paradigm shift. In particular, a severely parsimonious learner can issue conjectures that have wide variance in size because the only restriction on the size of the conjectures is that they be within a computable factor of the minimal size program for the function being learned. Now for a function with large minimal size program (together with a high growth computable "fudge" factor), the requirement of severe parsimony leaves the scope for conjectures to vary greatly in size. What seems to be needed is that the smallest size conjecture and the largest size conjecture on a function do not vary too much. This need motivates the notion of non-revolutionary identification.

Definition 28. Let $\mathbf{M}$ and $f \in \mathcal{R}$ be given. Then $\mathrm{ProgSet}(\mathbf{M}, f) = \{\mathbf{M}(f[n]) \mid n \in N \wedge \mathbf{M}(f[n]) \neq ?\}$.

Definition 29. Let $a, b \in N \cup \{*\}$.

(a) $\mathbf{M}$ is *non-revolutionary* just in case there exists a recursive h such that, for each $f \in \mathcal{R}$, $\max(\mathrm{ProgSet}(\mathbf{M}, f)) \leq h(\min(\mathrm{ProgSet}(\mathbf{M}, f)))$.
(b) $\mathbf{NrEx}_b^a = \{\mathcal{S} \mid (\exists \mathbf{M})[\mathbf{M} \text{ is non-revolutionary and } \mathcal{S} \subseteq \mathbf{Ex}_b^a(\mathbf{M})]\}$.

We consider the comparison between $\mathbf{Ex}_b^a$, $\mathbf{MEx}_b^a$, $\mathbf{SpEx}_b^a$ and $\mathbf{NrEx}_b^a$ for various values of a and b. To begin with, the following proposition immediately follows from the definition.

Proposition 30. $\mathbf{Ex}_0^a \subseteq \mathbf{NrEx}_0^a$.

We first consider the case when it is possible for severely parsimonious identification to diagonalize against $\mathbf{NrEx}$. The next theorem shows that there are collections of functions for which a severely parsimonious machine can identify an error free program if it is allowed up to 1 mind change, but for which even a finite variant program cannot be identified by any non-revolutionary machine even if an unbounded number of mind changes are allowed.

Theorem 31. $\mathbf{SpEx}_1^0 - \mathbf{NrEx}_*^* \neq \emptyset$.

Proof. We will construct an acceptable programming system ψ and a class C_ψ such that $C_\psi \in (\mathbf{SpEx}_1^0 - \mathbf{NrEx}_*^*)$. Since the classes $\mathbf{SpEx}_1^0$ and $\mathbf{NrEx}_*^*$ are acceptable programming system independent, we have the theorem.

Let **ZERO** denote the everywhere 0 function.

Let $C_\psi = \{\mathbf{ZERO}\} \cup \{f \mid \min(\{x \mid f(x) \neq 0\}) = \mathrm{MinProg}_\psi(f)\}$.

It is easy to see that, for all ψ, $C_\psi \in \mathbf{SpEx}_1^0$.

We now construct a ψ such that $C_\psi \notin \mathbf{NrEx}_*^*$.

Let g be defined as follows.

$$g(0) = 1$$

$$g(j+1) = 2 \cdot g(j) + 3$$

Note that the $\mathrm{card}(\{p \mid g(j) < p < g(j+1)\}) = g(j) + 2$.

Let $\psi_{g(j)} = \varphi_j$. This makes ψ an acceptable programming system.

Let $\psi_0 = \mathbf{ZERO}$, the everywhere 0 function.

Let f_p denote the function,

$$f_p(x) = \begin{cases} 0, & \text{if } x < p; \\ p, & \text{otherwise.} \end{cases}$$

Note that for $p \neq p'$, $f_p \neq^* f_{p'}$.

For p such that $p > 0$, and p is not in the range of g, let $\psi_p = f_p$.

Now, for each j, at least one of f_p, $g(j) < p < g(j+1)$, belongs to C_ψ (since there are $g(j) + 2$ such f_p's and thus at least one of them is not computed by any ψ program $\leq g(j)$). It follows that C_ψ contains infinitely many f_p's.

We now show that $C_\psi \notin \mathbf{NrEx}_*^*$. Suppose by way of contradiction that $\mathbf{M}$ witnesses $\mathbf{NrEx}_*^*$ identification of C_ψ. Then since $\mathbf{M}$ witnesses $\mathbf{NrEx}_*^*$ identification of $\{\mathbf{ZERO}\}$, there exists a z such that $\mathbf{M}(\mathbf{ZERO}[z]) \neq ?$. Let h be an increasing function such that, for all $f \in \mathcal{R}$, $\max(\mathrm{ProgSet}(\mathbf{M}, f)) \leq h(\min(\mathrm{ProgSet}(\mathbf{M}, f)))$. It follows that for all $p > z$ and $m > z$, $\mathbf{M}(f_p[m]) \leq h(\mathbf{M}(\mathbf{ZERO}[z]))$. But there are only finitely many programs $\leq h(\mathbf{M}(\mathbf{ZERO}[z]))$, and infinitely many f_p, such that $p \geq n$ and $f_p \in C_\psi$. Thus, $\mathbf{M}$ cannot $\mathbf{Ex}^*$-identify all $f_p \in C_\psi$. $\quad\square$

As a corollary to Proposition 30 and Theorems 23 and 31 we have the following.

Corollary 32. *Suppose* $\mathbf{I} \in \{\mathbf{Ex}, \mathbf{MEx}, \mathbf{SpEx}\}$. *Then,*
$\mathbf{I}_b^a \subseteq \mathbf{NrEx}_d^c \iff (b = 0) \wedge (a \leq c)$.

We now consider cases in which there are collections of functions that can be identified by non-revolutionary machines but cannot be identified by other strategies introduced in this paper.

As a corollary to Proposition 30 and results from the previous sections, we have the following.

Corollary 33. *Suppose* $n \in N$.

(a) $\mathbf{NrEx}_0^{n+1} - \mathbf{Ex}_*^n \neq \emptyset$.
(b) $\mathbf{NrEx}_0^0 - \mathbf{SpEx}_*^* \neq \emptyset$.
(c) $\mathbf{NrEx}_0^0 - \mathbf{MEx}_n^* \neq \emptyset$.

Additionally, our proof of Theorem 25 also shows that the following result holds.

Theorem 34. $\mathbf{NrEx}_{i+1}^0 - \mathbf{Ex}_i^* \neq \emptyset$.

As a corollary to the above theorem and Part (a) of Corollary 33, we have the following relationship between $\mathbf{NrEx}_b^a$ and $\mathbf{Ex}_d^c$ for various values of a, b, c, d.

Corollary 35. $\mathbf{NrEx}_b^a \subseteq \mathbf{Ex}_d^c$ iff $a \leq c$ and $b \leq d$.

Since for $n \in N$ and $a \in N \cup \{*\}$, $\mathbf{NrEx}_n^a \subseteq \mathbf{Ex}_n^a \subseteq \mathbf{MEx}^a$, the only case left to consider is $\mathbf{NrEx}_*^a$ versus $\mathbf{MEx}_*^b$. The next theorem helps settle this question; it shows that there are collections of functions that can be identified by non-revolutionary machines but cannot be identified in the nearly minimal sense even if the number of errors allowed in the final program is large but bounded. The proof, omitted for lack of space, is surprisingly a bit complex.

Theorem 36. For $n \in N$, $\mathbf{NrEx}_*^0 - \mathbf{MEx}_*^n \neq \emptyset$.

As a corollary we have,

Corollary 37. $\mathbf{NrEx}_b^a \subseteq \mathbf{MEx}_d^c \iff (d = *) \wedge (c \geq a) \wedge [(b \neq *) \vee (c = *)]$.

5   Severe Parsimony with Bc and Fex

We now extend the notion of severe parsimony to behaviorally correct identification and vacillatory identification. We first introduce these two criteria.

Definition 38. [11, 3] Let $a \in N \cup \{*\}$.

(a) **M** $\mathbf{Bc}^a$-*identifies* f (written: $f \in \mathbf{Bc}^a(\mathbf{M})$) just in case, $(\overset{\infty}{\forall} n)[\varphi_{\mathbf{M}(f[n])} =^a f]$. We define the class $\mathbf{Bc}^a = \{S \subseteq \mathcal{R} \mid (\exists \mathbf{M})[S \subseteq \mathbf{Bc}^a(\mathbf{M})]\}$.
(b) **M** $\mathbf{Fex}^a$-*identifies* f (written: $f \in \mathbf{Fex}^a(\mathbf{M})$) just in case there exists a nonempty finite set D of a-error programs for f such that for all but finitely many n, $\mathbf{M}(f[n]) \in D$. We define the class $\mathbf{Fex}^a = \{S \subseteq \mathcal{R} \mid (\exists \mathbf{M})[S \subseteq \mathbf{Fex}^a(\mathbf{M})]\}$.

The next definition adapts the notion of severe parsimony to $\mathbf{Bc}^a$-identification and $\mathbf{Fex}^a$-identification.

Definition 39. Let $a \in N \cup \{*\}$.

(a) $\mathbf{SpBc}^a = \{S \subseteq \mathcal{R} \mid (\exists \mathbf{M})[\mathbf{M}$ is severely parsimonious on S and **M** $\mathbf{Bc}^a$-identifies $S]\}$.
(b) $\mathbf{SpFex}^a = \{S \subseteq \mathcal{R} \mid (\exists \mathbf{M})[\mathbf{M}$ is severely parsimonious on S and **M** $\mathbf{Fex}^a$-identifies $S]\}$.

The following proposition is immediate.

Proposition 40. $(\forall a \in N \cup \{*\})[\mathbf{SpBc}^a = \mathbf{SpFex}^a]$.

The $a = 0$ case of the following theorem can be easily handled with a trick of Barzdin and Podenieks [3] and the $a = *$ case with a trick of Case and Smith [11]; however, the proof of the other cases is non-trivial (we omit the proof due to lack of space).

Theorem 41. $\mathbf{SpFex}^a = \mathbf{SpEx}^a$.

6 Future Work

Besides the promised handling of the cases of language learning and of slightly less conservative, non paradigm-shifting criteria in which the fudge factor functions h are allowed to be limiting-recursive, it would be interesting to investigate models of paradigm shifts in relation to massive changes in program control structure [23, 24, 27] and to connect paradigm shifts to the need, in some cases, for training sequences [1].

Acknowledgements

We are grateful to Raghu Raghavan who suggested to the second author to look at the phenomenon of paradigm shift in science. The authors' discussion of the difficulties of formalizing paradigm shift eventually led to the present paper. Research partially supported by a grant from the Australian Research Council.

References

1. D. Angluin, W. Gasarch, and C. Smith. Training sequences. *Theoretical Computer Science*, 66(3):255–272, 1989.
2. G. Baliga, J. Case, S. Jain, and M. Suraj. Machine learning of higher order programs. *Journal of Symbolic Logic*, 59(2):486–500, 1994.
3. J. M. Barzdin and K. Podnieks. The theory of inductive inference. In *Mathematical Foundations of Computer Science, High Tatras, Czechoslovakia*, pages 9–15, 1973.
4. L. Blum and M. Blum. Toward a mathematical theory of inductive inference. *Information and Control*, 28:125–155, 1975.
5. M. Blum. A machine independent theory of the complexity of recursive functions. *Journal of the ACM*, 14:322–336, 1967.
6. J. Case. The power of vacillation in language learning. Technical Report 93-08, University of Delaware, 1992. Expands on the article in *Proceedings of the Workshop on Computational Learning Theory*, Morgan Kauffman, 1988; journal article under revision.
7. J. Case, S. Jain, and S. Ngo Manguelle. Refinements of inductive inference by Popperian and reliable machines. *Kybernetika*, 30:23–52, 1994.
8. J. Case, S. Jain, and A. Sharma. On learning limiting programs. *International Journal of Foundations of Computer Science*, 3(1):93–115, 1992.
9. J. Case, S. Jain, and A. Sharma. Vacillatory learning of nearly minimal size grammers. *Journal of Computer and System Sciences*, 49(2):189–207, October 1994.
10. J. Case, S. Jain, and M. Suraj. Not-so-nearly-minimal-size program inference. In Klaus P. Jantke and Steffen Lange, editors, *Algorithmic Learning for Knowledge-Based Systems*, volume 961 of *Lecture Notes in Artificial Intelligence*, pages 77–96. Springer-Verlag, 1995.
11. J. Case and C. Smith. Comparison of identification criteria for machine inductive inference. *Theoretical Computer Science*, 25:193–220, 1983.
12. K. Chen. Tradeoffs in inductive inference of nearly minimal sized programs. *Information and Control*, 52:68–86, 1982.
13. R. Freivalds. Minimal Gödel numbers and their identification in the limit. *Lecture Notes in Computer Science*, 32:219–225, 1975.

14. M. A. Fulk and S. Jain. Approximate inference and scientific method. *Information and Computation*, 114(2):179–191, November 1994.

15. E. M. Gold. Language identification in the limit. *Information and Control*, 10:447–474, 1967.

16. S. Jain. On a question about learning nearly minimal programs. *Information Processing Letters*, 53(1):1–4, January 1995.

17. S. Jain and A. Sharma. Restrictions on grammar size in language identification. In David Powers and Larry Reeker, editors, *Proceedings MLNLO'91, Machine Learning of Natural Language and Ontology, Stanford University, California. Document **D91-09**, DFKI: Kaiserslautern FRG, 1991.*, pages 87–92, March 1991.

18. S. Jain and A. Sharma. Prudence in vacillatory language identification. *Mathematical Systems Theory*, 1994. To Appear.

19. Thomas Kuhn. *The Structure of Scientific Revolutions*. University of Chicago Press, Chicago, 1970.

20. S. Lange and P. Watson. Machine discovery in the presence of incomplete or ambiguous data. In K. Jantke and S. Arikawa, editors, *Algorithmic Learning Theory*, volume 872 of *Lecture Notes in Artificial Intelligence*, pages 438–452. Springer-Verlag, Berlin, Reinhardsbrunn Castle, Germany, October 1994.

21. M. Machtey and P. Young. *An Introduction to the General Theory of Algorithms*. North Holland, New York, 1978.

22. H. Putnam. Probability and confirmation. In *Mathematics, Matter, and Method*. Cambridge University Press, 1975.

23. G. Riccardi. *The Independence of Control Structures in Abstract Programming Systems*. PhD thesis, SUNY/ Buffalo, 1980.

24. G. Riccardi. The independence of control structures in abstract programming systems. *Journal of Computer and System Sciences*, 22:107–143, 1981.

25. H. Rogers. Gödel numberings of partial recursive functions. *Journal of Symbolic Logic*, 23:331–341, 1958.

26. H. Rogers. *Theory of Recursive Functions and Effective Computability*. McGraw Hill, New York, 1967. Reprinted, MIT Press 1987.

27. J. Royer. *A Connotational Theory of Program Structure*. Lecture Notes in Computer Science 273. Springer Verlag, 1987.

28. N. Shapiro. Review of "Limiting recursion" by E.M. Gold and "Trial and error predicates and the solution to a problem of Mostowski" by H. Putnam. *Journal of Symbolic Logic*, 36:342, 1971.

Probabilistic language learning under monotonicity constraints

Léa Meyer

Institut für Informatik und Gesellschaft
Albert-Ludwigs-Universität Freiburg
79098 Freiburg, Germany

Abstract. The present paper deals with probabilistic identification of indexed families of uniformly recursive languages from positive data under various monotonicity constraints. Thereby, we consider strong-monotonic, monotonic and weak-monotonic probabilistic learning of indexed families with respect to class comprising, class preserving and exact hypothesis spaces and investigate the probabilistic hierarchies of these learning models. Earlier results in the field of probabilistic identification established that - considering function identification - each collection of recursive functions identifiable with probability $p > \frac{1}{2}$ is deterministically identifiable (cf. [16]). In the case of language learning from text, each collection of recursive languages identifiable from text with probability $p > \frac{2}{3}$ is deterministically identifiable (cf. [14]), but when dealing with the learning models mentioned above, we obtain probabilistic hierarchies highly structured without a "gap" between the probabilistic and deterministic learning classes. In the case of exact probabilistic learning, we are able to show the probabilistic hierarchy to be dense for every mentioned monotonicity condition. Considering class preserving weak-monotonic and monotonic probabilistic learning, we show the respective probabilistic hierarchies to be strictly decreasing for probability $p \to 1$, $p < 1$. These results extend previous work considerably (cf. [16], [17]). For class comprising weak-monotonic learning as well as for learning without additional constraints, we can prove that probabilistic identification and team identification are equivalent. This yields discrete probabilistic hierarchies in these cases.

1 Introduction

Many fields in Machine Learning are concerned with investigating and formalizing human learning processes in order to utilize the results in designing computer programs. In particular, children's ability to learn their mother tongue on the base of incomplete and ambiguous information motivated various abstract learning models which try to reflect the special quality of language acquisition. A well studied approach in this field is the theory of formal language learning first introduced by Gold (cf. [2]). The general situation investigated in *language learning in the limit* can be described as follows: An inductive inference machine, fed more and more information about a language to be inferred, has to produce hypotheses about this language. The set of admissible hypotheses is called hypothesis space. The information the learner is fed can consist of positive and negative examples or only positive ones. In this paper we consider only the latter case. The sequence of hypotheses has to converge to a hypothesis correctly describing the language to be inferred. With respect to potential applications we focuse our attention on indexed families of uniformly recursive languages. Learning of indexed families was first studied by Angluin (cf. [1]) and further investigated by Zeugmann and Lange, Kapur and other authors (cf. e.g. [18] for an overview). By observing the human ability to infer explanations of a phenomenon on the base of incomplete data we notice that people enlarge their learning power by accepting that the learning processes may fail with a certain probability. In general, the learning power is enhanced even if the probability has to be nearly one and decreases *strictly* with increasing probability. Now the question arises whether "natural" probabilistic learning models exist which reflect this ability.

Earlier work done in the field of probabilistic identification established that - considering function identification - each collection of recursive functions identifiable with probability $p > \frac{1}{2}$ is deterministically identifiable (cf. [16] or [14]). Another result - which concerned function identification with bounded mind changes - established that, for all $n \geq 2$, a collection of recursive functions exists which is identifiable with at most n mind changes with arbitrary high probability but not deterministically identifiable with at most n mind changes (cf. [16]). This result, however, does not yield a probabilistic hierarchy which is strictly decreasing with increasing probability. Furthermore, Wiehagen *et al.* [17] constructed a nonstandard hypothesis space $\mathcal{G}$ such that each infinite set of recursive functions, which is identifiable with respect to some acceptable Gödel-numbering, is identifiable with arbitrary high probability with respect to $\mathcal{G}$ but not deterministically identifiable with respect to $\mathcal{G}$. However, the hypothesis space $\mathcal{G}$ does not induce a "natural" deterministic learning class. Considering language learning from text, each collection of recursive languages identifiable from text with probability $p > \frac{2}{3}$ is deterministically identifiable (cf. [14]). Consequently, in the case of language learning as well, we loose too much certainty in order to gain learning power, although probabilistic identification is strictly more powerful than team identification (cf. [4]).

In the sequel we show that the question above can be answered affirmatively when dealing with probabilistic identification of indexed families under various monotonicity constraints with respect to hypothesis spaces with uniformly decidable membership. Monotonicity constraints were introduced in order to deal with a major problem arising when learning languages from text, namely to avoid *overgeneralization*, i.e., hypotheses that describe proper supersets of the language to be inferred. Learning devices which strictly avoid overgeneralization are called *conservative* learners (cf. [1], [8]). The notion of conservative learning has been refined by introducing various monotonicity constraints. In the strongest notion, the learner, fed a text for a language to be inferred, has to produce a chain of hypotheses such that $L_i \subseteq L_j$ iff L_j is guessed later than L_i. In this case, the learner is said to identify this language *strong-monotonically* (cf. [6]). Other natural approaches to monotonicity are defined and investigated in [8], [11], [15], [18]. In this paper, we consider strong-monotonic, monotonic and weak-monotonic or conservative probabilistic learning of indexed families $\mathcal{L} = (L_j)_{j \in \mathcal{N}}$. Thereby, we distinguish between *class comprising* learning, i.e., $\mathcal{L}$ has to be learnt with respect to some hypothesis space that has a range comprising $range(\mathcal{L})$; *class preserving* learning, i.e., $\mathcal{L}$ has to be inferred with respect to some hypothesis space having the same range as $\mathcal{L}$ and *exact* learning, i.e., $\mathcal{L}$ has to be learnt with respect to the space $\mathcal{L}$ of hypotheses. We obtain the following results: Considering exact probabilistic learning, we show with a new separation technique that the probabilistic hierarchy under each mentioned monotonicity condition is *not discrete*. This can be regarded as a completely new phenomenon in the field of probabilistic identification. In the case of class preserving conservative probabilistic learning, we show the probabilistic hierarchy to be strictly decreasing for increasing probability, i.e., for all $p \in [0,1)$ there exists an indexed family $\mathcal{L}$ and a $\tilde{p} \in [0,1)$, $\tilde{p} > p$ such that $\mathcal{L}$ is conservatively identifiable with probability $\tilde{p}$ with respect to a class preserving hypothesis space but not conservatively identifiable with probability $q > \tilde{p}$ with respect to any class preserving hypothesis space. The same result holds for class preserving monotonic probabilistic learning. For probabilistic identification with no additional constraint as well as for class comprising conservative probabilistic identification, we show that probabilistic identification and team identification are equivalent. This leads to discrete probabilistic hierarchies in these cases.

The results obtained allow the following conclusions. First, probabilistic learners are suitable to replace deterministic learners provided they fulfill monotonicity conditions and work with respect to class preserving or exact hypothesis spaces. Secondly, the investigated learning models could give a deeper insight into the nature of inductive learning processes.

2   Preliminaries

We denote the natural numbers by $\mathcal{N} = \{0, 1, 2, \ldots\}$. Let M_0, $M_1, \ldots$ be a standard list of all Turing machines and let φ_0, $\varphi_1, \ldots$ be the resulting acceptable programming system, i.e., φ_i denotes the partial recursive function computed by M_i. Let Φ_0, Φ_1, $\ldots$ be any associated complexity measure (cf. [13]). Furthermore, let $k, x \in \mathcal{N}$. If $\varphi_k(x)$ is defined, we say that $\varphi_k(x)$ converges and write $\varphi_k(x) \downarrow$; otherwise $\varphi_k(x)$ diverges and we write $\varphi_k(x) \uparrow$. In the sequel we assume familiarity with formal language theory (cf. [3]). Let Σ be any fixed finite alphabet of symbols and let Σ^* be the free monoid over Σ. Any subset $L \subseteq \Sigma^*$ is called a language. Let L be a language and $s = s_0, s_1, \ldots$ a finite or infinite sequence of strings from Σ^*. Define $rng(s) := \{s_k | k \in \mathcal{N}\}$. An infinite sequence $\tau = s_0, s_1, \ldots$ of strings from Σ^* with $rng(\tau) = L$ is called a *text* for L. By $text(L)$ we denote the set of all texts for L. For a text τ and a number x, let τ_x be the initial segment of τ of length $x+1$. By the canonical text kan^L for a non-empty recursive language L we denote the text of L defined as follows (cf. [7]). Let $s_0, s_1, \ldots$ be the lexicographically ordered text of Σ^*. Test whether $s_z \in L$ for $z = 0, 1, 2, \ldots$ until the first $z \in \mathcal{N}$ is found such that $s_z \in L$. Since $L \neq \emptyset$ there must be at least one such $z \in \mathcal{N}$. Set $kan_0^L = s_z$. For all $x \in \mathcal{N}$ define:

$$kan_{x+1}^L = \begin{cases} kan_x^L \cdot s_{z+x+1}, & \text{if } s_{z+x+1} \in L, \\ kan_x^L \cdot s, & \text{otherwise, where s is the last string in } kan_x^L. \end{cases}$$

In the sequel we exclusively deal with the learnability of indexed families of uniformly recursive languages defined as follows (cf. [1]). A sequence $\mathcal{L} = (L_j)_{j \in \mathcal{N}}$ is said to be an *indexed family* of uniformly recursive languages provided $L_j \neq \emptyset$ for all $j \in \mathcal{N}$ and there is a recursive function F such that for all $j \in \mathcal{N}$ and $s \in \Sigma^*$:

$$F(j,s) := \begin{cases} 1, & \text{if } s \in L_j, \\ 0, & \text{otherwise.} \end{cases}$$

In the following we refer to indexed families of uniformly recursive languages as indexed families for short. Let $\mathcal{L}$ be an indexed family. By $rng(\mathcal{L})$ we denote $\{L_j | j \in \mathcal{N}\}$. As in Gold (cf. [2]) we define an *inductive inference machine* (abbr. IIM) to be an algorithmic device working as follows. An IIM M takes as its input larger and larger initial segments of a text τ and it either takes the next input string, or it first outputs a hypothesis, i.e., a number encoding a certain computer program, and then requests the next input string. The set of all admissible hypotheses is called *hypothesis space*. As hypothesis space we always take an enumerable family of grammars $G_0, G_1, G_2, \ldots$ over the terminal alphabet Σ satisfying $rng(\mathcal{L}) \subseteq \{L(G_j) | j \in \mathcal{N}\}$. Furthermore, we require that membership in $L(G_j)$ is uniformly decidable for all $j \in \mathcal{N}$ and all strings $s \in \Sigma^*$. If an IIM M outputs a number j, we are interpreting this number to be the index of the grammar G_j, i.e., M guesses the language $L(G_j)$. Let ρ be a finite sequence of strings from Σ^* and let $j \in \mathcal{N}$ be a hypothesis. Then j is said to be *consistent* with ρ iff $rng(\rho) \subseteq L(G_j)$. For a hypothesis space $\mathcal{G} = (L(G_j))_{j \in \mathcal{N}}$ we use $rng(\mathcal{G})$ to denote $\{L(G_j) | j \in \mathcal{N}\}$.

Let τ be a text for a recursive language L and let $x \in \mathcal{N}$. By $M(\tau_x)$ we denote the last hypothesis M outputs when fed τ_x. If there is no such hypothesis then $M(\tau_x)$ is said to be $\perp$. The sequence $(M(\tau_x))_{x \in \mathcal{N}}$ is said to *converge in the limit* to the number j iff either there exists some $n \in \mathcal{N}$ with $M(\tau_x) = j$ for all $x \geq n$, or $(M(\tau_x))_{x \in \mathcal{N}}$ is finite and its last member is j. Let $\mathcal{G} = (G_j)_{j \in \mathcal{N}}$ be a hypothesis space. M is said to *converge correctly on τ with respect to $\mathcal{G}$* iff $(M(\tau_x))_{x \in \mathcal{N}}$ converges in the limit to j with $L(G_j) = L$. Now we define learning in the limit (cf. [2]).

Definition 1. [2] Let $\mathcal{L}$ be an indexed family, let L be a language, and let $\mathcal{G}$ be a hypothesis space. *An IIM M CLIM-identifies L from text with respect to $\mathcal{G}$ iff M converges correctly with respect to $\mathcal{G}$ on every text τ for L.*

M CLIM-identifies $\mathcal{L}$ with respect to $\mathcal{G}$ iff, for each $L \in rng(\mathcal{L})$, M CLIM-identifies L from text with respect to $\mathcal{G}$.

Let $CLIM$ denote the collection of all indexed families for which there are an IIM M and a hypothesis space $\mathcal{G}$ such that M $CLIM$-identifies $\mathcal{L}$ with respect to $\mathcal{G}$.

The prefix C in $CLIM$ is used to denote *class comprising* learning, i.e., that $\mathcal{L}$ can be learned with respect to some hypothesis space comprising $rng(\mathcal{L})$. By LIM we denote the collection of all indexed families $\mathcal{L}$ that can be learned in the limit with respect to a *class preserving* hypothesis space $\mathcal{G}$, i.e., $rng(\mathcal{L}) = rng(\mathcal{G})$. The empty prefix for LIM is denoted by ε. If an indexed family $\mathcal{L}$ has to be inferred with respect to $\mathcal{L}$ itself, then we replace the prefix C by E, i.e., $ELIM$ is the collection of indexed families that can be learned exactly in the limit. We adopt this distinction for all the learning types defined below.

Next we define conservative (cf. [1]), weak-monotonic, monotonic and strong-monotonic inference (cf. [6], [15]).

Definition 2. [1], [6], [15] Let $\mathcal{L}$ be an indexed family, let L be a language, and let $\mathcal{G}$ be a hypothesis space. *An IIM M is said to identify a language L from text with respect to $\mathcal{G}$*

1. *conservatively*
2. *strong-monotonically*
3. *monotonically*
4. *weak-monotonically*

iff M $CLIM$-identifies L from text with respect to $\mathcal{G}$ and for every text τ for L as well as for all $x, k \in \mathcal{N}$, $k \geq 1$ with $M(\tau_x) \neq \bot$ the corresponding condition is satisfied:

1. if $M(\tau_x) \neq M(\tau_{x+k})$ then $rng(\tau_{x+k}) \not\subseteq L(G_{M(\tau_x)})$
2. $L(G_{M(\tau_x)}) \subseteq L(G_{M(\tau_{x+k})})$
3. $L(G_{M(\tau_x)}) \cap L \subseteq L(G_{M(\tau_{x+k})}) \cap L$
4. if $rng(\tau_{x+k}) \subseteq L(G_{M(\tau_x)})$ then $L(G_{M(\tau_x)}) \subseteq L(G_{M(\tau_{x+k})})$

If M identifies L from text with respect to $\mathcal{G}$ conservatively, strong-monotonically, monotonically and weak-monotonically, respectively, then M is said to $C\mu$-identify L from text with respect to $\mathcal{G}$ for $\mu \in \{COV, SMON, MON, WMON\}$.

M $C\mu$-identifies $\mathcal{L}$ with respect to $\mathcal{G}$ iff, for each $L \in rng(\mathcal{L})$, M $C\mu$-identifies L from text with respect to $\mathcal{G}$.

By $CCOV, CSMON, CMON$ and $CWMON$, we denote the set of all indexed families $\mathcal{L}$ for which there are an IIM M and a hypothesis space $\mathcal{G}$ such that M $C\mu$-identifies $\mathcal{L}$ with respect to $\mathcal{G}$.

Let $\mathcal{L}$ be an indexed family, let $\mathcal{G}$ be a hypothesis space, let $L \in rng(\mathcal{L})$, let $\tau \in text(L)$, and let $\mu \in \{COV, SMON, MON, WMON\}$. If M converges correctly on τ with respect to $\mathcal{G}$ and $(M(\tau_x))_{x \in \mathcal{N}}$ satisfies the condition μ, then M is said to $C\mu$-*converge correctly on* τ *with respect to* $\mathcal{G}$.

Let $j, n \in \mathcal{N}$. $(M(\tau_x))_{x \in \mathcal{N}}$ is said to $C\mu$-*converge to the number* j *up to* n iff $(M(\tau_x))_{x \in \mathcal{N}}$ satisfies the condition μ for all $x, k \in \mathcal{N}$, $k \geq 1$ with $x + k \leq n$ and $M(\tau_n) = j$.

Next we define team identification of indexed families (cf. [4]). Recall that a team of IIMs is defined to be a multiset of IIMs.

Definition 3. Let $\mathcal{L}$ be an indexed family, let L be a language, let $\mathcal{G}$ be a hypothesis space, and let $n \in \mathcal{N}$. A team of IIMs $M_1, \ldots, M_n$ $CLIM_{team}(n)$-*identifies L from text with respect to* $\mathcal{G}$ iff, for every $\tau \in text(L)$, there exists a $j \in \{1, \ldots, n\}$ such that M_j converges correctly on τ with respect to $\mathcal{G}$.

A team of IIMs $M_1, \ldots, M_n$ $CLIM_{team}(n)$-identifies $\mathcal{L}$ iff $M_1, \ldots, M_n$ $CLIM_{team}(n)$-identifies each $L \in rng(\mathcal{L})$ from text.

Let $CLIM_{team}(n)$ denote the collection of all indexed families $\mathcal{L}$ for which there are a team $M_1, \ldots, M_n$ and a hypothesis space $\mathcal{G}$ such that $M_1, \ldots, M_n$ $CLIM_{team}(n)$-identifies $\mathcal{L}$ with respect to $\mathcal{G}$.

Lange and Zeugmann [9] showed that the learning power in the LIM-case does not depend on the hypothesis space the learner may use, i.e., $CLIM = ELIM$. Similarly we can prove that $CLIM_{team}(n) = ELIM_{team}(n)$ for all $n \in \mathcal{N}$.

Recall that the notion of team learning defined in 3 is equivalent to a stronger notion (cf. [4]). Thereby, for any language L to be inferred there has to be a team member which $CLIM$-identifies L from every text $\tau \in text(L)$ with respect to the given hypothesis space.

The next definition concerns *probabilistic inductive inference machines* (abbr. PIM).

A PIM is an IIM which has the possibility to flip a t-sided coin and to base the choice of the next hypothesis not only on the text seen so far but additionally on the outcome of the coin flip. We assume P to *behave well*, i.e., P flips the coin each time it requests a new input string. More formally, a PIM P is an IIM equipped with a t-sided coin oracle. An oracle c is an infinite sequence $c_0, c_1, \ldots$ where $c_i \in \{0, \ldots, t-1\}$. By c^n we denote the initial segment $c_0, \ldots, c_n$ of c for all $n \in \mathcal{N}$.

Let c be an oracle. We denote the deterministic IIM defined by running P with oracle c by P^c. Intuitively, P^c, fed a text τ for a language to be learned, outputs the hypothesis j on τ_x if P outputs j on τ_x under the condition that the first $x + 1$ flips of the t-sided coin were c^x. Thus, we can interpret the probabilistic IIM P as a collection $\{P^c | c \in \{0, \ldots, t-1\}^\infty\}$ of IIMs. Instead of $P^c(\tau_x)$ we often write $P^{c^x}(\tau_x)$. Remark that each PIM equipped with a t-sided coin is equivalent to a PIM equipped with a two-sided coin (cf. [14]). For the sake of readability we define now a simplified version of *infinite computation trees* (cf. [14]). For a probabilistic IIM P equipped with a t-sided coin and a text τ for a recursive language L, we define $T_{P,\tau}$ to be the t-ary tree representing all possible outputs of P when fed τ. The nodes of $T_{P,\tau}$ correspond to the hypotheses P outputs and the edges correspond to the coin flips. Consequently, the paths of $T_{P,\tau}$ correspond to the sequences $(P^c(\tau_x))_{x \in \mathcal{N}}$ where $c \in \{0, \ldots, t-1\}^\infty$. Let $x \in \mathcal{N}$. The level x of the tree $T_{P,\tau}$ is defined to be the finite sequence $(P^s(\tau_x))_{s \in \{0, \ldots, t-1\}^x}$ where $\{0, \ldots, t-1\}^x$ is lexicographically ordered. Let $x \in \mathcal{N}$. By T_{P,τ_x} we denote the subtree of $T_{P,\tau}$ consisting of the first $x + 1$ levels from $T_{P,\tau}$. A path $(P^c(\tau_x))_{x \in \mathcal{N}}$ is said to *contain* a $j \in \mathcal{N}$ iff there exists an $m \in \mathcal{N}$ with $P^{c^m}(\tau_m) = j$.

Now let Pr denote the canonical Borel-measure on the Borel-σ-algebra on $\{0, \ldots, t-1\}^\infty$. For more details about probabilistic IIM's, measurability and infinite computation trees we refer the reader to Pitt (cf. [14]).

Definition 4. Let $\mathcal{L}$ be an indexed family, let L be a language, let $\mathcal{G}$ be a hypothesis space, and let $p \in [0,1]$. A PIM P $CLIM_{prob}(p)$-*identifies* L *from text with respect to* $\mathcal{G}$ iff the following holds for every text τ for L:

$$Pr(\{ c \in \{0, \ldots, t-1\}^\infty \mid P^c \text{ converges correctly on } \tau \text{ w.r.t. } \mathcal{G} \}) \geq p.$$

A *PIM* P $CLIM_{prob}(p)$-identifies $\mathcal{L}$ from text with respect to $\mathcal{G}$ iff P $CLIM_{prob}(p)$-identifies each $L \in rng(\mathcal{L})$ from text with respect to $\mathcal{G}$.

Let $CLIM_{prob}(p)$ denote the collection of all indexed families for which there are a PIM P and a hypothesis space $\mathcal{G}$ such that P $CLIM_{prob}(p)$-identifies $\mathcal{L}$ with respect to $\mathcal{G}$.

There are two natural ways to define monotonic notions of team- and probabilistic learning (cf. [5]). It is possible to claim that the monotonic requirement has to be fulfilled from every machine in the team or from every path in the infinite computation trees or we can restrict this demand to the converging team members or paths. In this paper we restrict ourselves to the second notion and refer the reader to [5] or [12] for a comparison of the learning power of the two notions.

Definition 5. Let $\mathcal{L}$ be an indexed family, let L be a language, let $\mathcal{G}$ be a hypothesis space, let $n \in \mathcal{N}$, let $p \in [0,1]$, and let $\mu \in \{COV, WMON, MON, SMON\}$.

1. *A team $M_1, \ldots, M_n$ of IIMs $C\mu_{team}(n)$-identifies L from text with respect to $\mathcal{G}$* iff, for every text τ for L, there exists a $j \in \{1, \ldots, n\}$ such that M_j $C\mu$-converges correctly on τ with respect to $\mathcal{G}$.

A team $M_1, \ldots, M_n$ of IIMs $C\mu_{team}(n)$-identifies $\mathcal{L}$ with respect to $\mathcal{G}$ iff $M_1, \ldots, M_n$ $C\mu_{team}(n)$-identifies each $L \in rng(\mathcal{L})$ from text with respect to $\mathcal{G}$.

2. *A PIM P $C\mu_{prob}(p)$-identifies L from text with respect to $\mathcal{G}$* iff the following condition holds for every text τ for L:

$$P(\{\, c \in \{0, \ldots, t-1\}^\infty \mid P^c \ C\mu - converges\ correctly\ on\ \tau\ w.r.t.\ \mathcal{G}\ \}) \geq p.$$

A PIM P $C\mu_{prob}(p)$-identifies $\mathcal{L}$ with respect to $\mathcal{G}$ iff P $C\mu_{prob}(p)$-identifies each $L \in rng(\mathcal{L})$ with respect to $\mathcal{G}$.

The collections $C\mu_{team}(n)$ and $C\mu_{prob}(p)$ are defined as usual.

Lange and Zeugmann [7] showed that weak-monotonic learning and conservative learning are equivalent. We can adopt their proof to show that $\lambda WMON_{prob}(p) = \lambda COV_{prob}(p)$ and $\lambda WMON_{team}(n) = \lambda COV_{team}(n)$ for all $n \in \mathcal{N}$, $p \in [0,1]$ and $\lambda \in \{\varepsilon, E, C\}$. In the sequel we deal with the notions $\lambda COV_{team}(n)$ and $\lambda COV_{prob}(p)$.

For $\mu \in \{LIM, COV, MON, SMON\}$ and $\lambda \in \{\varepsilon, E, C\}$ we denote the corresponding probabilistic hierarchy by $< \lambda\mu_{prob}(p) >_{p\in[0,1]}$.

- Let $(p_n)_{n\in\mathcal{N}}$ be a sequence of real numbers with $p_n \in [0,1]$ and $p_{n+1} < p_n$ for all $n \in \mathcal{N}$. The probabilistic hierarchy $< \lambda\mu_{prob}(p) >_{p\in[0,1]}$ is said to be *discrete with breakpoints at* p_n, $n \in \mathcal{N}$ iff $\lambda\mu_{prob}(p_{n+1}) \setminus \lambda\mu_{prob}(p_n) \neq \emptyset$ and $\lambda\mu_{prob}(p) = \lambda\mu_{prob}(p_n)$ for all $p_{n+1} < p \leq p_n$.
- $< \lambda\mu_{prob}(p) >_{p\in[0,1]}$ is said to be *strictly decreasing* iff, for all $p \in [0,1)$, there exists an indexed family $\mathcal{L}$ and a $\tilde{p} \in [0,1)$, $\tilde{p} > p$ such that $\mathcal{L} \in \lambda\mu_{prob}(\tilde{p})$ but $\mathcal{L} \notin \lambda\mu_{prob}(\tilde{p} + \epsilon)$ for all $\epsilon > 0$.
- $< \lambda\mu_{prob}(p) >_{p\in[0,1]}$ is said to be *dense* iff, for each $p, q \in [0,1]$, $p < q$, there exists a $r \in [0,1)$, $p < r < q$, with $\lambda\mu_{prob}(p) \subset \lambda\mu_{prob}(r) \subset \lambda\mu_{prob}(q)$ and all the inclusions are proper.

3 Discrete probabilistic hierarchies

In the first section of this paper we show the probabilistic hierarchy to be discrete for probabilistic learning without additional constraints as well as for class preserving conservative probabilistic learning.

Theorem 6. $< CLIM_{prob}(p) >_{p\in[0,1]}$ *and* $< CCOV_{prob}(p) >_{p\in[0,1]}$ *are discrete with breakpoints at* $\frac{1}{n}$, $n \in \mathcal{N}$.

The proof of this theorem divides into two steps. First, we show that probabilistic identification is equivalent to team identification in the considered cases.

Lemma 7. *Let $n \in \mathcal{N}$ and $\frac{1}{n+1} < p \leq \frac{1}{n}$. Then*

- $CLIM_{prob}(p) = LIM_{team}(n)$,
- $CCOV_{prob}(p) = CCOV_{team}(n)$.

For the details of the proof of Theorem 6, we refer the reader to the appendix.

Wiehagen *et al.* [17] showed that there exists a nonstandard hypothesis space $\mathcal{G}$ such that each infinite set of recursive functions, which is identifiable with respect to some acceptable Gödel-numbering, is identifiable with arbitrary high probability with respect to $\mathcal{G}$ but not deterministically identifiable with respect to $\mathcal{G}$. From the proof of the first part of Lemma 7 (see appendix), we can conclude that this result is not transferable to probabilistic learning of indexed families.

Corollary 8. *Let $\mathcal{L}$ be an indexed family and let $\mathcal{G}$ be a hypothesis space. If $\mathcal{L}$ is $CLIM_{prob}(p)$-identifiable with probability $p > \frac{1}{2}$ with respect to $\mathcal{G}$, then $\mathcal{L}$ is deterministically identifiable with respect to $\mathcal{G}$.*

4 Dense probabilistic hierarchies

In this section we investigate exact probabilistic identification and show the probabilistic hierarchy to be dense for every mentioned monotonicity condition. This goal requires to separate the probabilistic learning classes in a very strict way. There are two separation techniques often used in the setting of indexed families, namely diagonalization and reducing the halting problem to a given learning problem. The latter technique was introduced and investigated by Lange and Zeugmann (cf. [10]). An analysis of this technique shows that it is too "strong" for our purpose, since the indexed families constructed with this tool in general are not exactly conservatively identifiable with a probability $p > \frac{1}{2}$. Consequently, we had to search a separation technique which is "weaker" than the reduction to the halting problem but "strong" enough to avoid exact deterministic identification. In the proof of the following theorem we develop such a technique.

Theorem 9. *Let $c, d, n \in \mathcal{N}$ such that $\frac{c}{d} > \frac{1}{2}$ and $gcd(c, d) = 1$, and let $n \geq 1$. Then*

$$ESMON_{prob}(\frac{c}{d \cdot n}) \setminus \bigcup_{0 < \epsilon \leq 1 - \frac{c}{d \cdot n}} ECOV_{prob}(\frac{c}{d \cdot n} + \epsilon) \neq \emptyset$$

Proof. The proof divides into two steps. First let $c, d \in \mathcal{N}$ such that $\frac{c}{d} > \frac{1}{2}$ and $gcd(c, d) = 1$, and let $n = 1$. Let $k \in \mathcal{N}$ and define

- $L_k := \{a^k b^m | m \in \mathcal{N}\}$
- $L_k' := \begin{cases} L_k, & \text{if } \varphi_k(k) \uparrow, \\ \{a^k b^m | m \leq \Phi_k(k)\}, & \text{if } \varphi_k(k) \downarrow. \end{cases}$

The following alternative definition of L_k' shows that L_k' is recursive.

- If $\Phi_k(k) > n - 1$ then $a^k b^n \in L_k'$.
- If $\Phi_k(k) \leq n - 1$ then $a^k b^n \notin L_k'$.

The key idea of the proof can be described as follows. We define an indexed family $\mathcal{L}_{\frac{c}{d}} = (L_{<k,j>})_{k,j \in \mathcal{N}, j \leq c-1}$ such that the following holds.

- If $\varphi_k(k) \uparrow$ then all the languages $L_{<k,j>}$ for $j \in \{0, \ldots, c-1\}$ are infinite and equal to L_k.

- If $\varphi_k(k) \downarrow$ then exactly $2c - d$ of the languages are finite and equal to L'_k, the others are infinite and equal to L_k. The indices $\{j_1 \ldots, j_{2c-d}\} \subset \{0, \ldots, c - 1\}$ of the finite languages depend only on the value of $\varphi_k(k)$.

Obviously, $\mathcal{L}_{\frac{c}{d}}$ is strong-monotonically identifiable with probability $\frac{2c-d}{c}$ when each $< k, j >, j \le c - 1$ is guessed with probability $\frac{1}{c}$. But since the empty hypothesis $\perp$ can play the role of an index of a finite language as long as we have no information about $\varphi_k(k)$ we can prove $\mathcal{L}_{\frac{c}{d}}$ to be strong-monotonically identifiable with probability at least $\frac{c}{d}$. Intuitively, the identifying PIM guesses each $< k, j >$ with probability $\frac{1}{d}$ and $\perp$ with probability $\frac{d-c}{d}$. Now we have to precise how to choose the indices of the finite languages. For that purpose we define a surjective, total recursive function mod_{2c-d}^c. Set

$$M_{2c-d}^c = \{S | S \subset \{0, \ldots, c - 1\}, |S| = 2c - d\}.$$

Let $cod_{2c-d}^c : M_{2c-d}^c \to \{0, \ldots, \binom{c}{2c-d} - 1\}$ be an effective encoding of M_{2c-d}^c. Then define $mod_{2c-d}^c : \mathcal{N} \to \{0, \ldots, \binom{c}{2c-d} - 1\}$ by setting

$$mod_{2c-d}^c(y) := x \text{ iff } x \in \{0, \ldots, \binom{c}{2c-d} - 1\} \land y \equiv x \bmod \binom{c}{2c-d}$$

for all $y \in \mathcal{N}$. Obviously mod_{2c-d}^c is total recursive, surjective and $mod_{2c-d}^c(y)$ encodes a subset of $\{0, \ldots, c - 1\}$ of cardinality $2c - d$ for each $y \in \mathcal{N}$.

Now we are ready to define $\mathcal{L}_{\frac{c}{d}}$ more formally. Let $< , > : \mathcal{N} \times \{0, \ldots, c - 1\} \to \mathcal{N}$ be an effective encoding of the set $\{(x, y) | x, y \in \mathcal{N}, y \le c - 1\}$. For $k, j \in \mathcal{N}, j \le c - 1$ define $L_{<k,j>} \subseteq \{a^k b^m | m \in \mathcal{N}\}$ as follows. Let $k, j \in \mathcal{N}$.

$$L_{<k,j>} := \begin{cases} L'_k, & \text{if } \varphi_k(k) \downarrow \land j \in (cod_{2c-d}^c)^{-1}(mod_{2c-d}^c(\varphi_k(k))), \\ L_k, & \text{if } \varphi_k(k) \downarrow \land j \notin (cod_{2c-d}^c)^{-1}(mod_{2c-d}^c(\varphi_k(k))), \text{ or } \varphi_k(k) \uparrow. \end{cases}$$

Then $\mathcal{L}_{\frac{c}{d}} = (L_{<k,j>})_{k,j \in \mathcal{N}, j \le c-1}$ is an indexed family since

- $a^k b^n \in L_{<k,j>}$ for all $j \le c - 1$ if $\Phi_k(k) > n - 1$,
- $a^k b^n \in L_{<k,j>}$ for all $j \le c-1$ with $j \notin (cod_{2c-d}^c)^{-1}(mod_{2c-d}^c(\varphi_k(k)))$ if $\Phi_k(k) \le n - 1$,

and "$\Phi_k(k) \le n - 1$" is uniformly decidable for all $k, n \in \mathcal{N}$. Let $k \in \mathcal{N}$. If $\varphi_k(k) \downarrow$ then the languages with the indices $< k, j >$ with $j \in mod_{2c-d}^c(\varphi_k(k))$ are finite and equal to $\{a^k b^m | m \le \Phi_k(k)\}$. The other languages are infinite and equal to $\{a^k b^m | m \in \mathcal{N}\}$. Remark that it is not decidable whether a language $L \in \mathcal{L}_{\frac{c}{d}}$ is finite or not. We have to show now that $\mathcal{L}_{\frac{c}{d}}$ has the desired properties.

To prove $\mathcal{L}_{\frac{c}{d}} \in ESMON_{prob}(\frac{c}{d})$ we define a PIM P equipped with a $d - sided\ coin$. Let $L \in rng(\mathcal{L})$, let τ be a text for L, and let $x \in \mathcal{N}$. We can assume that τ_x is an initial segment of $\{a^k b^m | m \in \mathcal{N}\}$ for some $k \in \mathcal{N}$. Let $s \in \{0, \ldots, d - 1\}^\infty$ be an oracle.

PIM P: On input τ_x, P^{s^x} works as follows.

- If $s^1 = j$ with $j \in \{0, \ldots, c - 1\}$ then distinguish the following cases.

- If $< k, l >$ is not consistent with τ_x for some $l \leq c - 1$ then output $< k, i >$ with i being the least natural number $\leq c - 1$ such that $< k, i >$ is consistent with τ_x.
- If $< k, l >$ is consistent with τ_x for all $l \leq c - 1$ then set $P^{s^z}(\tau_x) = < k, j >$.
- If $s^1 = j$ with $j \in \{c, \ldots, d - 1\}$ then test whether $\Phi_k(k) \leq x$.
  If this is the case, then output $< k, j >$ with j being the least natural number in $(cod^c_{2c-d})^{-1}(mod^c_{2c-d}(\varphi_k(k)))$. Otherwise output $\perp$.

Obviously, this PIM identifies $\mathcal{L}_{\frac{c}{d}}$ strong-mononically with probability $\frac{c}{d}$.

It remains to show that $\mathcal{L}_{\frac{c}{d}} \notin ECOV_{prob}(p)$ for all $p > \frac{c}{d}$. Assume the converse and let $\epsilon > 0$ with $\mathcal{L}_{\frac{c}{d}} \in ECOV_{prob}(\frac{c}{d} + \epsilon)$. Let P be the identifying PIM and assume that P is equipped with a two-sided coin. We define a procedure $\mathcal{I}$ which computes for each $k \in \mathcal{N}$ a natural number $j \in \{0, \ldots, \binom{c}{2c-d} - 1\}$ such that $j \neq mod^c_{2c-d}(\varphi_k(k))$. Let $k \in \mathcal{N}$ and let kan^{L_k} be the canonical text for L_k. Recall that $L_k \in \mathcal{L}_{\frac{c}{d}}$.

In Stage n, $\mathcal{I}$ works as follows:

If $\Phi_k(k) \leq n - 1$ then set $\mathcal{I}(k) = j$ where j is the least number in $\{0, \ldots, \binom{c}{2c-d} - 1\}$ with $j \neq mod^c_{2c-d}(\varphi_k(k))$. Otherwise compute $T_{P,kan^{L_k}_n}$ and define for all $j \in \mathcal{N}$, $j \leq c - 1$:

$$p^n_j = Pr\{(c \in \{0, 1\}^\infty | (P^{c^x}(kan^{L_k}_x))_{x \in \mathcal{N}} \; ECOV-converges \; to \; < k, j > \; up \, to \, n)\}$$

Test if $\sum_{j=0}^{c-1} p^n_j > \frac{c}{d}$. If not then request another input string and go to stage $n + 1$. Otherwise there exists a $z > 0$ with $\sum_{j=0}^{c-1} p^n_j = \frac{c}{d} + z$. Let $S = \{j_1, \ldots, j_{2c-d}\}$ be a subset of $\{0, \ldots, c - 1\}$ of cardinality $2c - d$ and define:

$$m_S = \sum_{s=1}^{2c-d} p^n_{j_s} + (1 - \frac{c}{d} - z).$$

Now we define $\mathcal{I}(k)$ to be the least natural number $l \in \{0, \ldots, \binom{c}{2c-d} - 1\}$ such that $m_{(cod^c_{2c-d})^{-1}(l)} < \frac{c}{d} + \epsilon$.

Now we have to prove the following two claims:

Claim 1: The procedure $\mathcal{I}$ terminates for each $k \in \mathcal{N}$.

1. p^n_j is computable for all $j, n \in \mathcal{N}$, $j \leq c - 1$ and there exists an $n \in \mathcal{N}$ with $\sum_{j=0}^{c-1} p^n_j > \frac{c}{d}$ since $\mathcal{L}_{\frac{c}{d}}$ is assumed to be in $ECOV_{prob}(\frac{c}{d} + \epsilon)$.
2. Let $n \in \mathcal{N}$ with $\sum_{j=0}^{c-1} p^n_j > \frac{c}{d}$. Then there exists a subset $S = \{j_1, \ldots, j_{2c-d}\}$ of $\{0, \ldots, c - 1\}$ with $m_S < \frac{c}{d} + \epsilon$. Assume the converse, i.e., $m_S \geq \frac{c}{d} + \epsilon$ for each subset S of $\{0, \ldots, c - 1\}$ of cardinality $2c - d$. Then

$$\sum_{\{S | S \subset \{0, \ldots, c-1\}, |S| = 2c-d\}} m_S \geq \binom{c}{2c-d} \cdot (\frac{c}{d} + \epsilon).$$

From the definition of m_S and the equation $\sum_{j=0}^{c-1} p^n_j = \frac{c}{d} + z$, we obtain $\frac{c}{d} + z - \frac{d}{c}z \geq \frac{c}{d} + \epsilon$. This is a contradiction to $\frac{d}{c} > 1$.

Consequently, $\mathcal{I}$ is effective and outputs the code number of a subset of $\{0, \ldots, c-1\}$ of cardinality $2c - d$ for all $k \in \mathcal{N}$.

<u>Claim 2</u>: Let $k \in \mathcal{N}$ with $\varphi_k(k) \downarrow$. Then

$$\mathcal{I}(k) \neq mod^c_{2c-d}(\varphi_k(k)).$$

Let $k \in \mathcal{N}$ with $\varphi_k(k) \downarrow$. Let $S_k = \{j_1, \ldots, j_{2c-d}\}$ such that $\{L_{<k,j_1>}, \ldots, L_{<k,j_{2c-d}>}\}$ is exactly the set of the finite languages. Let $n \in \mathcal{N}$ such that $\mathcal{I}$ stops in Stage n. Then either $\Phi_k(k) \leq n - 1$ and thus $\mathcal{I}(k) \neq mod^c_{2c-d}(\varphi_k(k))$ by definition of $\mathcal{I}$ or $\Phi_k(k) > n - 1$. In the latter case, $kan_n^{L_k} = kan_n^{L'_k}$ and $\mathcal{I}(k) = l$ with $m_{(cod'_{2c-d})^{-1}(l)} < \frac{c}{d} + \epsilon$. Obviously, all paths not summed up in m_{S_k} do not converge conservatively on $kan^{L'_k}$ since these paths contain at least one index of L_k in $T_{P,kan_n^{L'_k}}$. Since $\mathcal{L}_{\frac{c}{d}}$ is assumed to be in $ECOV_{prob}(\frac{c}{d} + \epsilon)$, the finite language L'_k has to be conservatively identified with probability $p \geq \frac{c}{d} + \epsilon$. Consequently, m_{S_k} has to be $\geq \frac{c}{d} + \epsilon$ and we can conclude that $\mathcal{I}(k) \neq mod^c_{2c-d}(\varphi_k(k))$.

Now we are able to prove the desired separation. Define $F : \mathcal{N} \times \mathcal{N} \to \mathcal{N}$ by setting $F(k, x) := \mathcal{I}(k)$ for all $k, x \in \mathcal{N}$. Then F is recursive since $\mathcal{I}$ is recursive and there exists some $k_0 \in \mathcal{N}$ such that $\varphi_{k_0}(x) = \mathcal{I}(k_0)$ for all $x \in \mathcal{N}$ and hence $\varphi_{k_0}(k_0) = \mathcal{I}(k_0) \in \{0, \ldots, \binom{c}{2c-d} - 1\}$. Consequently, $mod^c_{2c-d}(\varphi_{k_0}(k_0)) = \varphi_{k_0}(k_0)$ and hence $mod^c_{2c-d}(\varphi_{k_0}(k_0)) = \mathcal{I}(k_0)$, a contradiction to Claim 2. Thus, $\mathcal{L}_{\frac{c}{d}} \notin ECOV_{prob}(\frac{c}{d} + \epsilon)$.

For the second part of the proof let $n \geq 2$ and $c, d \in \mathcal{N}$ with $\frac{c}{d} > \frac{1}{2}$. Let $\mathcal{L}_{\frac{c}{d}}^{mod}$ be the indexed family from the first part of this proof and let $\mathcal{L}_{n-1}^q$ be the indexed family defined in the proof of Theorem 5 (see appendix). Then $\mathcal{L}_{\frac{c}{d}}$ is strong-monotonically identifiable with probability $\frac{c}{d}$ but not conservatively identifiable with an higher probability and $\mathcal{L}^{n-1}$ is strong-monotonically identifiable with probability $\frac{1}{n}$ but not $CLIM_{prob}(p)$-identifiable with a higher probability. We define the indexed family which witnesses the desired separation by combining these two indexed families without reducing the complexity of neither of them so that the corresponding probabilities can be multiplicated. More formally, define the indexed family $\mathcal{L}^{n-1} \otimes \mathcal{L}_{\frac{c}{d}}$ over the terminal alphabet $\Sigma = \{1, a, b\}$ as follows. Let $<, , >$ be an effective encoding of $\mathcal{N} \times \mathcal{N} \times \{0, \ldots, c-1\}$ and set

$$L_{<i,k,j>} := L_i^q \cup L_{<k,j>}^{mod}$$

for all $i, k, j \in \mathcal{N}$, $j \leq c - 1$. Intuitively, a PIM can not identify $\mathcal{L}^{n-1} \otimes \mathcal{L}_{\frac{c}{d}}$ conservatively with a probability $p > \frac{c}{d \cdot n}$ since it has to guess <u>independently</u> indices for languages from $\mathcal{L}^{n-1}$ and $\mathcal{L}_{\frac{c}{d}}$, respectively. We ommit the formal proof here since it is a combination of the methods used to prove Theorem 6 and 9.

□

From Theorem 9 we get the desired problisitic hierarchies:

Corollary 10. $< E\mu_{prob}(p) >_{p \in [0,1]}$ is dense for every $\mu \in \{COV, MON, SMON\}$.

In particular, we can conclude that $E\mu_{prob}(p) \neq E\mu$ for all $p < 1$ and for all $\mu \in \{COV, MON, SMON\}$. For $p = 1$ however, there is no difference between probabilistic and deterministic learning, i.e., $\lambda\mu_{prob}(1) = \lambda\mu_{prob}(1)$ for all $\lambda \in \{\varepsilon, E, C\}$

and $\mu \in \{COV, MON, SMON\}$.

In the first section we investigated the connection between probabilistic identification of indexed families with respect to class comprising hypothesis spaces and the corresponding notions of team identification. The theorem above shows that there is no such connection when we consider exact probabilistic learning under monotonicity conditions. However, all the languages $\mathcal{L}_{\frac{c}{d}}$ for $\frac{c}{d} > \frac{1}{2}$ defined in Theorem 9 are strong-monotonically identifiable from a team of two IIM's. The following theorem shows by using some familiar diagonalization argument that exact strong-monotonic probabilistic learning is much stronger than exact conservative team learning.

Theorem 11. *There exists an indexed family $\mathcal{L}$, $\mathcal{L} \in LIM$ with:*

$$\mathcal{L} \in \bigcup_{0 < \epsilon < 1} ESMON_{prob}(1 - \epsilon) \setminus \bigcup_{n \in \mathcal{N}} ECOV_{team}(n)$$

Proof. Since the used diagonalization tool is well known we only give a sketch of the proof. For $k \in \mathcal{N}$ set $A_k := \{a^k\}$ and $\mathcal{A} = (A_k)_{k \in \mathcal{N}}$. Construct an indexed family $\mathcal{L}_0 = (L_i)_{i \in \mathcal{N}}$ with $rng(\mathcal{L}_0) = \{A_k | k \in \mathcal{N}\}$ such that for every language A_k, $k \in \mathcal{N}$ there are finite sections $N_{k,1}, N_{k,2}, \ldots$ of $\mathcal{N}$ with $|N_{k,j}| \uparrow \infty$ for $j \to \infty$ and $L_m = A_k$ for all $m \in N_{k,j}$, $j \in \mathcal{N}$ (cf. for example [17]). By diagonalyzing against all Turing machines $(M_t)_{t \in \mathcal{N}}$ we force each Maschine M_t to overgeneralize on almost all languages A_k, $k \in \mathcal{N}$ by enlarging the language $L_m \in \mathcal{L}_0$, $L_m = A_k$ iff M_t guesses m on the canonical text for A_k, $t \leq k$ and M_t did not guess an index n with $L_n = A_k$ before. $\quad\square$

5 Strictly decreasing probabilistic hierarchies

The first theorem in this section shows that the separation tools developped in Lange and Zeugmann (cf. [10]) can also be used to separate learning classes in the case of class preserving probabilistic identification under monotonicity conditions.

Theorem 12. $ESMON_{prob}(\frac{1}{2}) \setminus \bigcup_{0 < \epsilon \leq \frac{1}{2}} COV_{prob}(\frac{1}{2} + \epsilon) \neq \emptyset$

Proof. Define $\mathcal{L} = (L_{<k,j>})_{k,j \in \mathcal{N}}$ which witnesses the desired separation as follows (cf. [10]). Let $k \in \mathcal{N}$. Define $L_{<k,0>} := \{a^k b^m | m \in \mathcal{N}\}$. For $j > 0$ set $L_{<k,j>} := L_{<k,0>}$ if $\Phi_k(k) > j$ and $L_{<k,j>} := \{a^k b^m | m \leq d\}$ if $\Phi_k(k) \leq j$, where $d = max(2\Phi_k(k) - j, 1)$. Obviously $\mathcal{L}$ is an indexed family and $\mathcal{L} \in ESMON_{prob}(\frac{1}{2})$.

To show that $\mathcal{L} \notin \bigcup_{0 < \epsilon \leq \frac{1}{2}} COV_{prob}(\frac{1}{2} + \epsilon)$ we only sketch the proof since it is similar to the proof of Lange and Zeugmann (cf. [10]) who showed that $\mathcal{L} \notin COV$. Let P a PIM which identifies $\mathcal{L}$ conservatively with $p > \frac{1}{2}$, let $L \in rng(\mathcal{L})$, let τ be a text for L, and let $T_{P,\tau}$ the infinite computation tree. Let $k \in \mathcal{N}$ such that $rng(\tau) \subseteq \{a^k b^m | m \in \mathcal{N}\}$. Since $L_{<k,0>}$ is assumed to be conservatively identifiable with probabability $p > \frac{1}{2}$ there exists some level m_0 such that

$$Pr\{(c \in \{0,1\}^{\infty} \mid \exists m \leq m_0 \text{ with } rng(\tau_{m_0+1}) \subseteq L(G_{P^{c^m}(\tau_m)}))\} > \frac{1}{2}.$$

Then $\varphi_k(k) \uparrow$ or $\Phi_k(k) \leq m_0$. Thus, we could solve the halting problem and consequently $\mathcal{L} \notin \bigcup_{0 < \epsilon \leq \frac{1}{2}} COV_{prob}(\frac{1}{2} + \epsilon)$.

$\square$

Using this separation tool, we show now that the probabilistic hierarchies in the case of class preserving conservative and monotonic probabilistic learning are strictly decreasing.

Theorem 13. $< COV_{prob}(p) >_{p \in [0,1]}$ and $< MON_{prob}(p) >_{p \in [0,1]}$ are strictly decreasing.

Proof. Let $n \in \mathcal{N}$, and let $p_n = \frac{n}{n+1}$ for all $n \geq 2$. Let $n \in \mathcal{N}$, $n \geq 2$. We show that an indexed family $\mathcal{L}_{p_n}$ exists such that $\mathcal{L}_{p_n} \in COV_{prob}(p_n) \setminus COV_{prob}(p_n + \epsilon)$ for all $\epsilon > 0$. Let $< , >$ be an effective encoding of $\mathcal{N} \times \mathcal{N}$ and $k, j \in \mathcal{N}$. Set $L_{<k,0>} = \{a^k b^m | m \in \mathcal{N}\}$.

- If $\Phi_k(k) > j$, then set $L_{<k,j>} = L_{<k,0>}$.
- If $\Phi_k(k) \leq j$ and $j = z\Phi_k(k) + r$ for some $z \in \mathcal{N} \setminus \{0\}$, $r \in \{0, \ldots, \Phi_k(k) - 1\}$, then set $L_{<k,j>} =$

  - $\{a^k b^m | m \leq \Phi_k(k)\} \cup \{a^k b^{\Phi_k(k)+z}\}$ if $z \in \{1, \ldots, n\}$, $r = 0$,
  - $\{a^k b^m | m \leq \Phi_k(k) - r\} \cup \{a^k b^{\Phi_k(k)+z}\}$ if $z \in \{1, \ldots, n\}$, $r \in \{1, \ldots, \Phi_k(k) - 1\}$,
  - $L_{<k,0>}$ if $j \geq n + 1$, $r \in \{1, \ldots, \Phi_k(k) - 1\}$.

Obviously, $\mathcal{L}_{p_n} = (L_{<k,j>})_{k,j \in \mathcal{N}}$ is an indexed family. Let $k \in \mathcal{N}$ such that $\varphi_k(k) \downarrow$. Then for each language $L = L_{<k, z_0 \phi_k(k) + r>}$, $z_0 \in \{1, \ldots, n\}$, $r \in \{1, \ldots, \phi_k(k) - 1\}$, $L_{<k, z \phi_k(k)>}$ is not an overgeneralizations of L for $z \neq z_0$. Thus, we can prove $\mathcal{L}_{p_n}$ to witness the desired separation by using the technique sketched in Theorem 12.

To prove the second part of the theorem, let $p_n = \frac{3n}{3n+1}$ for all $n \in \mathcal{N}$, $n \geq 1$. Let $n \in \mathcal{N}$, $n \geq 1$. We define an indexed family $\mathcal{L}_{p_n}$ such that $\mathcal{L}_{p_n} \in MON_{prob}(p_n)$, $\mathcal{L}_{p_n} \notin MON_{prob}(p_n + \epsilon)$ for all $\epsilon > 0$. Let $< , >$ be an effective encoding of $\mathcal{N} \times \{0, \ldots, 3n-1\}$ and $k, j \in \mathcal{N}$, $j \leq 3n - 1$. Let $k, j \in \mathcal{N}$. Set $L_{<k,0>} = \{a^k b^m | m \in \mathcal{N}\}$.

- If $\varphi_k(k) \uparrow$ then set $L_{<k,j>} = L_{<k,0>}$ for all $j \leq 3n - 1$.
- If $\varphi_k(k) \downarrow$, $j = 3z + r$ for some $z \in \{0, \ldots, n-1\}$ and $r \in \{0, 1, 2\}$ then set

$$L_{<k,j>} = \{a^k b^m | m \leq \Phi_k(k)\} \cup M_{z,r}$$

where

$$M_{z,r} := \begin{cases} \{a^k b^{2z + (\Phi_k(k)+1)}\}, & \text{if } r = 0, \\ \{a^k b^{2z + (\Phi_k(k)+2)}\}, & \text{if } r = 1, \\ \{a^k b^{2z + (\Phi_k(k)+1)}, a^k b^{2z + (\Phi_k(k)+2)}\}, & \text{if } r = 2. \end{cases}$$

Then $\mathcal{L}_{p_n} = (L_{<k,j>})_{k,j \in \mathcal{N}, j \leq 3n-1}$ is an indexed family and witnesses the desired separation.

$\square$

Finally, the following remains open. We conjecture that there exists an indexed family which is strong-monotonically identifiable with probability $p = \frac{2}{3}$ with respect to some class preserving hypothesis space but not strong-monotonically identifiable with a larger probability with respect to any class preserving hypothesis space. However, we suppose this to be the best result possible in the case of class preserving strong-monotonic probabilistic learning.

Notes and Comments In the previous work we gave a complete picture of exact probabilistic learning under monotonicity constraints and some results on class preserving and class comprising probabilistic learning. Further work will establish the probabilistic hierarchies for the cases not considered in this paper.

The author wishes to thank Thomas Zeugmann for suggesting the topic and helpful discussion. Furthermore, I wish to thank Britta Schinzel and Arun Sharma for helpful comments.

References

1. Angluin, D. (1980): Inductive Inference of formal languages from positive data, Information and Control 45, 117-135.
2. Gold, E.M., (1967): Language identification in the limit, Information and Control 10, 447-474.
3. Hopcroft, J., Ullman, J. (1979): Introduction to Automata Theory, Languages and Computation, Addison-Wesley Publ. Company.
4. Jain, S, Sharma, A. (1993): Probability is more powerful than team for language identification, in: Proc. of the 6th ACM Conf. on Comp. Learning Theory, Santa Cruz, July 1993, 192-198, ACM Press.
5. Jain, S., Sharma, A. (1995): personal communication.
6. Jantke, K.P., (1991): Monotonic and non-monotonic inductive inference, New Generation Computing 8, 349-360.
7. Lange, S, Zeugmann, T. (1992): Types of monotonic language learning an their characterisation, in: Proc. of the 5th ACM Conf. on Comp. Learning Theory, Pittsburgh, July 1992, 377-390, ACM Press.
8. Lange, S., Zeugmann, T. (1993): Monotonic versus non-monotonic language learning, in: Proc. 2nd Int. Workshop on Nonmonotonic an Inductive Logic, Dec. 1991, Rheinhardsbrunn, (G. Brewka, K.P.Jantke, P.H.Schmitt, Eds): Lecture Notes in AI 659, S. 254-269, Springer-Verlag, Berlin.
9. Lange, S., Zeugmann, T. (1993): Language learning in the dependence on the space of hypotheses, in: Proc. of the 6th ACM Conf. on Comp. Learning Theory, Santa Cruz, July 1993, 127-136, ACM Press.
10. Lange, S., Zeugmann, T. (1993): The learnability or recursive languages in dependence on the hypothesis space, GOSLER-Report 20/93, FB Mathemathik, Informatik und Naturwissenschaften, HTWK, Leipzig.
11. Lange, S., Zeugmann, T., Kapur, S. (1995): Monotonic and Dual Monotonic Language Learning, Theoretical Computer Science, to appear.
12. Meyer, L. (1995): Probabilistic learning of indexed families, Institutsbericht, Institut für Informatik und Gesellschaft, Freiburg, to appear.
13. Machtey, M, Young, P. (1978): An Introduction to the General Theory of Algorithms, North Holland, New York.
14. Pitt, L. (1985): Probabilistic Inductive Inference, PhD thesis, Yale University, 1985, Computer Science Dept. TR-400.

15. Wiehagen, R.: A Thesis in Inductive Inference, in: Proceedings First International Workshop on Nonmonotonic and Inductive Logic, December 1990, Karlsruhe, (J. Dix, K. P. Jantke, P. H. Schmitt, Eds.), Lecture Notes in Artificial Intelligence, Vol. 534, 184-207, Springer-Verlag, Berlin.
16. Wiehagen, R., Freivalds, R., Kinber, E.B. (1984): On the Power of Probabilistic Strategies in Inductive Inference, Theoretical Computer Science 28, 111-133.
17. Wiehagen, R., Freivalds, R., Kinber, E.B. (1988): Probabilistic versus deterministic Inductive Inference in Nonstandard Numberings, Zeitschr. f. math. Logik und Grundlagen d. Math. 34, 531-539.
18. Zeugmann, T., Lange, S. (1995): A Guided Tour Across the Boundaries of Learning Recursive Languages, in: Algorithmic Learning for Knowledge-Based Systems (K.P. Jantke and S. Lange, Eds.), Lecture Notes in Artificial Intelligence Vol. 961, 193-262, Springer-Verlag, Berlin.

Appendix We have to prove Theorem 6 and Lemma 7.

1. Theorem 6:
   $< CLIM_{prob}(p) >_{p\in[0,1]}$ and $< CCOV_{prob}(p) >_{p\in[0,1]}$ are discrete with breakpoints at $\frac{1}{n}$, $n \in \mathcal{N}$.
2. Lemma 7:
   Let $n \in \mathcal{N}$ and let $\frac{1}{n+1} < p \le \frac{1}{n}$. Then
   - $CLIM_{prob}(p) = LIM_{team}(n)$,
   - $CCOV_{prob}(p) = CCOV - LIM_{team}(n)$.

Proof. (of Lemma 7) Let $\mathcal{L}$ be an indexed family, $\mathcal{G}$ a hypothesis space, $n \in \mathcal{N}$ and $\frac{1}{n+1} < p \le \frac{1}{n}$. Obviously $LIM_{team}(n) \subseteq CLIM_{prob}(p)$ and $CCOV_{team}(n) \subseteq CCOV_{prob}(p)$.

To prove the first part of the lemma, assume $\mathcal{L} \in CLIM_{prob}(p)$ with respect to $\mathcal{G}$. Let P be the identifying probabilistic IIM. In the case of function identification, Pitt showed by *counting converging paths* that for each collection of recursive functions identifiable with probability $p > \frac{1}{n+1}$, there exists a team $M_1, \ldots, M_n$ of IIMs with the following property. For each function f to be inferred there exists a $j \in \{1, \ldots, n\}$ such that M_j, fed a text for f, outputs an infinite sequence of finite lists of hypotheses and converges to a list containing at least one hypothesis which is correct for f. Considering language learning of indexed families from text, there is no difficulty in adopting this proof. Therefore, we ommit the details here and refer the reader to Pitt (cf. [14]).

Assume now that there exists a team $M_1, \ldots, M_n$ of IIMs with the following property. For all $L \in rng(\mathcal{L})$ and $\tau \in text(L)$ there exists a $j \in \{1, \ldots, n\}$ such that M_j, fed τ, outputs an infinite sequence of finite lists of hypotheses and converges to a list which contains at least one hypothesis correct for L with respect to $\mathcal{G}$. Notice that all indices in the lists will be interpreted as indices of languages in $rng(\mathcal{G})$. We define a team $M_1', \ldots M_n'$ of IIMs such that $M_1', \ldots M_n'$ $CLIM_{team}(n)$-identifies $\mathcal{L}$ with respect to $\mathcal{G}$. Let $L \in rng(\mathcal{L})$, let τ be a text for L and let $x \in \mathcal{N}$.

IIM M: On input τ_x, M_j' works as follows.

Simulate M_j on τ_x. If M_j outputs $\perp$ then output $\perp$ and request the next input string. If $M_j(\tau_x) = \{j_1, \ldots, j_m\}$, then delete the hypotheses $\{j_{l_1}, \ldots, j_{l_s}\}$ from the list which are not consistent with τ_x. Compare the remaining hypotheses $\{j_{k_1}, \ldots, j_{k_{n-s}}\}$ as follows. If there exists some $i \in \mathcal{N}$, $i \leq m - s$ with $L(G_{j_{k_i}}) \cap \{1, \ldots, x\} \subseteq L(G_{j_{k_l}}) \cap \{1, \ldots, x\}$ for all $l \in \mathcal{N}$, $l \leq m - s$, then output j_{k_i} for the least i with this property and request the next input string. Otherwise output nothing and request the next input string.

Then M'_j is computable since $\mathcal{G}$ is uniformly decidable and M'_j converges correctly on τ with respect to $\mathcal{G}$ iff M_j converges to a finite list of hypotheses containing at least one correct hypothesis for L. Consequently, $M'_1, \ldots M'_n$ $CLIM_{team}(n)$-identifies $\mathcal{L}$ with respect to $\mathcal{G}$ and thus $\mathcal{L} \in LIM_{team}(n)$ since $CLIM_{team}(n) = LIM_{team}(n)$ for all $n \in \mathcal{N}$. This part of Lemma 7 has independently been proven by Jain and Sharma (cf. [5]). For the second part of the lemma we refer the reader to [12].

$\square$

Proof. (of Theorem 6) Let $n \in \mathcal{N}$ and let $\frac{1}{n+1} < p \leq \frac{1}{n}$. By applying Lemma 7 we can conclude that $CCOV_{prob}(p) = CCOV_{prob}(\frac{1}{n})$ and $CLIM_{prob}(p) = CLIM_{prob}(\frac{1}{n})$. It remains to show that $CCOV_{prob}(\frac{1}{n}) \setminus CLIM_{prob}(\frac{1}{n}) \neq \emptyset$. To prove this, we deal with the corresponding notions of team learning. It is a well known result in inductive inference that each family $\mathcal{L}$ of recursive languages which contains an infinite language L and all finite subsets of L is not identifiable in the limit from text (cf. [2]).

Let $n \in \mathcal{N}$. We construct indexed families $\mathcal{L}^{n-1} \in CCOV_{team}(n+1)$, $\mathcal{L}^{n-1} \notin CLIM_{team}(n)$ generalizing this idea. Let $(\, , \,) : \mathcal{N} \times \mathcal{N} \setminus \{0\} \to \mathcal{N}$ be an effective encoding of $\mathcal{N} \times \mathcal{N} \setminus \{0\}$, i.e., the set of all ordered tupels with second component $\neq 0$. Since we can identify this set with the set of the positive rational numbers Q^+ by interpreting $(a, b) = \frac{a}{b}$, we can define a natural ordering on the tupels by setting $(a, b) \leq (c, d)$ iff $ad \leq cb$. For the sake of readability we restrict ourselves to the case $n = 3$. Let $<\, , \,>$ an effective encoding of $\mathcal{N} \times \mathcal{N}$. Define now for all $k, j \in \mathcal{N}$:

$$- \quad L_{<0,k>} = L_{<k,0>} := Q^+,$$
$$- \quad L_{<k,j>} := \begin{cases} \{\, (a,b) \mid (a,b) \leq (k,1)\,\}, & \text{if } j = 1, \\ \{\, (a,b) \mid (a,b) \leq (kj-1,j)\,\}, & \text{if } j > 1. \end{cases}$$

For $k, j \in \mathcal{N}$ the language $L_{<k,1>}$ corresponds to the set of all positive rational numbers which are less or equal to k and the language $L_{<k,j>}$ corresponds to the set of positive rational numbers less or equal to $k - \frac{1}{j}$. Define $\mathcal{L}^2 = (L_{<k,j>})_{k,j \in \mathcal{N}}$. $\mathcal{L}^2$ is an indexed family, since $(a, b) \leq (c, d)$ is uniformly decidable. The proof that $\mathcal{L}^2$ witnesses the desired separation is omitted. It is easy to see how this construction can be generalized to $n > 3$. For example, let $n = 4$. Then add the languages $\{(a, b) \mid (a, b) \leq (kn - j, nj)\}$ to $\mathcal{L}^2$ for all $k, j, n \in \mathcal{N}$, $k, j, n \geq 1$.

$\square$

Noisy Inference and Oracles

Frank Stephan

Institut für Logik, Komplexität und Deduktionssysteme, Universität Karlsruhe,
76128 Karlsruhe, Germany, email ⟨fstephan@ira.uka.de⟩. Supported by the
Deutsche Forschungsgemeinschaft (DFG) grant Me 672/4-2.

Abstract. A learner noisily infers a function or set, if every correct item is
presented infinitely often while in addition some incorrect data ("noise") is
presented a finite number of times. It is shown that learning from a noisy
informant is equal to finite learning with K-oracle from a usual informant.
This result has several variants for learning from text and using different
oracles. Furthermore, partial identification of all r.e. sets can cope also with
noisy input.

1 Introduction

Many scientific or mathematical problems are only solved numerically and the correctness of the solution depends on the computer power available. Scientists therefore have to trust the data, which may be incorrect; they can not wait until better
computer are available 10 years later. So they make up their current theories from
uncertain data.

Modeling the development of science as a long process, it has to be taken into
account that errors in today's simulation-data are discovered in 10 or 20 years, when
the experiments will be done using more powerful computers, which e.g. enable to
work with smaller grids and higher precision. Discovering an error results in a revision
of the theory, if necessary. So there is an infinite sequence of data, where each correct
item, say each correct outcome of a given simulation process, occurs infinitely often,
while the incorrect items only occur a finite number of times; from this sequence of
data scientists generate a finite sequence of theories; the last of these theories should
be correct.

In inductive inference, the topic of exploration is typically modeled by a function
or a set to be learned. And a given simulation is modeled as a pair (x, y) where x is
the input and y the output. The supplied information (x, y) is correct iff $f(x) = y$.
The sequent theories guessed by the scientists are modeled as programs, which are
intended to compute f. There are various approaches to inference from faulty data
[2, 5, 7, 17]; Jain [7] distinguishes three basic types of concepts for learning in the
limit from faulty data: (a) the learner receives some faulty data together with the
information on the concept to be learned, (b) all data is correct but some information
on the concept is never presented and (c) the combination of both concepts.

Many concepts of learning from faulty data have the disadvantage, that it is
impossible to define the object to be learned only from the input to the learner. If
e.g. in case (a) the informations $(0, 0)$ and $(0, 1)$ are both supplied to the learner,
then it is impossible to know which one is correct, i.e., whether $f(0) = 0$ or $f(0) = 1$.
The same holds if according to (b) no statement of the form $(0, y)$ is made at all.

The learner therefore has to overcome this gap by a priori knowledge about f, e.g. that always $f(0) = f(1)$ and $f(1)$ is specified uniquely on the information supplied to the learner.

The model considered here solves this problem by presenting the correct information infinitely often while the incorrect one occurs only finitely often, i.e., $f(x) = y$ iff (x, y) occurs infinitely often on the learner's input-tape. During the inference process, the learner still has the problem not to know whether the current input is correct, but in the limit it turns out which data is correct and which is incorrect; so the learner needs less a priori knowledge for learning in the limit.

Each correct item is presented to the learner infinitely often, but in addition the learner has to cope with some incorrect information, called the noise. Thus the noisy inference considered here can be put into Jain's first category (a), i.e., learning with additional faulty information. So noisy text in this context are a combination of the intrusion texts as defined by Osherson, Stob and Weinstein [17, Exercise 5.4.1 E] which may contain finite additional false words and the fat texts [17, Section 5.5.4] in which each item appears infinitely often. Learning from texts and learning from fat texts are equivalent models [17, Proposition 5.5.4 A]. But the intrusion texts are more restrictive than noisy texts as defined below since the class $\{\{0\}, \{1\}\}$ can be learned from very noisy text but not from intrusion texts. Now the concepts are presented in detail:

Definition 1. A *noisy informant* for a function f is an infinite sequence T such that every pair $(x, f(x))$ occurs infinitely often in this sequence while for each x pairs (x, y) with $y \neq f(x)$ occur only finitely often. A noisy informant for a set is a noisy informant for its characteristic function.

A *noisy text* for a set L is an infinite sequence $T = \{w_i\}_{i \in \omega}$ in which every $x \in L$ occurs infinitely often, i.e., $(\forall x \in L)(\exists^\infty i)[w_i = x]$, while only finitely often some $x \notin L$ occurs, i.e., $(\forall^\infty i)[w_i \in L]$.

An IIM M infers $\mathcal{L}$ noisily (from text or informant), iff for every $L \in \mathcal{L}$ and on every noisy text/informant $T = \{w_i\}_{i \in \omega}$ for L, M converges to an index for L, i.e., iff $M(w_0 w_1 \ldots w_n) = e$ for some index e for L and for almost all n. These criteria are denoted by NoisyTxt and NoisyInf.

A *very noisy text* for a set L is an infinite sequence T such that $x \in L$ iff x occurs infinitely often in T. A *very noisy informant* is a very noisy text for the graph of a function. Every noisy text is also very noisy but not vice versa.

A further important concept of learning theory in this paper is that of learning withoug mindchanges: An IIM learns *finitely* (FIN) a language or function iff it makes exactly one guess during the inference process and this guess is correct. Osherson, Stob and Weinstein [17] give an overview and further details on inductive inference.

The main recursion-theoretic definitions and notations can be found in the books of Odifreddi [16] and Soare [18]. Nevertheless some basic facts are included for the convenience of the reader:

A set is recursive enumerable (r.e.) iff there is an algorithm which outputs a sequence just containing all elements of the set, i.e., which outputs a text T of the set – this text may contain the symbol $\#$ to avoid undefined output in the case of $\emptyset$. RE denotes the class of all r.e. sets, REC that of all recursive functions.

A set A is Turing reducible to B ($A \leq_T B$) if A can be computed via a machine which knows B, i.e., which has an infinite database which supplies for each x the information whether x belongs to B or not. Such a database is called an *oracle* and the question "$x \in B$?" a *query* to B. The class $\{A : A \equiv_T B\}$ is called the Turing degree of B where $A \equiv_T B$ means that both, $A \leq_T B$ and $B \leq_T A$ hold. Given two sets A and B, the Turing degree of the join $A \oplus B = \{2x : x \in A\} \cup \{2x + 1 : x \in B\}$ is the least upper bound of the Turing degrees of A and B. K denotes the halting problem, i.e., the set $\{x : \varphi_x(x) \downarrow\}$. This notion can be relativized: $A' = \{x : \varphi_x^A(x) \downarrow\}$ is the halting problem relative to A where φ_x^A is the x-th recursive function equipped with the oracle A. Also an IIM may use an oracle, e.g., FinTxt[A] denotes the class of all families of languages learnable finitely via an IIM which uses the oracle A.

A set A has high Turing degree if $K' \leq_T A'$, i.e., if the halting problem relative to K can be solved using the halting problem relative to A. The high Turing degrees are also the degrees of the sets A such that there is a function f computable in A which dominates every recursive function g, i.e., which satisfies $(\forall^\infty x)\,[g(x) < f(x)]$. Some kind of counterpart are the hyperimmune-free degrees: they are the degrees of all sets A such that any function f computable relative to A is dominated by a recursive function, i.e., $(\forall f \leq_T A)\,(\exists g \in \text{REC})\,(\forall x)\,[f(x) \leq g(x)]$.

The 1-generic sets are those that either meet or strongly avoid each recursive set of strings: If A is 1-generic and W is a recursive set of strings, then there is either some $\sigma \in W$ with $\sigma \preceq A$ ("A meets W") or there is some $\sigma \notin W$ with $\sigma \preceq A$ and $\tau \notin W$ for all $\tau \succeq \sigma$ ("A strongly avoids W"). In this definition, "recursive" may be replaced by "r.e." without changing the concept. The interested reader may find more information about 1-generic sets in Jockusch's paper [10] or Soare's book [18, A.VI.3.6-9].

Section 2 deals with learning from noisy informant; this concept can be identified with finite learning from informant: NoisyInf = FinInf[K]. This connection relativizes and motivates looking for similar relations w.r.t. noisy learning and oracles. Further it provides an easy characterization for the inference degrees of noisy inference — the inference degree of an oracle A is $\{B : \text{NoisyInf}[B] = \text{NoisyInf}[A]\}$ [4]. In particular section 3 provides many connections for learning from noisy text, but it does not find an equivalence between noisy learning and an already well-known concept. Section 4 looks for connections between the text and informant version of noisy learning. Section 5 considers the case, where the family to be learned is uniformly recursive. Section 6 deals with partially identification. Osherson, Stob and Weinstein [17] showed that the class of all r.e. sets is partially identifiable from text; the same holds for noisy text and noisy informant, but not for very noisy text.

2 Inference From Informant

The main result of this section is, that finite learning from informant with K-oracle equals learning from noisy informant. This relation motivates the study of connections between noisy inference and finite inference with oracles.

Theorem 2. FinInf[K] = NoisyInf.

Proof. NoisyInf $\subseteq$ FinInf[K]: Assume that M is a recursive IIM which learns a family $\mathcal{L}$ of sets from noisy informant. A string σ is called α-consistent iff

$$(\forall x < |\alpha|)\,[((x,y) \text{ occurs in } \sigma) \;\Rightarrow\; y = \alpha(x)].$$

Now the following FinInf[K] IIM N infers $\mathcal{L}$:

$$N(\alpha) = \begin{cases} e & \text{if } e = N(\sigma\tau) \text{ for some string } \sigma \text{ of length up to } |\alpha| \\ & \text{and for all } \alpha\text{-consistent strings } \tau; \\ ? & \text{otherwise, i.e., there is no such } \sigma. \end{cases}$$

In short: N searches — using K-oracle — some kind of locking sequence σ and then outputs $e = M(\sigma)$.

Assume now that on the inference of U, $N(\alpha)$ outputs $e = N(\sigma)$ for some $\alpha \preceq U$. Let $w_{(x,y)} = (x, U(x))$ for all x, y. Now $\sigma w_0 w_1 w_2 \ldots$ is a noisy informant for U and thus M has to converge on this informant to a correct index. Since all strings $\tau_n = w_0 w_1 \ldots w_n$ are α-consistent, $e = N(\sigma\tau_n)$ and e is an index for U. Thus the first guess is already correct and no mindchange is necessary.

So it remains to verify that N always converges. Assume that N does not converge, i.e., for every σ and every $\alpha \preceq U$ there is an α-consistent τ with $M(\sigma\tau) \neq M(\sigma)$. Let $\sigma_0 = (0,0)$. For $n = 1, 2, \ldots$, there are $(U(0), U(1), \ldots, U(n))$-consistent strings τ_n such that

$$M(\sigma_n) \neq M(\sigma_{n-1}) \quad \text{where}$$
$$\sigma_n = \sigma_{n-1}\,(0, U(0))\,(1, U(1)) \ldots (n, U(n))\,\tau_n.$$

It follows that $T = \lim_n \sigma_n$ is a noisy informant for U and that M diverges on T, a contradiction. Thus N infers every $U \in \mathcal{L}$ and NoisyInf $\subseteq$ FinTxt[K].

FinInf[K] $\subseteq$ NoisyInf: Let N^K be a FinInf[K] IIM for some family $\mathcal{L}$. A string α is called σ-consistent iff for all $x < |\alpha|$ the pair $(x, \alpha(x))$ occurs in σ at least as often as any other pair (x, y). Now

$$M(\sigma) = \begin{cases} N^{K_{|\sigma|}}(\alpha) & \text{for the shortest } \sigma\text{-consistent } \alpha \\ & \text{which satisfies } N^{K_{|\sigma|}}(\alpha)\!\downarrow\,\neq\,? \text{ within } |\sigma| \text{ steps.} \\ ? & \text{otherwise, i.e., there is no such } \alpha. \end{cases}$$

M NoisyInf infers $\mathcal{L}$. $\qquad\qquad\qquad\qquad\qquad\qquad\qquad\qquad\qquad\qquad\qquad\qquad\square$

It is easy to see that the proof holds as well for learning functions as well for learning r.e. sets. Further the proof relativizes. Since FinInf[A] $\subseteq$ FinInf[B] $\Leftrightarrow$ $A \leq_T B$ [4, Theorem 6.36], the relativized version of this theorem also characterizes the inference degrees for noisy informant. In the non-relativized world, NoisyInf is between FinInf and LimInf.

Corollary 3.
(a) NoisyInf[A] $=$ FinInf[A'].
(b) NoisyInf[A] $\subseteq$ NoisyInf[B] *iff* $A' \leq_T B'$.
(c) FinInf $\subset$ NoisyInf $\subset$ LimInf.

While for sets the definitions of noisy informant and very noisy informant are equivalent (data (x, y) with $y > 1$ can be ignored), this equivalence does not hold in the field of inferring functions. But there remains a connection:

Theorem 4. *If $\mathcal{L}$ can be learned from noisy informant and some K-recursive function f bounds all functions $g \in \mathcal{L}$, then $\mathcal{L}$ can also be learned from very noisy informant.*

Proof. Let M be an IIM which infers $\mathcal{L}$ from noisy informant and let f_s be a uniform recursive sequence of functions which approximate f in the limit: $(\forall x)\,(\forall^\infty s)\,[f(x) = f_s(x)]$. Since f only has to be an upper bound, w.l.o.g. the f_s approximate f from below.

Every very noisy informant $T = w_0 w_1 \ldots$ for $g \in \mathcal{L}$ can be translated into a new noisy informant $T' = v_0 v_1 \ldots$ as follows:

$$v_s = \begin{cases} w_s & \text{if } w_s = (x, y) \text{ and } y \leq f_s(x); \\ \# & \text{otherwise.} \end{cases}$$

Also in T' every pair $(x, g(x))$ occurs infinitely often since $(x, g(x))$ occurs infinitely often in T, $g(x) \leq f(x)$ and therefore $g(x) \leq f_s(x)$ for almost all s. On the other hand, if $y > f(x)$, then $y > f_s(x)$ for all x and therefore (x, y) never occurs in T'. Further if $y \leq f(x)$ and $y \neq g(x)$, then (x, y) occurs only finitely often in T and therefore also only finitely often in T'. Thus T' is a noisy informant for g. Since this translation is computable and can be done on all finite initial segments of T, M can infer g from T'. □

The converse does not hold. For example the family $\{e 1^e 0^\infty : e \in \omega\}$ can be learned from very noisy informant, but it has no bound on $f(0)$ at all. On the other hand, the condition, that f is K-recursive can not be weakened, since the family

$$\{0^x y 0^\infty : x \in \omega \wedge 1 \leq y \leq f(x)\}$$

can be learned from very noisy informant iff some K-recursive function majorizes f.

3 Inference From Text

Locking sequences are an important tool in learning from text. Therefore it is useful to define them also for inference from noisy text. Let M be an IIM which infers L. σ is called a locking sequence for L iff

- $M(\sigma) = e$ with $W_e = L$ and
- $M(\sigma \tau) = M(\sigma)$ for all $\tau \in L^*$.

Since $L = W_e$, σ is also called a locking sequence for the index e. The proof, that a locking sequence exists, is almost identical to the one in the case of learning from text and is therefore omitted. The next two theorems make use of this fact.

Theorem 5. *Let $\mathcal{L} \in$ NoisyTxt. Then there is a recursive IIM which learns $\mathcal{L}$ from noisy text and for each $L \in \mathcal{L}$ there is a unique index e for L such that every noisy text T has a locking sequence $\sigma \preceq T$ with $M(\sigma) = e$.*

Proof. The proof is similar to the locking-sequence-hunting construcion of [17, Proposition 4.3.6A]. Let M be an given IIM; the new IIM N is defined inductively. Given the input $w_0 w_1 \ldots w_n$, let m denote the maximal number such that either $N(w_0 w_1 \ldots w_m) \neq N(w_0 w_1 \ldots w_{n-1})$ or $N(w_0 w_1 \ldots w_m) = ?$, further $m = 0$ if $n = 0$; note that $0 \leq m \leq n$. Now N looks for the first string σ such that

- $\sigma \in \{w_0, w_1, \ldots, w_n\}^*$ and $|\sigma| \leq n$.
- $range(\sigma) \subseteq W_{e,n}$ for $e = M(\sigma)$.
- $M(\sigma) = M(\sigma\tau)$ for all $\tau \in \{w_m, w_{m+1}, \ldots, w_n\}^*$ with $|\tau| \leq n$.

If such a σ exists, $N(w_0 w_1 \ldots w_n) = e$, otherwise $N(w_0 w_1 \ldots w_n) = ?$. The verification is similar to the in the proof of [17, Proposition 4.3.6A]; only the second condition is due to the fact, that a noisy text $w_0 w_1 \ldots$ for some $L \in \mathcal{L}$ may contain finitely many elements w_i outside L. $\qquad \Box$

Learning from text is impossible, if the language contains an infinite set and all its finite subsets. The following theorem shows, that learning from noisy text is even more restrictive:

Theorem 6. *If $L' \subset L$ then $\{L', L\} \notin$ NoisyTxt.*

Proof. Let M be an IIM which infers at least L and has a locking sequence σ for L. Further let $w_0 w_1 \ldots$ be an enumeration of L' in which every element of L' occurs infinitely often. Now $\sigma w_0 w_1 \ldots$ is a noisy text for L', but since $e = M(\sigma)$ is an index for L and $M(\sigma w_0 w_1 \ldots w_n) = e$ for all n (by $w_0, w_1, \ldots \in L$), M does not infer L' from noisy text. $\qquad \Box$

The severe restriction from Theorem 6 contrasts the fact, that if the sets to be learned are the graphs $\mathcal{G}$ of a set of functions, then there is no difference between noisy and non-noisy text, so learning from noisy text is in general not so restrictive as learning from noisy informant.

Theorem 7. *Let $\mathcal{G}$ be a the set of the graphs of some set of total recursive functions. Then $\mathcal{G} \in$ NoisyTxt $\Leftrightarrow \mathcal{G} \in$ LimTxt.*

Proof. If $w_0 w_1 \ldots$ is a noisy text for the graph of a function g, then it contains only finitely many (x, y) with $y \neq g(x)$ while each pair $(x, g(x))$ occurs infinitely often in $w_0 w_1 \ldots$. There is a k such that all w_i with $i \geq k$ are of the form $(x, g(x))$ for some x. So $w_k w_{k+1} w_{k+2} \ldots$ is text for $graph(g)$ which is not noisy. Some IIM M infers $\mathcal{G}$ from text. The following IIM N infers $\mathcal{G}$ from noisy text:

On input $w_0 w_1 \ldots w_n$, N searches the least $m \leq n$ such that the information $w_m, w_{m+1}, \ldots, w_n$ is not contradictory, i.e.,

$$(\forall i, j) [m \leq i \leq j \leq n \wedge w_i = (x, y) \wedge w_j = (x, z) \Rightarrow y = z],$$

and then N outputs $M(w_m w_{m+1} \ldots w_n)$.

For almost all n, this m (depending on n) coincides with k and therefore

$$(\forall^\infty n)\,[N(w_0 w_1 \ldots w_n) = M(w_k w_{k+1} \ldots w_n)].$$

Thus N on the noisy text $w_0 w_1 \ldots$ and M on the text $w_k w_{k+1} \ldots$, both converge to the same index for $graph(g)$. □

Some families of functions can be inferred in the limit, but are not in FinInf[A] for any oracle A. The family

$$\{f : (\forall^\infty x)\,[f(x) = 0]\} \in \mathrm{LimInf} - \mathrm{FinInf}[A]$$

is an example. So their graphs are LimTxt and NoisyTxt learnable, but not FinInf[A] and FinTxt[A] learnable for any oracle A. Therefore inference from noisy text is not contained in finite inference relative to any oracle:

Corollary 8. NoisyTxt $\not\subseteq$ FinTxt[A] *for all oracles A.*

So in contrary to the case of the informant, the classes FinTxt[K] and NoisyTxt do not coincide. Indeed Theorem 11 will show, that FinTxt[A] and NoisyTxt are incomparable for all oracles A. Since Theorem 11 also studies the connections FinTxt[A] $\subseteq$ NoisyTxt[B] it is worth to look first at the inference degrees with respect to learning from noisy text:

Theorem 9. *The following holds for all oracles A and B:*
(a) *If A is r.e. then* NoisyTxt[A] $\subseteq$ NoisyTxt[B] $\Leftrightarrow A \leq_T B$.
(b) *If $A, B \geq_T K$ then* NoisyTxt[A] $\subseteq$ NoisyTxt[B] $\Leftrightarrow A' \leq_T B'$.
(c) NoisyTxt[A] = NoisyTxt *iff $A \leq_T K$ and A has recursive or 1-generic degree.*

Proof. (a): Obviously $A \leq_T B \Rightarrow$ NoisyTxt[A] $\subseteq$ NoisyTxt[B] holds. For the converse consider the family $\mathcal{L}$ consisting of the r.e. set A and all sets $\{x\}$ with $x \notin A$. The IIM $M(w_0 w_1 \ldots w_n)$ outputs an index of the set

$$\begin{array}{ll} \{w_n\} & \text{if } w_n \notin A; \\ A & \text{otherwise, i.e., if } w_n \in A. \end{array}$$

M is obviously A-recursive; further if $w_0 w_1 \ldots$ is a noisy text for $\{x\}$, then $w_i = x$ for almost all i and M converges to an index for $\{x\}$. If $w_0 w_1 \ldots$ is a noisy text for A then $w_i \in A$ for almost all i and the M almost always outputs the same index for A.

On the other hand, assume that M is B-recursive and infers $\mathcal{L}$. A has a locking sequence σ. If $x \notin A$, then M converges on σx^∞ to an index of $\{x\}$, thus $M(\sigma x^n) \neq M(\sigma)$ for some n. If $x \in A$, then $M(\sigma x^n) = M(\sigma)$ for all n since σ is a locking sequence for A. In short

$$x \in A \iff (\forall n)\,[M(\sigma x^n) = M(\sigma)]$$

and the r.e. set A is co-r.e. relative to B. Thus $A \leq_T B$.

(b): Let $A, B \geq_T K$, $A' \leq_T B'$ and $\mathcal{L} \in$ NoisyTxt[A] via M. W.l.o.g. for every $L \in \mathcal{L}$

and every noisy text T for L, there is some locking sequence $\sigma \preceq T$ for M. The set of all locking sequences σ for some W_e is recursive in A' by the formula

$$E = \{(\sigma, e) : (\forall \tau \in W_e^*)\,[M(\sigma\tau) = M(\sigma)]\}$$

Thus E has a B-recursive approximation E_s; further A has an B-recursive approximation A_s. Now the new B-recursive IIM N infers $L \in \mathcal{L}$ from the text $w_0 w_1 \ldots$ as follows:

$N(w_0 w_1 \ldots w_n)$ searches for the first m such that $w_m, w_{m+1}, \ldots, w_n \in W_{e_m}$ and $e_m \in E_n$ for $e_m = M^{A_n}(w_0 w_1 \ldots w_m)$.

There is a first m such that $w_n \in W_e$ for all $n \geq m$, $w_0 w_1 \ldots w_n$ is a locking sequence for W_e and $M^A(w_0 w_1 \ldots w_m) = e$. For all sufficiently large n, $M^{A_n}(w_0 w_1 \ldots w_m) = e$, $(w_0 w_1 \ldots w_m, e) \in E_n$ and for all $i < n$ with $e_i = M^{A_n}(w_0 w_1 \ldots w_i)$, either $(w_0 w_1 \ldots w_i, e_i) \notin E_n$ or some $w_j \notin W_{e_i}$ where $i \leq j \leq n$. Thus $N(w_0 w_1 \ldots w_n) = e$ for almost all n and also N infers $\mathcal{L}$.

For the other way round, let C be a retraceable set of degree A', which is co-r.e. in A. Now let $\mathcal{L}$ consist of the sets

$$\begin{aligned}\{x, 0\} &\quad \text{iff} \quad x > 0 \text{ and } x \in C,\\ \{x\} &\quad \text{iff} \quad x > 0 \text{ and } x \notin C.\end{aligned}$$

Further C_s denotes a A-recursive approximation of C. Now given any input σ, let $x(\sigma)$ denote the last $y > 0$ which occurs in σ, i.e., $x(\sigma) = y \Leftrightarrow \sigma \in \omega^* y 0^*$. If $\sigma \in 0^*$ then $x(\sigma) = 0$. Now $M(\sigma)$ outputs an index of the set

$$\begin{aligned}\{x(\sigma), 0\} &\quad \text{if } x(\sigma) \in C_{|\sigma|}\\ \{x(\sigma)\} &\quad \text{otherwise.}\end{aligned}$$

If T is a noisy text for $\{0, x\}$ or $\{x\}$, then $x(\sigma) = x$ for almost all $\sigma \preceq T$. Further $x \in C_{|\sigma|}$ iff $x \in C$ for almost all $\sigma \preceq T$. Thus $\mathcal{L} \in \text{NoisyTxt}[A]$ via M.

Thus $\mathcal{L} \in \text{NoisyTxt}[B]$ via some B-recursive N. If $x \in C$ then there is a locking sequence σ such that $N(\sigma\tau) = e$ for some index e of $\{0, x\}$ and all $\tau \in \{0, x\}^*$. On the other hand if $x \notin C$ then N converges on every text σx^∞ to an index for $\{x\}$. Thus

$$x \in C \Leftrightarrow (\exists \sigma)\,(\exists e)\,(\forall n)\,[0 \in W_e \wedge N(\sigma x^n) = e].$$

Therefore C is r.e. in B'; since C is retraceable, C is even recursive in B' and $A' \leq_T B'$ follows.

(c): The proof of this fact is similar to that of [13, Theorem 9.5] concerning LimTxt inference degrees. $\qquad\square$

Theorem 9 also holds with LimTxt instead of NoisyTxt [13, Theorems 9.2, 9.4 and 9.5]. So it is likely, that the structures of the LimTxt and NoisyTxt inference degrees coincide and the following conjecture holds:

Conjecture 10. $\text{NoisyTxt}[A] \subseteq \text{NoisyTxt}[B] \Leftrightarrow \text{LimTxt}[A] \subseteq \text{LimTxt}[B]$.

The next result deals with the relation between $\text{FinTxt}[A]$ and $\text{NoisyTxt}[B]$.

Theorem 11. $\operatorname{FinTxt}[A] \subseteq \operatorname{NoisyTxt}[B] \Leftrightarrow K \leq_T B \wedge (A \oplus K)' \leq_T B'$.

Proof. The proof consists of three parts:
(a) If $\operatorname{FinTxt} \subseteq \operatorname{NoisyTxt}[B]$ then $K \leq_T B$.
(b) If $\operatorname{FinTxt}[A] \subseteq \operatorname{NoisyTxt}[B]$ then $(A \oplus K)' \leq_T B'$.
(c) If $(A \oplus K)' \leq_T B'$ and $K \leq_T B$ then $\operatorname{FinTxt}[A] \subseteq \operatorname{NoisyTxt}[B]$.

(a): Let $\mathcal{L}$ contain K plus all sigletons $\{x\}$ with $x \notin K$. There is a recursive function f such that
$$W_{f(x)} = \begin{cases} K & \text{if } x \in K; \\ \{x\} & \text{if } x \notin K. \end{cases}$$
Now the FinTxt IIM waits for the first x to appear on the input, outputs the guess $W_{f(x)}$ and terminates. The proof of Theorem 9:(a) shows that $\mathcal{L} \in \operatorname{NoisyTxt}[B]$ only if $K \leq_T B$.

(b): Let $\operatorname{FinTxt}[A] \subseteq \operatorname{NoisyTxt}[B]$. Let C be a retraceable set of degree $(A \oplus K)'$ which is co-r.e. in $A \oplus K$. So $\overline{C}$ is the domain of the partial function $\psi^{A \oplus K}$. Let U_y contain all x such that the computation of $\psi^{A \oplus K}v(x)$ terminates within y steps and equals to that relative $A \oplus K$: whenever an odd number $2z+1$ is queried, then either $z \in K_y$ or $z \notin K$. Furthermore, all queries are made to numbers below y. Note that $U_y \subseteq \overline{C}$. Further each $x \notin C$ is in almost all sets U_y. The sets U_y are uniformly co-r.e. in A and there is a recursive function h such that $\overline{U_y} = W_{h(y)}^{\{z \in A : z < y\}}$. Now let $\mathcal{L}$ consist of the sets
$$\begin{array}{ll} \{2x, 1, 3, 5, 7, \ldots\} & \text{iff } x \in C, \\ \{2x, 2y+1\} & \text{iff } x \in U_y. \end{array}$$
First $\mathcal{L} \in \operatorname{FinTxt}[A]$ is shown. The IIM waits until the even number $2x$ and an odd number $2y+1$ are in the input. Then it outputs the index $f(x, y)$ where
$$W_{f(x,y)} = \begin{cases} \{2x, 2y+1\} & \text{if } x \in U_y, \text{ i.e., if } x \notin W_e^{\{z \in A : z < y\}}; \\ \{2x, 1, 3, 5, 7, \ldots\} & \text{otherwise, i.e., if } x \in W_e^{\{z \in A : z < y\}}. \end{cases}$$
The function f is A-recursive and queries A only below y. $f(x, y)$ contains a table of $A(0), A(1), \ldots, A(y)$ and first enumerates $2x$ and $2y+1$ into $W_{f(x,y)}$. Then the machine emulates the enumeration of $W_{h(y)}^{\{z \in A : z < y\}}$ until x is enumerated into this set; if this happens then all odd numbers are enumerated into $W_{f(x,y)}$. So the IIM guesses $\{2x, 2y+1\}$ if $x \in U_y$ and guesses $\{2x, 1, 3, 5, 7, \ldots\}$ if $x \notin U_y$, in particular if $x \in C$. Thus $\mathcal{L} \in \operatorname{FinTxt}[A]$ and $\mathcal{L} \in \operatorname{NoisyTxt}[B]$ via some B-recursive M.

If $x \in C$ then M infers $V_x = \{2x, 1, 3, 5, 7, \ldots\}$ and V_x has a locking sequence. If $x \notin C$, then $x \in U_y$ for some y. Then M infers $\{2x, 2y+1\}$ and V_x has no locking sequence since $\{2x, 2y+1\} \subset V_x$. So the equivalences
$$x \in C \Leftrightarrow V_x \text{ has a locking sequence}$$
$$\Leftrightarrow (\exists \sigma)(\exists e)(\forall \tau \in V_x^*)[M(\sigma\tau) = e \wedge |W_e| > 2]$$
hold. Thus C is r.e. in B'. Since C is retraceable, $C \leq_T B'$ and $(A \oplus K)' \leq_T B'$.

(c): If $B \geq_T K$ and $(A \oplus K)' \leq_T B'$, then $\operatorname{NoisyTxt}[A \oplus K] \subseteq \operatorname{NoisyTxt}[B]$. So it remains to show that $\operatorname{FinTxt}[A] \subseteq \operatorname{NoisyTxt}[A \oplus K]$.

Let $\mathcal{L} \in \operatorname{FinTxt}[A]$. Form the definition of finite learning follows, that there are A-recursive functions f, g such that for every $L \in \mathcal{L}$:

- If $D_{f(i)} \subseteq L$ then $W_{g(i)} = L$;
- There is some i with $D_{f(i)} \subseteq L$.

Such a sequence can be obtained by A-recursively enumerating all strings σ on which a given FinTxt[A] IIM M outputs some $e \neq ?$. Then for the i-th such string σ_i, let $D_{f(i)} = range(\sigma_i)$ and $g(i) = M(\sigma_i)$. W.l.o.g. $\mathcal{L} \neq \{\emptyset\}$ and therefore $D_{f(i)} \neq \emptyset$ for all i. Now the following IIM N infers $\mathcal{L}$ from noisy text:

- For all $i \leq |\sigma|$, N calculates c_i which is the maximal number y such that every $x \in D_{f(i)}$ occurs y times in σ.
- N finds the least i with $c_i \geq c_j$ for all $j \leq |\sigma|$.
- N outputs $g(j)$ for the least j with $D_{f(j)} \subseteq W_{g(i)}$ and $D_{f(i)} \subseteq W_{g(j)}$.

In a given text T for L, only finitely often, say k times, occurs some $x \notin L$. On the other hand each $x \in L$ occurs infinitely often in T. There is a minimal j with $D_{f(j)} \subseteq L$ and $W_{g(j)} = L$. Every $x \in D_{f(j)}$ occurs at least $k + 1$ times in almost all $\sigma \preceq T$, thus for almost all $\sigma \preceq T$, the i computed in the second step satisfies $W_{g(i)} = L$. Then $D_{f(j)} \subseteq W_{g(i)}$ and $D_{f(i)} \subseteq W_{g(j)}$ and further that j is the minimal index with this property. So $N(\sigma) = j$ for almost all $\sigma \preceq T$ and N infers $\mathcal{L}$ from noisy text. $\square$

So the only relation is FinTxt[K] $\subset$ NoisyTxt[K] and there is no equivalent statement to FinInf[K] = NoisyInf. The family

$$\{\omega - \{i\} : i \in \omega\}$$

is learnable from very noisy text but not FinTxt[A] learnable for any oracle A. On the other hand there is a nice characterization of FinTxt[K] using monotonicity notions:

Kapur [11] introduced (in the restricted context of section 5) the notion of strongly dual monotonic inference, i.e., whenever the IIM makes a mindchange from e to e', then the guessed language must be more special: $W_{e'} \subseteq W_e$. Jain and Sharma [8] and Kinber and Stephan [12] generalized this and other notions of monotonic inference to learning r.e. languages. While the class FinTxt[K] can not be characterized in terms of noisy inference, it turned out to be equivalent with strongly dual monotonic inference without oracle.

Theorem 12. $\mathcal{L} \in$ FinTxt[K] *iff* $\mathcal{L}$ *can be learned via a recursive and strongly dual monotonic machine.*

4 Informant Versus Text

It follows immediately from the definition that every family of r.e. sets, which is learnable from text, is also learnable from informant. But this does not hold in the case of noisy inference, since the definitions of noisy text and noisy informant do not match so good as in the standard case. So the following holds:

Theorem 13. NoisyInf[A] *and* NoisyTxt[B] *are incomparable for all oracles A and B.*

Proof. The family $\{\emptyset, \Sigma^*\}$ is finitely learnable from noisy informant, but not learnable from noisy text by Theorem 6.

The family mentioned to prove Corollary 8 is in NoisyTxt[B] for all oracles B, but not in FinInf[A'] for any oracle A, in particular not in NoisyInf[A]. □

So it is better to look for inclusions which hold under additional constraints. The first is to consider very noisy text versus (very) noisy informant; note that in the case of characteristic functions of sets, there is no difference between noisy and very noisy informant. Given a noisy informant $T = (w_0, b_0), (w_1, b_1), \ldots$ for a set L, the sequence T containing all w_i with $b_i = 1$ is a very noisy text for L: w_i occurs in T' infinitely often iff $(w_i, 1)$ occurs in T infinitely often iff $w_i \in L$. Thus one can translate every (very) noisy informant into a very noisy text and simulate the IIM learning from very noisy text. Thus the following theorem holds (and also relativizes to every oracle):

Theorem 14. *Every class of sets learnable from very noisy text is also learnable from noisy informant.*

While NoisyInf[A] $\not\subseteq$ NoisyTxt[B] for all oracles A and B, there is a connection if the IIM learns from text without any noise:

Theorem 15. NoisyInf[A] $\subseteq$ LimTxt[B] $\Leftrightarrow$ $A' \leq_T B'$.

5   Learning Uniformly Recursive Families

Angluin [1] introduced the concept of learning, where the class $\mathcal{L}$ to be learned must have a uniformly recursive representation. Zeugmann's Habilitationsschrift [19] gives an overview on this field of learning theory. This notion is very restrictive, therefore the results, in particular the relativization, are different from those in section 3.

Theorem 16. *For a uniformly recursive family $\mathcal{L} = \{L_i\}$ the following is equivalent:*
(a) $(\forall i, j)[L_i \subseteq L_j \Rightarrow L_i = L_j]$.
(b) $\mathcal{L}$ *is exactly learnable from noisy text.*
(c) $\mathcal{L}$ *is class preserving learnable from noisy text.*
(d) $\mathcal{L}$ *is class comprising learnable from noisy text.*

Proof. (b $\Rightarrow$ c) and (c $\Rightarrow$ d) are obvious. Further (d $\Rightarrow$ a) follows from Theorem 6.

(a $\Rightarrow$ b): Let $\mathcal{L}$ fulfill the requirement from (a). It has to be shown that $\mathcal{L} \in$ NoisyTxt via an IIM that outputs the indices relative to the numbering $\{L_i\}$. For each σ and i let $error(\sigma, i)$ denote the number of $w \in \sigma$ with $w \notin L_i$. Now

$$M(\sigma) = \begin{cases} i & \text{if } i \text{ is the smallest } j \leq |\sigma| \text{ such that every } x \leq error(\sigma, j) \\ & \text{with } x \in L_j \text{ occurs at least } error(\sigma, j) \text{ times in } \sigma; \\ ? & \text{if there is no such } j \leq |\sigma|. \end{cases}$$

Let T be a noisy text for $L \in \mathcal{L}$. If $L_i \neq L$ then there are $x \in L - L_i$ and $y \in L_i - L$. x occurs infinitely often in T while the y occurs only finitely often in T, say k times. Every sufficient large initial segment $\sigma \preceq T$ contains x more than $x + y + k$ times, thus $error(\sigma, i) > x + y + k$. Since $y \leq error(\sigma, i)$ and y occurs less than $error(\sigma, i)$ times in L_i, $M(\sigma) \neq i$.

Now let i be the minimal index of L, i.e., i is the minimal j with $L = L_j$. For almost all $\sigma \preceq T$, $M(\sigma) \notin \{0, 1, \ldots, i-1\}$. Only finitely often, say k times, occurs some element outside L in T. Thus $error(\sigma, i) \leq k$ for all $\sigma \preceq T$. Further all $x \in L_i$ with $x \leq k$ occur in all sufficient long $\sigma \preceq T$ at least $k + 1$ times, thus $M(\sigma) = i$ for almost all $\sigma \preceq T$ and M converges to i. $\qquad\square$

It is easy to see that Theorem 6 holds also in a relativized world, i.e., that for any oracle A, $L \subset L' \Rightarrow \{L, L'\} \notin \mathrm{NoisyTxt}[A]$. Since the avoidance of inclusions is the only restriction to $\mathcal{L}$ and this restriction can not be overcome, oracles do not help to increase the learning power:

Theorem 17. *If $\mathcal{L}$ is a uniformly recursive family which is $\mathrm{NoisyTxt}[A]$ learnable for some oracle A, then $\mathcal{L}$ is already learnable from noisy text without any oracle.*

This is a consequence of $\mathcal{L}$ being uniformly recursive; there is even no greatest inference degree since by Theorem 11, $\mathrm{NoisyTxt}[A] \subset \mathrm{NoisyTxt}[A']$ holds for all oracles A.

Theorem 18. *For a uniformly recursive family $\mathcal{L} = \{L_i\}$ the following is equivalent:*
(a) $(\forall i)(\exists D)(\forall j)[D \subseteq L_j \Leftrightarrow L_i = L_j]$.
(b) $\mathcal{L}$ *is exactly* $\mathrm{FinTxt}[K]$ *learnable.*
(c) $\mathcal{L}$ *is class preserving* $\mathrm{FinTxt}[K]$ *learnable.*
(d) $\mathcal{L}$ *is class comprising* $\mathrm{FinTxt}[K]$ *learnable.*

Proof. (b $\Rightarrow$ c) and (c $\Rightarrow$ d) are obvious.

(a $\Rightarrow$ b): Let $\mathcal{L}$ fulfill the requirement from (a). The $\mathrm{FinTxt}[K]$ IIM asks on input σ with range D always iff D has two incomparable extensions in $\mathcal{L}$. Or more formally, the IIM asks the query

$$(\exists i, j, x)[D \subseteq L_i \wedge D \subseteq L_j \wedge (x \in L_i - L_j \vee x \in L_j - L_i)].$$

Since D is a fixed finite set, the query is K-recursive. By condition (a) after finite time the query receives a negative answer. Then the IIM has only to output the first index i with $D \subseteq L_i$; this index exists since σ is part of a text of some language L_i.

(d $\Rightarrow$ a): If $\mathcal{L}$ is class comprising $\mathrm{FinTxt}[K]$ learnable, then for each L_i there is some string σ such that the $\mathrm{FinTxt}[K]$ IIM M makes a guess, which of course is correct, say $M(\sigma) = i$. Therefore if $D = range(\sigma) \subseteq L_j$ then $L_j = L_i$ since σ is also an initial segment of some text for L_j and there is no mindchange possible after M suggested L_i; i.e., i is an index for L_j. $\qquad\square$

The degree-structure of the FinTxt and FinInf inference degrees relative to learning uniform recursive families of sets is different from the degree structure of learning arbitrary families of r.e. sets. Fortnow et al. [4, Theorem 6.36] showed that the latter coincides with the Turing degrees.

Theorem 19. *Let* F[A] *be the set of all functions* f *which are majorized by an* A-*recursive function and for which the set* $\{(x, y) : y < f(x)\}$ *is r.e.; further consider the inference degrees with respect to learning uniformly recursive families. Now the following is equivalent:*

(a) $F[A] \subseteq F[B]$.
(b) $\text{FinTxt}[A] \subseteq \text{FinTxt}[B]$.
(c) $\text{FinInf}[A] \subseteq \text{FinInf}[B]$.

Proof. (a $\Rightarrow$ b): Let $F[A] \subseteq F[B]$ and $\mathcal{L} = \{L_i\}$ be a uniformly recursive family. W.l.o.g. if $i \neq j$ then $L_i \neq L_j$. Now for each i let $w_{i,x} = x$ if $x \in L_i$ and $w_{i,x} = \#$ otherwise ($x \notin L_i$). Further let $f_A(i)$ be the first x such that $M(w_0 w_1 \ldots w_x) \neq ?$. Certainly $range(w_0 w_1 \ldots w_x) = \{y \in L_i : y \leq x\} \not\subseteq L_j$ for every set $L_j \neq L_i$. Thus f_A dominates the function $f_{\mathcal{L}}$ given by

$$f_{\mathcal{L}}(i) = \min\{x : (\forall j \in \omega - \{i\})(\exists y \leq x)[y \in L_i - L_j]\}.$$

Clearly $\{(i, y) : y < f_{\mathcal{L}}(i)\}$ is an r.e. set and $f_{\mathcal{L}} \in F[A]$. From the hypothesis (a) follows, that a B-recursive function f_B majorizes $f_{\mathcal{L}}$. The new IIM M works as follows:

$$M(\sigma) = \begin{cases} i & \text{if } i \leq |\sigma| \text{ and } (\forall x \leq f_B(i))[x \in L_i \Leftrightarrow x \in range(\sigma)]; \\ ? & \text{otherwise.} \end{cases}$$

Since $\{x \in L_i : x \leq f_B(i)\} \not\subseteq L_j$ for all $j \neq i$, the i in the expression is unique and M is well-defined. Whenever M infers L_i then M outputs ? until it has seen all elements in $\{x \in L_i : x \leq f_B(i)\}$; then it begins to output its only guess i. So $\mathcal{L} \in \text{FinTxt}[B]$ via M.

(b $\Rightarrow$ c): Note that $\mathcal{L} \in \text{FinInf}[A] \Leftrightarrow \mathcal{L}' = \{L \oplus \overline{L} : L \in \mathcal{L}\} \in \text{FinTxt}[A]$. Thus $\mathcal{L} \in \text{FinInf}[A] \Rightarrow \mathcal{L}' \in \text{FinTxt}[A] \Rightarrow \mathcal{L}' \in \text{FinTxt}[B] \Rightarrow \mathcal{L} \in \text{FinInf}[B]$ and therefore $\text{FinInf}[A] \subseteq \text{FinInf}[B]$.

(c $\Rightarrow$ a): This is shown by contraposition, let $f \in F[A] - F[B]$ and let the A-recursive function f_A majorize f. Since f has a recursive approximation from below, the family

$$\mathcal{L} = \{D : (\exists i \in D)[D \subseteq \{i, i+1, i+2, \ldots, i+f(i)\}]\}$$

is uniformly recursive. M finitely infers $\mathcal{L}$ relative to A as follows:

- If $\sigma = 0^i 1\tau$ and $|\tau| > f_A(i)$ then M outputs an index for $\{x < |\sigma| : \sigma(x) = 1\}$.
- Otherwise M makes no guess, i.e., $M(\sigma) = ?$.

On the other hand assume that $\mathcal{L} \in \text{FinInf}[B]$ via N and let

$$f_B(i) = \min\{|\tau| : N(0^i 1\tau) \neq ?\}.$$

Since no B-recursive function majorizes f, there is some i with $f_B(i) < f(i)$. Thus there is $D \in \mathcal{L}$ such that $i = \min(D)$ and inferring D, N makes its guess before seeing whether $i + f(i) \in D$ or not. N fails to infer either $D \cup \{i + f(i)\}$ or $D - \{i + f(i)\}$, but both sets are in $\mathcal{L}$. □

Corollary 20. *For the inference degrees of* FinTxt *or* FinInf *learning uniformly recursive families, the following holds:*
(a) *All oracles of hyperimmune-free degree are in the least inference degree.*
(b) *All 1-generic oracles are in the least inference degree.*
(c) *If A is r.e., then A's inference degree is below that of B iff $A \leq_T B$.*
(d) $\{A : A \geq_T K\}$ *is the greatest inference degree.*

Proof. (a): If A is of hyperimmune-free degree then $F[A] = F[\emptyset]$ since any A-recursive function is majorized by a recursive one. Thus all sets of hyperimmune-free degrees belong to the least inference degree.

(b): Let A be a 1-generic set. Consider any $f \in F[A]$ and let the A-recursive function $f_A = \{e\}^A$ majorize f. The set

$$B = \{\eta : (\exists x) [\{e\}^\eta(x)\!\downarrow < f(x)]\}$$

is r.e.; since $\{e\}^A(x)\!\downarrow \geq f(x)$, no string in B is a prefix of A. Since A is 1-generic, there is a string $\sigma \preceq A$ such that no extension of σ is in B. Now let

$$g(x) = \{e\}^\eta(x) \text{ for the first } \eta \succeq \sigma \text{ such that } \{e\}^\eta(x)\!\downarrow \text{ within } |\eta| \text{ steps.}$$

g is recursive and majorizes f. Thus $f \in F[\emptyset]$, i.e., $F[A] = F[\emptyset]$.

(c): Let A_s be a recursive enumeration of A and $F[A] \subseteq F[B]$. Now

$$f(x) = \begin{cases} s & \text{for the first } s \text{ with } x \in A_s; \\ 0 & \text{otherwise } (x \notin A, \text{ i.e., there is no such } s); \end{cases}$$

is a function in $F[A]$ and some B-recursive function g majorizes f. Then $x \in A \Leftrightarrow x \in A_{g(x)}$ and $A \leq_T B$.

(d): The greatest degree can only contain degrees $A \geq_T K$ since K is r.e.; so it remains to show that $F[A] \subseteq F[K]$ for all oracles A. But this follows from the fact, that each function $f \in F[A]$ is already K-recursive since $\{(x,y) : y < f(x)\}$ is an r.e. set. □

Theorem 21. FinTxt$[K] \subset$ NoisyTxt *in the context of uniformly recursive families.*

Proof. Assume that $\mathcal{L}$ satisfies the condition (a) of Theorem 18. Then $\mathcal{L}$ also satisfies condition (a) of Theorem 16: If $L_i \subseteq L_j$ then there is some $D \subseteq L_i$ such that all $L_j \supseteq D$ are equal to L_i. Then in particular, $L_i = L_j$.

The family $\mathcal{L} = \{\omega - \{i\} : i \in \omega\}$ of all sets whose complement has cardinality 1 witnesses that the inclusion in proper. □

6 Behavioural Correct and Partial Identification

Behavioural Correct identification means that an IIM outputs an infinite sequence of hypothesis which almost all compute the correct function or generate the correct set. It turns out that learning functions from noisy informant, there is no difference between behavioural correct and explanatory inference (NoisyInf):

Theorem 22. *The following three items are equivalent for any class* $\mathcal{L} \subseteq$ REC:
(a) $\mathcal{L}$ *can be learned finitely from informant using K-oracle.*
(b) $\mathcal{L}$ *can be learned in the limit from noisy informant.*
(c) $\mathcal{L}$ *can be learned behavioural correct from noisy informant.*

NoisyBC denotes the concept of infering behaviourly correct from noisy text. The non-inclusion FinTxt $\nsubseteq$ NoisyTxt does not generalize behaviourly correct inference:

Theorem 23. FinTxt $\subset$ NoisyBC.

Proof. Let M infer finitely a class $\mathcal{L}$ of languages from text, in particular M guesses ? until it outputs a guess e and then keeps this output e for ever. Now consider N given by

$$N(w_0 w_1 \ldots w_n) = M(w_m w_{m+1} \ldots w_n) \text{ for the maximal } m \leq n$$
$$\text{with } M(w_m w_{m+1} \ldots w_n) \neq ?$$

and let $w_0 w_1 \ldots$ be a noisy text for L. Since there is a maximal k with $w_k \notin L$, each sequence $w_m w_{m+1} \ldots$ with $m > k$ is a text for L. In particular for all $n \geq m$, $M(w_m w_{m+1} \ldots w_n)$ is either ? or an index for L. Since N outputs $M(w_m w_{m+1} \ldots w_n)$ for the maximal m such that $M(w_m w_{m+1} \ldots w_n) \neq ?$, these m satisfy $m > k$ for allmost all input $w_0 w_1 \ldots w_n$; then $w_m, w_{m+1}, \ldots, w_n \in L$ and since M finitely learns L, $M(w_m w_{m+1} \ldots w_n)$ is always an index for L.

   The properness of the inclusion follows from NoisyTxt $\nsubseteq$ FinTxt (Corollary 8) and the obvious fact that NoisyTxt $\subseteq$ NoisyBC.   □

Osherson, Stob and Weinstein [17, Exercise 7.5A] introduced the notion of partial identification from text and showed that the family of all r.e. languages can be learned from text under this criterion. The concept directly transfers to noisy learning:

Definition 24. A machine M partially identifies $\mathcal{L}$ from noisy text iff for every $L \in \mathcal{L}$ and every noisy text T for L there is a unique index e such that M outputs e infinitely often on input T and $W_e = L$. Partial identification from very noisy text and very noisy informant is defined analogously.

Let REC denote the class of all total recursive functions and RE that of all r.e. sets. The result of Osherson, Stob and Weinstein generalizes for learning from very noisy informant and from noisy text:

Theorem 25. REC *is partially identifiable from very noisy informant.*
RE *is partially identifiable from noisy informant.*
RE *is partially identifiable from noisy text.*

While RE is partially identifiable from noisy text, RE is not partially identifiable from very noisy text as the following example shows:

Example 26. *Let $\mathcal{L}$ contain all sets $\{x, x+1, x+2, x+3, \ldots\}$.*
$\mathcal{L}$ *is partially identifiable from very noisy text.*
$\mathcal{L} \cup \{\emptyset\}$ *is not partially identifiable from very noisy text.*

Acknowledgments I would like to thank John Case, Susanne Kaufmann and Efim Kinber for helpful discussions, proofreading and introducing me to noisy inference.

References

1. ANGLUIN, D. (1980), Inductive inference of formal languages from positive data, *Information and Control* **45**, pp. 117–135.
2. BALIGA, G., JAIN, S., AND SHARMA, A. (1992), Learning from Multiple Sources of Inaccurate Data, *in* "Proceedings of the International Workshop on Analogical and Inductive Inference in Dagstuhl Castle, Germany", October 1992, pp. 108–128.
3. BLUM, M., AND BLUM, L. (1975), Towards a mathematical theory of inductive inference, *Information and Control*, **28**, pp. 125–155.
4. FORTNOW, L., GASARCH, W. I., JAIN, S., KINBER, E., KUMMER, M., KURTZ, S., PLESZKOCH, M., SLAMAN, T., SOLOVAY, R., STEPHAN, F. C. (1994), Extremes in the degrees of inferability. *Annals of Pure and Applied Logic*, **66**, pp. 231–276.
5. FULK, M., AND JAIN, S. (1989), Learning in the presence of inaccurate information, *in* "Proceedings of the 2nd Annual ACM Conference on Computational Learning Theory," Santa Cruz, July 1989, pp. 175–188, Morgan Kauffmann Publishers.
6. GOLD, E.M. (1967), Language identification in the limit, *Information and Control* **10**, pp. 447–474.
7. JAIN, S. (1994), Program Synthesis in the Presence of Infinite Number of Inaccuracies, *in* "Proceedings of the 5th Workshop on Algorithmic Learning Theory", October 1994,
8. JAIN, S., AND SHARMA, A. (1994), On monotonic strategies for learning r.e. languages, *in* "Proceedings of the 5th Workshop on Algorithmic Learning Theory", October 1994, pp. 349–364.
9. JANTKE, K.P. (1991) Monotonic and non-monotonic inductive inference, *New Generation Computing* **8**, pp. 349–360.
10. JOCKUSCH, C. (1981) Degrees of generic sets. *London Mathematical Society Lecture Notes 45*, pp. 110–139.
11. KAPUR, S. (1992), Monotonic language learning, *in* "Proceedings of the 3rd Workshop on Algorithmic Learning Theory", October 1992, Tokyo, JSAI, pp. 147–158.
12. KINBER, E., AND STEPHAN, F. (1995), Language Learning from Texts: Mind Changes, Limited Memory and Monotonicity, *Information and Computation*, to appear. An extended extract appears in "Proceedings of the 8th Annual ACM Conference on Computational Learning Theory," Santa Cruz, July 1995.
13. KUMMER, M., AND STEPHAN, F. (1993) On the structure of degrees of inferability, *in* "Proceedings of the 6th Annual ACM Conference on Computational Learning Theory," Santa Cruz, July 1993, pp. 117–126, ACM Press, New York.
14. LANGE, S., ZEUGMANN, T., AND KAPUR, S. (1992), Monotonic and dual monotonic language learning, GOSLER-Report 14/94, TH Leipzig, FB Mathematik und Informatik, August 1992.
15. SCHÄFER, G. (1995), Some results in the theory of effective program synthesis – learning by defective information. *Lecture Notes in Computer Science 225*, pp. 219–225.
16. ODIFREDDI, P. (1989), "Classical Recursion Theory", North-Holland, Amsterdam.
17. OSHERSON, D., STOB, M., AND WEINSTEIN, S. (1986), "Systems that Learn, An Introduction to Learning Theory for Cognitive and Computer Scientists," MIT-Press, Cambridge, Massachusetts.
18. SOARE, R. (1987), "Recursively Enumerable Sets and Degrees", Springer-Verlag, Heidelberg.
19. ZEUGMANN, T. (1993), Algorithmisches Lernen von Funktionen und Sprachen. Habilitationsschrift, Technische Hochschule Darmstadt, Fachbereich Informatik.

Simulating Teams with Many Conjectures

Bala Kalyanasundaram[1] and Mahendran Velauthapillai[2]

[1] Department of Computer Science, University of Pittsburgh, Pittsburgh, PA 15260, USA
[2] Department of Computer Science, Georgetown University, Washington, DC 20057, USA

Abstract. This paper is concerned with the algorithmic learning where the learner is allowed to make finite but bounded number of mind changes. Briefly, in our learning paradigm, a learner is given examples from a recursive function, which the learner attempts to learn by producing programs to compute that function. We say that a team is successful if at least one member of the team learns the target function. The problem, given two teams with bounded number of learners and mind changes whether one team can provably learn more than the other team has been open for the last fifteen years. This paper makes significant progress toward a complete solution of this problem. In the case of error-free learning, this paper solves the open problem. Finally, in the case of EX learning our result shows that there is no team with $a \geq 0$ mind changes whose learning power is exactly equal to a single learner with bounded $b(\neq a)$ number of mind changes. In the case of PEX learning we have a positive answer.

1 Introduction

This paper is concerned with the algorithmic learning using a single and team of learners. The learners are allowed to make finite but bounded number of mind changes. The learners are given examples from a total recursive function, which they attempt to learn by producing programs to compute that function. If at least one learner is successful in producing a program that computes the recursive function, we say the team has successfully learned the function. The problem, given two teams whether one team can simulate the other team *optimally* has been open for the last fifteen years. The first part of this paper makes significant progress toward a complete solution of this problem. The second part makes significant progress towards understanding the structure of the classes of function these learners

In what follows, we introduce the necessary terminology and review the relevant literature. For an introduction to the topic of inductive inference, see [1]. The interest in the field shown by computer scientists is essentially due to artificial intelligence considerations [2]. We now proceed to develop notation and to discuss the fundamental concepts behind inductive inference.

Members of N , the natural numbers, will serve as program names. $\varphi_0, \varphi_1, \cdots$ is an *acceptable programming system* [18] containing all and only the partial recursive functions of a single argument. The acceptability means that certain natural properties hold for the chosen enumeration of the partial recursive functions. Program i computes the function φ_i. Symbols f and g will be used to denote recursive functions for which no program for computing them is yet known. We use $\subseteq$ (respectively $\subset$) to denote *subset* (respectively *proper subset*). The learning will be performed by *inductive inference machines* (abbreviated: IIM) that accepts the graph of a recursive function as input and output programs intended to compute the function generating the input. Suppose an IIM M is given the graph of f as input. We may suppose without loss of generality that f is given in its natural order $(f(0), f(1), \cdots)$ to M [5]. M will output a (possibly infinite) sequence of programs $p_0, p_1, \cdots$, each of which may or may not compute f. M is said to converge on input from f (written: $M(f)\downarrow$) iff *either* the sequence $p_0, p_1, \cdots$ is finite and nonempty *or* there is an n such that for all $n' \geq n$, $p_{n'} = p_n$. $M(f)\downarrow p_n$ means that *either* the sequence of output programs is finite with length $n+1$ *or* all but the first n programs in the sequence are precisely p_n. $M(\sigma)$ denotes the most recent output, if any, produced by M on input from the finite sample σ.

Gold [15] introduced a criterion of successful inference called "identification in the limit". This notion will be called EX identification. An IIM M EX-*infers* f (written: $f \in EX(M)$) iff $M(f)\downarrow p$ and $\varphi_p = f$. Each IIM will EX-infer some set of recursive functions. EX denotes the class of such sets, e.g. $EX = \{S \mid (\exists M)[S \subseteq EX(M)]\}$. EX stands for "explain," a term consistent with the philosophical motivations for the study of inductive inference, see [6].

For EX inference, the machine must produce a program that is correct on all inputs. This makes the inference more difficult, or perhaps as suggested in [22], impractical. A partial recursive function ψ is an n-*variant* of a recursive function f (written: $\psi =^n f$) iff the cardinality of $(\{x \mid \psi(x)\uparrow\} \cup \{x \mid \psi(x)\downarrow \neq f(x)\}) \leq n$. ψ is a *finite variant* of f (written: $\psi =^* f$) iff $(\{x \mid \psi(x)\uparrow\} \cup \{x \mid \psi(x)\downarrow \neq f(x)\})$ is finite. For any $e \in N \cup \{\star\}$, an IIM M EX^e-*infers* f (written: $f \in EX^e(M)$) iff $M(f)\downarrow p$ and $\varphi_p =^e f$. Similarly, for any $e \in N \cup \{\star\}$, $EX^e = \{S \mid (\exists M)[S \subseteq EX^e(M)]\}$. Note that $EX^0 = EX$. $EX^\star$ inference was introduced in [5] and EX^e inference, for $e \neq 0, \star$, was introduced in [6].

Although counting the number of mind changes an IIM makes before converging is not an abstract measure of the complexity of inference [12], it does provide a reasonable estimate for implemented inference systems. Consequently, the number of mind changes made by inference machines has received considerable attention [6,7,9,14,15]. A subscript b on the class name indicates a success criterion where the IIM converges after no more than b changes of conjecture. If $b = \star$ then the IIM is allowed finitely many mind changes. Formally, for $e, a \in N \cup \{\star\}$, an IIM M EX_a^e-infers f (written: $f \in EX_a^e(M)$) iff $M(f)\downarrow p$ in at most a changes of conjecture (mind changes) and $\varphi_p =^e f$. For $e, a \in N \cup \{\star\}$, $EX_a^e = \{S \mid (\exists M)S \subseteq EX_a^e(M)\}$. Consequently, $EX = EX_\star$. A fundamental relationship between anomalies and mind changes is given by: $EX_a^e \subseteq EX_b^{e'}$ iff $[e \leq e'$ and $a \leq b]$ [6].

The Blums [5] constructed two IIMs which inferred classes whose union was not inferrible by any IIM. Subsequently, this result was extended to arbitrarily large finite unions [21]. A set of functions S is inferred by m members $(m \leq n)$ of the team $M_1, M_2, \cdots, M_n$ if for each $f \in S$ there is at least m distinct IIM's (say $M_{i_1} \ldots M_{i_m}$) from the team such that $f \in EX(M_{i_j})$ [21]. For $e, a \in N$, $[m, n]EX_a^e$ denotes the class of sets that can be learned by m out of the n IIMs.

The goal of this paper is to find an informative and nontrivial predicate P such that $[1, m]EX_a^e \subseteq [1, n]EX_b^{e'}$ iff $P(m, n, e, e', a, b)$ holds. We call this the "6 parameter " problem, which has been open for the last fifteen years. In this paper we obtain some positive partial results that makes significant progress towards a complete solution. We derive a simple predicate for $P(m, n, 0, 0, a, b)$. In addition to this, we also show that we can trade mind changes for additional members without altering the learing power only if we are dealing with errors of commission. We now describe a model of learning (see [8,16]) that will make the above mentioned result more formal. In the case of team learning with success rate being m out of n, the team is considered to be successful in learning a target function f if at least m member of the team produce programs that compute f correctly. Under this notion, it is conceivable that some of the remaining $n - m$ members of the team may not *participate* in the learning process by not producing a program for the target function. Furthermore, it is also possible that some of the remaining $n - m$ *participating* members could produce programs that compute f incorrectly. A program is said to compute f incorrectly if it either produces a wrong result for some input (*error of commission*) or does not halt on some input (*error of omission*). We define *Popperian* type EX-inference, denoted by PEX, to be an EX-inference where every *participating* members of the team produce programs that halt on every input (i.e, no errors of omission).

2 Previous Results

Here we present results from [14] that are most recent, that made progress towards solving the "6 parameter" problem.

The next theorem gives a precise characterization of single machine simulating a team with a errors. Note the simulating team can reduce the errors by increasing its mind changes.

Theorem 1. $(\forall m > 1)$ $(\forall e, e', a \in N)$ $\left[[1, m] EX_0^e \subseteq EX_a^{e'} \text{ iff } a \geq 2(m - 1) \text{ and } e' \geq e + \left\lfloor \frac{e(m-1)}{a - (2m-3)} \right\rfloor \right]$

The next theorem completely characterizes the "5 parameter problem", where a single machine is simulating a team of machines with errors and mind changes.

Theorem 2. $(\forall m > 1)$ $(e, e', a, b \in N)$, $\left[[1, m] EX_a^e \subseteq EX_b^{e'} \right]$ if and only if $e' \geq e$ and $b \geq \left\lfloor \frac{e(m-1)}{e'-e+1} \right\rfloor (a + 1) + 2ma + \left\lfloor \frac{a}{e'-e+1} \right\rfloor a + 2(m - 1)$

However the proof techniques used in proving the above results do not hold when the simulation is done by a team. In fact when there are more than one machine involved in the simulation, they can cooperate among themselves in a very complicated way to do the simulation. Hence the diagonalization proofs, which show the simulation is optimal also gets complicated. Next we will present one result from [14] which has a partial solution to the above problem. Here one team with no errors and no mind changes is being simulated with another team.

Theorem 3. $(\forall m > n > 0)(\forall a \in N)$ $\left[[1, m] EX_0^0 \subseteq [1, n] EX_a^0 \text{ if and only if } a \geq \lceil 2m/n \rceil - 2 \right]$

3   Main Results

In this section we present a new result which makes a significant progress towards solving the "6 parameter problem". Here we consider a team of n machines simulating another team of m ($m > n$) machines with a mind changes. The $n = 1$ is a special case, since there is only one machine in the simulation, there can be no cooperation. Therefore the general result that we obtained does not specialize to the case $n = 1$. The $n = 1$ result follows from Theorem 2 which we state for completeness.

Theorem 4. ($\forall m > 1$) ($a, b \in N$), $[[1, m]EX_a \subseteq EX_b]$ if and only if $b \geq \lceil 2ma + 2(m-1) \rceil$

The next theorem considers simulating a team of m machines with a mind changes with a team of n machines. The theorem characterizes how many mind changes are required by the team of n machines to do the simulation optimally. Clearly, the following theorem characterize the predicate $P(m, n, 0, 0, a, b)$.

Theorem 5. ($\forall m > n > 1$)($\forall a, b \in N$) $[[1, m]EX_a^0 \subseteq [1, n]EX_b^0$ if and only if $b \geq \lceil 2(a+1)m/n \rceil - (a+2)]$

Proof. $\Rightarrow$

Let $m > n \geqslant 1$ and $a, b \in N$. We will prove the contrapositive: if $b < \lceil 2(a+1)m/n \rceil - (a+2)$ then $[1, m]EX_a^0 - [1, n]EX_b^0 \neq \emptyset$. Using n-ary recursion theorem we will construct a set S of recursive functions such that $S \in [1, m]EX_a^0$ and $S \notin [1, n]EX_b^0$. That is, we will construct a team of size m which will $[1, m]EX_a^0$-identify S and display an f in S such that any team of size n will not $[1, n]EX_b^0$-identify f. So our goal is to find such an $f \in S$. First we will describe S and then construct an $f \in S$. The following is an intuitive description of S, a set of recursive functions. Given a $f \in S$ there will be $m - 1$ other recursive functions in S which will have the same initial segment as f. In that common initial segment there will be at most $m(a+1)$ special integers one of which will describe f. It is important to note that the construction of f proceeds in stages. There will be at most $a + 1$ stages. If ever any one of the stages fail to terminate, we would have the required f. For example if stage zero fails to terminate, then the initial segment of f will have at most m special integers, and if stage (1) fails to terminate the initial segment of f will have at most $2m$ special integers etc. We will choose the special integers to be odd integers. Formally, $f \in S$ if and only if the following two conditions hold.

1. $f(x)$ is odd for no more than $m(a+1)$ distinct values of x (it will have at most $(a+1)$ blocks of m odd values).
2. There exists x and j such that $f(x) = 2j + 1$ and $\varphi_j = f$.
3. There will be no more than $m - 1$ odd numbers past this x.

We will construct IIMs $M_1', \cdots, M_m'$ such that for each $f \in S$ there is an i in the range $1 \leq i \leq m$ such that $f \in EX_a^0(M_i')$. For any $f \in S$, i^{th} member of the above team on input f executes the following algorithm.

Begin M_i'

1. Wait for the ith odd integer, say k.
2. Output $(k-1)/2$.
3. Set $i = i + m$ goto step (1).

End M_i'

By the definition of S, for any $f \in S$ one of the $m(a+1)$ special integers in f will describe f. Also, by the definition of S no IIM will make more than a mind changes. Therefore $S \in [1, m]EX_a^0$. Now we will show that $S \notin [1, n]EX_b^0$. Let $M_1, \cdots, M_n$ be any IIMs. We will construct an f such that, $f \in S$ and for $1 \le i \le n$, $f \notin EX_b^0(M_i)$. Without loss of generality we can assume that, each M_i (for $1 \le i \le n$) outputs at most $b+1$ guesses. From now on the word team will refer to the IIMs, $M_1, \cdots, M_n$. Given a program $\alpha_{j,k}$, we will abbreviate $\varphi_{\alpha_{j,k}}$ by $f_{j,k}$. Using a $m(m+1)(a+1)/2$-ary recursion theorem and a finite extension argument we construct functions $f_{j,k}$ $j \in \{1, \cdots, m\}$ and $k \in \{1, \cdots, j\}$. For $j \in \{1, \cdots, m\}$, and $k \in \{1, \cdots, j\}$ let $\sigma_{j,k}$ denote the largest initial segment of $f_{j,k}$ constructed so far. Let $x_{j,k}$ denote the largest value in the domain of $\sigma_{j,k}$. Note that at any instance, the team can have at most n valid programs. In phase 0, you do initializations.

Phase 0. Initialize. Set $x_{1,1} = 0$, $\sigma_{j,k} = \emptyset$, and $\sigma_{1,1}(x_{1,1}) = 2\alpha_{1,1} + 1$. We will use variables $i_1, \cdots, i_n$ to keep track of the last program output by the IIMs $M_{i_1}, \cdots, M_{i_n}$, respectively. Extend $\sigma_{1,1}$ with more and more values of 0's until $M_i(\sigma_{1,1})$ defined for some $1 \le i \le n$. Let i_1 be that i. Let $q_{i_1} = M_{i_1}(\sigma_{1,1})$. Throughout this proof q_i will denote the current guess of M_i (for $1 \le i \le n$) on the portion f defined so far. We are mostly interested in initial segments on which the team changes its mind. We use variables $k_1, k_2, \cdots, k_m$ to keep track of on which initial segments the team changes its mind. Since the first mind change was on $\sigma_{1,1}$, we set $k_1 = 1$. Note that the team has output one program.
End Phase 0

In phase 1, suppose there are j valid programs, using n-ary recursion theorem you construct $j+1$ identical initial segments such that on each initial segment team would output the j valid programs. Now extend the $j+1$ initial segments $j+1$ ways, the team is forced to output a new program on one of these segments (one of team members may have to change its mind). The following algorithm executed in stages will yield the desired f. Each Phase is divided into Stages. If some Stage fails to terminate we would have the desired f.

Phase 1. Construct m identical initial segments such that the M team on that segment outputs m programs.

For $j = 2$ to m do Begin stage j
1. Set $\sigma_{j,k} = \sigma_{j-1,1}$ for $k = 1$ to j (initialize $\sigma_{j,k}$)
   Define $\sigma_{j,k}(x_{j,k} + 1) = 2\alpha_{j,k} + 1$ for $k = 1$ to j (place special integers)
2. Simultaneously execute step (a) and (b) below until condition (A) is satisfied (force a mind change).
   (a) For $k \in \{1, \cdots, j\}$ simultaneously extend $\sigma_{j,k}$ with more and more values of $2k - 2$ (each $\sigma_{j,k}$ starts with the same initial segment and branch out differently)

(b) Look for the least $k \in \{1, \cdots, j\}$ such that $M_i(\sigma_{j,k}) \notin \{q_1, \cdots, q_n\}$ for some $1 \leq i \leq n$, where $q_1, \cdots, q_n$ are the current guess by each team member.

3. Set $\sigma_{l,k_l} = \sigma_{j,k_j}$ for $l = 1, \cdots, j-1$ (update all the previous segments on which the M team changed its mind.)

Condition (A). There exists $k \in \{1, \cdots, j\}$ and an $1 \leq i \leq n$ such that $M_i(\sigma_{j,k}) \notin \{q_1, \cdots, q_n\}$. Let k_j be least such k and i_j be the corresponding i, set $q_{i_j} = M_{i_j}(\sigma_{j,k_j})$.

For each j, one member of the team changes its mind on σ_{j,k_j}. Otherwise there exists a j for which condition (A) is not satisfied. Then by clause (a) in step (2) the functions $f_{j,1}, \cdots, f_{j,j}$ are total and distinct. Also by clause (b) in step (2) for each $i \leq n$, for all $k \leq j$, $M_i(f_{j,k})$ has converged to program q_i. If $j > n$ then the team has only n valid guesses, since there are j distinct functions, there exists a j_0 such that the team cannot identify f_{j,j_0}. If $j \leq n$ then the team has output only $j - 1$ guesses. Since there are j distinct functions there exists a j_1 such that f_{j,j_1} is not identified by the team. By the construction each of the above functions belongs to S. Hence the desired f would be either f_{j,j_0} or f_{j,j_1}.
End step j.

Note that if and when the above loop terminates, $k_1, \cdots, k_m$ are now defined. σ_{1,k_1}, $\sigma_{2,k_2}, \cdots, \sigma_{m,k_m}$ all have the same initial segment on which team has output m programs. Also, each initial segment contains exactly m special integers.
End Phase 1

Phase 2. Using the initial segments, force the team to output $m - n$ programs by diagonalization. We have to diagonalize against n programs, variable *count* is used to keep track of how many programs we have diagonalized against so far.
Let $D = \{q_1, \cdots, q_n\}$, $count = 0$.

For $j = 1$ to $m - 1$ do begin stage j

1. Set $x = x_{j,k_j}$.
2. Simultaneously execute step (a) , (b) and (c) for $s = 1, 2, \ldots$ until condition (B) or (C) is satisfied.
(a) Set $\sigma_{j,k_j}(x + s) = 0$.
(b) Look for a y in the set $\{x + 1, \cdots, x + s\}$ on which $\varphi_q(y)$ is convergent where $q \in D$.
(c) See if there exists an i such that $M_i(\sigma_{j,k_j}) \notin \{q_1, \cdots, q_n\}$.

Condition (B). There exists $q \in D$ and a point y such that $\varphi_q(y) \downarrow$. Then set $D = D - \{q\}$, $count = count + 1$ and

$$\sigma_{j+1,k_{j+1}}(z) = \begin{cases} 2 - 2\varphi_q(z), & \text{if } z = y; \\ \sigma_{j,k_j}(z), & \text{if } x_{j+1,k_{j+1}} \leq z \leq x_{j,k_j} \wedge z \neq y. \end{cases}$$

IF *count* $= n$ **then**

Extend $\sigma_{j+1,k_{j+1}}$ with more and more 0's until $M_i(\sigma_{j+1,k_{j+1}}) \notin D$ for some $i \leq n$. If such an extension is not found then $f_{j+1,k_{j+1}}$ is a total recursive function and $M_i(f_{j+1,k_{j+1}}) \downarrow = q_i$ for all $i \leq n$. Also, by construction $\varphi_{q_i} \neq f_{j+1,k_{j+1}}$, for all $1 \leq i \leq n$. Hence $f_{j+1,k_{j+1}} \notin [1,n]EX_a^0$. By the construction of $\sigma_{j+1,k_{j+1}}$ above, $f_{j+1,k_{j+1}} \in S$. Therefore, the desired f would be $f_{j+1,k_{j+1}}$. Suppose there exists some i such that M_i changes its mind on some extension of $\sigma_{j+1,k_{j+1}}$, set $q_i = M_i(\sigma_{j+1,k_{j+1}})$, $count = count - 1$ and $D = D \cup \{q_i\}$.

End If

Condition (C). If there exists an $i \leq n$ such that $M_i(\sigma_{j,k_j}) \notin D$. Then set $D = D - \{q_i\}$, $q_i = M_i(\sigma_{j,k_j})$, $count = count - 1$, $D = D \cup \{q_i\}$ and

$$\sigma_{j+1,k_{j+1}}(z) = \sigma_{j,k_j}(z) \quad \text{for} \quad x_{j+1,k_{j+1}} \leq z \leq x_{j,k_j}$$

End step j
End Phase 2

Suppose the above for loop does not terminate, then there exists a j for which Condition (B) and (C) are not satisfied. By clause (a) in step (2) f_{j,k_j} is a total recursive function. Let $f = f_{j,k_j}$. By clause (c) in step (2) $M_i(f)$ converges to q_i, and by clause (b) each q_i computes a finite function. Hence $f \notin [1,n]EX_b^0$, by construction of σ_{j,k_j} $f \in S$, therefore we have the desired f. Suppose the above loop terminates, then the team outputs $m - n$ programs. Now in Phase 1, the team guessed m programs, hence the team has guessed a total of $2m - n$ programs.

Phase 3. The team has only one valid program for the segment σ_{m,k_m}. By using $m - 1$ new special integers and construction similar to phase 1, we can construct m identical segments ($m - 1$ new and σ_{m,k_m}) and force the team to output $m - 1$ new programs. Using diagonalization techniques used in Phase 2, you can force the team to output $m - n$ programs. Now using a new special integer (in this phase we have used only $m - 1$, this is the left over one) we can force a new mind change. Hence we have forced the team to produce $2m - n$ new programs. Note at the end of Phase 2, the team has produced $2m - n$ programs and the function we constructed had m special integers. At this point in Phase 3, the team has output $2(2m - n)$ programs and the function we have constructed has $2m$ special integers. Therefore with $(a + 1)m$ special integers, we can force the team to output $(a + 1)(2m - n)$ programs.

End Phase 3

Now there are n members in the team, hence in the best case there is a member of the team which has guessed $\lceil (a + 1)(2m - n)/n \rceil$ programs. i.e. $\lceil 2(a + 1)m/n \rceil - (a + 1)$ programs, hence $\lceil 2(a + 1)m/n \rceil - (a + 2)$ mind changes. Hence if $b < \lceil 2(a + 1)m/n \rceil - (a + 2)$ then $[1,m]EX_a^0 - [1,n]EX_b^0 \neq \emptyset$.

($\Leftarrow$) Due to page limitations we now present a sketch of the proof that $[1,m]EX_a^0 \subseteq [1,n]EX_b^0$ if $b \geq \lceil 2(a + 1)m/n \rceil - (a + 2)$. Let T be the target learning team that $[1,m]EX_a^0$ identifies every function from the class S. We construct a team M that successfully simulates T and $[1,n]EX_b^0$ identifies every function from the class S. Let $f \in S$ be the target function under consideration.

The members of the team M take turn in producing their programs. So for the ease of presentation, we consider only the production of M's programs without associating it to any particular member. Each time a member of T produces a program (mind change or otherwise) the learner M responds with a program too. Since T (and respectively M) is a team with exactly m (respectively n) learners, at most m (respectively n) programs will be currently active. M's programs compute in such a way that each follow distinct active programs of T. It is the case that the earlier programs of M have precedent over the later one while trying to follow some program of T. Many other purely technical details such as Freivalds *bootstrapping* technique on how to achieve this has been omitted from this abstract.

We now describe the worst-case scenario for M. Initially T produces m programs and seeing this M produces m programs where only the last n programs are active. Now m programs of T follow different paths one after another. For the first n programs of T following different paths, no new programs are produced by M. For the remaining, $m - n$ programs following different paths, M must issue $m - n$ new programs. So, total number of programs issued by M is $2m - n$. This process is repeated $a + 1$ times. As a consequence, for a successful simulation M must issue $(a + 1)(2m - n)$. Since the team size of M is n, the number (b) of mind changes issued by at least one member of M is not less than $\left\lceil \frac{(a+1)(2m-n)}{n} \right\rceil - 1$. Simplifying the term, we get $b \geq \lceil 2(a+1)m/n \rceil - (a+2)$. ⊠

The following theorem was proved in [14].

Theorem 6. $(\forall m > 1)$ $[1, m]EX_0^0 \subseteq EX_a^0$ *if and only if* $a \geq 2(m-1)$.

Observe that for various values of m the number of mind changes (a) necessary for the simulating IIM is $2(m - 1)$, which is even. That is $[1, 2]EX_0^0 \subseteq EX_a^0$ for $a \geq 2$ and $[1, 3]EX_0^0 \subseteq EX_a^0$ for $a \geq 4$ etc. This raises the following question. A single IIM with odd mind chages, what can it simulate? The next theorem answers this question.

Theorem 7. *Let* $m = 3, 5, 7, \cdots$. *Then* $[2, m]EX_0^0 \subseteq EX_a^0$ *if and only if* $a \geq (m-2)$

Proof. $\Leftarrow$ Let m be an odd number. Let $S \in [2, m]EX_0^0$, then there exits $M_1, M_2, \cdots M_m$ IIM's (call them "team") such that for every $f \in S$, two IIM's in the team will output a correct program the first time that computes f. We will constrcut an IIM M such that M will simulate the team such that it will output no more than $m - 1$ programs ($m - 2$ mind changes). Let $p_1, \cdots, p_n$ be programs, the program $(p_1, \cdots, p_n)$ is defined as follows: on any input x; run programs $p_1, p_2, \cdots, p_n$ in parallel until one of them halt, output this value. Obviously if none of them halt the value is undefined.

Let $f \in S$ the IIM M on input f executes the following algorithm.

Begin M

1) Feed the team with more and more input from f. Two members of the team must output two programs p_1 and p_2. M outputs (p_1, p_2).

2) M continues to watch (p_1, p_2) while receiving more and more input from f. The following events can occur.

   e1) (p_1, p_2) outputs a wrong value, this implies one of p_1 or p_2 is wrong. Without loss of generality assume p_1 is wrong. M waits for the team to produce p_3 (this must happen since the team must produce two correct programs) and it outputs (p_2, p_3) and continues to watch (p_2, p_3).

   e2) M finds out bothe p_1 and p_2 are wrong. We will not deal with this event since it is a sub event (easier) than (e1) above.

   e3) The team outputs p_3 and p_4. Since we assume that (e2) does not occur, M outputs (p_1, p_2, p_3, p_4) and continues watching it. If (e2) occured M would output (p_3, p_4), clearly this is much less complicated than the other events for M to deal with.

3) Suppose at some point M's output is $(q_1, q_2, \cdots, q_r)$, if event (e1) happens M will trade one program for another and has used one of its alloted mind changes. If event (e2) happens M has to accormodate two additional programs (say s_1, s_2) and produce $(q_1, q_2, \cdots, q_r, s_1, s_2)$. Note that event (e2) is the worst case for M, since it has to deal with more programs.

4) Since $m > 1$ and an odd number $m = 2n + 1$ for some n. Since we are focusing on (e2) events M's first n guesses would be $(p_1, p_2), (p_1, \cdots, p_4), \cdots (p_1, p_2, \cdots, p_{2n})$.

5) Now M will look for two programs to converge and agree out of $p_1, p_2, \cdots, p_{2n}$. If two converges and agrees and the values are correct M does nothing. If the value is wrong it will remove them from further consideration. If two does not converge and agree, the team must produce last program. In which case M will output $(p_1, p_2, \cdots, p_{2n}, p_{2n+1})$. This is the worst of the three scenarios. So now will focus on the program $(p_1, p_2, \cdots, p_{2n}, p_{2n+1})$.

6) From now on M will look for two programs to agree, and if the values are wrong it will remove them from further consdideration. This can happen at most $n - 1$ times. It has a total of $2n + 1$ programs, It can remove a maximum of $2n - 2$ programs, since there must be 3 left over and two of them must be correct.

7) It step (4) M had n guesses, step (5) 1 guess and step (6) $n - 1$ guesses. Total of $2n$ guesses, i.e. total of $m - 1$ guesses, i.e. $m - 2$ mindchanges.

End M

Proof: $\Rightarrow$

Let $m > 1$ odd. We prove the contrapositive: if $a < (m - 2)$ $[2, m]EX_0^0 - EX_a^0 \neq \emptyset$. Using n-ary recursion theorem we will construct a set S of recursive functions such that $S \in [1, m]EX_0^0$ and $S \notin EX_a^0$. That is, we will construct a team of size m which will $[2, m]EX_0^0$-identify S and display an f in S such that any IIM will not EX_a^0-identify f. So our goal is to find such an $f \in S$. First we will describe S and then construct an $f \in S$. The following is an intuitive description of S, a set of recursive functions. Given a $f \in S$ there will be $m - 1$ other recursive functions in S which will have the same initial segment as f. In that common initial segment there will be at most m special integers two of which will describe f. We choose the special integers to be odd integers. It is important to note that the construction of

f proceeds in stages. If ever any one of the stages fail to terminate, we would have the required f. Formally, $f \in S$ if and only if the following two conditions hold.

1. $f(x)$ is odd for no more than m distinct values of x
2. There exists x, y and i, j such that $f(x) = 2i + 1$ and $\varphi_i = f$, $f(y) = 2j + 1$ and $\varphi_j = f$.

We will construct IIMs $M'_1, \cdots, M'_m$ such that for each $f \in S$ there is an i in the range $1 \leq i \leq m$ such that $f \in EX^0_0(M'_i)$. For any $f \in S$, i^{th} member of the above team on input f executes the following algorithm.

Begin M'_i

1. Wait for the ith odd integer, say k.
2. Output $(k-1)/2$.

End M'_i

By the definition of S, for any $f \in S$ there exists two special integers in f that will describe f. Therefore $S \in [2, m]EX^0_0$. Now we will show that $S \notin EX^0_a$ for $a < (m-2)$. Let M any IIM. We will construct an f such that, $f \in S$ and $f \notin EX^0_a(M)$. Given a program α_j, we will abbreviate φ_{α_j} by f_j. Using a m-ary recursion theorem and a finite extension argument we construct functions f_j for $j \in \{1, \cdots, m\}$. For $j \in \{1, \cdots, m\}$ let σ_j denote the largest initial segment of f_j constructed so far. Let x_j denote the largest value in the domain of σ_j. In phase 0, we do initializations.

Phase 0. Initialize.

Set $x_1 = 0$, $\sigma_1 = \emptyset$, $\sigma_1(x_1) = 2\alpha_1 + 1$, $\sigma_1(x_1 + 1) = 2\alpha_2 + 1$.
Set $x_2 = 0$, $\sigma_2 = \emptyset$, and $\sigma_2(x_2) = 2\alpha_1 + 1$. $\sigma_2(x_2 + 1) = 2\alpha_2 + 1$. So far σ_1 and σ_2 have the same initial segments.
Extend σ_1 and σ_2 with more and more values of 0's until $M(\sigma_1)$ defined say q. Note that M has output one program.
End Phase 0

Assume $m = 2n + 1$ for some n. In phase 1, using n-ary recursion theorem we construct n pairs of recursive functions so that we will have $2n$ indentical initial segments. Here we will force M to output $n-1$ programs. If ever any of the construction fails to terminate we will have the desired f.

Phase 1. Construct $2n$ identical initial segments such that M on that segment outputs n programs.

For $j = 3$ to $2n - 1$ by step 2 do Begin stage j
1. Set $\sigma_j = \sigma_{j-2}$ (initialize σ_j), $\sigma_{j+1} = \sigma_{j-2}$ (initialize σ_{j+1}).
2. Define $\sigma_j(x_j + 1) = 2\alpha_j + 1$, $\sigma_j(x_j + 2) = 2\alpha_{j+1} + 1$ (place special integers)
3. Define $\sigma_{j+1}(x_j + 1) = 2\alpha_j + 1$, $\sigma_{j+1}(x_j + 2) = 2\alpha_{j+1} + 1$ (σ_j and σ_{j+1} are identical initial segments)
4. Set $\sigma'_j = \sigma_{j-2}$ (initialize σ'_j), $\sigma'_{j+1} = \sigma_{j-2}$ (initialize σ'_{j+1}).
5. Define $\sigma'_j(x_j + 1) = 2\alpha'_j + 1$, $\sigma'_j(x_j + 2) = 2\alpha'_{j+1} + 1$ (place special integers)

6. Define $\sigma'_{j+1}(x_j + 1) = 2\alpha'_j + 1$, $\sigma'_{j+1}(x_j + 2) = 2\alpha'_{j+1} + 1$ (σ'_j and σ'_{j+1} are identical initial segments)

7. Simultaneously execute step (a) and (b) below until condition (A) is satisfied (force a mind change).
   (a) simultaneously extend σ_j, σ_{j+1} with more and more values of zeros and σ'_j, σ'_{j+1} with more and more values of twos (start with the same initial segment and branch out differently)
   (b) Look for a mind change for M on σ_j or σ'_j.

   Condition (A). $M(\sigma_j) \neq M(\sigma_{j-2})$ or $M(\sigma'_j) \neq M(\sigma_{j-2})$.

8. With out generality assume M changed its mind on σ_j (otherwise rename the initial segments) Set $\sigma_l = \sigma_j$ for $l = 1, \cdots, j - 1$ (update all the previous segments on which the M changed its mind.)

If condition (A) is not satisfied. then by clause (a) in step (2) the functions f_j, f_{j+1} are identical and total, also f'_j, f'_{j+1} identical and total. But f_j and f'_j are distinct. Also by clause (b) in step (2) $M(f_j)$ has converged to program (say q). Also $M(f'_j)$ has converged to the same program q. But f_j and f'_j are distict functions by construction. Hence q cannot identify both. Hence the desired f would be either f_j or f'_j.
End step j.

Note that if and when the above loop terminates,
$\sigma_1, \sigma_2, \cdots, \sigma_{2n}$ all have the same initial segment on which team has output n programs. Also, each initial segment contains exactly $2n$ special integers.
End Phase 1

Phase 2. Using the initial segments, force M to output $n - 1$ programs by diagonalization. Let the last program output by M be q.

For $j = 1$ to $2n - 2$ by step 2 do begin stage j

1. Set $x = x_j$ (note x_j is the largest value in the domain of σ_j).
2. Simultaneously execute step (a) , (b) and (c) for $s = 1, 2, \ldots$ until condition (B) or (C) is satisfied.
   (a) Set $\sigma_j(x + s) = 0$, $\sigma_{j+1}(x + s) = 0$.
   (b) Look for a $y \in \{x + 1, \cdots, x + s\}$ on which $\varphi_q(y)$ is convergent.
   (c) See if $M(\sigma_j) \neq q$.

Condition (B). There exists y such that $\varphi_q(y) \downarrow$. Then set for all $l > j + 1$

$$\sigma_l(z) = \begin{cases} 2 \dot{-} 2\varphi_q(z), & \text{if } z = y; \\ \sigma_j(z), & \text{if } x_l \leq z \leq x_j \wedge z \neq y. \end{cases}$$

Extend σ_{j+2} and σ_{j+3} with more and more 0's until $M(\sigma_{j+2}) \neq q$. If such an extension is not found then f_{j+2} and f_{j+3} are total recursive functions, and $M(f_{j+2}) \downarrow = q$. Also, by construction $\varphi_q \neq f_{j+2}$, and $\varphi_q \neq f_{j+3}$. Hence $f_{j+2} \notin EX_a^0$. By the construction of σ_{j+2} and σ_{j+3}

above, $f_{j+2} \in S$ and $f_{j+3} \in S$. Therefore, the desired f would be f_{j+2}. Suppose M changes its mind on some extension of σ_{j+2}, set $q = M(\sigma_{j+2})$.

Condition (C). If there exists an extension σ_j such that $M(\sigma_j) \neq q$. Then set $q = M(\sigma_j)$ and for all $l > j+1$

$$\sigma_l(z) = \sigma_j(z) \text{ for } x_l \leq z \leq x_j$$

End step j
End Phase 2

Suppose the above for loop does not terminate, then there exists a j for which Condition (B) and (C) is not satisfied. By clause (a) in in step (2) f_j is a total recursive function. Let $f = f_j$. By clause (c) in step (2) $M(f)$ converges to q, and by clause (b) q computes a finite function. Hence $f \notin EX_a^0$, by construction of σ_j $f \in S$. Therefore we have the desired f. Suppose the above loop terminates, then M outputs $n-1$ programs. Now in Phase 1, the M guessed n programs, hence the team has guessed a total of $2n-1$ programs.

Phase 3. The M has only one valid program for the segment σ_{2n-1} and σ_{2n} (which are indetical). Notice we have one more program left (used $2n$ out of $2n+1$) By construction similar to phase 1, we can construct two program such that σ_{2n-1} and one of the new ones go in one direction and σ_{2n} and the other new one go in another direction. This will force one more mind change.
End Phase 3

Now we have forced M to output a total of $2n$ programs; i.e $m-1$ program; i.e. $(m-2)$ mind changes; hence if $a < (m-2)$ $S \notin EX_a^0$

⊠

Corollary 8. $\forall n \geq 2$ $[2, n]EX_0^0 \subseteq EX_{n-2}^0$.

Proof. Note that when n is odd the above result is true. When n is even, you can trade one program for one mind change. That is, the same proof for Theorem 8 can be used to prove this.

⊠

This naturally leads us to the next question: Given $i \geq 0$ is there some $m \geq n$ such that the team $[n, m]EX_0^0 = EX_i^0$. Using results in [9,10,11,13], it is not hard to deduce a *no* answer for the above mentioned question for the cases $i = 0, 1$. We now prove the result for the general case.

Theorem 9.
a) *For $(i \geq 1)$ $(a, b \in N)$ and $(a \leq b)$ $EX_i \subseteq [a, b]EX_0^0$ if and only if $a/b \leq 1/(i+1)$.*
b) *If $a/b \leq 1/(i+1)$ then $[a, b]EX_0^0 - EX_i \neq \emptyset$.*

Proof. (Part a) ⇐ First from Theorem 5 observe that $EX_i \subseteq [1, i+1]EX_0^0$. Next it is easy to show that if $a/b \leq 1/(i+1)$ then $[i, i+1]EX_0^0 \subseteq [a, b]EX_0^0$. Hence if $a/b \leq 1/(i+1)$ then $EX_i \subseteq [a, b]EX_0^0$.
⇒ Notice that EX_i^0-type of learning can survive a diagonalization tree with $i+1$ stages (see [7]). Hence we can diagonalize against i groups of a programs from the

team. Hence if the team has to succeed it must be able to output a total of $ia + a$ programs. The total allowed is b, hence $ia + a \leq b$. This implies that $a/b \leq 1/(i+1)$. Using techniques from [10,11] it is not hard to prove the second part. $\boxtimes$

From the above theorem its easy to observe that a single IIM with mind changes and any team with zero mind changes can never be equal. Naturally this raises the following question: is there a single IIM with mind changes have the same power as some team with mind changes? Formally, given $i \geq 0$ is there some $m \geq n$ and $a \geq 0$ such that $[n, m]EX_a^0 = EX_i^0$. The following theorem shows that the answer to this question is *no*.

Theorem 10.
a) For $a, b, i, j \in N$ and $(a \leq b)$ $[a, b]EX_i \supseteq EX_j$ if and only if $a/b \leq (i+1)/(j+1)$.
b) If $a/b \leq (i+1)/(j+1)$ then $[a, b]EX_i - EX_j \neq \emptyset$.

Proof. We omit the details of this proof for lack of space. $\boxtimes$

On the other hand, the following theorem shows that the Theorem 9 is false if we are dealing with only errors of commission (i.e., PEX-type learning).

Theorem 11. For $(i \in N), [1, i+1]PEX_0 = PEX_i$.

Proof. We omit the details of this proof for lack of space. $\boxtimes$

Note that it is easy to extend the above result to include mind changes for the team.

4 Conclusions

Simulation of team of m IIM's with another team of n machines was studied. Theorem 5 indicates that if team of m machines with a mind changes can only be simulated with team n machines if and only if team of n machines are allowed $\lceil 2(a + 1)m/n \rceil - (a + 2) \rceil$ mind changes. We have not completely succeeded in our goal of characterizing the trade-offs between a bounded number of anomalies, a bounded number of mind changes and a fixed number of inference machines. for example, our results do not address the simulation issue when teams are allowed anomalies. We have compared teams of learners with single IIM with mind changes (Theorem 7). In Theorem 9, 10 we proved that the learning power of an IIM with (say a) mind changes, can never be equal to any team with mind changes (say $b \geq 0$) provided $b \neq a$. But for PEX learning we have a positive answer. From our results we can conclude that mind changes can be traded for number of machines without affecting the learning power only if you are dealing with errors of commission.

References

1. Angluin, D., and Smith, C.H. (1983), *Inductive inference: Theory and Methods*, *Computing Surveys*, 15, 237-269.

2. Angluin, D., and Smith, C.H. (1987), *Inductive inference*, in *Encyclopedia of Artificial Intelligence* (S. Shapiro), pp. 409-418, Wiley, New York.

3. Barzdin, J.A.(1974), *Two theorems on the limiting synthesis of functions*, in *Theory of Algorithms and Programs* (Barzdin, Ed.), Vol. 1, 82-88, Latvian State University, Riga, USSR.

4. Barzdin, J.A., and Freivalds, R.V. (1972), *On the prediction of general recursive functions*, *Soviet Math. Dokl.*, 13, 1224-1228.

5. Blum, L., and Blum, M, (1975), *Toward a mathematical theory of inductive inference*, *Information and Control*, 28, 125-155.

6. Case J., and Smith, C.H. (1983), *Comparison of identification criteria for machine inductive inference*, *Theoretical Computer Science*, 25, 193-220.

7. R. Daley, and B. Kalyanasundaram, *Capabilities of Probabilistic Learners with Bounded Mind Changes*, In *Proceedings of the 1993 Workshop on Computational Learning Theory*, 1993, 182-191.

8. R. Daley, and B. Kalyanasundaram, *Use of reduction arguments in determining Popperian FINite learning capabilities*, In *Proceedings of Algorithmic Learning Theory*, 1993, 173-186.

9. R. Daley, and B. Kalyanasundaram, *Probabilistic and Pluralistic Learners with Mind Changes*, In *Proceedings of Mathematical Foundations of Computer Science*, 1992, 218-226.

10. R. Daley, B. Kalyanasundaram, and M. Velauthapillai, *Breaking the probability 1/2 barrier in FIN-type learning*, In *Proceedings of the 1992 Workshop on Computational Learning Theory*, 1992, 203-217.

11. R. Daley, L. Pitt, M. Velauthapillai, and T. Will, *Relations between probabilistic and team one-shot learners*, In *Proceedings of the 1991 Workshop on Computational Learning Theory*, 1991, 228-239.

12. Daley, R.P., and Smith, C.H. (1986), *On the complexity of inductive inference*, *Information and Control*. 69, 12-40.

13. R.V. Freivalds, *Finite Identification of General Recursive Functions by Probabilistic Strategies*, Akademie Verlag, Berlin, 1979.

14. R.V. Freivalds, C.H. Smith, and M. Velauthapillai, *Trade-off among Parameters Affecting Inductive Inference*, *Information and Computation* (1989), 82, 323-349.

15. Gold, E. M., *Learning Identification in the Limit*, *Information and Control*, vol 10, 1967, pp. 447-474.

16. Jantke, K. P. and Beick, H. R. (1981), *Combining postulates of naturalness in inductive inference*, *Electron. Inform. Kebernet.* 17,465-484.

17. S. Jain, and A. Sharma, *Finite learning by a team*, In *Proceedings of the 1990 Workshop on Computational Learning Theory*, 1990, 163-177.

18. Machtey, M., and Young, P. (1978), *An Introduction to General Theory of Algorithms*, *North-Holland*, New York.

19. L. Pitt, *Probabilistic inductive inference*, *J. ACM* 36(2), 1989, 383-433.

20. L. Pitt, and C. Smith, *Probability and plurality for aggregations of learning machines*, *Information and Computation* 77(1), 1988, 77-92.

21. C. H. Smith, *The Power of Pluralism for Automatic Program Synthesis*, *Journal of the Association for Computing Machinery*, vol 29, 1982, pp. 1144-1165.

22. L. G. Valiant, *A theory of Learnable*, *Communications of the ACM*, vol 27, 1987, pp.1134-1142.

23. R. Wiehagen, R. Freivalds, and E. Kinber, *On the power of probabilistic strategies in inductive inference*. *Theoretical Computer Science*, 1984, 111-113.

Complexity of Network Training for Classes of Neural Networks

Charles C. Pinter

Bucknell University, Lewisburg PA 17837, USA

Abstract. It is known that the problem of training certain specific, very simple neural networks is NP-complete. While such results suggest that training is equally hard for larger, as well as differently configured networks, this conclusion is by no means self-evident. The main result of this paper is that it is NP-complete to train *any specific architecture* or class of architectures. On the other hand, it is also shown that a simple 4-node network (with two hidden and two output units) can be trained in polynomial time if the target network function is assumed to be surjective. This remains true for networks of any size, on the condition that the number of ouput units is at least equal to the number of units in the first computing layer. Thus, with a mild restriction placed on the class of target functions, training certain large networks may be easier than training smaller ones.

1 Introduction

Considerable enthusiasm has been generated by the success of feedforward neural networks in learning a variety of tasks, ranging from the classification of proteins to discovering grammatical rules. It is sobering to know that the general problem of training neural networks is NP-complete; this makes it all the more important to explore those special cases and restricted classes of problems for which training can be achieved in polynomial time.

The most important intractability results which have been obtained apply to specific, usually very simple networks, for which the training problem is shown to be NP-complete. Examples of these are the 3-Node network of Blum and Rivest [4], the 2-Cascade network of Lin and Vitter [8], and the shallow networks investigated by Judd in [7]. From such results one immediately deduces that the following "universal" network training problem is NP-complete: Given any network architecture α and any set S of training examples, determine if there exists a network for the architecture α, so that the network produces output consistent with the training examples.

It is probably not surprising that this last problem in NP-complete given its great generality. At the other extreme, the intractability results of [4], [7] and [8] are very specific; they apply only to those network architectures which are described in these studies. The first aim of this paper is to fill a gap at this point in the theory: We show that it is NP-complete to train *any specific architecture* or class of architectures.

While such a conclusion might be conjectured on the basis of studies such as [4], [7] and [8], the conclusion is by no means self-evident. As stated in [4], "these results do not imply that training is necessarily hard for networks other than those specifically mentioned". In fact, we show in Section 5 that a network obtained by slightly modifying the 3-Node network of [4]— by adjoining a second output node and requiring that the target function be a surjection—can be trained in polynomial time. An analogous result holds for any network if the number of output units is at least equal to the number of units in the first computing layer. Thus, with a relatively mild restriction placed on the class of target functions, training certain large networks may be easy.

This study is confined to fully-connected multilayer neural networks with linear threshold units. The results are sufficiently general, however, that with some modifications they can be made to apply to many other connectionist schemes as well. Our main intractability result applies to multilayer networks in which every layer has at least two nodes. A second intractability result applies to all networks with one hidden layer.

2 Definitions and Fundamental Notions

For the purposes of this paper, a *network architecture* is a directed, acyclic graph whose nodes can be grouped in "layers" so that every node is connected by an edge to each node of the next layer. By a *network* we mean an assignment of linear threshold functions to the nodes of the graph. The network then computes a function which is a composite of the node functions, as described next:

If $g_1, \ldots, g_k$ are functions from a set X to a set Y, we denote by $g = (g_1, \ldots, g_k)$ the following function: For $x \in X$,

$$g(x) = (g_1(x), \ldots, g_k(x))$$

Then g is a function from X to Y^k called an *array* of functions. We shall be dealing in this paper with composite functions f of the form

$$f = f_p \circ \ldots \circ f_2 \circ f_1 \tag{1}$$

such that for each $i = 1, \ldots, p$

$$f_i = (f_{i1}, \ldots, f_{ik_i})$$

All the component functions f_{ij} are assumed to be linear threshold functions. The functions $f_1, \ldots, f_p$ are called the *layers* of f. The function f defined above is said to be of *type* $(k_1, \ldots, k_p)$ because for each $i = 1, \ldots, p$, the i-th layer is an array of k_i functions. Note that each f_i is a function from $\{0,1\}^{k_{i-1}}$ to $\{0,1\}^{k_i}$.

The network architecture corresponding to f is then also said to be of type $(k_1, \ldots, k_p)$: It has p layers, and for $i = 1, \ldots, p$, there are k_i nodes in the i-th layer.

Remark. One slightly unconventional aspect of our definition is that we are counting only the "computing" nodes, and not the input nodes. Thus, the "first layer" refers here to the first computing layer. We assume that every first-layer function is a binary function of n binary variables.

Any function h determines a partition of its domain such that two elements x and y belong to the same class of the partition iff $h(x) = h(y)$. If h happens to be a linear threshold function, so that its range is $\{0, 1\}$, the partition determined by h has two classes, separated by a hyperplane.

If h is an array of functions from X to Y, say

$$h = (h_1, \ldots, h_k)$$

then each class of the partition determined by h is the k-fold intersection of a class of the partition for h_1, a class of the partition for h_2, ..., a class of the partition for h_k. If $h_1, \ldots, h_k$ are linear threshold functions with a common domain $X = \{0, 1\}^n$, then as noted above, the partition for each h_i has two classes separated by a hyperplane P_i. So, the partition corresponding to h divides X into 2^k categories determined by the mutually intersecting planes $P_1, \ldots, P_k$.

A useful consequence of this fact is the following: If f is the composite (1), whose first-layer function is f_1, and if elements x and y are in the same class of the partition of f_1, then $f(x) = f(y)$. [Indeed, f is of the form $\phi \circ f_1$; so $f_1(x) = f_1(y)$ implies $\phi(f_1(x)) = \phi(f_1(y))$]. Now, a *training example* is a pair $(x, label)$ where *label* is equal to the desired output value $f(x)$; it follows from the previous sentence that if elements x and y are in the same class of the partition for f_1, they have the same label. In brief, the partition determined by the first-layer function of f has the following property:

(*) Elements residing in the same class of the partition are labeled alike.

Example 1. Consider the architecture $\alpha = (2, 1)$. This is the 3-Node network architecture studied in [4]. It has a hidden layer with 2 nodes, and a second layer with one output node. There are n binary input variables. Suppose a training algorithm for this network is presented with a set of training examples. Each is either a *positive* example (if the desired output is 1), or a *negative* example (if the desired output is 0). For clarity, positive examples will be labeled $+$ and negative examples will be labeled $-$. Imagine that the training algorithm produces a solution, that is, a composite function f consistent with all the examples. As explained previously, the first layer of f induces a partition of $\{0, 1\}^n$ into 4 quadrants; by (*), each quadrant contains either $+$ points only, or $-$ points only.

Blum and Rivest in [4] consider the special case where the output function is restricted to be the logical "AND" function. In the resulting partition, all the $+$ points are confined to a single quadrant. In this case, the training problem for the network is equivalent to the following:

QUADRANT.

Instance: A set S of training examples, each one labeled either $+$ or $-$.
Question: Do there exist two planes which partition S in such a way that one quadrant contains only $+$ points, and the remaining quadrants contain only $-$ points?

It is proved in [4] that this problem is NP-complete. In the next Section we will be using, as our reference problem for deriving the intractability of network training, a variant of QUADRANT. In this variant we allow *three* labeling categories, positive, negative and "neutral"; thus, each example is labeled either $+$, $-$ or ν (neutral). Since three labels are allowed, we name the problem:

3LABEL.
Instance: A set S of training examples, each one labeled $+$, $-$ or ν.
Question: Do there exist two planes that partition S in such a way that one quadrant contains all the $+$ points, the quadrant opposite this one contains all the ν points, and the $-$ points are confined to the remaining two quadrants?

Theorem 1. *3LABEL is NP-complete.*

The proof is exactly the one given in Blum and Rivest [4] for QUADRANT. Bear in mind that the ν quadrant does not have to contain examples labeled ν; however, it cannot contain examples labeled $+$ or $-$.

3 Separating $\{0,1\}^n$ by Hyperplanes

This Section is devoted mainly to proving two lemmas which play an important role in the sequel. They are based on ideas introduced in [4]. First, some helpful terminology:

Suppose S is a subset of $\{0,1\}^n$ and λ is a function from S to $\{+,-,\nu\}$. Then the pair $\mathbf{S} = (S,\lambda)$ is called a *labeled set.* If $\mathbf{S} = (S,\lambda)$ and $\mathbf{S}' = (S',\lambda')$, then $\mathbf{S} \subseteq \mathbf{S}'$ means that $S \subseteq S'$ and $\lambda \subseteq \lambda'$. Moreover, if $S \subseteq \{0,1\}^n$ and $S' \subseteq \{0,1\}^{n+k}$, then $S \subseteq S'$ means that $x \in S \Rightarrow x0^k \in S'$.

Let $\mathbf{S}$ be a labeled set. We will say that a partition of $\{0,1\}^n$ *separates* $\mathbf{S}$ if each class of the partition contains only points of S with the same label; that is, only $+$ points, only $-$ points, or only ν points.

$\mathbf{S} \subseteq \{0,1\}^n$ means that $S \subseteq \{0,1\}^n$.

Lemma 2. *If* $\mathbf{S} \subseteq \{0,1\}^n$ *is a labeled set, there is a labeled set* $\mathbf{S}' \subseteq \{0,1\}^{n+3}$ *such that* $\mathbf{S} \subseteq \mathbf{S}'$ *and the following is true: If* $\mathbf{S}$ *can be separated by two planes in the manner prescribed by 3LABEL, then* $\mathbf{S}'$ *can be separated in the same way. Moreover, if two planes separate* $\mathbf{S}'$, *they do so in the manner prescribed by 3LABEL.*

Proof. Let $\mathbf{S}$ be a labeled subset of $\{0,1\}^n$. Add three new variables x_{n+1}, x_{n+2} and x_{n+3}, thereby expanding $\{0,1\}^n$ to $\{0,1\}^{n+3}$. Each point x in $\{0,1\}^n$, (hence in particular each x in S) is identified with $x000$. Extend $\mathbf{S}$ to $\mathbf{S}'$ by adjoining seven new labeled points in $\{0,1\}^{n+3}$:

New $+$ points: $0^n 101$, $0^n 011$, $0^n 000$
New $-$ points: $0^n 100$, $0^n 010$, $0^n 001$, $0^n 111$

The new points may be identified with points on a cube by disregarding the n leading 0s. (See Figure 1)

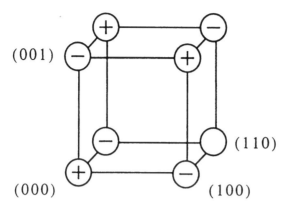

Fig. 1.

Now suppose S can be separated by two planes P_1 and P_2 as prescribed in 3LABEL. Let the equations of the planes be:

$$P_1 : a_1x_1 + \cdots + a_nx_n = -1/2$$

$$P_2 : b_1x_1 + \cdots + b_nx_n = -1/2$$

(We have multiplied each of the equations by a constant so the term on the right is $-1/2$. In case of a 0 constant term, we may shift the plane infinitesimally parallel to itself so as to avoid passing through the origin.) We define planes P_1' and P_2' in $\{0,1\}^{n+3}$ as follows:

$$P_1' : a_1x_1 + \cdots + a_nx_n + x_{n+1} + x_{n+2} - x_{n+3} = -1/2$$

$$P_2' : b_1x_1 + \cdots + b_nx_n - x_{n+1} - x_{n+2} + x_{n+3} = -1/2$$

The equations P_1' and P_2' classify the points $x000$ of S exactly as P_1 and P_2 do. If we denoted by $\mathbf{a}$ and $\mathbf{b}$ the vectors of coefficients of P_1' and P_2' respectively, here is what P_1' and P_2' do to the new points:

$$\mathbf{a} \cdot 0^n 101 = 0 > -1/2 \quad ; \quad \mathbf{b} \cdot 0^n 101 = 0 > -1/2$$

$$\mathbf{a} \cdot 0^n 011 = 0 > -1/2 \quad ; \quad \mathbf{b} \cdot 0^n 011 = 0 > -1/2$$

$$\mathbf{a} \cdot 0^n 111 = 1 > -1/2 \quad ; \quad \mathbf{b} \cdot 0^n 111 = -1 < -1/2$$

$$\vdots$$

This shows that each of the seven new points of S' is relegated by P_1' and P_2' to the correct quadrant. Thus, the planes P_1' and P_2' separate S' as prescribed in 3LABEL.

Suppose now that planes Q'_1 and Q'_2 separate S'; their restrictions to the cube shown in Figure 1 must separate the labeled points into quadrants. Notice that no single plane can separate the + from the − points of the cube, nor is it possible for two planes to confine the − points of the cube in one quadrant. Thus, any planes Q'_1 and Q'_2 which separate S' must do so as prescribed in 3LABEL. □

Lemma 3. *If* S $\subseteq \{0,1\}^n$ *is a labeled set, there is a labeled set* S'' $\subseteq \{0,1\}^{n+2}$ *such that* S $\subseteq$ S'' *and the following is true: If two planes* P_1 *and* P_2 *separate* S, *then there are* $k-2$ *additional planes* $P_3, \ldots, P_k$ *such that* $P_1, \ldots, P_k$ *separate* S''. *Moreover, if any* k *planes* $P_1, \ldots, P_k$ *separate* S'', *then exactly two of these planes, say* P_1 *and* P_2, *separate* S.

Remark. Any plane P in $\{0,1\}^{n+2}$ is identified with its restriction to $\{0,1\}^n 00$, hence with a plane in $\{0,1\}^n$.

Proof. Add two new variables x_{n+1} and x_{n+2}, thereby extending $\{0,1\}^n$ to $\{0,1\}^{n+2}$. Identify each point $x \in \{0,1\}^n$, (and in particular each x in S) with the point $x00 \in \{0,1\}^{n+2}$. Select $k-2$ points of the form $x11$, no two of which are to be neighbors (that is, to share a common edge of the hypercube), and label these points −. Let these points be denoted by $y_3, \ldots, y_k$. Finally, label all the neighbors of $y_3, \ldots, y_k$ as +. The set consisting of S together with the new labeled points is S''.

If P_1 and P_2 are planes in $\{0,1\}^n$, they may be extended to planes P'_1 and P'_2 in $\{0,1\}^{n+2}$ by adding two terms $a_{n+1}x_{n+1}$ and $a_{n+2}x_{n+2}$ to their equations. The coefficients a_{n+1} and a_{n+2} are very large, so that any point $x11$, $x01$ or $x10$ is on the positive side of both planes. Next, for $i = 3, \ldots, k$, P_i is a plane in $\{0,1\}^{n+2}$ which separates the corner y_i from its neighbors; thus, y_i is the only point on the negative side of P_i.

Finally, if $Q_1, \ldots, Q_k$ are any planes in $\{0,1\}^{n+2}$ which separate S'', then $k-2$ of the planes, say $Q_3, \ldots, Q_k$ are required to separate the corners $y_3, \ldots, y_k$ (labeled −) from their neighbors (labeled +). This leaves two of the planes, Q_1 and Q_2, to separate S. □

4   Intractability of Training Multilayer Networks

Let $\alpha = (k_1, k_2, \ldots, k_p)$ be a network architecture; such a network has k_p output functions, where $k_p \geq 1$. Thus, an output of the network is a k_p-tuple of 0s and 1s, that is, an element of $\{0,1\}^{k_p}$. Since the label attached to an example x is the intended value $f(x)$, labels also are elements of $\{0,1\}^{k_p}$. (Here, we shall not use +, − and ν as labels). So, a training example is a pair $(x, \lambda(x))$ where $x \in \{0,1\}^n$ and $\lambda(x) \in \{0,1\}^{k_p}$. If S is a set of training examples, we say that a network f is *consistent with* S if $f(x) = \lambda(x)$ for every x in S. We are now in a position to state the training problem:

TRAINING NETWORKS OF TYPE α. (TRAINα)
Instance: A set **S** of training examples.
Question: Is any network of type α consistent with **S**?

We will show next that for every architecture α, provided that there are at least two nodes on every level, the training problem for α is NP-complete.

Theorem 4. *Let $\alpha = (k_1, k_2, \ldots, k_p)$ where $k_i > 1$ for $i = 1, \ldots, p$. The problem "TRAINING NETWORKS OF TYPE α" is NP-complete.*

Proof. The proof is by reduction from 3LABEL. That is, it will be shown that from any instance of 3LABEL one can construct an instance of TRAINα such that the instance of TRAINα has a solution iff the instance of 3LABEL has a solution.

Let **S** be a set of points in $\{0,1\}^n$, each point labeled either 11, 01 or 00. (We shall think of 11 as $+$, 01 as $-$, and 00 as ν.) We begin by extending **S** to the set **S'** of Lemma 2. Then we extend **S'** to the set **S''** of Lemma 3. (Note: $k = k_1$ is the number of nodes in the first layer of α.)

Suppose we are given a solution for 3LABEL. That is, we are given two planes P_1 and P_2 which separate **S** as prescribed in 3LABEL. (See Figure 2).

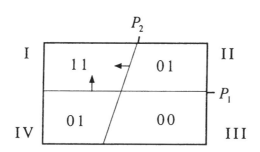

Fig. 2.

Let P_1' and P_2' be the extensions of P_1 and P_2 given in Lemma 2. Let $P_1'', P_2'', \ldots, P_k''$ be the planes given by Lemma 3. With these planes we associate linear threshold functions $f_{11}, \ldots, f_{1k}$ in the obvious manner:

$$f_{1i}(x) = 1 \text{ iff } x \text{ lies on the positive side of } P_i''. \tag{2}$$

As a consequence, if we number the quadrants I - IV as in Figure 2, the following are true for all points $x \in S'$: From (2),

x in Quadrant I implies $f_{11}(x) = f_{12}(x) = 1$
x in Quadrant II implies $f_{11}(x) = 1$ and $f_{12}(x) = 0$
x in Quadrant III implies $f_{11}(x) = f_{12}(x) = 0$
x in Quadrant IV implies $f_{11}(x) = 0$ and $f_{12}(x) = 1$.

Moreover (see Figure 2), the points of S' are labeled as follows:
If $x \in$ Quadrant I, its label is $\lambda(x) = 11$; if $x \in$ Quadrant III, then $\lambda(x) = 00$.
For points x in Quadrants II and IV, $\lambda(x) = 01$. It follows that for all $x \in S'$,

$$\lambda(x) = (f_{11}(x) \wedge f_{12}(x),\ f_{11}(x) \vee f_{12}(x)) \tag{3}$$

where $\wedge$ and $\vee$ are the logical "AND" and "OR" respectively.

Now consider the points $y_3, \ldots, y_k$ which were labeled in the course of applying Lemma 3. All we need to recall about them here is this: First, for $i = 3, \ldots, k$, y_i is the only point lying on the negative side of P_i, while all the other points of S'' lie on the positive side of P_i. Thus,

$$f_{1i}(y_i) = 0, \text{ and for all } x \neq y_i \text{ in } S'',\ f_{1i}(x) = 1 \qquad (i = 3, \ldots, k) \tag{4}$$

The only other thing we need to know about $y_3, \ldots, y_k$ is that they are all labeled 01, whereas their neighbors are labeled 11.

It follows that for all x in S'',

$$\lambda(x) = (f_{11}(x) \wedge f_{12}(x) \wedge \ldots \wedge f_{1k}(x),\ f_{11}(x) \vee f_{12}(x) \vee \neg f_{13}(x) \vee \ldots \vee \neg f_{1k}(x)) \tag{5}$$

where $\neg$ designates logical negation. [This is clear for points x in S' from (3) and (4). From (4), it is immediate for $y_3, \ldots, y_k$, which are labeled 01. For the neighbors of $y_3, \ldots, y_k$ it is true because, from the proof of Lemma 3, $f_{11}(x) = f_{12}(x) = 1$ for all labeled points $x \notin S'$.]

We now draw our argument to a close. We assign the following functions to the first two nodes of Layer 2 of the network:

$$f_{21} = y_{11} \wedge y_{12} \wedge \ldots \wedge y_{1k} \quad,\quad f_{22} = y_{11} \vee y_{12} \vee \neg y_{13} \vee \ldots \vee \neg y_{1k} \tag{6}$$

where $y_{11} = f_{11}(x), y_{12} = f_{12}(x), \ldots, y_{1k} = f_{1k}(x)$. So by (5), (f_{21}, f_{22}) produces the required network output.

Finally, this output value is "channeled through" to the output layer as follows: The first two nodes of every layer are assigned identity functions, so that for $j = 3, \ldots, p$

$$f_{j1} = f_{21} \text{ and } f_{j2} = f_{22} \tag{7}$$

(In each of f_{j1} and f_{j2}, all but one of the weights are set to 0). From (5), (6) and (7),

$$\lambda(x) = (f_{p1}(x),\ f_{p2}(x)) \tag{8}$$

for every x in S'', where f_{p1} and f_{p2} are the first two output nodes of the network. All remaing nodes are set to "constant 0". So we have a solution for TRAINα.

Conversely, suppose we are given a solution for TRAINα, where the labeled set is S''. Layer 1 of this solution determines planes $P_1, \ldots, P_k$ which separate S''. By Lemma 3, exactly two of the planes, say P_1 and P_2, separate S'. Then by Lemma 2, P_1 and P_2 separate S in the manner prescribed by 3LABEL. So we have a solution for 3LABEL. $\qquad\qquad\qquad\square$

Theorem 4 shows that it is intractable to train any specific architecture α, (where only the number n of input variables may vary). It is more useful, however, to consider classes of architectures, where the height and breadth of networks may increase with the number n of input variables. That is, we may consider families of architectures $\alpha = (k_1, \ldots, k_p)$ where p and the parameters k_i are all bounded by polynomials in n. The proof of Theorem 4 shows that training for any such family is NP-complete.

5   Intractability of Training Two-layer Networks

In [4], Blum and Rivest show that it is NP-complete to train networks of type $(r, 1)$, that is, 2-layer networks with $r \geq 2$ nodes in the intermediate layer and one output node, with the restriction that the output node computes the logical "AND" function. We begin by showing that the restriction is not needed.

Theorem 5. *If $\alpha = (r, 1)$ where $r \geq 2$, TRAINα is NP-complete.*

Proof. We begin by remarking that Lemmas 2 and 3 are true also in the case where examples are labeled only $+$ and $-$ (that is, there is no ν label). The statement of Lemma 2 is then modified so the planes which separate S do so not as prescribed by 3LABEL, but as prescribed by QUADRANT. The proofs of the lemmas are unaffected by this change. It is this version of the lemmas that we will be referring to in the present proof.

The argument is by reduction from QUADRANT. Let S be a labeled set of points in $\{0, 1\}^n$; each point is labeled $+$ or $-$. We begin by extending S to the set S' of Lemma 2, then we extend S' to the set S'' of Lemma 3.

Suppose we are given a solution for QUADRANT, that is, a pair of planes P_1 and P_2 which separate S as prescribed by QUADRANT. Let P_1' and P_2' be the extensions of P_1 and P_2 given in Lemma 2, and then let $P_1'', \ldots, P_r''$ be the planes given in Lemma 3. With these planes we associate linear threshold functions $f_{11}, \ldots, f_{1r}$ as follows:

$$f_{1i}(x) = 1 \text{ iff } x \text{ lies on the positive side of } P_i'' \tag{9}$$

Reasoning *mutatis mutandis* as in the proof of Theorem 4, (with points in Quadrants I - IV now labeled, respectively, as 1, 0, 0 and 0), it follows that for every x in S'', the function $f_{11} \wedge f_{12} \wedge \ldots \wedge f_{1r}$ gives the desired output.

Conversely, if we are given a solution for TRAINα where the labeled set is S'', then the first layer of the solution determines a partition of S'' by r planes. By Lemma 3, exactly two of these planes separate S', so by Lemma 2, the planes separate S as prescribed in QUADRANT. $\square$

When combined with Theorem 4, Theorem 5 shows that it is NP-complete to train any two-layer network $\alpha = (r, s)$ whose first layer has more than one node. (A network whose first layer has a single node can be trained in polynomial time, as its input is divided into two classes by a linear separator.)

6 Training Networks which have a Layer with One Node

This Section is devoted to a discussion of the only case which Theorems 4 and 5 leave unresolved: The case of a network with more than two layers, in which at least one layer has a single node. We begin by introducing another separation problem:

It has already been seen that training the 3-Node network—when the output node is restricted to the "AND" function—is equivalent to QUADRANT. If the output node for the same kind of network is restricted to the XOR function, the training problem is equivalent to:

XQUAD
Instance: A set S of training examples, each one labeled either + or −.
Question: Do there exist two planes which separate S in such a manner that the + points lie in two opposite quadrants, and the − points are confined to the other two quadrants?

Interestingly, this problem has so far resisted efforts to prove that it is NP-complete. We will show in this Section that if XQUAD is NP-complete, so is TRAINα for every α, and conversely. [This is true even when α has a layer with only one node.] The proof is modeled after our proof of Theorem 4, but we require a modified version of Lemma 2. (Here, a "labeled set" is a set whose every point is labeled + or −.)

Lemma 6. *If* $S \subseteq \{0,1\}^n$ *is a labeled set, there is a labeled set* $S' \subseteq \{0,1\}^{n+6}$ *such that* $S \subseteq S'$ *and the following is true: If* S *can be separated by two planes as prescribed in XQUAD, then* S' *can be separated in the same way. Moreover, if two planes separate* S', *they do so in the manner prescribed by XQUAD.*

Proof. Let S be a labeled subset of $\{0,1\}^n$. Add six new variables $x_{n+1}, \ldots, x_{n+6}$, thereby expanding $\{0,1\}^n$ to $\{0,1\}^{n+6}$. Let C_1 denote the cube determined by x_{n+1}, x_{n+2} and x_{n+3}, and let C_2 denote the cube determined by x_{n+4}, x_{n+5} and x_{n+6}. Now we extend S to a labeled set S' by adding labeled points as follows: First, we add seven points lying in C_1; they are the points shown in Figure 1. Then we add seven more labeled points lying in C_2; they are similar to those of Figure 1, except that the signs are changed; (+ points are labeled − in C_2, and − points are labeled + in C_2.) The remainder of the proof is very similar to that of Lemma 2:

Suppose S can be separated by two planes P_1 and P_2 as prescribed in XQUAD. We form planes P_1'' and P_2'' in $\{0,1\}^{n+6}$ as follows: If SUM_1 and SUM_2 denote the left halves of the equations for P_1' and P_2' in the proof of Lemma 2, then:

$$P_1'': \quad SUM_1 - x_{n+4} - x_{n+5} + x_{n+6} = -1/2$$

$$P_2'': \quad SUM_2 - x_{n+4} - x_{n+5} + x_{n+6} = -1/2$$

From the proof of Lemma 2, the labeled points in S and in C_1 are classified as required. One easily verifies that the labeled points in C_2 are also separated as required.

If a pair of hyperplanes Q_1 and Q_2 separate S', their restrictions to C_1 and C_2 separate the positive from the negative points in those cubes. The only way two planes can separate the labeled points in C_1 is for one quadrant to contain all the + points; then the two quadrants adjacent to this one contain the − points of the cube. In C_2 the opposite is true: One quadrant must contain all the − points, and the quadrants adjacent to this one contain all the + points. Thus, Q_1 and Q_2 separate S' in such a way that two opposite quadrants contain the + points, and two opposite quadrants contain the − points. □

Theorem 7. *If XQUAD is NP-complete, so is TRAINα for every α*

Proof. Since we already know that TRAINα is NP-complete when α has two or more nodes in every layer, as well as when α has only two layers, we will assume that α has at least 3 layers, including a layer with a single node. It may be assumed without loss of generality that the layer with a single node is the output layer.

Our proof will be a reduction of XQUAD to TRAINα. Let S be a set of points in $\{0,1\}^n$, each point labeled + or −. Extend S to the set S' of Lemma 6, then extend S' to the set S'' of Lemma 3.

Suppose we are given two planes P_1 and P_2 which separate S as prescribed by XQUAD. Then P_1' and P_2' are their extensions given by Lemma 6, and $P_1'', \ldots, P_k''$ are the planes given by Lemma 3. Let $f_{11}, \ldots, f_{1k}$ be linear threshold functions given by:

$$f_{1i}(x) = 1 \text{ iff } x \text{ lies on the positive side of } P_i'' \tag{10}$$

Now, in the second layer of the network we define f_{21} and f_{22} as follows:

$$f_{21} = f_{11} \wedge f_{12} \quad \text{and} \quad f_{22} = \neg f_{11} \wedge \neg f_{12}$$

and in the third layer of the network we define f_{31} by

$$f_{31} = f_{21} \vee f_{22}$$

It is not hard to verify that f_{31} produces the required output (namely, the XOR of f_{11} and f_{12}). If the architecture includes layers above Layer 3, the first node in every such layer is reserved to compute an identity function, so that for $j = 4, \ldots, p$,

$$f_{j1} = f_{31}$$

In particular, the output node f_{p1} produces the required output.

The converse is *mutatis mutandis* as in Theorem 4. □

7 Training for Surjections in Polynomial Time

In this Section it is shown that any network can be trained in polynomial time if the number of output units is at least equal to the number of units in the first computing layer—and if the target network function is assumed to be surjective.

In this discussion we will not be interested in solving the *decision problem* for network training (that is, does there exist a network f consistent with a set S of examples), but rather, we wish to solve the *search problem*:

If there exists a surjective network consistent with S, find it in polynomial time; if there is no such network, determine this fact in polynomial time.

The fact that this can be done, for any architecture $\alpha = (r, \ldots, r)$ and for any labeled set of examples, is not so much a theorem as an observation. We illustrate it with an example.

Example 2. Consider the 4-Node architecture $\alpha = (2, 2)$; it has a hidden layer with 2 nodes, and an output layer with 2 nodes. Since there are two output nodes, there are four possible output values: 00, 01, 10 and 11. The first layer of such a network determines a partition of the domain $\{0, 1\}^n$ into 4 quadrants which separate S: Since there are 4 output values, each of the 4 quadrants contains points labeled with a different output value.

It should now be clear how the 4-Node network can be trained in polynomial time: Let the 11 and 10 points be relabeled as $+$ points, and the 01 and 00 points as $-$ points. Then use a polynomial time algorithm to find a single plane P_1 separating the $+$ from the $-$ points. If this is unsuccessful, label the 11 and 00 points as $+$ (and the remaining points as $-$), or alternatively, label the 11 and 01 points as $+$ (and the remaining ones as $-$). Two of these combinations will yield separating planes if two such planes exist. If two planes cannot be found in this manner, they don't exist.

Finally, the output layer computes two linear threshold functions of two binary variables; even using trial and error they can be found in constant time.

Note that in this example the number n of input nodes is variable but the number of computing nodes is fixed. The same is true for the networks studied in [4] and [8]: The number of nodes above the input layer remains constant.

The method of Example 2 generalizes readily to architectures of the form $\alpha = (r, \ldots, r)$ for any size of r and any number of layers. We omit the details, which are fairly obvious.

The chief difference between the (hard) loading problem of Example 1 and the (easy) loading problem of Example 2 is that, in Example 1, the two separating hyperplanes must be found simultaneously, whereas in Example 2 they may be found consecutively. The example described in this Section is only one problem in a diverse class of network training problems which are easy because they allow the separating hyperplanes to be found consecutively. Undoubtedly, this class of problems is worth investigating further. In this regard, it should be noted that positive solutions to the network loading problem are few and limited. Other efforts to find positive results have concentrated on using some narrowly defined class of networks ([1], [8], [6]), restricting the distribution of examples ([2]), or strengthening the learning algorithm by allowing queries ([3], [6]).

8 Conclusion

It has been known for some time that the problem of training certain simple, very specific neural networks is NP-complete. In this paper we have undertaken the task of extending these results to broad classes of networks. Our study is confined to fully-connected multilayer neural networks with linear threshold units. For networks of this kind, we have shown that it is NP-complete to train any specific architecture or class of architectures, provided that each layer has more than one node. Moreover, we have extended a result of Blum and Rivest [4], by showing that it is NP-complete to train any two-layer network whose hidden layer has more than one node. (There may be a single node in the output layer.)

We believe that by using the methods of our paper, with the results of DasGupta et al. [5], it is possible to extend our results to networks with piecewise linear activation units. As for networks with sigmoid activation units, although it is widely conjectured that training such networks is NP-complete, very little progress has yet been made toward proving this.

References

1. Baum, E.B.: On learning a union of halfspaces. Journal of Complexity 6 (1990) 67-101
2. Baum, E.B.: A polynomial time algorithm that learns two hidden unit nets. Neural Computation 2 (1990) 510-522
3. Baum, E.B.: Neural net algorithms that learn in polynomial time from examples and queries. IEEE Trans. on Neural Networks 2 (1991) 5-19
4. Blum, A.L., Rivest, R.L.: Training a 3-node neural network is NP-complete. *Machine Learning: From Theory to Applications*, Springer-Verlag (1993) 9-28
5. DasGupta, B., Siegelmann, H., Sontag, E.: On a learnability question associated with neural networks with continuous activations. Proc. of the 7th Annual ACM Conference on Computational Learning Theory (1994) 47-56
6. Golea, M., Hancock, T., Marchand, M.: Learning nonoverlapping perceptron networks from examples and membership queries. Machine Learning 16 (1994) 161-183
7. Judd, J.S.: On the complexity of loading shallow neural networks. Journal of Complexity 4 (1988) 177-192
8. Lin, J.H., Vitter, J.S.: Complexity results on learning by neural nets. Machine Learning 6 (1991) 211-230

Learning Ordered Binary Decision Diagrams*

Ricard Gavaldà and David Guijarro

Department of Software (LSI)
Universitat Politècnica de Catalunya
Pau Gargallo 5
08028 Barcelona, Spain
{gavalda,guijarro}@lsi.upc.es

Abstract. This note studies the learnability of ordered binary decision diagrams (obdds). We give a polynomial-time algorithm using membership and equivalence queries that finds the minimum obdd for the target respecting a given ordering. We also prove that both types of queries and the restriction to a given ordering are necessary if we want minimality in the output, unless P=NP. If learning has to occur with respect to the optimal variable ordering, polynomial-time learnability implies the approximability of two NP-hard optimization problems: the problem of finding the optimal variable ordering for a given obdd and the Optimal Linear Arrangement problem on graphs.

1 Introduction

The representation of boolean functions as ordered binary decision diagrams (obdds) has received great attention recently. This representation has nice computational properties for fixed variable ordering, such as the existence of a minimum canonical form and efficient algorithms for elementary boolean operations, satisfiability, equivalence testing, and minimization. See [5] for some of the algorithms and a survey of the uses of obdd in fields such as digital system design, combinatorial optimization, and mathematical logic.

A major problem of the obdd representation is that the size of the obdd for a function varies greatly with the variable ordering chosen. The problem of finding an ordering that minimizes the size is usually approached with heuristics. This practice has been often supported by claims that the problem is NP-hard, although a formal proof has been given only very recently ([4], see also [11]).

This note studies the learnability of boolean functions in terms of obdds using membership and equivalence queries. We present an algorithm that, given an ordering, outputs the minimum obdd with that ordering in time polynomial in the size of this obdd (call it n) and the number of variables (call it m). For simplicity, this result is first obtained via a reduction to the problem of learning deterministic finite automata. Using Schapire's algorithm for dfa [10], this yields an algorithm

---

* This research was supported in part by the ESPRIT Working Group NeuroCOLT (nr. 8556), by the ESPRIT Project ALCOM II (nr. 7141), and by DGICYT (project nr. PB92–0709).

making nm equivalence queries and $O(n^2m^2)$ membership queries. Then we specialize our algorithm to obdds and reduce these bounds to n and $O(n^2m + nm\log m)$, respectively.

Furthermore, we show that we need both types of queries for polynomial-time learning at all, and learning the minimum obdd with respect to *the best* ordering is not possible unless P=NP. This is a consequence of the NP-hardness result in [4] for the problem of computing an optimal ordering for a given obdd. However, it is still open whether this optimization problem admits any polynomial-time approximation algorithm. We observe that learnability of obdds implies that there is some algorithm that finds solutions for this problem within a polynomial of the optimum. The same result holds for the Optimal Linear Arrangement problem [7], whose (non)approximability remains as an important question.

A related result on learnability of restricted branching programs is given by Raghavan and Wilkins in [9]. They show that minimum read-once branching programs are learnable in polynomial time with membership and equivalence queries. But in their context, "read-once" means that each variable is tested once in the whole branching program, while the "read-once" restriction in obdds means once along each path. Hence our results are incomparable. Learning obdds with respect to the best ordering looks like the smallest natural generalization of both their result and our result.

2   Definitions

All our *strings* are defined over the boolean alphabet $\{0, 1\}$. By $|x|$ we mean the length of string x. The symbol λ denotes the empty string. To simplify our exposition, lowercase letters late in the alphabet (typically, w, x, y, and z) are used to denote strings, and those early in the alphabet (a, b, and c) to denote bits.

We represent boolean functions by means of *Binary Decision Diagrams*, in short *bdds* and also called *branching programs*. A bdd is a directed acyclic graph with a single root and two sinks. The two sinks are labelled **acc** and **rej**, and each non-sink node is labelled with a variable v_i. Also, every non-sink node has exactly two outgoing edges, labelled 0 and 1. If D is the bdd and q one of its nodes, by $\delta_D(q, a)$ we mean the endpoint of the edge leaving q and labelled with a.

A bdd on variables $v_1, v_2, \ldots v_m$ computes a boolean function $\{0, 1\}^m \to \{0, 1\}$ in the natural way: For a string $a_1 a_2 \cdots a_m$, start at the root and, whenever in a node labelled v_i, follow the edge labelled by bit a_i. The value of the function is 1 if and only if this path ends in the **acc** node. More often, we view a bdd as accepting a language (a subset of $\{0, 1\}^m$); for a bdd D, this language is denoted by $L(D)$.

The number of nodes of a bdd D is written as $|D|$ and called its *size*.

Let π be an ordering of $\{1, \ldots, m\}$, that is, a one-to-one function from $\{1, \ldots, m\}$ to itself. For a string $x = a_1 a_2 \ldots a_m \in \{0, 1\}^m$, $\pi(x)$ is the string $a_{\pi(1)} a_{\pi(2)} \cdots a_{\pi(m)}$. This definition is extended to a language $L \subseteq \{0, 1\}^m$ by $\pi(L) = \{\, \pi(x) \mid x \in L \,\}$. The identity ordering is denoted by *id*.

For an ordering π and a bdd D, we say that D is a π-*ordered bdd*, or $\pi-obdd$, if the labels of the nodes along any path in D are consistent with the ordering π. That is, if v_i precedes v_j in a path of D, then $\pi^{-1}(i) < \pi^{-1}(j)$. Note that this definition prevents any path from checking a variable more than once. An *ordered bdd*, or *obdd*, is one that is a π-obdd for *some* π, that is one that is consistent with some ordering.

Our definition of deterministic finite automaton (dfa) is standard. Just to fix notation, we specify an acceptor dfa M by a tuple $(Q, \{0, 1\}, q_0, \delta, F)$, where Q, q_0, δ, and F are the set of states, the initial state, the transition function, and the set of final states, respectively.

Our results are proved in Angluin's model of exact learning [1, 2]. We assume that a teacher has a *target* boolean function, or equivalently, a target language $L^\star \subseteq \{0, 1\}^m$. The goal of the learning algorithm is to produce an obdd accepting exactly $L^\star$ by asking queries about $L^\star$ to the teacher; it will be crucial whether this obdd must respect a predefined variable ordering or not, and we will make it clear every time.

The learning algorithm can ask the teacher two types of queries:

- *Membership* queries: Given a bit vector $x \in \{0, 1\}^m$ the teacher answers YES if $x \in L^\star$ and NO otherwise.
- *Equivalence* queries: Given an obdd D, the teacher answers YES if $L(D) = L^\star$ and a pair (NO,x) where x is the *counterexample*, a string of length m in the symmetric difference of $L^\star$ and $L(D)$.

The running time of the algorithm is taken with respect to the worst-case choice of counterexamples, and is measured as a function of two parameters: m and the size of the smallest obdd accepting $L^\star$ (possibly, the smallest respecting some given ordering π if so specified). The second parameter is usually denoted by n. We say that a learning task is achievable in polynomial time meaning that some learning algorithm completes it in time polynomial in these two parameters for any target boolean function. We also say that we have min-learnability if the algorithm outputs the minimum size obdd.

We assume without loss of generality that learning algorithms know m in advance; otherwise, they ask an initial equivalence query with the empty set and define m to be the length of the counterexample received. Parameter n is initially unknown.

3 Learning Obdds with a Given Ordering

In this section we show that it is possible to learn the minimum π-obdd computing the target function when the ordering π is given.

We do this by reducing this learning problem to the well-studied problem of learning dfa. In fact, we take an *arbitrary* algorithm to learn dfa and show that, with an adequate interface to a teacher for π-obdds, it can be used to learn the minimum π-obdd.

To do this, note that there are two differences between obdds and dfa accepting a subset of $\{0, 1\}^m$: one, that the dfa must check the bits of the input string in sequential order while an obdd can use another ordering (though the same in every path); two, the dfa must look at all bits while the obdd can "skip" some if they are not relevant for the result. The following definitions and lemmas deal with both problems.

Definition 1. Let D be any obdd using any ordering. Then $\pi(D)$ is the obdd obtained by replacing, in each node, a label v_i with the label $v_{\pi(i)}$.

Fact 2. $|\pi(D)| = |D|$ and $L(\pi(D)) = \pi(L(D))$.

Definition 3. For a dfa M, $D(M)$ is the minimum id-obdd accepting $L(M)$. For an id-obdd D, $M(D)$ is the minimum dfa accepting $L(D)$. For any language $L \subseteq \{0, 1\}^m$, $M(L)$ and $D(L)$ are the minimum dfa and minimum id-obdd accepting L, respectively.

Lemma 4. *(i)* If $L(M) \subseteq \{0, 1\}^m$, then $|D(M)| \leq |M|$; *(ii)* $|M(D)| \leq 2(m-2)\cdot|D|$.

Proof. For (i), note that the dfa can be turned into an equivalent id-obdd just labelling every node at distance i from the initial state with variable v_{i+1}; no conflicts can appear in this labelling provided that M really accepts a subset of $\{0, 1\}^m$.

For (ii), the only problem is that in an id-obdd D there may be edges linking a node labelled with v_i to a node labelled with v_j, with $j > i+1$. To transform D into a dfa, it is enough to add a chain of $j - i - 1$ states that simply skip over $j - i - 1$ bits of input. There are at most $2|D|$ edges, and each edge requires at most $m - 2$ intermediate new states. The rej and acc nodes become the unique sink and final states of the dfa. □

(In fact, a finer count that $m \cdot |D|$ is enough in (ii); see the evaluation of the number of membership queries in Theorem 14.)

Fact 5. *M(D) and D(M) can be computed in polynomial time.*

With this notation and facts we can describe the reduction of obdd learning to dfa learning.

Theorem 6. *Assume that there is an algorithm that learns dfa in polynomial time, using $\#equ(n, m)$ equivalence queries and $\#mem(n, m)$ membership queries. Then there is an algorithm that receives an ordering π as input and learns the minimum $\pi-obdd$ for the target function in polynomial time, using $\#equ(2mn, m)$ equivalence queries and $\#mem(2mn, m)$ membership queries.*

Proof. Let $L^\star \subseteq \{0, 1\}^m$ be the target language and A be the claimed algorithm for learning dfa. The learning algorithm for $\pi-$obdds simulates A learning $\pi^{-1}(L^\star)$ by answering queries as follows:

- Membership query "$x \in \pi^{-1}(L^\star)$?" is replaced with "$\pi(x) \in L^\star$?";
- Equivalence query "$L(M) = \pi^{-1}(L^\star)$?" is replaced with "$L(\pi(D(M))) = L^\star$?" (i.e., transform M into an equivalent id-obdd, then permute its node labels following π and ask the resulting obdd as an equivalence query.) By Fact 2, both queries are equivalent. If a counterexample w is obtained, give counterexample $\pi^{-1}(w)$ to A.

Note that all the time needed for these replacements is a small polynomial of the size of their arguments.

When A terminates giving some dfa M, minimize $\pi(D(M))$ and output it.

The correctness of the algorithm is clear using again Fact 2. Let us evaluate, for example, the number of equivalence queries made by this algorithm. Similar arguments work for the number of membership queries and the time complexity.

We simulate A on $\pi^{-1}(L^\star)$, so we make at most $\#equ(|M(\pi^{-1}(L^\star))|, m)$ equivalence queries. Let $D^\star$ be the minimum π−obdd accepting $L^\star$. By Lemma 4, we have that $|M(\pi^{-1}(L^\star))| \leq 2(m-2) \cdot |\pi^{-1}(D^\star)| \leq 2(m-2) \cdot |D^\star|$, hence the claimed bound. □

Several algorithms for exact learning of dfa are known. A first algorithm by Angluin [1] was improved by Schapire [10]. Schapire's algorithm uses at most n equivalence queries and $O(n^2 + n \log m)$ membership queries to learn n-state dfa if the length of the longest counterexample does not exceed m. Plugging this algorithm into Theorem 6 we obtain:

Corollary 7. *There is an algorithm that, given an ordering π, outputs the minimum π−obdd for the target function in polynomial time, using $2nm$ equivalence queries and $O(n^2 m^2)$ membership queries, where n is the size of that π−obdd.*

4 Reducing the Number of Queries

In this section we present a modification of Schapire's algorithm that substantially decreases the number of queries used to learn an obdd. In particular, the number of equivalence queries of the new algorithm is bounded above by the π−obdd-size of the target concept, and independent of the number of variables. This is especially important as in many situations equivalence queries are expensive to answer. For example, in the standard transformation of an equivalence-query learner into a PAC-learner [1, 2], the sample size used by the latter is quadratic in the number of queries of the former.

We describe the algorithm assuming that the required order π is the identity. Other orders are handled by bit permutations as explained in the proof of Theorem 6.

We need some definitions and facts from Schapire's algorithm, and assume some familiarity with it. We repeat them here but we direct the reader to [1, 10] for full details.

Definition 8. An *observation table* consistent with $L^\star \subseteq \{0, 1\}^\star$ is a triple (S, E, T) where $S, E \subseteq \{0, 1\}^\star$ and T is a function $\{0, 1\}^\star \times \{0, 1\}^\star \mapsto \{0, 1\}$, such that for every $x \in S \cdot (\lambda + 0 + 1)$ and every $e \in E$, $T(x, e) = 1$ iff $xe \in L^\star$.

For every string x, we define a function $row(x)$ with domain E by $row(x)(e) = 1$ if $xe \in L^\star$, 0 otherwise. We will use $row(x)$ mostly (but not only) for $x \in S$.

An observation table is *closed* if for every $w \in S\{0, 1\}$ there is some $u \in S$ such that $row(w) = row(u)$.

Schapire's algorithm maintains an observation table (S, E, T) consistent with the target language. Whenever the table is closed, a dfa $M(T)$ is built out of the table and asked as an equivalence query. Each element in S is used as a representative of the state it reaches in the target dfa.

Fact 9. *The observation table maintained by Schapire's algorithm satisfies the following:*

1. *for every different w and w' in S, $row(w) \neq row(w')$.*
2. *$x \in S$ implies $|x| \leq m$.*

The difference in size between the minimum dfa and the minimum obdd for the target is in the number of states that are introduced just to skip irrelevant input bits. Inside the observation table, these states translate into *blind* rows.

Definition 10. Given an observation table (S, E, T), we say that a function $row(w)$ ($w \in S$) is *blind* if $row(w0) = row(w1)$.

Fact 11. *Suppose that Schapire's algorithm has at some moment an observation table $O = (S, E, T)$ and that at a later moment it has table $O' = (S', E', T')$. Let row and row' be the respective row functions. Then:*

1. *for every $x, y \in S$, $row(x) \neq row(y)$ implies $row'(x) \neq row'(y)$ (distinct rows never become equal again).*
2. *for every $x \in S$ if $row(x)$ is non-blind then $row'(x)$ is also non-blind.*

This follows immediately from the fact that Schapire's algorithm never deletes any entry from its observation table.

The reduction in the number of equivalence queries is based on checking the following property, that we call *self-consistency*. The intuitive meaning of this property is the following. Suppose that a string $w \in S$ leads to a non-blind state $row(w)$ in $M(T)$. If we append more and more bits to the end of w, we may visit some blind states $row(x_1)$, $row(x_2)$, ... of $M(T)$ until another non-blind state $row(w')$ is reached again. In principle, w and every x_i may be completely different, but we are guessing that after appending i bits to the end of w we really end up in the same state of the target dfa as x_i. Self-consistency states that this guess is not obviously wrong: it is not disproven by just trying a string of i zeros and the current set of experiments E.

Definition 12. Let $O = (S, E, T)$ be a closed observation table. We say that O is *self-consistent* if the following occurs for every $w \in S$ with a non-blind row and every $a \in \{0, 1\}$: Assume that in the obdd obtained from O we have $\delta(w, a) = w'$, with w' a non-blind row in T. Note that all states between $row(w)$ and $row(w')$ are blind. Then, for every i with $1 \leq i < |w'| - |wa|$:

1. let x be the state where the evaluations of strings $wa0^i0$ and $wa0^i1$ end; then $row(wa0^i0) = row(wa0^i1) = row(x)$, and
2. for every $\forall b, b' \in \{0, 1\}$ $row(wa0^ibb') = row(xb')$.

Lemma 13. *If a closed observation table O is consistent with target concept L^* but not self-consistent, then we can find a counterexample.*

Proof. If self-consistency fails then there is an i such that at least one of the following two cases is true:

1. $row(wa0^i b) \neq row(x)$ for some $b \in \{0, 1\}$: $wa0^i b$ and x reach the same state in the dfa associated to the observation table, but there is some $e \in E$ such that exactly one of $wa0^i be$ and xe is in L^*. Hence, $wa0^i be$ is a counterexample.
2. $row(wa0^i b) \neq row(x)$ for some $b \in \{0, 1\}$: by the same argument, $wa0^i b$ is a counterexample for the current obdd.
3. $row(wa0^i bb') \neq row(xb')$ for some $b, b' \in \{0, 1\}$: then, again with the same argument, $wa0^i bb'$ is a counterexample.

$\square$

We modify Schapire's algorithm filtering unnecessary equivalence queries. More precisely, whenever Schapire's algorithm poses an equivalence query, we test whether the observation table is self-consistent. If this is not the case, by Lemma 13 we can find a counterexample using a membership query instead. This way we keep the number of equivalence queries bounded above by obdd-size. The new bound on membership queries follows from the fact that obdds accept fixed-length languages, and hence a large fraction of membership queries can be answered NO right away.

Theorem 14. *There is an algorithm that, given the ordering π, outputs the minimum $\pi-obdd$ for the target function in polynomial time, using n equivalence queries and $O(n^2 m + nm \log m)$ membership queries, where n is the size of that $\pi-obdd$ and m is the number of variables.*

Proof. Run Schapire's algorithm. Membership queries are passed to the teacher if their length is m, others are answered NO.

Whenever Schapire's algorithm asks an equivalence query with a dfa that accepts a string not in $\{0, 1\}^m$, we supply a NO answer with that string as a counterexample. So we let pass only the equivalence queries accepting subsets of $\{0, 1\}^m$. Note that dfa accepting these languages are dag's where all paths from the root to a given state have the same length (except for the sink); we call this length the *level* of the state.

To solve these equivalence queries, we first check self-consistency of the hypothesis. If self-consistency fails, we get a counterexample by Lemma 13 and skip the equivalence query. Otherwise, the equivalence query is passed to the teacher.

Correctness of this algorithm is clear since Schapire's algorithm is correct. Let us bound first the number of equivalence queries it makes.

Consider two consecutive equivalence queries that we pass to the teacher. Let O and O' be their respective observation tables and let nr and nr' be the corresponding number of non-blind rows. We argue first that $nr < nr'$; then, using that Schapire's algorithm never surpasses the minimum number of states, the number of equivalence queries is bounded by the number of non-blind states that of the minimum target dfa, which, in turn, coincides with the number of states of the minimum $\pi-obdd$.

Suppose for the sake of contradiction that $nr \geq nr'$, using Fact 11 we know that $nr > nr'$ is impossible (a non-blind row remains non-blind forever). This leaves $nr = nr'$ as the only case.

The only possibility now is that, since the obdds associated to O and O' will have the same number of states, the transition function changes. Let u, u' and wa be the strings involved in one of these transition function changes, i.e., w, u, and

u' are in S, $row(w)$, $row(u)$ and $row(u')$ are non-blind, $row(u) \neq row(u')$, and wa leads to u in O but to u' in O'.

There are three cases:

1. $|u| > |u'|$. For $i = |u'| - |wa|$, self-consistency of O' implies that $row'(wa0^i) = row'(u')$ and this implies that $row(wa0^i) = row(u')$, but $i < |u| - |wa|$, so self-consistency implies that $row(wa0^i0) = row(wa0^i1)$. But if $row(u')$ is non-blind then $|u'| = m$ and $|u| > m$ which contradicts Fact 9.

2. $|u| = |u'|$. A similar argumentation yields $row(u) = row(u')$ which is a contradiction with the assumption that u and u' were involved in a transition function change.

3. $|u| < |u'|$. For $i = |u| - |wa|$, self-consistency of O together with the fact that $row(u)$ is non-blind, implies that $row(wa0^i0) \neq row(wa0^i1)$. But this contradicts self-consistency in O', namely that $row'(wa0^i0) = row'(wa0^i1)$.

Now we have proved $nr < nr'$ for any consecutive closed and self-consistent observation tables O and O', and hence that the number of equivalence queries does not exceed n.

For the membership queries: Schapire's algorithm makes membership queries at two moments: after a counterexample is found (either with an equivalence query or the use of Lemma 13), in order to find an experiment that distinguishes two previously equal rows; and all other membership queries, used to fill new entries (rows or columns) of the observation table. Additionally, we make membership queries to test self-consistency.

In our case, the number of the first type of queries is $O(nm \log m)$, because our target dfa has at most $2mn$ states, and finding the right experiment for the counterexample costs only $\log m$ membership queries, as described in [10].

For the other kind of membership queries: Define S_i and E_i to be the subsets of of the final S and E containing only strings of length i. Note that a string is introduced in E_{m-i} only to distinguish two rows indexed by strings of length i that looked equal before; therefore $|E_{m-i}| \leq |S_i|$. Only strings of length m are queried, and for every $w \in S$ there are rows indexed by w, $w0$, and $w1$. So the number of queries used to fill the table is at most

$$3 \cdot \sum_{i=0}^{m} |S_i| \cdot |E_{m-i}| \leq 3 \cdot \sum_{i=0}^{m} |S_i|^2.$$

To bound $|S_i|$, observe that there are two types of states in level i of the target dfa: some non-blind states corresponding to nodes in the target obdd, and some blind states corresponding to edges that cross level i. Let a and b be the number of each. Now, to have a nodes at level i there must be at least $a - 1$ distinct nodes in previous levels; for b edges to cross this level, there must be at least b distinct nodes in previous levels. Therefore $a + \max\{a - 1, b\} \leq n$, which implies $|S_i| = a + b \leq n$.

Hence, the number of membership queries used to fill the observation table is at most $3 \cdot \sum_{i=0}^{m} |S_i|^2 \leq 3(m + 1)n^2$.

Finally, to bound the number of queries used to check self-consistency, let R_i be the set of non-blind rows at level i of the final hypothesis. For each $w \in R_i$, we make at most $4m|E_{m-i}|$ queries, so the number of queries for this purpose is

$$\sum_{i=0}^{m} |R_i| \cdot 4m|E_{m-i}| \leq 4m \sum_{i=0}^{m} |R_i| \cdot |S_i| \leq 4m \cdot n \cdot \sum_{i=0}^{m} |R_i| = 4n^2 m.$$

This concludes the proof. □

5 Negative Results

Using adversary arguments, one can show that both types of queries, membership and equivalence, are necessary for learning at all.

Theorem 15. *Obdds are not learnable with membership queries alone or with equivalence queries alone, even with respect to any fixed ordering.*

Proof. For membership queries alone, the standard adversary argument using the class of all singleton sets shows that exponentially many membership queries are needed.

For equivalence queries alone, we observe that a learning algorithm for obdds and any fixed ordering yields an algorithm that learns dfa accepting fixed-length languages, and recall that no such algorithm exists as shown by Angluin [3]. Strictly speaking, it is not enough to appeal to the proof in [3]: we should show that the class of witness dfa provided by Angluin is still hard to learn under any permutation of input bits.

Instead, we reduce the problem as follows: to learn a target $L^* \subseteq \{0,1\}^m$ run the learner for π−obdds over $\pi^{-1}(L)$, and transform its output first into an $id - obdd$ (by renaming variables), then into a dfa. This yields the minimum dfa in polynomial time. □

Furthermore, if no order is given to the learner and we want it to find the best ordering, learning is computationally hard.

Theorem 16. *There is no polynomial-time algorithm that learns minimum-size obdds with membership and equivalence queries, unless $P = NP$.*

Proof. Assume that there is such a learning algorithm. Then, given an obdd, we can find in polynomial time the variable ordering that minimizes its size by running the learning algorithm; the theorem follows as this problem is NP-complete [4].

The process is as follows: given an obdd O, run the learning algorithm; membership queries are solved by evaluating them over O; equivalence queries are be solved in polynomial time using the algorithm of Fortune, Hopcroft, and Schmidt [6], which works even if the two obdds use different variable orderings. □

With the same argument we can show: suppose we have a polynomial-time learning algorithm that does not necessarily output the optimum obdd, but is guaranteed to output a polynomial approximation to it (this is the standard definition of learning). Then, we can use it to build an approximation algorithm for the obdd minimization problem whose performance ratio is polynomial.

Actually, the implication is true for another NP-hard optimization problem called Optimal Linear Arrangement or OLA. This result is essentially the observation that the reduction from OLA to obdd-minimization in [4] is approximation-preserving.

Definition 17. [7] The *Optimal Linear Arrangement* problem (OLA) is defined as follows:

INSTANCE: Undirected graph $G = (V, E)$, positive integer K.

QUESTION: Is there a one-to-one function $f : V \mapsto \{1, 2, \ldots, |V|\}$ (a linear arrangement) such that $cost_G(f) = \sum_{(u,v) \in E} |f(u) - f(v)| \leq K$?

Theorem 18. *If boolean functions are learnable in terms of obdds (with respect to the best ordering, but not necessarily in minimal form) then OLA can be approximated within a polynomial.*

Proof. We show that the reduction from OLA to finding optimal variable orderings in obdds is approximation-preserving up to a polynomial.

Given an undirected graph $G = (V, E)$, let n and m be $|V|$ and $|E|$ respectively. We deal w.l.o.g. with the case where the graph is connected and hence $m \geq n - 1$. The reduction in [4] produces from G an obdd o with the following properties:

1. o has more than n variables, but the optimum ordering always belongs to a set of easily described orderings with $n!$ elements, called "blockwise orderings" in [4].
2. For every variable ordering that is not blockwise we can easily find a blockwise one that gives equal or smaller size.
3. There is a bijection between the set of possible arrangements of G and blockwise orderings of the variables in o. Hence, every possible arrangement $f : V \mapsto \{1, 2, \ldots, |V|\}$ of G gives an obdd o_f equivalent to o.
4. Given G and f, it is easy to compute o_f and vice-versa.
5. There is a constant c such that, for every f, the following is satisfied:

$$|o_f| = cn^2 m^2 + cost_G(f).$$

6. Therefore, if f^* is the cheapest arrangement for G and o^* the smallest obdd equivalent to o, we have

$$|o^*| = |o_{f^*}| = cn^2 m^2 + cost_G(f^*).$$

Now assume that there is an algorithm that minimizes obdds up to some polynomial p. Run this algorithm on the input graph G and obtain an obdd o'. By property 2 we can assume that o' is blockwise-ordered, that is, it is $o_{f'}$ for an arrangement f'. Compute f' and output it as an approximation to the optimal linear arrangement.

Indeed, using properties 5 and 6 we have

$$cost_G(f') = |o'| - cn^2 m^2 \leq p(|o^*|) - cn^2 m^2 = p(cost_G(f^*) + cn^2 m^2) - cn^2 m^2.$$

Since any linear arrangement has cost at least $m \geq n - 1$, this is within some polynomial of $cost_G(f^*)$. □

Acknowledgments

We thank Christoph Meinel for pointing us to the work [4], Ingo Wegener for providing us with a copy, Hans Ulrich Simon and an anonymous referee for very helpful comments, and Josep Díaz for posing the question of learning obdds.

References

1. D. Angluin: "Learning regular sets from queries and counterexamples". *Information and Computation* **75** (1987), 87–106.
2. D. Angluin: "Queries and concept learning". *Machine Learning* **2** (1988), 319–342.
3. D. Angluin: "Negative results for equivalence queries" *Machine Learning* **5** (1990), 121–150.
4. B. Bollig and I. Wegener: *Improving the variable ordering of OBDDs is NP-complete.* Technical Report # 542, Universität Dortmund (1994).
5. R.E. Bryant: "Symbolic boolean manipulation with ordered binary decision diagrams". *ACM Computing Surveys* **24** (1992), 293–318.
6. S. Fortune, J. Hopcroft, and E. Schmidt: "The complexity of equivalence and containment for free single variable program schemes". *Proc. 5th Intl. Colloquium on Automata, Languages, and Programming.* Springer-Verlag Lecture Notes in Computer Science 62 (1978), 227–240.
7. M. Garey and D. Johnson: *Computers and intractability: a guide to the theory of NP-completeness.* Freeman 1979.
8. J. Gergov and C. Meinel: "On the complexity of analysis and manipulation of Boolean functions in terms of decision graphs". *Information Processing Letters* **50** (1994), 317–322.
9. V. Raghavan and D. Wilkins: "Learning μ-branching programs with queries". *Proc. 6th COLT* (1993), 27–36.
10. R.E. Schapire: *The Design and Analysis of Efficient Learning Algorithms.* MIT Press, 1992.
11. S. Tani, K. Hamaguchi, and S. Yajima: "The complexity of the optimal variable ordering problems for shared binary decision diagrams". *Proc. 4th Intl. Symposium ISAAC'93.* Springer Verlag Lecture Notes in Computer Science 762 (1993), 389–398.

Simple PAC learning of simple decision lists

Jorge Castro[1] and José L. Balcázar[2] *

[1] Dept. Llenguatges i Sistemes Informàtics, Universitat Politècnica de Catalunya
Email: castro@lsi.upc.es
[2] Dept. Llenguatges i Sistemes Informàtics, Universitat Politècnica de Catalunya
Email: balqui@lsi.upc.es

Abstract. We prove that $\log n$-decision lists —the class of decision lists such that all their terms have low Kolmogorov complexity— are learnable in the simple PAC learning model. The proof is based on a transformation from an algorithm based on equivalence queries (found independently by Simon). Then we introduce the class of simple decision lists, and extend our algorithm to show that simple decision lists are simple-PAC learnable as well. This last result is relevant in that it is, to our knowledge, the first learning algorithm for decision lists in which an exponentially wide set of functions may be used for the terms.

1 Introduction: simple PAC learning

In Valiant's original model of learning, "PAC learning", [8], one has to learn a target concept with high probability, in polynomial time (and, a fortiori, from a polynomial number of examples) within a certain error, under all probability distributions on the examples. This last requirement, to learn under all distributions, is a strong one. Many concept classes are not known to be polynomially learnable or known not to be polynomially learnable if RP $\neq$ NP, although some such concept classes are polynomially learnable under some fixed distributions. However, learning under one single, fixed distribution (frequently the uniform distribution, or products of it) may be too restrictive to be useful.

Li and Vitányi proposed in [4] the simple PAC learning model, aiming at a compromise between practicality —in the sense that more concept classes are learnable— and usefulness, understood as the ability to learn under a wide and interesting class of distributions. Roughly speaking, simple PAC learning model replaces the condition of learning under all distributions, as in Valiant's original model, by the request of learning under all simple distributions, assuming that the samples are obtained according to the "universal" distribution.

Simple distributions form a wide class that properly include all enumerable ones. Specifically, they are those multiplicatively dominated by the universal enumerable distribution m. This distribution assigns high probabilities to low Kolmogorov complexity examples. As we will see later, these properties of m have nice consequences with regard to PAC learning under simple distributions.

* Work supported in part by the EC through the Esprit BRA Program (project 7141, ALCOM II, and Working Group 8556, NeuroColt) and by the spanish DGICYT.

With the new model, Li and Vitányi [4] developed a theory of learning for simple concepts —concepts with low Kolmogorov complexity— that intuitively should be polynomially learnable. In fact, they showed several examples that strengthen this intuition. Here we extend their results to encompass also the case of the $\log n$-decision lists (explicitly left open there) and the simple decision lists introduced here.

Following [6], here a decision list f over n Boolean variables is a sequence of terms $f_1 \ldots f_t$; each term f_i, for $i = 1, \ldots, t - 1$, is a pair $\langle fm_i, fb_i \rangle$ where fm_i is a monomial and fb_i is either 0 or 1. The last term f_t is always $\langle 1, fb_t \rangle$. The value of a decision list f on a setting of the n Boolean variables is defined to be fb_i, where i is the least number such that fm_i is satisfied by the assignment. The class of k-decision lists consists of all decision lists f for which each monomial fm_i has at most k literals. Rivest gave in [6] an algorithm for learning k-decision lists, for each constant k. The class of $\log n$-decision lists includes all decision lists f over n Boolean variables such that each term f_i of f of f has Kolmogorov complexity $O(\log n)$. Simple decision lists (our main target concept) will be defined later.

Our results are based on an algorithm for exact learning of decision lists, via equivalence queries. It works under the assumption that a set G, including all the terms of the target list, is known, and runs in time polynomial in the cardinality of G. Equivalently, the set of candidate functions to appear in the terms of the list must be known and of polynomial size to get a polynomial time learning algorithm. Our first description of this algorithm appears in the unpublished technical report [3], and we describe it again below for the sake of completeness; however, it was independently anticipated in [7] (but both descriptions differ somewhat). Furthermore, as the references and discussion there indicate, an algorithm for predicting decision lists had been discovered earlier by Littlestone.

From this learning algorithm, we can solve the simple PAC learning problem for $\log n$-decision lists, stated as open in [4] (see also page 308 of [5]). Further work will allow us to extend the result to simple decision lists. The main contributions of this paper, beyond that algorithm, are its adaptation to the simple PAC setting and the identification of the strictly more general, but still simple PAC learnable, class of the simple decision lists.

2 Preliminaries

We follow sections 5.5 and 5.6 of [5] and section 2 of [4]. In this paper we work with a discrete sample space S. The elements of S are called examples. A concept c is a subset of S. Abusing notation, we use c and the characteristic function $f : S \longrightarrow \{0, 1\}$ of c interchangeably for the concept $c \subseteq S$ and for the syntactic representation of c. For a concept c, we denote by $l(c)$ the minimum length of the representations of c. A concept class C is a set of concepts. Fixed f as the target concept, a learning algorithm draws examples from the sample space S according to a fixed but unknown probability distribution P. Each example e comes with a label that shows the value of $f(e)$.

For instance, in our case, each concept is a subset of $\{0, 1\}^n$, represented by a decision list which must compute the characteristic function of that set (our "target function"); furthermore, the list must obey the diverse restrictions imposed in each section of the paper.

Definition 1. A concept class C is PAC learnable iff there exists a learning algorithm A such that, for each $f \in C$ and ϵ $(0 < \epsilon < 1)$, algorithm A always halts within time and number of examples $p(l(f), 1/\epsilon)$, for some polynomial p, and outputs a concept $h \in C$ which satisfies

$$\text{Prob}(P(h \neq f) < \epsilon) > 1 - \epsilon.$$

Note that the PAC learning model requires that the algorithm learns under all distributions (the distribution P in the definition is unknown). We can also define, in a natural way, PAC learning under a class Δ of distributions: simply requiring definition 1 only on distributions from Δ.

It can be proved that there exists an universal enumerable distribution, denoted by **m**, that multiplicatively dominates each enumerable distribution. It can be shown that $\mathbf{m}(x) = 2^{-K(x)+O(1)}$, where $K(x)$ denotes the Kolmogorov complexity of x. The universal distribution has many important properties. Under **m**, easily describable objects have high probability, and complex objects have low probability. Our work is centered in learning under simple distributions:

Definition 2. A distribution P is simple iff it is multiplicatively dominated by the universal distribution. That is, there exists a constant c, such that for all x,

$$c\mathbf{m}(x) \geq P(x).$$

It can be shown that simple distributions properly include enumerable ones and that there is a distribution which is not simple [4]. The following theorem relates learning under simple distributions with learning under the universal distribution **m**.

Theorem 3 [4]. *A concept class C is PAC learnable under the universal distribution* **m**, *iff it is PAC learnable under simple distributions, provided that in the learning phase the set of examples is drawn according to* **m**.

In [4] it is shown how to exploit this completeness theorem to obtain new learning algorithms. Now, we define

Definition 4. A concept class C is simple-PAC learnable iff it is PAC learnable under **m**.

In order to take advantage of sampling under **m**, most applications of simple PAC learning work for specific subsets of representations, characterized by some condition; usually, an upper bound on the Kolmogorov complexity of either some parts of the representation itself, or of the elements of the concepts represented. In many cases, this bound allows one to prove that an initial phase of sampling is likely to provide some initialization values from which the learned representation is then extracted. However, with negligible but positive probability, this initial sampling may lead to output representations that do not fulfill the defining condition. This issue is discussed further below, in the light of our concrete example.

We assume the reader knows the exact learning and the learning via queries models (see [1] and [2]). In particular, we will work with the learning via equivalence queries model. Roughly speaking, in this model the learning algorithm has to produce in polynomial time a representation of the target concept, doing a polynomial number of equivalence queries. An equivalence query asks whether a representation given by the algorithm correctly represents the target concept. Equivalence queries are answered by a teacher affirmatively —when the query correctly represents the target concept— or with a counterexample that proves the difference.

A PAC learning algorithm can be obtained from an algorithm that learns via equivalence queries by means of a now standard transformation (see [1] and [2]):

Theorem 5. *Let C be a concept class. If C is learnable via equivalence queries then C is PAC learnable.*

3 Learning decision lists

Let $f = f_1 \ldots f_t$ be a decision list with $f_i = \langle fm_i, fb_i \rangle$, for $i = 1, \ldots, t-1$, and $f_t = \langle 1, fb_t \rangle$. Let $G = \{g_1, \ldots, g_s\}$ be a set of terms with $g_i = \langle gm_i, gb_i \rangle$ for $i = 1, \ldots, s$, and let us assume that $\{f_1, \ldots, f_t\} \subseteq G$.

We consider the following algorithm *Learn_Dlist* that, knowing the set G, tries to learn f doing equivalence queries. Here E denotes a set of labeled examples according to f, obtained from previous queries. Although described differently, the algorithm is essentially the same as that of [7]; however, our version was developed independently [3].

function Learn_Dlist (G) ret g : decision_list
$E := \emptyset$
$g :=$ Group_list(G, E)
Ask the equivalence query $g = f$?
while the teacher does not reply "yes" do
    Let e be the new counterexample
    Let $g_l = \langle gm_l, gb_l \rangle$ be the first term of g such that $gm_l(e) = 1$
    $E := E \cup \langle e, \overline{gb_l} \rangle$
    $g :=$ Group_list(G, E)
    Ask the equivalence query $g = f$?
endwhile
return g
endfunction

Since the algorithm does not stop unless the equivalence query has been answered positively, whenever it stops it has correctly learned the target decision list.

The core of the algorithm is the function *Group_list*. Intuitively, this function returns a decision list g by grouping all terms of G according to their behaviors on E. Given a labeled example $\langle e, b \rangle$ of E and a term g_i of G, we say that $\langle e, b \rangle$ is a consistency (resp. an inconsistency) of g_i iff $gm_i(e) = 1$ and $gb_i = b$ $(gb_i = \overline{b})$. Each term g_i of G appears in g placed in the first group of terms with the following property: each inconsistency of g_i is a consistency of some term in a previous group. The function *Group_list* is formally defined as follows (here ++ denotes list concatenation):

function Group_list (G', E) **ret** g : decision_list
for all $i = 1, \ldots, s$ **do**
    Let C_i be the set of labeled examples $\langle e, b \rangle \in E$
    such that $gm_i(e) = 1$ and $gb_i = b$
    (* let us call C_i the consistency set of the term g_i *)
    Let I_i be the set of labeled examples $\langle e, b \rangle \in E$
    such that $gm_i(e) = 1$ and $gb_i = \bar{b}$
    (* let us call I_i the inconsistency set of the term g_i *)
endfor
$g :=$ nul_list
while $G' \neq \emptyset$ **do**
    Let $Newgroup$ be the list of terms of G' such that their inconsistency
    sets are empty. It does not matter the order in the list
    $g := g \mathbin{++} Newgroup$
    $G' := G' - \{\text{terms of } Newgroup\}$
    for all $g_i \in G'$ **do**
        for all $g_j \in Newgroup$ **do**
            $I_i := I_i - (I_i \cap C_j)$
        endfor
    endfor
    (* consistent examples of terms in $Newgroup$ have been erased
       from the inconsistency sets *)
endwhile
return g
endfunction

Assuming that *Group_list* halts, each time that it is called it generates a new list g, in such a way that $g = gr(g, 1) \mathbin{++} \cdots \mathbin{++} gr(g, k)$, where $gr(g, 1)$ –the first group of g– is a list of terms having no inconsistencies in E, and in general, $gr(g, i+1)$ is a list of terms whose inconsistencies in E are included in the union of the consistency sets of terms in previous groups. Now, we are ready to prove the following lemma

Lemma 6. *Assuming that G includes all terms of f, the algorithm Learn_Dlist halts and learns f in time polynomial in s, where s is the cardinality of G.*

Proof. We have just to prove that *Learn_Dlist* runs in time polynomial in s. We proceed by steps.

Fact 1. The function *Group_list* halts in time polynomial in s and the cardinality of E.

We show that $Newgroup$ is always non empty. At the beginning of the process of *Group_list*, the set G' is G and includes all terms $f_1, \ldots, f_t$ of the target list f. The first group $gr(g, 1)$ is always nonempty because f_1 does not have inconsistencies. Let us suppose that $gr(g, i)$ is the last group constructed and $G' \neq \emptyset$. Either, all terms of f are already in a group, or there exists a term of f in G'. In the first case, the term $f_t = \langle 1, fb_t \rangle$ of f is in a group. As each example of E is either consistent or inconsistent for f_t, we may conclude that all inconsistency sets of terms in G' have already been erased. So, *Newgroup* is G'.

In the second case, let f_{σ_i} the first term of f that belongs to G'. As E is a set of examples of f, the inconsistency set of f_{σ_i} is empty because all its inconsistencies in E are included in the union of the consistency sets of $f_1, \ldots, f_{\sigma_i-1}$ that, by hypothesis, belong to previous groups. So, f_{σ_i} belongs to *Newgroup*. $\square$

Fact 2. The decision list g returned by *Group_list* has at most $t+1$ groups of terms, where t is the number of terms of f.

Using ideas from above it can be shown the following: $f_1 \in gr(g, 1)$, so $f_2 \in gr(g, 1) \cup gr(g, 2)$ and, in general, $f_i \in gr(g, j)$ and $j \leq i$. So, $f_t = \langle 1, fb_t \rangle \in gr(g, j)$ and $j \leq t$. Now the result is clear. $\square$

Fact 3. Let g_i be a term of G and let $gr(g, \sigma_i)$ be the group of g_i before processing *Group_list*. Let $gr(g, \mu_i)$ be the group of g_i after processing *Group_list*. It holds that $\sigma_i \leq \mu_i$.

When a new counterexample is put in E the inconsistency set of g_i cannot decrease. A contradiction appears if we suppose $\sigma_i > \mu_i$ for some $1 \leq i \leq s$. $\square$

Fact 4. The term g_l has to change of group by processing *Group_list*.

Let us suppose that $g_l \in gr(g, i)$ before processing *Group_List*. Note that the last counterexample e will be put in the inconsistency set of g_l and will not be put in the consistency sets of terms in $gr(g, j)$ with $j < i$. Now, by fact 3, it is clear that g_l has to change of group by processing *Group_List*. $\square$

Fact 5. Each term g_i changes of group at most t times.

It is a consequence of facts 2 and 3. $\square$

Fact 6. The function *Learn_Dlist* halts in time polynomial in s.

By facts 4 and 5, the *while* instruction of *Learn_Dlist* is processed at most st times. Now, by fact 1 we get the result. $\square$

Now, let us suppose that f is a $\log n$-decision list. The following lemma says that, drawing examples under the universal distribution, with high probability a set G including all terms of f can be obtained in polynomial time.

Lemma 7. *Let f be a $\log n$-decision list and let $f_i = \langle fm_i, fb_i \rangle$ for $i = 1, \ldots, t$ be the terms of f. Let c be a constant such that for all $i = 1, \ldots, t$, it holds $K(fm_i) < c \log n$. Let ϵ be a real number such that $0 < \epsilon < 1$. There exists an integer n_c depending only on c such that for all $n \geq n_c$, if we draw n^{c+2}/ϵ examples according to m, with probability greater than $1 - \epsilon$ a set G including all terms of f can be obtained in time $O(n^{2(c+2)}/\epsilon^2)$.*

Proof. The idea is from [4] (see also [5]). If we draw n^{c+2}/ϵ examples according to m, it holds the following,

Fact. For all $n \geq n_c$, where n_c is an integer depending only of c, with probability greater than $1 - \epsilon$ all examples of the following form will be drawn.

For each monomial m over n variables with $K(m) < c \log n$: the example vectors 0_m, defined as the vectors that satisfy m and have 0 entries for all variables not in m; the example vectors 1_m, defined as the vectors that satisfy m and have 1 entries for all variables not in m.

This fact is shown in the proof of theorem 3 of [4]. Now, we obtain the set G with the following procedure:

Draw n^{c+2}/ϵ examples according to m. Let E be this set of examples.
$G := \emptyset$
for each pair of examples in E do
    Let m be the monomial which contains x_i if both examples have '1' in
    position i, contains $\bar{x}_i$ if both examples have '0' in position i, and does
    not contain variable x_i otherwise $(1 \leq i \leq n)$
    $G := G \cup \{\langle m, 0 \rangle, \langle m, 1 \rangle\}$
endfor

Let us call this procedure *Get_set*. Using the fact above, it is clear that *Get_set* satisfies the lemma. □

Finally, we are ready to show simple pac-learning for $\log n$-decision lists. Let f be as in lemma 3.2 and let t_L be the time of *Learn_Dlist* running on a set that includes all terms of f. With probability at least $1 - \epsilon$, the algorithm

    Get_set(G)
    Let $s \in O(n^{2(c+2)}/\epsilon^2)$ be the cardinality of G
·   Simulate Learn_Dlist for $t_L(s)$ steps

learns f exactly. Removing the equivalence queries in the standard way (as in the proof of theorem 2.5, see [1] and [2]) we obtain a pac-learning algorithm, say A, with the following property,

$$\text{Prob}\left(\text{m}(g_A \neq f) < \epsilon\right) \geq$$
$$\text{Prob}\left(\text{m}(g_A \neq f) < \epsilon \,\middle|\, \{f_1, \ldots, f_t\} \subseteq G\right) \cdot \text{Prob}\left(\{f_1, \ldots, f_t\} \subseteq G\right) >$$
$$(1 - \epsilon)(1 - \epsilon) \geq 1 - 2\epsilon$$

where g_A denotes the output list of A. Therefore, we have shown

Theorem 8. *Let $\mathcal{D}_c$ be the class of $\log n$-decision lists having all their terms Kolmogorov complexity bounded by $c \log n$. The $\mathcal{D}_c$ classes are simple PAC learnable.*

4 Interlude: improper learning

Some comments are in order here. We have imposed no time restriction on the Kolmogorov complexity of the monomials appearing in the decision list. Assume for a moment that a polynomial time bound is imposed; then PAC learnability would follow automatically from Rivest's algorithm [6]. Indeed, as indicated in that paper (see section 5.3), Rivest's algorithm only depends on being able to loop in polynomial time over the set of all functions potentially appearing in the terms (expressed there as a polynomial bound on the size of that set, somewhat inexactly, since the algorithm has to cycle over all of them in polynomial time).

This approach requires, however, another subtle condition: namely, proper learning. Indeed, if all monomials can be produced deterministically in polynomial time, as in the case of polynomially time-bounded Kolmogorov complexity, then the consistent list obtained by Rivest's algorithm achieves learning, as follows from the Occam razor theorem (see [6]). But, without that time bound, we no longer have proper learning, in the sense that the outcome of the initialization phase might be (with low probability) completely arbitrary, and thus there is no guarantee that the output of whatever computations are based on it consists only of $O(\log n)$-complex monomials. For instance, for any fixed, arbitrary, set of monomials (of the right size), there is a (small but) positive probability that the initialization sampling phase gives precisely that set.

And even for highly likely successful initializations, a number of spurious monomials, completely arbitrary, are nearly surely obtained, cannot be sifted out in polynomial time, and may find their way to sneak into the final outcome. The longer the initialization phase, the more of these will show up.

This fact holds in many other known cases of simple PAC learning, such as in learning $\log n$-DNF's, which does not reduce through initial sampling to Valiant's (Occam-razor-like) algorithm for k-DNF's: simple PAC learning of simple concepts is usually not proper, since nonsimple representations of simple concepts have a positive probability of being obtained.

As a consequence, in our case, Rivest's algorithm cannot be used to learn after the initialization phase; it can be used, of course, to find a consistent decision list, which is not necessarily "one of a few", however, since essentially any decision list representing the target, whether simple or not, may be obtained. Therefore the Occam razor theorem cannot be used to prove that learnability is achieved in this manner.

Our way out has been to avoid the Occam razor theorem, heading for another known way to reach PAC algorithms: the transformation from an equivalence query algorithm. This allows us also to consider separately the sampling oriented towards an initialization and the sampling oriented to check progress in the learning phase, so that the huge sampling needed for an extremely high confidence does not hinder the algorithm by throwing in lots of "nonsimple" monomials.

5 Simple decision lists

This section nontrivially extends the previous results to simple decision lists. These are based on the simple DNF's defined in [4], where they are argued to represent a rather general class of boolean functions. Simple decision lists generalize them, so that the class they define is still larger.

The interest of simple decision lists is that there is an exponentially large repertoire of choices for each term: instead, the simplicity lies in the structural compatibility between the different terms, as made precise below in the definition of simple decision list. This contrasts with the previously studied cases here and in [7], where the set of available functions must be polynomial in size in order to get a polynomial time learning algorithm.

Here, instead, the simplicity condition is structural, and refers to the functions actually appearing in the decision list, and to the order in which they appear (and this is where they depart from simple DNF's). The precise definition of simple DNF's appears in [4] and is omitted here, as is the comparison with simple decision lists. (Actually, once the precise generalization of simple DNF's is found, adapting the previously described algorithm is easy, specially after investing some time in searching for the clearest proof of the main lemma below.) For a boolean vector v, denote $v^{(j)}$ the vector obtained by flipping the j-th bit of v.

Definition 9. A decision list f, with $f_i = \langle fm_i, fb_i \rangle$ for $i = 1, \ldots, t$, is c-simple if there are boolean vectors v_i, $i = 1, \ldots, t$, with $K(v_i) \leq c \log n$, such that v_i satisfies fm_i, and for all j,

1. $v_i^{(j)}$ does not satisfy any fm_k with $k < i$, and
2. if $f(v_i^{(j)}) = f(v_i)$ then $v_i^{(j)}$ satisfies fm_i.

Arguing here as in the previous sections, in a polynomially large sample, with high probability, all the vectors v_i and $v_i^{(j)}$ appear, together with their respective values under f. More precisely, there is a constant $c' \geq c$ such that if $K(v_i) \leq c \log n$, then $K(v_i^{(j)}) \leq c' \log n$. Our main lemma now is that the simplicity condition allows us to characterize, in terms of these values, that with high probability are known, which variables may or may not appear in each monomial. Namely:

Lemma 10. Variable x_j belongs to monomial fm_i iff $f(v_i^{(j)}) \neq f(v_i)$.

Proof. By the first simplicity condition, the evaluation of f on $v_i^{(j)}$ does not stop at any fm_k with $k < i$; therefore, $f(v_i^{(j)}) = fb_k$ with $k \geq i$. However, v_i does satisfy fm_i. If $x_j \in fm_i$, flipping the j-th value of v_i ensures that $v_i^{(j)}$ does not satisfy fm_i, and by the second condition we get $f(v_i^{(j)}) \neq f(v_i)$. And if $x_j \notin fm_i$, flipping the j-th value of v_i has no effect and we get $f(v_i^{(j)}) = fb_i = f(v_i)$. □

Now the specific algorithm goes as follows. On inputs n and ϵ,

draw (according to m) an initial sample E of size $s = n^{c'+2}/\epsilon$;
$G := \emptyset$;
for each $\langle v, b \rangle \in E$ do
    check that all $v^{(j)}$ are in E (otherwise move to next v);
    $m := \emptyset$;
    for each j do
        if $f(v^{(j)}) \neq f(v)$ then add x_j to m
    $G := G \cup \{\langle m, 0 \rangle, \langle m, 1 \rangle\}$
endfor

Arguing as before, with probability $1 - \epsilon$ we obtain in this manner a set G including all the terms of f, and we can use it to initialize the same PAC simulation of Learn_Dlist as in the previous section. In this way we get:

Theorem 11. For all constants c, the class of c-simple decision lists is simple PAC learnable.

6 Conclusions

Li and Vitányi gave in [4] several examples of simple PAC learning. The outline of their proofs is the following. First a certain property P —that depends on the class C they try to learn— is shown to happen with high probability drawing examples under m. Second, assuming that property P happens, a PAC learning distribution-free algorithm —frequently an Occam algorithm— for C is given. However, the Occam algorithm required is usually different from known Occam algorithms for the non-simple case. This is due to the fact, as analyzed here, that the learning is likely to be improper, with a large number of nonsimple hypothesis being output with (small but) positive probability, thus preventing the Occam razor theorem to apply.

This work shows that, in some cases, a learning via equivalence queries algorithm may be easier to get than a pure pac-learning distribution-free or an Occam one, giving rise to the similar scheme:

1. With high probability get property P.
2. Assuming P, try a learning via equivalence queries algorithm for C.

This allows for closing the explicitly stated open problem of simple PAC learning $\log n$-decision lists, as well as to extend the approach to a broad class of decision lists that is no longer constrained by a polynomial number of possible functions at each term.

Acknowledgements

We thank Ricard Gavaldà and Hans Ulrich Simon for useful discussions and sharing opinions, and John Shawe-Taylor for organizing a workshop on query learning where parts of this work were presented, as well as the participants in the workshop for their useful feedback. Likewise, to the referees that forced us to an interesting deeper analysis of the improperness of most simple PAC learning algorithms, and of its consequence for the Occam razor theorem.

References

1. Angluin, D.: Learning regular sets from queries and counterexamples. Information and Computation 75 (1987) 87–106
2. Angluin, D.: Queries and concept learning. Machine Learning 2 (1988) 319–342
3. Castro, J.: A note on learning decision lists. Report de Recerca LSI-95-2-R, Dept. LSI, UPC (1995)
4. Li, M. and Vitányi, P.: Learning simple concepts under simple distributions. SIAM Journal of Computing 20 (1991) 911–935
5. Li, M. and Vitányi, P.: An introduction to Kolmogorov complexity and its applications. Springer-Verlag (1993)
6. Rivest, R.: Learning decision lists. Machine Learning 2 (1987) 229–246
7. Simon, H.U.: Learning decision lists an trees with equivalence queries. In Second European Conference, EuroCOLT'95, Barcelona (1995) 322–336. Lecture Notes in Artificial Intelligence.
8. Valiant, L.G.: A theory of the learnable. Comm. ACM 27 (1984) 1134–1142

The Complexity of Learning
Minor Closed Graph Classes

Carlos Domingo[1] and John Shawe-Taylor[2]

[1] Dept. of Computer Science,
Tokyo Institute of Technology,
Meguro-ku, Ookayama, Tokyo 152,
Japan
Email: carlos@cs.titech.ac.jp
[2] Dept of Computer Science,
Royal Holloway,
University of London,
Egham, Surrey TW20 0EX,
England
Email: john@dcs.rhbnc.ac.uk

Abstract. The paper considers the problem of learning classes of graphs closed under taking minors. It is shown that any such class can be properly learned in polynomial time using membership and equivalence queries. The representation of the class is in terms of a set of minimal excluded minors (obstruction set). Moreover, a negative result for learning such classes using only equivalence queries is also provided, after introducing a notion of reducibility among query learning problems.

1 Introduction

This paper considers the problem of identifying a very broad series of classes of graphs, namely those closed under taking graph minors. Such sets of graphs have been studied for a number of years by graph theorists, most notably in a series of papers by Robertson and Seymour (see for example among other papers [11, 13, 12, 15, 14]). The classes of graphs that are closed under taking minors are very common. Examples are the planar graphs, graphs which can be embedded in 3-dimensional space without knots, graphs which can be embedded in 3-dimensional space without interlocking cycles, graphs with genus, bounded treewidth or pathwidth, etc. In some cases there are no known algorithms for testing for membership in these classes, though the general theory of graph minors ensures that such algorithms must exist. One way of viewing our results is a general method of learning such algorithms.

The key result obtained by Robertson and Seymour showed that for any class of graphs closed under taking minors, there is a *finite* set of minimal minors not in the class. This set is called the obstruction set of the class. Any such class can therefore be characterized as the set of graphs which do not contain any member of the obstruction set as a minor. For the example of planar graphs the obstruction set consists of the two non-planar graphs, K_5 and $K_{3,3}$. Hence, in this case the result is equivalent to the famous Kuratowski theorem that a graph is planar if and only if it does not contain one of these two graphs as a minor. In general there are no efficient algorithms for computing the obstruction set of a class of graphs, and in some cases of interest (e.g. the set of graphs embeddable in 3-space such that no cycle forms a knot) the obstruction set is not yet known.

This paper shows that any graph class that is closed under taking minors can be exactly identified using the learning protocol of equivalence and membership queries. The learning algorithm delivers the obstruction set of the class using a number of queries that is polynomial in the size of the minimal representation and the size of the largest counterexample.

Once the obstruction set has been constructed, there are well developed algorithms for deciding whether a given graph has a member of the obstruction set as a minor. These algorithms are at worst cubic in the number of vertices in the graph, but exponential in the size of the obstruction set. Hence, the representation fails to be polynomially evaluable in its own size but, once it is fixed, is polynomially evaluable in the size of the graph which is being evaluated. This technical point will not be relevant to our learning algorithm, since we will not need to evaluate the representations on any examples. In summary, our learning algorithm uses membership and equivalence queries to "learn" an algorithm that is known to exist, but which we do know how to build.

On the other hand, it is also showed that when restricting the learner to use only equivalence queries, such polynomial time learning algorithm does not exist. We introduce a notion of reducibility between query learning problems needed for the proof. Using previous negative results for Monotone DNF formula [2, 6] the lower bound for learning minor closed graphs classes using only equivalence queries can be pushed up to $\Omega(n^{\log n})$.

In the next section we will review the definitions and results of the theory of graph minors and of learning theory that we will need. This will lead into Section 3 containing our main positive results. Section 4 contains the definition of reduction and the negative results. Finally, the conclusion indicates how the results can be generalized and highlights questions that remain unresolved.

2 Definitions and Known Results

A graph G comprises a set of nodes VG and a set of edges $EG \subseteq VG \times VG$, which is symmetric and antireflexive. We say that a graph H is a one-step minor of a graph G, denoted $H \prec_1 G$, if H is obtained from G by one of the following operations:

1. deletion of one edge;
2. by deletion of one vertex together with all edges incident with the vertex; or
3. by identifying two adjacent vertices into a single vertex, that is adjacent to all the vertices adjacent to either of the two identified vertices.

The minor relation (denoted $\preceq$) is the transitive reflexive closure of the relation $\prec_1$.

A class of graphs $\mathcal{G}$ is minor closed if $G \in \mathcal{G}$ and $H \preceq G$ imply that $H \in \mathcal{G}$.

For a minor closed class of graphs $\mathcal{G}$, the obstruction set of $\mathcal{G}$, denoted $\mathrm{ob}(\mathcal{G})$, is the set of minimal elements in the relation $\preceq$ in the complement of $\mathcal{G}$. Hence, for each graph G, $G \in \mathcal{G}$ if and only if there is no $H \in \mathrm{ob}(\mathcal{G})$ that is a minor of G.

Robertson and Seymour proved Wagner's conjecture that for every minor closed class of graphs, the obstruction set is finite. Their theorem states.

Theorem 1. *[5] For every minor closed class of graphs $\mathcal{G}$ the obstruction set $\mathrm{ob}(\mathcal{G})$ of $\mathcal{G}$ is finite.*

Corollary 2. *Every minor closed class of graphs is decidable.*

In fact the situation is much better than being simply decidable. Efficient algorithms have been devised for testing whether a fixed given graph is a minor of a graph G, which are polynomial in $|G|$.

Theorem 3. *[5] For every graph H, there exists an $O(n^3)$ algorithm, that given a graph G, tests whether H is a minor of G.*

Corollary 4. *Given the obstruction set $\mathrm{ob}(\mathcal{G})$ of a minor closed class of graphs $\mathcal{G}$, we can test whether a graph G is a member of the class in $O(|G|^3)$ time.*

In the case of classes that do not contain all planar graphs, the complexity can be improved using results about graphs of bounded treewidth [5].

Proposition 5. *Given the obstruction set $\mathrm{ob}(\mathcal{G})$ of a minor closed class of graphs $\mathcal{G}$ that does not contain all planar graphs, we can test whether a graph G is a member of the class in $O(|G|)$ time.*

We can relax our definition of graph and our minor relation fixing the labels of the vertices in our graphs.

Definition 6. A graph G_L is say to be labeled if we have a fixed labeling in its vertices that allow us to exactly recognize each vertex and therefore each edge.

We must also redefine our minor relation in order to fit it with labeled graphs.

Definition 7. Let G_L and H_L be two labeled graphs. We say that G_L is a labeled minor of H_L (denoted by $G_L \preceq_L H_L$) iff the set of edges of G_L is contained in the set of edges of H_L.

Thus, we can also consider classes of labeled graphs closed under the "labeled minor relation" previously defined. This classes will be represented by a finite obstruction set of labeled graphs. A labeled graph will be in the class iff it does not have any of the "forbidden" graphs of the obstruction set as a labeled minor.

The notion of query learning was introduced by Angluin in 1987 [1]. In this paper we follow the modified learning framework defined by Watanabe [17] and extended in [18] . In order to specify our learning problem we have to determine both a concept space and a way of representing the concepts. The formal object known as a *representation class* is, informally, a triple (R, c, Σ) where R is a set of valid representations, c a semantic function from R to the concept space and a Σ is an alphabet for the concepts represented by R. Thus, for each representation $r \in R$, the concept $c(r) \subseteq \Sigma^*$ is the concept represented by r. Whenever c and Σ are implicitly understood we will use R as an abbreviation for the whole class.

Throughout the paper we will work with the class of concepts $\mathcal{G}$ of graphs closed under taking minors. We can represent a class $\mathcal{G}$ by a finite set of minimal excluded minors. We call this representation class R_{ob}. The representation of the classes of graphs closed under taking minors will thus be in terms of their obstruction set. Hence, we consider the finite sets of graphs which form an antichain in the 'is a minor' relation. The corresponding class of graphs is obtained by taking the complement of the set of graphs which have at least one graph from the set as a minor.

For proving our negative result we also need to make use of two more representation classes. First, we consider the representation class of Monotone formulae in disjunctive normal form (DNF). A Boolean formula is said to be monotone if all the literals in the formula appear positively. We denote this representation class by $R_{monoDNF}$. The other representation class will be the labeled obstruction set representing minor closed graph classes of labeled graphs. We call this representation class R_{ob_L}.

When we are talking about query learning, we need to define the communication protocol between the *Teacher* and the *Learner*. A protocol is a set of queries. We will use through the paper two kind of queries, membership and equivalence queries [1].

Thus, we will say that the class R is learnable in polynomial time using queries from a protocol Q if there exists an algorithm S that learns any $r \in R$ from any Teacher T answering from Q in time bounded polynomially in the size of the smallest representation and the length of the longest answer given by T.

In the following section we will use a protocol with both queries, membership and equivalence. In Section 4 we restrict our protocol to have only equivalence queries.

3 Learning minor closed classes

The main positive result of this paper can now be stated.

Theorem 8. *The representation class R_{ob} is learnable in polynomial time using membership and equivalence queries.*

Proof. The algorithm which identifies the obstruction set is as follows. Note that the algorithm is always working with an obstruction set which is too small and so has a hypothesis class which is too big. Hence the equivalence queries always deliver a negative counterexample. In addition, when added to the set Obstruct, it is a minimal member of the complement of $\mathcal{G}$ in the minor relation. Hence, Obstruct is always a subset of the complete obstruction set.

```
Obstruct := {};
While Not EquivalenceQuery(Obstruct, CounterExample) Do Begin
    /* CounterExample is the negative counterexample returned by
       the equivalence query */
    Repeat
      Minors := OneStepMinors(CounterExample);
      /* Minors is the set of minors obtained from CounterExample
         by one step e.g. one edge deletion, etc.        */
      Smaller := False;
      Repeat
        Select G from Minors;
        If MembershipQuery( G ) Then
              /* i.e. G is a positive example  */
              Minors := Minors - { G }
        Else Begin
              CounterExample := G;
              Smaller := True;
        End;
      Until Smaller Or (Minors = {});
    Until Not Smaller;
    Obstruct := Obstruct + { CounterExample };
  End;
  Return ( Obstruct );
```

Observe that if the graph $G \preceq H$ with $G \neq H \in$ Obstruct, we must necessarily have $G \in \mathcal{G}$, since $G \notin \mathcal{G}$ would imply that H was not minimal in the complement of $\mathcal{G}$. We will prove by induction that at every stage the set formed by the set Obstruct $\cup \{$CounterExample$\}$ form an antichain in the relation $\preceq$, which represents a class $\mathcal{G}($Obstruct $\cup \{$CounterExample$\})$ which contains the class $\mathcal{G}$. This is certainly true at the start of the algorithm, since $\mathcal{G}(\emptyset)$ is the class of all graphs. Assume that it is true at some later iteration of the loop. If the equivalence query succeeds, then the algorithm has successfully identified the obstruction set. If it fails the counterexample CounterExample generated must be a negative example, since we have $\mathcal{G}($Obstruct$) \supseteq \mathcal{G}$. Hence also Obstruct $\cup \{$CounterExample$\}$ form an antichain in the relation $\preceq$, since $G \succeq H \in$ Obstruct implies CounterExample $\notin \mathcal{G}($Obstruct$)$, while $G \preceq H \in$ Obstruct implies $G \in \mathcal{G}$ by the observation above. The other stage at which CounterExample is updated is in the inner loop after a membership query fails on a graph G which is a one step minor of CounterExample. Since Obstruct $\cup \{$CounterExample$\}$ formed an antichain and $G \preceq$ CounterExample, no element of Obstruct is a minor of G. Similarly, $G \preceq H \in$ Obstruct implies $G \in \mathcal{G}$ by the observation. It follows that the set Obstruct $\cup \{G\}$ also forms an antichain. But as $G \notin \mathcal{G}$ we also have $\mathcal{G}($Obstruct $\cup \{G\}) \supseteq \mathcal{G}$ as required.

In order to estimate the complexity of the algorithm, note that each iteration of the outer loop extends the set Obstruct by one element, and so the number of iterations is equal to the number of elements in the obstruction set. For each new counterexample, each execution of the inner loop reduces its size by either one edge, or at least one vertex. Hence the number of iterations of that loop is linear in the size of the counterexample. Finally, the innermost loop is executed a number of times that is at most equal to the size of the counterexample. Hence, the time complexity of the two inner loops is at most quadratic in the size of the counterexample. By being more selective about the one step minors considered and taking into account that if an edge/vertex cannot be deleted at one step the same edge/vertex cannot be deleted at the next, these two inner loops can be made to run in time linear in the size of the counterexample. □

Corollary 9. *The class of all classes of graphs that are closed under taking minors represented by obstruction sets can be learned using equivalence and membership queries.*

Proof. By the theorem, we can use the equivalence and membership queries to construct the obstruction set of the class, which is thus uniquely identified. □

Note that the obstruction set can then be used to determine membership of a given graph G in the class, in time that is $O(|G|^3)$, by Corollary 4. Further by Proposition 5, the test for membership can be made in $O(|G|)$ time, if the class does not contain all planar graphs.

4 Equivalence queries are not enough

In this section we restrict our learner to use only one type of queries, equivalence queries. We want to show that using such a restricted model there is no polynomial time learning algorithm for graphs classes closed under taking minors.

In [2] a general proof technique called approximate fingerprints is shown. When you can show that a representation class has the approximate fingerprint property this implies that there is no polynomial time algorithm for learning that representation class using only equivalence queries. Furthermore, Gavaldà [7] proved that the converse also holds. If a representation class is not learnable then it has the fingerprints property. Several negatives results have been proved using this technique. We will make explicit use of one of them and an improvement.

Theorem 10. *[2] There is no polynomial time algorithm that exactly identifies all Monotone DNF formulas using only equivalence queries.*

The following corollary of the previous theorem will allow us to improve the lower bound:

Corollary 11. *[6] There is no $O(n^{\log n})$ algorithm for exact identification of all Monotone DNF formulas using only equivalence queries.*

Our goal will be to reduce our learning problem to the problem of learning Monotone DNF formulas. In the following subsection we introduce the notion of reduction we will use for the proof.

4.1 Reduction between query learning problems

A general notion of reduction among representation classes that preserves polynomial predictability was introduced in [10]. Since our model of learning is different the reduction must be redefined in order to make it useful for the current framework.

Assume we have a learning algorithm L_2 that exactly identifies the representation class R_2 using polynomial number of equivalence queries. We would like to construct a reduction from the representation class R_1 to R_2 that allows us to build an algorithm L_1 which exactly identifies representation class R_1 using the same number of equivalence queries. The algorithm L_1 will entail running L_2, but whenever L_2 asks an equivalence query, L_1 transforms the query to an equivalence query in R_1. Thus, our reduction should provide a function g (called the *representation transformation*) which maps representations from R_2 to R_1. Moreover, when L_1 receives a counterexample there must exist a second transformation f (the *word transformation*) which maps this counterexample into a counterexample to be passed back to L_2. If the reduction (transformations f and g) fulfills some requirements the algorithm L_1 using the efficient algorithm L_2 for R_2 is an efficient learning algorithm for R_1, preserving the number of equivalence queries. However, we are not always able to transform the equivalence queries for representations R_2 into equivalence queries for R_1. Thus, g may be only a partial function. In the cases when g is undefined the algorithm L_1 must be able to answer by itself with a counterexample consistent with any target concept represented in R_1.

Since we want to use the transformation for proving a non-learnability result, we only need to preserve the number of queries. In fact, we do not really care about the time complexity of the transformations f and g, as far as they are computable and length preserving within a polynomial. Below we give the formal definition of the reduction.

Definition 12. [10] A function h all of whose inputs and outputs are either words or natural numbers (encoded in unary notation) is called *polynomial length preserving* if there is a fixed polynomial q such that all inputs to the function h of length at most l produce outputs of length at most $q(l)$.

Definition 13. Let (R_1, c_1, Σ_1) and (R_2, c_2, Σ_2) be a pair of representation classes. With respect to this pair, a *word transformation* is a function $f : \Sigma_1^* \mapsto \Sigma_2^*$ and a *partial representation transformation* is a partial function $g : R_2 \mapsto R_1$. here

Definition 14. The representation class R_1 *reduces to* the representation class R_2 (denoted by $R_1 \trianglelefteq R_2$) iff there is a polynomially length preserving word transformation f and a polynomially length preserving partial representation transformation g such that the following two conditions hold:,

1. When g is defined for an $r_2 \in R_2$, $w_1 \in c_1(g(r_2))$ iff $f(w_1) \in c_2(r_2)$.
2. When g is undefined for an $r_2 \in R_2$ it must be possible to compute a word $w \in \Sigma_2^*$ such that for any $r \in R_2$ for which g is defined, $w \in c_2(r)$ iff $w \notin c_2(r_2)$.

Lemma 15. *For all representation classes R_1 and R_2, if $R_1 \trianglelefteq R_2$ and R_2 is exactly learnable using polynomial number of equivalence queries, the R_1 is exactly learnable using at most the same number of queries.*

Proof. (sketch) The efficient algorithm L_2 for R_2 is used as a subroutine by the algorithm L_1 for R_1 as indicated above. When L_2 asks an equivalence query, L_1 attempts to transform it using the function g. If successful it uses the result as the hypothesis for its own equivalence query in R_1 and returns the image of the resulting counterexample under the map f to L_2, otherwise it generates the word guaranteed by the second condition of Definition 14. This is a good counterexample since the algorithm is being required to learn a representation which is in the domain of g. The algorithm will terminate when for some $r \in R_2$, the hypothesis $g(r)$ given by L_1 as an equivalence query receives the answer "yes". In this case L_1 has successfully identified the target concept as $g(r)$. □

Lemma 16. *The reduction is transitive, i.e., if $R_1 \trianglelefteq R_2 \trianglelefteq R_3$, then $R_1 \trianglelefteq R_3$.*

Proof. (sketch) The only problem in composing the reduction functions is the case when $g_1 : R_2 \to R_1$ is not defined for some $g_2(r)$. But the guaranteed $w \in R_2$ can be mapped back to a counterexample for r using f_2. □

4.2 Monotone DNF are reducible to Minor Closed Graphs Classes

In the previous section we defined a notion of reduction among query learning problems. Now, we want to make use of this notion to reduce Monotone DNF formulae to Obstruction sets.. Unfortunately, we have not found any straight way to make this reduction. Therefore, we might use an intermediate representation class, Labeled Obstruction Sets which was previously defined in the second section.

Lemma 17. $R_{monoDNF} \trianglelefteq R_{ob_L}$.

Proof. The reduction we will show below is actually a reduction from the negations of Monotone DNF formulae to R_{ob_L}. However, the problem of learning the negations of a hypothesis class is clearly equivalent to learning the class itself.

Let ob_L be an arbitrary obstruction set of t labeled graphs with at most n vertices and at most k actual edges out of m possible. We first show how to transform this obstruction set into a Monotone DNF formulae. We consider formulae over m variables, V_m. Since we are working with labeled graphs we can exactly identify each edge. Therefore, each edge corresponds to a variable and one graph will correspond to the assignment with precisely those variables corresponding to its edges set true. Moreover, each graph of the obstruction set will give one term of the formula. This transformation is computable and polynomially preserves the length of the obstruction set. It is also a total function, so we do not have to consider the problem of the function being partial. Hence, this defines our representation transformation g.

Let $a \in \{0,1\}^m$ an assignment for a boolean formulae over V_m. We can build a labeled graph with n vertices and m possible edges such that the edge e_i appears in the graph iff $a_i = 1$. This will be our word transformation f which is also clearly computable and length preserving. To check the first condition for a reduction, consider the negation of a Monotone DNF formula $\phi = g(Ob)$ for some obstruction set Ob of labeled graphs. The formula ϕ is not satisfied by an assignment a iff the term obtained from the assignment is a a superset of at least one of the terms of the formula. But the graph $f(a)$ is not contained in the class defined by Ob iff the set of edges of $f(a)$ is a superset of at least one of the graphs in the obstruction set. $\qquad\square$

Lemma 18. $R_{ob_L} \trianglelefteq R_{ob}$.

Proof. We first define the function f which maps a labeled graph into a corresponding unlabeled graph. Let G_L be a labeled graph with n vertices $\{v_1, \ldots, v_n\}$. We call the vertices of G_L the principal vertices. Let v_i be one the principal vertices of G_L. We add to v_i one edge and at the other side of this new edge, we add the complete graph K_{n+i+1} by one of its vertices. This defines the graph $f(G_L)$ and hence the word transformation f from labeled graphs to unlabeled graphs. Note that the size of $f(G_L)$ is polynomial in the size of G_L. Thus, f is polynomially length preserving. We claim that the principal vertices of G_L can be uniquely identified in $f(G_L)$. They will be the n vertices with at most n incident edges. It will be useful later to consider to particular labeled graphs. Let G_0 be the graph obtained after applying f to the labeled graph with n vertices and no edges. G_0 will be the graph containing n components, the i-th component comprising a complete graph on $n+i+1$ vertices linked by an edge to a vertex of degree 1. Similarly, consider the graph $G_* = f(K_n)$. Note that a graph H is the image of a labeled graph iff the following holds: $G_0 \preceq H \preceq G_*$. Hence, if $f^{-1}(H)$ is undefined, either $G_0 \npreceq H$ or $H \npreceq G_*$.

The inverse transformation f^{-1} from unlabeled graphs to labeled graphs is only partially defined, since f is not onto. Nevertheless, we will use $f' = f^{-1}$ in the construction of our representation transformation. In fact we slightly extend the domain of f' to include those graphs satisfying $H \npreceq G_*$, by mapping these graphs to G_*. Hence, for an obstruction set Ob of unlabeled graphs, g is defined provided each element of Ob is in the domain of f'. In this case we define $g(Ob)$ by applying f' elementwise. Note that for any labeled graphs G_L and H_L, $G_L \preceq_L H_L$ iff $f(G_L) \preceq f(H_L)$. Furthermore, since $f(G_L) \preceq G_*$ for all G_L, $H \npreceq G_*$ implies $H \npreceq f(G_L)$ for all G_L. This means that the presence of such an H in the obstruction set Ob will have no influence on whether $f(G_L) \in c_{ob(Ob)}$. Hence, when g is defined, it satisfies the first condition of the reduction.

To complete the proof, we must show that when g is not defined we can satisfy the second condition. For g not to be defined on an obstruction set Ob, there must be at least one graph $H \in Ob$ which is not in the domain of f', that is $G_0 \npreceq H$. We must construct an unlabeled graph C such that, for any obstruction set Ob' for which g is defined, $C \in \mathcal{G}(Ob')$ iff $C \notin \mathcal{G}(Ob)$. For any G_L, $G_0 \preceq f(G_L)$ implies that $f(G_L) \npreceq H$ (otherwise we contradict the assumption that $G_0 \npreceq H$, by the transitivity of the minor relation). Nevertheless, H is minor of itself (by definition of the minor relation) and therefore $H \notin \mathcal{G}(Ob)$ but $H \in \mathcal{G}(Ob')$ for any Ob' for which g is defined. Thus, in this case H itself is the word that satisfies the second condition of the reduction. □

Now we are ready for stating our main negative result:

Theorem 19. *There is no algorithm that exactly identifies the representation class R_{ob} using $\mathcal{O}(n^{\log n})$ equivalence queries.*

Proof. Suppose there is one. By transitivity of the reduction(Lemma 16) we contradict Corollary 11. Notice that in Lemma 18 we restrict the number of edges in our graphs to be a fixed constant. Thus, when applying the reductions we are also restricting the number of literals in each term of the Monotone DNF formulae. However, the same negative result of Corollary 11 holds even if we restrict the number of literals per term to be a fixed constant. For more details about this we refer the reader to [6]. □

5 Conclusions

Our results show that the learning protocol of membership and equivalence queries can be used to construct the obstruction set of a class of graphs closed under taking minors using time polynomial in the size of the obstruction set and the length of the longest counterexample. There are no known efficient algorithms for constructing the obstruction set even for simply defined classes. The algorithm can therefore also throw light on this open problem. Moreover, we show that membership are essential to the algorithm. In order to show this we introduce a notion of reducibility among query learning problems. The same notion can be easily modified to show that membership alone are not also enough for learning this class of graphs. Therefore, the protocol used in the algorithm is minimal.

The results presented here can be generalized to any other partial order $\preceq$ on graphs as long as the defined class contains a finite number of obstructions, the number of immediate predecessors in the ordering is polynomial in the size of the graph and as long as we can check for any fixed H and an arbitrary G whether $H \preceq G$ in time polynomial in $|G|$. Examples of such partial orders are the immersion order and more generally the so-called Robertson and Seymour posets [8].

Note also that we do not need to restrict ourselves to graphs. Consider the set of all binary n-bit strings with the ordering being the monotonicity ordering. A string s can be characterized by monomial $m(s)$ containing the 1 coordinates. The set of strings t satisfying $s \preceq t$ in the ordering are precisely those satisfying the monomial $m(s)$. Hence, the set of strings determined by an obstruction set S are those satisfying the negation of the disjunctive normal form,

$$\bigvee_{s \in S} m(s).$$

In this case Theorem 8 is the well-known result that monotone DNF formulae are learnable using membership and equivalence queries [1].

One might be tempted to conjecture that all classes that can be learned by equivalence and membership queries satisfy this poset property. The poset structure would be defined in terms of the expressive power of the class $\mathcal{H}$ of functions considered. Hence, for inputs x and y, we would define,

$$x \preceq y \Leftrightarrow f(x) = 0 \Rightarrow f(y) = 0,$$

for all $f \in \mathcal{H}$. A counterexample to this conjecture is provided by the languages recognized by DFA's, , since for any pair of strings x, y there exist DFA's A and B, such that $A(x) = 0 = B(y)$ and $A(y) = 1 = B(x)$. Hence, x and y are not in the relation $\preceq$, which is thus the identity relation. This means that every string not in a language has to be specified which in turn implies that the obstruction set is not always finite.

Some other classes of functions satisfying the poset structure have been proved to be learnable only with membership queries, as read-once monotone formulas [3] or 2-monotonic positive boolean functions [9]. However, in our case equivalence queries are essential for our algorithm as well as membership queries.

Our learning strategy is known more generally as "Closure Algorithm" for learning intersection-closed concept classes. It is easy to see that the algorithm is robust to noise in the counterexample using the same proof techniques developed in [4].

Our algorithm seems to be strongly representation dependent, meaning that we can learn such a broad class of graphs because is represented by the finite set of obstructions. An interesting open problem is investigating the complexity of learning minor closed graphs classes represented by a formula in Monadic Second Order Logic [5]. We conjecture that the same result does not hold for that representation since is more concise.

6 Acknowledgments

Section 2 was developed together with Hans Bodlaender and James Abello [16]. Thanks to them for useful discussions on early drafts of the paper. The authors would like also to thank Osamu Watanabe and Ricard Gavaldà for helpful comments and interesting conversations while working on the topic.

References

1. D. Angluin. Queries and Concept Learning, *Machine Learning*, 2 (1988) 319–342.
2. D. Angluin. Negative results for equivalence queries. *Machine Learning*, 5 (1990) 121-150.
3. L. Hellerstein, and M. Karpinski. Learning read-once formulas with membership queries. *Proc. of the 2nd COLT*, San Mateo, CA, (1989), 162-174.
4. P. Auer, N. Cesa-Bianchi On-Line Learning with Malicious Noise and the Closure Algorithm *Proc. of the 5th International Workshop on Algorithmic Learning Theory*, LNAI, 872 (1994) 229-247. *To appear in Annals of AI and Mathematics*
5. H.L. Bodlaender. A Tourist Guide through Treewidth, *Acta Cybernetica*, 11 (1993).
6. C. Domingo. Improved Fingerprints, *Unpublished Manuscript*, (1994).
7. R. Gavaldà. On the Power of Equivalence Queries. *Proc. of the First European Conference in Computational Learning Theory*, (1993), 193-203.
8. M.R. Fellows and M.A. Langston. Exploiting RS-posets: Constructive algorithms from nonconstructive tools. Preprint, Feb. 1989.
9. K. Makino and T. Ibaraki. A Fast and Simple Algorithm for Identifying 2-Monotonic Positive Boolean Functions *Technical Report of IEICE, COMP94-46* (1994) 11-20.
10. L. Pitt and M. K. Warmuth, Prediction-Preserving Reducibility *Journal of Computer Science*, 41, (1990), 430-467.
11. N. Robertson and P.D. Seymour. Graph minors. I. Excluding a forest. *J. Comb. Theory Series B*, 35 (1983) 39–61.
12. N. Robertson and P.D. Seymour. Graph minors. III. Planar tree-width. *J. Comb. Theory Series B*, 36 (1984) 49–64.
13. N. Robertson and P.D. Seymour. Graph minors. II. Algorithmic aspects of tree-width. *J. Algorithms*, 7 (1986) 309–322.
14. N. Robertson and P.D. Seymour. Graph minors. V. Excluding a planar graph. *J. Comb. Theory Series B*, 41 (1986) 92–114.
15. N. Robertson and P.D. Seymour. Graph minors. IV. Tree-width and well-quasi-ordering. *J. Comb. Theory Series B*, 48 (1990) 227–254.
16. John Shawe-Taylor, Carlos Domingo, Hans Bodlaender and James Abello, Learning Minor Closed Graph Classes with Membership and Equivalence Queries, *NeuroCOLT Technical Report* NC-TR-94-014, 1994.
17. O. Watanabe. A formal study of learning via queries. *Lecture Notes in Computer Science 443: Proceedings of the 17th ICALP*,M.S.Paterson, ed., Springer-Verlag, (1990) 139-152.
18. O. Watanabe. A framework for polynomial time query learnability *Math. Systems Theory*, 27 (1994) 211–229.

Technical and Scientific Issues of KDD
(or: Is KDD a Science?)

Yves Kodratoff
CNRS, LRI, Bât. 490,
Univ. Paris-Sud, F-91405 Orsay.

Each time a new set of techniques develops, the same pattern of behavior appears inside the world of scientists. They tend to divide in two groups. The conservative one claims that the old techniques were good enough to take care of all problems. The enthusiastic one jumps on the new techniques, develop them, start formalizing them, and, when this stage is achieved, the conservatives start appreciating the new technique, and acknowledge it as a new scientific field. I have several example in mind of this process. The most striking is Statistics which is nowadays becoming even somewhat doctrinal, while, still in the seventies, proper research work was done under the name of Probability Theory, and Statistics was just a "bunch of techniques". More controversial examples, still at present, are Artificial Intelligence (AI) and Fuzzy Set Theory, still widely despised by many orthodox scientists. Both slowly gather scientific recognition by some of the more adventurous people of the conservative group, mainly under the pressure of their applications.

Since **Knowledge Discovery in Databases** (KDD) is born barely some five years ago, it is not surprising that many still claim that it is not a Science but only an engineering topic. During the winter of 95, I presented KDD to French AI specialists. I shown how many new tasks are brought to the fore when doing KDD. To my deep surprise, many of them reacted negatively, telling me that I missed to show why KDD is a new scientific field, that, as was said of Statistics thirty years ago, it is nothing but "a bunch of techniques". The purpose of this paper is to address this question, and more generally to try convincing even the conservative scientists that KDD is indeed a part of Science.

We shall define what KDD is, and we shall analyze its several tasks, especially those that set up new problems to be solved by forthcoming scientific research, not simply by putting together existing techniques.

1 - A DEFINITION OF KDD

Let us follow Fayyad et al. (1995) to define **Data Mining** (DM) as using any kind of algorithm in order to find patterns into the data. DM is thus one step of the more complex process of KDD, which aims at transforming the data (or the information) into knowledge, through a process that begins by accessing the data, follows by mining it, and ends in interpreting it. The algorithms used by DM are usually of two different kinds. They can be more "numeric" oriented, and they stem from Statistics. They can be more "symbolic" oriented, and they stem from **Machine Learning** (ML). In this way, KDD makes use of DM without caring much about the origin of the pattern extractor, it is a KDD problem to make sense of the obtained patterns. Some DM techniques have been concerned by this problem in the past, they can be seen as precursors of KDD.

We must thus insist on the fact that KDD takes care of the whole process of transforming data into knowledge. The word **"knowledge"** itself is obviously badly defined unless a user can define what "makes sense" for him. The KDD process is therefore user and goal oriented. The same user, working in different contexts to achieve different goals, may have different definitions of what is meaningful and useful to him. On the other hand, KDD is supposed to take care of huge amounts of data, thus making automation unavoidable. One touches here *the first paradoxical feature of KDD*. On the one hand it is user-oriented, and the user must be included in the loop which extracts knowledge from the data. On the other hand, the amounts of data are so large that full automation is necessary. This contradiction contains the essence of all the scientific problems issuing from KDD whose role is to manage these contradictory needs.

The goal of all existing techniques, ML, Statistics, but also **Database Management Systems** and **Visualization Systems** is obviously to help the user in handling his data, thus all of them can claim that they have been trying to solve for ever the same problems as KDD does. They have been however developed by very different scientific communities, for some good reasons.

People in Databases are concerned with an efficient management of the data in collecting, updating and retrieving it. The resulting languages, such as SQL queries, are rigorous and efficient, but tend to be hard to use. Moreover, Databases are concerned with deductive queries only (what can I deduce from the data?) and not at all by inductive ones (what can I induce, or learn, or guess from the data?).

Statisticians are also concerned with rigor and efficiency and they obtain strong results that are all biased by this concern. Their results are usually hard to understand (one says that Data Analysis often produces more data than it started from, making it quite difficult for a non-specialist to understand them), and can be even misleading when a non statistician wishes to interpret naively the results of his statistical packages. Statisticians, as opposed to people in Databases, are interested in deductive as well as in inductive reasoning, and one can discover statistically significant previously unknown information from their results. The data they are exclusively dealing with are numeric data.

People in ML address a quite different problem. They are concerned almost exclusively by induction, they do use deduction, but only a tool that can help the overall inductive process. They take into account the concern for comprehensibility: a field expert should understand the results provided by a ML program with fairly little effort. They are dealing usually with symbolic and numeric data, even though they historically begun by using pure symbolic data. Symbolic means here (numbers are indeed symbols!) that the data have a semantics different from the one of numbers. This symbolic data shows relationships expressed by "part-of", "is-a", etc. relations. For instance, expressing that the concept "dolphin" is a ("is-a" relationship) kind of "mammal". This fact, and the inheritance on the properties of a mammal to a dolphin (for instance, one knows even without having met any instance of this behavior, that she-dolphins milk their babies). Some relations have to be expressed by theorems. For instance, expressing that almost all sons have a mother and a father, establishes a relation between the concepts of "son", "mother", and "father" which would be very difficult to describe in a numeric way. These relationships and theorems are often called **domain knowledge**, or **background knowledge**, and part of ML efforts have been to include explicit background knowledge in the inductive process, while Statistics includes it implicitly. Yet another concern of ML is the one of bias. Induction is a very biased process, depending heavily on context, and making explicit the bias of each of the learning programs is an integral part of the ML research program.

With such different concerns, it is quite normal that the three above scientific fields have been evolving in different directions. The *second paradoxical feature of KDD* is that it demands to use in a coordinated way those three scientific fields of various concerns. One cannot seriously argue that one has "just to merge" them. In particular, they evolved knowledge representations that catch different aspects of reality, and that are almost impossible to reconcile without losing the strength of the concerned field. Taking care of these divergent knowledge representations without losing too much efficiency is one of the major problems of KDD, and it has been almost ignored up to now [an exception is found in Lindner and Morik (1995), a similar problem is dealt with in Kodratoff and Vrain (1993)].

It follows that, from a technical point of view, KDD can be seen as standing in the center of a triangle formed by Statistics, ML, and Database management as figure one below illustrates.

Let us now describe the third paradoxical feature of KDD. Statistics, ML and Databases are all three under the pressure of the technical demands, and all three have some links some Cognitive Science. However, it is clear that Databases are strongly user driven. Statistics are also widely used, while ML has found of the order of 100 applications over the world, which is not negligible, but very little as compared to the applications of its two companion domains. On the contrary, many ML specialists have been concerned by the relevance of Cognitive Science, even if this trend has not been enough developed in the past. KDD should put into existence links that are still very weak, and unify those links in such a way that, for instance, one does not start building specific links between Statistics and Cognitive Sciences, but between KDD and Cognitive sciences. This is what we call *third paradoxical feature of KDD* by which KDD is supposed to create and unify the links between existing technologies, the industrial demands, and human ways of

Databases

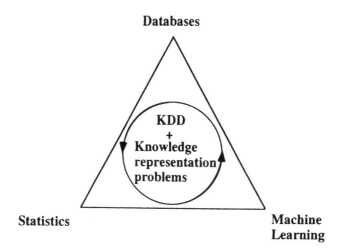

Statistics   **Machine
                                   Learning**

*Figure 1. KDD must merge together Databases, Statistics, and ML which evolved very
different knowledge representation schemes, and which have very different concerns.*

reasoning. The main problem it meets in achieving this goal is the hard problem of **goal-oriented
data mining**. The aim of KDD is to include the user's goals and needs in a ML program, a
statistical package, a DB query. This is implies usually specific **bias** that will lead for industrial
uses, and relative to a human understander. These bias are very implicit in the DBMS and the
statistical packages, somewhat more studied in ML. In none of these fields, however, are solved
the three following problems:

    - express explicitly the induction bias and measure their impact on the result of the learning
systems. This is a problem for DM research.

    - express explicitly the goals of the user. This is typically a cognitive problem since very
often users can hardly express their real goals in words. One needs to analyze their actions to
discover their real goals. This is the issue of interestingness, a topic often dealt with in the KDD
literature.

    - express explicitly what a user can understand of the results of the DM process. This is the
issue of comprehensibility, again a cognitive problem.

    - express the link between a bias (it is often very syntactic) and the user's definitions for
interestingness and comprehensibility, once they are known, since they are usually described in an
entirely different language than the one of the bias.

In other words, KDD can be again seen as central to a kind of triangle, as drawn by figure 2
below.

2 - KNOWLEDGE REPRESENTATION ISSUES

Putting BD into ML.
First/zeroth order problem.
Missing values (use KDD itself to recreate missing values?).

3 - PUTTING STATISTICS INTO ML

Statistics require a model, which is hard to find automatically to feed in the ML system.

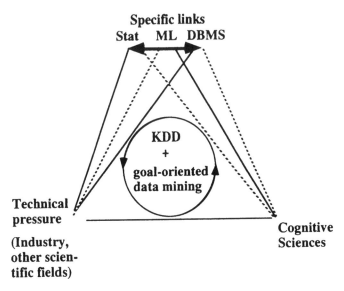

Figure 2. KDD is central to academic research, industry needs, and human understanding. This generates a need for solving the problem of goal-oriented data mining.

4 - PUTTING ML IN STATISTICS

explicit bias: adapting them to the user's needs and goals.
using explicit background knowledge
Definition of background knowledge
    relative to the base
    relative to the data
        classical knowledge (ontology, relations)
        segmentation of data (due to large sets considered)
        reliability of data
        usefulness of extracted knowledge

5 - DEALING WITH ML WEAKNESSES

    cleaning
    pre-clustering

6 - COMPREHENSIBILITY NEED DUE TO INTERACTIVE SYSTEM

        Visualization. A s counter-example to popular belief, when the hidden units are not all connected, i.e., that the NN presents some structure, the visualization of the results obtained by the NN is quite possible. In that case, one can say that NN provides comprehensible results.
    Summarization
    Explanations. Categories of human comprehensible knowledge

7 - INTERESTINGNESS & USEFULNESS

8 - COGNITIVE ISSUES

Elicitation by the analysis of user's actions rather than user's discourse.
User's goal included in the DM software.
User's ability to understand used to post-process the results of DM software.

9 - THEORY

Complexity
Probably Approximately Comprehensible (PACo) theory of learning
Probably Approximately Interesting (PAI) theory of learning

Bibliography

Fayyad et al. (1995)
Lindner and Morik (1995) Lindner G., Morik K. "Coupling a Relational Learning Algorithm with a Database System," Workshop notes of "Statistics, ML, and KDD," Heraklion April 1995.
Kodratoff, Y., Vrain C. "Acquiring first-order knowledge about air-traffic control," Knowledge Acquisition, 5:1-36, 1993.

Analogical Logic Program Synthesis Algorithm That Can Refute Inappropriate Similarities

Ken SADOHARA[1] and Makoto HARAGUCHI[2]

[1] Department of Systems Science Tokyo Institute of Technology
4259 Nagatsuta, Midori-ku Yokohama, 227 Japan
E-mail:sadohara@sys.titech.ac.jp
[2] Division of Electronics and Information Engineering
Hokkaido University N13-W8, kita-ku, Sapporo, 060 Japan
E-mail:makoto@db.huee.hokudai.ac.jp

Abstract. This paper presents an algorithmic learning theory for analogical synthesis of logic programs from their examples. An analogical synthesizer is defined as a kind of inductive inference machine that uses analogy. More precisely speaking, it synthesizes target programs from their examples, given a source program to which the target programs should be similar. One of the difficulties in realizing an efficient analogical synthesizer is to distinguish useless and inappropriate similarities from the other. A similarity is inappropriate if every similar program with respect to the similarity is not correct. If our synthesizer cannot refute such similarities then it would waste computational resources without succeeding to find a desired program.

To cope with this hard problem on analogical synthesis, this paper first applies the notion of refutably inferable class of linear programs, and obtains a basic synthesizer. It has a function of refuting inappropriate similarities. Secondly this paper investigates another method of refuting inappropriate similarities, using an analogous technique that has been employed for theorem proving with abstraction. Incorporating this method into the basic synthesizer, we obtain a more efficient one.

All the synthesizers presented in this paper are proved to identify a similar correct program in the limit, given a source program.

1 Introduction

This paper concerns a new algorithmic learning theory for analogical reasoning of logic programs that is a kind of Logic Program Synthesis from examples (LPS). LPS is a framework for synthesizing a logic program that can explain given examples correctly and has been widely studied by many authors [4, 14, 11, 2]. Most LPS systems construct target programs in a huge search-space and are not so efficient. Some researchers [15, 13, 8] have already pointed out analogy might be helpful to improve LPS systems. Any LPS system using analogy assumes a source program and tries to find a correct program [3] in a space of programs that are similar to the source program. The use of analogy has been therefore

---
[3] A correct program means a program which can explain given examples correctly.

considered useful to reduce the search-space of LPS systems. To refer to such LPS using analogy, we use the term Analogical Logic Program Synthesis (ALPS).

Although ALPS is expected to have such an advantage of efficiency, no studies have proved that the use of analogy really achieves it. Furthermore, there exists a criticism that analogy makes LPS more difficult, for ALPS systems must find not only a correct program but also a similarity. The systems must determine which program is appropriate as a source program and how the correct program is similar to the source program. Even if we admit such a disadvantage, we believe that ALPS is worth investigating because of another role of analogy that is pointed out in [1]. It is the role as a device to shift a bias. A bias is a tendency to select a class of programs from the class of correct programs. Therefore, an ALPS system inheriting the role of analogy enables us to lead the system to identify a desired program, depending on which source program we feed the system. In the case of ordinary LPS systems, a user is supposed not to refuse an unintended program produced by the system, as long as it is correct. If the user further wants to obtain a desired program, he or she has to ask the system designer to change the system's hypothesis space to another one not containing the unintended correct program. Therefore, it is preferable that the system's hypothesis space can be altered depending on users' intention. ALPS systems might be able to perform such an alteration because a source program given by a user biases their hypothesis space. For example, let us consider programs for sorting lists. An ALPS system might be able to identify *insert-sort* program rather than *naive-sort* program, provided we give the system a source program whose structure is similar to *insert-sort*.

Whereas ALPS is worth investigating as mentioned above, very few studies based on a firm theoretical basis have been established. We need a theory for ALPS to analyze various problems on ALPS as precisely as possible and to have a perspective to obtain an efficient ALPS algorithm. From this viewpoint, we have proposed a theory of ALPS and an ALPS algorithm in our previous paper [12]. However, the algorithm is too inefficient to be practical. The purposes of this paper are to consider a crucial problem that makes the algorithm inefficient and to resolve it. To understand the problem, let us look into the search-space of the algorithm. The algorithm must search for a similarity as well as a correct program. In fact, the algorithm searches a two-dimensional space. One dimension is for selecting an appropriate similarity, and the other is for choosing a correct program. Any similarity forms a subspace of similar programs with respect to the similarity. It should be noted here that, if the subspace does not contain any correct program, the corresponding similarity is never useful to purchase a desired correct program. In this sense, a similarity is said to be inappropriate if every program in the subspace defined by the similarity is not correct. To prevent our ALPS algorithm from searching such useless subspaces, the algorithm is expected to decide whether a similarity is inappropriate or not. However, our previous algorithm has not taken the problem of inappropriateness into account, since the decision problem of the inappropriateness seems to be undecidable in general. Consequently, we have designed the algorithm so that it searches even the useless subspaces. This makes our previous ALPS algorithm extremely inefficient.

This paper, on the other hand, proposes two methods to cope with the difficult problems as mentioned above.

First we apply the notion of refutably inferable class of programs, which is introduced by Mukouchi and Arikawa [5]. An LPS algorithm is said to refutably infer a class of programs if the algorithm can effectively decide whether there exists no correct program in the class. Moreover, a class of programs is said to be refutably inferable if there exists an LPS algorithm that refutably infers the class. If every subspace formed by every similarity is refutably inferable then every inappropriate similarity can be refuted. To this end, we adopt the class of linear programs with at most $n \geq 0$ clauses, which is proved to be refutably inferable by Mukouchi and Arikawa. For the class of programs, we present an LPS algorithm that refutably infers every subspace by every similarity. Needless to say, it can work as a method of refuting every inappropriate similarity.

Second we analyze our notion of similarities, and extract a property based on which we have another method to refute inappropriate similarities. It is more efficient than the first method, although it can not refute every inappropriate similarity.

Incorporating these two methods, we obtain an ALPS algorithm for the class of linear programs with at most $n \geq 0$ clauses that can refute inappropriate similarities. We believe that this algorithm can be a basis for future practical ALPS algorithms.

2   Preliminaries

In this section, we briefly review various notions concerning logic programs and introduce some notations. For further details of logic programs, see [3].

For any finite set Σ of function symbols and any finite set Π of predicate symbols, we call the pair $\langle \Sigma, \Pi \rangle$ a *vocabulary*, where constant symbols are treated as function symbols with arity zero. Throughout this paper, we assume a set $\mathcal{V}$ of countably many variables, and a set $\mathcal{C}$ of countably many constant symbols whose elements never appear in any vocabulary. The proof of the later result assumes the existence of a potentially unbounded number of constant symbols which do not appear in the relevant program. This is why we need the set $\mathcal{C}$. We call the elements of $\mathcal{C}$ *special constants*. The use of the special constants has close analogue in the use of logic interpreters such as PROLOG: queries are permitted to use constant symbols which are not employed in a program. In this setting, our assumption seems to be appropriate.

Given a vocabulary V, we define terms, substitutions, atoms and literals constructed from V, $\mathcal{V}$ and $\mathcal{C}$ as usual. A finite set $\{A, \neg B_1, \ldots, \neg B_n\}$ of literals is called a *definite clause*, which is denoted by $A \leftarrow B_1, \ldots, B_n$ in some cases. For any definite clause $C = A \leftarrow B_1, \ldots, B_n$, head($C$) denotes the positive literal A and body(C) denotes the set of atoms $\{B_1, \ldots, B_n\}$. The symbol $\square$ denotes the empty clause. In this paper, we consider only logic programs which are finite sets of definite clauses.

Next we define the notions of subsumption and reduction of clauses which originate from Plotkin [7]. A definite clause C *subsumes* a definite clause D $(C \succeq D)$ iff there exists a substitution θ such that $C\theta \subseteq D$. A definite clause C *properly subsumes* a definite clause D $(C \succ D)$ iff $C \succeq D$ and $D \nsucceq C$. Two definite clauses C and D are called *equivalent* $(C \sim D)$ iff $C \succeq D$ and $D \succeq C$. This relation is an equivalence relation which defines a partition on definite clauses. Every set of equivalent clauses is called a *equivalence class*. A definite clause C is called *reduced* iff for any $C' \subseteq C$, $C' \sim C$ implies $C = C'$. Two definite clauses are called *variants* iff they are equal up to renaming variables. It is proved by Plotkin [7] that if two equivalent clauses both are reduced then they are variants. A logic program P *subsumes* a logic program Q $(P \succeq Q)$ iff for any clause C in Q, there exists a clause D in P such that $D \succeq C$.

For any vocabulary $V = \langle \Sigma, \Pi \rangle$, $\text{Trm}(V)$ denotes the set of terms constructed from Σ, V and C. Similarly, $\text{Sub}(V)$ and $\text{Atm}(V)$ denote the set of substitutions constructed from $\text{Trm}(V)$, the set of atoms constructed from $\text{Trm}(V)$ and Π respectively. Furthermore, $\text{Cls}(V)$ denotes the set of reduced representatives of all equivalence classes on the clauses constructed from V and V. It follows from the definition that for any clauses $C, D \in \text{Cls}(V)$, $C \sim D$ implies $C = D$.

For any set of clauses S, $V(S)$ denotes the vocabulary $\langle \Sigma, \Pi \rangle$, where Σ and Π are the set of function symbols and the set of predicate symbols occurring in S respectively. When we consider several logic programs, we assume that their vocabularies are disjoint.

For any logic program P, $\mathcal{B}(P)$ denotes the *Herbrand base of P*, which is the set of ground atoms in $\text{Atm}(V(P))$. A mapping $T_P : 2^{\mathcal{B}(P)} \rightarrow 2^{\mathcal{B}(P)}$ is defined as follows. For any $I \subseteq \mathcal{B}(P)$,

$$T_P(I) = \left\{ A \in \mathcal{B}(P) \;\middle|\; \begin{array}{l} \text{There exists a ground instance } A \leftarrow B_1, \ldots, B_n \\ \text{of a clause in } P \text{ such that } \{B_1, \ldots, B_n\} \subseteq I \end{array} \right\}$$

Then,

$$T_P \uparrow 0 = \emptyset$$
$$T_P \uparrow n = T_P(T_P \uparrow (n-1)) \text{ for any positive integer } n$$
$$T_P \uparrow \omega = \bigcup_{n<\omega} T_P \uparrow n \text{ for the first transfinite ordinal } \omega$$

$\mathcal{M}(P)$ denotes the *least Herbrand model of P*. It is known that $\mathcal{M}(P) = T_P \uparrow \omega$.

For any mapping ϕ, $\mathcal{D}(\phi)$ denotes the domain of ϕ, and $\phi|S$ denotes the restriction of ϕ to $S \cap \mathcal{D}(\phi)$ for any set S. The image of partial mapping ϕ is defined as $\phi(S) = \{\phi(e) \mid e \in S \cap \mathcal{D}(\phi)\}$ for any set S.

For any substitution $\{X_1/t_1, \ldots, X_n/t_n\}$, if each t_i $(1 \leq i \leq n)$ is a special constant in C then we call it a C-*substitution*. A ground substitution θ is *grounding substitution of a clause* C if $C\theta$ is a ground clause.

For any set S, $\sharp S$ denotes the cardinality of S.

3 Analogical Logic Program Synthesis

In this section, after introducing similarities between logic programs, we formalize the ALPS. Then we introduce a class of the similarities and present an ALPS algorithm for the class. Furthermore, we point out a crucial difficulty in obtaining a practical ALPS algorithm. The contents of this section are based on our previous paper [12], and a result on a more general class of similarities and a more general ALPS algorithm are presented.

Similarities between logic programs are defined as follows.

Definition 1. Let P and Q be logic programs. Let ϕ be a partial mapping from $\mathcal{B}(Q)$ to $\mathcal{B}(P)$. Q is *similar to P w.r.t.* ϕ if

$$\phi(T_Q(I)) \subseteq T_P(\phi(I))$$

for any $I \subseteq \mathcal{B}(Q)$.

The above definition is equivalent to the condition that for any $A \in \mathcal{D}(\phi)$, if A is supported[4] by $I \subseteq \mathcal{B}(Q)$ in Q, then $\phi(A)$ is supported by $\phi(I)$ in P. Intuitively speaking, ϕ preserves logical implications at the ground level. As a result, any computational trace of Q can be simulated by P, provided the trace is successfully mapped. To sum up, the similarities are defined as homomorphisms which partially preserve computational traces. Our notion of the similarities is closely related to the notion of abstraction in [6]. Examples of the similarities are illustrated later.

Using the similarities between logic programs defined above, we define the ALPS as follows.

Definition 2. Let V be a vocabulary. The set $\mathrm{Cls}(V)$ is called a *hypothesis language* and the set of ground atoms in $\mathrm{Atm}(V)$ is called an *observational language*.

Let L_h be a hypothesis language and L_o be an observational language. The set $M \subseteq L_o$ is called a *model of L_h*. For a model M of L_h and a ground atom $\alpha \in L_o$, if $\alpha \in M$ (resp., $\alpha \in M^c$) then $\langle \alpha, \text{true} \rangle$ (resp., $\langle \alpha, \text{false} \rangle$) is called a *fact from M*, where M^c means $L_o \setminus M$. For a model M of L_h, a *presentation of M* is a sequence $\langle \alpha_1, V_1 \rangle, \langle \alpha_2, V_2 \rangle, \ldots$ of facts from M such that $\{\alpha_i \mid \langle \alpha_i, \text{true} \rangle\} = M$ and $\{\alpha_i \mid \langle \alpha_i, \text{false} \rangle\} = M^c$. For sets $T, F \subseteq L_o$, a model M is said to be *consistent with $\langle T, F \rangle$* if $T \subseteq M$ and $F \subseteq M^c$ hold. Furthermore, for sets $T, F \subseteq L_o$, a program P is said to be *consistent with $\langle T, F \rangle$* if $\mathcal{M}(P)$ is consistent with $\langle T, F \rangle$.

Definition 3. Let L_h be a hypothesis language and L_o be an observational language. For any presentation of any model M of L_h, an *LPS algorithm for L_h* is a effective procedure that reads one fact at a time and once in a while produces as output a logic program consisting of clauses in L_h. An LPS algorithm $\mathcal{A}$ is

---

[4] We say that a ground atom $A \in \mathcal{B}(Q)$ is supported by $I \subseteq \mathcal{B}(Q)$ in Q if there exists a ground instance C of a clause in Q such that $\mathrm{head}(C) = A$ and $\mathrm{body}(C) \subseteq I$.

said to *converge to a program* P if $\mathcal{A}$ eventually produces P and never again produces a different program.

For a logic program P, a class $\mathcal{CP}$ of logic programs consisting of clauses in L_h and a class Φ of partial mappings from L_o to $\mathcal{B}(P)$, an LPS algorithm $\mathcal{A}$ for L_h is called an *ALPS algorithm for P, $\mathcal{CP}$ and Φ* if the following condition holds: for any presentation of any model M of L_h, $\mathcal{A}$ converges to a program $Q \in \mathcal{CP}$ such that $\mathcal{M}(Q) = M$ and Q is similar to P w.r.t. a mapping in Φ whenever there exists such a program in $\mathcal{CP}$.

For obtaining an ALPS algorithm, we introduce a class of partial mappings between Herbrand bases. For any mapping ϕ in the class, it is decidable whether a program Q is similar to a program P w.r.t. ϕ.

Definition 4. Let V_1 and V_2 be vocabularies. For total mappings $\phi^T : \mathrm{Trm}(V_1) \to \mathrm{Trm}(V_2)$ and $\phi^A : \mathrm{Atm}(V_1) \to \mathrm{Atm}(V_2) \cup \{\perp\}$ satisfying the following conditions, the pair $\langle \phi^T, \phi^A \rangle$ is called a *substitution-preserving mapping from V_1 to V_2*, where the symbol '$\perp$' does not appear in any vocabulary and $\phi^A(e) = \perp$ means that ϕ^A is not defined for e.

1. ϕ^T and ϕ^A are computable.
2. For any element $e \in V \cup C$, $\phi^T(e) = e$.
3. For any atom $A \in \mathrm{Atm}(V_1)$, $\phi^A(A\theta) = \phi^A(A)\phi^S(\theta)$, where for any substitution $\theta = \{X_1/t_1, \ldots X_n/t_n\} \in \mathrm{Sub}(V_1)$, $\phi^S(\theta) = \{X_1/\phi^A(t_1), \ldots, X_n/\phi^A(t_n)\}$.

In what follows, ϕ^T and ϕ^A are denoted by ϕ if there exists no confusion.

We should notice the following. Firstly, for any atom A and any substitution θ, $\phi(A) = \perp \Leftrightarrow \phi(A\theta) = \perp$ holds from the condition 3. That is, if ϕ is defined to an atom A then ϕ is also defined to any generalization of A and to any specialization of A. Secondly, if A is a ground atom then no variable occurs in $\phi(A)$. Therefore, for any program P and Q, and any substitution-preserving mapping ϕ from $V(Q)$ to $V(P)$, $\phi|\{A \in \mathcal{B}(Q) \mid \phi(A) \neq \perp\}$ is a mapping from $\mathcal{B}(Q)$ to $\mathcal{B}(P)$. In what follows, we may use the restriction without any notice if there exists no confusion.

For example, let us consider the following logic programs *append, plus, insert-sort*[5] and *natural-number*.

$$plus = \begin{cases} \texttt{plus(0, X, X)} \leftarrow \\ \texttt{plus(s(X), Y, s(Z))} \leftarrow \texttt{plus(X, Y, Z)} \end{cases}$$

$$append = \begin{cases} \texttt{append([], X, X)} \leftarrow \\ \texttt{append([A|X], Y, [A|Z])} \leftarrow \texttt{append(X, Y, Z)} \end{cases}$$

$$natural\text{-}number = \begin{cases} \texttt{nn(0)} \leftarrow \\ \texttt{nn(s(X))} \leftarrow \texttt{nn(X)} \end{cases}$$

$$insert\text{-}sort = \begin{cases} \texttt{sort([],[])} \leftarrow \\ \texttt{sort([A|X],Y)} \leftarrow \texttt{sort(X,Z),insert(Z,[A],Y)} \end{cases}$$

---

[5] The clauses for the definition of **insert** is omitted.

Then the following mapping ϕ_1 is a substitution-preserving mapping from $V(append)$ to $V(plus)$ and the following mapping ϕ_2 is a substitution-preserving mapping from $V(insert\text{-}sort)$ to $V(natural\text{-}number)$.

$$\phi_1([]) = 0$$
$$\phi_1([A|B]) = s(\phi_1(B))$$
$$\phi_1(\text{append}(A,B,C)) = \text{plus}(\phi_1(A), \phi_1(B), \phi_1(C))$$

$$\phi_2([]) = 0$$
$$\phi_2([A|B]) = s(\phi_2(B))$$
$$\phi_2(\text{sort}(A,B)) = \text{nn}(\phi_2(A))$$
$$\phi_2(\text{insert}(A,B,C)) = \perp$$

For instance, $\phi_1(\text{append}([], [a], [a])) = \text{plus}(0, s(0), s(0))$, $\phi_2(\text{sort}([2,1],[1,2])) = \text{nn}(s(s(0)))$.

For any substitution-preserving mapping ϕ from V_1 to V_2, we extend ϕ as follows. For any $S \subseteq \text{Atm}(V_1)$, $\phi(S) = \{\phi(A) \mid A \in S \text{ and } \phi(A) \neq \perp\}$, and for any $C \in \text{Cls}(V_1)$,

$$\phi(C) = \begin{cases} \phi(\text{head}(C)) \leftarrow B_1, \ldots, B_n & \text{if } \phi(\text{head}(C)) \neq \perp \\ \perp & \text{otherwise} \end{cases},$$

where $\{B_1, \ldots, B_n\} = \phi(\text{body}(C))$. For any $Q \subseteq \text{Cls}(V_1)$, $\phi(Q) = \{\phi(C) \mid C \in Q \text{ and } \phi(C) \neq \perp\}$. For example, $\phi_1(append) = plus$ and $\phi_2(insert\text{-}sort) = natural\text{-}number$.

The next proposition follows from the definition.

Proposition 5. *Let V_1 and V_2 be vocabularies, and ϕ be a substitution-preserving mapping from V_1 to V_2. For any definite clauses $C, D \in \text{Cls}(V_1)$ such that $C \succeq D$, the following holds.*

1. *$\phi(C) = \perp$ if and only if $\phi(D) = \perp$.*
2. *If $\phi(C) \neq \perp$ and $\phi(D) \neq \perp$ then $\phi(C) \succeq \phi(D)$.*

For substitution-preserving mappings, we obtain the following result.

Theorem 6. *Let Q and P be logic programs, and ϕ a substitution-preserving mapping from $V(Q)$ to $V(P)$. Q is similar to P w.r.t. ϕ iff $P \succeq \phi(Q)$ holds.*

Proof. (if part) For any $I \subseteq \mathcal{B}(Q)$ and any $A \in \phi(T_Q(I))$, there exists a clause $C \in Q$ and a grounding substitution $\theta \in \text{Sub}(V(Q))$ of C such that $\phi(\text{head}(C)\theta) = A$ and $\text{body}(C)\theta \subseteq I$. By the assumption, there exist a clause $D \in P$ and a substitution $\sigma \in \text{Sub}(V(P))$ such that $D\sigma \subseteq \phi(C)$. Thus, $\text{head}(D)\sigma\phi(\theta) = \phi(\text{head}(C)\theta) = A$ and $\text{body}(D)\sigma\phi(\theta) \subseteq \phi(\text{body}(C)\theta) \subseteq \phi(I)$. This means $A \in T_P(\phi(I))$.

(only-if part) We prove it by contraposition. Assume there exists a clause $C \in Q$ such that $D \not\succeq \phi(C)$ for any clause $D \in P$. Then, there exists a grounding C-substitution $\theta \in \text{Sub}(V(P))$ of $\phi(C)$ such that for any clause D in P and any grounding substitution $\sigma \in \text{Sub}(V(P))$ of D, $D\sigma \not\subseteq \phi(C)\theta$. Therefore, $\phi(\text{head}(C))\theta \notin T_P(\phi(\text{body}(C))\theta)$. On the other hand, there exists a ground substitution $\mu \in \text{Sub}(V(Q))$ such that $\theta\mu$ is a grounding substitution of C. If we assume $I = \text{body}(C)\theta\mu$ then $\phi(\text{head}(C)\theta\mu) = \phi(\text{head}(C))\theta \in \phi(T_Q(I))$ and $\phi(I) = \phi(\text{body}(C))\theta$. This means $\phi(T_Q(I)) \not\subseteq T_P(\phi(I))$. □

For example, we can easily confirm the following similarities: *append* is similar to *plus* w.r.t. ϕ_1 and *insert-sort* is similar to *natural-number* w.r.t. ϕ_2.

For any programs P, Q and any substitution-preserving mapping ϕ from $V(Q)$ to $V(P)$, $P \succeq \phi(Q)$ is decidable. Because $P \succeq Q$ is decidable [10] for any programs P, Q. Therefore, we obtain the following enumerative algorithm $\mathcal{ALPS}_1$. Figure 1 illustrates how $\mathcal{ALPS}_1$ searches a two-dimensional search-space by hypotheses and substitution-preserving mappings.

Procedure $\mathcal{ALPS}_1(P, \{Q_i\}_{i \in N}, \{\phi_j\}_{j \in N})$;
begin
$\quad i := 1; j := 1; n := 1;$
$\quad S_{true} := \emptyset; S_{false} := \emptyset;$
$\quad$ **repeat**
$\qquad$ *read-store*(S_{true}, S_{false});
$\qquad$ **if** $P \not\succeq \phi_j(Q_i)$ **or**
$\qquad\quad Q_i$ is not consistent with $\langle S_{true}, S_{false} \rangle$
$\qquad$ **then begin** $j := j - 1; i := i + 1;$ **end;**
$\qquad$ **else** output Q_i and ϕ_j;
$\qquad$ **if** $j < 0$ **then begin**
$\qquad\quad n := n + 1; j := n; i := 1;$
$\qquad$ **end;**
$\quad$ **forever;**
end.

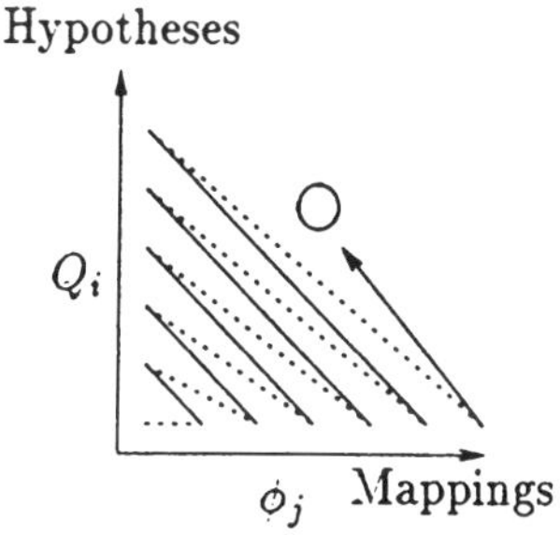

Hypotheses

Q_i

ϕ_j Mappings

Fig.1.

Procedure read-store (S_{true}, S_{false});
begin
$\quad \langle \alpha, V \rangle := $ *read-fact*;
$\quad$ **if** $V = $ true **then** $S_{true} := S_{true} \cup \{\alpha\}$;
$\quad$ **else** $S_{false} := S_{false} \cup \{\alpha\}$;
end.

For the algorithm, we obtain the following theorem easily.

Theorem 7. *Let L_h be a hypothesis language and L_o be an observational language. Let P be a logic program, $\mathcal{CP} = \{Q_i\}_{i \in N}$ a class of programs consisting of clauses in L_h and $\Phi = \{\phi_j\}_{j \in N}$ a class of substitution-preserving mappings from $V(L_h)$ to $V(P)$. $\mathcal{ALPS}_1(P, \mathcal{CP}, \Phi)$ is an ALPS algorithm for P, $\mathcal{CP}$ and Φ if for any finite sets $T, F \subseteq L_o$ and any program $Q \in \mathcal{CP}$, whether Q is consistent with $\langle T, F \rangle$ or not is effectively decidable.*

$\mathcal{ALPS}_1$, however, uses dovetailing in order to search the two-dimensional search-space and this search-strategy makes the algorithm impractical. To remove the difficulty, we now look more carefully into the search-space. Any substitution-preserving mapping forms a subspace of similar programs w.r.t. the mapping. If there exists no correct program in the subspace, the mapping is said to be inappropriate. The inappropriateness is formally defined as follows.

Definition 8. Let L_h be a hypothesis language, L_o be an observational language and $M \subseteq L_o$ be a model of L_h. Let P be a logic program, $\mathcal{CP}$ a class of programs consisting of clauses in L_h. A partial mapping ϕ from L_o to $\mathcal{B}(P)$ is said to be *inappropriate* if every program in CP which is similar to P w.r.t. ϕ is not consistent with $\langle M, M^c \rangle$.

The subspace formed by an inappropriate mapping is useless because every effort to find a solution in the subspace is in vain. In addition, in the case where the subspace is infinite, it is problematic since an algorithm might search the useless subspace infinitely without switching to another subspace. This is why $\mathcal{ALPS}_1$ uses dovetailing. If we have a method of decision whether mappings are inappropriate or not then we can obtain a better ALPS algorithm which does not have to use the dovetailing. The remainder of this paper concerns this method.

4   A Refutably Inferable Algorithm for a Class of Linear Programs

In this section, we give an LPS algorithm that converges to a correct program if the program is in a given class of programs, otherwise it refutes the class and terminates.

Such an algorithm is introduced by Mukouchi and Arikawa [5]. It is defined as follows.

Definition 9. Let L_h be a hypothesis language and CP be a class of programs consisting of clauses in L_h. An LPS algorithm $\mathcal{A}$ for L_h is said to *refutably infer* CP if $\mathcal{A}$ satisfies the following condition: for any presentation of any model M of L_h, if there exists a program $Q \in CP$ such that $\mathcal{M}(Q) = M$, then $\mathcal{A}$ converges to $Q' \in CP$ such that $\mathcal{M}(Q') = \mathcal{M}(Q)$, otherwise $\mathcal{A}$ produces 'refutation' sign and terminates. A class CP is said to be *refutably inferable* if there exists an LPS algorithm for L_h that refutably infers CP.

Mukouchi and Arikawa [5] showed an algorithm that refutably infers the class of length bounded EFSs with at most $n \geq 0$ clauses. As they pointed out, their arguments for the class are valid for the class of linear programs with at most $n \geq 0$ clauses. Linear programs are defined as follows.

Definition 10. A clause $A \leftarrow B_1, \ldots, B_n$ is *linear* if $|A\theta| \geq |B_i\theta|$ for any substitution θ and any $i = 1, \ldots, n$. A program P is *linear* if clauses in P are all linear.

In the above definition, $|A|$ denotes the total number of occurrences of variables and function symbols in A. According to the literature [17], for any atom A and B, and any substitution θ, $|A\theta| \geq |B\theta|$ holds if and only if $|A| \geq |B|$ and $o(X, A) \geq o(X, B)$ for any variable X, where $o(X, A)$ is the number of all occurrences of X in A. Therefore it is decidable whether a definite clause is linear or not.

For any linear clause, we obtain the following result.

Proposition 11. *For any linear clause C, the following holds.*

1. C *is reduced.*
2. *For any substitution θ, $C\theta$ is linear.*

In the remainder of this section, we consider an algorithm that refutably infers the class of linear programs with at most $n \geq 0$ clauses. Whereas Mukouchi and Arikawa's algorithm is a simple enumerative method, our algorithm makes use of the contradiction backtracing algorithm and the notion of refinements of clauses developed by Shapiro [14]. We begin by defining a refinement operator for linear clauses.

In this and all subsequent section, we fix a vocabulary $\langle \Sigma, \Pi \rangle$ and denotes the set of linear clauses in $\mathrm{Cls}(\langle \Sigma, \Pi \rangle)$ by $\mathcal{LC}$ and the set of ground atoms in $\mathrm{Atm}(\langle \Sigma, \Pi \rangle)$ by L_o. For any $n \geq 0$ and any $H \subseteq \mathcal{LC}$, H^n denotes the set $\{P \subseteq H \mid \sharp P = n\}$ and $H^{\leq n}$ denotes $\bigcup_{i=0}^{n} H^i$. Furthermore, for any $\ell \geq 0$ and any $S \subseteq \mathcal{LC}$, $S(\ell)$ denotes the set $\{C \in S \mid \ell \geq |\mathrm{head}(C)|\}$.

Definition 12. A mapping $\rho : \mathcal{LC} \to 2^{\mathcal{LC}}$ is called a *refinement operator for $\mathcal{LC}$* if $\forall C \in \mathcal{LC} \ \forall D \in \rho(C)$, $C \succ D$ holds and $\rho(C)(\ell)$ is computable for any $\ell \geq 0$.

For any refinement operator ρ and any clauses $C, D \in \mathcal{LC}$, we define an ordering $C \succ_\rho D$ iff there exists a finite chain $C = C_0, C_1, \ldots, C_n = D$ such that $C_{i+1} \in \rho(C_i)$ for any $0 \leq i \leq n-1$. In addition, we define an ordering $C \succeq_\rho D$ iff either $C \succ_\rho D$ or $C = D$ holds for any refinement operator ρ and any clauses $C, D \in \mathcal{LC}$,

We can see the following result for refinement operators for $\mathcal{LC}$.

Proposition 13. *For any refinement operator ρ for $\mathcal{LC}$, the following holds.*

1. *For any $C, D \in \mathcal{LC}$, $C \succ_\rho D$ implies $|\mathrm{head}(D)| \geq |\mathrm{head}(C)|$.*
2. *There exists no infinite descending chain $C_0, C_1, C_2, \ldots$ such that $C_i \in \rho(C_{i+1})$ for any $i \geq 0$.*

For instance, there exists the following refinement operator ρ_0 for $\mathcal{LC}$.

Definition 14. For any $C, D \in \mathcal{LC}$, $D \in \rho_0(C)$ iff one of the following conditions holds:

1. D and $C \cdot \{X/Y\}$ are variants, where X and Y are distinct variables occurring in C.
2. D and $C \cdot \{X/f(X_1, \ldots, X_n)\}$ are variants, where $f \in \Sigma$ is a function symbol with arity n, X is a variable occurring in C and all X_i's $(1 \leq i \leq n)$ are distinct variables not occurring in C.
3. D and $C \cup \{\neg B\}$ are variants, where $\neg B \notin C$, $|\mathrm{head}(C)| \geq |B|$ and $o(X, \mathrm{head}(C)) \geq o(X, B)$ for any variable $X \in \mathcal{V}$.
4. $C = \square$ and $D = p(X_1, \ldots, X_n) \leftarrow$, where $p \in \Pi$ is a predicate symbol with arity n and all X_i's $(1 \leq i \leq n)$ are distinct variables.

Proposition 15. ρ_0 *is a refinement operator for $\mathcal{LC}$.*

For this refinement operator ρ_0, we obtain the following result.

Theorem 16. *For any clause $C, D \in \mathcal{LC}$, $C \succ D$ if and only if $C \succ_{\rho_0} D$.*

Proof sketch. (if part) It follows from the definition of refinement operators.

(only-if part) Using Proposition 11, we can generalize Theorem 4 in [9] and obtain the following. (1) For any clauses $C, D \in \mathcal{LC}$ such that $C \neq D$, $\exists \theta \ C\theta = D$ implies $C \succ_{\rho_0} D$.

In addition, we can obtain the following. (2) For any clauses $C, D \in \mathcal{LC}$, $C \subset D$ implies $C \succ_{\rho_0} D$. Because for any $1 \leq i \leq n - 1$, we see $C \cup R_i$ is a reduced linear clause by Proposition 11 and $C \cup R_{i+1} \in \rho_0(C \cup R_i)$ by the third condition in the definition of ρ_0, where $D \setminus C = \{A_1, \ldots, A_n\}$ and $R_i = \{A_1, \ldots, A_i\}$ for any $1 \leq i \leq n$.

By adding (1) and (2) we complete the proof. □

We can see that ρ_0 is complete for $\mathcal{LC}$ in the sense of Shapiro [14], i.e. $\square \succeq_\rho C$ for any clause $C \in \mathcal{LC}$. However, the result says a stronger property of ρ_0, which is called strong completeness by Van der Laag and Nienhuys-Cheng [16]. We mention the usefulness of the property in the next section.

Next we introduce a notion corresponding to Shapiro's [14] notion of the source set of a marking.

Definition 17. Let ρ be a refinement operator for $\mathcal{LC}$ and m a finite set of clauses in $\mathcal{LC}$. For any $H \subseteq \mathcal{LC}$, H_ρ^m denotes the set

$$\{C \in H \mid C \notin m \text{ and } \forall D \in H, \ D \succ_\rho C \Rightarrow D \in m\}$$

Intuitively speaking, m means a set of false clauses and H_ρ^m means the set of maximal clauses with respect to $\succ_\rho$ which are not false. For H_ρ^m, the following holds.

Proposition 18. *Let ρ be a refinement operator for $\mathcal{LC}$ and m a finite set of clauses in $\mathcal{LC}$. For any $H \subseteq \mathcal{LC}$ and any $l \geq 0$, the following holds.*

1. *The set $H_\rho^m(l)$ is a finite set and computable.*
2. *For any $C \in H(l)$, if $C \notin m$ holds then there exists $D \in H_\rho^m(l)$ such that $D \succeq_\rho C$.*

Now we present an algorithm that can refutably infer $H^{\leq n}$ for any $n \geq 0$ and any $H \subseteq \mathcal{LC}$. In the following algorithm, we assume a refinement operator ρ for $\mathcal{LC}$. The procedure contradiction-backtrace $(H_\rho^m(l), S_{true}, S_{false})$ in the algorithm is Shapiro's *contradiction backtracing algorithm* [14]. The procedure returns a false clause in $H_\rho^m(l)$, i.e. a clause $C \in H_\rho^m(l)$ such that head$(C)\theta \in S_{false}$ and body$(C)\theta \subseteq S_{true}$ for some grounding substitution θ of C.

Procedure $\mathcal{RILPS}(n, H)$;
begin
    $S_{true} := \emptyset$; $S_{false} := \emptyset$; $m := \{\square\}$;
    read-store (S_{true}, S_{false});

$$\textbf{while } S_{true} = \emptyset \textbf{ do begin} \qquad\qquad (1)$$

    output {};

    read-store (S_{true}, S_{false});

end;

$T_0 := S_{true}$; $F_0 := S_{false}$;

for $k = 1$ **to** n **do begin**

  $\ell_k := \max\{|\alpha| \mid \alpha \in T_{k-1}\}$;

  repeat $\qquad\qquad\qquad\qquad\qquad\qquad\qquad\qquad\qquad\qquad (2)$

      $P :=$ make-consistent-program $(H, m, k, \ell_k, S_{true}, S_{false})$;

      while $P \neq$ 'refutation' **and** P is consistent with $\langle S_{true}, S_{false} \rangle$ **do begin**

         output P; read-store (S_{true}, S_{false});

      end;

    until $P =$ 'refutation';

    $T_k = S_{true}$; $F_k = S_{false}$;

  end;

  output 'refutation';stop;

end.

Procedure make-consistent-program $(H, m, k, \ell_k, S_{true}, S_{false})$;

begin

  while $S_{false} \cap \mathcal{M}(H_\rho^m(\ell_k)) \neq \emptyset$ **do begin** $\qquad\qquad\qquad (3)$

    $C :=$ contradiction-backtrace$(H_\rho^m(\ell_k), S_{true}, S_{false})$;

    $m := m \cup \{C\}$;

  end;

  if $\exists P \subseteq H_\rho^m(\ell_k)$, $\sharp P = k$ **and** $S_{true} \subseteq \mathcal{M}(P)$ $\qquad\qquad (4)$

  then return(P); **else return**('refutation');

end.

We should notice that for any program $P \subseteq \mathcal{LC}$ and any ground atom $A \in L_o$, whether $A \in \mathcal{M}(P)$ holds or not is decidable [17]. Thus for any finite sets $T, F \subseteq L_o$, whether P is consistent with $\langle T, F \rangle$ or not is also decidable.

    For the algorithm, we obtain the following results.

Lemma 19 (Mukouchi et al. [5]). *Let H be a subset of $\mathcal{LC}$ and $n \geq 1$ be an integer. Let $T \subseteq L_o$ be a nonempty finite set, $F \subseteq L_o$ a finite set and $\ell = \max\{|A| \mid A \in T\}$. If any $P \in H^{n-1}$ is not consistent with $\langle T, F \rangle$, then any $P' \in H^n \setminus H^n(\ell)$ is not consistent with $\langle T, F \rangle$.*

Lemma 20. *The procedure make-consistent-program$(H, m, k, \ell_k, S_{true}, S_{false})$ returns 'refutation' sign iff any $Q \in H^k(\ell_k)$ is not consistent with $\langle S_{true}, S_{false} \rangle$.*

Proof sketch. (if part) It is clear because the while-loop (3) always terminates and the condition (4) never holds by the assumption.

    (only-if part) It suffices to show that the condition (4) holds if there exists a program $Q \in H^k(\ell_k)$ which is consistent with $\langle S_{true}, S_{false} \rangle$. Let Q be $\{C_1, \ldots, C_k\}$. Then by Proposition 18, for any $1 \leq i \leq k$, there exists $C_i' \in H_\rho^m(\ell_k)$ such that $C_i' \succ_\rho C_i$ since $C_i \notin m$. Let P be $\{C_1', \ldots C_k'\} \subseteq H_\rho^m(\ell_k)$. Clearly, $S_{true} \subseteq \mathcal{M}(Q) \subseteq \mathcal{M}(P)$ and this completes the proof. $\qquad \square$

Theorem 21. *For any $n \geq 0$ and any $H \subseteq \mathcal{LC}$, $\mathcal{RILPS}(n, H)$ refutably infers the class $H^{\leq n}$.*

Proof sketch. By mathematical induction on k, we can show that if T_k and F_k are defined then any program in H^k is not consistent with $\langle T_k, F_k \rangle$ as follows. (i) In case $k = 0$, it is clear because T_0 is not empty and $\mathcal{M}(\{\}) = \emptyset$. (ii) In case $k \geq 1$, we assume that T_k and F_k are defined. Then we see that T_{k-1} and F_{k-1} are also defined, and by induction hypothesis, any program in H^{k-1} is not consistent with $\langle T_{k-1}, F_{k-1} \rangle$. By Lemma 19, any program in $H^k \setminus H^k(\ell_k)$ is not consistent with $\langle T_{k-1}, F_{k-1} \rangle$. Since $T_{k-1} \subseteq T_k$ and $F_{k-1} \subseteq F_k$, any program in $H^k \setminus H^k(\ell_k)$ is not not consistent with $\langle T_k, F_k \rangle$. In addition, by Lemma 20, any program in $H^k(\ell_k)$ is not consistent with $\langle T_k, F_k \rangle$.

In case there exits a correct program $P \in H^{\leq n}$, let k be $\sharp P$. Then by the above result, T_k and F_k is not defined. This means that and either loop (1) or (2) never terminates and the algorithm converges to a correct program.

In case there exists no correct program in $H^{\leq n}$. By Lemma 20, after the procedure make-consistent-program returns 'refutation' n times, $\mathcal{RILPS}(n, H)$ outputs 'refutation' sign and terminates. $\qquad\Box$

5 Refuting inappropriate similarities

In this section, we illustrate how the algorithm $\mathcal{RILPS}(n, \mathcal{LC})$ refutes inappropriate similarities. In addition, we consider a case that inappropriate similarities are refuted more easily using a property of our notion of similarities.

Definition 22. Let ϕ be an substitution-preserving mapping and P a logic program. The set $\{C \in \mathcal{LC} \mid \phi(C) = \bot \text{ or } \exists D \in P, D \succeq \phi(C)\}$ is denoted by $\mathcal{LC}[P, \phi]$.

We see that $\mathcal{LC}[P, \phi]^{\leq n}$ is the set of programs in $\mathcal{LC}^{\leq n}$ which are similar to P w.r.t. ϕ. Therefore if the algorithm $\mathcal{RILPS}(n, \mathcal{LC}[P, \phi])$ refutes $\mathcal{LC}[P, \phi]^{\leq n}$ then ϕ is inappropriate. In the following, we illustrate how the algorithm refutes $\mathcal{LC}[P, \phi]^{\leq n}$ for a concrete program P and a concrete mapping ϕ.

Let us consider a case that an ALPS algorithm synthesizes *plus* given *append* as a source program. Let a substitution-preserving mapping ϕ_3 from $V(plus)$ to $V(append)$ be as follows.

$$\phi_3(0) = []$$
$$\phi_3(s(A)) = [[] | \phi_3(A)]$$
$$\phi_3(plus(A, B, C)) = append(\phi_3(C), \phi_3(B), \phi_3(A))$$

For example, $\phi_3(plus(0, s(0), s(0))) = append([[]], [[]], [])$.
Then we can see $\mathcal{LC}[append, \phi_3] = \{C \in \mathcal{LC} \mid C_1 \succeq C \text{ or } C_2 \succeq C\}$ because of Proposition 5, where

$$C_1 = plus(X, X, 0) \leftarrow$$
$$C_2 = plus(s(Z), Y, s(X)) \leftarrow plus(Z, Y, X)$$

and $\mathcal{LC}$ denotes the set of linear clauses in $\mathrm{Cls}(\mathrm{V}(plus))$. If we denotes the set of maximal clauses $\{C \in \mathcal{LC}[P, \phi] \mid \forall D \in \mathcal{LC}[P, \phi] \; D \not\succ C\}$ by $\phi^{-1}(P)$ then $\phi_3^{-1}(append) = \{C_1, C_2\}$.

Now we illustrate how the algorithm $\mathcal{RILPS}(2, \mathcal{LC}[append, \phi_3])$ refutes the class $\mathcal{LC}[append, \phi_3]^{\leq 2}$ when the algorithm uses the refinement operator ρ_0 for $\mathcal{LC}$. First we should notice that by virtue of the strong completeness of ρ_0, $\mathcal{LC}[append, \phi_3]_{\rho_0}^m = \phi_3^{-1}(append)$ holds when $m = \emptyset$. That is, using ρ_0, any clause in $\mathcal{LC}[P, \phi]$ is reachable from a clause in $\phi^{-1}(P)$ on account of the strong completeness. After reading the fact $\langle plus(0, s(0), s(0)), true\rangle$, the algorithm sets k to 1 and ℓ_k to 6. Then the procedure make-consistent-program returns 'refutation' sign because neither $\mathcal{M}(C_1)$ nor $\mathcal{M}(C_2)$ are consistent with $\langle S_{true}, S_{false}\rangle$. Therefore the algorithm sets k to 2. However the procedure make-consistent-program returns 'refutation' sign again because $\mathcal{M}(\{C_1, C_2\})$ is not consistent with $\langle S_{true}, S_{false}\rangle$. Thus the algorithm $\mathcal{RILPS}(2, \mathcal{LC}[append, \phi_3])$ refutes $\mathcal{LC}[append, \phi_3]^{\leq 2}$ and ϕ_3 is inappropriate.

By the way, there exists another easier way of decision whether ϕ_3 is inappropriate or not. This method is based on the following property of our notion of similarities.

Theorem 23 (Sadohara et al. [12]). *Let P and Q be logic programs. Let ϕ be a partial mapping from $\mathcal{B}(Q)$ to $\mathcal{B}(P)$. If Q is similar to P w.r.t. ϕ then $\phi(\mathcal{M}(Q)) \subseteq \mathcal{M}(P)$.*

On account of this theorem, we see that every similar program w.r.t. ϕ_3 never proves $A = plus(0, s(0), s(0))$. Because $\phi_3(A) = append([[]], [[]], []) \notin \mathcal{M}(append)$. Therefore there exists no correct program in $\mathcal{LC}[append, \phi_3]^{\leq 2}$ and ϕ_3 is inappropriate. In this way, the ALPS algorithm can decide that a mapping ϕ is inappropriate whenever the algorithm finds a ground atom $A \in S_{true}$ such that $\phi(A)$ is not proved by a given source program.

6 An ALPS Algorithm for a Class of Linear Programs

On the basis of arguments in the preceding two sections, we show the following ALPS algorithm for the class of linear programs with at most $n \geq 0$ clauses that can refute inappropriate similarities.

Procedure $\mathcal{ALPS}_2(n, P, \{\phi_i\}_{i \in N})$;
begin
   $S_{true} := \emptyset$; $S_{false} := \emptyset$; $m := \{\Box\}$; $i := 1$;
   read-store (S_{true}, S_{false});
   while $S_{true} = \emptyset$ **do begin**
      output $\{\}$ and ϕ_i;
      read-store (S_{true}, S_{false});
   end;
   repeat
      $T_0 := S_{true}$; $F_0 := S_{false}$;

if $\phi_i(A) = \perp$ or $\phi_i(A) \in \mathcal{M}(P)$ for all $A \in S_{true}$ then begin
  for $k = 1$ to n do begin   (1)
    $\ell_k := \max\{|\alpha| \mid \alpha \in T_{k-1}\};$
    repeat
      $P := $ make-consistent-program $(\mathcal{LC}[P, \phi_i], m, k, \ell_k, S_{true}, S_{false});$
      while $P \neq$ 'refutation' and P is consistent with $\langle S_{true}, S_{false}\rangle$ do
        begin
          output P and ϕ_i; read-store $(S_{true}, S_{false});$
          if $\phi_i(A) \neq \perp$ and $\phi_i(A) \notin \mathcal{M}(P)$ for some $A \in S_{true}$
          then exit the for-loop (1)
        end;
      until $P = $ 'refutation';
      $T_k := S_{true};\ F_k := S_{false};$
    end;
  end;
  $i := i + 1;$
 forever;
end.

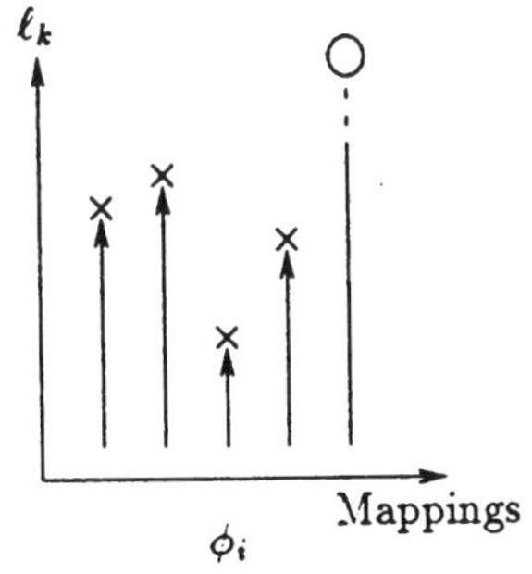

Fig. 2.

Theorem 24. *Let P be a logic program and $\Phi = \{\phi_i\}_{i \in N}$ a class of substitution-preserving mapping from $V(\mathcal{LC})$ to $V(P)$. $\mathcal{ALPS}_2(n, P, \Phi)$ is an ALPS algorithm for P, $\mathcal{LC}^{\leq n}$ and Φ.*

Proof sketch. $\mathcal{LC}[P, \phi_i]^{\leq n}$ is the set of programs in $\mathcal{LC}^{\leq n}$ which are similar to P w.r.t. ϕ_i. Furthermore, the algorithm $\mathcal{RILPS}(n, \mathcal{LC}[P, \phi_i])$ refutably infers $\mathcal{LC}[P, \phi_i]^{\leq n}$ for any $i \geq 1$, and this completes the proof. □

Figure 2 illustrates how the algorithm $\mathcal{ALPS}_2(n, P, \Phi)$ searches a collection of subspaces $\mathcal{LC}[P, \phi_1]^{\leq n}, \mathcal{LC}[P, \phi_2]^{\leq n}, \ldots$.

7 Conclusions

We have presented a theory of ALPS and showed an enumerative ALPS algorithm. From the consideration of the algorithm, we pointed out a crucial difficulty in obtaining a practical ALPS algorithm, namely refuting inappropriate similarities. To refute such similarities, we have investigated two methods. One is based on the fact that the class of linear programs with at most $n \geq 0$ clauses is refutably inferable. The other is based on a property of our notion of similarities. Incorporating these two methods, we have obtained another ALPS algorithm for the class of linear programs with at most $n \geq 0$ clauses that can refute inappropriate similarities.

There remain future researches such as the implementation of the ALPS algorithm and experiments to show the usefulness of ALPS.

References

1. Bipin Indurkhya. On the role of interpretive analogy in learning. In *Proc. 1st Internat. Workshop on Algorithmic Learning Theory*, pages 174–189, 1990.
2. Hiroki Ishizaka. Model inference incorporating generalization. *Journal of Information Processing*, 11(3):206–211, 1988.
3. J.W. Lloyd. *Foundations of Logic Programming*. Springer-Verlag, second edition, 1987.
4. Stephen Muggleton. Inductive logic programming. In *Inductive Logic Programming*, pages 3–27. ACADEMIC PRESS, 1992.
5. Yasuhito Mukouchi and Setsuo Arikawa. Towards a mathematical theory of machine discovery from facts. *Theoretical Computer Science*, 137:53–84, 1995.
6. David A. Plaisted. Theorem proving with abstraction. *Artificial Intelligence*, 16:47–108, 1981.
7. G.D. Plotkin. A note on inductive generalization. In *Machine Intelligence 5*, pages 153–163. Edinburgh University Press, 1970.
8. Luc De Raedt and Maurice Bruynooghe. Interactive concept-learning and constructive induction by analogy. *Machine Learning*, 8:107–150, 1992.
9. J.C. Reynolds. Transformational systems and the algebraic structure of atomic formulas. In *Machine Intelligence 5*, pages 135–153. Edinburgh University Press, 1970.
10. J.A. Robinson. A machine-oriented logic based on the resolution principle. *Journal of the Association for Computing Machinery*, 12:13–41, Mach. 1965.
11. Céline Rouveirol. Extension of inversion of resolution applied to theory completion. In *Inductive Logic Programming*, pages 64–92. ACADEMIC PRESS, 1992.
12. Ken Sadohara and Makoto Haraguchi. Analogical logic program synthesis from examples. In *Proc. 8th European Conference on Machine Learning*, Lecture Notes in Artificial Intelligence Vol. 914, pages 232–244. Springer-Verlag, 1995.
13. Seiichiro Sakurai and Makoto Haraguchi. Towards learning by abstraction. In *Proc. 2nd Internat. Workshop on Algorithmic Learning Theory*, pages 288–298, 1991.
14. Ehud Y. Shapiro. Inductive inference of theories from facts. Technical Report 192, Yale University Computer Science Dept., 1981.
15. Birgit Tausend and Siegfried Bell. Analogical reasoning for logic programming. In *Inductive Logic Programming*, pages 397–408. ACADEMIC PRESS, 1992.
16. Patrick R.J. van der Laag and Shan-Hwei Nienhuys-Cheng. Subsumption and refinement in model inference. In *Proc. 6th European Conference on Machine Learning*, pages 95–114. Springer-Verlag, 1993.
17. Akihiro Yamamoto. Procedural semantics and negative information of elementary formal system. *J. Logic Programming*, 13:89–97, 1992.

Reflecting and Self-Confident
Inductive Inference Machines*

Klaus P. Jantke

Hochschule für Technik, Wirtschaft und Kultur Leipzig (FH)
Fachbereich Informatik, Mathematik & Naturwissenschaften
P.O.Box 66, 04251 Leipzig, Germany
janos@informatik.th-leipzig.de

Abstract. Reflection denotes someones activity of thinking about one-self as well as about one's relation to the outside world. In particular, reflecting means pondering about ones capabilities and limitations. Reasoning about ones competence is a central issue of reflective behaviour. Reflection is a key issue of recent artificial intelligence.

There is investigated the problem of automated reasoning about the competence of inductive inference machines. Reflective inductive inference machines are those which are able to identify whether or not some information presented exceeds its learning capabilities. An inductive inference machine is self-confident, if it usually trusts in its ability to solve the learning problem on hand. It is reflecting and self-confident, if it normally believes in its power, but recognizes problems exceeding its competence. The problem is formalized and studied within the setting of inductively learning total recursive functions. There is a crucial distinction of immediately reflecting inductive inference machines and those which need an a priori unknown amount of time for reasoning about its competence.

The core result is a characterization of problem classes solvable by reflective inductive inference machines. Roughly speaking, for a given problem class $U \subseteq \mathcal{R}$, one may develop a reflecting and self-confident inductive inference machine, if and only if the development of such a machine is not necessary at all, as the problem class can be reasonably extended such that reflection turns out to be unnecessary. A derived result exhibits that, in contrast to intuition, there is no difference in power between reflecting and immediately reflecting inductive inference machines.

The ultimate goal of the present paper is to contribute to a better understanding of the reflection problem in artificial intelligence. The present paper is intended to be a launching pad for this endeavor.

* The work has been partially supported by the German Federal Ministry for Research and Technology (BMFT) within the Joint Project (BMFT-Verbundprojekt) **GOSLER** on **Algorithmic Learning for Knowledge-Based Systems** under contract no. 413-4001-01 IW 101 A. A preliminary version of the approach and some basic results has been printed as GOSLER Report # 24/94, September 1994.

1 Motivation

The development of knowledge-based systems is an exciting area of research and applications. With the growing complexity of application domains for AI systems, there is a growing need for control. But simultaneously, the growth in complexity makes AI systems less controlable. This bears abundant evidence of the need for computer support in system supervision and even for computer self-control.

Reflection denotes someones activity of thinking about oneself as well as about one's relation to the outside world. In particular, reflecting means pondering about ones capabilities and limitations. Reasoning about ones competence is a central issue of reflective behaviour.

According to the importance of reflection for artificial intelligence, there had been launched an ESPRIT Basic Research Action P3178 entitled REFLECT on Knowledge Level Reflection: Specifications and Architectures. The interested reader is directed to [vHABS+92] and [vHW92], in this respect. The present approach has also been based on a critical inspection of the basic REFLECT publications [vHABS+92], [vHW92], and [Kar94] known to the author.

Essentially, there is a need for reflective AI systems which "know" about its competence, i.e. both its power and its limitations. Obviously, the research into reflective AI systems is one of the most fundamental and challenging areas of recent artificial intelligence research. The ESPRIT Basic Research Action RE-FLECT comprised a remarkable research capacity towards reflecting systems in artificial intelligence (cf. [vHABS+92]).

The state of the art is still unsatisfactory, and most AI systems are not reflecting at all. This bears witness to the need of research endeavours into the essentials of automating reflective behaviour.

In well-formalized areas of theoretical computer science, one may even formally demonstrate and prove that reflection has a remarkable impact on the power of those systems being reflective. In recursion theory, for instance, versions of the recursion theorem (cf. [Rj67], [MY74]) represent reflection. One of the most impressive and powerful tools using reflection is the so-called operator recursion theorem (cf. [Cas74], [Cas94]).

However, reflection remains one of the most difficult issues of artificial intelligence. In particular, there is not much knowledge about reflecting learning algorithms which know explicitly about its competence. A learning algorithm should be called reflecting, if either it is able to solve a learning problem faced to or it can discover the fact that a particular problem on hand is exceeding its capabilities. It seems highly desirable to equip learning algorithms with the ability of reflection. Basically, there are two different approaches: Pessimistic algorithms usually assume to be unable to solve a given learning problem. In particular cases, they recognize its competence to solve a problem finally. Optimistic algorithms originally trust in its ability to solve problems. To them, reflection means to reject unsolvable problems after a certain time of pondering.

Algorithms of the latter type behave somehow self-confidently. In the present paper, we decided to investigate the phenomenon of reflection and self-confidence in a well-understood and widely formalized area of learning theory to come up with precise and formally verified results. The area under consideration is recursion-theoretic inductive inference. Our ultimate goal is to contribute to a better understanding of the reflection problem in artificial intelligence. The present paper is intended to be a launching pad for this endeavor.

2 Notions and Notations

We adopt most notions and notations from recursion theory. [Rj67] and [MY74] are excellent references in this respect. Only a few abbreviations will be used. $I\!N$ describes the set of natural numbers. Recursive functions are defined upon $I\!N$. For arbitrary arity $n \in I\!N$, the class of total recursive and partial recursive n-ary functions is denoted by $\mathcal{R}^n$ and $\mathcal{P}^n$, respectively. The upper index $n = 1$ will be usually dropped. Functions to be learned will be presented by sequences of input/output examples. Those sequences will be presented with respect to some underlying ordering. For simplicity, we consider only repetition-free and complete sequences of natural numbers, i.e. permutations of the standard ordering $X_0 = \{0, 1, 2, \ldots\}$. The collection of all those orderings is denoted by $\mathcal{F}(I\!N)$. As models of computability, we except every approach which may be formalized by any acceptable programming system. Those programming systems are usually called GÖDEL numberings. All those GÖDEL numberings of the n-ary partial recursive functions are collected in $G\ddot{o}^n$. Again, the upper index $n = 1$ will be usually dropped. Particular GÖDEL numberings are denoted by φ. Given any $\varphi \in G\ddot{o}$, every index $i \in I\!N$ describes some partial recursive function $\varphi_i \in \mathcal{P}$. For any function $f \in \mathcal{P}$ and any argument $x \in I\!N$, the notation $f(x) \downarrow$ means that f is defined on x. Otherwise, one writes $f(x) \uparrow$. $\mathcal{R}$ and $\mathcal{P}$ may be generalized to $\mathcal{TF}$ and $\mathcal{PF}$ denoting the class of all total resp. partial functions from $I\!N$ into $I\!N$ which do not need to be computable. It follows the underlying learning scenario:

Any total recursive function $f \in \mathcal{R}$ (the object to be identified eventually) is presented according to some arrangement $X \in \mathcal{F}(I\!N)$ of arguments, i.e. f is specified in the limit by $((x_0, f(x_0)), (x_1, f(x_1)), (x_2, f(x_2)), (x_3, f(x_3)), \ldots)$. Initial seqments $((x_0, f(x_0)), \ldots, (x_n, f(x_n)))$ of such a sequence are abbreviated by $f_X[n]$. Furthermore, one may assume any bijective encoding of these initial segments. For simplicity, we consider $f_X[n]$ as a natural number uniquely encoding the corresponding finite list of input/output examples. In dependence on the class of admissible information arrangements X, we choose different encoding to get surjective mappings. This allows us to view inference algorithms as partial recursive functions getting fed in information about some target function $f \in \mathcal{R}$ to be learned as natural numbers encoding $f_X[0], f_X[1], f_X[2], f_X[3], \ldots$. If one restricts the attention to the standard arrangement $X_0 \in \mathcal{F}(I\!N)$ of arguments, only, the index X may be dropped to simplify the notation to $f[0], f[1]. f[2], \ldots$. An algorithm $S \in \mathcal{P}$ is said to learn some function $f \in \mathcal{R}$, if in processing any admissible sequence of information $f_X[0], f_X[1], f_X[2], \ldots$, it is generating a sequence of hypotheses $S(f_X[0])$, $S(f_X[1])$, $S(f_X[2])$, ... which stabilizes after finitely many mistakes on some $a = S(f_X[n])$ describing the target function f correctly, i.e. meeting $\varphi_a = f$ with respect to some underlying GÖDEL numbering $\varphi \in Gö$. This is formalized as below, where

$$\lim_{n \to \infty} h_n = \begin{cases} a & : \quad \exists m \in I\!N \; \forall k \geq m \; (\, h_k = a \,) \\ \uparrow & : \quad otherwise \end{cases}$$

is the formalization of convergency invoked.

Note that we are not going to justify GOLD–style inductive learning within the present paper. The interested reader may consult some surveys like [AS83] and [KW80], some easy introductions like [Jan89] and [JL89], some larger collections of topical results like [BB75] and [JB81], and some recent publications like [Ang92] and [Wie92], in this respect.

In the sequel, we are introducing so-called identification types comprising classes of functions uniformly learnable in some sense. The first two notions are standard (cf. [JB81], [AS83], for instance); they are only inclosed here to keep the paper on hand self-contained. The main contribution of the present paper is, technically speaking, the introduction of new identification types for formalizing reflective inductive inference. There are a couple of results relating these new identification types to the hierarchy of types known before.

Definition 1

Assume any GÖDEL numbering $\varphi \in Gö$. Any class $U \subseteq \mathcal{R}$ is said to be learnable in the limit w.r.t. φ on arbitrary arrangements of information

if and only if

$$\exists S \in \mathcal{P} \; \forall f \in U \; \forall X \in \mathcal{F}(I\!N) \; \forall n \in I\!N$$

$$S(f_X[n]) \downarrow \quad \wedge \quad \exists a \in I\!N \; (\, a = \lim_{n \to \infty} S(f_X[n]) \downarrow \; \wedge \; \varphi_a = f \,)$$

For any given $S \in \mathcal{P}$, $LIM_\varphi^{arb}(S)$ denotes the maximal class of learnable total recursive functions with respect to φ.

$$LIM_\varphi^{arb} = \{\, U \mid \exists S \in \mathcal{P} \, (U \subseteq LIM_\varphi^{arb}(S)) \,\} \qquad \qquad \square$$

Definition 2

Assume any GÖDEL numbering $\varphi \in Gö$. Any class $U \subseteq \mathcal{R}$ is said to be learnable in the limit w.r.t. φ on the standard arrangement of information

if and only if

$$\exists S \in \mathcal{P} \; \forall f \in U \; \forall n \in I\!N$$

$$S(f[n]) \downarrow \quad \wedge \quad \exists a \in I\!N \; (\, a = \lim_{n \to \infty} S(f[n]) \downarrow \; \wedge \; \varphi_a = f \,)$$

For any given $S \in \mathcal{P}$, $LIM_\varphi(S)$ denotes the maximal class of learnable total recursive functions with respect to φ.

$$LIM_\varphi = \{ U \mid \exists S \in \mathcal{P} (U \subseteq LIM_\varphi(S)) \} \qquad \qquad \square$$

It is folklore that these concepts do not depend on $\varphi \in G\ddot{o}$ at all. Instead of LIM_φ^{arb} and LIM_φ above, the notations LIM^{arb} and LIM are sufficient. In particular, it holds $LIM^{arb} = LIM$. (Note that the identification type LIM is called GN in the early Latvian publications, and it is named EX by most US American authors.)

These basic concepts together with a huge amount of modifications and specializations are frequently used in learning theory (cf. [AS83] and [KW80], e.g.).

3 Former Formalizations of Reflection

There is no concept of reflecting inductive inference strategies for learning recursive functions, so far. But there is some related work. Here, we are sketching the two most appropriate approaches known to the author: reliable inductive inference machines and inductive inference machines that can refute spaces of hypotheses. The latter approach has been investigated in two different versions. For the lack of space, the presentation will be quite brief. The interested reader is directed to the original literature mentioned.

3.1 Reliable Inductive Inference

The study of *reliable* inductive inference strategies was the subject of ELIANA MINICOZZI's Ph.D. thesis (cf. [Min76], [BB75]). Lateron, THOMAS ZEUGMANN has been able to characterize reliable inductive inference in terms of *general recursive operators* (cf. [Zeu83]). Together with EFIM B. KINBER, he derived further generalized results in [KZ85].

Here, we are briefly sketching the motivations and formalizations of reliable inductive inference. The intention is to compare these older concepts to our new approach to reflecting inductive inference strategies. This is particularly important, as we are still cruising for appropriate formalizations.

It is one of the serious problems of GOLD–style inductive inference that one does not know, in general, whether or not a particular learning process has been completed successfully. Therefore, if some learning strategy stabilizes on some incorrect hypothesis, this may be erroneously interpreted as reaching the ultimate learning goal. The difficulty is that the consistency of hypotheses is undecidable, in general. This crux of inductive learning has motivated the introduction and investigation of reliable inductive inference strategies. Those distinguished strategies should never stabilize on information sequences outside of its learning competence. Note that reliability as explained and formalized below is a property to be defined on limiting presentations, i.e. on infinite sequences of information units to be presented piecewise. Below, the class $Q \subseteq PF$ indicates the potential source of those unrepresentative information sequences possibly exceeding a strategy's competence.

In [LW94], only finite information segments may be called unrepresentative. This careful distinction is essential, as it is the key difference between the approaches in [MA93] and [LW94]. STEFFEN LANGE and PHIL WATSON provide a discussion of this issue in [LW94].

Definition 3

Assume any GÖDEL numbering $\varphi \in G\ddot{o}$. Any class $U \subseteq \mathcal{R}$ is said to be learnable w.r.t. φ by a *reliable* inductive inference strategy within $Q \subseteq PF$ on arbitrary arrangements of information

if and only if

$$\exists S \in P \; \forall f \in U \; \forall X \in \mathcal{F}(I\!N) \; \forall n \in I\!N$$

$$\exists a \in I\!N \; (\; a = \lim_{n \to \infty} S(f_X[n]) \downarrow \; \wedge \; \varphi_a = f \;) \quad and$$

$$\forall g \in Q \setminus LIM(S) \; (\; \lim_{n \to \infty} S(g_X[n]) \uparrow \;)$$

The identification type is denoted by $REL^{arb}[Q]$ and defined via $REL^{arb}[Q](S)$ similar to the concepts above. □

Note that we have tuned the notations to our needs. So far, reliable inductive inference on the distinguished arrangement $X_0 \in \mathcal{F}(I\!N)$ has not been investigated. The following relationship between fundamental identification types is known (cf. [Min76], [BB75]).

Theorem 1   [Minicozzi and Blum/Blum]

$$REL^{arb}[PF] \; = \; REL^{arb}[P] \; \subset \; REL^{arb}[TF] \; \subset \; REL^{arb}[\mathcal{R}] \; \subset \; LIM$$

The reader may compare this to the approaches to reflecting inductive inference strategies and to the results derived in the sequel. In the author's opinion, reliable inductive inference does not meet the intention of inductive inference machines "knowing" about their limitations, as only infinite information sequences are expressing a machine's relinquishment.

3.2   Refuting Spaces of Hypotheses

Motivated by KARL POPPER's work (cf. [Pop63], [Pop65]), YASUHITO MUKOUCHI and SETSUO ARIKAWA have introduced what they call *inductive inference machines that can refute hypothesis spaces* (cf. [MA93]) for learning formal languages. The intention is to characterize inductive inference strategies and their corresponding power which are even more trustable than reliable strategies. Those distinguished strategies are requested to recognize information which exceeds its learning power. To refute a space of hypotheses is just a derived decision referring to the learning scenario in which such an inductive inference strategy is used.

As YASUHITO MUKOUCHI and SETSUO ARIKAWA deal with indexed families of recursive languages, the formalisms invoked in [MA93] are substantially different from those underlying the present work. Therefore, we restrict ourselves to an intuitive introduction of their concepts and results, only. For more details, the interested reader may consult the paper [MA93] already referred to.

The problem under consideration is to learn formal languages from positive data. Any language is presented in the limit by a sequence of exactly all its words. Such a sequence is called a *text*. At each moment, only a finite initial segment of a text can be accessed. A strategy generates hypotheses by processing initial segments of texts. These hypotheses are interpreted w.r.t. some effective enumeration of formal languages, where membership is uniformly decidable. A strategy learns successfully, if and only if it stabilizes on a correct hypothesis (cf. our definition of LIM above). The family of all language classes uniformly learnable in this sense forms an identification type denoted by $LIM.TXT$. If the admissible strategies are obeyed to behave reliably as formalized above, the corresponding identification type is called $REL.TXT$. Those classes of formal languages identifiable as introduced in [MA93] are collected in a new identification type denoted by $REF.TXT$. An inductive inference machine of the $REF.TXT$ type learns as usual. But if it gets fed any unrepresentative sequence of information, i.e. one which does not describe any language of the target class, it refutes the input after processing some finite part. The result corresponding to the one mentioned above is

Theorem 2   [Mukouchi/Arikawa]

$$REF.TXT \quad \subset \quad REL.TXT \quad \subset \quad LIM.TXT$$

Learning from *informant* is only briefly touched. In contrast to text, an informant about some language is any complete sequence of examples and counterexamples labelled accordingly. The corresponding identification type is called $REF.INF$. There is a figure in [MA93] implicitly containing the following result.

Theorem 3   [Mukouchi/Arikawa]

$$REF.TXT \quad \subset \quad REF.INF$$

There is a couple of further results in [MA93], and it is worth reading this first paper in its area. For our present purpose, the results mentioned here will do.

3.3   Justified Refuting Inductive Inference

Following [MA93], STEFFEN LANGE and PHIL WATSON have refined the approach towards learning formal languages in a somehow reflective way in [LW94].

The authors are investigation both *text* and *informant*. The key distinction from the work sketched above lies in the concept of unrepresentative information. The authors are characterizing those finite initial segments of information sequences unrepresentative, if there is no consistent concept in the whole concept class under consideration. The corresponding identification types[1] of classes of formal languages introduced in [LW94] are called $JREF.TXT$ and $JREF.INF$ below. There are formally slightly stronger versions which require to refute unrepresentative information *immediately*. We name the corresponding identification types $JREF^i.TXT$ and $JREF^i.INF$. There are the following basic results.

Theorem 4 [Lange/Watson]

$$JREF^i.TXT \;=\; JREF.TXT$$

$$JREF^i.INF \;=\; JREF.INF$$

Usually, the more expressive presentation of languages by both examples and counterexamples provides more learning power. Thus, the first result in [LW94] is especially interesting:

Theorem 5 [Lange/Watson]

$$JREF.TXT \;\#\; JREF.INF$$

In [LW94], there is a large number of further results worth to be studied.

4 Reflecting Inductive Inference Machines

Reflecting inductive inference machines are those which either learn successfully or detect that the information presented exceeds its learning capabilities.

Definition 4

Assume any GÖDEL numbering $\varphi \in G\ddot{o}$. Any class $U \subseteq \mathcal{R}$ is said to be learnable w.r.t. φ on the standard arrangement of information by an *immediately reflecting* inductive inference strategy

if and only if

$\exists S \in \mathcal{P} \; \forall f \in U \; \forall n \in I\!N$

$S(f[n]) \downarrow > 0 \quad \wedge \quad \exists a \in I\!N \; (\; a = \lim_{n \to \infty} S(f[n]) \downarrow \; \wedge \; \varphi_a = f \;)$

and

$\forall g \in \mathcal{R} \; \forall n \in I\!N \; (\; \forall f \in LIM(S) \; (\; g[n] \neq f[n] \;) \; \Rightarrow \; S(g[n]) = 0 \;)$

As above, the identification type is denoted by $REFL^i$ and defined via $REFL^i(S)$.

□

---

[1] We have slightly tuned the notations, for our purpose.

Given any learning problem solvable by some inductive inference machine $S \in \mathcal{P}$, an initial segment $g[n]$ is called unrepresentative, exactly if it holds $\forall n \in \mathbb{N} \, \forall f \in LIM(S) \, (\, g[n] \neq f[n] \,)$.

In the stronger version above, *immediately reflecting inductive inference machines* discover information exceeding its competence immediately when presented. The target concepts are defined as follows, where, for technical simplicity, we assume that all usual hypotheses are numbers greater than zero. Thus, we do not need a particular "refutation sign" like $\perp$ in [MA93], as the natural number 0 will do. The weaker version of reflecting behaviour of an inductive inference machine tolerates some more time for pondering before rejecting a piece of unrepresentative information. This approach seems much more intuitive. It will be formalized below.

Definition 5
Assume any GÖDEL numbering $\varphi \in G\ddot{o}$. Any class $U \subseteq \mathcal{R}$ is said to be learnable w.r.t. φ on the standard arrangement of information by a *reflecting* inductive inference strategy

if and only if

$$\exists S \in \mathcal{P} \, \forall f \in U \, \forall n \in \mathbb{N}$$

$$S(f[n]) \downarrow > 0 \quad \wedge \quad \exists a \in \mathbb{N} \, (\, a = \lim_{n \to \infty} S(f[n]) \downarrow \wedge \varphi_a = f \,)$$

and
$$\forall g \in \mathcal{R} \, \forall n \in \mathbb{N} \, (\, \forall f \in LIM(S) \, (\, g[n] \neq f[n] \,) \; \Rightarrow \; \exists m \geq n \, (\, S(g[m]) = 0 \,) \,)$$

The identification type is denoted by $REFL$ and defined via $REFL(S)$ similar to the concepts above. □

Analogously, one may define $REFL^{arb}$ and $REFL^{i^{arb}}$. As the formalization is straightforward, it may suffice to present only one of the definitions.

Definition 6
Assume any GÖDEL numbering $\varphi \in G\ddot{o}$. Any class $U \subseteq \mathcal{R}$ is said to be learnable w.r.t. φ by a *reflecting* inductive inference strategy

if and only if

$$\exists S \in \mathcal{P} \, \forall X \in \mathcal{F}(\mathbb{N}) \, \forall f \in U \, \forall n \in \mathbb{N}$$

$$S(f_X[n]) \downarrow > 0 \quad \wedge \quad \exists a \in \mathbb{N} \, (\, a = \lim_{n \to \infty} S(f_X[n]) \downarrow \wedge \varphi_a = f \,)$$

and
$$\forall X \in \mathcal{F}(\mathbb{N}) \, \forall g \in \mathcal{R} \, \forall n \in \mathbb{N}$$

$$(\, \forall f \in LIM(S) \, (\, g_X[n] \neq f_X[n] \,) \; \Rightarrow \; \exists m \geq n \, (\, S(g_X[m]) = 0 \,) \,)$$

The identification type is denoted by $REFL^{arb}$ and defined via $REFL^{arb}(S)$ similar to the concepts above. □

The first two identification types introduced here correspond to $JREF^i.INF$ and $JREF.INF$ as investigated before. Note that in learning total recursive functions, there does not exist a distinction like the one between text and informant in language learning.

These concepts specify a *self-confident version of reflection*. An inductive inference machine of this type assumes its ability to solve a given learning problem. Only in case some information presented exceeds the machine's competence, this is reflected, either immediately or past some time of pondering. One could also define a dual type of pessimistic reflection, where machines usually tend to resign from a learning task and only in some positive cases explicitly express its competence.

The first lemma makes some almost trivial consequence explicit. Informally speaking, if some inference machine S turns out to be a reflective one for some problem class U in the sense of $REFL^i$ or $REFL^{i^{arb}}$, it may be equivalently replaced by a total recursive machine.

Lemma 1

$$\forall S \in \mathcal{P} \, (\, \exists U \subseteq \mathcal{R} \, (\, U \subseteq REFL^i(S) \,) \; \Rightarrow$$

$$\exists S' \in \mathcal{R} \, (\, REFL^i(S) \subseteq REFL^i(S') \,) \,)$$

$$\forall S \in \mathcal{P} \, (\, \exists U \subseteq \mathcal{R} \, (\, U \subseteq REFL^{i^{arb}}(S) \,) \; \Rightarrow$$

$$\exists S' \in \mathcal{R} \, (\, REFL^{i^{arb}}(S) \subseteq REFL^{i^{arb}}(S') \,) \,)$$

The proof is almost trivial (cf. [Jan94]). There is no space and no need to present it.

Invoking a technique known from the proof that every inductive inference problem belonging to LIM has a total recursive solution, we get the following technically helpful result.

Lemma 2

$$\forall U \subseteq \mathcal{R} \, (\, U \in REFL \; \Rightarrow \; \exists S' \in \mathcal{R} \, (\, U \subseteq REFL(S') \,) \,)$$

$$\forall U \subseteq \mathcal{R} \, (\, U \in REFL^{arb} \; \Rightarrow \; \exists S' \in \mathcal{R} \, (\, U \subseteq REFL^{arb}(S') \,) \,)$$

Proof: Because of the strong similarity of both identification types, it should be sufficient to prove only one version of the lemma. For readability, we choose the syntactically simpler first version.

We assume any $\varphi \in G\ddot{o}$, any $U \in REFL$, and any $S \in P$ with an arbitrary problem class $U \subseteq REFL(S)$. One may fix any particular index j of S, i.e. $\varphi_j = S$. Furthermore, we assume an arbitrary abstract complexity measure ϕ compatible with φ as introduced in MANUEL BLUM's fundamental paper [Blu67].

Given any finite sample of input/output examples, it is uniformly possible to compute a GÖDEL number of the function of finite support being outside this sample identical to zero. For a convenient notation, $\langle \ldots \rangle$ denotes an arbitrary effective and bijective encoding of samples. One may assume that the encoding $\langle \ldots \rangle$ is compatible with the other encodings in use, i.e. for all initial segments $(x_0, f(x_0)), \ldots, (x_n, f(x_n))$, it holds $f_X[n] = \langle \{(x_0, f(x_0)), \ldots, (x_n, f(x_n))\} \rangle$. T is assumed to be any such compiler, i.e. for any sample $\{(x_0, y_0), \ldots, (x_n, y_n)\}$ and for any argument $x \in \mathbb{N}$

$$\varphi_{T(\langle \{(x_0,y_0),\ldots,(x_n,y_n)\} \rangle)}(x) = \begin{cases} y_m & : \quad y_m > 0 \wedge x = x_m \in \{x_0,\ldots,x_n\} \\ 0 & : \quad otherwise \end{cases}$$

Obviously, T is total recursive. For technical reasons, we assume that T is mapping onto the positive integers, only. Thus, 0 is not among its values.

For the following construction, one may choose any function $s \in \mathcal{R}$ with

$$\forall x \in \mathbb{N} \ (\ s(x+1) > s(x) > x \ )$$

s is used as a step counting function estimating computation time. The target inductive inference machine S' is easily defined as follows:

$$S'(f[n]) = \begin{cases} T(f[n]) & : \quad n = 0 \ \vee \\ & \quad \exists m \le n \ (\ \phi_j(f[m]) \le s(n) \wedge S(f[m]) = 0 \ ) \\ S(f[k]) & : \quad \forall m \le n \ (\ \phi_j(f[m]) \le s(n) \rightarrow S(f[m]) > 0 \ ) \\ & \quad \wedge \ k = \max\{ m \mid \phi_j(f[m]) \le s(n) \} \end{cases}$$

It remains to prove the key properties of S'. As this is quite simple, some sketches should suffice.

First, $S' \in \mathcal{R}$. This holds as the defining conditions are computable, they are exhaustive, and both S and T are defined in case they are called.

Second, $f \in REFL(S)$ implies $f \in REFL(S')$. If f belongs to the learning problem solvable by S, the inductive inference machine S is defined on every input, and it is converging to a correct index of f. As soon as $n \in \mathbb{N}$ is large enough to estimate some $\phi_j(f[m])$, all subsequent hypotheses are built according to the second defining case above. Thus, S' is footstepping S.

It remains to complete the second statement by investigating initial segments exceding the competence of S. In such a case, S' is repeating former hypotheses generated by S until S decides to generate the output 0. Whereas the hypotheses before may be incorrect, at this critical point S' guesses some function of finite support. If some function of finite support is really presented, it is identified by S' according to the first defining condition. Thus, $REFL(S')$ is the originally solvable problem class $REFL(S)$ enriched by the particular functions of finite support guessed intermediately. This completes the proof. $\square$

Note that the validity of the lemma results from an interplay of two basic phenomena: On the one hand, reflective inductive inference strategies as introduced are classifying input data in the limit. Therefore, past some unknown point in time, such an inference machines "knows" correctly how to process certain information provided. On the other hand, GOLD–style inductive inference machines can be slowed down and completed by repeating hypotheses generated before, whenever a computation is seemingly diverging. Dovetailing both processes as above yields the desired result.

The proof provides, as a side-effect, a corollary analogous to the first lemma:

Corollary 3

$$\forall S \in \mathcal{P} \ (\ \exists U \subseteq \mathcal{R} \ (\ U \subseteq REFL(S) \ ) \ \Rightarrow$$

$$\exists S' \in \mathcal{R} \ (\ REFL(S) \subseteq REFL(S') \ ) \ )$$

$$\forall S \in \mathcal{P} \ (\ \exists U \subseteq \mathcal{R} \ (\ U \subseteq REFL^{arb}(S) \ ) \ \Rightarrow$$

$$\exists S' \in \mathcal{R} \ (\ REFL^{arb}(S) \subseteq REFL^{arb}(S') \ ) \ )$$

The key insight is that there are no longer any unrepresentative initial segments. These auxiliary results have set the stage for a summary of results and discussion.

5 Limitations of Self-Confidence and Reflection

The corollary and the lemmata above yield the following characterization of the investigated identification types. For notational convenients, we introduce the concept of the set of initial segments belonging to some class of total recursive functions.

$$\alpha(U) \ = \ \{\ y_0 \ldots y_n \mid \exists f \in U \ \forall m \leq n \ (\ f(m) = y_m \ )\}$$

$$\alpha^{arb}(U) \ = \ \{\ (x_0, y_0) \ldots (x_n, y_n) \mid \exists f \in U \ \forall m \leq n \ (\ f(x_m) = y_m \ )\}$$

The following theorem is our characterization of the power and limitations of self-confident inductive inference machines which are either reflecting or immediately reflecting. This result does not mean that reflection is impossible. But it says that reflective behaviour can be guaranteed only in so remarkably restricted cases that it is always possible to enrich the problem class on hand to become complete with respect to initial segments. Doing so, the need for reflective behaviour formally disappears. For all classes of total recursive functions $U \subseteq \mathcal{R}$:

Theorem 6

$$U \in REFL^{i^{arb}} \quad \Longleftrightarrow$$

$$\exists U' \supseteq U \ (\ U' \in LIM^{arb} \ \wedge \ \alpha^{arb}(U') \ = \ (\ I\!N \times I\!N \ )^* \ )$$

$$U \in REFL \quad \Longleftrightarrow$$

$$\exists U' \supseteq U \ (\ U' \in LIM \ \wedge \ \alpha(U') \ = \ I\!N^* \ )$$

Proof: These statements are immediate consequences of the results above. Thus, technically speaking, Lemma 2 is the core result of this paper.

Given any class $U \in REFL^{i^{arb}}$ (or $REFL$), the desired extension results from any reflective learning machine S by building $U' = REFL^{i^{arb}}(S')$ (or $REFL(S)$, resp.) as in the proofs before. □

This is the key result of the present paper. It may be paraphrased as follows in a more technical and in a more problem-oriented form, respectively:

Interpretation I: *For any given problem class $U \subseteq \mathcal{R}$, one may develop a reflecting inductive inference machine, if and only if the class can be completed without loosing learnability such that all possible initial segments occur.*

Interpretation II: *For any given problem class $U \subseteq \mathcal{R}$, one may develop a reflecting inductive inference machine, if and only if the development of such a machine is not necessary at all.*

The core characterization result above has a corollary which seems to contradict the intuition considerably, although it is somehow similar to Theorem 4 above.

Theorem 7

$$REFL^{i^{arb}} = REFL^i = REFL^{arb} = REFL$$

Proof: By the characterization theorem, all these identification types are characterized by the possibility to complete problem classes with respect to initial segments. Thus, the equalities $REFL^{i^{arb}} = REFL^{arb}$ and $REFL^i = REFL$ are true, as the differences of the corresponding sets of initial segments are only technical in nature. Finally, it is sufficient to prove $REFL = REFL^{arb}$. As $REFL^{arb} \subseteq REFL$ holds by definition, this reduces to $REFL \subseteq REFL^{arb}$. For the proof, one may assume that any given problem class $U \in REFL$ is complete with respect to initial segments. A corresponding learning strategy S must belong to $\mathcal{R}$. From $LIM \subseteq LIM^{arb}$ follows the desired result. □

6 Conclusions

The results presented are quite easy and clear. However, these results are – to the author's knowledge – the first formally well-based results which explicitly characterize the power and limitations of reflective behaviour in artificial intelligence. They exemplify that algorithmic learning theory carries fundamental messages to the surrounding area of artificial intelligence. There are further efforts of the author to introduce artificial intelligence concepts into inductive inference for – after intensive disciplinary work on learning theory – returning messages to the artificial intelligence community. Monotonic reasoning (cf. [Jan91a], [Jan91b]) and case-based reasoning (cf. [Jan92], [SJL94], [JL95]) are recently two prototypical examples.

We confine our discussion to only two problem areas. First, we give a very brief interpretation and criticism of the results achieved so far. Second, we sketch a program of further research in the area of reflective inductive inference.

In the author's opinion, the results of the present paper carry at least the following messages:

1. There are classes of learning problems that can be solved by reflecting and self-confident mechanisms, i.e. it is reasonable to investigate reflection of learning algorithms and to develop and implement several versions of those strategies.
2. Learning problems which can be solved by reflecting and self-confident mechanisms as introduced above are very restricted. Therefore, for a majority of learning problems, this type of learning algorithms does not exist.
3. Whenever the strong form of reflection introduced can be implemented, it can be avoided by solving a more comprehensive learning problem which does not need any reflection.
4. In contrast to intuition, it does not provide more learning power, if one allows a reflective learning algorithm to spend more time on reasoning about its compentence.
5. In contrast to many other identification types, it does not matter whether or not a reflective and self-confident inductive inference mechanism knows in advance about the arrangement of information provided.

From the perspective of these interpretations, the results are raising a couple of research questions. Some of them are listed, for illustration. It is the author's strong belief that, on the one hand, investigating reflective systems behaviour is an exciting and relevant research area, both in artificial intelligence, in general, and in learning theory, in particular. On the other hand, developing a research program for a promising area is, at least partially, a problem of research in itself.

i   There may be different versions of formalizing reflective behaviour. These versions may result in a partial ordering with respect to expressiveness.
ii It may be a criterion for appropriateness of reflection concepts whether or not immediate reflection is stronger than unconstraint reflection.
iii It may be another criterion for appropriateness of reflection concepts whether or not there is a difference in learnability between cases where information is presented in an order known in advance and unrestricted cases.
iv It may be especially interesting and, perhaps, considerably more complex to investigate combinations of the latter two aspects.
v   If a certain type of reflection has been chosen, it is desirable to enrich learning mechanisms with a feature of recovering. In other words, if reflection yields the information that some information exceeds a learning mechanism's competence, there should be – if possible – some therapy, for instance, by changing the criterion of success.
vi If the view of diagnosis and therapy is adopted, it may be combined with some or all of the aspects mentioned before.

In every case, it is highly desriable to guide the choice of theoretical research problems in the present area by an intention to derive messages of a potential interest to a larger community.

The author gratefully acknowledges fruitful discussions both about the problem of reflective system's behaviour, in general, and the approach presented, in particular, with OKSANA ARNOLD, GUNTER GRIESER, and STEFFEN LANGE. In particular, several discussions with GUNTER GRIESER are partially reflected in the list of research problems presented above. Anonymous referees provided very helpful criticism.

References

[Ang92]   Dana Angluin. Computational learning theory: Survey and selected bibliography. In *ACM Symposium on Theory of Computing, STOC'92*, pages 351–368. ACM Press, 1992.

[AS83]   Dana Angluin and Carl H. Smith. A survey of inductive inference: Theory and methods. *Computing Surveys*, 15:237–269, 1983.

[BB75]   Leonore Blum and Manuel Blum. Toward a mathematical theory of inductive inference. *Information and Control*, 28:125–155, 1975.

[Blu67]   Manuel Blum. A machine-independent theory of the complexity of recursive functions. *Journal of the ACM*, 14:322–336, 1967.

[Cas74]   John Case. Periodicity in generations of automata. *Mathematical Systems Theory*, 8(1):15–32, 1974.

[Cas94]   John Case. Infinitary self-reference in learning theory. *Journal on Experimental and Theoretical AI*, 6(1):3–16, 1994.

[Gol67]   E Mark Gold. Language identification in the limit. *Information and Control*, 14:447–474, 1967.

[Jan89]   Klaus P. Jantke. Algorithmic learning from incomplete information: Principles and problems. In J. Dassow and J. Kelemen, editors, *Machines, Languages, and Complexity*, Lecture Notes in Computer Science, pages 188–207. Springer-Verlag, 1989.

[Jan91a]   Klaus P. Jantke. Monotonic and non-monotonic inductive inference. *New Generation Computing*, 8(4):349–360, 1991.

[Jan91b]   Klaus P. Jantke. Monotonic and nonmonotonic inductive inference of functions and patterns. In K.P. Jantke J. Dix and P.H. Schmitt, editors, *Nonmonotonic and Inductive Logic, 1st Int. Workshop*, Lecture Notes in Artificial Intelligence 543, pages 161–177. Springer-Verlag, 1991.

[Jan92]   Klaus P. Jantke. Case based learning in inductive inference. In *Proc. 5th Annual ACM Workshop on Computational Learning Theory, (COLT'92), July 27-29, 1992, Pittsburgh, PA, USA*, pages 218–223. ACM Press, 1992.

[Jan94]   Klaus P. Jantke. Towards reflecting inductive inference machines. GOSLER Report 24/93, HTWK Leipzig (FH), FB Informatik, Mathematik & Naturwissenschaften, September 1994.

[JB81]   Klaus P. Jantke and Hans-Rainer Beick. Combining postulates of naturalness in inductive inference. *EIK*, 17(8/9):465–484, 1981.

[JL89]   Klaus P. Jantke and Steffen Lange. Algorithmisches Lernen. In K.P. Jantke J. Grabowski and H. Thiele, editors, *Grundlagen der Künstlichen Intelligenz*, pages 246–277. Akademie-Verlag Berlin, 1989.

[JL95]   Klaus P. Jantke and Steffen Lange. Case-based representation and learning of pattern languages. *TCS*, 137(1):25–51, 1995.

[Kar94]   Werner Karbach. *MODEL-K: Modellierung und Operationalisierung von Selbsteinschätzung und -steuerung durch Reflexion und Metawissen*, volume 57 of *DISKI, Dissertationen zur Künstlichen Intelligenz*. infix, 1994.

[KW80]   Reinhard Klette and Rolf Wiehagen. Research in the theory of inductive inference by GDR mathematicians - a survey. *Information Sciences*, 22:149–169, 1980.

[KZ85]   Efim Kinber and Thomas Zeugmann. Inductive inference of almost everywhere correct programs by reliably working strategies. *Elektron. Inf.verarb. Kybern. (Journal of Information Processing and Cybernetics)*, 21(3):91–100, 1985.

[LW94]   Steffen Lange and Phil R. Watson. Machine discovery in the presence of incomplete or ambiguous data. In Setsuo Arikawa and K.P. Jantke, editors, *Algorithmic Learning Theory including Analogical and Inductive Inference, AII'94 & ALT'94*, LNAI, pages 439–453. Springer-Verlag, 1994.

[MA93]   Yasuhito Mukouchi and Setsuo Arikawa. Inductive inference machines that can refute hypothesis spaces. In K.P. Jantke, S. Kobayashi, E. Tomita, and T. Yokomori, editors, *Proc. 4th Workshop on Algorithmic Learning Theory, (ALT'93), November 8-10, 1993, Tokyo*, volume 744 of *Lecture Notes in Artificial Intelligence*, pages 123–136. Springer-Verlag, 1993.

[Min76]   Eliana Minicozzi. Some natural properties of strong identification in inductive inference. *Theoretical Computer Science*, 2:345–360, 1976.

[MY74]   Michael Machtey and Paul Young. *An Introduction to the General Theory of Algorithms*. North-Holland, 1974.

[Pop63]   Karl Popper. *Conjectures and Refutations*. Routledge and Kegan Paul, 1963.

[Pop65]   Karl Popper. *The Logic of Scientific Discovery*. Harper & Row, 1965.

[Rj67]   Hartley Rogers jr. *The Theory of Recursive Functions and Effective Computability*. McGraw-Hill, 1967.

[SJL94]   Yasubumi Sakakibara, Klaus P. Jantke, and Steffen Lange. Learning languages by collecting cases and tuning parameters. In Setsuo Arikawa and K.P. Jantke, editors, *Algorithmic Learning Theory including Analogical and Inductive Inference, AII'94 & ALT'94*, LNAI, pages 533–547. Springer-Verlag, 1994.

[vHABS+92] Frank van Harmelen, Hans Akkermann, Brigitte Bartsch-Spörl, Bert Bredeweg, Carl-Helmut Coulon, and Uwe Drouven. Knowledge-level reflection: Specifications and architectures. Esprit Basic Research Project P3178 REFLECT Report, University of Amsterdam, June 1992.

[vHW92]   Frank van Harmelen and Bob Wielinga. Knowledge-level reflection. In B. LePape and L. Steels, editors, *Enhancing the Knowledge Engineering Process*, pages 175–204. Elsevier Science Publ., 1992.

[Wie92]   Rolf Wiehagen. From inductive inference to algorithmic learning theory. In S. Doshita, K. Furukawa, K.P. Jantke, and T. Nishida, editors, *Proc. 3rd Workshop on Algorithmic Learning Theory, (ALT'92), October 20-22, 1992, Tokyo*, volume 743 of *Lecture Notes in Artificial Intelligence*, pages 13–24. Springer-Verlag, 1992.

[Zeu83]   Thomas Zeugmann. A-posteriori characterizations in inductive inference of recursive functions. *Elektron. Inf.verarb. Kybern. (Journal of Information Processing and Cybernetics)*, 19(10/11):559–594, 1983.

On Approximately Identifying Concept Classes in the Limit

Satoshi Kobayashi   Takashi Yokomori

Department of Computer Science and Information Mathematics,
The University of Electro-Communications,
1-5-1, Chofugaoka, Chofu, Tokyo 182, Japan,
e-mail:{satoshi,yokomori}@cs.uec.ac.jp

Abstract. In this paper, we introduce various kinds of approximations of a concept and propose a framework of approximate learning in case that a target concept could be outside the hypothesis space. We present some characterization theorems for approximately identifiability. In particular, we show a remarkable result that the upper-best approximate identifiability from *complete* data is collapsed into the upper-best approximate identifiability from *positive* data. Further, some other characterizations for approximate identifiability from positive data are presented, where we establish a relationship between approximate identifiability and some important notions in quasi-order theory and topology theory. The results obtained in this paper are essentially related to the closure property of concept classes under *infinite* intersections (or *infinite* unions). We also show that there exist some interesting example concept classes with such properties (including specialized EFS's) by which an upper-best approximation of *any* concept can be identifiable in the limit from positive data.

1 Introduction

Although computational learning theory has provided various kinds of frameworks for analysing the process of *learning* from a computational point of view, most of learning models take there the strong assumption that a target concept should be in a *fixed* class of concepts, called *hypothesis space*. While such a limitation of a target concept permits rigorous studies on the computational complexity of learning some fixed classes of concepts, it sometimes causes the divergence of learning process in practice when a target concept could be outside the hypothesis space.

One approach to overcome such difficulties is, as studied in [Muk93a], equipping a learner with the ability to refute the hypothesis space, in case that a target concept is not contained in it. Another one is permitting a learner to output an approximate concept, such as a minimal concept, when a target concept is outside the hypothesis space, which was recently studied by [Muk94] and [Sak91] using the framework of Gold's identification in the limit from positive data [Gol67]. This paper closely concerns the latter approach.

On the other hand, some interesting works attempting to generalize the Valiant's Probably Approximately Correct (or PAC) learning model [Val84] have been reported, where the target concept (or function) assumption is somehow weakened[PV88] [Hau92][KSS92]. In [KSS92], Kearns, et al. proposed an extended PAC learning model, called *agnostic learning*, in which we make no assumptions on the target concept (function). They provided some positive and negative results which outline the possibilities of agnostic learning. This paper can also be regarded as an attempt to investigate the possibilities of *agnostic learning* in the framework of *identification in the limit*.

In this paper, we introduce various kinds of approximations of a concept. Based on those notions, we propose a framework for analyzing the approximate learnability in case that a target concept could be outside the hypothesis space. We present some characterization theorems for approximate identifiability. In particular, we show a remarkable result that the upper-best approximate identifiability from *complete* data is collapsed into the upper-best approximate identifiability from *positive* data. Further, many interesting characterizations for approximate identifiability from positive data are presented, where we establish relationships between approximate identifiability and some important notions in quasi-order theory or topology theory. The results obtained in this paper are essentially related to the closure property of concept classes under *infinite* intersections (or *infinite* unions). We also show that there exist some rich and interesting example concept classes with such properties (including specialized EFS's) by which an upper-best approximation of *any* concept can be identifiable in the limit from positive data.

2 Preliminaries

2.1 Fundamental Definitions and Notations

A *universal set* U is a recursively enumerable set. A subset of U is called a *concept*, and a set of concepts is called a *concept class*. The set of all concepts over U is denoted by 2^U. For any concept L, we also regard L itself as a *characteristic function* from U to $\{0,1\}$ such that for any $w \in U$, $L(w) = 1$ iff $w \in L$. For any concept class $\mathcal{C}$, the complementary class of $\mathcal{C}$ is defined to be $\{U - L \mid L \in \mathcal{C}\}$ and is denoted by $\mathcal{C}mp(\mathcal{C})$. By $\subseteq$ ($\subset$), we denote the inclusion (proper inclusion) relation. A concept class $\mathcal{C}$ has *an infinite ascending (descending) sequence* iff there exists an infinite sequence of concepts $L_1, L_2, \ldots$ in $\mathcal{C}$ such that $L_1 \subset L_2 \subset \cdots$ ($L_1 \supset L_2 \supset \cdots$).

A binary relation $\leq$ is a *quasi-order* on U iff for each a, b, c in U, the following properties hold:

(1) $a \leq a$ (reflexivity),
(2) if $a \leq b$ and $b \leq c$, then $a \leq c$ (transitivity).

In case $a \leq b$ and $b \leq a$, we say that a and b are *equivalent with respect to* $\leq$. We write $a < b$ iff $a \leq b$ and $b \not\leq a$. In case $a \not\leq b$ and $b \not\leq a$, we say that a and b are *incomparable*. We know the following fundamental fact.

Lemma 1. Let S be an infinite set of nonequivalent elements with respect to a quasi-order on U. Then, S contains either an infinite linearly ordered sequence or an infinite set of pairwise incomparable elements.

Wa say that a quasi-order $\leq$ on U is a *well quasi-order* ([Kru72]), iff the following conditions hold:

(1) there exists no infinite sequences $w_1, w_2, \ldots$ of elements in U such that for any positive integer i, $w_{i+1} < w_i$ holds,

(2) there exists no infinite sets of pairwise incomparable elements in U.

We say that a concept L is *a lower (an upper) set with respect to* $\leq$ iff for any w_1 and w_2 in U such that $w_1 \leq w_2$ ($w_2 \leq w_1$), $w_2 \in L$ implies $w_1 \in L$. The concept class consisting of all concepts that are upper sets with respect to a quasi-order $\leq$ is called an *upper-closed class with respect to* $\leq$, and is denoted by $Cls(\leq)$.

For any concept class C, we define a *quasi-order induced by* C, denoted by $\leq_C$ as follows: for any w_1, w_2 in U,

$$w_1 \leq_C w_2 \text{ iff } \forall L \in C \, (w_1 \in L \text{ implies } w_2 \in L).$$

Example 1. Let Σ be a finite alphabet and Σ^* be the set of all words over Σ. In this example, we consider Σ^* as a universal set. We define $w_1 \leq_{sp} w_2$ iff w_2 is a supersequence of w_1. The subsequence order $\leq_{sb}$ is defined by : $w_1 \leq_{sb} w_2$ iff w_2 is a subsequence of w_1. By SPC and SBC, we denote the upper-closed classes with respect to $\leq_{sp}$ and $\leq_{sb}$, respectively. Then, $\leq_{SPC}$ and $\leq_{SBC}$ coincide with $\leq_{sp}$ and $\leq_{sb}$, respectively. □

2.2 Topological Spaces

Let X be a non-empty set and T be any class of subsets of X. Then we define

$$\bigcup T = \{x \mid x \in A, \text{ for some } A \in T\},$$
$$\bigcap T = \{x \mid x \in A, \text{ for every } A \in T\}.$$

For an empty class, we define $\bigcup \emptyset = \emptyset$ and $\bigcap \emptyset = X$.

A class T of subsets of X is closed under *finite unions (finite intersections)* iff for any finite subclass G of T, $\bigcup G$ ($\bigcap G$) is contained in T as an element. A class T of subsets of X is closed under *infinite unions (infinite intersections)* iff for any (possibly infinite) subclass G of T, $\bigcup G$ ($\bigcap G$) is contained in T as an element.

Let X be a non-empty set. A class T of subsets of X is called a *topology* on X iff it satisfies the following conditions:

(1) T is closed under infinite unions,

(2) T is closed under finite intersections.

A *topological space* (X, T) consists of two objects; a non-empty set X and a topology T on X. The sets in the class T are called *open sets* of topological space (X, T). An element in X is called a *point*. A *closed set* in a topological space (X, T) is a set whose complement is an open set.

If A is a subset of X, then its *closure*, denoted by $Cs(A)$, is the intersection of all closed supersets of A. If A is a subset of X, then its *interior*, denoted by $It(A)$, is the union of all open subsets of A.

For any open set A of a topological space (X, T), a class G of open subsets of X is called an *open cover* of A iff each point in A belongs to at least one element in G. A subclass of an open cover which is itself an open cover is called a *subcover*. An open set A is said to be *compact* iff every open cover of A has its finite subcover.

2.3 Fundamentals for Identification in the Limit

Throughout this paper, let U be a universal set. For a given concept L, *a positive presentation of L* is an infinite sequence $\sigma = w_1, w_2, \ldots$ such that $\{w_i \mid i \geq 1\} = L$. In case of $L = \emptyset$, a positive presentation of L is an infinite sequence of a special symbol # such that $\# \notin U$. A *negative presentation* of L is defined to be a positive presentation of $U - L$. For a given concept L, *a complete presentation of L* is an infinite sequence $\gamma = (w_1, l_1), (w_2, l_2), \ldots$ of pairs on $U \times \{0, 1\}$ such that $\{w_i \mid i \geq 1\} = U$ and γ contains $(w, 1)$ iff $w \in L$. An element w such that $(w, 1)$ (respectively, $(w, 0)$) appears in γ is called a *positive example* (respectively, a *negative* example) in γ.

Let $\mathbf{N}$ be the set of all positive integers. A class $C = \{L_i\}_{i \in \mathbf{N}}$ of concepts is *an indexed family of recursive concepts* (or, *indexed family*, for short), iff there exists a recursive function $f : \mathbf{N} \times U \to \{0, 1\}$ such that

$$f(i, w) = \begin{cases} 1 & if \ w \in L_i, \\ 0 & otherwise. \end{cases}$$

Let L be any concept in C. We say that an algorithm M *identifies L in the limit from positive data* iff for any positive presentation of L, the infinite sequence, $g_1, g_2, g_3, \ldots$, of integers produced by M converges to an integer n such that $L = L_n$. An indexed family C is *identifiable in the limit from positive data* iff there exists an algorithm M such that M identifies every concept in C in the limit from positive data. Identifiability from complete data and negative data is defined in a similar manner.

Note that an indexed family C may contain an empty concept $\emptyset$ in our framework, where the following fundamental results on the identifiability from positive data hold as in the original framework[Ang80].

A finite subset T of L_i in C is a *finite tell-tale* of L_i iff for any L_j in C, $T \subseteq L_j$ implies $L_j \not\subset L_i$. Angluin showed an important result on a characterization of the identifiability in the limit from positive data.

Theorem 2. [Ang80] An indexed family C is identifiable in the limit from positive data iff there exists an effective procedure that on any input i enumerates a finite tell-tale of $L_i \in C$. □

We say that an indexed family C has *infinite elasticity* iff there exist an infinite sequence $w_0, w_1, w_2, \ldots$ of elements in U and an infinite sequence $L_1, L_2, \ldots$ of concepts in C such that, for any $k \geq 1$, $\{w_0, w_1, \ldots, w_{k-1}\} \subseteq L_k$ and $w_k \notin L_k$ hold. An indexed family C has *finite elasticity* iff C does not have infinite elasticity. An indexed family C has *finite thickness* iff for any w, the cardinality of the set $\{L \in C \mid w \in L\}$ is finite. The finite thickness is a sufficient condition for the finite elasticity.

Theorem 3. [Wri89][MSW90] An indexed family C is identifiable in the limit from positive data if C has finite elasticity. □

As is proved in [MS93], various kinds of operations on concept classes preserve the property of finite elasticity. Let C be a concept class. By $Intsct(C)$, we denote the smallest class that contains $C \cup \{\emptyset\}$ and is closed under finite intersections. Later we will use the next lemma.

Lemma 4. [KY94a] Let C be an indexed family which has finite elasticity. Then, $Intsct(C)$ has finite elasticity. □

2.4 A Framework of Approximate Learning

Let C be a concept class and X be a concept (not always in C). A concept $Y \in C$ is called a C-upper approximation of a concept X iff $X \subseteq Y$ and for any concept $C \in C$ such that $X \subseteq C$, $C \not\subseteq Y$ holds. A concept $Y \in C$ is called a C-upper-best approximation of a concept X iff $X \subseteq Y$ and for any concept $C \in C$ such that $X \subseteq C$, $Y \subseteq C$ holds. A concept $Y \in C$ is called a C-lower approximation of a concept X iff $Y \subseteq X$ and for any concept $C \in C$ such that $C \subseteq X$, $Y \not\subseteq C$ holds. A concept $Y \in C$ is called a C-lower-best approximation of a concept X iff $Y \subseteq X$ and for any concept $C \in C$ such that $C \subseteq X$, $C \subseteq Y$ holds. By $\overline{C}X$ ($\underline{C}X$), we denote the C-upper-best (C-lower-best) approximation of a concept X.

C has upper approximation property (u.a.p.) iff for any concept X, there exists a C-upper approximation of X. C has upper-best approximation property (u.b.a.p) iff for any concept X, there exists a C-upper-best approximation of X. Similarly, C has lower approximation property (l.a.p.) iff for any concept X, there exists a C-lower approximation of X. C has lower-best approximation property (l.b.a.p.) iff for any concept X, there exists a C-lower-best approximation of X.

Then, we have the following.

Lemma 5. A concept class C has u.b.a.p. iff C is closed under infinite intersections.

Proof. For proving the if part, assume that C is closed under infinite intersections. Let S be any concept. We have $\mathcal{F} = \{C \in C \mid S \subseteq C\} \neq \emptyset$, since $U = \bigcap \emptyset \in C$. Let $X = \bigcap \mathcal{F}$. Then, we have $S \subseteq X$. Further, for any concept $C' \in C$ such that $S \subseteq C'$, $X \subseteq C'$ holds, since $C' \in \mathcal{F}$. Therefore, $X \in C$ is C-upper best approximation of S. Hence, C has u.b.a.p.

Conversely, let us assume C has u.b.a.p., and consider any subclass $\mathcal{F}$ of C. Let $X = \bigcap \mathcal{F}$ and define $Y = \overline{C}X$. From the assumption, we have $Y \in C$.

By definition, $X \subseteq Y$ holds. We will show that $Y \subseteq X$ as follows.

Assume that there exists an element u such that $u \in Y$ and $u \notin X$. Then, by the definition of X, we have that there exists a concept $A \in \mathcal{F}$ such that $u \notin A$. For the concept A, we have $X \subseteq A$ and $Y \not\subseteq A$, which contradicts the fact that Y is the C-upper-best approximation of X. Therefore, we have $Y \subseteq X$.

Hence, $X = Y \in C$ holds. This completes the proof. □

In a similar manner, we have the following.

Lemma 6. A concept class C has l.b.a.p. iff C is closed under infinite unions. □

These results imply that concept classes with u.b.a.p. and l.b.a.p. satisfy the definition of topology on U. We will present some topological characterizations of approximate identifiability from positive data in section 4.

Furthermore, it is easy to see the followings.

Lemma 7. If a concept class C with $U \in C$ ($\emptyset \in C$) has no infinite descending (ascending) sequences, then C has u.a.p. (l.a.p.) □

Let C be an indexed family and L be a (possibly non-recursively enumerable) concept. We say that an algorithm M *identifies C-upper (C-upper-best) approximation of L in the limit from positive data* iff for any positive presentation of L, the infinite sequence, $g_1, g_2, g_3, ...$, of integers produced by M converges to some positive integer n such that L_n is C-upper (C-upper-best) approximation of L. A concept class C_1 is *upper (upper-best) approximately identifiable in the limit from positive data by an indexed family C_2* iff there exists an algorithm M such that M identifies C_2-upper (C_2-upper-best) approximation of any concept $L \in C_1$ in the limit from positive data.

We say that an algorithm M *identifies C-lower (C-lower-best) approximation of L in the limit from positive data* iff for any positive presentation of L, the infinite sequence, $g_1, g_2, g_3, ...$, of integers produced by M converges to some positive integer n such that L_n is C-lower (C-lower-best) approximation of L. A concept class C_1 is *lower (lower-best) approximately identifiable in the limit from positive data by an indexed family C_2* iff there exists an algorithm M such that M identifies C_2-lower (C_2-lower-best) approximation of any concept $L \in C_1$ in the limit from positive data.

In a similar manner, the upper(-best) or lower(-best) approximate identifiability in the limit from complete data and from negative data is defined.

The following notion of *M-finite thickness* was introduced by Sato and Moriyama ([SM93]). An indexed family C satisfies *MEF-condition*, iff for any nonempty finite set $T \subseteq U$ and any $L_i \in C$ with $T \subseteq L_i$, there exists a C-upper approximation L_j of T such that $L_j \subseteq L_i$. An indexed family C satisfies *MFF-condition*, iff for any nonempty finite set $T \subseteq U$, the cardinality of $\{L_i \in C \mid L_i \text{ is a } C\text{-upper approximation of } T\}$ is finite. An indexed family C has *M-finite thickness* iff C satisfies both MEF- and MFF-conditions.

Mukouchi presented an interesting result on a sufficient condition for the upper approximate identifiability from positive data using the following lemma.

Lemma 8. [Muk94] Let C be an indexed family which satisfies MEF-condition and has finite elasticity, let $L \subseteq U$ be a nonempty concept, and let $L_n \in C$ be a concept.
(a) If $L \subseteq L_n$, then there exists a C-upper approximation $L_j \in C$ of L such that $L_j \subseteq L_n$.
(b) If L_n is a C-upper approximation of L, then there exists a finite subset T of L such that L_n is a C-upper approximation of T. □

Theorem 9. [Muk94] If an indexed family C has M-finite thickness, finite elasticity, and U as an element, then 2^U is upper approximately identifiable in the limit from positive data by C. □

Further, Sato and Moriyama presented the following result.

Theorem 10. [SM93] If an indexed family C has M-finite thickness and every concept in C has a finite tell-tale, C is identifiable in the limit from positive data. □

3 A Characterization of Upper-Best Approximate Identifiability from Positive Data

In the rest of the paper, we argue on the issue of upper-best approximately identifying the class 2^U in the limit by some indexed family. In this section, we present a

characterization theorem for such an approximate identifiability from positive data.
By Theorem 2 and Theorem 10, we have the following.

Theorem 11. Let C be an indexed family with u.b.a.p. Then, the followings are equivalent.
(1) C is identifiable in the limit from positive data.
(2) Every concept in C has a finite tell-tale. □

The following is a characterization for the upper-best approximate identifiability from positive data.

Theorem 12. Let C be an indexed family with u.b.a.p. Then, the followings are equivalent.
(1) 2^U is upper-best approximately identifiable in the limit from positive data by C.
(2) 2^U is upper-best approximately identifiable in the limit from complete data by C.
(3) C has finite elasticity.
(4) C has no infinite ascending sequences.

Proof.
(1)⇒(2) : Immediately from the definition.
(2)⇒(4) : Assume that C has an infinite ascending sequence $\tilde{L}_1 \subset \tilde{L}_2 \subset \tilde{L}_3 \subset \cdots$ and let $\mathcal{F} = \{\tilde{L}_i \mid i \geq 1\}$. The condition (2) implies that there exists an algorithm M which upper-best approximately identifies 2^U in the limit from complete data with respect to C. In the following, $\sigma = w_1, w_2, \ldots$ is a positive presentation of U such that for any $i, j \ (\geq 1)$ with $i \neq j$, $w_i \neq w_j$ holds.

We will define an infinite sequence $\tilde{L}_{p_0}, \tilde{L}_{p_1}, \ldots$ of concepts in $\mathcal{F}$ and an infinite sequence $(w_1, l_1), (w_2, l_2), \ldots$ of pairs on $U \times \{0, 1\}$ fed to M as follows:

Stage 0 : $n_0 = 0$; $p_0 = 0$; $\tilde{L}_{p_0} = \emptyset$; initialize M;
Stage i ($i \geq 1$) :
    (i) Let $\tilde{L}_{p_i}$ be a concept in $\mathcal{F}$ such that $\tilde{L}_{p_i} - (\tilde{L}_{p_{i-1}} \cup \{w_1, \ldots, w_{n_{i-1}}\}) \neq \emptyset$;
    (ii) Additionally feed M a sequence,
        $(w_{n_{i-1}+1}, \tilde{L}_{p_i}(w_{n_{i-1}+1})), (w_{n_{i-1}+2}, \tilde{L}_{p_i}(w_{n_{i-1}+2})), (w_{n_{i-1}+3}, \tilde{L}_{p_i}(w_{n_{i-1}+3})), \cdots$
        of pairs on $U \times \{0, 1\}$ until the outputs of M converges to some index g_i;
    (iii) Let n_i be the total number of pairs fed to M up to this point;
    (iv) Go to Stage $i + 1$;

At the first step of each ith $(i \geq 1)$ stage, $\tilde{L}_{p_i}$ can be defined, since $\tilde{L}_1 \subset \tilde{L}_2 \subset \tilde{L}_3 \subset \cdots$ is an infinite sequence and the cardinality of $\{w_1, \ldots, w_{n_{i-1}}\}$ is finite. At the second step of each ith $(i \geq 1)$ stage, the output of M converges to some index g_i, since for any concept L, M can identify a C-upper-best approximation of L in the limit. Further, $\tilde{L}_{p_i} - \{w_1, \ldots, w_{n_{i-1}}\} \subseteq L_{g_i} \subseteq \tilde{L}_{p_i}$ holds for each $i \geq 1$, since at the ith stage, the set of all positive examples in a complete presentation fed to M contains $\tilde{L}_{p_i} - \{w_1, \ldots, w_{n_{i-1}}\}$ and is contained in $\tilde{L}_{p_i}$. Therefore, we have for each $i \geq 1$, $L_{g_{i+1}} - L_{g_i} \supseteq \tilde{L}_{p_{i+1}} - \{w_1, \ldots, w_{n_i}\} - \tilde{L}_{p_i} \neq \emptyset$. Thus, M changes its conjectures infinitely many times.

Then, we define a language L_* using the infinite sequence τ_∞ which is fed to M in the definition above: $w \in L_*$ iff $(w,1)$ belongs to τ_∞. (Recall that L_* may not be recursively enumerable.) We have that the C-upper-best approximation of L_* can not be identifiable in the limit from the complete presentation τ_∞ by M, since M on input τ_∞ changes its conjectures infinitely many times. This is a contradiction.
$(4) \Rightarrow (3)$: Assume that C has infinite elasticity. Then there exists an infinite sequence $w_0, w_1, w_2, ...$ of elements in U and an infinite sequence $L_1, L_2, ...$ of concepts in C such that for any $k \geq 1$, $\{w_0, w_1, ..., w_{k-1}\} \subseteq L_k$ and $w_k \notin L_k$ hold. Let us define concepts $L_i' = \bigcap\{L_j \mid j \geq i\}$ $(i \geq 1)$. We have that for each $i \geq 1$, $L_i' \in C$, since C is closed under infinite intersections by Lemma 5. It is easy to see $L_1' \subset L_2' \subset L_3' \subset \cdots$, which implies that C has an infinite ascending sequence. This completes the proof.
$(3) \Rightarrow (1)$: Note that u.b.a.p. of C implies M-finite thickness of C. Therefore, we obtain this implication immediately from Theorem 9. □

Corollary 13. 2^U is upper-best approximately identifiable in the limit from complete data by an indexed family C iff 2^U is upper-best approximately identifiable in the limit from positive data by C.

Proof. Note that the upper-best approximate identifiability requires the u.b.a.p. of C. □

Thus, it is remarkable that the upper-best approximate identifiability from *complete* data is collapsed into the upper-best approximate identifiability from *positive* data. By duality, we have the following.

Theorem 14. Let C be an indexed family with l.b.a.p. Then, the followings are equivalent.
(1) 2^U is lower-best approximately identifiable in the limit from negative data by C.
(2) 2^U is lower-best approximately identifiable in the limit from complete data by C.
(3) $Cmp(C)$ has finite elasticity.
(4) C has no infinite descending sequences. □

Further, by Theorem 12, Theorem 14, Lemma 7, we have the following.

Corollary 15. If 2^U is upper-best (lower-best) approximately identifiable in the limit from complete data by an indexed family C, then $C \cup \{\emptyset\}$ $(C \cup \{U\})$ has l.a.p. (u.a.p.) □

Example 2. Consider an alphabet $\Sigma = \{a, b\}$, and an indexed family C_1 consisting of languages $L_0 = \emptyset$, $L_1 = \Sigma^*$, $L_2 = \{a^j \mid j \geq 1\} \cup \{b\}$ and $L_i = \{a^j \mid 1 \leq j \leq i\}$ $(i \geq 3)$. Note that C_1 is closed under infinite intersections and infinite unions, thus C_1 has u.b.a.p. and l.b.a.p. by Lemma 5 and Lemma 6. It holds that C_1 has infinite ascending sequence. However, each language $L_i \in C_1$ has a finite tell-tale T_i, where $T_0 = \emptyset$, $T_1 = \{bb\}$, $T_2 = \{b\}$ and $T_i = L_i$ $(i \geq 3)$. Therefore, by Theorem 11 and Theorem 12, we have that C_1 is identifiable in the limit from positive data, but 2^U is not upper-best approximately identifiable in the limit from complete data by C. On the other hand, by Theorem 14, 2^U is lower-best approximately identifiable in the limit from negative data by C_1 since C_1 has no infinite descending sequences. □

Theorem 16. Let C be an indexed family which has M-finite thickness and finite elasticity. Then, 2^U is upper-best approximately identifiable in the limit from positive data by $Intsct(C)$.

Proof. First we will show the closure property of $Intsct(C)$ under infinite intersections. It suffices to show that for any infinite subclass $\mathcal{F}$ of C with $\bigcap \mathcal{F} \neq \emptyset$, $\bigcap \mathcal{F}$ can actually be constructed by a finite intersection of concepts in C.

Let $\mathcal{F} = \{L_1, L_2, ...\}$, $L = \bigcap \mathcal{F}$, and $w_1, w_2, ...$ be some enumeration of elements in L. By Lemma 8 (a), for each $L_i \in \mathcal{F}$, there exists a concept $L_i' \in C$ such that $L \subseteq L_i' \subseteq L_i$ and L_i' is a C-upper approximation of L. Let $\mathcal{F}' = \{L_i' \mid L_i \in \mathcal{F}\}$, then we have $L = \bigcap \mathcal{F}'$. Furthermore, by Lemma 8 (b), for each $L_i' \in \mathcal{F}'$, there exists a finite subset F_i of L such that L_i' is a C-upper approximation of F_i. Thus, we can define a function $h : \mathbf{N} \to \mathbf{N}$, by $h(k) = min\{j \mid L_k'$ is a C-upper approximation of $\{w_1, w_2, ..., w_j\}\}$.

In case that $h(k)$ is bounded by some positive integer n, L can be represented by some finite intersection, since C has M-finite thickness.

Consider the case that $h(k)$ is not bounded by any positive integer. Then, there exists an infinite sequence $k_1, k_2, ...$ with $k_1 < k_2 < \cdots$ and $h(k_1) < h(k_2) < \cdots$. By the definition of $h(k)$, for each L_k', there exists a concept $L_k'' \in C$ such that $\{w_1, ..., w_{h(k)-1}\} \subseteq L_k''$ and $L_k'' \subset L_k'$. We have $w_{h(k)} \notin L_k''$, since L_k' is a C-upper approximation of $\{w_1, ..., w_{h(k)}\}$. Then, the infinite sequences $w_{h(k_1)}, w_{h(k_2)}, ...$ and $L_{k_1}'', L_{k_2}'', ...$ satisfy the condition of infinite elasticity, which is a contradiction.

Therefore, $Intsct(C)$ is closed under infinite intersections.

We will complete the proof of the theorem. By Lemma 4, we have that $Intsct(C)$ has finite elasticity. Hence, by Lemma 5, Theorem 12 and the closure property of $Intsct(C)$ under infinite intersections, the claim holds. □

Corollary 17. Let C be an indexed family which has finite thickness. Then, 2^U is upper-best approximately identifiable in the limit from positive data by $Intsct(C)$.

Proof. Note that the finite thickness of C implies the finite elasticity and the M-finite thickness of C. □

Example 3. The class $\mathcal{PAT}$ of pattern languages has finite thickness ([Ang80]). Therefore, 2^U is upper-best approximately identifiable in the limit from positive data by $Intsct(\mathcal{PAT})$.

In order to give another interesting example, let us consider the group on integers by +(addition) and the class $\mathcal{Plus}$ consisting of all its subgroups and $\emptyset$. By a well known result in group theory, we have that $\mathcal{Plus}$ is closed under infinite intersections. Further, it holds that $\mathcal{Plus}$ has finite thickness. Therefore, 2^U is upper-best approximately identifiable in the limit from positive data by $\mathcal{Plus}$. □

We show that there exist rich classes by which 2^U is upper-best approximately identifiable in the limit from positive data. Elementary formal systems (EFS's, for short), originally introduced by Smullyan [Smu61], are a kind of logic system where we use string patterns instead of terms in first order logic. For more detailed definition or theoretical results on learning EFS's, refer to [ASY92],[Shi94].

By $\mathcal{LB}$, we denote the class of all length bounded EFS's. By $\mathcal{LB}^{\leq n}$, we denote the class of length bounded EFS's with at most n axioms. We denote, by $L(\mathcal{LB})$

$(L(\mathcal{LB}^{\leq n}))$, the class of all languages defined by EFS's in $\mathcal{LB}$ ($\mathcal{LB}^{\leq n}$) with a fixed unary predicate symbol. It is known that $L(\mathcal{LB})$ coincides with the class of context sensitive languages.

Theorem 18. [Shi94] For any $n \geq 1$, $L(\mathcal{LB}^{\leq n})$ have finite elasticity. □

Lemma 19. [SM93] For any $n \geq 1$, $L(\mathcal{LB}^{\leq n})$ have M-finite thickness. □

Theorem 20. For any $n \geq 1$, 2^U is upper-best approximately identifiable in the limit from positive data by $Intsct(L(\mathcal{LB}^{\leq n}))$. □

4 Topological Characterizations for Approximate Identifiability

In this section, we focus on the concept classes which have u.b.a.p. and l.b.a.p. We give some topological characterizations of the upper-best approximate identifiability from positive data for such classes. We then present a characterization theorem of concept classes by which 2^U is both upper-best and lower-best approximately identifiable in the limit from complete data.

We begin by the next fundamental lemma.

Lemma 21. For any concept class C, the followings are equivalent.
(a) C has u.b.a.p. and l.b.a.p.
(b) C is an upper-closed class for some quasi-order on U.

Proof.
(a)⇒(b) : It suffices to show $C = Cls(\leq_C)$.

Consider any concept $L \in C$ and any elements w_1 and w_2 in U such that $w_1 \leq_C w_2$ and $w_1 \in L$. By the definition of $\leq_C$, we have $w_2 \in L$. Therefore, L is an upper set with respect to $\leq_C$. Hence, $L \in Cls(\leq_C)$, which implies $C \subseteq Cls(\leq_C)$.

It is only left to show $Cls(\leq_C) \subseteq C$. Consider any concept $L \in Cls(\leq_C)$ and a concept subclass $\mathcal{G}_1 = \{A \in C \mid A \subseteq L\}$. From the assumption (a) and Lemma 6, $\bigcup \mathcal{G}_1 \in C$ holds. Therefore, it suffices to show $L = \bigcup \mathcal{G}_1$. By definition, we have $\bigcup \mathcal{G}_1 \subseteq L$. We will prove $L \subseteq \bigcup \mathcal{G}_1$.

Consider any element $w \in L$ and a concept subclass $\mathcal{G}_2 = \{A \in C \mid w \in A\}$ ($\neq \emptyset$, since $U = \bigcap \emptyset \in C$ holds by the assumption (a) and Lemma 5). From the assumption (a) and Lemma 5, we have $\bigcap \mathcal{G}_2 \in C$. By the definition of $\mathcal{G}_2$, it is easy to see that for any w' in $\bigcap \mathcal{G}_2$, $w \leq_C w'$ holds. Therefore, we have $\bigcap \mathcal{G}_2 \subseteq L$, since L is an upper set with respect to $\leq_C$ and contains w. Hence, $\bigcap \mathcal{G}_2 \in \mathcal{G}_1$ holds, which implies $w \in \bigcup \mathcal{G}_1$. This completes the proof.

(b)⇒(a) : We only show here that C has u.b.a.p. The dual argument can be applied to the proof for the existence of lower-best approximations. Let $\leq$ be a quasi-order under consideration. By Lemma 5, it suffices to show that C is closed under infinite intersections.

It is clear that C contains U and $\emptyset$ as elements. Let $\mathcal{F}$ be any non-empty subclass of C such that $\bigcap \mathcal{F} \neq \emptyset$. We can show $\bigcap \mathcal{F} \in C$ as follows.

Let x be an element in $\bigcap \mathcal{F}$ and y be an element in U such that $x \leq y$. By $x \in \bigcap \mathcal{F}$, we have $x \in A$ for each $A \in \mathcal{F}$. Therefore, it holds that $y \in A$ for each $A \in \mathcal{F}$, since each $A \in \mathcal{C}$ is an upper set with respect to $\leq$. Hence, we have $y \in \bigcap \mathcal{F}$, which implies that $\bigcap \mathcal{F}$ is an upper set with respect to $\leq$. Therefore, $\bigcap \mathcal{F} \in \mathcal{C}$ holds from the assumption (b). This completes the proof. □

Lemma 22. Let $\mathcal{C}$ be a concept class with u.b.a.p. and l.b.a.p., and consider topological spaces $\mathcal{T}_1 = (U, \mathcal{C})$ and $\mathcal{T}_2 = (U, Cmp(\mathcal{C}))$. Then, the followings hold.
(1) For topological space $\mathcal{T}_1$, $\forall X \subseteq U$ $It(X) = \underline{\mathcal{C}}X$.
(2) For topological space $\mathcal{T}_2$, $\forall X \subseteq U$ $Cs(X) = \overline{\mathcal{C}}X$.

Proof. Immediately from the definitions of closure and interior operations. □

Theorem 23. Let $\mathcal{C}$ be an indexed family with u.b.a.p. and l.b.a.p., and consider a topological space $\mathcal{T}_1 = (U, \mathcal{C})$. Then, the followings are equivalent.
(1) 2^U is upper-best approximately identifiable in the limit from complete data by $\mathcal{C}$.
(2) 2^U is upper-best approximately identifiable in the limit from positive data by $\mathcal{C}$.
(3) $\mathcal{C}$ is identifiable in the limit from positive data.
(4) Each concept in $\mathcal{C}$ has a finite tell-tale.
(5) $\mathcal{C}$ has finite elasticity.
(6) $\leq_{\mathcal{C}}$ is a well quasi-order.
(7) Every open set in $\mathcal{T}_1$ is compact.

Proof.
(1)⇔(2) : From Theorem 12.
(2)⇒(3) : From the definition of upper-best approximate identifiability.
(3)⇒(4) : From Theorem 2.
(4)⇒(6) : We first prove that there exists no infinite sequences $w_1, w_2, w_3, \ldots$ such that for any $i \geq 1$, $w_{i+1} <_{\mathcal{C}} w_i$. Assume otherwise and consider the set $S = \{w_1, w_2, w_3, \ldots\}$ such that for any $i \geq 1$, $w_{i+1} <_{\mathcal{C}} w_i$. We define $L = \{w \in U \mid \exists w' \in S (w' \leq_{\mathcal{C}} w)\}$ and $L_i = \{w \in U \mid w_i \leq_{\mathcal{C}} w\}$ for each $i \geq 1$. By Lemma 21, $\mathcal{C}$ is the upper-closed class with respect to $\leq_{\mathcal{C}}$. Therefore, we have $L \in \mathcal{C}$ and $L_i \in \mathcal{C}$ since L and L_i $(i \geq 1)$ are upper sets with respect to $\leq_{\mathcal{C}}$. Then, we can show that L does not have any finite tell-tales as follows.

Assume that L has a finite tell-tale T. Let n be the minimum index of the elements $w_j \in S$ such that $\forall w \in T$ $w_j \leq_{\mathcal{C}} w$. We have $T \subseteq L_n \subset L$, which contradicts the definition of finite tell-tale. Therefore, there exists no infinite sequences $w_1, w_2, w_3, \ldots$ such that for any $i \geq 1$, $w_{i+1} <_{\mathcal{C}} w_i$.

We then prove that there exists no infinite sets of incomparable elements with respect to $\leq_{\mathcal{C}}$. Assume otherwise and consider an infinite set $S = \{w_1, w_2, \ldots\}$ of incomparable elements with respect to $\leq_{\mathcal{C}}$. Define $L = \{w \in U \mid \exists w' \in S (w' \leq_{\mathcal{C}} w)\}$ and $L_i = \{w \in U \mid \exists w' \in \{w_1, \ldots, w_i\} (w' \leq_{\mathcal{C}} w)\}$, for each $i \geq 1$. In a similar manner, we can prove that $L \in \mathcal{C}$, $L_i \in \mathcal{C} (i \geq 1)$ and L has no finite tell-tales. This is a contradiction.
(6)⇒(7) : Assume that an open set $L \in \mathcal{T}_1$ is not compact. Then, the next fact holds.

Fact 1 : There exists an open cover $\mathcal{G}$ of L, whose any subcover of L is not finite.

It is clear that L is not empty. We will define an infinite sequence $\mathcal{F}_0, \mathcal{F}_1, \dots$ of concept classes and an infinite sequence $w_1, w_2, \dots$ of pairwise non-equivalent elements with respect to $\leq_C$ as follows:

Stage $0 : \mathcal{F}_0 = \emptyset$ (empty *class*);
Stage i $(i \geq 1)$:
    Find an element $w_i \in (L - \bigcup \mathcal{F}_{i-1})$;
    Find a concept $L_i \in \mathcal{G}$ containing w_i;
    Let $\mathcal{F}_i = \mathcal{F}_{i-1} \cup \{L_i\}$;
    Go to stage $i + 1$.

It is easy to show by Fact 1 that at each stage $i \geq 1$, w_i and L_i are well-defined and satisfy $w_i \in L_i$ and $\forall j < i\,(w_i \notin L_j)$. We have that for any i and j with $j < i$, $w_j \not\leq_C w_i$. Therefore, for any i and j with $i \neq j$, w_i and w_j are not equivalent with respect to $\leq_C$. Thus, by Lemma 1 and the relation $w_j \not\leq_C w_i (j < i)$, there exists either an infinite descending sequence or an infinite set of pairwise incomparable elements with respect to $\leq_C$ in $\{w_1, w_2, w_3, \dots\}$, which is a contradiction.

(7)$\Rightarrow$(5) : Assume that C does not have finite elasticity. Then there exist an infinite sequence $w_0, w_1, w_2, \dots$ of elements in U and an infinite sequence $L_1, L_2, L_3, \dots$ of concepts in C such that for any $k \geq 1$, $\{w_0, \dots, w_{k-1}\} \subseteq L_k$ and $w_k \notin L_k$ hold.

Consider a concept $L_i' = \bigcap_{j \geq i} L_j$ for each $i \geq 1$. We have $L_i' \in C$ for each $i \geq 1$, since C is closed under infinite intersections by Lemma 5. Furthermore, $L' = \bigcup_{i \geq 1} L_i' \in C$ holds, since C is closed under infinite unions by Lemma 6. Notice that the following fact holds.

Fact 2 : $L_1' \subset L_2' \subset \dots \subseteq L'$, $w_i \notin L_i'$ $(i \geq 1)$ and $\{w_0, w_1, \dots\} \subseteq L'$.

The concept class $\{L_i' \mid i \geq 1\}$ is an open cover for L'. Then, from the assumption (7), there exists a finite subcover $\mathcal{F}$ of $\{L_i' \mid i \geq 1\}$ for L'. Let n be the maximum index of L_j' in $\mathcal{F}$. Then, by the Fact 2, we have $\bigcup \mathcal{F} \subseteq L_n' \subset L'$, which is a contradiction.

(5)$\Rightarrow$(2) : By Theorem 9. $\qquad\qquad\qquad\qquad\qquad\qquad\qquad\qquad\qquad\qquad\qquad\Box$

By duality, we have the following.

Theorem 24. Let C be an indexed family with u.b.a.p. and l.b.a.p. and consider a topological space $T_2 = (U, Cmp(C))$. Then, the followings are equivalent.
(1) 2^U is lower-best approximately identifiable in the limit from complete data by C.
(2) 2^U is lower-best approximately identifiable in the limit from negative data by C.
(3) C is identifiable in the limit from negative data.
(4) Each concept in $Cmp(C)$ has a finite tell-tale.
(5) $Cmp(C)$ has finite elasticity.
(6) $\leq_{Cmp(C)}$ is a well quasi-order.
(7) Every open set in T_2 is compact. $\qquad\qquad\qquad\qquad\qquad\qquad\qquad\qquad\qquad\Box$

Example 4. By Theorem 23 (Theorem 24), we have that 2^U is upper-best (lower-best) approximately identifiable in the limit from positive data (negative data) by $\mathcal{SPC}$

(by $\mathcal{SBC}$), since $\leq_{\mathcal{SPC}}$ ($\leq_{\mathcal{SBC}}$) is a well quasi-oder([Hai69]). On the other hand, 2^U is not upper-best (lower-best) approximately identifiable in the limit from complete data by $\mathcal{SBC}$ (by $\mathcal{SPC}$), since there exists an infinite descending (ascending) sequence with respect to $\leq_{\mathcal{SBC}}$ ($\leq_{\mathcal{SPC}}$).

Another interesting example is derived from a well known result in [Kru60] that quasi-order $\leq_{tree}$ of finite trees by homeomorphic embedding is a well quasi-order. Thus, we have that any concept on finite trees is upper-best approximately identifiable in the limit from positive data by $Cls(\leq_{tree})$. □

By By Theorem 23 and Theorem 24, it is easy to see the following.

Theorem 25. 2^U is both upper-best and lower-best approximately identifiable in the limit from complete data by an indexed family $\mathcal{C}$ iff the following conditions hold:
(1) the cardinality of $\mathcal{C}$ is finite,
(2) $\mathcal{C}$ is closed under finite intersections and finite unions. □

5 Concluding Remarks

In this paper, we have shown some characterization theorems for the approximately identifiable classes from positive and from complete data. Some comparisons between our approximation framework and that of the rough set theory, proposed by [Paw91], are discussed in [KY94b].

Our definition of the *upper-best* approximate identifiability from positive data is a special case of the *strong-minimally inferability from positive data* in [Muk94] (equivalent to the notion of the *upper* approximate identifiability from positive data in this paper), where he presented a *sufficient* condition for such an identifiability. In this paper, we have presented some *necessary and sufficient* conditions for the *upper-best* approximate identifiability from positive data and shown the equivalence between the upper-best approximate identifiability from *complete* data and that from *positive* data. Further, we have introduced the dual notions of those learning models, and presented their characterizations.

These results are closely related to the closure property of concept classes under *infinite* intersections (or *infinite* unions). We have also presented that some interesting concept classes with such properties are upper-best approximately identifiable in the limit from positive data. Further results on such concept classes will be discussed in the future works.

Acknowledgement

We would like to thank Noriyuki Tanida for his helpful comments and suggestions. This work was supported in part by Grants-in-Aid for Scientific Research No.07780310 from the Ministry of Education, Science and Culture, Japan.

References

[Ang80] D. Angluin. Inductive inference of formal languages from positive data. *Information and Control*, vol.45, pp.117-135, 1980

[ASY92] S. Arikawa, T. Shinohara and A. Yamamoto. Learning Elementary Formal Systems. *Theoretical Computer Science*, **95**, pp.97-113, 1992

[Gol67] E. Mark Gold. Language identification in the limit. *Information and Control*, vol.10, pp.447-474, 1967

[Hai69] L. H. Haines. On Free Monoids Partially Ordered by Embedding, *Journal of Combinatorial Theory*, **6**, pp.94-98, 1969

[Hau92] D. Haussler. Decisin Theoretic Generalizations of the PAC model for Neural Net and Other Learning Applications. *Information and Computation*, Vol. 100, No. 1, pp.78-150, 1992

[Kru60] J. B. Kruskal. Well-Quasi-Ordering, the Tree Theorem and Vazsonyi's Conjecture. *Trans. Amer. Math. Soc.*, **95**, pp.210-225, 1960 (May)

[Kru72] J. B. Kruskal. The Theory of Well-Quasi-Ordering: A Frequently Discovered Concept. *Journal of Combinatorial Theory (A)*, **13**, pp.297-305, 1972

[KSS92] M. J. Kearns, R. E. Schapire and L. M. Sellie. Toward Efficient Agnostic Learning, *Proc. of 5th Annual Workshop on Computational Learning Theory*, pp.341-351, 1992

[KY94a] S. Kobayashi. and T. Yokomori. Families of Noncounting Languages and Its Learnability from Positive Data. Technical Report CSIM 94-03, University of Electro-Communications, September, 1994

[KY94b] S. Kobayashi and T. Yokomori. An Extended Rough Set Theory Toward Approximate Learning of Formal Languages. *Proc. of International Workshop on Rough Sets and Soft Computing*, pp.482-489, 1994

[KY94c] S. Kobayashi and T. Yokomori. Some Characterizations of Approximately Identifiable Language Classes. Technical Report CSIM 94-06, Department of Computer Science and Information Mathematics, University of Electro-Communications, December, 1994

[MS93] T. Moriyama and M. Sato. Properties of Language Classes with Finite Elasticity. *Proc. 4th Workshop on Algorithmic Learning Theory*, Lecture Notes in Artificial Intelligence **744**, pp.187-196, 1993

[MSW90] T. Motoki, T. Shinohara and K. Wright. The correct definition of finite elasticity: corrigendum to identification of unions. *Proc. of 4th Workshop on Computational Learning Theory*, pp.375-375, 1991

[Muk93a] Y. Mukouchi and S. Arikawa. Inductive Inference Machines That Can Refute Hypothesis Spaces. *Proc. of 4th Workshop on Algorithmic Learning Theory*, Lecture Notes in Artificial Intelligence **744**, Springer-Verlag, pp.123-136, 1993

[Muk94] Y. Mukouchi. Inductive Inference of an Approximate Concept from Positive Data, in *Proc. of 5th International Workshop on Algorithmic Learning Theory*, Lecture Notes in Artificial Intelligence **872**, Springer-Verlag, pp.484-499, 1994

[Sak91] A. Sakurai. Inductive Inference of Formal Languages from Positive Data Enumerated Primitive-Recursively, *Proc. of 2nd Workshop on Algorithmic Learning Theory*, pp.73-83, 1991

[SM93] M. Sato and T. Moriyama. Inductive Inference of Length Bounded EFS's from Positive Data, in preparation, 1993

[Paw91] Z. Pawlak. Rough Sets : Theoretical Aspects of Reasoning about Data. Kulwer Academic Publishers, 1991

[PV88] L. Pitt and L. G. Valiant. Computational Limitations on Learning from Examples, *Journal of the ACM*, Vol. 35, No. 4, pp.965-984, October 1988

Application of Kolmogorov Complexity to Inductive Inference with Limited Memory

Andris Ambainis*
University of Latvia
and
Riga Institute of Information Technology
e-mail: ambainis@cclu.lv

Abstract. We consider inductive inference with limited memory[1].
We show that there exists a set U of total recursive functions such that
- U can be learned with linear long-term memory (and no short-term memory);
- U can be learned with logarithmic long-term memory (and some amount of short-term memory);
- if U is learned with sublinear long-term memory, then the short-term memory exceeds arbitrary recursive function.

Thus an open problem posed by Freivalds, Kinber and Smith[1] is solved. To prove our result, we use Kolmogorov complexity.

1   Introduction

There are two kinds of complexity in inductive inference (and learning in general):

- the complexity of computations necessary for learning;
- the complexity of learning itself;

There are some complexity measures that better reflect the complexity of computations and some measures that better reflect the complexity of learning. Several attempts to separate these two kinds of complexity have been made.

For space (memory) complexity such separation was done by Freivalds, Kinber and Smith[1]. They proposed to consider two kinds of memory: long term memory and short term memory.

Inductive Inference Machine (IIM) uses long term memory to remember portions of input it has seen and, perhaps, other necessary information. In addition to this long term memory, IIM has short term memory that can be used for computations. Each time when IIM reads new input data, this memory is automatically cleared, so it cannot be used for remembering information.

---

* Mailing adress: Andris Ambainis, Institute of Mathematics and Computer Science, University of Latvia, Raina bulv. 29, Riga,LV-1459, Latvia. The author was supported by Latvian Science Council Grant No.93.599, Riga Institute of Information Technology, and scholarship "SWH izglītībai, zinātnei un kultūrai" from Latvian Education Foundation.

Freivalds, Kinber and Smith[1] have proved that, if a set of functions U is learnable, then U is learnable with linear long term memory and no short term memory. (Short term memory is not needed because it appears that, in this case long term memory is sufficient for carrying out all the computations.)

However, if sublinear bound on long term memory is imposed, short term memory becomes necessary. Freivalds, Kinber and Smith[1] proved that there exists a set of functions that can be learned with sublinear long term memory but requires linear short term memory in this case. However, an open question remained:

How many short term memory do we need if we are learning with sublinear long term memory? Is it possible to find examples when learning with sublinear long term memory requires amount of short term memory exceeding any rapidly increasing function?

We answer this open question in affirmative. We prove that there exists a set of total recursive functions that is learnable with sublinear (logarithmic) long term memory but amount of short term memory needed to learn this set of functions exceeds any recursive function.

To prove our result, we consider the set of all recursive functions with low Kolmogorov complexity. (The set of all such functions that the Kolmogorov complexity of $f(0) \dots f(n-1)$ is at most $2 \log_2 n + C$ for all n and some fixed C.)

2   Definitions

We shall consider inductive inference of recursive functions in Gold's model[2].

Inductive Inference Machine (IIM) is an algorithmic device which receives as input the values of some function $f(0), f(1), \dots$ and outputs the sequence of conjectures $h_1, h_2, \dots$. Each conjecture is a program in some acceptable programming system[6, 5].

IIM M *EX-identifies (learns)* a function f if the sequence of conjectures converges to program h which computes the function f.

IIM M identifies a set of functions U if it identifies each function $f \in U$. A set of functions U is called identifiable(learnable) if there exists IIM which identifies U. The collection of all identifiable sets is denoted EX.

We consider the version of this model introduced in [1].

In this model IIM has two types of memory: ·

1. *Long term memory.* It can be used to remember parts of the input IIM has seen and, perhaps, some other information (previous conjectures, etc.).
2. *Short term memory.* It is cleared each time when IIM begins reading new value of function $f(n)$. It can be used for computations.

The separation of two types of memory is necessary, because sometimes IIM may need to perform very space consuming computation to decide which bits of the input it is necessary to keep in long term memory. Without short term memory, such computation artificially enlarges the amount of long term memory needed by IIM.

IIM identifies (learns) a set of functions U with $g(n)$ long term and $h(n)$ short term memory if it identifies U and uses at most $g(n)$ bits of long term and $h(n)$ bits of short term memory on the first n bits of $f(0)f(1)\ldots$ for any $f \in U$ and all $n \in \mathbb{N}$. The collection of all sets that are identifiable with $g(n)$ long term and $h(n)$ short term memory is denoted $EX : g : h$. The collection of all sets that are identifiable with $g(n)$ long term memory and no restrictions on short term memory is denoted $EX : g$.

3 Results

Theorem 1 *There exists a set of recursive functions U such that:*

1. *U is learnable with linear long term memory(and no short term memory);*
2. *U is learnable with logarithmic long term memory;*
3. *For arbitrary recursive function $g(n)$ set U is not learnable with sublinear long term memory and $g(n)$ short term memory.*

Proof. We shall use Kolmogorov complexity[3, 4].

Informally, *Kolmogorov complexity* of a word $x_1 \ldots x_n$ where $x_1, \ldots, x_n \in \{0, 1\}$ is the length of smallest program which outputs word $x_1 \ldots x_n$. For more formal definitions, see [3, 4]. It is well known that

Proposition 1 *Kolmogorov complexity of a word 0^n is less that $\log_2 n + C$ for some constant C.*

Proof. We can take a program which consists of number n and instructions to write n zeros. We need $\log_2 n$ bits to record n and C bits to record instructions where C does not depend on n. □

Now, we define the set U. It consists of all recursive functions f such that

1. For all x $f(x)$ is equal to 0 or 1;
2. There exists only finite number of such x that $f(x) \neq 0$;
3. For each n Kolmogorov complexity of the word $f(0)f(1)\ldots f(n-1)$ is at most $2\log_2 n + C$ where C is the constant from Proposition 1.

1. U is learnable with linear long term memory(and no short term memory).
   It is well known that the set of all functions of finite support (all functions such that $f(x) \neq 0$ only for finitely much x) is EX-learnable. U is subset of this set and, hence, is EX-learnable, too. Freivalds, Kinber and Smith[1] have proved that each EX-learnable set is learnable with linear long term memory and no short term memory.
2. U is learnable with logarithmic long term memory;
   Consider an Inductive Inference Machine which, for each n, after reading $f(0)\ldots f(n-1)$ constructs all possible programs with length at most

$2 \log_2 n + C$ and simulates all them in parallel step by step. Simulation continues until a program outputing $f(0) \ldots f(n-1)$ is found, then learning machine records the text of this program in memory. (If such program does not exist, then, according to definition of U, $f \notin U$.) After reading $f(n)$ IIM takes the program from memory, executes it and obtains $f(0) \ldots f(n-1)$. So, if $f \in U$, our machine always knows the values of $f(0) \ldots f(n)$ and uses memory which is only logarithmic from amount of input information.

Conjectures are computed from $f(0) \ldots f(n)$ in the same way as in usual algorithm for the learning of functions of finite support. (We can use this algorithm because, if $f \in U$, then our machine always knows all the values $f(0) \ldots f(n)$ that it has received as input.)

3. U is not learnable with sublinear long term memory and $g(n)$ short term memory, for any recursive $g(n)$.

We prove this proposition by the way of contradiction. Let us assume that there exists an Inductive Inference Machine M which learns U with $h(n)$ long term and $g(n)$ short term memory where $h(n) = o(n)$ and $g(n)$ is recursive. The values of $f(x)$ can be 0 or 1. Hence, each value of $f(x)$ is 1 bit and $f(0) \ldots f(n)$ are $n+1$ bits.

From $h(n) = o(n)$ we have that there exists a number N such that for all $n \geq N$ $h(n) < \frac{n}{2}$.

Consider a program consisting of numbers k, n, l such that $N < 2^k \leq n$ and l is equal to 0 or 1 and following instructions:

Step 1. Take all possible sequences $f(0) \ldots f(2^{k+1})$ where $f(0) = \ldots = f(2^k - 1) = 0$ and $f(2^k), \ldots, f(2^{k+1}) \in \{0,1\}$ in lexicographical ordering. For each of these sequences $f(0) \ldots f(2^{k+1})$ simulate IIM M until one of following results is obtained:

(a) M uses more than $g(n)$ short term memory on $f(0) \ldots f(n-1)$ for some n,

(b) M gets in infinite loop,

(c) M reads $f(0) \ldots f(2^{k+1})$, writes down something in long term memory and tries to read $f(2^{k+1} + 1)$.

In cases (a) and (b) set $f_0(0) = f(0), \ldots, f_0(2^{k+1}) = f(2^{k+1})$ and $f(x) = 0$ for $x > 2^{k+1}$ and go to step 4.

In case (c) we write down $f(0) \ldots f(2^{k+1})$ and bits written by M into long term memory.

Step 2. If, during all simulations no cases (a) and (b) occur, look through the values of possible sequences $f(0) \ldots f(2^{k+1})$ and corresponding memory bits of M and find two sequences $f_1(0) \ldots f_1(2^{k+1})$ and $f_2(0) \ldots f_2(2^{k+1})$ such that M writes down the same bits after reading these two sequences.

(Such sequences certainly exist, because there are 2^{2^k+1} possible sequences $f(0) \ldots f(2^{k+1})$. Each such sequence contains $2^{k+1} + 1$ bits of information. From $2^{k+1} + 1 > 2^k > N$ we have that

$$h(2^{k+1} + 1) < \frac{2^{k+1} + 1}{2}$$

and $h(2^{k+1}+1) \leq 2^k$. So, M can use only 2^k bits of long-term memory while working on $f(0)\ldots f(2^{k+1}+1)$. It means that M can store in its memory only 2^{2^k} different messages after reading $f(0)\ldots f(2^{k+1}+1)$. As the number of possible messages is less than the number of possible sequences, we have that there are two sequences on which M writes in its memory the same message.)

Step 3. If $l = 0$, take $f_0(x) = f_1(x)$ for $x \leq 2^{k+1}$ and $f_0(x) = 0$ for $x > 2^{k+1}$. If $l = 1$, take $f_0(x) = f_2(x)$ for $x \leq 2^{k+1}$ and $f_0(x) = 0$ for $x > 2^{k+1}$.

Step 4. Output $f_0(0)\ldots f_0(n)$.

The length of this program is $\log_2 n + \log_2 k + D$ where D is some constant. ($\log_2 n$ bits for storing the value of n, $\log_2 k$ bits for storing the value of k and D bits for storing the instructions.)

We take as k such number that $2^k > N$ and $\log_2 k + D < \log_2 2^k + C$ where C is the constant from Proposition 1.

Proposition 2 *The function $f_0(0)\ldots$ computed by program above (for fixed l) belongs to U.*

Proof. Evidently, all $f_0(x)$ are 0 or 1. All $f_0(x)$ are 0 for $x > 2^{k+1}$, hence there is only a finite number of such x that $f_0(x) \neq 0$. It remains to prove that Kolmogorov complexity of $f_0(0)\ldots f_0(n)$ is at most $2\log_2 n + C$.

If $n < 2^k$, then $f_0(0)\ldots f_0(n)$ is the word consisting of $n + 1$ zeros and its complexity is at most $\log_2 n + C$ according to Proposition 1. If $n \geq 2^k$, then $f_0(0)\ldots f_0(n)$ is output of the program described above and the length of that program is $\log_2 n + \log_2 k + D < 2\log_2 n + C$. $\square$

Let us consider two cases:

(a) There exists such sequence $f(0)\ldots f(2^{k+1})$ that $f(0) = \ldots = f(2^k-1) = 0$ and $f(2^k),\ldots f(2^{k+1}) \in \{0,1\}$ and on it M uses too much memory (more than $g(n)$ short term memory) or goes into infinite loop.

Then, one of such sequences is $f_0(0)\ldots f_0(2^{k+1})$. It means that M does not identifies f_0 with $h(n)$ long term and $g(n)$ short term memory. But $f_0 \in U$.

(b) Such sequence does not exist.

We take functions f_1 and f_2 from the described program. $f_1(x) = f_2(x) = 0$ for $x \geq 2^{k+1}+1$. After reading $f_1(0)\ldots f_1(2^{k+1})$ and $f_2(0)\ldots f_2(2^{k+1})$ IIM M has the same information in its long term memory. So, it works in the same way on two different functions f_1 and f_2 and, hence, M does not identify at least one of f_1 and f_2. But, both f_1 and f_2 belong to U.

In both cases we obtain that M does not identify some function from U. It is in contradiction with the assumption that M identifies U.

So, we have proved that U is not learnable with sublinear long term memory and $g(n)$ short term memory, for arbitrary recursive $g(n)$.

Theorem is proved. $\square$

Using similar method (and the same set U) we can prove

Theorem 2 *There exists a set of recursive functions U such that*

1. $U \in EX : n + c \log_2 n : 0$;
2. $U \in EX : c_1 \log_2 n + c_2$ for some c_1, c_2;
3. $U \notin EX : n - g(n) : h(n)$ for arbitrary $g(n)$ such that $\lim_{n \to \infty} g(n) = +\infty$ and arbitrary recursive $h(n)$.

Proof sketch. The proof is, in general, similar to the proof of Theorem 1. The main difference is as follows:

Instead of fixing the length of sequence $f(0) \ldots f(2^k)$ a priori, we construct a program which searches, through sequences of increasing length, looking for examples on which IIM works incorrectly and we analyze Kolmogorov complexity of this program. □

So, we see that the set U is learnable using logarithmic long term memory. But, if we try to learn it with realistic (recursive) amount of used short term memory, we need to remember all or almost all input information (we can learn it with $n - c$ bits of long term memory for constant c). Learning with $n - g(n)$ long term memory and recursive amount of short term memory is impossible even if $g(n)$ is growing to infinity very slowly (even if $g(n)$ is growing slower that arbitrary recursive function). Even very small decrease in used long term memory leads to enormous increase in computational complexity (short term memory and computation time, too).

Possible directions for future work are obtaining the consequences of this result and determining whether similar results hold for other learning models.

4 Acknowledgements

I would like to thank Rūsiņš Freivalds, Juris Smotrovs and several anonymous referees for their useful comments.

References

1. [FKS93] R. Freivalds, E. Kinber and C. Smith, *On the impact of forgetting on learning machines*, Proceedings of the 6-th ACM COLT, 1993, pp. 165-174. To appear in *Information and Computation*.
2. [Gol67] E. M. Gold, *Language identification in the limit*, Information and Control, vol. 10(1967), pp. 447-474
3. [Kol65] A. N. Kolmogorov, *Three approaches to the quantitative definition of 'information'*, Problems of Information Transmission, vol.1 (1965), pp. 1-7
4. [LV93] M. Li, P.Vitanyi, *Introduction to Kolmogorov complexity and its applications*, Springer, 1993
5. [MY78] M. Machtey and P. Young, *An Introduction to the General Theory of Algorithms*, North-Holland, New York, 1978
6. [Rog67] H. Rogers, *Theory of Recursive Functions and Effective Computability*, McGraw-Hill, New York, 1967. Reprinted by MIT Press, Cambridge, MA, 1987.

Author Index

Springer-Verlag
and the Environment

We at Springer-Verlag firmly believe that an international science publisher has a special obligation to the environment, and our corporate policies consistently reflect this conviction.

We also expect our business partners – paper mills, printers, packaging manufacturers, etc. – to commit themselves to using environmentally friendly materials and production processes.

The paper in this book is made from low- or no-chlorine pulp and is acid free, in conformance with international standards for paper permanency.

Lecture Notes in Artificial Intelligence (LNAI)

Lecture Notes in Computer Science